Practice Evaluation for the 21st Century

WILLIAM R. NUGENT

University of Tennessee

JACKIE D. SIEPPERT

University of Calgary

WALTER W. HUDSON

Late of Florida State University

BROOKS/COLE

THOMSON LEARNING

Australia • Canada • Mexico • Singapore • Spain
United Kingdom • United States

BROOKS/COLE

THOMSON LEARNING™

Helping Professions Executive Editor: Lisa Gebo
Editorial Assistant: Sheila Walsh
Marketing Manager: Caroline Concilla
Marketing Assistant: Megan Hansen
Signing Representative: Jim Gaughan
Project Editor: Lisa Weber
Print Buyer: April Reynolds
Permissions Editor: Stephanie Keough-Hedges

Production Service: Buuji, Inc.
Copy Editor: Linda Ireland/Buuji, Inc.
Illustrator: Buuji, Inc.
Cover Designer: Ross Carron
Cover Printer: RR Donnelley & Sons,
 Crawfordsville
Compositor: Buuji, Inc.
Printer: RR Donnelley & Sons, Crawfordsville

Wadsworth/Thomson Learning
10 Davis Drive
Belmont, CA 94002-3098
USA

For more information about our products, contact us:
Thomson Learning Academic Resource Center
1-800-423-0563
http://www.wadsworth.com

International Headquarters
Thomson Learning
International Division
290 Harbor Drive, 2nd Floor
Stamford, CT 06902-7477
USA

UK/Europe/Middle East/South Africa
Thomson Learning
Berkshire House
168-173 High Holborn
London WC1V 7AA
United Kingdom

Asia
Thomson Learning
60 Albert Street, #15-01
Albert Complex
Singapore 189969

Canada
Nelson Thomson Learning
1120 Birchmount Road
Toronto, Ontario M1K 5G4
Canada

Library of Congress
Cataloging-in-Publication Data
Nugent, William R.
  Practice evaluation for the 21st century / William R.
Nugent, Jackie D. Sieppert, Walter W. Hudson.
    p. cm.
  Includes bibliographical references and index.
  ISBN 0-534-34867-X
    1. Social service—Evaluation.   2. Social
  service—Data processing.   3. Evaluation
  research (Social action programs)   I. Sieppert,
  Jackie D. (Jackie Dale)   II. Hudson, Walter W.
  III. Title.
HV41 .N84 2001
361.3'068'4—dc21   00-062160

Contents

Preface

This book was written to provide a comprehensive and self-contained textbook for courses in practice evaluation. The science and technology of practice evaluation are now routinely taught to students who seek professional and academic degrees in many allied human services disciplines and professions, including social work, psychology, counseling, and psychiatry. Despite the success of this work over the past 20 years, pedagogical materials have not kept pace with the expansion of evaluation technology to make it more practice relevant and more readily available for practical use following the completion of professional training. This text is designed to address current curricular deficits and to provide instructors, students, and practitioners with an enhanced evaluation technology that will fruitfully serve them well into the 21st century. Specifically, this book is designed to:

- Serve as a classroom text for instructors who teach client assessment and practice evaluation courses in all human services disciplines and professions (i.e., social work, psychology, school counseling, family therapy, pastoral counseling, etc.)

- Provide new and updated client assessment and practice evaluation methods that are not presently available in other currently available texts

- Introduce new assessment and evaluation methods that never before have been available through any other source

- Provide instructors, students, and practitioners with practical assessment and evaluation techniques and tools that are more suited to the conduct and evaluation of practice on a regular or even day-to-day basis

- Provide all human services organizations and practitioners a completely automated assessment and evaluation system that is based on the most up-to-date network-driven database technology

Although there are a number of fine books currently on the market that cover practice evaluation, none do so in the context of a complete assessment and evaluation technology as does this book.

This book is written in three parts. Part I covers single-case design methodology. As is done in many texts, we cover some basic single-case designs that are, in our opinion, most well suited for use in real-world practice. We do this within the context of working with clients in everyday practice in a managed care environment, not within a context of doing scientific research. These two contexts—that of modern-day practice and that of scientific research—are different, and some practice evaluation texts develop practice evaluation within a scientific context. This contextual development should help the student as well as the practitioner better understand how practice evaluation can fit very nicely within the modern practice environment. We also present methods for analyzing single-case design data, some of which are new and have yet to appear in any other source. Some of these methods are so new that we have provided Appendix A that covers technical issues germane to the statistical basis of these new methods. This appendix is for the reader who is familiar with statistics and mathematics and who is concerned with the logical, mathematical, and statistical basis for these methods. The appendix is not for the typical person reading this book, and someone can read through the book without ever looking at this appendix and not miss any of the important content for actually doing assessment and evaluation work. We also cover methods for aggregating and analyzing single-case designs for program evaluation. Again, much of this material has not appeared anywhere else. We believe that this material makes this book a source of cutting-edge practice evaluation methodology.

Part II of the book covers measurement in practice. We address the role of measurement in practice as well as some issues related to applied measurement in the context of today's managed care environment. We then present a number of short-form and multidimensional assessment tools that can be used in a wide range of practice settings for doing client assessment. Some of these assessment tools have appeared in previous books and journal articles, while others are new. These measures cover an incredibly wide range of areas in which clients will have problems. These measures were designed not only to aid practitioners in assessing the problems faced by their clients but also to serve as tools for evaluating the severity of clients' problems across time. This makes these measures particularly well suited to repeated measurement and single-case designs. These measures are presented and discussed, and sample copies are included in Appendix B. We also present, and answer, a number of questions commonly asked about these measures and their use in practice.

Part III of the book presents a professional version of a computer program that can be downloaded free from the Brooks/Cole website at **http://helpingprofessions.wadsworth.com/nugent/cass**. This software can be used to manage a practice, whether a practitioner works privately or as only one of many practitioners in a large human service organization. This program is called Computer Assisted Social Services, or CASS for short. CASS is an incredibly powerful program that enables practitioners to manage virtually their entire practice. CASS can be used to manage case notes, keep track of client contacts, manage professional tasks that need to be done in work with clients, as well as help to accomplish many other practice-related chores. The CASS program also contains a training module that can be used to score several of the short-form and multidimensional scales discussed in the book and to help practitioners learn to construct single-case designs. The training portion of the program also includes an option called CAAP that enables someone to complete a number of the scales discussed in this book by using a computer. CAAP presents items from these scales to a person on screen, scores the scales, and presents the scores obtained by the respondent on screen along with brief interpretations of the meaning of the scores. The program as downloaded will enable the user to use either CASS or CAAP to score a limited number of the CASS scales.

The CASS and CAAP software are examples of some of the powerful technological tools that are being developed that will help practitioners to use the assessment and evaluation technology and methods presented in the first two parts of this book. This software was developed by our coauthor Walter Hudson, who died of cancer in August of 1999. This software and the associated scales are still published and owned by WALMYR Publishing, PO Box 12217, Tallahassee, FL, 32317; phone number (850) 383-0045. The purpose of including these materials with this book is to help the reader to learn the practice evaluation methods presented in the book as well as to appreciate the power of the new technologies being developed to aid practitioners in the conduct of their daily work with clients. In the past, scoring credits were available from WALMYR Publishing that could be used to make the scoring options in the CASS and CAAP software more permanent parts of these programs. Since Walter's death, however, these scoring credits have not been available, though they may be available again at some point in the future.

This combination of single-case design methodology, applied measurement tools, and computer software provides a powerful assessment and evaluation technology that can be used by instructors to teach the necessary material students need to conduct practice evaluation in today's managed care environment. It also provides students with a textbook that gives them all the resources they need not only to learn client assessment and practice evaluation methods, but also to take with them and use in their everyday work with clients. In short, this book is a teaching device that doubles as an everyday guide to doing practice evaluation and simultaneously provides almost all of the tools students will need to do practice evaluation once they are in the field.

A lot has happened since we planned and started to write this book. By far the most significant was Walt's death. We cannot adequately express our sadness and sense of loss at his passing, nor can we fully express the deep gratitude that we have for all of the things we learned from our experiences with Walt. He was one of the most well spoken persons we have ever met, and certainly one of the friendliest. As a mentor, he was unsurpassed. We are deeply sad that he is not here to see the successful completion of this book. We had originally intended for Walt to be the senior author of this book. However, we have done a significant amount of work on the book since his passing, and many of the ideas that appear in the book he never saw. Because of this, while we hope to continue to receive the same positive support we have seen in our prepublication reviews, we decided that if the book is criticized we should take the lion's share of the blame. Therefore, we have placed Walt's name third on the list. Many of the chapters were written by Walt, and we have made few changes to those chapters other than attempts to make our different writing styles consistent. Much of this preface was taken from the prospectus for this book that was written primarily by Walt. This has been done in an effort to honor his memory and the work of inestimable value that he did for the profession of social work. We dedicate this book to the memory of Dr. Walter Hudson—friend, colleague, and mentor.

We would also like to express our tremendous gratitude to the many people who helped make this book possible. The people at Brooks/Cole—Lisa Gebo, Joanne VonZastrow, and all of the other folks—have been just fantastic. They really hung in there with us through the many difficult times that occurred during the writing of this book. We also want to thank the many reviewers who took their valuable time to read and comment on early drafts of this book: Rafael Engel, University of Pittsburgh; Judith Gonyea, Boston University; Holly Ackerman, Tulane University; Kevin Corcoran, Portland State University; Bruce D. Friedman, Michigan State University; Bruce Thyer, University of Georgia; Barbara Shank, University of St. Thomas.

The comments and suggestions that they made were very valuable and have made this book better as a result. We also want to thank the many colleagues (too numerous to name) who looked over drafts of chapters and gave us very useful feedback and criticism. We want to express special gratitude to Myrna Hudson, the widow of Walter Hudson. Myrna worked closely with us to finalize the book in the aftermath of Walt's death. Her efforts and support were extremely helpful and are greatly appreciated. Finally, we would like to thank our families, including parents, spouses, and children. Our parents helped us to get where we are through their work and sacrifices for our educations. Our spouses and children helped us by supporting us throughout this long endeavor. We could not have done this without the help and support of all of you. Give yourselves a hearty round of applause!

William R. Nugent   Jackie Sieppert
May 2000   May 2000

1

Introduction

This book provides a complete and self-contained assessment and evaluation technology for use by all human services professionals in service delivery, educational, and research settings. It contains several components that, together, make up a complete system for evaluating client problems, assisting with initial diagnosis and treatment planning, monitoring client progress over time, evaluating the effectiveness of practice or service delivery on a case-by-case basis, conducting program level evaluations of organizational service delivery efforts, and conquering all of your most demanding outcome-oriented quality assurance problems. The book introduces a conceptual framework called the **empirical practice model** or EPM, and this first chapter is designed to provide a foundation and overview of that model or perspective.

The empirical practice model, as a system, is presented to you as a theory of human problems, a theory of empirical practice, a collection of tools and procedures, guidelines for decision making, computer software with which to deliver the entire system, and many examples and illustrations to explain how to use the EPM system. This chapter provides an overview of the entire system as a rather large thumbnail sketch, and the remainder of the book provides the detailed information for each component.

OVERCOMING BAD VIBES

The overriding purpose of this book is to provide you with information, ideas, and tools that will help you to become a better practitioner, supervisor, or administrator. It also aims to help these three principal organizational actors to work together more effectively and to better understand each other's unique practice needs and perspectives. It is therefore extremely important to recognize that the empirical practice model is not *owned* by any group or level of organizational actors; it must be used and shared by all practitioners within the organization.

It is unfortunate that the evaluation of practice has too often been imposed from the top down—on one group of practitioners by another—within the human service organization. Such a practice often generates considerable discontent and ill will, and the results of the evaluation efforts are often disappointing or even useless. It must be understood from the outset that practice evaluation is a professional obligation and not an administrative fiat.

Although practice evaluation is a professional obligation, it has too often been treated as a device that is hostile toward and critical of those who bear the burden of delivering services to clients. That is not what this book is about. To the contrary, the empirical practice model that is presented in this book is designed to assist and help the service delivery practitioner and to help all practitioners within the organization to become more effective in their efforts.

Despite this overarching purpose of the book, the very notion of "practice evaluation" instantly conjures up discussion and consideration of topics such as accountability and quality assurance monitoring. Such concepts have too often been presented and advanced as harsh devices, and it is important to overcome the tendency to regard them in such lights. Instead, we shall define them very carefully, and in doing that we shall make them our professional allies rather than our enemies or critics. The next step is to define and therefore understand these concepts so that you can use them to support your service delivery efforts.

ACCOUNTABILITY AND EFFECTIVENESS

Human services professionals at all levels within service delivery organizations and institutions have always been accountable in some fashion. Our fondest hope has been that the services we provide are effective in the most important sense of the term—we help people solve or alleviate the problems they want us to help them solve. Despite our best efforts and our noblest ambitions, early efforts to be accountable and to demonstrate effectiveness were often disappointing or even downright inadequate (e.g., Fischer, 1973). Even so, this has not lessened the press for accountability and demonstrations of effectiveness. To the contrary, the press for accountability has grown larger and more intense.

In the United States, the entire profession of medicine has been pressured into what became known at the end of the 20th century as the managed care model of practice. Managed care in the field of medicine is two ventures packaged into one system. First, and foremost, *it is a cost containment system*. It is also a quality assurance mechanism in which the objective is to provide high-quality and completely adequate medical services at the lowest cost possible.

Managed care in the human services professions and disciplines is not so different from that in medicine. If there is any human services mandate for the 21st century, it is that we all must become more accountable and that we must do so by demonstrating the ability to deliver services that really do help clients solve or alleviate the problems for which they seek help. In the past we did not know how to do that because we did not have an effective evaluation technology. Now we do have such technology, and its development and use have led to what the remainder of the book will refer to as the *empirical practice model* or EPM.

Two Definitions of Effectiveness

Although there are many ways to view the concept of accountability, the only one that occupies any serious consideration in the various human services professions is one that is based on the concept of effective service delivery. Unfortunately, there has been a great deal of confusion about the concept of effectiveness because it has at least two meanings. One of those meanings is attached to the notion that effective service delivery consists of providing services, treatment, and/or interventions that are commonly regarded (for whatever reason) as the most appropriate. This view of effectiveness is one that focuses entirely on *what we do*—what services we provide, how many cases we carry, how many visits we make, what theories or service protocols we use, and so on. This view of effectiveness focuses entirely on the *interventive behavior* of the practitioner, agency, and service delivery system.

The second, and entirely different, view of effectiveness focuses exclusively on *outcomes*—did the client's problem(s) get solved, or did the client improve in some important and significant way? This second definition of effectiveness can be tied to the concept of change. In this regard, we assert the first rule of the empirical practice model.

The First Rule of EPM

There is and can be no such thing as effectiveness until there is measurable positive change in the client's problem.

The simple notion that effectiveness is defined in terms of *desired positive change* is radical, imminently reasonable, and strangely difficult to grasp. If the client seeks improved housing, there must first be a change in housing—and it must be a change for the better. If a client seeks help with alleviating depression (or marital discord, family conflict, peer relationship problems, problems at work, unemployment, suicidal ideation, fearfulness, aggression, partner abuse, or any of a score of other problems), effective service delivery is evidenced only when there is desired positive change in the level(s) of the problem(s) for which the client has sought help. Parenthetically, it is the use of the concept of desired positive change that defines us as members of a value-driven profession.

Three Definitions of Accountability

Accountability is not new. It has been around since the earliest days of recorded history, and it is not going to go away. The most common form of accountability is the one used in commerce and industry. If we bought 10 yards of cloth, did we in fact get 10 yards of cloth? For our purposes, this ancient (and still used) form of accountability can be called *commercial resource accountability* (CRA). We have been very successful with accountability in this arena because we all have to account for the way we expend commercial resources. We have made superb use of computers and other tools to get this job done. This form, however, is not the type of accountability with which we are concerned here.

A second form of accountability that is important to us as human services professionals can be termed *service resources accountability* (SRA). With this form, we are vitally concerned with *professional behavior*—what services we provide, how many cases we carry, how many visits we make, what theories or service delivery protocols we use, and so on. It is here that we seek novel and often untested forms of service delivery, define them as preferred, desired, or even mandated care protocols, and then use computers and other devices to monitor their delivery. This is the area of human services practice and administration to which we have given the greatest attention in the application of computer and information management technology.

The part of SRA that significantly overlaps with CRA has been enormously successful and will continue to be so. Yet, there is considerable disappointment with these forms of accountability because often they are not practice relevant, and thus far they have failed to provide meaningful results in terms of effectiveness monitoring and improved quality of client care. A third form of accountability, however, defined as *service outcome accountability* (SOA), focuses on detecting or measuring desired positive change. It does not matter what we do—what professional behavior we engage in; what does matter is the demonstration of desired change or the lack thereof. As professional caregivers, our service behaviors do matter, of course—we should not engage in service delivery behaviors that do not result in desired change, or at least have a good probability of producing desired change. From an SOA perspective, however, the nature of any specific interventive behavior does not matter unless it produces desired change.

THE FUNDAMENTAL EQUATION
OF THE EMPIRICAL PRACTICE MODEL

At this point we have defined the concept of effectiveness in terms of the concept of desired change, and we have defined service outcome accountability or SOA as a system that captures and uses information about such change—about outcomes. It is therefore a simple matter to build a very elegant model of SOA for use in the empirical practice model through use of the language of elementary mathematics. We begin by defining an outcome variable, often spoken of as a dependent variable. First, we define the concept of a *client problem*, or *CP*, as measured (or understood) at some point in time, t_1. We shall denote this measure (or understanding) of the client's problem at t_1 as CP_1. In an effort to improve the client's lot in life (i.e., to help her or him solve a problem), we shall *do something* (i.e., engage in some form of service delivery behavior) and then look at the same client problem, or *CP*, as measured (or understood) at some point in time, t_2. When we do that, we hope that we can see some improvement (desired change) from t_1 to t_2. That is, we hope that the client's problem as measured (or understood) at time t_2, CP_2, is much improved relative to CP_1. This provides us with a simple definition of desired change:

$$\Delta CP = CP_1 - CP_2 \qquad (1.1)$$

where Δ stands for "difference" or "change."

We have now defined the left side of our service outcome accountability (SOA) or empirical practice model; now we turn to the right side of the equation. That is where what we do—our service behaviors—matters. If we denote these service behaviors as $X_1, X_2, \ldots X_n$, signifying the fact that there are potentially many different service behaviors in which we engage for our client, we can complete the model (or equation) by expressing desired change as a function of our caregiving behavior. That is, the model is fully specified by writing:

$$\Delta CP = CP_1 - CP_2 = f(x_1, x_2, \ldots x_n) + e \qquad (1.2)$$

or, in even more succinct form, as:

$$\Delta CP = f(x_i) + e, \qquad i = 1, 2, \ldots n \qquad (1.3)$$

where the term $f(x_i)$, or $f(x_1, x_2, \ldots x_n)$, indicates that the change in the client's problem(s) is a function of (i.e., is related to) the caregiving behaviors $x_1, x_2, \ldots x_n$ in which we engage, and the letter e indicates that there are some things that affect client change that are unpredictable and over which we have no control. Thus, Equation 1.3, $\Delta CP = f(x_i) + e$, is a shorthand way of saying that the change in the client's problem(s) is related to the $i = 1, 2, 3, \ldots n$ caregiving behaviors in which we engage as well as to other unpredictable and uncontrollable factors.

The beauty of Equation 1.3 is its elegant simplicity and the fact that it serves two purposes. First, it is a model for research that addresses the question, "Are the caregiving services (behaviors) actually related to desired change?" Second, it becomes the EPM mandate that says, "Desired change must be shown to be a function of caregiving behavior." The term e in the model represents "error" (or residual) and merely notes the fact that perfect prediction or explanation is simply not possible. For those who do not like (or have difficulty understanding) mathematical models, the model of Equation 1.3 expresses an incredibly simple idea: *The positive change in our clients' problems should be at least in part a result of what we do to help them.* And this leads us to the second rule of EPM.

The Second Rule of EPM

The scientific and professional basis for EPM resides in the fact that measured positive change in the client's problem is shown to be a function of the services that were provided.

In summary, we can rather easily capture information about the presence and degree of client change. That measured change represents the left side of the empirical practice model shown in Equation 1.3. Moreover, we can also quite easily capture information about the services that were provided to a client, as shown in the righthand side of Equation 1.3. The second rule of EPM, however, requires that the left side of this equation be a function of the right side—in other words, that what is on the right side (our interventive behaviors) caused the left side (the desired changes in the client's problem[s]).

No doubt, professional interventive behavior is not the only influence that will produce change in a measured client problem. There are many factors in the environment that may operate to enhance or even harm the client's potential for positive change, and those factors should be taken into account. Thus, it is a simple matter to denote these environmental factors as E_1, E_2, . . . E_k, to signify the fact that there are potentially many different environmental influences that can affect client change. There are also many internal, or maturational, factors that may operate to cause change in the client's problem. We can denote the internal factors as I_1, I_2, . . . I_m. Thus, we can create another model (or equation) by expressing desired change as a function of the environment and of natural internal (maturational) forces, such that:

$$\Delta\ CP = CP_1 - CP_2$$
$$= f\ (E_1,\ E_2,\ .\ .\ .\ E_k) + f\ (I_1,\ I_2,\ .\ .\ .\ I_m)$$

or

$$\Delta CP = f\ (E_j) + f\ (I_l) + e \qquad\qquad (1.4)$$

where $j = 1, 2, . . . k$; and $l = 1, 2, . . . m$.

It will come as no surprise to see that we can combine the models of Equations 1.3 and 1.4 to produce a much richer model to account for both:

$$\Delta CP = f\ (x_i) + f\ (E_j) + f\ (I_l) + e \qquad\qquad (1.5)$$

where $i = 1, 2, . . . n; j = 1, 2, . . . k; l = 1, 2, ... m$. The final model of Equation 1.5 merely asserts that client change is in part due to professional interventive behavior (X_i), in part due to environmental (E_j) and internal forces (I_l), and that it must include an error term (e) to represent the fact that perfect prediction or explanation is simply impossible.

For some very good reasons (the details of which are too complex to be discussed here), we can largely ignore the models of Equations 1.4 and 1.5 and proceed with the empirical practice model of Equation 1.3, which says that positive client change must be in part a function of professional caregiving behavior if we are to make the claim that we are providing "effective" interventions.

COST BENEFIT ANALYSIS

Cost benefit analysis is a true siren song to nearly all rational thinkers. How could it be otherwise? The logic is compelling, and the appeal is nearly irresistible—define a benefit, look at the cost of obtaining it, compute a cost benefit ratio, compare the result to other cost benefit ratios similarly obtained, and select the best available ratio as indicating the preferred mode of service delivery.

Despite its enormous appeal, cost benefit analysis has been exceedingly difficult to accomplish in the human services and will continue to be so until we begin to understand and use the concept of measured change (ΔCP) as defined earlier. In short, we must define the concept of a *benefit* as:

$$Benefit = CP_2 - CP_1 = \Delta CP \qquad (1.6)$$

Suppose, for example, that a social service agency uses three different strategies to treat family violence. A first step would be to define three benefits, B_1, B_2, and B_3, where

$$B_i = CP_{i2} - CP_{i1} = \Delta CP_i, \, i = 1, 2, 3 \qquad (1.7)$$

and to compute that value for each client in each treatment group. We could then compute the average cost benefit ratio for each approach to treating family violence. It would then be a simple matter to compare results for the three service delivery strategies. Of course, there is more to it than this, but the keynote of success (and failure if we continue to ignore it) is the ability to actually measure, at a minimum, the values of CP_1 and CP_2 with accuracy, reliability, and validity. In summary, the major reasons for prior failures of cost benefit analyses arise from inadequate definitions of *benefit* and the failure to use reliable and valid measurement tools.

There are, of course, many different ways to conceptualize the notion of "benefit" (political benefits, planning benefits, technological benefits, training benefits, etc.), but the focus here is on a discussion of service outcome accountability that ultimately drives all other considerations. We can now take the concepts discussed thus far and look more closely at the *empirical practice model*.

EMPIRICAL PRACTICE MODEL

For purposes of this book, we shall define the *empirical practice model* (EPM) as a form of practice that uses Equation 1.3 and some additional tools of science to enhance the quality of service delivery, treatment, or therapy with the aim of increasing the likelihood of a more *positive outcome* (ΔCP) for the client.

Empirical practice refers to practice, as opposed to research. Moreover, the entire corpus of EPM is based entirely on three fundamental procedures:

1. Measure the client's problem(s).
2. Measure the client's problem(s) repeatedly over time.
3. Assess the extent to which positive change in the client's problem(s) is associated with the intervention.

The core elements of EPM are as simple, and as complicated, as implied by these three procedures. The first procedure implies that we must learn a great deal about applied measurement theory, and that is a topic that comprises a substantial part of this book—we shall explain in considerable detail how to accurately measure clients' problems. The second procedure implies that we must at a minimum use some form of nonexperimental time-series design to monitor progress, and the third procedure implies that some kind of manipulation of treatment may be required. We must structure services in such a manner that we can compare the across-time profile of the client's problem *in the absence* of services with the across-time profile of the client's problem *during* services. The second and third innovations are covered in detail in Part II of this book, but the following text provides a brief introduction to them.

A Simple Monitoring Design

Figure 1.1 illustrates the first two elements or innovations of EPM. This is the case of a hypothetical 28-year-old woman who sought help with depression following abandonment by her husband and a subsequent divorce. In this case we have no information about the nature of the treatment given to the client, and there is no indication that the treatment was manipulated. All measures of the client's problem were made *during* service provision. All that we see are the results of measuring the client's level of depression, doing that repeatedly over time on a weekly basis, and a simple graph of those results. Yet, this simple graph is worthy of serious thought and consideration.

The first thing to notice is the use of the *generalized contentment scale* or GCS (Hudson, 1997) to measure the client's level of depression. It is for that reason that the vertical axis of the graph is labeled as "GCS Scores." Higher scores on the GCS are indicative of depression of greater magnitude, and vice versa. The second very conspicuous feature of the graph is that the client completed the GCS scale once a week and that she made steady improvement in reducing the level of her depression, as evidenced by her decreasing GCS scores. *We see in this simple graph a dramatic illustration of positive change.* Equally important, we see in this simple illustration two of the core ingredients of EPM—measure the client's problem, and do so repeatedly over time.

In the next chapter you will come to know the time-series graph of Figure 1.1 as a simple monitoring, or B, design. Its enormous power resides in the fact that it can dramatically document the progress that a client makes in solving the problem for which he or she has sought professional help. Does this

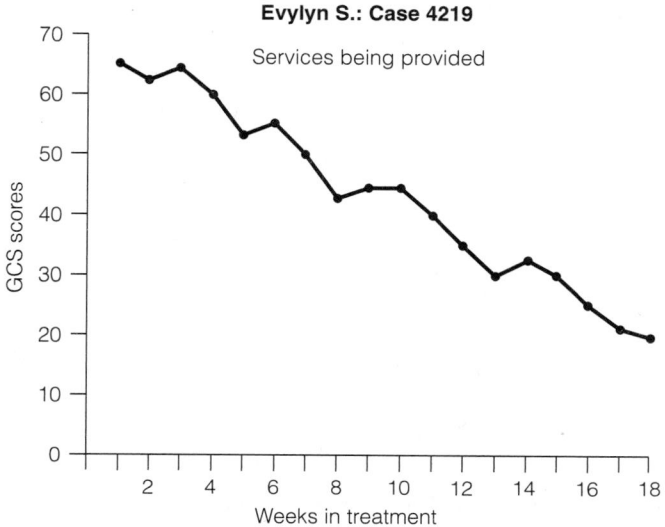

FIGURE 1.1 Single-case data for Evylyn S.

kind of evidence measure up to the first rule of EPM? Absolutely! Does it measure up to the second rule of EPM? Absolutely *not!*

The simple monitoring design shown in Figure 1.1 provides virtually no information about the effectiveness of the services provided to the client. The reason is that no effort was made to compare the client's across-time problem profile without any services with the client's across-time problem profile during service provision. The dramatic improvement shown by this client could be due to the services provided, or it could be due to one or more external events—she met a new friend, she got a promotion on her job, she just got better over time, and so on. Positive change could be completely accounted for by one or more of the factors in the model of Equation 1.4—that is, by environmental or internal factors as opposed to the services provided.

However, consider the hypothetical case of Adelio M. shown in Figure 1.2. The significant difference between this figure and Figure 1.1 is that we now have performed at least a rudimentary manipulation of the intervention. We have a pretreatment profile of the client's problem that we can compare with an across-time profile of the client's problem obtained during treatment. That makes all the difference! Since Adelio M.'s GCS scores do not begin to show a decrease until treatment starts, we now have some basis for claiming that it was the treatment that was responsible for the dramatic positive change.

In order to understand the simple graph shown in Figure 1.2, it is important to know that the first three measures of Adelio M.'s depression were obtained while he was undergoing assessment and waiting to be assigned a counselor. The first one was obtained when Adelio walked into the clinic, the second during his second visit (when assessment was underway, but before

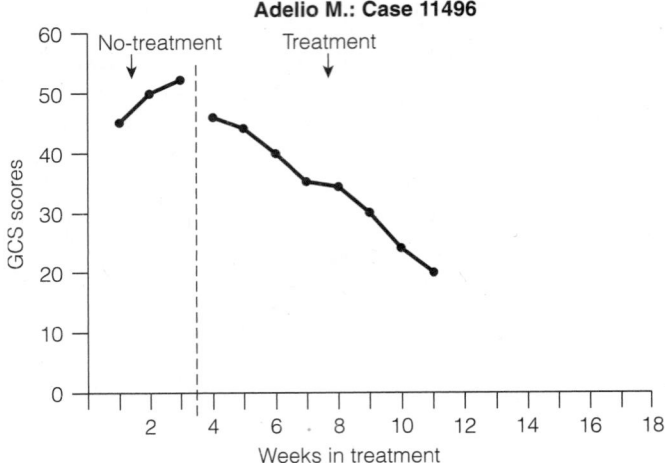

FIGURE 1.2 Single-case data for Adelio M. This figure shows a basic manipulation of treatment—a no-treatment period followed by a treatment period.

treatment started), and the third on his third visit immediately before the assigned counselor initiated treatment. In short, Adelio did not receive any professional treatment during the first two weeks following his initial contact with the agency. The first three measures shown in Figure 1.2 can be described as a *no-treatment (or baseline) period* (or phase) for Adelio.

As implied by the structure of the graph in Figure 1.2, a counselor was assigned to Adelio's case and the treatment for his depression began during the third week, and treatment was continued for the subsequent 8 weeks as shown in the graph. The 8-week period of contact and work with the client can be described as the *treatment period* (or phase) for Adelio.

The logic and the data speak to us rather forcefully. During the baseline or no-treatment period, Adelio M. received no services other than assessment, and he made no progress; in fact, he got worse. During the treatment period, Adelio received the treatment provided by his counselor, and he made steady improvement. The evidence is simple and suggestive—there was no improvement in the absence of treatment, and when treatment was provided there was consistent positive change. The logic and the data lead us to the conclusion that it was the services provided by the counselor that helped Adelio to overcome a serious problem with depression. The logic and the data are compelling in suggesting to us that $\Delta CP = f(X_i)$ and that we have abided the first *and* second rules of EPM. But who is, or should be, convinced of this—and who should not be convinced?

Before we turn to this question, note that you have now seen the two most useful time-series designs in the whole of the empirical practice model—the simple designs shown in Figures 1.1 and 1.2. Moreover, these two designs form a powerful basis for helping practitioners to improve service delivery to clients, for helping supervisors to guide and direct that work, and for helping administrators to evaluate an entire program of services and to dramatically report and describe the success of everyone's efforts. Mastering and using these two designs while employing reliable and valid measures of clients' problems conquers the most important challenges of quality assurance, and this is incredibly easy to do.

Although much more needs to be said and understood about these two simple designs and the task of measuring the client's problem, the material covered thus far forms the solid core for a full implementation of the empirical practice model within nearly any practice setting, agency, or human service organization. (Exceptions will be discussed in later chapters.) The remainder of this book will demonstrate how to achieve such results on a routine and regular basis. But for now, let us return to the question of who should and should not be convinced of the evidence and claims for the effectiveness of service delivery.

SCIENTIST AND PRACTITIONER

Almost any well-trained scientist would tell you that the logic and data that are illustrated and presented in Figure 1.2 are neither compelling nor convincing of the claim that it was the services provided that caused Adelio M.'s improvement. Moreover, there are specific and compelling reasons for that assertion. On the other hand, any well-trained and long-experienced practitioner would tell you in no uncertain terms that the evidence speaks for itself. The data in Figure 1.2 are an unmistakable demonstration of the effectiveness of delivered services, and complaints to the contrary are scientific nitpicking. Both the scientist and the practitioner would be correct.

Herein lies one of the oldest and fiercest conflicts in the whole of human services—the battle *royale* between scientist and practitioner. This conflict has served for entirely too many decades as a major barrier to mutual understanding and productive collaboration between scientists and practitioners, and it must be resolved. The simple truth is that both are correct (and both are wrong) because the "correctness" of their arguments is completely role-dependent.

Consider a patient's visit to a physician. The physician examines the patient carefully, notes all the symptoms, takes some throat cultures, and on the basis of laboratory tests concludes that the patient has a bad case of strep throat. The physician then prescribes some antibiotics along with some palliatives and behavioral recommendations concerning work, rest, and diet and sends the patient home to mend. Two weeks later the physician notes during a follow-up visit that the fever and nausea are gone and there is no lingering evidence of the presence of streptococcus. The patient "got well."

The physician has not used the elementary experimental design illustrated in Figure 1.2 but, instead, has used the simpler monitoring design shown in

Figure 1.1. The physician measured the patient's problem at t_1 (the first office visit) and again at t_2 (the second office visit) and made note of the clear and dramatic improvement. If asked whether this was compelling evidence that the antibiotics did the trick, the physician would likely retort, "Absolutely." A biological scientist, however, would likely retort, "Absolutely *not*." The physician's situation is the same as that of a practicing human services professional. So who is right and who is wrong—physician or scientist? Both are right (and wrong), depending on their roles.

Practitioner Role

The physician has three fundamental obligations to the patient and to her colleagues as a member of a self-regulated profession. Her first duty is to accurately evaluate the nature and severity of the patient's problem (to collect some data with which to render a diagnosis). Her second duty is to engage in professional behavior that is known to have a high likelihood of producing a desired outcome (prescribe the antibiotics). Her third duty is to determine whether there was positive change (the patient got well). The physician, like the human services professional, is duty-bound to fulfill the first rule of EPM—to measure her client's problem repeatedly over time.

The physician is *not* duty-bound to scientifically *prove* that it was the antibiotics that actually caused the demise of the streptococcus that invaded the patient's body and produced the illness that was displayed in the detected symptoms. However, she (like the human services professional) is duty-bound to administer treatments (engage in professional behavior) that are known by scientifically credible evidence to have a high likelihood of producing positive change. This leads to the third rule of EPM.

The Third Rule of EPM

Human services practitioners are required by the ethics of their profession to learn about and use those services or interventions that have been shown through credible scientific evidence to have a high likelihood of producing desired positive change.

Scientist Role

In the example of the physician's treatment of strep throat, it is unquestionably the duty of the scientist to demonstrate that it was indeed the antibiotics that got rid of the infection. That is a very big and difficult job, and the rules for demonstrating that the treatment was indeed the cause of the improvement are different—much more demanding and stringent. For the scientist, the logic and data presented in Figure 1.2 are not strong enough to rule out a host of other possible sources of the change observed in Amelio M.'s depression (remember the terms $f(E_j)$ and $f(I_l)$ in Equation 1.4). These data are not even remotely convincing for the scientist, and the logic is certainly not very compelling. The scientist (in medical or human services) is not responsible for the care, treatment, and delivery of services to specific patients or clients. The scientist *is* responsible for developing and validating, through the use of credible methods and evidence, the diagnostic and interventive knowledge base that will be passed on for use by the practitioner. The methods and rules for doing that are very stringent; the scientist's colleagues are acutely aware of those rules and methods, and the scientist's evidence, methods, and claims are rightly placed under painfully close scrutiny.

Role Dependency in Science and Practice

In both the medical and the human services professions and disciplines, the lines between practice and research are very clear. The practitioner is responsible for the delivery of effective treatment, services, or interventions, and the scientist is responsible for the knowledge base that must be provided to the practitioner. The rub comes when the knowledge base is weak, incomplete, or has significant gaps—or when someone tries to be both scientist *and* practitioner simultaneously.

The rules of evidence that are deemed appropriate and acceptable are entirely dependent on the role that is played by the user of those rules. The rules of evidence appropriate for use by the practitioner are not appropriate or acceptable for the scientist. Similarly, the rules of evidence required of the scientist are not appropriate for the practitioner. Two critical points help to resolve the old and rather unproductive battle between scientists and practitioners:

1. When one occupies the role of practitioner, one is duty-bound to pursue *the goals of practice*—the provision of services, care, and treatment to clients. The rules of evidence that are used and needed to demonstrate that one has achieved a goal of practice may be entirely adequate and acceptable for the practitioner (and her or his practice colleagues) but be, to some extent, inadequate for the scientist.

2. When one occupies the role of scientist, one is duty-bound to pursue *the goals of science*—and that means one must convince the scientific community that one has done that. The rules of evidence required to fulfill the role of scientist can, and often do, represent very good science but very poor practice.

The considerable role ambiguity and confusion that arises in this regard does so largely because of the woefully incomplete knowledge base that is needed for use of the EPM. In the face of incomplete knowledge, the practitioner often becomes interested in the scientific problems of developing better treatments or services for use in practice. Similarly, the scientist often becomes invested in issues of practice in order to develop and pursue the goals of science. Evidence produced by the practitioner may demonstrate good practice but also constitute lousy science. Similarly, the evidence produced by the scientist may demonstrate good science but be seen as poor practice. As noted by Thomas (1978), it is all but impossible to simultaneously conduct both superb practice and superb science.

The great benefit of understanding these important differences is simple enough. The evidence of effectiveness produced by the practitioner may feed and stimulate, but not satisfy, the scientist, and the evidence produced by the scientist may feed and stimulate, but not satisfy, the practitioner. As for reducing role ambiguity, it is useful to pose two questions:

1. If I am pursuing a goal of practice, am I using rules of evidence that will satisfy my obligations to my clients and my professional colleagues in the practice community?
2. If I am pursuing a goal of science, am I using rules of evidence that will satisfy the requirements of my colleagues in the scientific community?

The purpose of this book is not to teach you how to *do science*—other books do that quite well. The purpose of this book is to explain how *some* of the tools of science can be used to conduct and improve the quality of practice and to demonstrate effectiveness in providing services to clients.

THE ROLE OF FEEDBACK

Chapters 4 and 5 will cover single-case time-series designs in more detail, but here an overview of their use is presented. From a practice perspective, the most important use of these designs is *not* to determine whether it was a treatment or service that was responsible for an achieved positive change. Rather, the most valuable application of these designs is to use them to provide feedback information to the practitioner that will help him or her to shape or modify the treatment or service delivery plan. This core feature of their use provides the single most important benefit of the empirical practice model as a device for enhancing the effectiveness of practice. It is essential to understand this at the beginning, which is why it is illustrated in this first chapter.

Feedback: An Illustration

Elementary time-series data provides its most powerful benefit when used to provide us and our clients with feedback information about problem-solving progress or the lack of it. In order to see how such feedback can be used for treatment planning purposes, we shall look at the progress of Tommy J. who is being treated for severe reactive depression following the death of his 16-year-old son who was killed in a head-on automobile collision. The first graph (see Figure 1.3) shows that we have administered the GCS once a week for the first three weeks of treatment.

Please note: Though the data in Figure 1.3 come from a hypothetical case, you may still have some rather strong professional reactions to the graphs that you will see. Please take notice of them for later discussion because this may be a suicidal client.

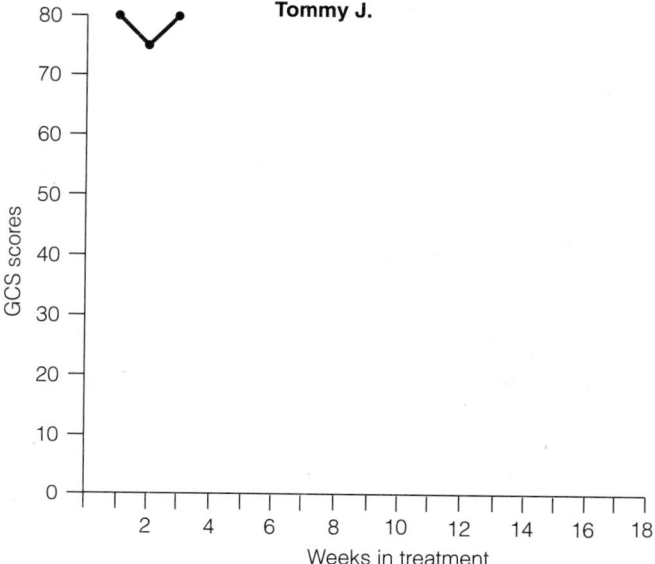

FIGURE 1.3 Single-case data for Tommy J.

The Beginning In the first three-week period of contact with the client, we see that, hardly out of the intake, assessment, and planning phase of treatment, the practitioner has little more than a good picture of the severity of the client's problem. Yet, the picture given to us by the graph in Figure 1.3 provides a great deal of important information. The depression score exceeds 70 in all three administrations, and the practitioner would therefore be concerned about *a possible suicide attempt* (the reason for that is explained in Hudson, 1997). At this point, the practitioner likely has a well-formulated treatment plan, has been implementing it in an effort to reduce Tommy's depression, and hopes very soon to begin seeing some progress in alleviation of the severity of the depression. Although there may be a well-formulated treatment plan in place, we do not know what it is and therefore will not discuss it at this point. For our purposes, we note in Figure 1.3 that the depression for Tommy J. is very severe and that there is no evidence of improvement over the first three weeks. Perhaps that is not of major concern because, one might argue, the treatment has not yet had a chance to take effect and produce improvement. That having been said, however, the continuation of Tommy's severe depression, as evidenced by the continued high GCS scores, *is critical feedback to the social worker.*

The treatment or service package being delivered in this case may very well not yet have had time to produce a decline in the level of Tommy J.'s depression. When Tommy comes in for his fourth session, however, the practitioner will ask him to once again complete the GCS scale. When he does that, the practitioner will update the graph shown in Figure 1.3 and thereby capture information about whether and to what extent there has been any improvement in the client's problem.

Although we will show the results of this treatment effort by examining seven different graphs (Figures 1.3 through 1.9), it is important to recognize that the practitioner will be using only one graph, updated each time the client completes the assessment scale, to monitor the specific problem that is being addressed. We have broken this progression into seven different graphs only to illustrate what we mean by the notion of feedback and to thereby recognize the important, even central, role that it plays in the use of the empirical practice model.

Let us now return to Tommy J. and look at Figure 1.4 to see if he has made any progress. Obviously, the fourth week has not been a good one for Tommy. His GCS score, in fact, is a little higher than before despite the fact that we had hoped to see at least some small beginning improvement. It still may be premature to expect positive change for Tommy because it often takes some measure of time and effort to make a noticeable dent in cases of this nature. We may therefore decide that our best course of action is to continue with the treatment plan that we have developed and see what will develop during the next week.

Although we must be "fair" in making any judgments about the effectiveness of the service or treatment, we note again that we have a serious problem on our hands—a possible suicidal client. Thus, although we can be "generous" in our judgments about the efficacy of treatment in a theoretical sense, neither the practitioner nor the client can afford any excesses in complacency. In short, we should be mindful of the third rule of EPM in our continuing efforts to help Tommy with his serious problem with depression. Let us see how he does next week.

Still No Improvement   Week five (Figure 1.5) shows that the apparent upward trend we saw at the end of the previous week did not continue. That is good to see. However, the level of depression for Tommy J. is still very high, and there is no evidence to suggest that the treatment is having a positive effect.

Once again, it may be our best judgment that changing the treatment plan might be premature (though in this case a continuation of "more of the same" may be a breach of the practitioner's duties to provide an appropriate "standard of care" for the client; Bongar et al., 1998). Success in severe cases of depression often takes time, and this case may well be no exception. Nonetheless, there should now be some cause for concern about the effectiveness of the treatment given that five weeks have gone by, there has been no change, and there is such great potential for a critical event in the life of this client.

Despite our growing concerns about the efficacy of the treatment plan, let us continue the treatment and see what develops by the next session with the client. If we see a very large or even clinically significant turn for the better, we will be encouraged about the clinical decisions made thus far. The results are shown in Figure 1.6.

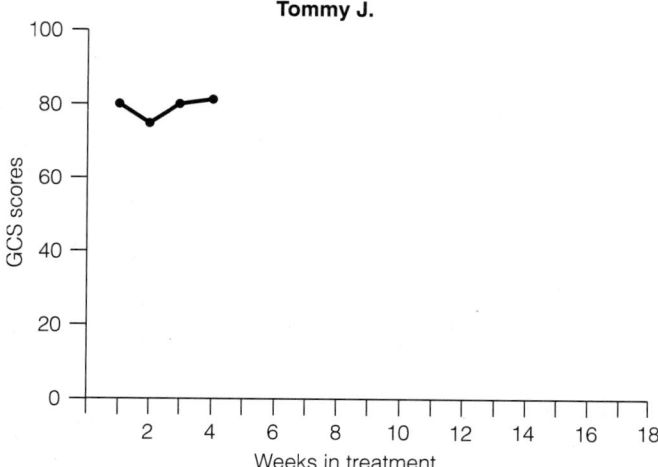

FIGURE 1.4 Single-case data for Tommy J.

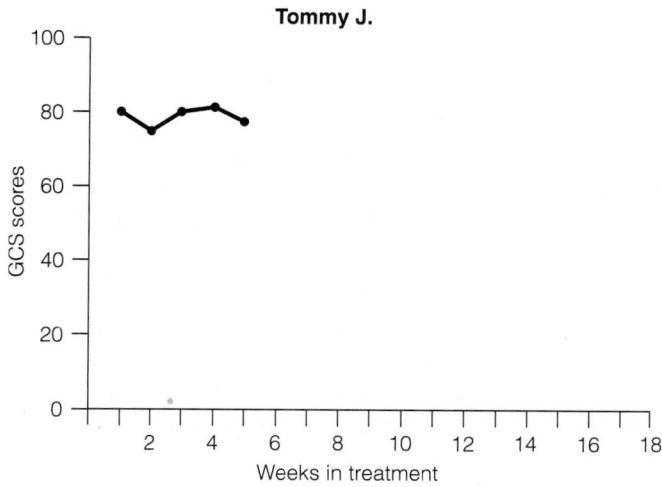

FIGURE 1.5 Single-case data for Tommy J.

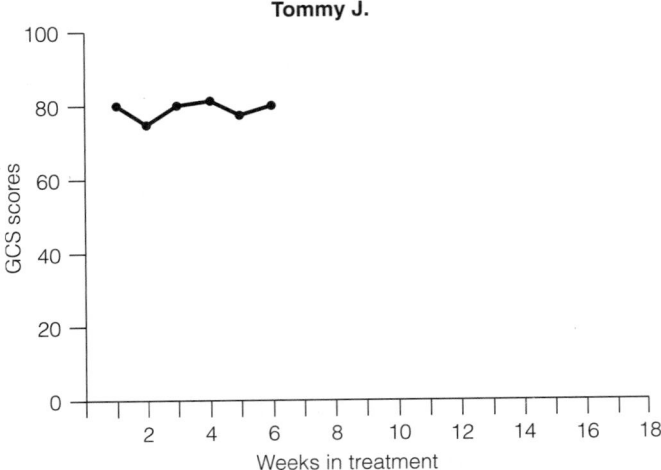

FIGURE 1.6 Single-case data for Tommy J.

When Shall We Change the Treatment? We can now clearly see what is perhaps the single most important feature of using time-series data as a feedback mechanism. We have seen no improvement in the level of depression after six weeks of working with Tommy J. Those who adhere very strongly to a short-term treatment model will interpret these data as demanding immediate reassessment of the treatment plan and may feel that a change in treatment was mandated much earlier. Those who adhere to long-term treatment models will see the same data very differently. That is not the point at all. The critical point is that *we must react to time-series feedback information.*

> Routine feedback information showing no positive change in the level of severity or level of the problem will eventually dictate a change in treatment regardless of your theoretical orientation. There is no need to quibble amongst ourselves over what is the correct theory.

We have no intention of discussing what might be the appropriate intervention or theoretical orientation to use with clients. Use of the empirical practice model does not require it, and such matters are best covered by texts devoted to methods and techniques of treatment. In the case of Tommy J., however, the practitioner did make a major change in the treatment plan, and we can now look at the next period to see if that change in the treatment had any positive effect.

Evidence of Positive Change The evidence shown in Figure 1.7 is much more encouraging. We can now see a very definite positive change in the level of the client's depression, which strongly suggests that the change in treatment (whatever it may have been) was a good one.

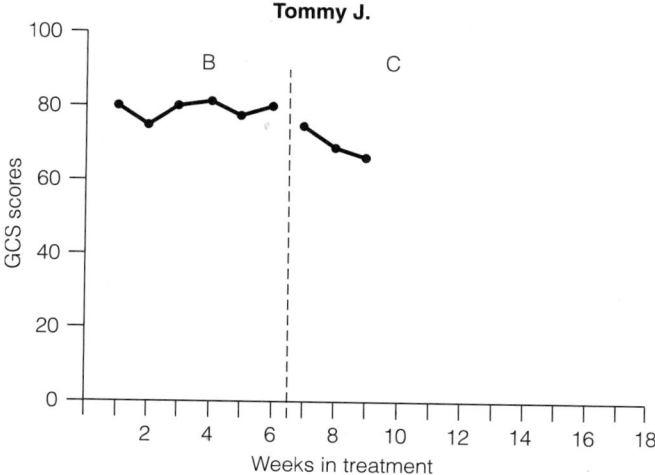

FIGURE 1.7 Single-case data for Tommy J.

As discussed earlier in this chapter, the human services scientist would quickly assert that the evidence in Figure 1.7 is virtually worthless if it is used in an attempt to scientifically validate the treatment as being responsible for the observed positive change in this case. We are not attempting to pursue a goal of science, however, and therefore we do not assume the responsibility of conducting our work with sufficient rigor to persuade our scientific colleagues of any such claims about the causal impact of the intervention.

To the contrary, we are pursuing a goal of practice; our primary responsibility is not to the scientific community, but to our client and our professional colleagues who share our practice-related goals. If our scientific colleagues cannot understand and appreciate that practice concern and orientation, that is their problem and not ours. Our first duty is to the client, and not to science. Admittedly, we have a duty to select treatments in accord with the third rule of EPM, but that is a shared responsibility—our scientific colleagues must first provide the scientifically validated interventive knowledge base. We, of course, have to learn about and use validated treatment techniques. Let us now look at the next period to see whether the downward trend has continued.

Making Use of Anomalous Changes In the graph shown in Figure 1.8 we see that the downward trend in the level of depression has continued, but we note also the conspicuous spike that occurred during week 13. Such anomalous spikes are referred to as *critical incidents;* we must check them out and note the results in the record. In this case, Tommy J. encountered a serious and bloody automobile accident on the highway, and the event of being confronted with that tragedy flooded him with the pain of his son's death. The subsequent drop

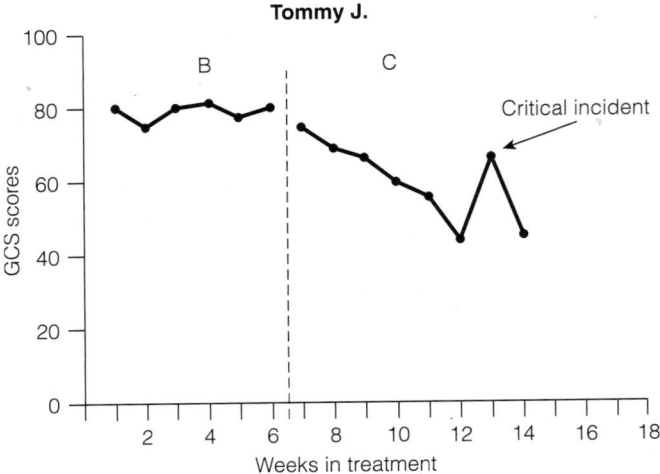

FIGURE 1.8 Single-case data for Tommy J.

in level of depression suggests that his setback was transient. Now let us wrap up this case by looking at the results at the time the case was closed.

The Final Picture for Tommy J.   The overall picture for Tommy J. cannot be seen until we near the end of treatment and begin termination. Once there, as seen in the graph in Figure 1.9, the result is pleasing. Despite the desirability of obtaining the final picture of success, the most important role of using time-series monitoring is the feedback that it provides on a weekly basis. That feedback function dramatically supports the critical work of treatment planning and of making appropriate changes to the treatment of choice.

THE PROMISE OF THE EPM

The promise of the empirical practice model is simple, clear, and direct. If the practitioner will learn and then actually use the methods of the EPM, *we guarantee that he or she will improve as a practitioner in terms of producing more frequent and much larger positive outcomes or benefits for his or her clients.* There is, in fact, research evidence supporting this claim (Slonim-Nevo & Anson, 1998). If we are wrong, write to us, show us the data that supports and documents the failure, and we will publicly retract this claim. *We also guarantee that if you learn about the methods of EPM but do not actually use them, they will not work!*

Because of the high promise and easily mastered technology of EPM, we have a profound moral and professional obligation to teach it and use it in virtually every professional service organization that pretends (in the best sense of the word) to offer a benefit to clients. That we are not doing this points to the

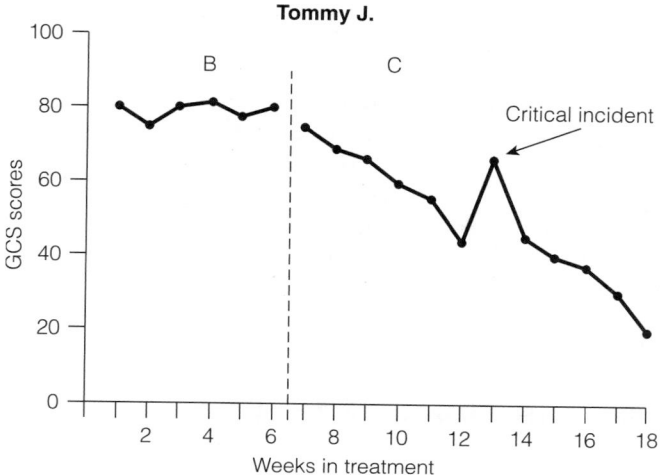

FIGURE 1.9 Single-case data for Tommy J.

fact that we are professionally delinquent in providing adequate services to our clients—worldwide!

The EPM for Everyone

It may appear that the empirical practice model is designed primarily for use by practitioners—those who must actually provide the services, treatments, or interventions to clients. Indeed, it is a fundamentally important *direct practice* tool, but it is also much more than that. It takes little imagination to see how a collection of outcome-oriented graphic reports such as those shown in the figures in this chapter can be an enormous aid to *supervisors,* who can see at a mere glance the nature and extent of progress (or lack thereof) for any client, with respect to any problem, at any specified point in time. It also takes little imagination to recognize how *administrators, program evaluators, and policy makers* may capitalize on the use of this model. An agency that adopts the empirical practice model and uses it consistently with clients will quickly develop an incredible database of outcome-oriented findings with respect to different clients, with different problems and circumstances, who have received different services. Managerial, planning, and evaluation personnel can then aggregate, sort, and organize agencywide information in order to support the work of guiding, managing, and administering social services. Chapters 11 and 12 in Nurius and Hudson (1993) address these tasks in considerable detail, and the process has been automated in the *Computer Assisted Social Services (CASS)* software (Hudson, 1996) that will be presented and discussed later in this book.

The history of information acquisition and management is stamped hard with a pattern that practitioners the world over know very well: Most demands for evaluation and service delivery information are imposed on practitioners by managers from the top down; little is ever done by way of soliciting practitioner input or judgment; and the results often are useless to both the administrator and the practitioner. The consequence has been a historical battle between the top and the bottom levels of entirely too many agencies—each accusing the other of being irrelevant, ignorant, insensitive, or at least unappreciative. The empirical practice model may help to mend this enormous gulf between these critical groups of organizational actors by securing information that is useful to everyone in the organization—those at the top and those at the bottom. A significant portion of this book will explain how to accomplish that.

A HUMAN PROBLEM THEORY

Nearly all of the assessment scales, unidimensional and multidimensional, that are described or discussed in this book are designed to measure a separate and distinct problem in personal or social functioning. Each scale (measurement tool) is viewed, by analogy, as being similar to a thermometer. A thermometer will measure the temperature of an object, but it will provide no information about the source, cause, or origin of the heat. A thermometer will inform a physician of the presence of a fever, but it is useless in giving information about what caused the fever.

The assessment scales we describe and recommend in this book perform very much like a thermometer. They do a good job of indicating that a client has a problem in an area addressed by one of the scales and of indicating how serious that problem may be; however, none of the scales provide any information whatsoever about the source or cause of the problem(s) they measure.

To continue the analogy, a thermometer is theoretically based only in the sense that it is interpreted from the theory of molecular motions (statistical thermodynamics). A thermometer is completely atheoretical with respect to theories about the causes of a particular temperature change. Similarly, the measurement tools we recommend in subsequent chapters are theoretical with respect to the definition and measurement of problems in personal and social functioning, but they are completely atheoretical with respect to theories about the cause and control of those problems.

For purposes of description, consider the theory of molecular motion as a microtheory and a theory about the causes of heat and heat transfer as a macrotheory. (We recognize that physicists may complain of our abuse of thermodynamics.) The microtheory of molecular motion is useful in studying the behavior of thermometers. Likewise, the basic elements of a microtheory that are presented for the definition and measurement of problems in living are useful for understanding the theoretical orientation of the assessment scales and how they function as measurement devices. No effort is made in this book to develop or defend a macrotheory about the cause or origin of personal and social problems. For example, the assessment scales we describe and use will not help you to understand why family members assault one another should you wish to construct a theory of family violence. On the other hand, several of the assessment scales will provide valuable information about the severity of problems in the area of family violence.

A microtheory about personal and social problems is best created and understood within the context of first examining the basic approach to measurement that was used in the development of the many different scales we describe. The approach is straightforward and consists of little more than asking respondents to report the relative frequency of occurrence of the behavior, affect, or perception that is represented by the content of a specific scale item. For example, the fourth item of the GCS scale (a measure of clinical depression) states, "I have crying spells," and the respondent is asked to report how frequently that behavior occurs on a scale from 1 to 7, where 1 = None of the time and 7 = All of the time. The item scores obtained from the items comprising the GCS are summed and linearly transformed in order to obtain a total score that ranges from 0 to 100. If the obtained GCS score is both reliable and valid, we can claim that we have measured something called "depression," but we cannot yet claim that we have measured a personal adjustment problem. The following microtheory about human problems provides a basis for making the claim that we have measured a human problem.

The core ingredients of the microtheory of human problems consist of two fundamental axioms. These axioms state:

1. Human problems do not exist until someone defines them.
2. All human problems are defined in terms of a value base.

Two major implications of these axioms must always be kept in mind when using the problem-oriented measurement scales to evaluate problems in living. The first is that any conclusion about the presence of any personal or social functioning problem or disorder is always based on the value position of the person who draws the conclusion. That is, a problem does not exist until someone defines it, and problems are always defined in terms of someone's value position. This means that it is entirely possible, and not at all uncommon, for a practitioner to conclude that a client has a problem in some well-defined area of functioning but for the client to claim otherwise. Discrepancies of this nature can arise for at least two reasons: (1) the practitioner and client may be using different data, or the assessment scale may not be reliable and valid, and (2) the practitioner and the client may be using different value positions to draw conclusions about the presence of a problem in personal or social functioning.

The latter difficulty is especially important and can be illustrated with a familiar example. Traffic courts frequently refer people to human services professionals for the treatment of alcohol abuse that has come to the court's attention because of charges for driving a vehicle while intoxicated. The practitioner may administer the Multi-Problem Screening Inventory or MPSI scale (Hudson, 1990) to the client and obtain a high score on the alcohol abuse subscale, say, a score of 47. Under these circumstances, the practitioner will conclude that the client has a drinking problem, and the court has already arrived at that conclusion (which was the basis for the referral in the first place). The client, on the other hand, may strongly assert that he or she does not have a drinking problem ("I can hold my liquor with the best of them!") and is seeking help only because it was mandated by the court as a way to avoid stiff penalties. The facts in this case are indisputable, but the conclusions differ because the client and the practitioner are evaluating the facts from different value positions.

The second implication of the microtheory about problems in living has to do with the task of establishing clinical cutting scores for a particular assessment scale. In a very serious way, this task addresses the question of "How big is 'big'?" In other words, how large must a score be on a particular scale in order to properly conclude that the client has a clinically significant problem in the area being assessed? The use of the word *properly* in this context must be understood—at core, the method for establishing clinical cutting scores is one that is based entirely on the consensual judgment of experienced practitioners.

This means, quite clearly, that using the clinical cutting scores provided for an assessment scale involves an implicit decision to abide by the consensual judgments of those colleagues who participated in the establishment of the clinical cutting scores. It is also a recognition that those consensual judgments emerged from adherence to a common set of values with respect to the definitions of "clinically significant" problems in each of the areas of personal and social functioning represented by the particular scale.

This microtheory of human problems has many other implications that cannot be discussed here. The major purpose for stating it is to alert users of the assessment scales described in this book to the fact that the clinical cutting scores of such measures are by no means rigid points that discriminate the "sick" from the "well" or the "functional" from the "dysfunctional." At best, they are guidelines that practitioners can use to make well-guided decisions about the severity of client problems in a wide range of areas concerning personal and social functioning. Practitioners must, however, exercise their own professional judgments whenever they have a strong basis for departing from the typical prescriptions that are offered for interpretation of assessment scale scores.

THE ROLE OF MEASUREMENT

None of the foregoing will come to any fruition unless we find some way to actually measure a client's problem. In fact, there are many ways to measure a client's problem (Nurius & Hudson, 1993), but the empirical practice model uses primarily one approach—the short-form unidimensional assessment scales designed for use in repeated administrations with clients. The empirical practice model also makes use of more comprehensive multidimensional assessment scales, and those will be described later as assessment supports to describe client problems and conduct progress evaluations. However, the heart and soul of the empirical practice model is its use of short-form measures because of their efficiency and ease of use.

Chapter 11 provides information about the use and psychometric performance of many different short-form measurement scales that are readily available and were designed for use in assessing the severity or magnitude of a variety of personal and social problems. Each of the measurement tools described in Chapter 11 was designed for use by practitioners, service delivery personnel, and researchers who are in need of reliable and valid measures that describe the quality of personal and social functioning among individuals, couples, families, and small groups.

COMPUTERS AND THE EMPIRICAL PRACTICE MODEL

Virtually all of the materials described and discussed in this book can be employed and implemented with use of traditional paper-and-pencil methods. None of it is terribly difficult. Once you become acquainted with the empirical practice model and begin to incorporate it into your agency or practice, however, you will recognize additional uses of the information about your clients that you would like to implement. An example is the aggregation of client data for use in program evaluation. There are other uses as well that are all but impossible without the aid of computers. Thus, this book describes, illustrates, and makes use of the *Computer Assisted Social Services (CASS)* software, which includes a program called the *Computer Assisted Assessment Package (CAAP)* that is designed for use by your clients.

Chapters 17 through 22 of this book are devoted to use of the CASS and CAAP software and your computer. Computer analysis is quite easy once you learn about the many different features of the software and how best to put them to use. The CASS software implements all of the empirical practice methods described in this book, and more. However, we urge that you not rush into a computer implementation. Rather, read and make sure you understand the materials in the next several chapters, and then launch your use of the CASS software in your own practice.

PART I

Using Single-Case
Time-Series Designs

2

Designing for Effectiveness-Oriented Practice

In Chapter 1 we introduced the basic concepts and principles underlying the empirical practice model, or EPM. This model offers practitioners and human service agencies an incredibly powerful tool for evaluating the effectiveness of practice. Like the process of using any powerful tool, however, conducting useful practice evaluation does take some background work. One cannot simply say one is going to begin evaluating one's practice, and then start doing so without any background knowledge or preparation. In order to effectively conduct practice evaluation, you need to spend a bit of time developing fundamental knowledge about what the evaluation process looks like, how to plan for useful evaluation, how to conduct evaluation activities, and how to use the feedback offered by evaluation to improve service delivery.

This chapter provides the conceptual and practical foundations necessary for practitioners who wish to adopt an "effectiveness orientation" toward their practice. By necessity such an orientation is broad in scope, because the factors that influence and impinge upon practice are diverse. All practitioners are part of a larger context, one that includes norms, professional standards, administrative structures and tasks, financial restrictions, governmental regulations, and so on. The exact context may vary for specific human service practitioners, but in general we must all pay attention to a myriad of these details. The implication is that an "effectiveness orientation" must be sufficiently flexible to be used in a wide variety of situations and contexts. This demands a framework and technology that can be easily understood, implemented, modified, and guided.

In this chapter we present such a framework. It is a framework based on five levels of evaluation. These levels depend on the same general tasks and processes—setting goals and objectives or defining professional activities, for example. They differ, however, in the specific questions asked and the methodological techniques used to answer those questions. Although we will focus on the level of practice evaluation, it is hoped that after reading this chapter you will have a basic understanding of evaluation as a general process, and the linkages between practice and program evaluation.

Our first task is to briefly outline the levels of evaluation and the questions addressed by each level. This will be followed by a discussion of goals, program objectives, practice objectives, and activities. A brief discussion of how evaluation enhances decision making will also be presented. Next, we will discuss the importance of routine information collection and the techniques you can use to accomplish this task. Finally, we will suggest a set of practical questions and basic principles for effective information collection.

A BASIC EVALUATION TYPOLOGY

There are numerous models of evaluation available to guide both practitioners and human service agencies. Most incorporate a dual approach, one focusing on the evaluation of practice on a case level, the other focusing on evaluation of the programs professionals practice within the agency. Of course those in human services would ideally like to show effectiveness on both case and program levels. Indeed, to really establish the effectiveness of service delivery in human service programs, we *must* show effectiveness at both levels. This fact makes evaluation a central, increasingly important function of human service professionals and the agencies in which they work. In short, evaluation is *both* a micro and macro activity that should be routinely conducted on all aspects of professional practice.

Jacobs (1988) argues that useful evaluation requires models that can be modified to fit the needs of specific programs. This is accomplished by tailoring the questions and information collection along several fronts, such as determining the need for a program, establishing utilization patterns, monitoring resources, demonstrating progress toward program objectives, and identifying program impacts.

Jacobs (1988) also outlines a set of critical assumptions that underlie useful evaluation. These assumptions show the functions and roles of evaluation in any human service agency:

1. *Evaluation should be viewed as the systematic collection and analysis of program-related data.* It is used to understand how a program delivers services and/or what the consequences of services are for participants. It is both descriptive and judgmental of program merit, with an emphasis on developing an evaluation approach that fits the program.

2. *Evaluation is a necessary component to every program, irrespective of size, age, or orientation.* It encompasses a wide variety of perspectives and activities, some of which should be an integral part of every program's functioning. At a minimum programs should be able to articulate their beliefs, describe changes in program orientation, and document service delivery in order to provide feedback for improving program effectiveness. Evaluations can and should be movement builders.

3. *There are numerous legitimate purposes for evaluation.* All programs should be committed to providing effective services. Not all evaluations should attempt to determine service impact per se, however. Programs have natural life cycles, and evaluation questions should be consistent with and meaningful to different developmental stages. Conducting outcome evaluations on young programs, for example, is wasteful and premature.

4. *There are many legitimate audiences for evaluation.* Programs have multiple constituencies and stakeholders, each of whom have differing information needs, beliefs, and agendas. The audience to which an evaluation is directed shapes important decisions about data collection, analyses, and study dissemination. An important goal is to pursue evaluations helpful to the target audience(s) in question while recognizing this inherent multiplicity.

5. *Evaluation activities should not detract from service delivery.* Even though many demands for evaluation come from stakeholders external to programs, those demands do not have to be blindly accepted. Evaluations should be designed and implemented in ways consonant with and relevant to everyday service delivery. To the extent that this is not possible, evaluation requirements should be negotiated both within the program and between the program and external stakeholders. The goal is to achieve an optimal balance between methodological design and practice, and allocation of resources that minimizes conflict between service and evaluation. (Jacobs, 1988, pp. 49–50)

Gabor, Unrau, and Grinnell (1998) outline a simple typology that incorporates five different types of evaluations. Each type maintains its own set of critical questions that must be answered to achieve a useful and relevant evaluation. As such, these evaluation types are often mistakenly thought of as unique, isolated models. In reality, they form a loose hierarchy that is linked by definitions of problems that need to be addressed, the nature and intensity of professional activities, the logic of intervention, and accountability demands generated by clients, communities, and funders. The questions posed at lower levels of evaluation must be answered in order to successfully answer the questions posed at higher levels of evaluation. For example, we must be able to answer questions about a program's goals, objectives, and activities (evaluability assessment) in order to successfully answer questions about process or outcome. This also means that as the evaluation questions become more comprehensive and complex, the data sources and methodologies required to evaluate them become more comprehensive and complex. The practical result of this evaluation hierarchy and the linkages forged between each level is that those programs most successful at evaluating their efforts usually conduct evaluation activities on multiple levels at once. By this we mean that questions asked and information collected at one level will almost always facilitate understanding and decision making on other levels as well.

Table 2.1 shows the five types of evaluation described by Gabor et al. (1998). Each type of evaluation will be briefly discussed here. (For more detail regarding evaluation, see Gabor, Unrau, & Grinnell, 1998.)

Needs Assessment   These evaluations determine the presence of a social problem and identify potential solutions to that problem. They are best thought of as evaluations that take place before a service or program is designed or implemented. The information provided by a thorough needs assessment helps to plan a feasible, effectively targeted program. In addition to establishing the need for a given service, thorough needs assessments form the foundation upon which effective programs are evaluated at higher levels. Unfortunately, needs assessments (and the foundations they form) are often ignored in favor of "knee-jerk" political agendas and reactions to emerging social crises.

Evaluability Assessment   At this level of evaluation, the object is to develop or examine the specific program model that underlies a program's reaction to social problems identified during a needs assessment. The program model is often thought of as a flowchart that clearly identifies the logic behind the program—the program's mission, goals, objectives, activities, and so on. We should know, for example, what theoretical framework intervention is based on, how these theories are translated into concrete, measurable objectives, and how the activities of practitioners are linked to this theoretical framework. The tasks inherent in evaluability assessment essentially involve detailing the program's conceptualization and operations, and then determining whether the program accurately reflects this foundation.

Process Assessment   This type of evaluation seeks to identify and assess *how* service is delivered to clients. What exactly does the program do as it provides services? Who makes decisions about the services to be delivered, and how are these decisions made? What flow or path do clients follow as they receive services? What other activities do program personnel engage in, and how are these sequenced within the program's structures? In short, when a thorough process assessment tells us how services are delivered, this information may become useful when asking why clients do or do not make progress. This information also helps to answer questions about whether a program's services are efficient or cost-effective.

Outcome Assessment   Establishing client outcomes has long been a difficult and often ignored task in human services. We have faced incredible challenges in specifically defining positive client outcomes, and even more difficulty in

Table 2.1 A Typology of Evaluation in the Human Services

Type of Evaluation	Purpose	Questions Asked	Quantitative/Qualitative Data Required
Needs Assessment	To identify the presence of a social problem, and determine its critical characteristics and impacts	What social problems or issues are to be addressed?	The prevalence and severity of the problems or issues to be addressed
		What perceptions do relevant stakeholders (e.g., community residents, other service providers, funders, government) have about these issues?	Characteristics of potential client populations
	To identify a potential solution to the problem that is both feasible and likely to alleviate the problem		Opinions of community stakeholders about the social problem and how it should be resolved
		What types of services do these stakeholders view as important?	Patterns of existing service delivery, and the gaps found between programs
		What services are actually needed the most?	Potential costs of implementing the suggested solution, as well as the potential costs of not implementing it
		What characteristics need to be incorporated into any program meant to address these issues?	
Evaluability Assessment	To develop a program model that addresses the social problems identified in a needs assessment	What is the goal of this particular program?	The program's stated purpose or mission
		What objectives does the program hope to achieve?	Conceptual linkages between the program's goals and the client population to be served, the problem to be resolved, and the means by which the program hopes to achieve this goal
	To determine whether a program's goals and objectives are relevant and useful for conducting evaluation	What do the professionals in this program do to achieve its goals and objectives?	The program's organizational structure
		Is the logic and structure of this program sufficiently developed to allow adequate evaluation of the program?	The nature of and linkages between case-level practice objectives and macrolevel program objectives

Table 2.1 A Typology of Evaluation in the Human Services (continued)

Type of Evaluation	Purpose	Questions Asked	Quantitative/Qualitative Data Required
Process Assessment	To identify and assess the activities undertaken as part of professional intervention (either across an entire program or in relation to specific parts of a program) To monitor and measure the interventions applied to alleviate client problems	What are the characteristics of the program's clients? What are the staff numbers, training, and profile? What kinds of intervention are applied, in what ways? How much service is actually delivered to clients? How are decisions made regarding client flow? What administrative supports and procedures are in place? Do the activities described in the program's model actually take place as described?	Client demographics, assessments, and related information Staff profiles and activities Decision-making mechanisms and procedures Nature and levels of client assessment, intervention, and follow-up Program resources, infrastructure, and administrative procedures Client satisfaction with the program
Outcome Assessment	To document client change To document program effectiveness To demonstrate accountability to relevant stakeholders	Is the program meeting its stated objectives? What short- and long-term improvements are observed for these clients? How do these client outcomes compare to those for whom no service delivery occurred or who received other services? Are we able to establish a causal linkage between client outcomes and the program's intervention?	Individual client progress tracked over time (e.g., standardized measures, client interviews, etc.) Client outcomes aggregated across the program and collected over time Alternative explanations for client progress Control or comparison data for comparing client outcomes Client satisfaction with the program Reviews of client records and program documentation Stakeholders' perceptions regarding the program's accountability

Table 2.1 A Typology of Evaluation in the Human Services (continued)

Type of Evaluation	Purpose	Questions Asked	Quantitative/Qualitative Data Required
Efficiency Assessment	To document the level of resources expended to achieve an observed client outcome	What outcomes can be established for this program?	Outcome data as described above
		Can dollar figures be attached to these outcomes?	Nature and levels of resources provided to the program by funding sources (e.g., facilities, equipment, administrative time and supports, direct clinical time and supports, etc.)
		What resources were expended to achieve these outcomes?	
		What is the ratio of resources expended to the benefits estimated for this program?	Actual expenditures of these resources in the program
		Is the cost of this program reasonable given its demonstrated levels of success?	Comparative data regarding direct clinical costs versus administrative costs, capital costs, etc.
		How does the cost benefit ratio of this program compare to other similar programs?	Cost benefit ratios of this program
			Cost benefit ratios of other similar programs
		Are there ways to obtain the same outcomes with lower expenditures of resources (across the program or in specific components of the program)?	

actually measuring such outcomes. Despite these difficulties, outcome evaluation asks a very basic question that *must* be answered by all practitioners and programs. Is our intervention effective in achieving positive client outcomes? Answering this question is deceptively simple. We can often provide evidence that individual clients make significant progress toward achieving treatment or practice objectives. If most of our individual clients make significant progress toward their treatment objectives, we usually conclude that the overall program was successful. This certainly may be so, but to best establish outcome effectiveness we increasingly turn to methods of data aggregation and analysis. (One such method is discussed in Chapters 7 and 8 of this book.)

Efficiency Assessment The problem of defining client outcomes perhaps makes efficiency assessment the most difficult and underutilized type of evaluation in the human services. Many relevant client outcomes remain frustratingly complex and abstract, such that arriving at a measurable definition of those outcomes is almost impossible. This makes the act of attaching a dollar value or financial benefit to client outcomes an exceedingly delicate and difficult task. Of course, this makes calculation of a cost benefit ratio almost impossible as well. Efficiency assessments in the human services are often rudimentary; however, they can be conducted on a very basic level. With some evidence of client outcomes, we can make determinations about the relative costs of a program, compare its outcomes and costs to those of other programs, and make modifications within programs to increase the efficiency of service delivery.

THE ROLE OF GOALS, OBJECTIVES, AND ACTIVITIES

The types of evaluation and evaluation tasks most relevant to this book relate to evaluation of practice, not programs. It is important, however, to know that there is a direct bridge between micro levels of practice (direct treatment or service delivery) and macro practice (management, planning, and program operations). Human service professionals work within programs and agencies. In order for professionals to be effective, the programs or agencies must be well-conceptualized, provide sufficient resources and infrastructure, and provide the overall context for good practice to occur. In order to demonstrate effectiveness of programs, on the other hand, the professionals who provide service must accurately assess client problems, plan treatment, implement service delivery, and provide evidence of client progress. Effectiveness is therefore a blend of program and direct service delivery, of micro and macro practice.

Effective practice with clients should be linked conceptually to program goals and objectives. To clarify the relationship between practice and programs, we now turn to a brief discussion of the hierarchy of goals, objectives, and activities. This discussion will demonstrate how practitioners can describe their practice and client progress in measurable terms, and will demonstrate how doing so contributes to the establishment of overall program effectiveness.

Program Goals

Program goals are broad statements that describe what a specific program hopes to achieve in relation to specific social problems. They are essentially statements of intent, and are abstract to the point of not being measurable. The goal of the Cystic Fibrosis Stress Management Program (CFSMP) at a local hospital, for example, may be:

> To enable patients with cystic fibrosis to live full and productive lives within the boundaries set by their illness. The program seeks to strengthen the personal functioning and coping abilities of cystic fibrosis patients through the teaching of adaptive coping skills.

This goal is like most others. It identifies the social problem that the CFSMP addresses, and the population targeted for service delivery. At the same time the goal describes the desired state for its clients and the means by which it hopes to help clients achieve this state.

Program goals are important for a number of reasons. They are public statements that describe the very reason for the program's existence. This is particularly relevant to governmental and professional regulatory bodies, potential funders, and potential clients. At the same time, well-conceptualized program goals offer program staff a sense of belonging and direction. They tell the staff what the program hopes to achieve and facilitate thinking about how the staff's skills and activities relate to achieving the desired outcome of the program's activities. Yet they are also vague enough that program staff will have considerable flexibility to define how their own unique skills and activities fit within the broader framework. This is the true strength of program goals—they are both a clearly stated purpose and vague enough for program staff to attach personal meaning to what they do as professionals.

Program Objectives

Objectives are drawn logically from a program's goal. They are best thought of as concrete, measurable indicators used to tell when the results referred to in the program's goal are actually achieved. By being both concrete and measurable, objectives allow practitioners to say precisely the degree to which they have achieved program goals.

Since objectives are drawn from program goals, which are client-centered, it only makes sense that objectives should also be client-centered. This means that objectives need to refer to the presence or absence of client change for the social problem(s) being addressed by the program. They should also be: (1) meaningful or relevant in relation to the overall program goal; (2) specific and clearly worded; (3) measurable; and (4) directional in terms of clearly stating whether levels of the client's problem will increase or decrease (Gabor, Unrau, & Grinnell, 1998).

The notion of specifying all client problems in measurable terms can seem very daunting. Indeed, we often have to be creative and flexible when developing measurable objectives. It does help, however, to know that we can measure client problems in a number of ways. The simplest measurements often involve behavioral indicators. We could, for example, measure the incidence of arguments or positive parenting behaviors among divorcing parents. Another way to measure client problems is to assess knowledge. Do these parents know the impact of divorce and parental conflict on children? Do they know how child support payments are calculated? A third target of measurement is affect. An "affect" objective essentially measures feelings or attitudes and sets a target for changing these feelings or attitudes. Using the same example, our program might create objectives to increase divorcing parents' feelings of attachment to their children, or to decrease feelings of isolation or anger.

Think back to the goal of the Cystic Fibrosis Stress Management Program (CFSMP). The program's goal focused on enabling patients with cystic fibrosis to live full and productive lives. If we were to create relevant program objectives that were also specific, measurable, and directional, they might look like this:

1. To increase patients' knowledge of stress and its effects

2. To reduce the impact of stress on cystic fibrosis patients

3. To increase the sense of personal control for cystic fibrosis patients

Practice Objectives

Program and practice objectives are similar in one way. Both should be centered on client change. They differ, however, in focus. Program objectives are broader in scope, and focus on achievement of results across the entire program. Practice objectives, on the other hand, are based on individual clients or a case level of practice. These objectives are called by many names—treatment objectives, client goals, client targets, therapeutic goals, and so on. Regardless of what term is used, these objectives set an idividualized "state of being" that is desired for clients.

Just as program objectives are drawn logically from program goals, practice objectives should be drawn from program objectives. (A logical sequence or hierarchy should be emerging here.) This makes sense, as the interventions we attempt with any client should have some relationship to the results our program is trying to achieve. For example, think again of a program that seeks to reduce conflict among divorcing parents. Suppose the practitioner engages one of these parents in a way that teaches him or her conflict-avoiding behaviors and positive communication skills. If this parent does indeed meet the practice objectives (increased use of conflict-avoiding behaviors and positive communication skills), the practitioner has contributed toward the larger program goal of reducing conflict among divorcing parents through the program's services. It is the aggregation of positive results across practice objectives that provides evidence of achievement on program objectives.

Take one more example. A social worker in the Cystic Fibrosis Stress Management Program would certainly be aware of the program's objectives—increasing knowledge of stress, reducing the impact of stress, and increasing the sense of personal control. When working with a single client from this program, a pratitioner might form the following practice objectives:

1. To reduce Tara M.'s stress levels when experiencing medical intervention
2. To increase Tara M.'s sense of control when dealing with medical personnel
3. To increase Tara M.'s use of support systems available to cystic fibrosis patients

Practice objectives must be measurable. For each practice objective set by Tara and her social worker, a relevant, reliable, and valid measure should be identified and used routinely. These measures can be diverse, ranging from standardized scales, to measurement instruments constructed by the practitioner (see Chapter 16), to simple frequency or duration recordings of problems that the practitioner and client agree on. The point is, if achievement of the practice objective is not measured, it will be very difficult to argue success on either a practice or program level.

Practice Activities

Practice activities are the things we *do* as practitioners. We interview clients, offer individual counseling, conduct educational or therapeutic groups, make contact with others important to a case, complete paperwork, attend staff meetings, go to workshops, and participate in thousands of other activities. Each of these activities contributes to the quality and comprehensiveness of professional practice. Still, it is essential to remember that all of these activities should contribute in some way to achieving our client's practice objectives or the program's broader objectives. This means that there should again be a logical link between practice activities and the practice objectives agreed to with clients, and then to program objectives and the program goal. Although this is a simple and reasonable premise, it is often ignored or undervalued in human service agencies. There are many instances of activities performed in agencies that cannot be directly linked to what the program and its professionals are trying to achieve.

The social workers in the Cystic Fibrosis Stress Management Program, for example, may engage in many activities that are directly related to practice and program objectives. They might teach progressive muscle relaxation as a way to reduce stress, network with other service providers, provide individual counseling to CF patients, help patients learn the medical terminology being applied to their case, participate in service team meetings, review the latest research at the medical library, and so on. Each of these activities can be linked to a specific practice objective. These activities should facilitate clients' progress on the objectives set in their cases, and contribute to the practitioner's overall effectiveness.

Relationship Between Goals, Objectives, and Activities

Figure 2.1 shows the sequence of program goal, program objectives, practice objectives, and practice activities related to Tara's case in the Cystic Fibrosis Stress Management Program example. The figure highlights the logical flow that should exist between all of these aspects of program and practitioner functioning. If practitioners are unable to make the connection between practice activities and practice objectives, practice objectives and program objectives, or program objectives and program goals, service delivery will likely be compromised. Either practitioner activities will be misdirected in some way, or practitioners will be unable to establish their effectiveness or the effectiveness of the program. Conversely, if the program's practitioners are able to document success with their clients on a case-by-case level, they can start to build evidence that says the program's objectives are being met. This in turn helps to establish that the program is indeed meeting its goal.

Another way of portraying the relationship between all these goals, objectives, and activities is as a hierarchy (see Gabor, Unrau, & Grinnell, 1998, p. 100). The foundation of treatment services is based on two things. First is the full range of *activities professionals engage in* to facilitate client change. Thinking back to Chapter 1, this may be thought of as the part of practice that is concerned with professional behavior. This is a focus on process. As such, this foundation is the one on which we base *service resources accountability*—what services were provided, what caseload the therapist carried, how many sessions were held, how much time was spent in meetings or direct service contact, and so on. Assuming that we are able to adequately define and monitor these activities, it is very possible to evaluate the process of practice.

The second tier of the hierarchy, that of *practice objectives,* is what this book focuses on. In order to demonstrate effectiveness-oriented practice, practitioners must be able to define client outcomes in specific, measurable terms. By setting clear practice objectives and using valid measures to assess these objectives, practitioners can also demonstrate *service outcome accountability.* Without demonstrated client change in regard to the objectives set for clients, practitioners cannot demonstrate effectiveness. This is true first and foremost for practice evaluation on a case level. Because of the linkages between practice and program, however, the implication is also that programs will be unable to demonstrate effectiveness if their practitioners cannot do so. In short, an effectiveness-orientation to practice requires clear specification, measurement, and evaluation of both process and outcome—the activities engaged in to facilitate client change and the actual change observed for the client.

The discussion of the linkages between practice and program effectiveness has been brief, but many other sources provide more detail regarding the nature and process of evaluation (see, e.g., Alter & Evens, 1990; Gabor, Unrau, & Grinnell, 1998; Patton, 1996; Rossi & Freeman, 1993). We now turn to a discussion of the "glue" that holds the levels of evaluation together and

Program goal

To enable patients with cystic fibrosis to live full and productive lives within the boundaries set by their illness. The program seeks to strengthen the personal functioning and coping abilities of cystic fibrosis patients through the teaching of adaptive coping skills.

Program objectives

1. To increase patients' knowledge of stress and its effects
2. To reduce the impact of stress on cystic fibrosis patients
3. To increase the sense of personal control for cystic fibrosis patients

Practice objectives

1. To reduce Tara M.'s stress levels when experiencing medical intervention
   Measure: CFSMP Stress Knowledge Test
2. To increase Tara M.'s sense of control when dealing with medical personnel
   Measure: The Health Locus of Control Scale
3. To increase Tara M.'s use of support systems available to cystic fibrosis patients
   Measure: Frequency of use of CF Network services

Practice activities (examples)

1. Conduct intake interview and review patient history.
2. Present and discuss stress-related content in weekly stress management groups.
3. Teach progressive muscle relaxation in individualized sessions.
4. Make referrals to CF Network service providers, with telephone follow-up.
5. Hold weekly discussion of the case in service team meetings.
6. Teach medical terminology related to CF. Discuss strategies for dealing with medical personnel.
7. Administer measures during baseline phase. Repeat as necessary.
8. Provide reading material, audio stress management tapes, and other materials as required.

FIGURE 2.1 Logic of treatment conceptualization for Tara M. in the Cystic Fibrosis Stress Management Program

provides evidence of effectiveness. The glue is information. Information guides all aspects of professional practice, on both case and program levels. It ensures a common purpose for practitioners working within programs, provides understanding to a practitioner's assessment, shows whether intervention is working, and allows programs to monitor their functioning. In fact, information guides every aspect of planning, implementing, and evaluating both micro and macro practice.

The remainder of this chapter discusses issues and techniques relevant to obtaining reliable and valid information for guiding practice. This discussion also will be brief, as many books have been written on the topic of information and information management in the human services. Our comments center on the following: (1) the role of information in human services; (2) developing effective information structures; and (3) using information technology effectively.

The Role of Information in Human Services

Information is much more than just data. Data are raw facts, not yet summarized, analyzed, or interpreted. In order to obtain information, we have to take raw data—numbers of clients, client performance on outcome measures, program expenditures, and so on—and give meaning to them. This is accomplished by looking for patterns, gaps, anomalies, and other unique aspects of the data. We might, for example, examine program data for the last year to determine whether the numbers and types of clients served by our program have changed substantially. Such an act of summarizing and interpreting allows us to understand the stories and messages held within data. It also makes information come alive. Information is never static—it changes as data changes, shifts as our interpretations shift, and becomes more or less relevant as our decision-making needs evolve.

Useful information has a number of common characteristics. First, useful information must be accurate. This essentially refers to the degree to which the information reflects reality. If the available information suggests that a client is no longer experiencing suicidal ideation, for example, we would certainly hope that this picture is accurate. For obvious reasons, faulty information in this case could be disastrous. Unfortunately, information in the human services is not always accurate. Even though most practitioners and programs now make information collection a routine part of practice, there is often little attention to developing simple procedures to facilitate accurate information collection. One of the authors, for instance, once witnessed a health care professional completing a form meant to record worker activities. The form included areas in which to record things such as time spent with clients, contacts made with collateral persons, time spent doing administrative tasks, and so on. On the surface, completion of the form seemed to be going well; but the worker had forms for four or five days on the desk and had completed all of these at once, mostly from memory. In such cases, the information provided is certainly questionable.

It is important to note, however, that the professional in this case may not have been entirely at fault. Another critical quality of useful information is relevance. This criterion is especially critical for practitioners, who far too often are asked to provide data that holds no direct relevance for them. Such situations can develop when information systems are designed and imposed from above, without adequate consultation and consideration for those who provide direct services. In the case described, the professional probably saw no direct relevance to the data being provided. (Few of the professionals in that department ever looked at the monthly summaries provided by the information processing department of that particular hospital.) Examples like this illustrate that variables related to perceived relevance (such as prior planning, input from frontline workers, and staff training) are critical factors in successful information management (Benbenishty & Oyserman, 1995; Carrilio et al., 1985; Edwards & Reid, 1989; Fuchs, 1987; Johnson et al., 1977; Lyons et al., 1987; Mandell, 1989; Neugeboren, 1995; Palmer et al., 1991; Poertner & Rapp, 1987).

The precise attributes that make information relevant varies across agencies, programs, practitioners, and clients. Even within the same case, the exact information considered relevant often changes over time. These factors make information relevance difficult to define and assess in many cases. This is one reason that many poorly designed information systems focus primarily on professional activities or transactions. Knowing things like the number of clients served and the proportion of hours actually spent in direct service is certainly important, but such information tells us little about the performance or outcomes generated by practitioners or programs. In fact, it tells us little about how and why these activities may contribute to the successes that practitioners and programs achieve.

On a basic level, information relevance can be assessed relatively easily. Practitioners should be able to look at the data they are asked to provide and answer the following questions. Are these data client-centered in some fashion? Will understanding the data have a direct impact on my decision making? Do the benefits of understanding these data outweigh the effort or costs incurred in collecting it? How much of these data actually get translated into useful information? Can these data be easily interpreted and used? Is there a different set of data or procedures for interpretation that would generate better information with which to guide practice? These are the questions that should be asked in regard to any data or documentation as professionals strive to develop an effectiveness orientation toward their practice.

One final characteristic of useful information is worth noting. In order for information to be useful, it must be timely. This means that the data must be ready for interpretation, in an appropriate form, soon after the events to which the information applies have occurred. When determining whether an intervention should be discontinued, for instance, data regarding client progress must be available promptly. It must be as recent as possible to ensure that measurement of the targeted problem is accurate at the point of decision making. The information must not arrive after the time at which the decision must be made. Whittaker, Fine, and Grasso (1989), for example, found that systematic analysis of routinely collected agency data permitted them to detect, earlier than previously possible, shifts in patterns of child and family characteristics and referral sources that significantly aided their assessment of risk and their allocation of service resources.

Figure 2.2 shows a conceptualization of the information used in human services. The conceptualization inherent in the graphic in Figure 2.2 borrows from the conceptualization of treatment services of Gabor, Unrau, and Grinnell (1998). The similarity between this conceptualization of information use in human services and Gabor et al.'s (1998) conceptualization of treatment services is, in a sense, inevitable, since understanding and decision making at each level of service delivery should be based on accurate, relevant, and timely information.

The foundation of the model in Figure 2.2 is practice. The first level of information needs to relate to the activities of practitioners. At this level, the data collected and the interpretations developed are based on individual

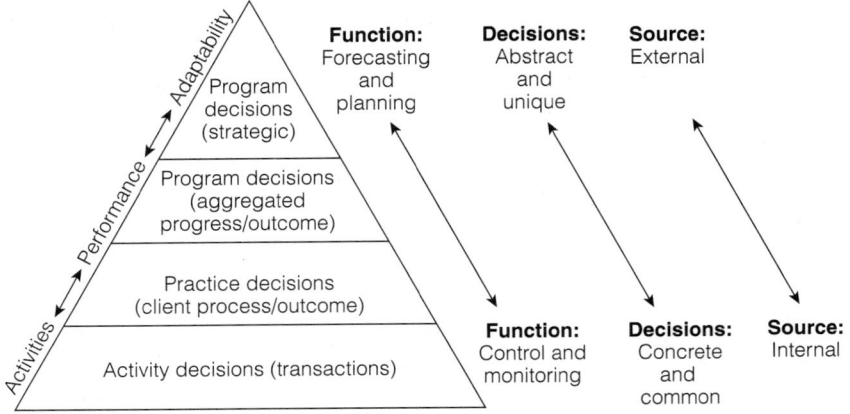

FIGURE 2.2 Conceptualizing information in human services.

transactions. How many clients did the practitioner see in the last week? How many direct client contact hours were logged? How many committee meetings did the practitioner have to attend, and how much time did this take? These are transactions based on professional behaviors and, as such, are a very basic measure of professional process. Making decisions using this kind of information can be relatively straightforward. The function of such information is simply to control and monitor the transactions that occur within a program or agency. The number of clients or practitioner workload is monitored (and hopefully regulated). Summaries are calculated and reported to show the average number of contacts required for each case, the average length of treatment services, the frequency of attrition among cases, the time required to perform administrative tasks, and so on. Such information is certainly useful. It provides a picture of what we actually *do* to deliver professional services. Unfortunately, this kind of information has all too often been used as the primary source for decision making in human service agencies, as the information is easily collected using simple internal procedures.

The second tier of information facilitates decision making in relation to direct practice decisions. This information relates to the practice objectives set for clients. It focuses not on professionals' behaviors, but on the process and outcomes displayed by clients. This is truly client-centered versus practitioner-centered information. What activities have clients themselves engaged in to facilitate change? What factors or experiences in each case have hindered progress? Most importantly, what outcomes can we document for particular clients? This information (related to practice decisions, as opposed to activities) represents the most important level of performance assessment for professionals. This is not because professional activities are unimportant; indeed, the opposite is true. The behaviors we engage in as professionals are critical to effective service delivery. As we argued in Chapter 1, however, behaviors are of no real consequence unless they contribute to desired change for clients.

The activities we engage in should have a definite probability of producing positive client outcomes. Therefore, the documentation of client outcomes forms the core of performance assessment. This level of information collection and use is the core focus of this text. Our intent is to provide techniques and tools that you may adopt to collect and use information for establishing practice effectiveness.

The final two levels of the information hierarchy shown in Figure 2.2 relate to broader program decisions. The first of these relates to aggregated process and outcome data, on a program level. It is here that program administrators use aggregated information to make decisions related to overall client utilization patterns, staff numbers, training needs, budget expenditures, fundraising, necessary modifications to existing services, and so on. In some ways the performance questions remain the same as those asked at the practice level, but they have a broader focus. Is this agency or program meeting its stated objectives? If so, what decisions need to be made to continue achieving this success, or what modifications would allow these objectives to be met more efficiently or more effectively? If not, what decisions are required to change the way services are conceptualized and delivered?

Since these questions are broader than those at the direct practice level, the information sought at the program level is broader as well. It is not that the questions are more difficult, or that program decisions are more complex than practice ones; the information required just differs in scope. The process of aggregating information across clients, practitioners, administrators, and programs can be tricky. At the same time, performance assessment at the program level demands additional information from outside the program itself. External stakeholders take on a much stronger role in making program decisions. For example, regulatory bodies may change the standards to which programs must adhere. Funders may decide to increase or decrease funding in specific areas, or request changes to the ways programs operate. Coalitions of service providers may be formed to address emerging community needs or to deliver services more efficiently. Information exchanges about such things are critical to an effective human service program, and reflect what has been called an "open system" organization.

The final level of information required is also program-related. It does not focus as much on program operations, however, as it does on program adaptability. Those responsible for the program must collect information that is useful for making long-term, strategic decisions about the program. This is a forecasting and planning function to ensure the program will maintain a viable and useful role in the future. Such information usually does not come from within the organization. Instead, it comes from developing an understanding of things like emerging social problems, changes in the patterns of existing social problems, political trends, demographics, economics, and so on. Such information is rarely clear, concrete, or neatly documented. It tends to be abstract, interrelated through complex "webs" of relationships, and quickly evolving. This makes the process of making strategic program decisions a bit like playing the role of a human services "futurist."

FINAL THOUGHTS ABOUT COLLECTING PRACTICE EVALUATION INFORMATION

We have discussed the nature of evaluation in human services and the kinds of information used to establish performance of programs and practitioners. In ending our discussion, we will pose a set of practical questions that must be answered in collecting practice evaluation information. The answers to these questions form the heart of subsequent chapters. Keep these questions in mind as you continue to read this book.

In simple terms, answering questions about practice effectiveness boils down to obtaining information about the process and outcome of practice. We need some basic information about the transactions (activities and interventions) we engage in as professionals in order to determine what we did that facilitated client change. More importantly, we need reliable and valid information about the outcomes (achievement of practice objectives) demonstrated by our clients.

Figure 2.3 shows a diagram portraying the practical steps and questions practitioners must answer as they evaluate a practice encounter. The diagram is simplified to provide an overview of the steps and questions that must be dealt with as practitioners evaluate their practice. Each question may be broken into many other questions concerning smaller details with which practitioners must be concerned.

Deciding upon answers to these questions can be confusing and overwhelming at first. Consider a seemingly simple question from the list in Figure 2.3 as one example. With a new client, the practitioner should ask what measures are available to monitor the practice objectives agreed to. The options available are diverse. Should the practitioner use some existing structured form already used by the organization? How about standardized assessment scales? Would a questionnaire of some type work? How might case note recordings contribute to measuring the achievement of practice objectives? The answers to these questions must be carefully considered. (Descriptions of these recording formats can be found in Nurius & Hudson, 1993.)

As you can see, there are many information-related questions that must be asked of every practice encounter. Many of these questions will be answered in the same way, based on the similarities of cases, organizational practices, regulatory standards, professional preferences, and so on. It does not matter that the same answers may be applied in many cases; the important part is the act of ensuring the questions are answered in every case.

The process of answering practice evaluation questions necessarily depends on the context set for practice. In particular, it incorporates input from a wide variety of the personnel in any program or agency and from the overall organizational context. Inevitably, however, the quality of practice information collected depends upon practitioners' commitment to routine data collection and analysis, and their ability to use such tools effectively. The remainder of this book focuses on providing you with these tools.

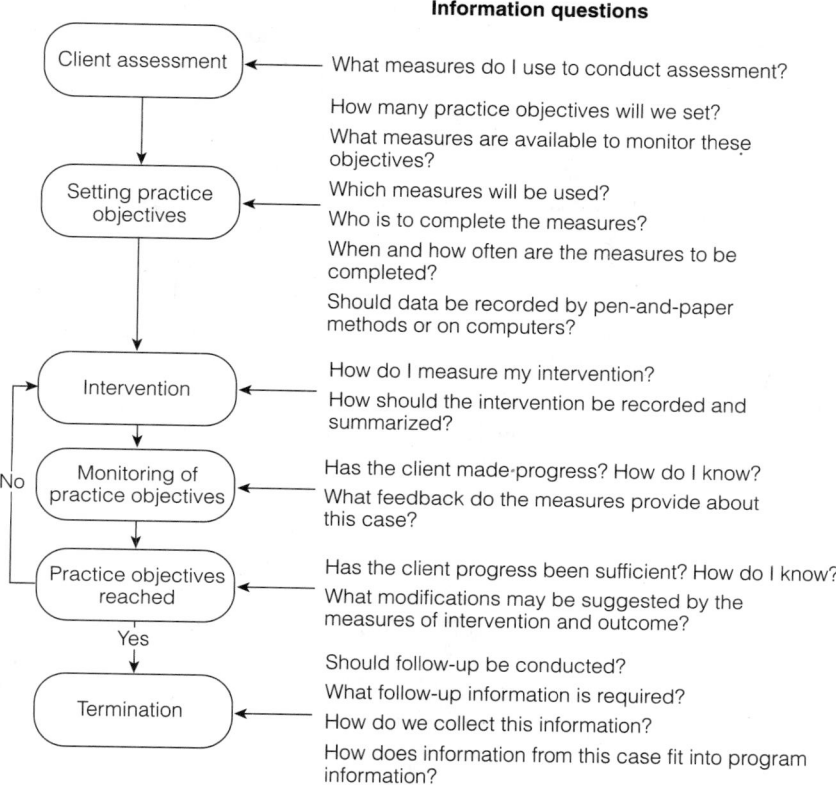

Information questions

Client assessment ← What measures do I use to conduct assessment?

How many practice objectives will we set?
What measures are available to monitor these objectives?

Setting practice objectives ← Which measures will be used?
Who is to complete the measures?
When and how often are the measures to be completed?
Should data be recorded by pen-and-paper methods or on computers?

Intervention ← How do I measure my intervention?
How should the intervention be recorded and summarized?

Monitoring of practice objectives ← Has the client made progress? How do I know?
What feedback do the measures provide about this case?

No

Practice objectives reached ← Has the client progress been sufficient? How do I know?
What modifications may be suggested by the measures of intervention and outcome?

Yes

Termination ← Should follow-up be conducted?
What follow-up information is required?
How do we collect this information?
How does information from this case fit into program information?

FIGURE 2.3 Practical information questions related to practice evaluation.

We would like to leave you with a few basic suggestions for establishing an effective routine for information collection. Consider these principles carefully, and discuss them within your organization. The product will be an improved organizational context, one in which information collection can be optimized.

- Any information collected should meet, first and foremost, the needs of frontline practitioners. They are the ones who have direct contact with clients and must make decisions about clients' cases. If documentation procedures and measures are imposed by other stakeholders, data collection will often fail, as practitioners may fail to buy into the process. If, on the other hand, good information is shaped and collected by practitioners, the information necessary for program evaluation will naturally evolve.

- Only data that are directly relevant to practice should be collected. There is a tendency to apply a "shotgun approach" to data collection—that is, to try to collect as much data as possible, without a plan for using the data, in the hope that it will prove useful in the future. This only serves to overwhelm both the practitioner and the client.

- If possible, the plan for data collection and analysis should be written, as this provides a definite plan to which the practitioner can refer on a routine basis. If circumstances change or the practitioner needs to refer to documentation after a case is closed, a formal record of empirical practice already exists.

- Practitioners need to be clear in the way they document their practice. Using well-defined practice objectives that clearly state what the practitioner is trying to achieve and identifying specific measures for assessing client progress provide a common language that aids in interpretation of cases and in learning across the organization and profession.

- Practitioners should consider using computer technology to assist with information collection. As will be shown later in this book, computers offer real advantages in storage capacity, speed of information retrieval, analysis options, ability to portray results graphically, and so on.

SUMMARY

The process of evaluating practice is part of a much larger context. This context relates to evaluation efforts on many levels and to the use of information to guide every aspect of practitioner and program functioning. Because of this, the prospect of adopting an "effectiveness orientation" toward practice can seem daunting to practitioners. The procedures for conceptualizing and using an effectiveness-based approach, however, do not have to be overly complex or burdensome.

It is useful to keep the object of evaluation efforts as simple and direct as possible. Practitioners should ask only for information that will be used in making decisions and should make sure that the information is related to achieving client objectives. They should ask themselves whether the information is indeed important for guiding practice decisions.

Once questions regarding the data to be collected are answered, the next task is to answer a few basic questions about information collection. What is to be measured? What kinds of recording forms or instruments are available to measure this information? Who is to conduct the measurements, and how often should this be done? Should the information be stored on pen-and-paper forms, or should computerized records be used? These are essentially commonsense questions. Once a plan has been created based on what needs to be measured and how measurement should occur, the results are recorded. This conceptually simple process is the hallmark of effective practice evaluation.

In this chapter we discussed the importance of measuring client problems over time. There has been a long-standing debate about the benefits and limitations of using single-system designs for such measurements in practice. The critics claim that single-system designs are arbitrary scientific methods imposed on practice. In the next chapter, we deal with this debate and explore the notion of single-system designs as science. We also offer an alternative perspective, one that views single-system designs not as a scientific imperative, but as a tool of practice.

3

N = 1 Designs in Science and Practice

In Chapter 1, we introduced you to the conceptual foundations, defining characteristics, and utility of using single-system designs. In Chapter 2, we discussed the linkages between single-system designs and the processes of evaluating your micro- and macro-level social work practice efforts. In this chapter, we now turn to a more detailed discussion of single-system designs as both science and practice. We specifically focus on using single-system designs not as a restrictive scientific framework, but as a tool that can enhance your ability to do and evaluate practice.

SOCIAL WORK AS SCIENCE
AND PRACTICE

There has been considerable debate about what has been called the "scientist-practitioner" model of social work practice. The advocates of this model (e.g., Bloom, Fischer, & Orme, 1999; Blythe, Tripodi, & Briar, 1994; Fischer & Corcoran, 1994; Thyer, 1996) seek to move the social work profession toward a practice model that has at its foundation the principles and tools of science. Bloom et al. (1999), for example, see scientific practice as the "combination of a sensitive and caring practitioner with the logical and empirical strengths of the applied social scientist" (p. 3). In this model, practice is seen as the science of professional action—action that merges up-to-date and relevant information, techniques that are demonstrably effective, objective evaluation, and the profession's own value base into a systematic way of resolving client problems. Together these functions combine with the practitioner's natural intuitiveness and creativity to create a complete social work professional. This professional is guided by a dual reality—a sense of humanity and caring along with the desire to objectively evaluate the effectiveness of her or his own practice efforts.

The scientist-practitioner model has been argued to hold a number of important implications for social work practitioners. First is the implicit message to those in the field that social work practice is science, and that science can be social work practice. That is, science and practice are to be considered as opposite sides of the same coin. Both sides are needed to produce a caring and effective social worker. Work with each client, therefore, needs to be considered not only as a research opportunity, but also as a research responsibility.

Second, it has been argued that scientific practice can be conducted using a generic problem-solving framework. Some proponents of this framework assert that science and practice are simply parallel processes based on the same steps and questions (Grinnell, Rothery, & Thomlison, 1993). The scientist or practitioner first identifies the problem to be addressed, and then clearly defines and specifies the nature of this problem. Next, alternatives for resolving the problem are generated, and strategies are selected to implement the alternatives. These alternatives are implemented, and then the results are evaluated and the findings disseminated. Throughout this process it is recognized that the problem-solving method is not linear and that the problem-solving steps are not separate entities. Instead, the entire process is seen as an iterative, interconnected process whereby each stage, with its associated activities, informs and directs the others.

The third implication for the practitioner from this model concerns accountability. Accountability is seen as the need for effectiveness on the part of practitioners, agencies, and the profession as a whole. Proponents of the scientific-practice framework argue that social workers need to evaluate their own practice in a way that demonstrates the value of their work to themselves, their clients, their agency, their funders, and to the profession. Fischer and Corcoran (1994), for example, define accountability as "a commitment (to) delivering effective service, which is fulfilled by conscientious monitoring and measurement of one's practice and the client's functioning" (p. 4).

Another implication of the scientist-practitioner model is that practitioners need to become skilled in the use of the technologies that drive the scientist-practitioner model. Core among these are single-system designs (which we have already discussed a bit) and standardized scales or measures that serve as clinical assessment instruments (which we talk more about later in this book). Standardized scales are measures that display a uniformity of procedures for administering and scoring (Jordan & Franklin, 1995). They have been well researched, and have been shown to produce scores with acceptable reliability and validity. This gives the practitioner some confidence in the measure's ability to produce scores that describe the problem being addressed, and permits the monitoring of change over the course of intervention. Best of all, standardized measures are available to measure a wide range of problems that clients bring to social workers, including relationships problems, problems with self-esteem, depression, health problems, eating disorders, anxiety disorders, violence and aggression, management style, and agency climate, among countless others. Based on their known performance characteristics and broad availability, standardized measures therefore become critical to the scientific practice model. Social workers are encouraged to identify reliable and valid measures for problems they encounter, and then use these instruments to monitor their clients' progress through intervention.

For many professionals the scientific-practice model is very appealing. It reflects the very principles by which many of us see professional social work being organized and conducted. Although the ideas proposed in the scientist-practitioner model are compelling, it is a model that has failed to gain wide acceptance in social work (Penka & Kirk, 1991; Robinson, Bronson, & Blythe, 1988). There are many, in fact, who continue to question the notion of science as the basis of practice. These criticisms are varied. Some argue, most notably from a constructivist or relativist position, that this model is based on a faulty and obsolete scientific paradigm. This model, it is said, is based on the assumption of a single, objective reality that can be observed and measured. The gist of this argument is that this assumption isolates the model from the abstract, often unobservable realities of clinical practice. The scientific-practice model, moreover, is thought to be based on a Western notion of the superiority of science as a way of knowing and a misguided faith in technology. It is argued that it is this technology that serves as a vehicle for robbing the clinical process of context, richness of language and client narrative, and ideological stances that consider phenomena such as oppression and patriarchy (Heineman, 1981; Witkin, 1991, 1996).

This "postmodernist" attack on the scientist-practitioner model can be seen as an instance of a broader and more general attack on empirical science (Laudan, 1990). It should be noted that the arguments that form the core of this attack, and the resulting conclusions about the epistemological basis of science, are not accepted by the majority of philosophers of science and contain a number of serious self-contradictions (Laudan, 1990; Wilber, 1998).

Related criticisms point to issues regarding assumptions about causality and generalization in science (Wakefield & Kirk, 1996). Because one of the tenets of science has to do with establishing causality, it is suggested that single-system designs enforce a pressure for practitioners to establish the linkages between their treatment and client outcome. This encourages the use of complex designs in which baseline and treatment phases are alternated in order to establish that client improvement is temporally and sequentially linked with treatment. Critics suggest that there are ethical, cost, and logistical difficulties in imposing such designs on practice. There are indeed problems with the fit between the conduct of practice and the conduct of scientific research that sometimes make it difficult, if not impossible, to use the more complex single-system designs (such as the ABAB or multiple baseline) in practice (Thomas, 1978). As we will discuss later, however, the fit between science and practice is not completely conflictual, and the use of the more complex single-system designs can often fit well within a practice context.

In terms of generalization, one of the hopes of scientist-practitioner advocates is that use of single-subject designs will provide data about which treatments work to treat which problems with which clients, under what conditions. Critics argue, however, that the development of such a knowledge base has proven somewhat elusive for the profession. Results from single cases have historically been difficult to aggregate on broader levels, even within agency settings. The product of this situation is that as a profession we have largely been unsuccessful in matching treatments to clients. Wakefield and Kirk (1996) argue that this process of client-treatment matching is scientifically untenable, due to problems associated with unknown representativeness of single clients, the uncontrollability of things such as the therapist–client relationship, and the unreplicability of specific instances of treatments. In our view this is an overly pessimistic position that ignores some of the major advances in the development of effective and replicable interventions, and of beginning knowledge about client characteristics that make clients more amenable to the interventions. For example, David Barlow and colleagues (Barlow, 1988; Barlow & Cerny, 1988; Craske & Barlow, 1993; Craske, Brown, & Barlow, 1991) have developed an intervention for panic disorder and have repeatedly shown that 80 to 90 percent of the persons who undergo this intervention are panic-free after completion, and as many as 78 percent of these persons who benefit from the treatment remain panic-free after five years. They have also found that marital distress may make clients less likely to benefit from this intervention procedure (Craske & Barlow, 1993). Similarly, Foa and colleagues (Foa, Grayson, Steketee, Doppelt, Turner, & Latimer, 1983; Foa, Steketee, Grayson, Turner, & Latimer, 1984; Riggs & Foa, 1993) have developed an extremely effective intervention for obsessive-compulsive disorder that seems to be moderated by depression. That is, clients who are depressed do not seem to benefit as much as clients who are not depressed or as much as clients who undergo this treatment after their depression has been successfully treated. This is the kind of information that is critical to the optimal matching of client and intervention procedure. Criticisms of single-case design methodology in terms of generalizability have also, in many cases, been overstated and ignore the powerful basis that replication creates for generalizability (Harris & Jenson, 1985; Johnston & Pennypacker, 1980; Kazdin, 1982, 1998; Neuliep, 1991). Johnston and Pennypacker (1980) give an excellent overview of the replication history of research on "time out" as an intervention procedure that establishes a strong basis for the generalizability of this intervention and that serves as a paradigmatic example of the use of replication for establishing generalizability.

A final criticism of the scientist-practitioner model is a practical one. Critics point out that even after years of promotion, single-system designs and standardized measures have not been used in social work to the extent once hoped for (Penka & Kirk, 1991; Robinson, Bronson, & Blythe, 1988). Critics suggest that even when those trained in the scientist-practitioner model are considered, it is still rare to find a social worker who practices using this scientific foundation. The reasons postulated for this are again varied. It is suggested that the scientific-practice model has failed to help demonstrate effectiveness of social work practice, that single-system designs necessary for demonstrating effectiveness are expensive and difficult to implement, and that the notion of accountability used in the scientist-practitioner model is narrow and misconstrued. Some point to an artificial emphasis on discrete variables, in that we try to measure distinct, isolated aspects of people and life events (Meyer, 1996). This serves to remove the connections and relationships between multiple problems, and lessens our ability to understand the complete phenomena being considered. They also point to the process of using quantitatively defined measures to measure these problems. The use of paper-and-pencil instruments, answer categories, and numbers, it is suggested, is contrary to the way practitioners think, feel, and work. Rather than focusing on the reality captured by such instruments, critics suggest that the client narrative is what practitioners favor and find useful to guide practice.

N = 1 DESIGNS AS TOOLS TO DO
AND ENHANCE PRACTICE

We firmly believe in the single-system designs and standardized measures encouraged by the scientist-practitioner model. They are valuable and integral tools for use in social work practice. At the same time, however, we also recognize the limitations imposed by the model. There are many distinct and important differences in the roles, methods, and purposes for conducting science and conducting practice. Quite simply, social work practitioners do not conduct basic science. Practitioners are not scientists; they have never occupied that role, and they (probably) will never do so. As a profession, we therefore encounter difficulties when trying to make practice fit into a scientific framework. Much more useful, in our eyes, is a practice model that focuses on doing practice while using scientific tools and methods, and scientifically validated interventions, to inform and enhance our practice efforts. This means that we can still strive toward scientific standards, and apply scientific methods to practice. The first consideration, however, should always be providing our clients with the best possible services. We can use the tools of science to accompany, inform, and enhance our service provision. Two of these tools simply happen to be single-subject designs and standardized measures. (Another set of useful tools that can be used to enhance practice is the critical thinking skills discussed by Gilovich [1991] and Gibbs & Gambrill [1999].)

The remainder of this chapter is dedicated to discussing two things. We will first compare the assumptions, procedures, and roles of science and practice. We will then outline a collaborative model of practice and science, one that shows how to use single-subject designs as a way to enhance practice, not determine it. We hope it proves to be a useful model for social workers.

THE NATURE OF SCIENCE VERSUS THE NATURE OF PRACTICE

Science has become a dominant force that shapes all aspects of our lives as we enter the 21st century. The stamp of "science" has become a symbolic seal of approval. For many people, especially in North America, science represents ideals of objectivity, progress, technology, knowledge, order, quality, and so on (Giere, 1991; Rosen, 1991). As such, science has become an important tool for establishing legitimacy. This began first in the natural sciences where advances in biology, medicine, chemistry, physics, and other areas have contributed significantly to our lifestyles and culture over the last century. More recently, however, social work and the other social sciences have felt the need to justify their role and purpose. We have therefore increasingly adopted science as one of the foundations for our profession. In order to think about a realistic and useful role for science in social work practice, it is necessary to compare differences in the purposes, roles, and methods of science and practice. The elements of these differences are summarized in the text that follows.

Order, Logic, and Generalization   Science has been defined as human beings' attempts to understand the reproducible and predictable aspects of the natural world (Rosen, 1991). As this definition implies, through "science" we try to find order and predictability in our world. This endeavor assumes that there are logical patterns and linkages that can be drawn from what often appears as a chaotic and random world around us. It assumes that there is at least some order and predictability in the universe, and that this order and predictability can be discovered and known by humans. We assume that there is at least some predictability to the world, including human behavior and social phenomena. Thus, the challenge for us is to find out, through empirical data and sound logic, how much predictability there is and to what extent we can use this predictability to control certain aspects of our existence (Rosen, 1991).

Good science is also thought to involve one or both of two types of logic. First, we might observe a phenomenon across multiple instances or across time, and then try to recognize consistent patterns and principles in our observations. This process is called induction or inductive reasoning (or logic). For example, we might record data about all the suicides in our state for five years. Suppose we had data from 1,000 such cases. We would try to identify common themes and factors in the data so that we could say something more general about suicide, such as "suicide is more common among males than females." In other words, we move from specific cases to general principles. The second type of logic used in science is the process of deduction, or deductive reasoning (or logic). In deductive logic, we begin with broad, general principles. From this foundation, we try to apply the general principles to specific cases and develop deductively valid predictions about the outcomes of experiments or observations (Giere, 1991; Rosen, 1991). We develop a priori hypotheses and then set about to test them. For instance, we might develop a hypothesis, based on a combination of general principles about suicidal behavior and the characteristics of a specific client, that the client may attempt to kill herself or himself over the next month. We would then use this speculation, arrived at through deductive reasoning, to guide our practice behavior with this client.

Regardless of whether the scientist uses inductive or deductive logic, the goal is often to identify general principles or generalizations. At the level of the individual client, the goal may be to clearly establish a functional relationship between the client's behavior and some aspect of her or his environment (Johnston & Pennypacker, 1980). In any case, phenomena that are totally unique in the sense of being nonreplicable are beyond the domain of what can be investigated through science (Rosen, 1991).

Social work practice involves the use of scientific generalizations. As a profession we would very much like to identify effective common criteria and procedures for assessing personal and social problems. We would also like to identify a range of interventions that can be applied effectively to these problems under a range of circumstances. Social work practice also involves the identification of functional relationships between environmental factors and the behavior of specific client systems. At a practical level, social work practice is based upon individual systems—either a specific individual person, a family, a community, or some other identifiable social entity. This means that most practitioners are first and foremost interested in individual client systems. In order to make sense of our client's problems, we need to recognize them as individuals and assess them as such. In order to build a relationship with them, we need to interact with them on a personal level. In order to effect change, we need to build a uniquely tailored intervention plan with our clients. Scientifically valid general principles, however, can critically inform the creation of treatment plans. A good example of the mixing of scientifically valid general principles regarding well-specified intervention methods with information unique to specific clients can be found in Barlow and Cerny (1988).

Data and Measurement   The conduct of science is based upon empirical evidence obtained through sensory experiences. The data we use in scientific endeavors are qualitative distinctions or consistencies found within these sensory experiences and/or quantitative aspects of these experiences. This fact has a number of consequences. Phenomena that cannot be observed in some manner through our senses are not amenable to study through scientific methods. This means that there is a whole category of questions that cannot be addressed through science. Questions about, for example, ethical principles, morals, and transcendental issues (such as "Does God exist?" and "Is there life after death?") fall into this category. We agree with Rosen (1991) who has argued that for these questions that are beyond the domain of science, there are many legitimate ways of attempting to find answers, including philosophy and religion.

In contrast to the conduct of science, social work practice deals with many issues and questions that cannot be answered by science. Ethical dilemmas exist, such as conflicts between a professional code of ethics and the demands placed on social workers by agencies or, perhaps, moral conflicts between treatment options (such as some forms of sex therapy) and social workers' moral sense of "right" and "wrong." Some clients may also bring problems that involve questions of values, morals, and/or transcendental issues. Science will in all probability be of little help in such instances.

In practice, the social worker needs to make many types of assessments. Some can be captured through direct observation of the behavior of client systems, through the use of standardized measurement scales, and through normal agency documentation. There are also those, however, that ultimately consist of professional opinions, evaluations, and judgments. For example, a social worker may have to make a judgment about a client's potential for making a suicide attempt. The social worker would use, most defensibly (Fremouw, Perczel, & Ellis, 1990), a number of standardized measures, structured interview methods, and collateral information to help gather as much information as possible. In the final analysis, however, the social worker has to combine this information and use his or her judgment to make a decision about the risk that the client poses to herself or himself and then act on this judgment call. Thus, science can inform the decision, but it cannot make it for the social worker. These types of critical judgments contribute to good practice.

One of the goals of science is to understand complex phenomena by modeling it as the interaction between a relatively small number of factors or variables. We attempt to learn about how the various factors interrelate by controlling and holding constant the environment in which the research is being done and the measurements are being taken. In this manner, the measurements that are obtained and the observations that are made are not influenced by the aspects of the environment that are held constant.

In practice, though, social workers rarely (if ever) have the same degree of control over the environment that a researcher can exert. Rather than isolating one or two variables for study, they usually have to assess and consider multiple, interrelated events or experiences. The self-deprecating actions and beliefs of a troubled teen, for instance, cannot easily be isolated from the relationships the teen has with others in her or his social environment. Nor can the social worker assume that he or she will be able to assess or measure the client's problem at regular intervals over a specific period of time. Some of the more significant problems that can hinder the regular use of measures in practice are such things as missed appointments, the inability to contact a client at a specific time, client noncompliance, and the premature termination of services. These types of uncontrollable factors can severely hinder the repeated measurement of clients' problems.

There are some variables that will be more difficult to operationalize and measure in practice. For example, measures for childhood internalizing disorders, such as anxiety or depression, have not been as well developed as measures of the same problems for adults. Developing criteria for assessing the presence and severity of these disorders can be difficult. One potential problem with existing measures of childhood internalizing disorders is that they are simply derivatives of approaches developed originally for adults (Kovacs &

Lohr, 1995). The world of practice is filled with such difficulties in operationalizing concepts and measuring client problems.

This discussion of measurement is not intended to suggest that measurement does not have a critical role in good practice. On the contrary, it is essential for good practice. In social work, there is a strong need for accurate and thorough information that can be used for developing treatment plans, selecting interventions, and evaluating practice efforts. Social workers need to recognize, however, the limits that currently exist in the measurement of human behavior, problems, and social phenomena. One of the critical measurement tasks they face in practice, therefore, is to learn about the variety of measurement options that are available, their respective strengths and weaknesses, how each can be selectively applied to best assess clients' problems, and how one can proceed when ready-made measures do not exist.

Ecology   Science attempts to isolate phenomena so that they can be better studied. This requires the control, through strong research design, of environmental factors. These factors are often called confounding variables, and they are considered to be a major road block in the conduct of good science. In many scientific endeavors, the goal is to control (by holding constant) all confounding variables and demonstrate that one variable is a cause of another. It is critical, therefore, that in establishing causality the scientist control the ecology (systemic factors) in which a phenomenon is embedded.

In practice, social workers rarely if ever are able to control the ecology in which a client's problem is embedded; in many cases, they must utilize aspects of the client's ecology. As noted, social workers are concerned primarily with individual systems, such as a single person, a family, or a community. The realities of practice, however, force them to also consider the interrelationships among these individual systems as possible targets of intervention or as allies to be used in the process of changing the client's problem. This means that they must assess the ecology of a client's problem and intervene with that ecological system when necessary. Thus, even if it were possible to control the ecology of the client's problem in the sense of holding it constant, as may be required by science, social workers would not want to do so because of the demands of providing services to their client.

This potential reliance upon ecology as a target of change or as an ally of change can pose problems in terms of any attempt to demonstrate that a causal relationship exists between the services provided and the client's positive outcomes. By the nature of the profession, social workers often need to utilize the very range of factors that they simultaneously need to hold constant in order to establish causality. This means that they may experience great difficulty in demonstrating that their interventions were the cause of clients' improvements.

Practice Contexts   One last set of factors distinguishes science from practice. Social work practice is shaped and impacted by the realities of being an applied profession. The conflicts created by the differing demands of doing science and doing practice have been well described by Thomas (1978). We work in a practice context that consists of complex human problems presented to us in our own work contexts, which can include large caseloads, intense agency pressures to serve large numbers of clients, and a dearth of resources. That is, we work in field settings, not science laboratories. This creates conflicts between the rules of science and the realities of practice. Conducting practice and determining its effectiveness is beset with ongoing methodological concerns that many scientists never have to face. We often run into situations, for instance, in which it would be impossible, for political, ethical, and legal reasons, to randomly assign clients to experimental versus control groups. We will probably never be in a situation in which we can randomly select clients with whom to work. Moreover, social work practitioners face many situations for which outcome measures may be limited or nonexistent, sample sizes too small, or client attrition uncontrollable. To correct such methodological shortcomings can be expensive, complex, and time-consuming, if possible at all. Again, it is our position that science and practice are to some extent in conflict due to unique purposes, roles, methods, and contexts. Using science as the sole foundation for practice therefore becomes problematic. We suggest a shift in thinking. This shift moves one toward viewing science as a set of tools consisting of many methods, techniques, and ways of thinking that can help the social worker to conduct and evaluate practice. In this view, science cannot claim to be the sole source of "truth." Rather, science can be understood as one source of data (albeit a very important one) that helps practitioners make sense of multiple "truths," including principles of ethics; moral codes and beliefs; managed care demands; social structures; agency politics, culture, and climate; and competing ideologies. Knowing how and when to apply the tools of science thus becomes critical in helping to make sense of any practice situation or context.

USING *N* = 1 DESIGNS TO CONDUCT AND ENHANCE SOCIAL WORK PRACTICE

We have learned that science is not practice, and practice is not science. Despite the differences between science and practice, however, science remains a powerful and important tool for assisting and informing practice. In particular, there are sufficient parallels between the logic of single-subject designs and social work practice to make single-system designs a dynamic, effective tool for informing and guiding practice. The use of single-subject designs encourages us to carefully identify and assess the target problems presented by the client. It also facilitates making our client central to her or his own treatment, as we negotiate and contract with the client to establish the goals of intervention. Single-subject designs also lend themselves to monitoring the client's progress through treatment, and to making adjustments when it is obvious that the service goals are not being reached. Finally, single-subject designs permit the evaluation of treatment, and are useful for suggesting appropriate points at which to terminate intervention. In short, these designs and the accompanying use of measurement are among the most powerful tools available for practitioners. Together they provide regular, objective feedback on the practice of social work. They tell us whether our clients have received the assistance they need to alleviate or eliminate the problems they presented to us. They give us the information we need to adapt our interventions, or to switch to alternate interventions when necessary. And although these designs may also be used for broader evaluative purposes, this must be considered a secondary benefit of the technology. The real benefit is improved practice.

To better understand this relationship between single-subject designs and practice, it is useful to examine a model of practice and the contributions that single-subject designs can make at each stage of the practice model. There are many practice models available in the literature. Since we are talking about using single-subject designs as a tool to facilitate and monitor change, though, it is useful to see where they fit into a practice model that focuses on change. Sheafor, Horejsi, and Horejsi (1994) present a five-phase model of the change process employed in social work. This model and the potential contributions made by single-subject designs to each phase of the change process are shown in Figure 3.1.

Intake and Engagement

This phase of the change process involves three distinct components. The first component is a preintake step. During this step, we must recognize that many clients have a history of involvement with professional helpers. Many clients, therefore, enter professional involvement with us with some trepidation, reluctance, anger, and/or resentment. It is important to set the stage for further involvement with the client by arranging a comfortable and private meeting area, presenting oneself as a professional, and considering all available client information. Next, the social worker and client must begin the engagement phase. This includes working toward the creation of an empathic, open, and collaborative relationship that is infused with a sense of promise and hope for the client. Finally, a formal intake process must occur. This is the first concrete-action stage. The practitioner and client must arrive at a consensus about why the client is seeking assistance (problem identification) and whether the agency-client match is appropriate. Assuming that this takes place, the process of defining roles and expectations for both the practitioner and the client begins.

At the intake and engagement phase, the contribution of single-subject designs is rather limited. Experience in clearly defining and assessing client problems can contribute to a briefer and more thorough identification period. There are also instances in which the measures that might become part of a single-system design are actually used by the agency or practitioner as a screening or diagnostic tool. The information gathered from this initial application of specific measures is used to gather background information that can assist the social worker in the decision about whether to refer this client elsewhere or proceed with intake. It can also give a sense of the urgency involved with

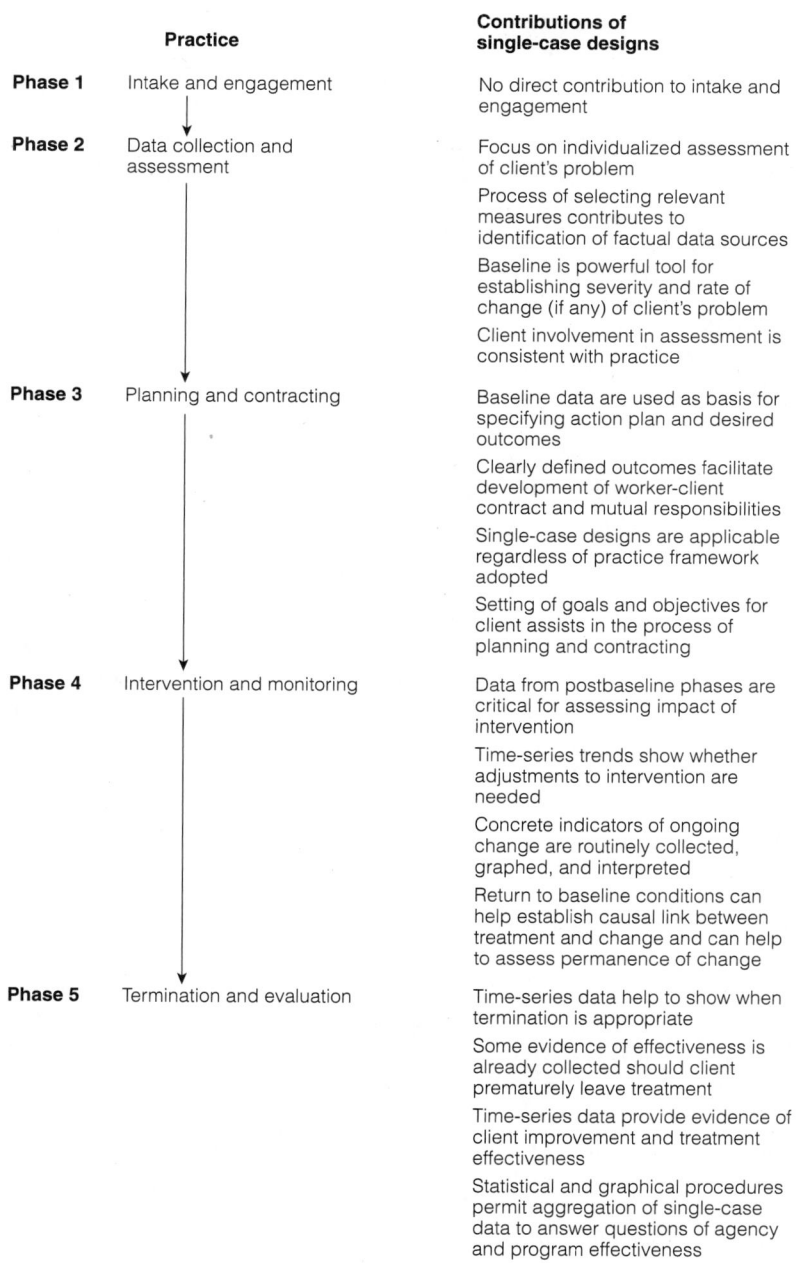

	Practice	Contributions of single-case designs
Phase 1	Intake and engagement	No direct contribution to intake and engagement
Phase 2	Data collection and assessment	Focus on individualized assessment of client's problem
		Process of selecting relevant measures contributes to identification of factual data sources
		Baseline is powerful tool for establishing severity and rate of change (if any) of client's problem
		Client involvement in assessment is consistent with practice
Phase 3	Planning and contracting	Baseline data are used as basis for specifying action plan and desired outcomes
		Clearly defined outcomes facilitate development of worker-client contract and mutual responsibilities
		Single-case designs are applicable regardless of practice framework adopted
		Setting of goals and objectives for client assists in the process of planning and contracting
Phase 4	Intervention and monitoring	Data from postbaseline phases are critical for assessing impact of intervention
		Time-series trends show whether adjustments to intervention are needed
		Concrete indicators of ongoing change are routinely collected, graphed, and interpreted
		Return to baseline conditions can help establish causal link between treatment and change and can help to assess permanence of change
Phase 5	Termination and evaluation	Time-series data help to show when termination is appropriate
		Some evidence of effectiveness is already collected should client prematurely leave treatment
		Time-series data provide evidence of client improvement and treatment effectiveness
		Statistical and graphical procedures permit aggregation of single-case data to answer questions of agency and program effectiveness

FIGURE 3.1 Contributions of single-system designs to social work practice.

Source: Based on and adapted from Sheafor, Horejsi, and Horejsi (1994).

the intake process. In general, however, many clients who come to see us feel both a sense of urgency and apprehension. Therefore, it is important to place good practice—relationship and trust building—above any desire to gather empirical data.

In realistic terms, the intake and engagement phase sets the stage for a productive implementation of a single-subject design. Successful engagement with the client begins the process of building mutual trust, communication, and expectations. It is the resultant relationship that allows the client to actively participate in the planning and implementation of a single-subject design. It is also the resultant relationship that forms the foundation for client understanding about the purpose and procedures employed in a single-subject design.

Data Collection and Assessment

The heart of this second phase is to generate the facts that help the practioner understand the client's problem and the factors that will contribute to or prevent change. In addition, we must identify potential resources that will be needed to fuel the change process. This phase consists of two distinct components. The first is data collection. The client's problem must be recognized as both similar to other problems experienced by clients who have been served by the agency in the past, and as a unique phenomenon being experienced by this particular person. Because the client's problem is individualized, it is also critical to have the client actively participate in decisions about what data are to be collected and how data collection will occur. Data collection may take many forms—direct observation, structured interview, formal testing procedures, rapid assessment scales, and so on. Finally, it is important to specifically focus data collection on the change process. The information generated needs to be relevant, appropriate for making decisions about the progress of treatment, and factual in nature.

The second component in this phase is assessment. Assessment is the interpretation of information (data) collected about the client's problem. The data are organized and summarized to get a concrete sense of what is known about the client's problem, and to identify specific targets of change. As in data collection, the client is expected to actively participate in the assessment process. Both the social worker and the client consider what needs to change and how to bring about that change. From this set of preliminary operationalizations, a preliminary plan for intervention will be formulated. In other words, working hypotheses about the client's problem and the proposed intervention(s) are generated. These hypotheses will be tested as the worker and client progress deeper into the change process.

Single-system designs have a great deal to offer this phase. One of the central tasks in the implementation of a single-system design is to develop an individualized assessment and intervention plan for a target problem (or target problems), which is consistent with the need for practice to be flexible. Social workers can use the elements of single-system designs to meet the need for both accurate assessment of the client's problems and accommodation of the diversity among clients and the problems they bring to the worker.

The major challenge for data collection and assessment is to answer the question, "Have the client's problems and the context underlying those problems been adequately and validly defined?" The search for answers to this question usually begins with general questions to the client about personal strengths and weaknesses, the social context of her or his problems, and personal, professional, or societal resources that might impact on the problems being addressed. This will give the practitioner a firm sense of what issues will become priorities for intervening with the client. One of the realities of practice, however, is that all of us approach problems with unconscious biases, conceptual schemas, and expectancies (Garb, 1998; Gilovich, 1991). It is therefore helpful to apply additional measures (such as standardized measures) that have been shown to validly assess the problems the practitioner has begun to identify. This serves two purposes. It supports (or challenges) the initial professional opinions and ideas about the case, and it serves as a vehicle for more clearly specifying and defining the key elements of the problem presented. First, we work toward selection of specific problems that will be the target of intervention. Then we engage in the process of selecting relevant measures that contribute to our understanding of the target problems. Finally, we get a concrete measure that provides factual data about the severity of these problems.

As we begin the helping process, it is often useful to get a sense of how our client's problem is changing. The application of measurement tools for data collection and assessment is, therefore, particularly useful if we are able to establish a pretreatment, or baseline, phase. Of course, there are many instances in which a baseline is not possible. A client who expresses suicidal ideation, for example, should not be assessed repeatedly over time before we intervene to prevent our client from acting on her or his suicidal thoughts. For many clients, however, assessment is strengthened by the information gained in a good baseline (see, e.g., Barlow & Cerny, 1988). We not only learn about how severe the client's problem is, but also get to see the direction and rate at which the problem is changing. All of this information is critical for the planning and contracting phase that is to follow and for later attempts to evaluate the effects of the interventions that are implemented.

Planning and Contracting

The third phase of the helping process involves formulating an actual plan of action that will lead to change in the problem(s) identified in the data collection and assessment phase. It also involves developing a formal or informal contract between the practitioner and client that outlines the roles and expectations of each in relation to the action plan.

The planning aspect of this phase is crucial to good practice. A good plan clearly specifies the exact changes the practitioner and client wish to accomplish. Long-term goals must be set for the client. Long-term goals present problems, though, because they are often global, do not maintain client motivation well, and are difficult to measure. Therefore, we also need short-term objectives for the client, objectives that Sheafor et al. (1994) call concrete, attainable, and measurable. The short-term objectives in fact provide a focus for ongoing intervention and monitoring. Finally, the practitioner and client must carefully detail the strategies for change that they will employ. Each activity is identified, along with a solid rationale about how that activity will contribute to the change desired.

Once long-term goals, short-term objectives, activities, and the conceptual linkages between them are clear, the practitioner and client are able to form a practice contract. This contract may or may not be formalized into a written plan. In good practice, however, it is a mutual agreement that outlines the problems to be addressed, specific assessment and monitoring procedures, mutual obligations on both the worker and client, timelines for the intervention, and logistical details such as schedules and locations for meetings.

Single-system designs are a useful tool in helping to focus the planning and contracting aspects of practice. The results from measures applied in the data collection and assessment phase can serve as the focal points for planning and contracting, particularly if the client has had an ongoing chance to discuss baseline data with the practitioner. Together the worker and client can discuss the severity of the problems assessed, and any fluctuations or trends apparent during the baseline phase. And together they can identify the long-term goals and short-term objectives that will form the basis of the action plan and the outcomes by which to judge success.

There are two other major contributions that a single-system design can make to planning and contracting. First, regardless of the practice framework adopted by the practitioner, a single-system design can be applied to the action plan that will be developed. Single-system designs are compatible and functional for an incredibly wide diversity of practice theories, models, and perspectives. The practitioner does not have to change his or her professional model to adopt the technologies favored by single-system designs. This gives both the practitioner and client great flexibility to decide what activities will become part of the action plan. Second, the development of clearly operationalized outcomes facilitates both the practitioner's and client's awareness and comfort with the action plan developed. The client can truly become integrated into the change process by shaping the goals and objectives that are selected as targets, and then helping to specify the action plan that will be followed. From the practitioner's perspective, the use of a single-system design is critical for clarifying the roles and responsibilities to be adopted, and the expectations to be laid out for the client. These are the keys to good practice planning and contracting.

Intervention and Monitoring

This phase of the helping process is the first in which the practitioner focuses on the action of social work. It represents the application of the worker's knowledge and skills in doing what is expected of her or him in the contract formed with the client. The worker must assist the client in performing her or his roles and activities, bring external resources or change agents to bear on the problem being addressed, monitor the client's progress, and ensure that any progress made is stabilized into a more permanent state for the client. These tasks break into three distinct components: intervention; monitoring; and stabilization.

When implementing an intervention, the practitioner is rarely the central factor in facilitating change. Social workers usually act as a catalyst; they are not the fuel that drives change—the fuel is found in clients' efforts, motivation, skills, knowledge, and responsibility. Social workers provide knowledge, and the encouragement and guidance to facilitate change. In this model, intervention can take many forms, depending on the practice context set by the client and agency. Intervention, for example, might include securing financial or child welfare assistance, social support, education, counseling, service coordination, policy analysis, lobbying, service brokering, client advocacy, research, and so on.

The monitoring component of this phase is critical to good practice. We each have a professional responsibility to continually assess the impact of what we do on behalf of our clients. Are we in fact being successful in our intervention? Through ongoing evaluation of our client's progress toward achievement of the contracted goals and objectives, we are able to get an immediate sense of the efficacy of our efforts. Just as importantly, if we discover that our intervention is not contributing to successful change, we can modify the intervention or abandon it in favor of another practice option.

Finally, in practice we concern ourselves with stabilizing the achievements made by our clients. One of the things we know about change in any system (remember that our profession takes a person-in-environment focus) is that change may cause disequilibrium. The natural tendency of any system is to restore itself to the previous state of equilibrium. Therefore, the practitioner's awareness and efforts are very important for stabilizing the changes accomplished by the client and/or the environment that impinges upon the client. It is perhaps in the intervention and monitoring phase of the helping process that single-system designs have the most to offer. By this point in the change process, the client and practitioner have selected target problems, collected baseline data if possible, and developed an action plan. Now that the intervention is being implemented, some key questions arise. Is the intervention having any impact on the target problems? How much change is occurring? And perhaps most importantly, are the changes those that we want to see?

By continuing to apply the selected measures over time and portraying these data within a single-system design, the practitioner and client can quickly and easily establish preliminary evidence about the initial impacts of intervention. The picture that emerges will show whether the severity of the client's problem is unchanged, decreasing, or increasing. We hope to see a trend that shows our client is improving as the action plan unfolds. Often, however, the intervention will have minimal impact on the client's problems. This should cause the practitioner to reconsider the nature of the intervention. In some cases, the intervention can actually exacerbate the client's situation. In this event, the practitioner needs to know this is happening immediately, so that the current intervention can be modified or abandoned. Administration of measurement tools at periodic intervals as part of a single-system design provides the timely information that is needed for such monitoring.

Single-system designs also contribute to monitoring through the assessment of how stable change has been for the client. A practitioner who is ethically and practically able to remove the intervention for a period of time can still continue to apply measurement tools to the client's target problems. This does two things for practice. In terms of monitoring, it shows whether the client's achievements have become stabilized. If they have, the practitioner has evidence to suggest that proceeding to a termination phase is appropriate. If the change is not stable, however, this suggests that the practitioner may need to reintroduce the intervention and focus on identifying and encouraging resources that will assist the client in making positive changes more than a temporary phenomenon. The return to a baseline phase also creates a stronger evaluation design. The return to baseline can contribute significantly to providing evidence of the efficacy of practice. This is an evaluative process discussed in more detail in the next section on the termination and evaluation phase.

Termination and Evaluation

The fifth and final stage of the change process concerns what happens when the practitioner nears the final stages of a practice encounter. The first task is to prepare for and complete termination. The practitioner must prepare the client for ending the mutual relationship and bonds that have developed as they worked together. This may involve dealing with any apprehension, anger, or other emotions felt by the client as they near completion of the helping process. It also involves, however, discussing with the client why termination is important and the rationale that explains why termination is occurring at this particular point in time.

The evaluation component of this phase is important for guiding and developing practice. On a direct level, it gives practitioners a final chance to examine their practice, and to ask whether their intervention was effective. They can review the contract formulated with the client, and reflect upon gaps in their efforts to assist the client, modifications that became necessary, and critical factors that may have contributed to their practice success and/or failure. Practitioners should not be afraid to recognize failure. The systematic study of intervention failures has led to the discovery of critical conditions under which a treatment works and does not work (see, e.g., Foa, Grayson, Steketee, & Doppelt, 1983; Foa, Grayson, Steketee, Doppelt, Turner, & Latimer, 1983). On a broader level, though, evaluation also takes a wider view. The agency will want to know if the services it delivers are effective, and whether any changes to its programs are required. It may also need to gather collective information in response to funders or accreditation bodies. This issue obviously relates to the notion of accountability we discussed earlier in this chapter.

Single-system designs can contribute significantly to decisions about termination. The trends and patterns shown in data collected as part of the design help to show whether in fact progress has been made in addressing the client's problems. Visual inspection of the baseline and intervention data will show, for example, whether a client's scores on a depression or marital satisfaction scale have improved to the point at which intervention may no longer be needed. This is particularly important if the client has reservations about her or his own ability to deal with the target problems once intervention has ended. The practitioner can discuss the data and graphs with the client, and point to concrete evidence that he or she has made significant process. From this basis, both can discuss the appropriateness of termination. Moreover, if the practitioner has been able to apply a second baseline phase, the data may show that changes to the targeted problems are stable. This helps to confirm for the client that he or she now has the capabilities and resources to face the problems without professional assistance.

The utility of any single-system design for evaluative purposes depends somewhat on the actual design applied to the practice situation. In the simplest single-system design (called a B design), for example, the practitioner monitors the client's target problem only while intervention is applied. Neither baseline data nor posttreatment (follow-up) data are collected. In such a design, we can only show that the client's problem improved during intervention. We do not know, however, if that problem was already improving before intervention, or whether the client's progress was lost once intervention ceased. This means that we know client improvement and intervention occurred simultaneously, but we cannot attribute this improvement to intervention. Too many other factors may have contributed to the change process. Other single-system designs are more useful for establishing the effectiveness of intervention. Some designs, for example, can show through sequential baseline and intervention phases that the client's problems remained unchanged before intervention, improved for the better during intervention, reverted somewhat during a second baseline phase, and improved again when intervention was applied a second time. Such trends in client scores are unlikely to be coincidental, thus giving the practitioner some evidence of the efficacy of the intervention. It should be noted that the evidence of intervention effectiveness provided by any single-system design is better than no concrete, systematically collected information at all.

Another benefit of single-system designs for determining practice effectiveness relates to one of the limitations of traditional group comparison (nomothetic) research (Nugent, 1996). We have discussed the impact of premature client termination on data collection and evaluation. It is common for clients to unilaterally terminate the helping process, which plays havoc with data collection geared toward widely separated points in time. When using a single-system design, though, data collection is an ongoing process that occurs on a regular basis. So when a client does terminate unexpectedly, the practitioner is left with at least a partially completed time-series data set. This is not an ideal situation, but the practitioner does have some information about the effectiveness of the intervention.

Finally, as a profession, social work is increasingly concerned with issues of accountability. Reductions in resource allocations, demands from funders for evidence of program value, and increasing competition from other disciplines are all putting pressure on social work to justify what it does. Single-system designs have great potential (largely unrealized to date) for providing information related to accountability.

It is a popular myth that while single-system designs have much to offer practice evaluation, they are of little value for the purposes of program evaluation. Program administrators can in fact benefit from single-system designs in many ways. Bloom, Fischer, and Orme (1999), for instance, suggest that administrators can learn from several types of information derived from single-system designs. This information includes: aggregated program data on client problems and strengths; data on the success of intervention with specific problems; data on the caseload performance of particular practitioners; and overall data on how well the program's practitioners are performing. The criticism of such data has long been that it is impossible to aggregate unique data from single cases into program- or agency-level data that can be meaningfully interpreted. There are relatively new procedures, however, that do help us aggregate the data from isolated practice cases into data sets that are useful for program evaluation. It is beyond the scope of this chapter to discuss the nature of these statistics here, but they are discussed more thoroughly later in this book.

SUMMARY

This chapter has focused on the differences between science and practice. We hope we have made it clear that science is not practice, nor is practice science! There are, however, scientific tools that can help practitioners do and enhance practice. One of the most powerful of these tools is the single-system design. Together the features of a single-system design—setting measurable client objectives, selecting valid and reliable outcome measures, and graphically displaying data collected from these measures over time—can contribute to the entire helping process. At each phase of the helping process, the tools offered by single-system designs can enhance practice. Moreover, the adaptable nature of single-system designs gives the practitioner considerable flexibility in deciding how to best apply them to any practice situation. This fact is what makes single-system designs a practice tool, not a restrictive scientific method.

4

**Monitoring and
Evaluating Clinical
Practice**

I n the last chapter, we described the valuable contributions that single-system designs can make to the conduct of effective practice. In this chapter, we provide more detail by offering concrete suggestions for using these designs to monitor and evaluate the progress that clients make. We begin by discussing the nature and purpose of client monitoring, including the most common questions that practitioners ask. We then provide a basic framework for realistically monitoring and evaluating client problems, and changes in those problems over time. We conclude this chapter with a discussion of specific single-system designs that allow practitioners to conduct a basic evaluation of a client's progress over time.

THE NATURE OF MONITORING
CLINICAL PRACTICE

Practitioners face difficult and complex dilemmas on a daily basis in their social work practice. Each working day they must assess the issues and needs brought to them by new clients, make decisions about the most appropriate interventions to assist their clients, and determine how well their clients are progressing through the treatment process. All of this is complicated by the demands imposed on them by the modern human service environment, with its growing administrative pressures and focus upon quality assurance. It often seems that practitioners must increasingly make critical observations, judgments, and decisions in a context that provides little guidance or time for such matters.

Social work practitioners possess unique combinations of professional experience, training, professional and personal skills, and intuition that make these professional tasks easier. These combinations are referred to as practice wisdom (Klein & Bloom, 1995) or cognitive maps (Ingram, 1986). They offer conceptual templates or guides for practice. That is, practitioners bring a specific set of beliefs, expectations, and knowledge to bear on client problems and their relationships with clients. Without such cognitive structures, they would operate in a relative vacuum—and obviously not be nearly as effective. Yet something more is needed. Practice wisdom and relationships with clients are not enough. First, we need to recognize the limitations of practice wisdom as a guide to practice (see, e.g., Dawes, 1994, especially chapters 2, 3, and 4; Garb, 1998; Gilovich, 1991). Second, research has shown that certain technical intervention procedures add significantly to the portion of change that clients experience that is attributable to our interpersonal skills and our relationship with our clients (see, e.g., Persons & Burns, 1986). Thus, we need a systematic way of examining our beliefs about the interventions we have selected, of testing our expectations about how the selected interventions will work, and of expanding our knowledge about the results of our practice efforts. Monitoring and evaluating our practice offers a means of doing these things. The process of monitoring and evaluating also allows us to collect ongoing information that answers questions about the accuracy of our assessments, inferences, judgments, and decisions. In other words, monitoring and evaluating helps us to build reliable and valid foundations that will expand upon the practice wisdom that we have accumulated.

It must be remembered, however, that we do not want to make practice fit the requirements of science but, rather, to make science fit the requirements of practice. It is useful to identify a few core questions that monitoring and evaluation may help us to answer. Nurius and Hudson (1993) offer five such questions, discussed in the text that follows. Each question relates to our everyday judgments, and each can be at least partially answered by the effective monitoring and evaluation of our practice.

Question number one: Have I validly and adequately defined the client's priority problems and the intervention context? This question is the foundation of our clinical assessment. We must use the information provided by our clients (both explicit and implicit) to formulate a strong sense of the problem areas that need to be addressed. For example, consider a hypothetical client named Dan T., a young man who lives in constant pain as a result of an industrial accident. Dan can no longer work. Among other issues, Dan displays signs of depression, extreme anxiety, and sexual dysfunction. In assessing Dan T.'s case, we would ask many questions about these issues. Which of these problems appears to be most severe, or most urgent? How recently did they appear? How closely do these issues mirror his bouts of physical pain? How are Dan's social relationships being affected, or are they perhaps affecting his problems? These questions that we ask, the observations and judgments that we make, and the final assessments that we make are in fact all examples of clinical measurement. Client monitoring and evaluation simply takes these assessments and measurements and enables us to conduct them in a more systematic way. That is, we identify the information required to make a thorough assessment and find the appropriate measures to collect this information. Then we conduct these measures, hopefully over a number of observations or points in time, so that we get a set of objective data that supplements our practice wisdom. We could, for example, have Dan T. complete a standardized instrument such as the Gate Control Pain Management Inventory (GCPMI; Hudson, Faul, & Sieppert, 1996) to measure his chronic pain and its effects. This instrument might tell us that he suffers from frequent skeletal, muscular, and abdominal/chest pain, but that the pain is most severe in muscular areas. Perhaps more importantly, the instrument might also tell us that pain is affected as much by social modifiers (mood, tension, etc.) as it is by physical modifiers. The instrument might also verify Dan's statements by showing that he is indeed depressed and anxious. In fact, his scores on a "suicidal thoughts" subscale might show that Dan requires immediate counseling regarding potential self-harm. Clearly this information would be invaluable in determining whether we have adequately defined the nature and range of Dan T.'s presenting problems.

Question number two: Is this client progressing? Often identifying and tracking change is difficult. Many judgments about client progress are based on personal observations, beliefs, and intuitions, and these are frequently (unfortunately) not valid (see Dawes, 1994, chapter 3; Garb, 1998). We all react to change on the basis of personal biases that are shaped by first impressions of clients, specific events in clients' lives or the client-worker relationship, or attributions about cause and effect that lead to erroneous assumptions. Client monitoring via a single-system design helps to identify change through a systematic process that compares relevant measurements of the client's problem(s) across time. By specifying target objectives along with the client, and then accurately measuring progress toward these objectives over time, we can simply but effectively monitor change for our clients in a manner less susceptible to personal errors of inquiry.

Question number three: Is the progress meaningful and sufficient? This question is one of degree. How far, in fact, has our client progressed toward the agreed-upon objectives? Is our client still at risk? Have our client's problems been stabilized, or have they decreased to a point that warrants cessation of treatment? As is probably obvious, answering such questions involves a process of comparison. We must compare ongoing measurements of client progress with both prior levels of the client's problem and with the goals set during the contracting phase of work with the client. Single-system designs contribute to answering the question of whether progress is meaningful and sufficient through the use of consistent and accurate measurements of the client's problems. We can visually review the development of change to help determine the practical significance of our client's progress. Such monitoring over time clearly traces the degree to which we are achieving, or not achieving, our client's goals.

Question number four: What attributions can I make about the cause of the observed progress (or lack of it)? We would all like to assume that our intervention directly led to improvements in the client's situation. Even if we observe improvement, however, it is risky to automatically conclude that our intervention caused changes in the client's problems. There are in fact many factors that can lead to change—changes in family status, newly formed relationships, normal developmental processes, resolution of crises, intervention by other persons (both professional and nonprofessional), and so on (Barlow, Hayes, & Nelson, 1984; Bloom, Fischer, & Orme, 1999; Kazdin, 1982). Careful monitoring of clinical practice, however, can assist us in showing the effects of intervention by establishing evidence for patterns of change. We discuss this more fully in the next chapter.

Question number five: What generalizations can I make about the future of this case or about other cases? While the previous question looks to causes of change, this question asks to what settings, cases, and treatments can we generalize the results we have obtained. This is a crucial question, as many of us tend to generalize far too easily. This is natural, as we try to extend the lessons of one case to our work on other cases. The monitoring and evaluation of clinical practice by single-system design methods will not automatically protect against this dangerous temptation. It will, however, force us to explicitly state client objectives, assessment procedures, and criteria for success. These help to make us aware of the idiosyncrasies of each case. Perhaps more importantly, they also allow us to replicate procedures and measures in systematic ways to build a body of evidence about the impacts of our practice (Barlow, Hayes, & Nelson, 1984). The successful replication of single-case design results can build a body of evidence that can support the applicability of specific intervention methods with clients in a range of settings (Harris & Jensen, 1985; Kazdin, 1998). Johnston and Pennypacker (1980) provide an excellent example of this with regard to the use of "time out" as a behavior control procedure.

By now it should be obvious that we believe monitoring and evaluation are powerful tools to improve practice. If we focus the monitoring and evaluation process on the five practical questions outlined here, it is clear that they have much to offer. What is required to make monitoring and evaluation truly useful, though, is a simple framework that puts practice needs ahead of scientific imperatives. The next section of this chapter provides such a framework.

THE SINGLE-SYSTEM FRAMEWORK

The following framework is a simple one. It is based on the fundamental procedures of the empirical practice model (EPM) introduced in Chapter 1. These procedures include: (1) measure the client's problem; (2) measure the client's problem repeatedly over time; and (3) manipulate the intervention. This fundamental model needs to be expanded upon a bit here, so that the concrete steps required to make single-system designs a practical part of everyday practice become clear. The single-system framework is based on the following four-step process:

1. Decide upon measurable client objectives.
2. Select appropriate measures to monitor progress toward these objectives.
3. Collect data over time by ongoing application of the measures.
4. Graph the results of this data collection so that it can be interpreted.

Deciding Upon Measurable Client Objectives

As indicated in Chapter 1, the first rule of EPM is that there can be no such thing as effectiveness until there is measurable positive change in the client's problem. This rule has a number of implications. First, we must have a thorough understanding of our client's problem and must know how we and the client want it to change. What is the nature of the problem? How severe are its effects? Is it deteriorating? How might we be able to intervene? All of these questions are related to the act of assessment. Second, we must then be in a position to highlight aspects of the client's problem that will serve as the targets of intervention. In other words, what is it about this problem that we can reasonably expect to change? Once this question is answered, we can measure change in the problem over time, $\Delta CP = CP_1 - CP_2$.

The act of setting measurable client objectives begins with developing a general sense of the client's problems. Clients often present a range of issues, concerns, or complaints. A single client, for instance, may bring up issues related to marital problems, financial difficulties, alcoholism, anger, and depression. Where do we start? In such cases, it is important to prioritize and then select one (or if absolutely necessary two or three) specific problems that will be targeted for change (Bloom et al., 1999). These targeted problems form the client objectives for our single-system design.

It is also important to remember that client objectives need to be something that we can reasonably expect to resolve. Grinnell, Gabor and Unrau (1997) suggest that client objectives must also be both comprehensive and precise. Each client objective must clearly explicate what is to be achieved, under what conditions, to what extent, and by whom. This is excellent advice, as any ambiguity leads to questions about the goals of intervention and how we will determine success. For example, imagine a hypothetical client named Bela T..Bela's presenting problem revolves around extreme anxiety and ambivalence related to her job. She reports constant restlessness, an inability to sleep, loss of appetite, deep feelings of resentment toward her job, and regular conflicts with coworkers. She tells the social worker that she wants to "fit in" better at work—a worthwhile goal, but not yet a useful client objective. After further inquiry, the worker discovers that Bela feels ill-equipped to fulfill her responsibilities at work. Her performance reviews have been sub-par, and she is constantly behind in completing her work. These issues are subsequently affecting every aspect of her work environment.

Together the social worker and Bela consider a range of possible objectives. Bela could ask for a transfer to a less technical and demanding job within the organization, pursue training that would make her job easier, or even move to another organization. She could also engage in more regular supervision sessions with her immediate supervisor. Bela T. tells the worker that she wants to stay at this organization, so together the two of them decide upon two client objectives. The first is to increase Bela's technical skills. They both agree that the worker will know this has been accomplished if Bela T. achieves at least an 80 percent average in two job-related courses at a local school of technology by the end of the year. The second client objective they decide on is to increase supervisor satisfaction with Bela's work over the next six months. This will be monitored by having bimonthly supervisory sessions with Bela's immediate supervisor, at which time the supervisor will complete a graphic rating scale assessing Bela's performance over the previous two weeks.

This example reminds us of a critical principle. Client objectives that are not measurable are useless. Developing client objectives is essentially a process of taking an abstract problem or issue and working with the client to clearly define this problem or issue in observable terms, and then deciding how it can be measured. Such a process is absolutely essential for any successful single-system design. Selecting appropriate measures is the topic of our second step.

Selecting Appropriate Measures

Monitoring progress toward client objectives cannot be successfully accomplished without the use of specific outcome indicators. These indicators are measures that the practitioner has carefully constructed, or more commonly chosen from a wide range of instruments professionally designed for that very purpose. Selecting appropriate measures is so important that Part II of this text is dedicated to discussing how practitioners can find or construct appropriate measurement tools. A few introductory comments are in order, though.

There are a number of options available for measuring progress toward client objectives. In practice, they boil down to four fundamental ways of measuring a client's problem: the *presence/nonpresence* of the problem, the *frequency* with which the problem occurs, the *duration* of the problem, and the *magnitude* of the problem (Nurius & Hudson, 1993). For instance, client problems can be measured as a dichotomy—the problem is either present or absent. A client is depressed or is not depressed; an objective is either achieved or it is not. Some problems lend themselves to frequency counts, such as the number of times a child hits his or her siblings, how often a client takes a prescribed medication, or the frequency of a client's self-affirming statements. Measures of duration focus on the length of an event or the length of time that passes between two events. Examples of duration measures include the length of time that a child's temper tantrums last; the duration of a headache; the length of time between social interactions or events (such as the length of time between a shy male's requests for a date with a young woman in whom he is interested); or the length of time that passes between a client's release from a residential program and the point in time that he or she experiences a relapse in a behavioral or mental health problem. Finally, magnitude measures record the level or severity of a phenomenon as judged by the client or an observer. These might include, for instance, scores on a self-efficacy scale, assessments of pain intensity, or self-assessments of the severity of depression. Regardless of the client's problem, the practitioner needs to select a measure that taps into one of these ways of measuring the problem.

The extent or severity of a client's problem cannot be considered measured until the practitioner identifies and adopts specific indicators. The key to creating a successful single-system design is to achieve an accurate picture of the client's functioning at any point in time. Deciding upon a measure of frequency, duration, and so on is not enough, however. Selecting appropriate measures must be matched with adoption of an appropriate measurement plan. This means that practitioners need to understand the standard measurement protocols and/or guidelines that have been developed for any existing instruments that are selected for use. It also requires that the specific measurement plan should be agreed upon so that both the social worker and client know who will do the measuring, when the measures are to be completed, and who can decide to alter the measurement plan. A lack of consistency or unexpected changes in the measurement plan should be considered potentially serious gaps in the information available to inform practice.

There are two basic types of measures available for single-system designs. Practitioners can create their own measures, a topic discussed in Chapter 16 of this book. There are in fact many practice situations and client issues for which previously constructed measurement instruments are not available or appropriate. This is often the case, for example, when working with children. There is a relative shortage of standardized instruments specifically designed for and validated with children. In these and similar circumstances, practitioners may be forced to develop their own simple measures. This can be a major undertaking, though not as daunting as it may sound provided that they understand the conceptual and practical foundations of constructing such instruments.

The empirical practice model relies heavily on the use of already existing short-form assessment scales. These scales are designed for swift completion and repeated administration over the course of service. More importantly, they have been carefully constructed and thoroughly tested to ensure they are capable of producing both reliable and valid indicators of the problems that clients face. These measures offer such high levels of efficiency, effectiveness, and ease of use that they are discussed in much more detail later in this book.

Collecting Data Over Time

The most powerful aspect of single-system designs is that they allow the social worker to monitor clients' problems over time. This longitudinal or time-series monitoring should be considered a vital source of information and feedback that supplements more traditional sources of feedback, such as case conferences and collateral contacts. This longitudinal or time-series information provides the social worker with a means of self-regulating practice, a source for making decisions about necessary corrections to treatment plans, and a powerful means of demonstrating client success.

The process of monitoring over time naturally implies that clients are asked to complete the selected measures on a regular basis. This is to be expected, as the primary value of the EPM lies in obtaining timely feedback to enhance practice. In short-term treatment, the measures should be completed consistently over short periods, once a week for example. In long-term treatment, the interval between measurements can be longer. If treatment is expected to last for up to six months, measurement every couple of weeks is probably about right. If the treatment is expected to last longer, however, the worker may want to have the measures completed once every three weeks or once a month.

Remember that the real purpose of collecting data over time is to provide the social worker with feedback. Data collection should not be made into a restrictive template that directs practice. The frequency and method of data collection should be as unobtrusive as possible and should make the information gained truly useful to both the worker and client. Information that is irrelevant or ignored is a waste of time and a detriment to good practice.

Graphing a Single-System Design

A number of single-system designs have already been graphed in this text. Obviously they are relatively simple to construct and use. We will review a few of the basic graphing principles, however, just to make sure practitioners are in a position to use these powerful tools. Many computer programs, such as Microsoft's PowerPoint and Corel's Presentations, enable practitioners to make graphs quickly and easily. Single-case design graphs can also be made using the CASS software that is described in Part III of this book.

The act of graphing a single-system design is really just a matter of plotting scores from the measures selected to monitor client objectives. These scores are placed visually on a chart that tracks the course of service over time. The simplest way to begin a single-system graph is to draw a graph with both a vertical and horizontal axis. The vertical axis is labeled and numbered to be consistent with the outcome measure selected, say scores (0–100) from the Generalized Contentment Scale (Hudson, 1997). The horizontal axis is labeled and numbered according to the duration or frequency of service, say days or weeks of treatment. Each time the selected measure is applied, the resulting score is plotted by drawing a data point at the right level along the vertical axis, directly above the appropriate point in time. Then the data points are connected across time. It is that simple. There are many examples of graphs for single-case designs in the figures throughout this book.

Graphing single-system designs can be done in a number of ways. One way is to draw the whole graph with pencil and paper. A slightly easier method is to have generic graphs printed in large quantities, and then fill in relevant labels and data points when required. As noted earlier, many computer programs can also produce quick and high-quality single-system graphs. Graphs can be created with most word processors and with any of the spreadsheet and graphics software now available. The graphs in this book were originally created using Corel's Presentations. There are software programs specifically designed to construct single-system designs. One such example is CASS, which will be discussed in more detail later. In any event, practitioners should select the method with which they are most comfortable and begin graphing single-system designs. Those who have not used such graphs before will be surprised at how powerful these simple visual representations can be for both the social worker and the client, as well as for supervisors and others interested in the outcomes for clients.

PHASES AND BASELINING

Now that we have described the basic single-system framework, we need to introduce two other concepts—the use of *phases* and the notion of *baselining*. These two methods allow us to manipulate treatment and to get at the heart of establishing the effectiveness of practice efforts.

The Concept of Phases

The true power of single-system designs lies in the use of phases. Phases are identifiable, distinct periods in a single-system design that correspond to specific episodes in the helping process. The act of monitoring a client's problem before any intervention is applied (such as during an assessment or waiting list period), for instance, is called a baseline phase. (More will be said about this shortly.) A distinct new phase in the design begins once a specific intervention is initiated with the client. Additional phases can be added to the design, as in the form of alternative interventions or a return to baseline periods or previously used interventions.

Each phase in a single-system design is normally assigned a letter of the alphabet to distinguish it from other phases. The baseline phase is called the "A" phase, representing a period of time during which no intervention is applied. Subsequent phases are lettered sequentially. For example, in the "B" phase, an intervention is applied for the first time. In a "C" phase, the B-phase intervention is stopped and a different intervention approach is used. Interventions can also be combined, and this practice strategy is symbolized in a single-system design by combining letters. For example, suppose that one decided to simultaneously use the two interventions that were used in B and C phases. The period during which both B and C phase interventions were used simultaneously would be labeled a "BC" phase. The specific single-case design is labeled by way of the phases used. For example, if one monitored a client's progress by using a baseline phase followed by a single treatment phase, the design would be called an "AB," or "A/B," design. If, after a baseline and first treatment period, one used a second, different treatment after the first one failed, one would be using an "ABC," or "A/B/C," design.

The use of phases does not imply that practitioners are limited to only one practice or intervention technique per phase. It does mean, though, that a specific measurable intervention, or combination of interventions or approaches, is applied per phase. This combination can take the form of a single-intervention package (such as Barlow and colleagues' intervention for panic disorder [Barlow & Cerny, 1988]), a few well-integrated and consistent practice techniques (such as the intervention methods comprising Beck's cognitive-behavioral treatment for depression [Young, Beck, & Weinberger, 1993]), or a whole treatment program (such as multisystemic therapy with delinquent adolescents [Henggler, Melton, & Smith, 1992]). Such freedom gives the practitioner great flexibility in applying single-system phases to practice. Any array of assessment and intervention techniques can be used in practice. As long as each phase is well defined and internally consistent, this array of tools and skills can be altered or combined in a wide variety of ways.

But why go to the work of splitting practice activities into phases and graphing the results? This juxtaposing of periods in which the worker does different things with the client is the heart of manipulating treatment. Manipulating treatment increases the worker's ability to make and interpret comparisons between measurements obtained in different phases. Baseline measurements give the worker an across-time profile of the client's problem(s) prior to, or in the absence of, any intervention. In subsequent intervention phases, observations continue to be made of the client's problem(s), and these measurements are compared to those from previous treatment phases or to baseline data. If the intervention is "working," then the client's problem would be expected to improve during the intervention periods relative to previous phases or the baseline period. That is, the client's problem would show differences indicating improvement during the treatment phase as compared to, for example, the baseline profile. The logic of this comparison is based on a critical assumption: the across-time pattern in the client's problem will be similar to that during baseline if nothing occurs to cause a change in the problem (Barlow et al., 1984; Bloom et al., 1999; Kazdin, 1982). The baseline pattern in the client's problem is extended into the next phase and is used as a prediction of what would have happened in terms of the client's problem in the absence of any intervention. Thus, any positive changes during intervention relative to the client's baseline functioning are suggestive of the effectiveness of the intervention used. There are ways to make an even stronger case for the effectiveness of an intervention, and these will be dealt with more directly in the next chapter. The analysis of single-case design data is covered in Chapter 6.

The Concept of Baselining

The concept of baselining is a fundamental, and at times misunderstood, component of single-system designs. Baselining refers to the practice of measuring the client's problem over a period of time before any intervention is implemented. It is in essence a period of observation or data collection that provides an across-time profile of the client's problem in the absence of any intervention. Baselining serves two fundamental functions. First, it can be an integral part of the assessment process. This should be no surprise, since the process of assessment involves working with the client to obtain information about the origin, severity, current status, and contexts related to her or his problem. The answers received draw a vivid picture of the client's situation and may suggest appropriate intervention approaches. Baselining simply adds another level of specificity to this natural part of the helping process. By applying reliable and valid measures to the client's problem during the baseline phase, a more thorough picture of the client's problem emerges.

Consider, for example, the case of a young woman named Tanya S. She entered a local family service agency, citing sadness and previous sexual abuse as issues with which she wanted help. Like many clients, however, she was vague and ambiguous when describing the nature and extent of these issues. As part of the assessment process, the intake worker asked Tanya S. to complete the Multi-Problem Screening Inventory (MPSI; Hudson, 1990). The instrument revealed that Tanya's major problems appeared to be depression, feelings of guilt, and drug use. The suicidal thoughts subscale showed that at the current time, suicidal ideation was very low and did not appear to be a critical issue. Tanya was asked to complete the same instrument a second time while on a brief waiting list. These repeated measurements confirmed that Tanya S.'s principal problems were depression, feelings of guilt, and drug use, and that she was currently not suicidal. When a counselor became available for Tanya, these problems were targeted for intervention.

This example highlights a critical aspect of using baselines in the assessment phase of practice. The procedures and data collected during a baseline phase are best considered one of many tools available to the practitioner. Baselining procedures are not a replacement for sound clinical judgment, interviewing skills, or other assessment techniques. Nor do they in themselves provide a complete assessment that is ready to be acted upon. Rather, baselining serves as a way to help structure the assessment process. The collection and recording of data during baselining offer a systematic method of observing the client's problems and determining their magnitude. It also gives initial information about how quickly these problems are changing. In short, baselining helps to make assessments more detailed and generally more complete.

The second primary purpose of baselining is to provide a basis for future comparisons of client functioning. The baseline profile of the client's problem is used as a reference basis against which to compare the treatment-phase profile of the client's problem. Any changes during treatment should contrast clearly and favorably against the baseline profile (Parsonson & Baer, 1986). In any practice situation, the practitioner makes an initial assessment of the client's problems, and then continually compares client progress with this initial assessment. Baselining does not alter this activity—it merely increases the precision with which it is done. It does so by offering systematic data collection procedures using sensitive and reliable measures over a period of time.

There are two methods of compiling baseline data. Each has a very different utility for the practitioner, and each serves as a valuable complement to the other. The first is known as a retrospective baseline. To construct a retrospective baseline, the client is asked to remember or recall the extent or nature of the problem at a specific point in the past. Using this past point in time as a reference, the client then completes the measure selected to assess the problem. There is some evidence to suggest that retrospective measures of client's problems are valid (Howard, Millham, Slaten, & O'Donnell, 1981; McMillan, Jongen, & Greenwood, 1996; Perneger, Etter, & Rougemont, 1997), though this evidence is by no means consistent (Ptacek, Smith, Espe, & Raffety, 1994; Simpura & Poikolainen, 1984). This technique obviously depends on the capacity of the client's memory and will be prone to the same limitations as any other methods that rely on memory. In general, however, it can help to highlight the client's problem at critical points in the past. This not only helps the client to express and understand the development of the problem, but it also gives the practitioner a stronger sense of the client's history. Retrospective baselines are perhaps most useful in situations in which it is not possible to delay treatment (such as in cases of suicidal risk).

Consider the following example. John B. is a new client who has sought help for feelings of insecurity and worthlessness. He says that right now he feels all right, but it is a constant struggle to convince himself that he is a good person. The practitioner might say, "John, I'd like you to think about some point in the past when you felt your worst. Now, thinking about that time, I'd like you to fill out the ISE [a self-esteem scale described in Chapter 11] for me." By having John B. complete the ISE retrospectively, the practitioner would obtain a sense about how John experienced his problem at its most severe. This would be both a useful basis for opening further dialogue with John and a point of comparison once treatment begins.

The practitioner might also say, "John, I'd like you to think about how you feel right now and fill in the ISE. I'd also like you to complete it once a week for the next two weeks. Then when you come back for our next meeting, we'll really get going on dealing with the issues you feel." By having John B. complete the ISE while other assessment activities are ongoing, the practitioner would be constructing a concurrent baseline. While retrospective baselines help identify historical patterns in a client's problem, concurrent baselines paint a picture of client functioning from the moment of intake through the introduction of intervention. They are the most common type of baselines used to help assess client problems, as they provide objective information about the current status of the client's problem and how it may be changing as assessment continues.

Regardless of whether a practitioner uses a retrospective or concurrent baseline, a few suggestions help make these baselines more effective for the practitioner. The first is that a single measurement during baseline is often misleading. The single measure that is obtained can be influenced by any number of things—the client's health that day, a sudden exacerbation of the problem, a chance interaction the client had just before coming to see the practitioner, and so on. Any of these could result in a higher (or lower) score than that which would be usual. This can give the practitioner a very misleading sense of the client's problem and lead him or her to later erroneously infer that the intervention has helped the client (a problem called regression to the mean; see Gilovich, 1991). It is therefore best to obtain more than a single baseline measurement so that a pattern can emerge in the data. This is sometimes not possible, of course; but it should be done if at all possible. In most cases, the practitioner should be able to obtain a couple of retrospective measures and a single concurrent measure, so that three baseline measurements will be available. As with all aspects of single-system designs, the practitioner must use his or her best clinical judgment and collect baseline data only with an eye toward how that data will be of use in working with this particular client.

Over two decades ago, Hersen and Barlow (1976) suggested that at least three baseline observations are required to identify any pattern in the client's problem. This remains good advice, though many would argue that even three baseline measures are too few (Parsonson & Baer, 1986). Client baselines often show frustratingly high levels of instability or fluctuation (again for any number of personal and external reasons). Relying on information provided by one or two data points is therefore somewhat risky, as any change observed could be misleading. As information is gained from the third data point and beyond, however, trends and fluctuations in the client's problem are easier to identify and interpret.

The best scenario for the practitioner is to obtain a stable baseline over the course of three or more measurements using a mix of retrospective and concurrent measurements if necessary. This is because stable baselines (i.e., those with no trend and little or no variability) are easier to interpret and understand. For example, a client who shows consistently high scores on the Index of Alcohol Involvement (see Chapter 11), as in Figure 4.1, is a client who: (1) has a clinically significant problem with alcohol that does not appear to be reactive to other factors; and (2) does not seem to be improving without intervention. Situations involving baselines that are not stable can be more difficult to interpret. For example, Figure 4.2 shows baseline data collected for Miles H., a client who expressed a great deal of dissatisfaction with the sexual relationship he shares with his wife of 15 years. Measures collected on the Index of Sexual Satisfaction (ISS) over a four-week period, however, showed considerable variation in Miles's feelings about this sexual relationship. Understanding the factors that lead to such dramatic variability in Miles H.'s satisfaction with his sexual relationship with his wife will require substantial clinical investigation. As will be seen in Chapter 6, a baseline such as that in Figure 4.1 makes the assessment of change between baseline and treatment much more straightforward than does a baseline such as that in Figure 4.2.

If the baseline data show a clear trend toward client improvement, questions emerge about the necessity of intervention. If the client's problem appears to be getting better without assistance, how does the social worker know that he or she should intervene? The worker may make things worse by slowing, or even reversing, the improving trend in the client's problem.

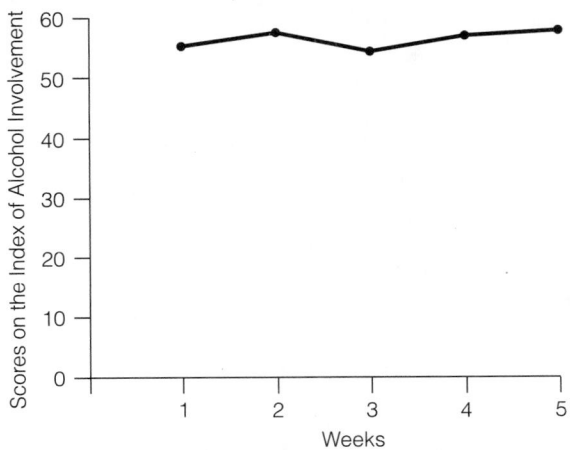

FIGURE 4.1 An example of a stable, easy-to-interpret baseline.

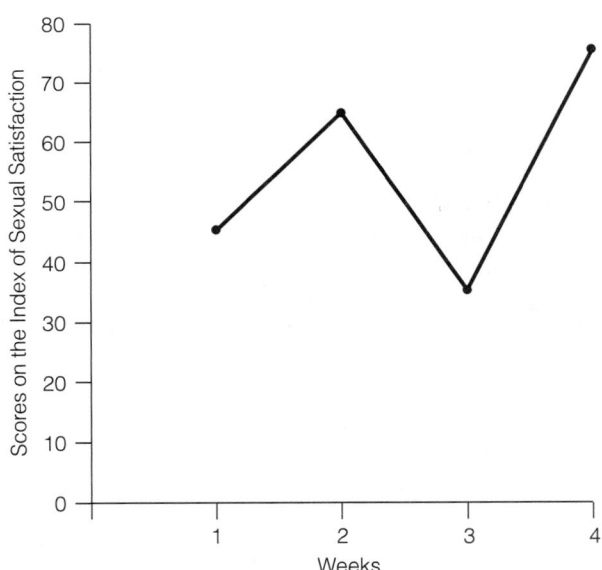

FIGURE 4.2 An example of a variable, more difficult-to-interpret baseline.

This brings us to the ethics of baselining. There are some who have vocally opposed the very existence of concurrent baselining, arguing that it is unethical to withhold treatment while baseline data are collected. We agree that strict adherence to baseline "rules" in the name of science or practice evaluation poses tremendous issues for good practice. It is simply inappropriate to automatically withhold intervention and collect baseline data to ensure a picture-perfect baseline period. This is one of the ways in which the demands of practice and the demands of science are in conflict (Thomas, 1978). We would argue, however, that if used with good clinical judgment and a sense of flexibility, baselines are a natural part of good social work practice. They can be as integral and ethical as any other aspect of practice.

The act of client assessment takes time, particularly if done thoroughly, and this time commitment is well suited to the use of baselines. In fact, a compelling argument can be made that a "rush to treatment" prior to a thorough and competent assessment is not only unethical but also a breach of a reasonable standard of care. If practitioners use their clinical judgment and collect baseline measures during the normal assessment process, a natural baseline is formed. This should not interfere with or lengthen the assessment process. In fact, it may both improve and shorten the process. In any event, assessment and baselining should occur during the same time span. If this is done, intervention can be introduced at exactly the same point it would be if a single-system design were not being applied.

There are circumstances under which the use of concurrent baselines is never acceptable. These most commonly occur when clients face emergency or crisis situations that involve potential harm. Many of these situations involve physical danger and life-threatening problems to the client, such as suicidal impulses or critical health issues. There are also cases in which a lack of intervention may increase the potential for the client to do harm to others. Most, if not all, of these cases present situations in which a concurrent baseline would be both unethical and, arguably, malpractice. Even here, though, the practitioner has options. The client may be asked to complete relevant baseline measures retrospectively. Although not as methodologically compelling as a concurrent baseline, data from a retrospective baseline can add information that is of use in evaluating the effects of interventions as well as demonstrating that the client has improved while under the social worker's care. Another option in these cases is to aggregate data across several clients, as we will discuss in Chapters 7 and 8. This aggregation allows the worker to use replication, a critically important procedure in the social sciences (Kazdin, 1998; Nueliep, 1991), to provide evidence of effective practice.

Baselines need to be approached with careful thought and sound rationales. Practitioners should keep in mind, though, that baselines are simply a specific form of collecting and recording data that is in reality similar to traditional practice approaches. We merely extend the traditional notion of assessment to include baseline measures. The procedures contained in baselining allow social workers to carefully observe changes in clients' problems over time. Just as importantly, the workers can then retrieve this information by pulling a client's graph from their files. With this retrieved information, they can review a client's progress with her or him, share the information with a clinical supervisor, and begin to aggregate the information to guide practice in other similar practice situations.

Finally, it must be remembered that baselining is more than a fancy tool to organize data. Baseline data also serve as a powerful vehicle for clients to gain a better understanding of their problems. It can be a uniquely empowering experience for clients to be active participants in problem assessment. Scores from baseline measures help clients understand the characteristics of their problems, and changes during the baseline period help to highlight trends or patterns in, as well as factors related to, their problems. Clients can often relate specific scores to events or external factors in their lives, a procedure called critical incident investigation, which gives a better awareness of the dynamics underlying their problems. By involving clients in baseline data collection, the practitioner offers them more control over their problems. Such involvement also helps to build a collaborative partnership between the worker and the client (Egan, 1990).

BASIC MONITORING DESIGNS

The following subsections discuss a number of single-system designs that are useful for monitoring practice. These designs generally focus on providing answers to the second and third practice questions posed in this chapter: Is this client progressing? and Is this progress meaningful and sufficient? In this sense, they help practitioners to be specific about a client's status at any point in time. These designs are presented as a tool to enhance practice, not as a scientific rulebook for social workers to follow. They cannot answer the final questions posed in this chapter, questions about causal linkages between intervention and client progress and about the generalizability of outcomes.

The B Design

This is the simplest and most basic single-system design for monitoring clinical practice. It consists of a single phase during which the practitioner repeatedly measures a client's targeted problems while intervention is applied. This implies that treatment can begin as soon as the client's problems are clearly identified, measures selected, and the intervention decided upon. This design fits very well with practice. Since there is no baseline period, there is no delay in starting the intervention. This lack of baseline measures, however, also means that no determination of causality can be made. This design is perfectly adequate if the questions the practitioner (or anyone else) wants to answer are "Is this client progressing?" and "Is the progress meaningful and sufficient?"

Consider the fictitious case of Tammy O. and her teenage son Michael. Tammy O. sought the help of a counselor because she and Michael seemed to be fighting constantly, and Michael's outbursts had been getting increasingly vocal and angry. Their caseworker quickly determined that Michael felt a deep sense of alienation from his mother and that Tammy was at a loss about how to rectify this situation. After some initial discussion, Tammy and Michael agreed with their caseworker's assessment that their primary task was to develop better communication skills. They both agreed, along with their caseworker, to use the Index of Family Relations (IFR; Hudson, 1997) as a measure for monitoring their progress in improving their relationship.

The caseworker decided upon a relatively simple intervention—instruction (and practice via role-plays) in conflict resolution and communication skills for both Tammy and Michael. The worker also chose to have both clients complete the IFR at the start of each session. Figure 4.3 shows the results tracked by the caseworker over time. These results clearly show that both Tammy and Michael made considerable progress over the 12 weeks of intervention and that this progress was substantial. It is important to remember, however, that these results do not enable the caseworker to demonstrate whether the weekly communication training sessions directly caused the observed improvements.

Figure 4.3 shows both the simplicity and the power of this basic monitoring design. By graphing the clients' IFR scores over time, the caseworker created a means of displaying her clients' progress. Such a graphical display is useful as a means of showing clients (as well as agency personnel and others) the extent to which they have progressed. Most importantly, however, these graphs act as a valuable source of feedback to enhance direct practice. The combination of assessments from a carefully selected outcome measure and graphs of these assessments over time gives the practitioner a quick, visual source of information that supplements other sources of information, such as verbal reports from clients and the worker's own clinical observations. This graphical feedback will, hopefully, show a rather steady and continuous improvement in clients' situations. It may also show, however, cases where clients fail to improve over time. It might even show cases where clients' situations deteriorate. In either of the last two situations, the practitioner will want to consider alternate intervention strategies.

The B design does not provide any substantial evidence that the intervention caused the client's progress because there are many uncontrolled factors that may have contributed to a client's progress other than the intervention used. This design does, however, provide concrete evidence of changes in clients' problems, and this is often a major practice evaluation task.

The BC and BCD Designs

The BC and BCD designs are sometimes called successive intervention designs. They are just like the B design, but with the addition of at least one extra phase in which a new intervention is introduced. This is most often done in cases where the expected improvements in the client's problem fail to develop with use of the first intervention. When a practitioner observes that there is no improvement, or only insufficient improvement, in a client's problem, he or she may decide to stop the first intervention and start a new one.

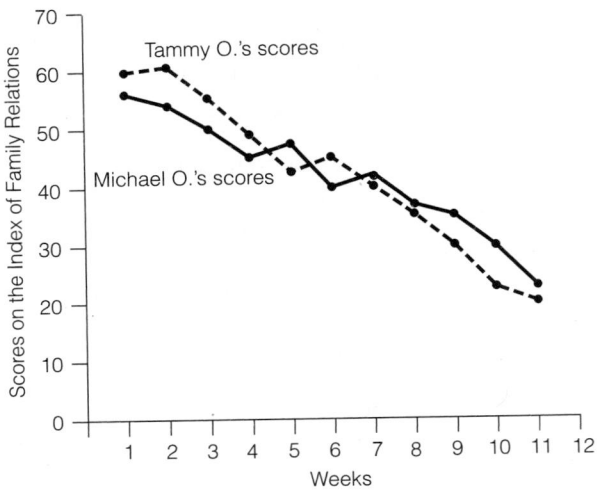

FIGURE 4.3 Tammy O. and Michael O.'s IFR scores over 12 weeks of treatment.

Figure 4.4 shows an example of such a case. This figure shows the case of Wayne Y., a client experiencing difficulty coping with a number of stresses in his life. His clinician determined that Wayne lacked effective stress management skills. Wayne and his clinician decided to use weekly applications of the Index of Clinical Stress (Hudson, 1997) as a measure of Wayne's stress levels. In the B phase, Wayne was taught progressive relaxation and a series of visualization exercises designed to help him relax when faced with stressful situations. It was apparent after four weeks, however, that Wayne was not making any progress.

Wayne Y.'s clinician decided to change interventions and began to teach Wayne the stress inoculation training program developed by Meichenbaum (Sundel & Sundel, 1999). This constituted the beginning of a C phase in this case. Regular use of the ICS was maintained, and the results graphed as before. Figure 4.4 shows that with the use of stress inoculation training, Wayne began to make progress. His stress scores started to decline, and by the end of 15 weeks he was functioning much better.

The BC and BCD designs have the same strengths and limitations of the B design. Their major strength lies in the provision of regular feedback to the practitioner—monitoring success, or the lack of it, over time. These designs can show only client progress, however. Like the B design, they do not control for extraneous factors that may affect the client's problems. In Wayne Y.'s case, for example, it may be tempting to conclude that the stress inoculation training caused Wayne's stress levels to decrease. Unfortunately, the BC or BCD designs do not provide evidence with qualities that support such inferences. A much more powerful design would be required to provide evidence that the stress inoculation training was a causal factor in the decrease in Wayne's stress levels.

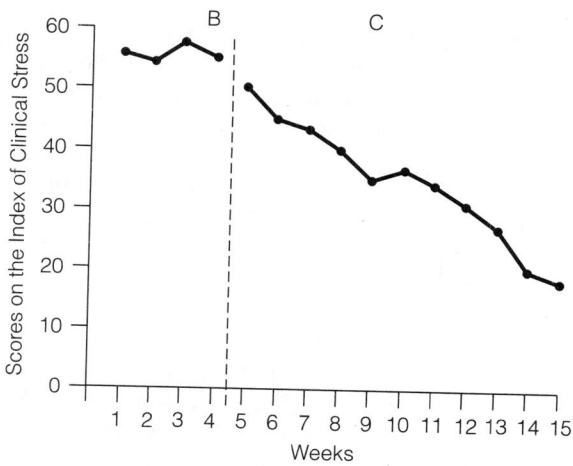

FIGURE 4.4 Wayne Y.'s scores over two different treatments.

The AB Design

The AB design has been referred to as the "basic" single-system design (Bloom et al., 1999). In order to use the AB design, the practitioner must be in a situation in which he or she can obtain a series of baseline measurements before intervention is implemented. After the baseline measurements are gathered, the practitioner starts treatment while simultaneously continuing to measure the client's problem. This second phase is called a treatment phase, and the data collected during treatment is called treatment phase data. The juxtaposition of baseline and treatment-phases creates the AB design.

Imagine that a clinician is helping a couple, Don and Karen C., with marital difficulties that they have encountered. The most salient difficulty that they complain about is relatively frequent verbal arguments. During the first meeting, the clinician has this couple remember the number of verbal arguments that they had the previous week. They remember three verbal arguments. This is an example of a retrospective measurement. Karen and Don will not be able to see the clinician again for two weeks. During this time, the clinician has the couple keep count of the number of verbal arguments that they have each day by recording them on a 3-inch by 5-inch index card. These counts are an example of concurrent baseline data. Two weeks later, the couple again meets with the clinician, and the practitioner initiates a marital therapy protocol and at the same time has the couple continue to keep count of the number of verbal arguments they have each day. The retrospective count obtained during their first meeting, together with the concurrent counts (all aggregated and plotted by week) obtained during the two weeks the couple were unable to see the clinician, comprise the A-phase, or baseline, data. The counts obtained during the provision of marital therapy comprise the B-phase, or treatment-phase data. The results of this AB evaluation are shown in Figure 4.5.

Figure 4.5 shows that the couple had a number of verbal arguments during baseline and that the weekly number of verbal arguments was somewhat variable. The weekly number of verbal arguments begins a gradual decline during treatment, and the variability in their arguments declines as well as treatment goes on. By the 12th week of treatment, the weekly number has dropped to zero, and between the 12th and 16th weeks, the numbers of verbal arguments remain quite low. These AB data clearly suggest that the couple experienced a decrease in the number of verbal arguments they had while receiving treatment from the clinician.

The addition of the baseline phase increases the power of this single-system design. The data in Figure 4.5 offer compelling evidence, from a clinical perspective, that the marital therapy may have been a causal factor in the decrease in the numbers of verbal arguments in which the couple engage. This evidence is, as discussed earlier, not compelling from a scientific perspective. However, given the conflicting demands of science and practice (Thomas, 1978), this may be, except in the most unusual cases, the strongest evidence that can be provided in the practice context.

Replicated AB Designs   Replication is central and critical to science (Kazdin, 1998) and can readily be carried out in practice. Some have argued that the replication of the simple AB design can build a scientifically compelling case for the effectiveness of an intervention (see Harris & Jenson, 1985). We discuss this issue further in Chapter 7. For now, we just want to alert the reader to the tremendous potential in using the simple AB design, and then replicating it across different clients, practitioners, settings, and/or other important social work practice factors, as a means of providing evidence for the effectiveness of intervention efforts.

SUMMARY

Even while we struggle with cutbacks in resources and the growth of quality assurance demands, we must continue to provide effective observations, judgments, decisions, and services in our practice. This is unquestionably one of the greatest challenges we face in practice as we enter the 21st century. One of the best ways of meeting this challenge is to approach client problems and intervention systematically. The simple four-step process involved in use of single-system designs offers a useful framework for doing this. The practitioner and client first agree upon measurable client objectives, and then collaboratively select appropriate measures that will document progress. Next, the practitioner uses these measures to collect data over time, and then graphs the results for interpretation. Although this process is most often discussed as a scientific process, it fits well with the exigencies of practice. It is relatively simple to

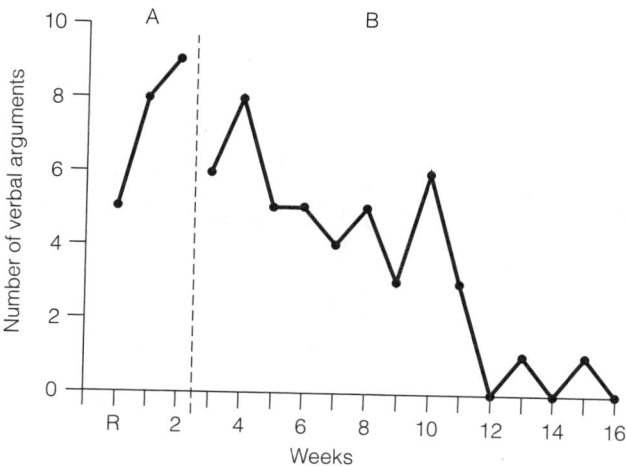

FIGURE 4.5 Don and Karen C.'s weekly numbers of verbal arguments both before and during treatment.

conceptualize, and it need not detract from the more traditional aspects of practice. This is what makes single-system designs such a viable tool for enhancing practice.

Perhaps the most powerful aspect of single-system designs is the use of phases and baselines. Together they give the practitioner great flexibility. A single-system design can be quickly implemented when client issues or environmental constraints force a rapid intervention response. In these cases, a simple B design will not only fit well with practice but will also enable the worker to provide concrete evidence of change in the client's problems. In many instances, however, practitioners will be able to use retrospective and/or concurrent baseline measurements to provide a pretreatment profile of the client's problems. Then the baseline and treatment phases can be juxtaposed to provide clinically compelling evidence for the effectiveness of the worker's practice efforts.

5

⚜️

Designs to Evaluate Practice

In the last chapter, we discussed the nature of client monitoring and the practical considerations involved in making monitoring successful. In this chapter, we extend those principles to look at single-system designs that effectively evaluate the effects of intervention—not just portray client improvement. To do this, a brief discussion of what we mean by evaluating practice is in order, as is a discussion of the concept of causality. Then we will point out some threats to the internal and external validity of evaluation designs, and suggest a few ways to improve an evaluative design. Finally, we will offer some basic evaluative single-system designs and discuss the practical considerations that must be dealt with in implementing evaluative single-system designs.

THE NATURE OF EVALUATING PRACTICE

In Chapter 4, we presented five core questions that need to be answered in any process of monitoring and evaluating practice. These questions lie at the heart of the empirical practice model (EPM). To review, these questions are as follows:

1. Have I validly and adequately defined the client's priority problems and the intervention context?

2. Is this client progressing?

3. Is the progress meaningful and sufficient?

4. What attributions can I make about the cause of the observed progress (or lack of it)?

5. What generalizations can I make about the future of this case or about other cases?

The basic monitoring designs and procedures offered in the last chapter focus primarily on answering the first two of these questions. The last three, however, require that further questions be answered (through systematic goal setting and data collection). In order to answer the third question—determining whether a client has made meaningful and sufficient progress—the practitioner must have contracted with the client in terms of setting objectives that are directly measurable. The fourth question is based on the extent to which we can attribute change in client problems to our intervention. This question then, focuses on the concepts of causality and internal validity (the degree to which we are confident that a treatment variable is the cause of change in an outcome variable). The fifth question of the EPM refers to the generalizations that we can make about the results of our intervention. We hope that these results will have significance and utility for predicting the future of this case or the other cases with which professionals deal. These are issues of external validity.

Let us consider an example of service effectiveness. A young woman named Karen B. enters professional treatment by virtue of a crisis call she made to a local suicide crisis line. Initial assessments done by crisis workers determined that Karen was suffering from severe depression that was associated with years of surviving physical and emotional abuse by her partner.

Karen B. was admitted to a local women's shelter, where she received counseling for her depression. She completed the GCS her first day of treatment and scored a 71, indicating a severe case of depression. Regular administration of the GCS suggested that Karen was making steady progress. After 12 weeks of counseling and other assistance from the shelter, Karen left the shelter, and her case was closed. Her GCS scores at that time suggested that Karen was no longer experiencing clinical levels of depression.

What do we know about the effectiveness of the counseling services delivered to Karen B.? There were no baseline measurements in this case, but we certainly get the overall impression that Karen's experience at the shelter was extremely positive. After all, in 12 weeks she went from being a severely depressed woman to one who showed no clinically significant levels of depression at all. A check with the case notes recorded by counselors supports this impression, as does Karen's own verbal reports to shelter staff.

In reality, we cannot definitively conclude that counseling led to Karen's reduced levels of depression. The data available in this case are simply inadequate to prove such a claim because there are other possible explanations for Karen's improvement. Perhaps she would have recovered on her own, or her improvements had actually started before she was admitted to the shelter. It could even be that some external factors, such as support from a few close friends, contributed to her progress. To rule out such possible explanations, we need to establish baseline trends, and then observe the impact of intervention. Just as importantly, we need to determine if other external circumstances or events contributed to Karen's improvement. In other words, to rigorously evaluate the impact of this practice situation, we need to find out if intervention actually caused the changes noted in Karen B. This process—one of determining causality—is the focus of this chapter.

Before we discuss single-system designs that help answer questions of causality, however, we need to discuss the concepts of causality, internal validity, and external validity in turn. First, let us examine the concept of causality.

ESTABLISHING CAUSALITY USING SINGLE-SYSTEM DESIGNS

What do we mean by causality? Many people use the term *cause* lightly, using it as a general description for things that we associate together. It is natural, for example, for social workers to say that our intervention "caused" positive change for a client, that reductions in welfare rates "cause" increases in the number of working poor, or that increased sexual violence on television "causes" corresponding increases in sexual violence in real life. These relationships may in fact be causal, but we are usually not in a position to draw definitive conclusions about such causality. Remember, the word *causality* implies "proof," and this is very difficult to establish in our social world. There are far too many unexplored and complicated factors that confound or confuse the relationships we examine.

Bloom, Fisher, and Orme (1999) outline a series of conditions that must be met if we are to fully establish causality in clinical cases (see also Kazdin, 1982). They are as follows:

1. *Temporal arrangement.* Changes in our client's targeted outcome must occur after intervention is applied, not before.

2. *Copresence.* We do not expect instantaneous change in our client's targeted outcomes once intervention is applied. Given a reasonable length of time during which intervention is applied, however, we should see changes begin to develop for the client.

3. *Contingent occurrence.* Client improvement should be associated with application of an intervention. If we see positive change for the client in the absence of intervention, it can be assumed that something else is causing changes for the client.

4. *Consistency of effects.* A clear pattern of copresence should emerge for the outcome measures. This means that repeated introduction of an intervention must consistently be associated with changes observed for our clients.

5. *Competing hypotheses.* To what extent have we ruled out other, rival explanations for the changes observed in client outcome? This involves a

systematic search both conceptually and practically to see if there are any other factors that are present at the same time as the intervention, and that might explain the results we have observed for our clients.

6. *Consistency over time.* The relationship that develops between our intervention and observed changes in client outcome should not fluctuate greatly over time. In other words, the relationship between intervention and outcome should appear to be stable for prolonged periods of time.

7. *Conceptual integrity.* This final test of causality is whether the emerging relationship between intervention and outcome makes sense conceptually or on the basis of practice wisdom. Does our existing knowledge base or practical experience somehow anchor the observed causal relationship in a conceptual framework that is plausible?

From a purely scientific perspective, the social work profession has tremendous, inherent difficulties in establishing causal relationships for many things we would like to understand. This is also true of the efficacy of intervention. We can often establish temporal arrangements, determine the copresence of intervention and client change, or verify that client progress is contingent upon application of an intervention. Due to the complex nature of social phenomena, however, we experience more difficulty in showing consistent effects of intervention, or in ruling out competing hypotheses. In fact, social work practice rarely involves situations that can be sufficiently controlled to permit causal attributions from a scientific perspective about the relationship between intervention and client outcomes.

We favor a practical approach to establishing causality. On a practical level, we need to recognize that most practice situations involve a wide range of circumstances and events that might hide, inflate, or modify the relationship between intervention and outcome. The challenge for us as practitioners is to construct a single-system design (or any other research method) that includes as many components as possible to rule out these other factors. If we can do so, we might reasonably conclude that client outcomes were achieved because of the intervention we applied.

One way of thinking about establishing causality in single-system designs is to think about the construction of these designs as a process of logical inference. Thyer (1993) labels this process the "principle of unlikely successive coincidences." In basic monitoring designs, for example, we cannot claim that it was intervention that led to observed changes for our clients. This is because it is possible that any number of rival hypotheses may account for observed changes. A purely random event, a coincidence, may account for improvements in client outcome. In single-system designs that are constructed to answer questions of effectiveness, however, we can control for rival hypotheses by demonstrating a series of unlikely coincidences. If a practitioner can demonstrate that intervention began, and then the client's problem improved, more than one time, then the likelihood of client improvement by coincidence is reduced. A pattern of two or more unlikely coincidences greatly reduces the plausibility of rival hypotheses, while supporting the effects of intervention. If a practitioner can demonstrate consistently that client outcomes improved only after intervention was initiated, he or she might reasonably conclude that a causal relationship between intervention and outcome has been approximated.

To work with the principle of unlikely coincidences, however, one must know how to construct single-system designs that control for these external hypotheses or factors. That is, we strive to construct single-system designs to be as rigorous as possible, so that the conclusions we draw are subject to few alternative explanations. These alternative explanations are called threats to internal validity, the topic of our next discussion.

Threats to Internal Validity

Internal validity is extremely important to the process of evaluating clinical practice. Even though the term may seem foreign, the questions it poses are simple. Internal validity refers to the extent to which a research design ensures that the introduction of an independent variable (if any) can be identified as the sole cause of change in a dependent variable (Grinnell & Unrau, 1997). For our purposes, for example, we question whether there are confounding circumstances or events that might detract from our ability to draw conclusions about the cause of change in client problems. If the answer is yes, it means that there may be alternative explanations beyond our intervention that helped the client make progress. Internal validity is critical to determining efficacy of practice, as it directly determines our ability to draw conclusions about whether our intervention led to change for clients. The following are considered to be the major threats to internal validity of single-system designs.

History   Was there any event or set of events that occurred outside of intervention that may be responsible for the client outcomes observed? These events have the potential to lead to observed change in clients. We can mistakenly interpret this change as being the product of our intervention, rather than the product of these outside events. Take, for example, a situation in which we wish to improve a client's parenting skills. We apply a pretest that indicates our client has very limited parenting skills prior to our intervention. After completing our intervention—an educational program designed to give clients increased knowledge of good parenting behaviors—posttest scores indicate that the client has shown a significant increase in parenting skills. Without our awareness, however, during the intervention period, the client also found an informal mentor through a local community agency. This mentor provided ongoing advice and modeling for our client to make the client a better parent. In this situation, four possibilities exist to explain our results. First, our intervention may have led to the achieved posttest scores. Second, the external mentoring may have led to the observed change in our client. Third, it may be the combined effect of our educational program and the mentoring that improved our client's parenting skills. Finally, another, completely unrecognized event may have contributed to client change.

Maturation   Did any psychological or physical process occur within the client that might have affected the outcome observed? This threat essentially refers to any cognitive, psychological, or physical developmental process experienced by the client over a period of time. The most obvious examples of maturation apply to children, adolescents, and perhaps the elderly. Suppose, for instance, that we wish to reduce the frequency of hitting behaviors in a child who has been referred to us for aggressive behavior. Since children inevitably mature at a rapid pace, conclusions about the effectiveness of our intervention may be clouded by the realization that this child may have undergone a natural developmental process that influenced the child's aggressive behavior.

Repeated Testing   Did the process of being repeatedly observed or tested influence the client's performance on outcome measures? If so, a repeated testing effect has occurred. Testing effects refer to the possibility that the client has reacted to the act of being measured, observed, or questioned. For the purposes of a single-system design, the primary concern with testing is the possibility that completing earlier measures will directly influence later measures. Suppose that we gave a client a test that examined his or her knowledge of elder abuse. Testing effects might have two influences in this case. The client might remember some of the items when given a subsequent posttest, thereby inflating his or her apparent knowledge levels at a later point. Alternatively, the client might do poorly on elder abuse pretests and, as a result, approach subsequent measures with a great deal of anxiety and apprehension. This in turn might cause the client to do even worse on the elder abuse posttests. The client's knowledge has not really declined in this case; the client has just been affected by the process of being tested.

Instrumentation   Are changes in the client's targeted outcome a product of errors in the measurement process? Possible errors include use of an outcome measure that is unreliable or invalid for the purpose for which it is being used. Perhaps someone who is observing client behaviors is using an unsystematic, inconsistent way of observing and recording those behaviors. Maybe the counselors are changed at some point during the intervention process, or a lone counselor decides to change his or her way of assessing client progress before intervention is completed. Finally, measurement of a client's problem may be situation-specific. An agorophobic's anxious reactions to being in public would obviously differ, for example, depending on whether we measured his or her anxiety at home or at our office. In any of these circumstances, there is a strong potential to obtain a flawed measure of client progress simply because we failed to measure accurately and consistently.

Attrition   Are the results of intervention distorted because some clients dropped out of treatment? This threat to internal validity is a concern when you are focusing on a group of clients. Clients drop out of treatment for a variety of reasons. Some find the intervention lacking, others are not motivated, and many have difficulty with things like transportation. Whenever individuals drop out of treatment, we can consider those who remain to be a different sample than those who have left. Unfortunately, we often do not know exactly how these two groups differ. Consider an example. A practitioner is working with a group of girls who enter a teen parenting program, the goal of which is to provide them with basic parenting, dietary planning, and financial skills. The practitioner, however, discovers that about 40 percent of the girls drop out of treatment before the midpoint of the program. It is possible that those girls who dropped out of the program were those who possessed the least developed skills, and that they found the program overwhelming. By observing only those who remained, we would obviously overestimate the value of this particular intervention.

Regression to the Mean   Did the client's performance on cognitive, psychological, or physical tests fluctuate naturally? Many such fluctuations are a part of the ebb and flow of life. On any measure, we all tend to perform around an average level, for us as individuals. There is therefore a tendency for an extreme performance level, both high and low, to regress or move toward this average or mean. A common example is that of clients who go to agencies because they have arrived at a crisis point in their life. Think of an adolescent named Maria E., for example. Maria E. enters treatment at a youth treatment center with extremely elevated levels of depression. At the intake interview, Maria is asked to complete the Generalized Contentment Scale (Hudson, 1997). Her score of 75 on this scale suggests that Maria is extremely depressed. On that basis, Maria E. is provided with counseling services for a period of eight weeks. At that time, the GCS produces a score of 53 for Maria. Can we assume that counseling has caused a significant improvement in Maria E.'s situation? Not necessarily! The improvement suggested by Maria's posttest may actually reflect the fact that Maria's depression was at an extreme level when she entered treatment, and that it naturally moved toward a more typical level regardless of the intervention.

Selection Bias   Is the observed outcome a product of particular characteristics that make this client or group of clients unique? Why do some clients seek assistance from counselors, while others do not? Are there regional, cultural, or other differences among clients that might help explain whether or not a particular outcome is achieved? In any of these instances, an observed cause–effect relationship may appear to exist within a single client or a group of clients when, in fact, these other factors may be making our results biased in some way of which we are unaware. For example, we might be trying to assess the impact of progressive muscle relaxation upon the frequency and severity of lower back pain for a client named Ivan R. Ivan R. is a middle-aged working individual who recently immigrated from an eastern European country. Baseline measures suggested that Ivan displays relatively low levels of pain frequency and severity. After treatment, these levels do not appear to have changed very much. As practitioners, however, we are unaware that there are significant cultural differences that lead individuals from some groups to express pain far more freely than others. It just so happens that Ivan hails from a cultural group that expresses pain far less frequently and vocally than others. This is a selection bias that will influence our results. It is also worth noting that this bias will affect the external validity of our outcomes as much as the internal validity.

Diffusion or Treatment Contamination Are the observed changes in our client's targeted outcome a product of a series or combination of treatments? Or has contact with other clients somehow influenced the course of intervention for this particular client? In single-subject designs, the first of these possibilities is the most prevalent concern. A series of interventions can usually not be seen as independent and unique. That is because earlier interventions often shape clients' reactions to subsequent interventions, and the two interventions together often interact in ways that we are completely unaware of. In a situation where a practitioner applies both cognitive restructuring and behavioral techniques to an anxious client, for instance, how might the two approaches impact the client? We do not know; therefore, inferences about causality are more difficult to make.

Threats to External Validity

External validity refers to how easily a research design allows us to generalize research findings to other groups and other situations (Grinnell & Unrau, 1997). Results with strong external validity will be results that are broadly applicable to external populations, settings, treatment variables, and measurement variables. External validity may therefore be thought of in terms of both population and environment. Bracht and Glass (1968) offer a useful distinction—they break external validity into both population validity and ecological validity, and set conceptual limits for the applicability of results for both other persons and other environments.

Threats to the external validity of single-system designs are multiple. Bloom, Fisher, and Orme (1999) provide an excellent summary of these threats, by listing them as follows:

1. *Differential independent (intervention) variables.* Any intervention applied to different clients or client systems in different settings by different practitioners will be different from the original intervention in varying ways and degrees. This reduces the likelihood of identical outcomes or results in comparison to the original case.

2. *Practitioner effects.* Different practitioners naturally have different attributes, varying in terms of beliefs, style, appearance, skills, and so on. These variations may influence client outcomes so that different practitioners

applying the same intervention can be expected to have varying effects on clients, including client success.

3. *Different dependent (target or outcome) variables.* Even with the same problem, there may be differences in how the target variables are conceptualized and operationalized (measured) across settings or by various practitioners. This again reduces the likelihood of achieving identical results across different populations and environments.

4. *Interaction of history and intervention.* If ecological or extraneous events occur at the same time as the intervention, they may be producing or influencing the observed outcome. To the extent that these ecological or extraneous factors vary across cases, generalization regarding outcomes and causal relationships will be limited.

5. *Measurement differences.* If differences exist across cases in how key phenomena (the problem, the intervention, the outcome) are operationalized or measured, there will likely be differences in the results.

6. *Differences in clients.* Just as practitioners differ, so do clients. Any number of client characteristics (age, race, gender, class, cognitive ability, belief systems, and so on) can potentially affect the extent to which the results can be generalized.

The key principle underlying generalizability is one of replication of findings. This is the extent to which we observe the same outcome for similar people, in similar circumstances, while applying similar interventions. This kind of replication is called direct replication, and obviously it provides a relatively strong basis for generalizability. External validity is often assumed, but not as frequently established as when a direct replication is done. We discuss replication in greater detail in chapter 7. Suffice it to say for now that replication is key to establishing generalizability.

BASIC EVALUATION DESIGNS

The single-system designs presented in the following pages are considered useful and effective for evaluating clinical practice. To varying degrees they offer design improvements over the basic monitoring designs. These improvements, such as manipulating treatment by starting it and then stopping it, simply increase our ability to control for threats to internal validity. In so doing, they also allow us to state, with a reasonable conviction based upon the principle of unlikely successive coincidences, that our client's stated objectives were achieved because of the intervention we applied.

The ABA Design

The ABA single-system design is a simple extension of the AB design discussed in the last chapter. As in the AB design, the practitioner is able to establish patterns in initial client functioning by use of baseline measurements. After the baseline is established, a B phase consisting of an intervention is applied to the client's problem. The strength of the ABA design, however, lies in the additional baseline or A phase that is implemented after intervention is given a chance to affect the problem at hand. The ABA design therefore allows the practitioner to compare progress across three distinct phases. If the intervention really does cause change in the client's targeted outcome, we would expect measurements during the intervention phase to move in the desired direction. Subsequently, however, when intervention is removed, measurements of the client's targeted outcome should tend to move back in the direction of the original baseline measurements. As such observations build over time, the sequence of unlikely successive coincidences supports the probability that our intervention is leading to client change.

Consider the case of Juanita H. and daughter Damita, for example. Juanita is a single mom who is experiencing difficulty in coping with her daughter's behavior at home. Damita appears to be acting out constantly; she displays frequent behaviors such as staying out until early morning, drinking excessively, using drugs, lying to her mother, and being verbally abusive to her siblings. The practitioner assigned to work with Juanita and Damita asks Juanita to complete the Child's Behavior Rating Scale (CBRS; Hudson, 1990). The CBRS is a rating scale that must be completed by a parent, guardian, or other responsible adult who has an intimate, firsthand knowledge of a child's behavior. The scale uses a behavioral problem checklist to assess the relative frequency of certain problematic behaviors, on a scale that ranges from 1 (never) to 5 (always). A large total score on the CBRS indicates that the child is exhibiting serious behavioral problems.

The practitioner implements a baseline phase during which Juanita H. completes two retrospective CBRS measures, then completes the CBRS concurrently and again twice the next two weeks, giving two retrospective and three concurrent baseline measures. As shown in Figure 5.1, the results indicate that Damita does indeed show frequent behavioral problems. On that basis, Juanita and Damita are asked to join a group run by the agency, the purpose of which is to foster effective parent-child communication and problem solving. Damita's behavior continues to be monitored during this group intervention. It soon appears that much of Damita's acting out behavior was related to feelings of isolation and uncertainty in connection with a new relationship that her mother had recently begun. Improved communication between mother and daughter seems to have the desired effect; after only five weeks, intervention is removed. At this point, a second baseline phase is started. As seen in the graph of CBRS scores, Damita then seems to revert back to many of her old ways.

This example highlights one of the major problems in the ABA design. In order to show that intervention causes change for our clients, we have to remove it. The second baseline phase is a powerful indicator of the effects of intervention, but it also creates an ethical dilemma. Is it appropriate to terminate a case with a baseline phase, just for the purpose of showing that treatment works? This is an important question. The assumption often made in the

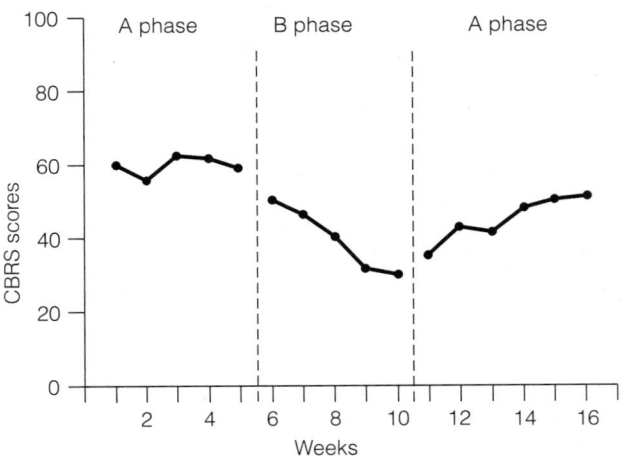

FIGURE 5.1 An example of an ABA single-case design.

use of this design is that intervention is removed, not after success is determined, but in order to establish patterns in outcome measures. If the intervention is indeed the cause of the changes in the client's problem, then once it is removed, the client's problems should return to or approach preintervention levels. In practice, ending a case with your client either unimproved or worse off is obviously unethical. You must never place the determination of causality above the ongoing need to assist your clients. For this reason, the ABA design should be used with extreme caution because of its potential implications for your client.

One way of handling the dilemma of removing treatment is to adopt a routine follow-up procedure for clients. The time period following treatment's natural completion can be considered as a second baseline phase during which the client's problems can continue to be monitored. This provides additional data for comparison, without the dangers of removing treatment. If the client's problem worsens, you then re-implement treatment. This serves to remind clients that you are concerned about their ongoing well-being. The ABA design, properly used, can fit well with practice.

The ABAB Design

The ABAB design is one of the most powerful evaluation designs. It is similar to the AB and ABA designs, but differs by the addition of a second intervention phase. To construct an ABAB design, the practitioner would start with a standard AB design, temporarily halt the intervention, and then resume it once again (essentially two AB designs glued together in sequence). The strength of the ABAB design is that it creates four "experimental conditions," two baseline and two intervention conditions. The patterns evident in data from each of the baseline phases can be compared to data patterns in the treatment phases to establish that change in client functioning occurs between baseline and treatment conditions.

Figure 5.2 illustrates a case study using an ABAB design. In this case study, the client, Matthew J., is being seen because he has been referred to his company's employee assistance program (EAP). The referral was made because Matthew seems to experience regular conflict with his coworkers at the workplace. The EAP worker assigned to the case asks Matthew J. to complete the Index of Peer Relations (IPR) during a brief assessment period—the initial A phase. After the severity of Matthew's peer relations difficulties become evident, a period of formal treatment is introduced. As the figure shows, this period of intervention has the desired effect, as represented by Matthew's rapidly declining IPR scores. To test the stability of Matthew's gains (and to determine something about the causal relationship between treatment and Matthew's progress), the EAP worker introduces a second A phase. The results show that Matthew's IPR scores again deteriorate, though they do not approach the severity noted when Matthew was first assessed. After sustaining the second A phase long enough to establish a clear pattern in Matthew's IPR scores, the EAP worker again invites Matthew to participate in formal treatment. At the close of this treatment, it is clear that Matthew J. is again relating much better to his coworkers.

The contribution ABAB designs make to establishing causality is made through the replication of patterns in our data. That is, if we can replicate the pattern of improving client outcome measurements when intervention is introduced, across two matched AB designs, it is unlikely that such results are a product of coincidence. Instead, changes in client functioning that are matched to two different periods of intervention lend credence to our premise that intervention has worked with this client.

It is important to note that applying the ABAB design is a labor-intensive procedure. It requires considerable lengths of time to implement correctly, and calls for considerable effort in terms of data collection and graphing. There are also situations in which removal of the intervention for any period of time is either inappropriate, impossible, or both. Therefore, it is wise to be cautious when thinking of using the ABAB design. Remember, the design should fit practice requirements, not the requirements of science.

The BAB Design

The BAB design is a very useful single-system design when it is not feasible to implement an initial baseline phase of observation. There are many reasons that it might not be feasible to implement the baseline phase. Perhaps there are ethical concerns (such as withholding treatment in crisis situations) or pragmatic reasons (assuming responsibility for a client who has already commenced treatment) that prevent implementation of a baseline. In these types of situations, the BAB design offers evidence of treatment effectiveness, without compromising practice integrity.

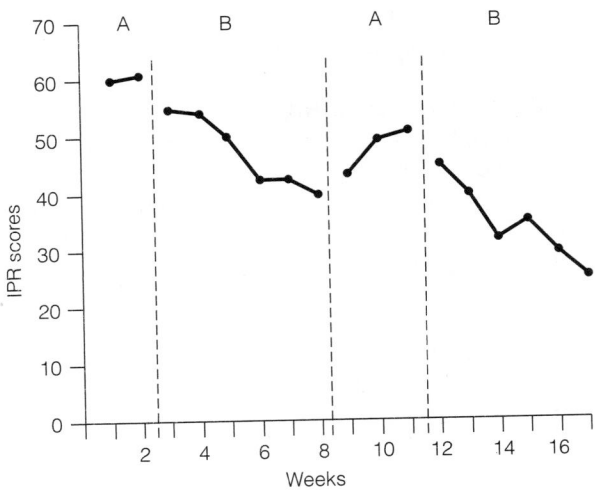

FIGURE 5.2 An example of an ABAB single-case design.

The BAB design is constructed by recording outcome measures repeatedly over time as soon as intervention begins (or at least as soon as possible). After this phase of intervention and ongoing measurement reaches a point at which the practitioner feels safe in removing the intervention, a baseline phase of monitoring is started. In this monitoring phase, the intervention is temporarily withheld in order to determine whether the client's functioning will stabilize, or whether deterioration occurs in the client's targeted problems. Assuming that the monitoring phase suggests that further intervention would be useful for the client, the intervention is reinstated, and the client's functioning is monitored during this second B phase.

Figure 5.3 shows an example of a BAB single-system design. In this case, a young man named Richard K. asked to speak to a counselor at a local family service agency. During the intake interview, Richard expressed very strong feelings of nervousness, anxiety, stress, and a general feeling of being out of control. These feelings, he said, started when his partner had unexpectedly become pregnant. He ended the interview by saying he simply did not know how to cope anymore.

The intake worker referred Richard K. to a practitioner named Lynne. Lynne recognized some urgency in Richard's feelings, and immediately began counseling him regarding his fears and feelings of stress. At the same time, Lynne asked Richard K. to complete the Index of Clinical Stress (ICS). The ICS is a scale that measures the degree of problems clients have with personal stress on a rather global level (Abell, 1986, 1991).

After eight counseling sessions with Lynne (and his partner), Richard K. was beginning to feel much better about the implications of impending fatherhood. As Figure 5.3 shows, his scores on the ICS dropped steadily during

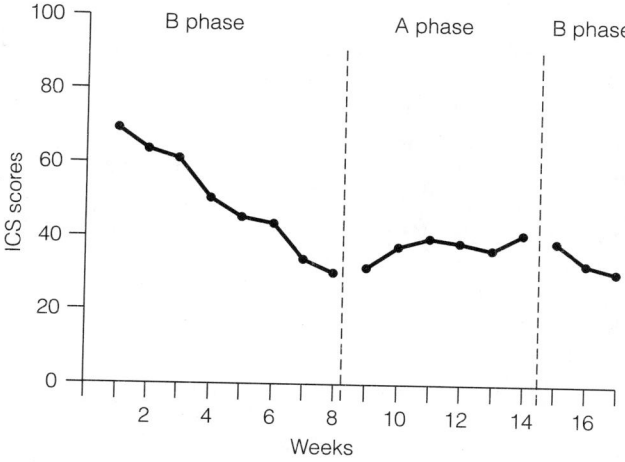

FIGURE 5.3 An example of a BAB single-case design.

this time. After eight sessions, Lynne felt it was time to assess whether it was time for Richard to leave treatment, and so a no treatment monitoring phase was introduced. Richard K. continued to complete the ICS and submitted each one to Lynne for review. After another six weeks, it was apparent that Richard had a few residual effects of the stress he was feeling, so Lynne asked him to come in for a few more sessions. After another three sessions, Richard and Lynne agreed that his stress was greatly reduced, and he was ready to take on fatherhood.

The obvious advantage of the BAB design is that there is no delay in service delivery while the practitioner monitors through an initial A phase. Intervention can begin immediately. It also offers some advantages over the ABA and ABAB designs. Unlike the ABA design, the BAB design does not require a final baseline phase. This is useful for two related reasons. First, contact with the client does not end on a phase that consists of simple monitoring—contact ends with a treatment phase. Second, we do not have to be as concerned about keeping clients motivated and "in touch" during a final A phase. The advantage that BAB designs have over the ABAB design is purely pragmatic. With one less A phase to complete before commencing our contact with the client, the BAB design is more efficient (and more palatable) in terms of time, effort, and data collection. In a very real sense, the BAB design is very well suited to use in practice

The BCBC Design

There is another single-system design that is worth noting for its potential contribution to establishing the efficacy of clinical practice. This is the BCBC design. In a BCBC design, the practitioner records measures of client functioning repeatedly over time for a single intervention (this is often an existing or routine intervention). Then the existing intervention is removed temporarily, so that a second intervention may be tried for a period of time. After another period of time, the initial intervention is reinstated, and the effect upon client functioning is observed. Finally, this first intervention is removed again, so that an additional period of the second intervention can be introduced. The pattern formed by these successive periods of parallel interventions, then, is one in which two periods of the first intervention (B) are interspersed by two periods of the second intervention (C).

Figure 5.4 shows an example of a BCBC single-system design. This is the case of Mansa R., a middle-aged man who has been sent to mandatory treatment after being charged with driving under the influence (DUI). Mansa's addiction's counselor decides that two interventions might be beneficial for Mansa—an educational program offered to all people convicted of a DUI charge, and individual counseling. At the same time, the counselor is not sure which of the two interventions might be most effective in reducing the likelihood that Mansa R. will again drive while intoxicated.

The counselor and Mansa agree to use the Index of Alcohol Involvement (IAI) as a measure of Mansa's progress. The IAI is an instrument that measures the degree of problems clients have with alcohol abuse (Hudson, MacNeil, & Dierks, 1993). It captures information that describes the extent to which alcohol constitutes a clinically significant personal or social problem for the individual. High scores indicate more serious problems with alcohol abuse. Treatment for Mansa R. begins with four weeks of attendance at the alcohol education program offered by the agency. This program focuses on exploring the personal and family impacts of alcohol abuse, and the social consequences of abuse (loss of employment, accidental deaths, etc.). Mansa immediately begins completing the IAI to record his progress in reducing his drinking behaviors.

After the four weeks, the alcohol education program breaks for a short period. The counselor notes that Mansa R.'s IAI scores have not declined very much, and asks Mansa to come in for individual counseling. Mansa does so for the next four weeks, and his IAI scores suggest that he is making steady progress. At that point, the alcohol education program starts up again, and Mansa attends the next four sessions in lieu of individual counseling. As Figure 5.4 shows, however, his IAI scores again seem to increase somewhat. Finally, contact with Mansa R. is completed by another four weeks of individual counseling with the addictions counselor.

What does Figure 5.4 tell us about the two different interventions used in Mansa R.'s case? In some ways, that question is difficult to answer. We do see that Mansa's IAI scores suggest that treatment worked. The pattern shown in the data also suggests that Mansa benefited more from individual counseling than he did the alcohol education program. There are, however, some difficulties in establishing causality. We cannot, for example, completely distinguish between the effects of the B intervention (educational program) and the C intervention (individual counseling). There may be carryover effects such that

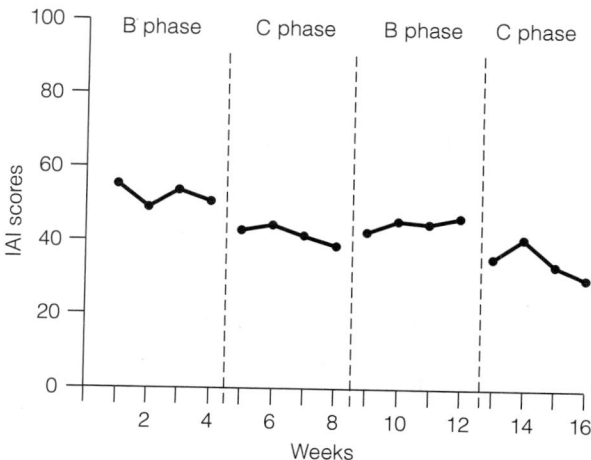

FIGURE 5.4 An example of a BCBC single-case design.

it is the combination of educational programming and individual counseling that helped Mansa R. make progress.

Still, the BCBC design is useful when a baseline phase is not desirable or possible. It does give a sense of the comparative effectiveness of two different interventions. The BCBC design also offers a mechanism for introducing and piloting several different interventions in order to determine which one is likely to be more effective (Thyer, 1993).

The Multiple Baseline Design

The final single-case design that we will discuss is the multiple baseline design. The multiple baseline design can be used to demonstrate that a treatment or program may have been a causal factor in the changes that a client experiences during the course of services. There are several forms of the multiple baseline (MBL) design. The first distinction that can be made is between the *MBL design across subjects (or persons)* and the *MBL design across behaviors*. In the MBL across persons design, the practitioner has two or more clients who are suffering from the same problem, measures their problem in the same manner, and uses the same intervention to treat the problem. Then the progress of each client is monitored as it is in AB single-case designs, except that *each of the clients has a baseline phase of differing length*. For example, suppose that three clients are treated for depression and that each client's depression is measured weekly using the Generalized Contentment Scale, one of the short-form measures discussed later in this book. The first client's baseline lasts for two weeks before treatment starts; the second client's baseline lasts for three weeks before treatment starts; and the third client's baseline lasts for four weeks before treatment starts. The implementation of treatment across these three clients is staggered in such a manner that each client has a baseline period of different length. *If the intervention causes changes in these clients' depression, then no change should be seen until treatment starts.* That is the fundamental idea in the MBL design: treatment is staggered across the clients, and if no changes are seen in any of the clients' problems until treatment starts, then this is compelling evidence from a scientific perspective, as well as a clinical perspective, that treatment has caused the observed changes (Barlow & Hersen, 1984; Bloom et al., 1999; Kazdin, 1982).

In an MBL design across behaviors, there is a single client who has problems with more than one behavior. Each problem behavior is measured; and the same treatment is applied in an effort to change each of the problem behaviors. For example, suppose that we have a client, Joe A., who has several "bad habits" at work that he needs to change: he is slow to respond to e-mail messages that he receives (often waiting several days before checking and answering them); he is slow to return phone calls (often waiting for several days to return a call); and he is slow to open and respond to regular mail that he receives (again, often waiting for several days before checking his office mail box and collecting, and responding to, the mail that he receives). Each problem could be measured, say, by having Joe count the number of days before he does each of these things (check and respond to e-mail, return phone calls, and check and respond to regular mail). The same intervention would be applied to each bad habit, but there would be baselines of different length before the intervention is initiated with one of the bad habits. For example, we might have a 7-day baseline period before starting the treatment to change the e-mail problem, a 14-day baseline before applying the intervention to the phone call return problem, and a 21-day baseline before applying the intervention to the problem with his response to regular mail.

There are two types of baselines that can be used: *concurrent* and *nonconcurrent* (or *natural*). With concurrent baselines, each baseline for each client, or each behavior, must be started at the same time. For example, in an MBL design across persons, the practitioner would have to start measuring each client's problem on the same day. In contrast, in a nonconcurrent, or natural, MBL design across persons, the baselines can be started at different times. For example, in a natural MBL design across persons with three clients, the baseline for the first client could be started on a Thursday at the beginning of June, the baseline for the second client on a Monday in September, and the baseline for the third client on a Friday in December (Barlow et al., 1984). This feature of the natural MBL design makes it very well suited for use in practice.

Let us use an example to illustrate this useful and powerful single-case design. Suppose that we want to determine whether a treatment we use for depression actually has an effect on our clients' levels of depression. Over a period of time we have three clients with whom we work in an effort to reduce their levels of depression. We begin working with the first client, Sally D., on January 30. We measure her level of depression near the end of our first meeting with her, and thereafter at the beginning of each weekly meeting with her, using the Generalized Contentment Scale (GCS). We treat her depression using a specific intervention, say Aaron T. Beck's cognitive-behavioral treatment approach to depression (Beck et al., 1979); and as a natural course of our work with Sally, we begin this treatment at the beginning of our third session with Sally. This results in a baseline phase with two data points, as seen in Figure 5.5. We continue our work with Sally through 12 treatment phase sessions, with the results shown in Figure 5.5. On May 1, we begin working with another depressed client, Tom H. As with Sally, we use the GCS to measure Tom's depression at each meeting. As a natural course of our work with Tom, we end up having three baseline measures over three weeks prior to starting the cognitive-behavioral treatment of Tom's depression. We continue this process during the 15 weeks of treatment, with the results shown in Figure 5.5.

On August 15, we begin working with Jose M., another depressed client. As with Sally D. and Tom H., we use the GCS to monitor Jose's depression. Jose M., however, misses his third and fifth planned meetings with us. As a result, we are not able to begin the cognitive-behavioral treatment with Jose until after we have four baseline data points spread over six weeks. We then continue the treatment over 14 weeks, with the resulting data shown in Figure 5.5.

Notice in Figure 5.5 that each client has a baseline period of different duration, the hallmark of a multiple baseline design. However, this differential baseline length was not planned. The different baseline lengths occurred as a natural part of the practice context. This is what makes the natural multiple baseline design, in contrast to the concurrent multiple baseline design, so compatible with practice. With the concurrent multiple baseline design, we would have had to have been working with Sally D., Tom H., and Jose M. *at the same time*. We would have needed to start each client's baseline at the same time, and then stagger treatment across these three clients. This would have required us to keep two of these clients in prolonged baseline periods. This necessity makes the concurrent multiple baseline design much less compatible with the practice context.

Notice also in Figure 5.5 that each client's depression does not appear to begin to diminish until treatment starts. This is the pattern that appears in multiple baseline designs if treatment causes the decrease in the clients' problems. In the multiple baseline design, if treatment causes the clients' problems to decrease, then the typical pattern is: (1) there is no improvement in any of the clients' problems during baseline, and (2) improvements in a specific client's problem begins immediately, and only, after treatment is initiated for the specific client. This is the data pattern that is shown in Figure 5.5. The multiple baseline design can be a powerful design for providing evidence that clients have improved during service provision and that the services provided were responsible for their improvement. The strength of the evidence for a causal relationship between treatment and clients' improvements *increases* as the number of clients in the multiple baseline design increases. For example, a stronger case for causality can be made with four clients in the MBL design than with three, with five clients in the MBL design than with four, and so on.

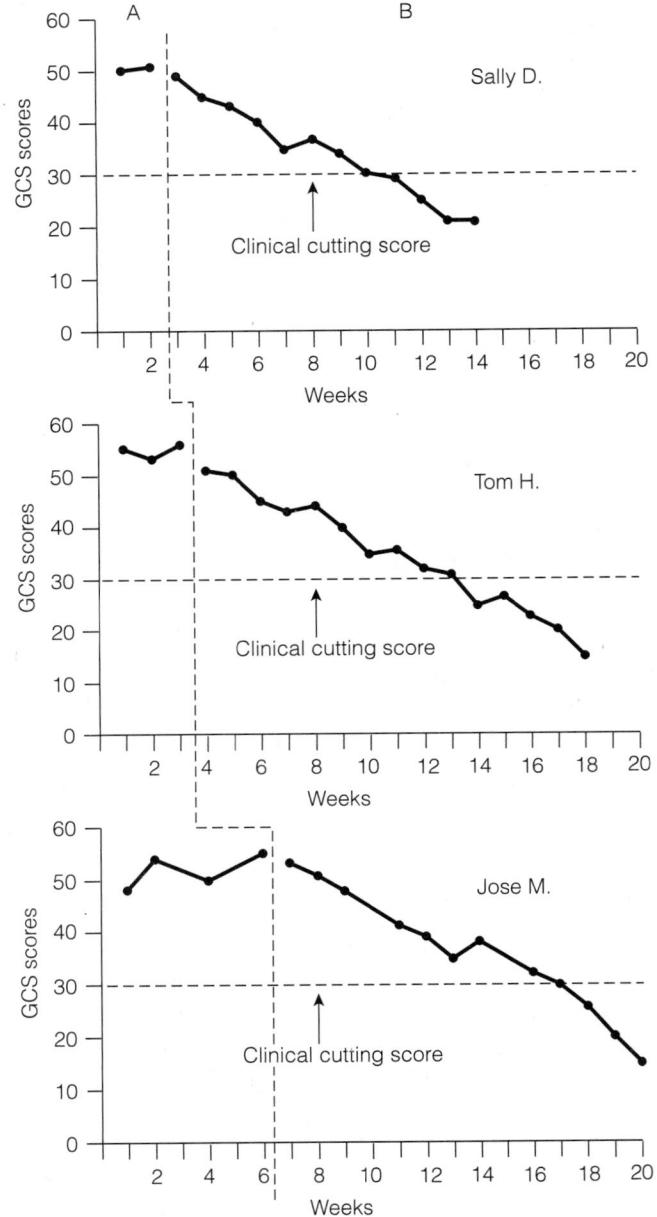

FIGURE 5.5 The data from a hypothetical natural multiple baseline design across three clients treated for depression.

SUMMARY

This chapter has dealt with the challenge of establishing the efficacy of clinical practice using single-system designs. Such a process involves adopting a systematic approach to constructing a single-system design. This approach is essentially a balancing act. On one hand, the practitioner must try to approximate causal relationships between intervention and outcome. This means that he or she must demonstrate: a temporal order in which outcome follows intervention; a definite relationship between intervention and outcome; and control for rival hypotheses that might offer alternative explanations for client outcome. This also means that the practitioner must strive to piece together single-system design components to control for threats to internal and external validity. On the other hand, the practitioner must ensure that ethical, professional, and pragmatic considerations are not put aside by the demands of scientific rigor. We forcefully recommend that practitioners take a pragmatic approach to implementing the designs presented in this chapter. They should use them creatively and whenever possible, but they must not jeopardize the integrity of their practice to fulfill the strict parameters of a specific design.

Most of the single-system designs discussed in this chapter share a common characteristic—the stopping of treatment at some point in the process of intervention. For most of the designs (ABA, ABAB, BAB), this entails stopping treatment so that client functioning can be monitored during a baseline phase. For the BCBC design, one of the treatments is stopped so that a second, alternative intervention can be introduced. This characteristic allows us to build arguments of practice efficacy by using the principle of unlikely successive coincidences. The multiple baseline design uses the baselines of differing length to control threats to internal validity. In short, these designs offer an effective mechanism for showing that social work works!

6

⚜

The Analysis of
Single-Case Design Data

In this chapter, we describe methods for analyzing single-case design data. First we briefly discuss some general issues in the analysis of data from single-case designs. We examine several terms that are important in the analysis of single-case design data: *level, mean, trend, variability*, and *overlap*. We define these terms and give examples using both contrived single-case data and examples from the literature. Then we discuss the meaning of *change* in level, mean, trend, and variability, as well as the important notion of *background variability*. We also discuss the role that overlap, or the lack thereof, plays in the determination of change between phases. We show examples of change between adjacent phases, again using both contrived data and examples from the literature. Finally, we lead the reader through visual analyses of single-case design data from several hypothetical practice evaluation studies.

VISUAL ANALYSIS AND STATISTICAL
ANALYSIS PROCEDURES

Two general sets of methods are used to analyze the data obtained in single-case design evaluations of interventions or programs: visual analysis procedures and statistical analysis procedures. Both sets of procedures have the same ultimate goal: the determination of change between adjacent phases. Visual analysis procedures rely on relatively general and subjective methods that involve nothing more than the visual inspection of graphic plots of single-case design data. Sometimes graphic aids, such as the use of trend lines, are used to facilitate visual analyses (Bailey, 1984; Parsonson & Baer, 1992; Rojahn & Schulze, 1985). Visual analysis methods are those most commonly used in single-case design methodology (Kazdin, 1982). Advocates of visual analysis procedures argue that if a change in client functioning is not obvious to the naked eye, then the change is of little or no practical importance. They further argue that a principal goal in single-case design research is the identification of intervention procedures that are powerful enough to produce large changes that are obvious to visual inspection (Parsonson & Baer, 1992).

Statistical analysis procedures involve any of a variety of descriptive and inferential statistical methods. The use of statistical procedures, especially inferential statistical methods, in the analysis of single-case design data is controversial. Probably one of the most significant (and somewhat controversial) issues concerns the possibility of autocorrelation in the time-series data that result from single-case design methods (Bloom, Fischer, & Orme, 1999; Huitema, 1986, 1988; Kazdin, 1982). When present in time-series data, autocorrelation can lead to biased tests of statistical significance and erroneous decisions concerning change in the outcome variable (Cook & Campbell, 1979; Gottman, 1981). Among the commonly discussed statistical procedures for use in single-case design methodology are various approaches to time-series analysis (Gottman, 1981; Ostrom, 1990). Some time-series methods require many more data points than are usually found in single-case design evaluations. In any case, inferential statistical methods are rarely used in single-case design methodology, and we will not discuss their use. There are a number of methodological, statistical, and philosophical issues involved in this controversy, and these issues are beyond the scope of this chapter. The interested reader is referred to Kratochwill and Levin (1992) for a discussion of issues related to the statistical analysis of single-case design data, and to Gottman (1981), Harvey (1990), McCleary and Hay (1980), and Ostrom (1990) for introductions to time-series analysis methods. More recently there has been a discussion of the use of statistical process control procedures for analyzing single-case design data. The interested reader is referred to Pfadt and Wheeler (1995), Pfadt et al. (1992), and Orme and Cox (2000).

CHARACTERISTICS OF SINGLE-CASE DESIGN DATA: DEFINITIONS AND REPRESENTATIONS

Level

There are several terms that we will use in our discussion. The first is *level*. Level refers to the magnitude of the outcome variable at a given point in time. For example, imagine that the dependent variable in a single-case design evaluation is "the number of times Johnny hits his sister each day." On Tuesday, Johnny's mother observes him hit his sister three times and records this on a 3-inch by 5-inch note card, which she later gives to the social worker. When the social worker plots on a graph the value of the dependent variable for Tuesday, the value plotted will be three, the level of the dependent variable for that particular day.

Mean

Mean refers to the arithmetic mean of the data points in a particular phase (or portion of a phase) of a single-case design. For example, suppose that Johnny's mother records the following numbers of times that Johnny hit his sister each of seven baseline days: 2, 3, 5, 4, 6, 7, and 9. The mean level of the dependent variable during baseline would be $[2 + 3 + 5 + 4 + 6 + 7 + 9] / 7 = 36/7 = 5.1$. This value could be represented on a single-case design graph by drawing a line at the value 5.1 across the phase. This line would be called the "phase mean line," or simply the "mean line."

Sometimes use is made of the "moving average" (Gottman, 1981). The moving average most often used in single-case design analyses is the average value of successive pairs of data points in a phase (Bloom et al., 1999). The moving average of the first two baseline data points for Johnny would be

$$\frac{2 + 3}{2} = 2.5$$

The remaining moving average values for Johnny's baseline data would be 4, 4.5, 5, 6.5, and 8.

Trend

Trend refers to the extent to which the level of the dependent variable changes systematically across the duration of a single-case design phase and is an indicator of the rate at which the dependent variable is changing across time. For example, Johnny's mother has reported the following daily numbers of times that Johnny hit his little sister during baseline: 2, 3, 5, 4, 6, 7, and 9. Notice that Johnny appears to be hitting his little sister more frequently as the baseline phase goes by. This systematic increase across time indicates a trend, in this case an increasing trend. When plotted on a graph, these data would appear as in Figure 6.1. Note how the increasing trend is visually apparent on the graph. Had Johnny's mother reported the numbers as 9, 7, 8, 8, 5, 4, and 2, then the trend in Johnny's hitting behavior would have been decreasing. This decreasing trend is shown in Figure 6.2. Sometimes trend is referred to as *improving* or *deteriorating*. These terms refer to whether or not the trend indicates that the client is getting better (an improving trend) or getting worse (a deteriorating trend).

There have been two procedures generally recommended for calculating an index to numerically represent the trend in a single-case design phase: the celeration line (Bloom & Fischer, 1982; Shinn, Good, & Stein, 1989) and ordinary least squares (OLS) regression analysis (Bloom, Fischer, & Orme, 1999).

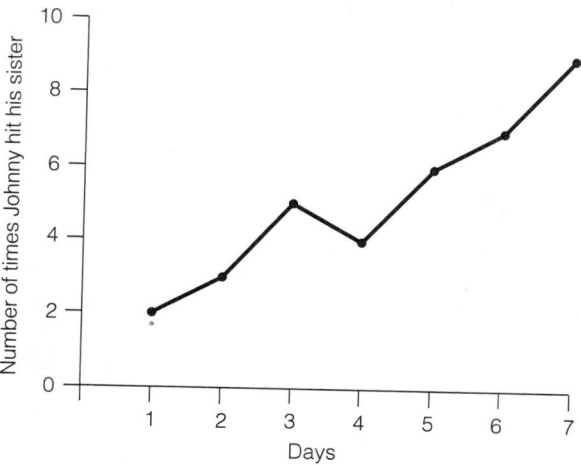

FIGURE 6.1 Single-case design data showing increasing (improving) trend.

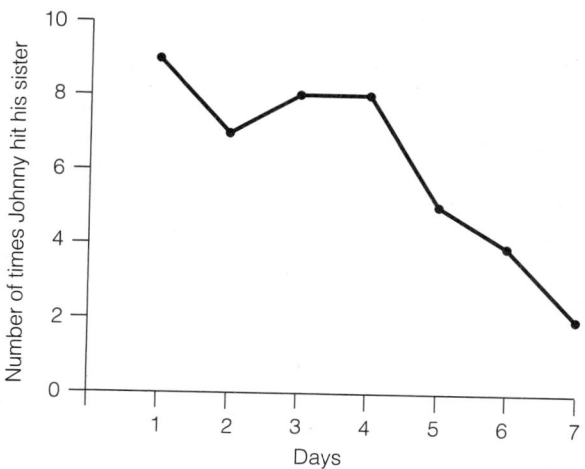

FIGURE 6.2 Single-case design data showing a decreasing (deteriorating) trend.

The celeration line approach requires nothing more complex than the computation of two means, plotting points to represent these means, drawing a line connecting the two means to visually represent the trend, and then using a formula to calculate a numerical estimate of the trend (Bloom & Fischer 1982; Bloom et al., 1999). The regression method can be applied using a computer program or an advanced calculator to obtain a regression estimate of the trend, and then using the estimated regression equation to draw a line representing the trend (Bloom et al., 1999). Thus, while not overly difficult, these two methods are somewhat complicated for easy use in practice.

As we prove in Appendix A (for those who justifiably say "show me"), there is a very simple procedure that can be used to represent the trend across a single-case design phase. The procedure is as follows:

1. Draw a line segment from the first data point through the last data point in the phase, with an arrow head at the end of the line segment indicating the direction of the trend. This arrow, which represents the average (and direction) of the trend across the phase and is called the *phase trend arrow* or *phase trend line*, is symbolized as $\vec{T}_{wm}$. This method is very simple to use and gives a defensible graphical representation of the trend of the client's problem across the phase.

2. If a numerical index of trend is needed, subtract the value of the first data point in the phase from the value of the final data point in the phase. This procedure provides an estimate of how much the client's problem changed across the phase. Let this difference be represented by ΔY, so

$$\Delta Y = Y_{final} - Y_{initial} \qquad (6.1)$$

where Y_{final} is the value of the final measurement in the phase, and $Y_{initial}$ is the value of the first measurement in the phase.

3. Subtract the time of the first measurement in the phase from the time that the final phase measure was obtained. This difference gives the length of time that elapsed between the first and last measures in the phase. Let this difference be represented by Δt , so

$$\Delta t = t_{final} - t_{initial} \qquad (6.2)$$

where t_{final} is the time that the final phase measure was obtained, and $t_{initial}$ is the time that the first phase measure was obtained.

4. Form the ratio

$$T_{wm} = \Delta Y/\Delta t \qquad (6.3)$$

where T_{wm} is the weighted average trend across the phase. This ratio, T_{wm}, is a numeric index representing the trend across the phase. In fact, as shown in Appendix A, this index gives an unbiased estimate of the weighted mean trend across the phase.

This method can be illustrated using the data in Figure 6.3. The final baseline measure is 9, and the first baseline measure is 2, so for baseline phase $\Delta Y = 9 - 2 = 7$. The time of the final baseline measure is the 7th day, while the time of the first baseline measure is the 1st day, so for baseline $\Delta t = 7 - 1 = 6$, and the trend for baseline is

$$T_{wm} = 7/6 = 1.167 \approx 1.2$$

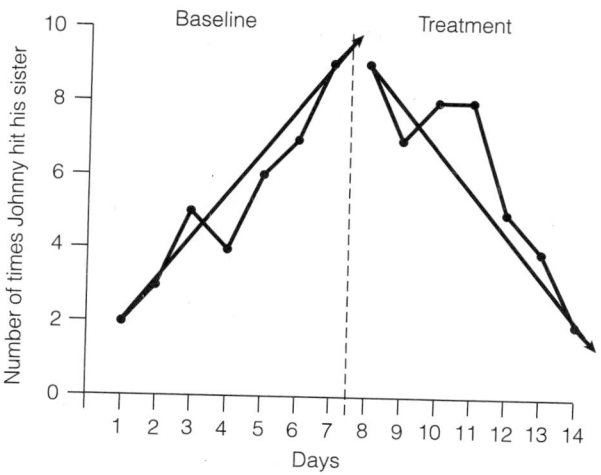

FIGURE 6.3 AB single-case design data with trend arrows drawn in.

which means that the dependent variable for this client was increasing, on average, at a rate of about 1.2 units (in this case, episodes of hitting) per day across the phase. Similarly, for treatment phase $\Delta Y = 2 - 9 = -7$ and $\Delta t = 14 - 8 = 6$, so $T_{wm} = -7/6 = -1.167 \approx -1.2$. This means that the dependent variable for this client was decreasing at an average rate of a little more than one dependent variable unit per day across the phase. The trend arrows for each phase in Figure 6.3 are drawn simply by connecting the first and last data points in each phase with a straight line headed by an arrow indicating the direction of the trend.

Limitations   The procedure discussed here produces a trend estimate, and a graphic representation, that represents trend in a *linear* manner. A major limitation of the use of linear trend representations, whether created using the procedure described here, the celeration line technique, or ordinary least squares regression procedures, is that extreme, outlying values of the dependent variable at the beginning or end of the phase can exert substantial influence on a trend estimate (McCleary & Welsh, 1992; Parsonson & Baer, 1992). This problem is illustrated in Figures 6.4 and 6.5. In Figure 6.4, the change between the first and second data points (6 units) is three times larger than the change between any other successive data points (2, 1, and 1) in the phase. Similarly, in Figure 6.5, the change between the next-to-last and last data points (6 units) is three times larger than the change between any other two successive data points in the phase (1, 2, and 1). These are examples of outlying observations at the beginning (Figure 6.4) and the end (Figure 6.5) of a phase.

The following additions to the procedure described earlier can be used to address this limitation and to provide an "adjusted" trend representation:

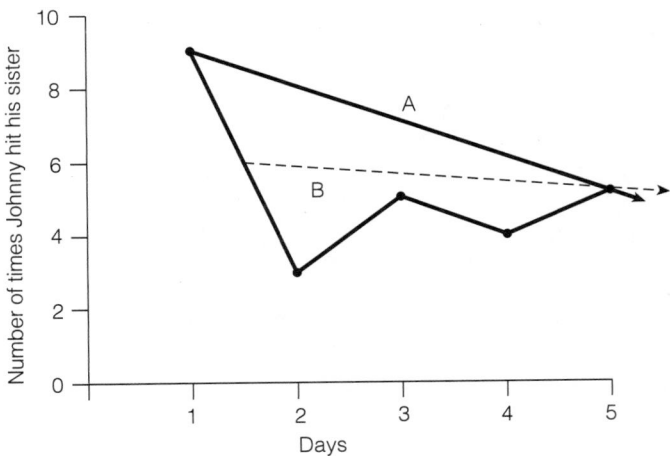

FIGURE 6.4 Single-case design phase with outlying first-phase data point.

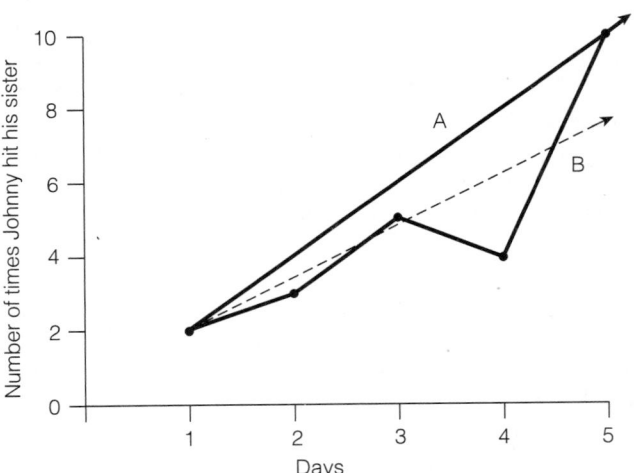

FIGURE 6.5 Single-case data with outlying last-phase data point.

(a) draw the weighted mean trend arrow, as in steps 1 through 4 of the procedure. Then, (b) visually inspect the graphed single-case design data. If the difference between the first and second data points in the phase is three (or more) times larger than the differences between any other successive data points in the phase, as in Figure 6.4, draw the trend line from the *midpoint* of the line segment connecting the first and second data points in the phase through the final data point in the phase (see rationale in Nugent, 2000). If the extreme point is the last data point in the phase, and the difference between the next-to-last and last data points in the phase is three (or more) times larger than the differences between any other successive data points in the phase, as in Figure 6.5, draw the trend line from the first data point in the phase through the *mid-point* of the line segment connecting the next-to-last and last data points in the phase. You can use a ruler (or some other straightedge device) to find the point that is the midpoint of the line segment connecting the first and second, or the next-to-last and last, data points in the phase.

   This procedure makes use of the moving average of the first two (or last two) data points to smooth the variability produced by the extreme data point (Gottman, 1981; Kazdin, 1982; Wheeler, 1995) and will produce a trend line that is less influenced by the unusual data point. This procedure has been used to produce the alternate trend lines (labeled B and shown as dashed arrows) in Figures 6.4 and 6.5. Notice how different the trend is as represented by the weighted mean trend, shown by the arrow labeled A, and the trend as represented by the dashed arrow B. If the extreme data point is the first in the phase, and you need a numerical index describing the trend, then you can compute an adjusted trend, T'_{wm}, from

$$T'_{wm} = \frac{Y_f - Y'_1}{t_f - t'_1} \tag{6.4}$$

where

$$Y'_1 = \frac{Y_1 + Y_2}{2} \text{ and } t'_1 = \frac{t_1 + t_2}{2}$$

If the extreme data point is the last in the phase, then the adjusted trend T'_{wm} can be computed from

$$T'_{wm} = \frac{Y'_f - Y_1}{t'_f - t_1}$$

where

$$Y'_f = \frac{Y_{n-1} + Y_n}{2} \text{ and } t'_f = \frac{t_{n-1} + t_n}{2} \tag{6.5}$$

The adjusted trend, as computed using Equation 6.4 and represented by the dashed arrow in Figure 6.4, is

$$T'_{wm} = \frac{5 - \dfrac{9 + 3}{2}}{5 - \dfrac{1 + 2}{2}} = \frac{5 - 6}{5 - 1.5} = -.29$$

and the adjusted trend in Figure 6.5, as computed by Equation 6.5 and represented by the dashed arrow, is

$$T'_{wm} = \frac{\dfrac{4 + 10}{2} - 2}{\dfrac{4 + 5}{2} - 1} = \frac{7 - 2}{4.5 - 1} = +1.4$$

A second limitation of the use of a linear trend representation is that *nonlinear*, or *curvilinear*, trends will not be well represented. This is illustrated in Figure 6.6. The dashed curve shows the nonlinear trend across the phase as represented by a quadratic regression model (with $R = .92$). The weighted mean trend arrow (labeled A) does not model the curvilinear nature of the trend across the phase. In particular, the mean trend arrow in Figure 6.6 fails to represent the *increasing* trend in the dependent variable across the second half of the phase.

Notice in Figure 6.6 how all of the data points (except the first and last) fall on the same side of the weighted mean trend arrow (labeled A in the figure). Also notice how neither the first nor last data points in the phase are substantially different from the phase data point next to them. If all (or nearly all) of the data points are on the same side of the phase trend arrow, but there is *not* an unusual data point at the beginning or end of the phase, then you can represent the trend in the phase as *nonlinear* by redrawing the trend as follows: (a) draw a line segment starting at the first phase data point and extending through the lowest (or highest) midphase data point. Put an arrow head at the end of this line segment indicating the direction of the trend over the first section of the phase; then (b) draw a second line segment that starts at the data point where the first line segment ended and that goes through the final data point in the phase. Put an arrow head at the end of this line segment indicating the direction of the trend over the latter part of the phase. The procedures in (a) and (b) in this paragraph should be used only if the trend line in the second portion of the phase crosses three or more data points (for reasons discussed later). If the use of (a) and (b) in this paragraph results in a trend line across the second part of the phase that crosses less than three data points, then the trend line across the first part of the phase should be drawn through the data point immediately preceding the lowest (or highest) data point. If more than one data point in the phase shares the same lowest (or highest) value, then the trend line across the first part of the phase should be drawn through the first of the data points with the lowest (or highest) values. Finally, if a numerical index of trend is needed, you can (c) calculate the "local" trends, that is, the trends over specific portions of the phase (Gottman, 1981), for the first and second parts of the phase by

$$\Delta Y^\star / \Delta t^\star = (Y_{f\star} - Y_{i\star})/(t_{f\star} - t_{i\star}) \tag{6.6}$$

where $Y_{f\star}$ is the final measure, made at time $t_{f\star}$, in the section of the single-case phase, and $Y_{i\star}$ is the first measure, taken at time $t_{i\star}$, in the section of the single-case phase.

An application of this procedure is shown in Figure 6.6. Notice that there are two data points (the fifth and seventh) that share the same "lowest" value; the local trend line across the first portion of the phase has been drawn through

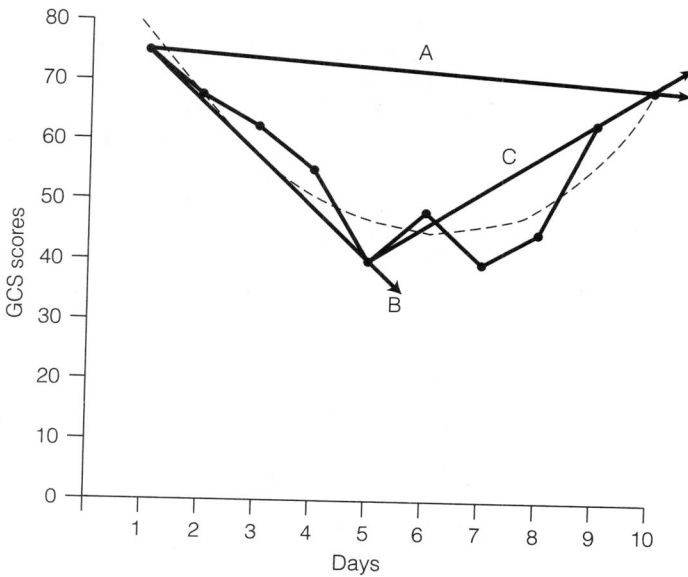

FIGURE 6.6 Single-case design phase with nonlinear trend.

the fifth data point, since this is the first of the two "lowest" data points that occur in the phase. Notice how the two local trend lines, labeled B and C, across the first and second parts of the phase do a better job of representing the nonlinear trend than does the weighted mean trend line. The weighted mean trend in the data in Figure 6.6 is $-.78$. In contrast, the local trend over the first half of the phase is -8.75, while the local trend over the second half of the phase is $+5.6$.

This addition to the procedure described earlier for estimating and drawing the trend in a single-case design phase is not perfect. It creates what is called a "quadratic" representation of the phase trend, and nonlinear trends can be more complicated than a quadratic (single-bend) curve. However, attempting to represent more complex trend curves, though merely an extension of the procedures described in (a) through (c), will most likely not be necessary in the vast majority of cases. Trend curves more complex than quadratic, such as cubic (two bends) or quartic (three bends), will probably show up only when there are larger numbers of data points in a phase, and larger numbers of phase data points (especially in baseline) will be the exception rather than the rule. Further, as the trend curve becomes more and more complex, the weighted mean trend will do a better and better job of representing the trend in the phase.

General Guidelines   The number of data points in a phase will constrain, to some extent, the method you use to represent trend. Let n indicate the number of data points in the phase. We recommend that you use the weighted mean trend line if $n \leq 3$, since there are too few data points to use any of the other procedures we have described. If $n = 4$, then you can use either the weighted mean trend line *or* the modified procedure that takes into account an unusual data point, whichever is most appropriate. If $n \geq 5$, then you can use any of the procedures described. When representing a nonlinear trend, the trend line in the second part of the phase must never be based on less than three data points, since doing so, as will be seen later, would make it impossible to represent the background variability around this second-phase trend line.

An important question concerns whether you should use a trend arrow to represent the data in a phase, or whether the phase mean should be used. In the latter case, you would use a line segment that marks the phase mean, as is done in statistical process control (Pfadt & Wheeler, 1995; Wheeler, 1995). You might think that if the trend is "really 0"—that is, in some way is "nonsignificant"—then the phase mean should be used. Parsonson and Baer (1986) made a number of points that bear on this issue. In their discussion of hypothetical baseline data for a young girl, they noted:

> A slow increasing trend in her likelihood to cross the street safely can be seen. In a 8-point baseline, that might be attributed to chance variation; on the other hand, *it is visible, and interpretation later will depend on what changes can be seen relative to this baseline.* Thus, it does not really matter whether the baseline is truly increasing; what matters is that any intervention applied after this baseline must produce increases that contrast to this *apparent* trend. . . . [A]ny useful intervention will produce effects clearly contrasting to it—and any intervention that cannot produce effects better than that need not be validated as functional, anyway: it will have no use in a pragmatic world. (p. 167, emphasis added)

The weighted mean trend arrow is a natural frame of reference against which to compare the data pattern in the next phase. The "significance" of the trend is less important than the fact that the trend exists and is represented by the trend line.

Variability

Variability refers to the extent to which the data in a particular phase (or set of phases) in a single-case design fluctuate or vary between observations. Visually, variability would be detected by data that "wiggle" or change a lot; the more (less) the wiggle, the greater (lower) the variability. Statistically, the variability would most commonly be measured by such indices as the range, standard deviation, or the variance (Bloom et al., 1999). The range is computed by subtracting the smallest value of the dependent variable in a phase from the largest value. The standard deviation and variance can most easily be computed using a personal computer or a calculator that has statistical keys.

For example, the range of Johnny's daily levels of hitting his little sister across the week's data given in Figure 6.1 is $9 - 2 = 7$, and the standard deviation (calculated on a hand calculator) is 2.4. Another example of variability in data is shown in Figure 6.7. This figure shows data from two phases of a

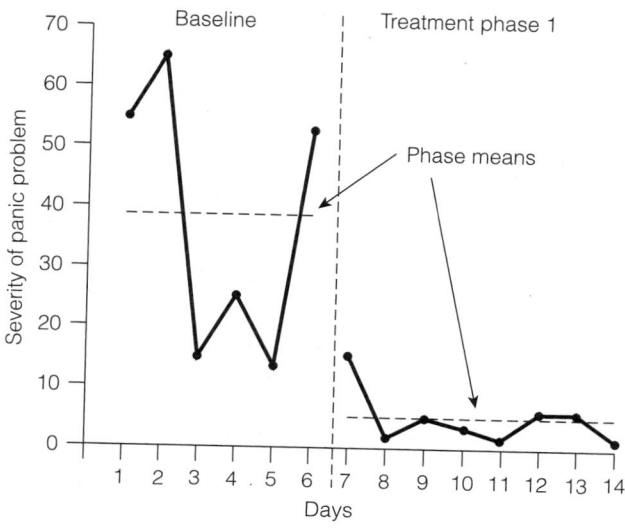

FIGURE 6.7 Baseline and first treatment phase data for intervention for panic disorder. Adapted from Nugent (1993a). Courtesy of the Haworth Press, Inc.

single-case design evaluation of a hypnotic intervention used for a client's problems with panic attacks conducted by one of the authors (see Nugent, 1993a, p. 52, Figure 2). The dependent variable was a measure of the severity of panic experienced by the client. Notice in Figure 6.7 how much the data wiggle or change from one data point to the next across the baseline phase. The range of these baseline data is 65 − 14 = 51, and the standard deviation is 22.02. In contrast, the data in the treatment phase in Figure 6.7 are much less variable, and this lower variability is visually apparent by its relative lack of wiggle compared with that in baseline. The range of these treatment-phase data is 16 − 3 = 13, and the standard deviation is 5.25.

Another method of representing variability numerically is the *average moving range*, a method used in statistical process control (Orme & Cox, 2000; Pfadt & Wheeler, 1995). The moving range is defined as the absolute value of the difference between two successive data points in a single-case design phase, $|y_i - y_{i+1}|$. For example, the baseline data in Figure 6.7 have the values 55, 64, 16, 26, 14, and 54. The data points for treatment phase are 16, 2, 5, 3, 2, 6, 6, and 2. The moving range between the first two data points is $|55 - 64| = 9$. The set of moving range values for the baseline data is 9, 48, 10, 12, and 40. You will notice that there are only five moving range values, which is one less than the number of data points in the phase (in this case, six). In general, if there are n phase data points, there will be $n − 1$ moving range values. The average moving range value for the baseline data in Figure 6.7 is

$$\frac{9 + 48 + 10 + 12 + 40}{5} = \frac{119}{5} = 23.8$$

(For practice, calculate the mean moving range for the treatment phase data in Figure 6.7. The answer is 4).

Pfadt and Wheeler (1995) and Wheeler (1995) discuss the use of the mean moving range in setting variation bounds in time-series data. They define a measure of variation called the *sigma unit*, which for time-series data such as that found in single-case designs is calculated by the formula

$$\sigma = sigma = (2.66 \times \bar{R})/3$$

where $\bar{R}$ is the average moving range. Two sigma units would be $2 \times \sigma$, and three sigma units would be $3 \times \sigma$. Pfadt and Wheeler (1995) and Orme and Cox (2000) discuss placing one-, two-, and three-sigma-unit bands above and below the phase mean line and then using these bands to decide if any changes between phases are meaningful. We will also make use of the sigma unit later in our recommendations for analyzing single-case design data, but in a somewhat different manner.

Background Variability

A central concept in the assessment of between-phase change in the analysis of single-case data is the notion of *background variability* (Barlow, Hayes, & Nelson, 1984). Background variability can be thought of as the "typical" or "usual" variability, relative to some basis such as a mean line (Wheeler, 1995) or a trend line (Gottman, 1981), inherent in the data in a particular phase. In visual analyses, assessments of change between phases are made relative to some representation of background variability. That representation may be informal and "in the eye of the beholder," such as in an "interocular test" (Gottman, 1981), or more formal such as in statistical analyses (Barlow et al., 1984; Barlow & Hersen, 1984; Bloom et al., 1999; Kazdin, 1982). The sigma unit, discussed earlier, can also be used to set graphical variation bounds representing the background variability in time-series data (Orme & Cox, 2000; Pfadt & Wheeler, 1995; Pfadt et al., 1992; Wheeler, 1995).

Overlap

This leads to the notion of *overlap*. Overlap usually refers to the extent to which the ranges of values of data points in two adjacent phases share common values (Kazdin, 1982). Look again at the data in Figure 6.3. The data points in baseline range from 2 to 9, and those in treatment phase range from 2 to 9. The data in these two adjacent phases overlap completely, since the two ranges of values completely match; that is, the baseline range of values (2 to 9) completely entails the treatment-phase range of values (also 2 to 9).

One problem with the notion of overlap as described here (which is how it is most often used) is that it does not take trend into account. Notice that in Figure 6.3, according to the traditional definition, the A- and B-phase data overlap completely. However, the trend of the dependent measure in baseline is *increasing*, while the trend during treatment phase is *decreasing*. A good definition of overlap should account for trend and at the same time lend itself to easy use by practitioners. We recommend the following method, inspired by procedures described by Bloom and Fischer (1982, pp. 468–471) and Wheeler (1995), to graphically represent background variability and assess overlap:

1. Find the phase data point *furthest* from the phase trend line. If the weighted mean trend line, or the trend line adjusted to reduce the influence of an outlying data point, has been used to represent the trend, then the data point furthest from this trend line will be used. If a nonlinear trend has been modeled, then the data point furthest from the local trend line across the *second* part of the phase will be used. This is why the local trend arrow over the second part of a phase should never be based on less than three data points, as noted earlier. *The distance between the trend line and this data point is used as an estimate of one sigma unit relative to the trend line.* The justification for the use of this distance as an estimate of one sigma unit relative to the trend line is given in Appendix A. As is proven in the appendix, the use of the data point furthest from the trend line as an estimate of one sigma unit will be, on average, a liberal estimate, overestimating the correct value of one sigma unit by about 13 percent (see Figure A.3 in Appendix A). It is also shown in Appendix A that positive autocorrelation (if present) in the single-case data will reduce the average overestimation of one sigma unit obtained using this method.

2. Draw a line parallel to the trend line and through this data point. Draw a second line, parallel to the first line and the same distance from the trend line as the first line, on the *opposite* side of the trend line. Extend these two lines, and the trend line, into the next phase. The region between the two lines parallel to the trend line represents the background variability *relative to the trend line*. The extension of this region into the next phase is the "extended region of background variability" from the preceding phase. The extended region of background variability represents the predicted area in which data points should fall *if the data pattern in the previous phase (or latter part of the previous phase) continues without any change.* This extension into the next phase serves as a basis of comparison for the actual data in the phase (Barlow et al., 1984; Bloom et al., 1999; Kazdin, 1982; Parsonson & Baer, 1986). Any data points in the subsequent phase that fall within the extended region of background variability from the preceding phase are defined as *overlapping* with the data in the previous phase. Any data points in the subsequent phase that fall outside of the extended region of background variability do *not* overlap with the data in the previous phase. Notice the difference between this definition of overlap and that traditionally used. This definition uses the trend line as a basis, while the traditional definition makes use of the maximum and minimum levels of the dependent variable within phases as a basis.

3. Draw another parallel line, *twice* as far from the trend line as the lines drawn in the previous step, on each side of the trend line. Extend these two lines into the next phase, just as in the previous step. These two lines are used as approximate two–sigma–unit bounds relative to the trend line and can be used as further assessment guides.

The procedures in steps 1 through 3 are merely an application of graphical methods of analysis of time-series data used by engineers in statistical process control, or SPC (Orme & Cox, 2000; Pfadt & Wheeler, 1995; Pfadt et al., 1992; Wheeler, 1995).

Look at Figure 6.8, a redrawn version of Figure 6.3. Weighted mean trend lines can be seen in the baseline and treatment phases. The fourth baseline measure is the data point farthest from the weighted mean trend line (about 1/4 of an inch as graphed in Figure 6.8), so a *heavy* dashed line has been drawn through this point parallel to the trend line. A similar heavy dashed line has been drawn on the upper side of (and the same distance from) the trend line. Both of these lines (as well as the trend line) have been extended into the treatment phase. The region in baseline phase between these heavy dashed lines represents the region of baseline background variability relative to the weighted mean trend arrow. The region between these lines that has been extended into treatment phase is the extended region of baseline-phase background variability relative to the baseline trend. Two lighter dashed lines have also been drawn, parallel to the trend line, that are twice as far from the trend line (about 1/2 of an inch) as are the first two parallel lines, and extended into treatment phase. These two lines represent approximate two sigma bounds relative to the trend line. As can be seen in Figure 6.8, the first treatment-phase data point falls within the extended region of baseline-phase background variability. By the definition of overlap given immediately above, the first treatment-phase data point overlaps with the baseline data pattern. No other treatment-phase data points overlap with the baseline data pattern.

BETWEEN PHASE CHANGE

Change in Level and Mean

Change in level refers to a shift or discontinuity in values of the dependent variable between adjacent phases of a single-case design (Kazdin, 1982). The change in level between phases refers to the difference in the value of the dependent variable from the end of one phase to the beginning of the subsequent phase. Similarly, a change in mean refers to a change in the mean levels of the dependent variable from one phase to the next.

Look again at Figure 6.7. Notice that the level of the last baseline measurement was 54, while the value of the first B-phase measure was 16. In this case, the change in level across the A/B-phase transition was $16 - 54 = -38$, with the minus sign indicating that the change in level represented a decrease

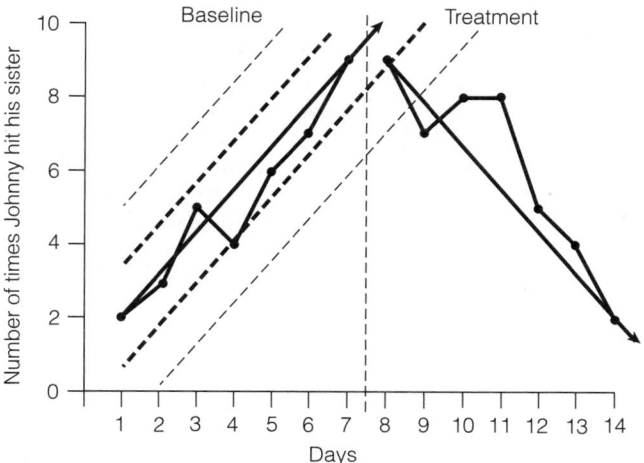

FIGURE 6.8 Figure 6.3 redrawn with region of baseline-phase background variability (dark dashed lines) and estimated two sigma lines (light dashed lines) drawn in.

relative to baseline. The level of the first treatment-phase measurement of the dependent variable was 38 units lower than the level at the final baseline measure. The mean level during the baseline phase of this study was

$$\frac{55 + 64 + 16 + 26 + 14 + 54}{6} = 38.2$$

The mean level during the B phase was

$$\frac{16 + 2 + 5 + 3 + 2 + 6 + 6 + 2}{8} = 5.25$$

Thus, the change in mean level between A and B phases was $5.25 - 38.2 = -32.95$, with the minus sign indicating that the change in mean represents a decrease relative to the baseline mean.

Change in Trend

Change in trend refers to between-phase differences in the rate at which the dependent variable changes across a phase. Figure 6.3 shows hypothetical data from an A/B single-case design evaluation with the trend arrows drawn in for both baseline and treatment phases. Notice that the trend arrow for baseline points upward, while the trend arrow for treatment phase points down. This illustrates a change in trend between baseline and treatment phases. This change is shown graphically by the two trend arrows in Figure 6.3. This change can also be quantified by using the trend computation methods discussed earlier. For the data in Figure 6.3, the baseline trend was computed to be +1.2, while the treatment trend was −1.2. This is a difference between baseline to treatment phase of

$$-1.2 - 1.2 = -2.4$$

The minus sign indicates that the change in trend is in a decreasing direction. If a decreasing direction indicates that the client is getting "better," then this change in trend is in an improving direction. However, if a decreasing trend indicates that the client is getting "worse" over time, then the change in trend is in a deteriorating direction.

Change in Variability

Change in variability refers to between-phase differences in the variability of the data in single-case design phases. For example, in Figure 6.7, the data in the baseline phase in this single-case design are quite variable. The standard deviation of these data is 22.02, and the average moving range is 23.8. In comparison, the variability of the data in B phase is rather small. In B phase, the data appear to cluster at a low level across the vast majority of the phase. The standard deviation of the B-phase data is about 4.68, and the average moving range is 4. Thus, the change in variability between these two phases is quite large.

Assessing Between Phase Change

The concepts of background variability and overlap provide a means of comparing the data patterns between two adjacent single-case design phases. The basic idea is to assess the extent to which the data pattern in the adjacent phase is "different" relative to both the pattern and the "typical" variability in the data in the previous phase (Barlow et al., 1984). *The greater the extent to which the data pattern in the subsequent phase diverges from the data pattern in the previous phase, in terms of magnitude and direction relative to the background variability in the previous phase, the greater the evidence for change between phases.* One important criterion often used in the assessment of between-phase differences is overlap: the less the data in the adjacent phase overlap with the data in the previous phase, the stronger the evidence for change (Barlow et al., 1984; Barlow & Hersen, 1984; Kazdin, 1982). This criterion implies the existence of a "unit of overlap" that might be used to more systematically assess the presence of change between phases.

The sigma unit relative to the trend line, discussed earlier, is one "unit of overlap" that might be used. Any data point that is more than one sigma unit away from the extended trend line, by definition, fails to overlap with the data pattern in the previous phase. Hence, the more sigma units a data point falls from an extended trend line, the farther it is from overlapping with the data pattern in the previous phase. This unit of overlap (i.e., the sigma unit), the extended region of background variability, the estimated two sigma bounds described earlier, and four detection rules from statistical process control (SPC) may be used to assess between-phase change. These SPC detection rules, and their rationale, have been discussed in detail by Wheeler (1995), and their use in the analysis of single-case design data has been discussed by Orme and Cox (2000), Pfadt et al. (1992), and Pfadt and Wheeler (1995). The SPC rules are:

1. Any data point that falls three or more sigma units away from the phase mean line is meaningfully different.

2. If two out of three consecutive data points fall two or more sigma units away from the phase mean line, they are meaningfully different.

3. If at least four out of five successive data points fall on the same side of, and more than one sigma unit away from, the phase mean line, then these data are meaningfully different.

4. If at least eight consecutive data points, or twelve of fourteen successive points, fall on the same side of the phase mean line, then these data are meaningfully different.

The purpose of using these rules in analyzing single-case data is to identify a change in the client's problem as measured by the outcome variable. This is simply a specific adaptation of the purpose of the detection rules in SPC, which is to detect a change in the underlying process that is generating the time-series data (Wheeler, 1995).

In the context of single-case design evaluations, any detection rules that are used should be sensitive enough to detect change, while at the same time being robust enough to detect change only when it is there. The rules should also recognize the context of the generally small number of phase measures that are found in most single-case design evaluations. The four detection rules that follow are adapted from Wheeler (1995) and appear to meet these criteria. They are recommended for use in assessing between-phase change:

Rule 1: *A significant change is indicated by a data point that falls more than two sigma units away from the extended trend line.* This rule says that data points that are more than one "overlap units" away from overlapping with the previous phase's data pattern are different enough to be regarded as "significantly different." This is a two-sigma-unit version of the three-sigma-unit rule (detection rule 1 in Wheeler, 1995) used in SPC. It is recommended, in lieu of the three-sigma-unit rule, so as to give a greater sensitivity to change (see Wheeler, 1995, Chapter 9, and section 4 of Chapter 10, including Figure 10.20). According to Figure 10.20 (with $k = 1$) in Wheeler (1995), this will give increased power while maintaining a relatively low probability of a type I error.

Rule 2: *Two of three data points falling more than two sigma units away from the extended trend line signify significant change.* This rule is an extension of Rule 1 and is an adaptation of SPC detection rule 2 in Wheeler (1995).

Rule 3: *Four of five data points on the same side of the extended trend line, and more than one sigma unit away from the extended trend line, signify significant change.* This is Wheeler's (1995) SPC detection rule 3, albeit stated in terms relative to the trend line as opposed to a line marking the phase mean. This rule says that four of five successive data points that fail to overlap with the previous phase's data pattern serve to signify the presence of significant change. A general guideline from this rule that is adapted to serve in the small n context of single-case design evaluations is that if all n data points in an adjacent phase (but the phase $n < 5$) fail to overlap with the data pattern in the previous phase, this is suggestive of significant change.

Rule 4: *Seven data points in a row that are on the same side of the extended trend line (but not necessarily more than one sigma unit away from the extended trend line) are indicative of significant change.* This is a less conservative version of Wheeler's (1995) SPC detection rule 4 (also see Grant & Leavenworth, 1980). A general guideline from this rule is that if the phase $n < 7$, and if *all n* of the phase data points are on the same side of the extended trend line, the pattern is suggestive of change. Clearly, as $n \rightarrow 7$, the evidence for change becomes stronger, and as n becomes smaller, the evidence becomes weaker.

These detection rules, and the procedures described earlier, should also be used in conjunction with critical incident recording and investigation (Bloom et al., 1999; Hudson, 1982).

Look again at Figure 6.8. The data in treatment phase show a clear trend away from the extended baseline trend line, suggesting a change in trend between baseline and treatment phase. As noted, only the first treatment-phase data point overlaps with the baseline data pattern. The final six data points in treatment phase lie beyond both the extended region of baseline background variability and the estimated two sigma bound. The characteristics of the data, and detection rule 2, clearly suggest that there is an important change between baseline and treatment phase in this contrived single-case design.

The methods, guidelines, and detection rules discussed here are not intended to comprise either a form of statistical significance testing or a means of assigning probability values to particular data patterns. They are, rather, intended as graphic aids and analysis tools to help you conduct visual analyses while preserving as much as possible the flexibility inherent in visual analysis approaches (Parsonson & Baer, 1992). Given the practice context, in most cases you will have precious few data points in a single-case design to use to evaluate your interventions. This means, in a statistical sense, that your analyses will be conducted in a low-power situation; that is, it will be harder to detect change than it would be if you had many more single-case data points. The use of the above four detection rules, as opposed to, say, the use of three sigma bounds as are used in SPC (Orme & Cox, 2000; Pfadt & Wheeler, 1995), or some decision rule based on statistical significance testing methods (Chow, 1996), will give you greater power to detect change (Wheeler, 1995). This increased power may lead you at times to find significant change when there was, in fact, *no* change (i.e., a type I error). This particular balance between type I errors and type II errors (i.e., missing important change when it is there) is much more acceptable in a practice evaluation context than in a research context (Posavac, 1998). The balance between type I and type II error rates must be different in the realm of practice and the realm of science because the demands of science place a greater emphasis on low type I error rates than the demands of practice evaluation (Posavac, 1998; Thomas, 1978).

Latency of Change

Another concept that is important when analyzing single-case design data is the notion of *latency of change* (Kazdin, 1982). Latency of change refers to the period of time that passes between the end of one phase (such as the end of a baseline phase) and the point in the subsequent phase when some type of change in the dependent variable first becomes noticeable. One way to utilize this concept is to look at the number of data points in the next phase that fall within the extended region of background variability from the preceding phase before subsequent phase data points begin to fall outside of the region. In Figure 6.8, notice that only the first treatment-phase data point falls within the extended region of baseline background variability. All other data points are beyond this region, and on the same side of the extended trend arrow. This suggests that there was a *delayed* change in Johnny's problem of hitting his sister. Thus, there was slight latency of change. This can be contrasted with the situation shown in Figure 6.9. Notice that all of the data points in treatment phase fall outside of the extended baseline background variability region, and all are on or beyond the estimated two sigma band. This figure therefore shows an immediate change. The *less* the latency of change there is in the single-case design data (that is, the quicker that change occurs) concomitant with the start of treatment, the more convincing the argument that treatment caused change (Barlow et al., 1984; Kazdin, 1982).

Permanent Versus Temporary Change

A change that remains intact throughout a single-case design phase is said to be *permanent*. In contrast, a change that disappears after a period of time is said to be *temporary*. The change in Johnny's hitting behavior shown in Figure 6.9 is permanent. All treatment phase data points remain outside of the extended region of baseline phase background variability. This is in contrast to the change shown in Figure 6.10. Notice how, in this figure, Johnny's hitting behavior changes immediately with the start of treatment but disappears by the fourth day of treatment. This is a temporary change.

ILLUSTRATIVE VISUAL ANALYSES

The visual analysis of single-case design data involves the use of all the methods we have discussed for looking at single-case data and comparing the data in adjacent phases. The data pattern that appears in one phase (such as baseline phase) is compared with the pattern observed in the next adjacent phase (such as a treatment phase), and decisions are made about whether any differences

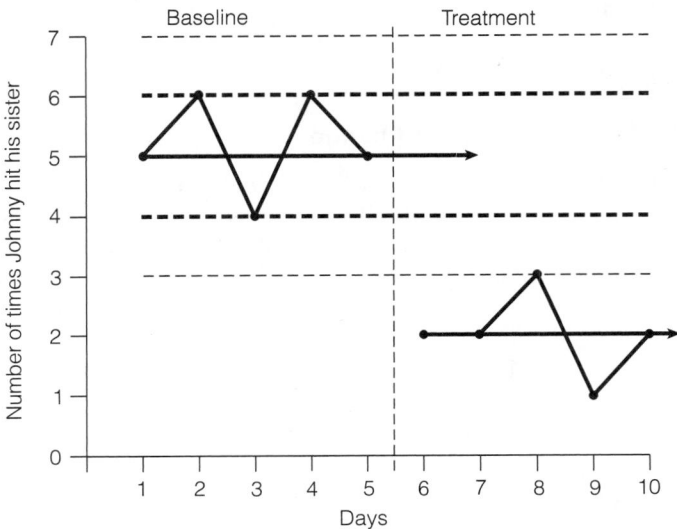

FIGURE 6.9 An example of an immediate and permanent change.

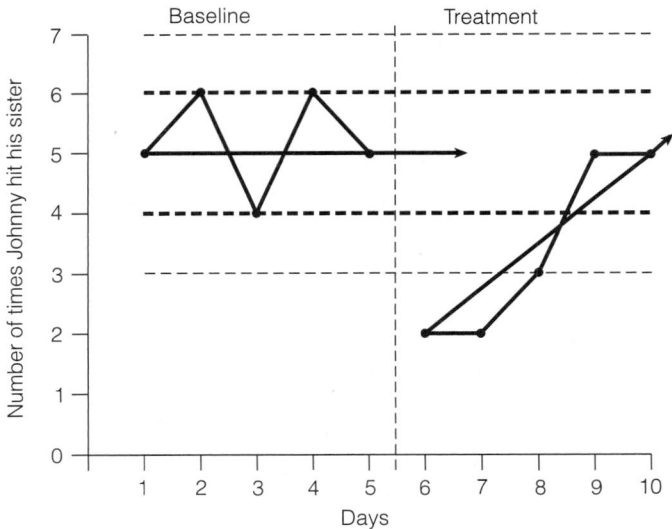

FIGURE 6.10 An example of an immediate but temporary change.

exist and, if so, how important those differences are. The data pattern in a previous phase is used to predict what would most likely have occurred in the next phase of the single-case design if nothing had occurred to alter the pattern in the previous phase (Bloom et al., 1999; Kazdin, 1982). The most fundamental comparison of this type is the comparison of a treatment-phase data

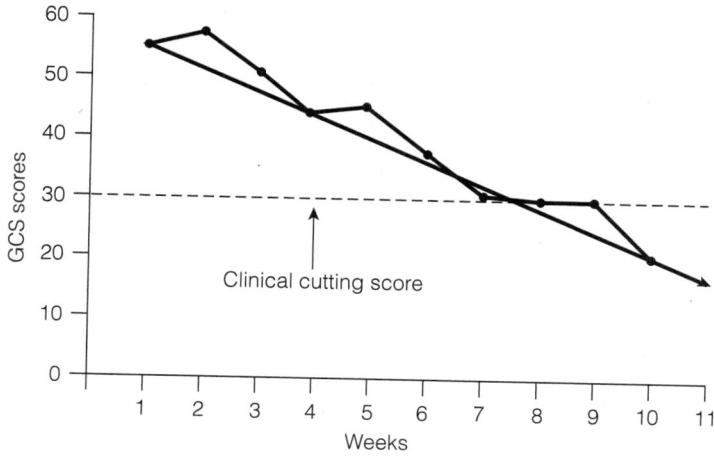

FIGURE 6.11 B design data for hypothetical client treated for depression.

pattern with a baseline data pattern. The baseline data pattern is used to predict how the data pattern would most likely have continued in the immediate future in the absence of any causal factors impacting on, and changing, the baseline pattern. The treatment-phase data pattern is compared with the baseline pattern, and against the background variability in the baseline pattern, and determinations are made about whether the treatment-phase pattern has changed relative to that in baseline (Barlow, Hayes, & Nelson, 1984). Visual inspection is made to determine whether there is any evidence of changes in level, mean, trend, variability, or some combination of these, as well as an assessment as to the latency of any change that is noticeable and whether this change is permanent. If there is visually apparent change, then this evidence is related to the evaluation question driving the single-case design study.

Following are illustrative analyses of several hypothetical single-case design studies of interventions. These hypothetical evaluations have been designed to illustrate applications of the methods we have described in this chapter.

Illustrative Analysis Number One

The first illustrative analysis is of hypothetical data from a B design used to evaluate the treatment of a client for depression. The B design data for this hypothetical client are shown in Figure 6.11. The practitioner measured the magnitude of this client's problem with depression on a weekly basis using the GCS. The phase trend line has been drawn in Figure 6.11, as has a dashed line indicating the clinical cutting score on the GCS. The important thing to note in this graph is that (1) the hypothetical client's GCS scores decrease over the course of the ten weeks of treatment, and (2) the final three GCS scores are at, or below, the clinical cutting score. There is no need to draw in the region of background variability or the estimated two sigma bounds, since this is a B design and there is no comparison possible between different phases. This hypothetical case nicely illustrates the simplicity of the analysis of data from a simple B design. It also illustrates how powerful a B design can be for providing compelling evidence that the client improved during the course of treatment. If your evaluation goal is simply to provide evidence that your client improved during the course of service provision—with no attempt to claim that the services provided were the *cause* of change—then the B design is all you need.

Illustrative Analysis Number Two

The second illustrative analysis is of hypothetical data from an AB design evaluation of another client's problem with depression. The data from this hypothetical evaluation are shown in Figure 6.12. The practitioner used the GCS to monitor this client's depression and assessed the magnitude of the client's depression on a weekly basis. In Figure 6.12, you can see a black, dashed arrow in baseline that represents not only the baseline trend line but also the region of baseline phase background variability and the estimated two sigma bounds. In this case, there is *no* variability in the client's GCS scores during baseline! Thus, the baseline trend line, the lines marking the region of baseline phase background variability, and the lines marking the two sigma bounds all fall on top of one another. This is the ideal type of baseline phase data, though it is not likely to occur in practice (Barlow et al., 1984; Bloom et al., 1999; Kazdin, 1982).

You will also notice in Figure 6.12 the solid black arrow marking the treatment phase trend. Notice that the trend in treatment phase is away from the extended baseline trend line and that all treatment-phase data points are beyond the region of baseline background variability as well as the estimated two sigma bounds. Further, the final treatment-phase data point falls below the clinical cutting score on the GCS. Thus, the data in Figure 6.12 provide compelling evidence that this hypothetical client improved during treatment. The data also suggest, rather strongly from a clinical perspective (though not convincingly from a scientific perspective), that treatment was responsible for the change experienced by this client.

We urge you to look through the social work and psychological literature for examples of AB data such as that shown in Figure 6.12. One example is given by Kazi and Wilson (1996). They evaluated the effects of services provided in an effort to reduce a young boy's problem with truancy. A second example is provided by Bradshaw (1996). In this case, an AB design was used to evaluate a cognitive-behavioral approach to working with clients with schizophrenia. In both cases, the baseline data were like that shown in Figure 6.12—there was no variability. In both cases, the treatment-phase data also showed marked changes relative to the baseline data.

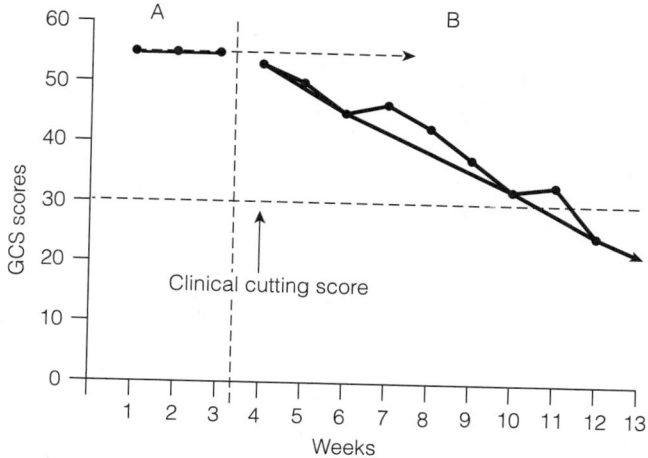

FIGURE 6.12 Hypothetical AB design data from an evaluation of treatment of a client's problem with depression.

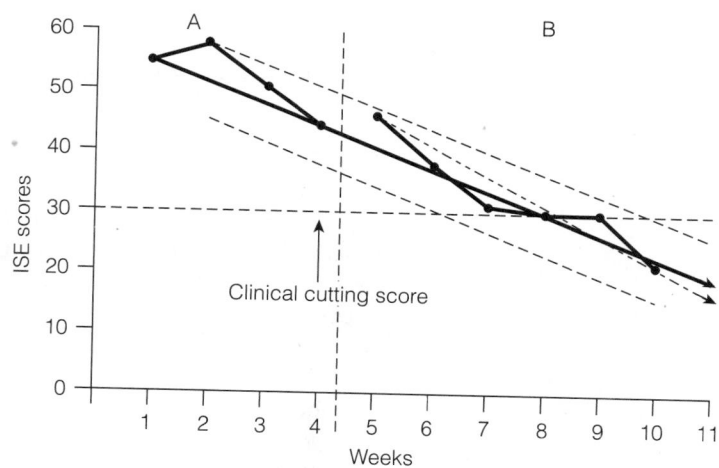

FIGURE 6.13 Hypothetical data from an AB design evaluation of an intervention for problems with self-esteem.

Illustrative Analysis Number Three

In this hypothetical case, an AB design was used to evaluate an intervention for problems with self-esteem. In this case, the practitioner used the ISE to monitor, on a weekly basis, the magnitude of the client's self-esteem problems. The data from this imaginary evaluation are shown in Figure 6.13. The black arrow in this figure represents the extended baseline-phase trend line, while the dashed black lines represent the extended region of baseline-phase background variability. The dashed black arrow represents the treatment-phase trend line. Notice that the data in baseline phase and treatment phase both show decreasing trends in ISE scores. Notice how similar the baseline- and treatment-phase trends are. Also notice that while the final three treatment-phase measures are at or below the clinical cutting score on the ISE, *all treatment phase data points fall within the region of extended baseline variability.* Thus, while the evidence clearly indicates that this client improved during service provision, it does not support treatment as being responsible for the client's improvement. Since the treatment-phase data fall within the extended region of baseline background variability, the results suggest that the treatment-phase data are a continuation of the baseline data pattern. This data pattern actually suggests that the client may have improved without any service provision, though there is no way of knowing for sure, since we do not have the data showing what would have happened had the client *not* received treatment. This example illustrates the problems that are brought on by missing data on the counterfactual (in this case, the data we would have obtained had the client *not* received treatment) when we are trying to make inferences about the effects of treatment (Gilovich, 1991).

Ilustrative Analysis Number Four

This analysis illustrates a hypothetical case in which treatment-phase data suggest that the chosen treatment is not working, so a new intervention is implemented. In this hypothetical case, an ABC design is used to evaluate the treatment of a client for depression. As in the earlier imaginary cases, the practitioner used the GCS on a weekly basis to monitor the magnitude of the client's depression. The data from this hypothetical evaluation are shown in Figure 6.14. In Figure 6.14, you can see a dashed black arrow that represents not only the extended baseline trend line, but also the extended region of baseline-phase background variability and the estimated two sigma bounds. This is similar to the data shown in Figure 6.12. There is no variability during baseline. You should notice in Figure 6.14 that the data in B phase appear to be an extension of the A-phase data. Whatever treatment is being used in the B phase does not appear to be making any difference in the client's problem with depression. This is an example of the feedback function that single-case designs can provide to the practitioner. Since the B-phase data appear to be a continuation of the A-phase data, the A and B phases can be combined into an extended baseline for purposes of analysis. This is why the dashed arrow has been extended through B phase and into C phase in Figure 6.14.

Given the lack of change in B phase, the practitioner implements a new intervention in the C phase. Notice that the C-phase data trend away from the extended baseline trend line, and that all C-phase data points fall outside the extended region of baseline phase variability and beyond the estimated two sigma bound (i.e., below the dashed black arrow). Notice also that the final

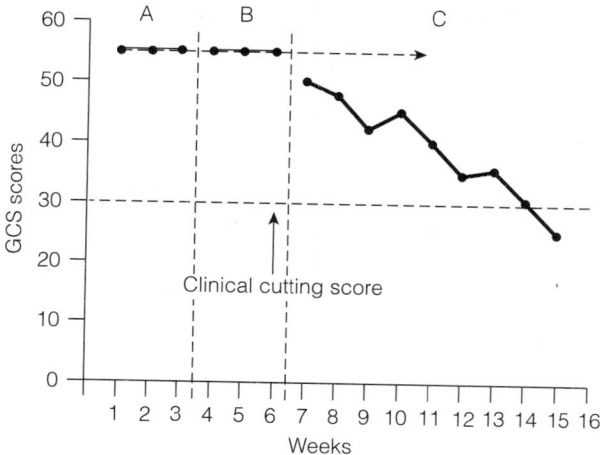

FIGURE 6.14 Hypothetical data from an ABC single-case design evaluation of service provision.

C-phase data point falls well below the clinical cutting score on the GCS. Thus, these data suggest that (a) the client's depression improved during service provision, and (b) the intervention used in C phase may have been responsible for the observed changes. This illustrative analysis is therefore similar to the second illustrative analysis described earlier.

Kazi and Wilson (1996) provide an example similar to that in this illustrative analysis. They report the results of an A/B/BC/C single-case design evaluation of an intervention for a female adolescent's truancy. In the B phase, the social worker implemented counseling sessions with the girl, her mother, grandmother, and boyfriend. The A- and B-phase data both showed a stable weekly school attendance rate of zero percent. The social worker then added a behavioral intervention to the counseling sessions. The behavioral component involved a reinforcement schedule for the girl's attending school. During this BC phase, the girl's school attendance jumped immediately to 40 percent and increased across the phase to 100 percent by the fifth week of the BC phase. The social worker then dropped the counseling sessions but continued the reinforcement for attending school (C phase), and the girl's school attendance remained at 100 percent. We urge you to look at the single-case design data that appear in the Kazi and Wilson (1996) article.

Illustrative Analysis Number Five

This hypothetical analysis is of A/B single-case design data, shown in Figure 6.15, from an evaluation of an intervention used with a male college student who experiences significant anxiety around females. This example involves an unusual baseline data point and shows how critical incident recording and investigation can facilitate the analysis of single-case design data. In this hypo-thetical evaluation, the outcome measure was the number of conversations with female college students initiated by the male college student. The practi-tioner had the young man keep a count, on a 3-inch by 5-inch index card, of the number of conversations he started with female college students each week. The data from the A/B design evaluation are shown in Figure 6.15. In this figure, you can see the solid black arrow indicating the baseline phase trend line. Notice how the trend line is drawn through the midpoint between the next-to-last and last baseline-phase data points. This was done because the dif-ference between the next-to-last and last data points in baseline was more than three times greater than the differences between any other two successive data points in the phase. The moving range values for the baseline data are 1, 1, and 4. Notice that the last moving range value—the difference between the values of the next-to-last and last baseline data points—is four times as large as either of the other moving range values. Here is where critical incident recording can help. The practitioner in this case inquired about the unusual data point and learned that the young man had attended a party at which a game called "get to know you bingo" was played. This game required participants to go around, introduce themselves, and learn something interesting about the other person so they could fill in the squares on a special bingo card. The young man reported that he introduced himself, with great difficulty, to four female col-lege students during the game. In contrast, he estimated that between 15 and 20 young female college students introduced themselves to him. Thus, the crit-ical incident information helps to place the final baseline-phase data point into a context that facilitates its interpretation. In this case, although it represents a large jump relative to the other data points in baseline, the jump is apparently due to an unusual environmental factor and does not appear to represent a sig-nificant improvement in the young man's ability to initiate conversations with female college students. Thus, the method for dealing with unusual data points in a phase, as described earlier in this chapter, was used to draw the baseline trend line in Figure 6.15.

The extended region of baseline phase background variability is shown by the heavy dashed lines, and the upper estimated two sigma bound by the lighter dashed line, in Figure 6.15. Notice that the extended baseline trend line shows a flat (and, hence, nonchanging) trend across baseline. The practitioner implemented an intervention involving social skills training and in vivo prac-tice with female college students during treatment phase. Notice that the treatment-phase trend line is in an increasing (and hence improving) direction and trends away from the extended baseline trend and region of baseline phase background variability. Also notice that all but the first treatment-phase data points fall above the upper estimated two sigma bound in Figure 6.15. Hence, by detection rule 2, discussed earlier, this data pattern clearly suggests that the young man's frequency of initiating conversations with female college students significantly increased relative to baseline during the course of treatment.

The reader may wonder how different the analysis of the data in Figure 6.15 would be if the method we described earlier in this chapter for representing

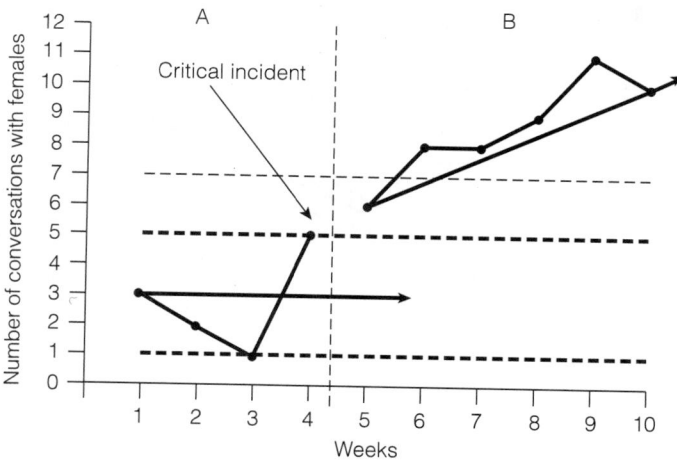

FIGURE 6.15 Hypothetical A/B design data from an evaluation of an intervention for social anxiety.

trend when an unusual data point appears at the end of a phase had not been used. In other words, how sensitive is this analysis to the way that the baseline trend is represented? The data in Figure 6.15 are shown again in Figure 6.16, but without the final baseline data point being treated as an unusual point. Notice in Figure 6.16 that the extended region of baseline background variability, represented by the dashed lines, is much wider than in Figure 6.15. This is because the large difference between the next-to-last and last baseline data points has not been smoothed by using the moving average of these two data points and by using the trend representation method we described earlier in this chapter. Notice now that the baseline trend is increasing (and hence improving) as opposed to being flat (and showing no-change). This difference is due to the final baseline data point. In Figure 6.15, the influence of this data point has been reduced by using the moving average of the next-to-last and last baseline data points to draw in the baseline trend line. In Figure 6.16, this influence has not been reduced. Thus, the baseline trend is, in this case, significantly dependent upon the method used to draw the baseline trend line. The size of the region of baseline phase background variability is also dependent upon the method used to draw in the baseline phase trend line.

Notice also that the treatment-phase trend line still trends away from the extended baseline phase trend line, but to a much smaller degree. Also notice that all six of the treatment-phase data points are on the same side of the extended baseline trend line, though all fall within the extended region of baseline phase background variability. Detection rule 4, discussed earlier, suggests that there is meaningful change, but this evidence is less compelling in Figure 6.16 than in Figure 6.15. This illustrates the influence that the last baseline-phase data point has in the analysis of the data in this hypothetical case and

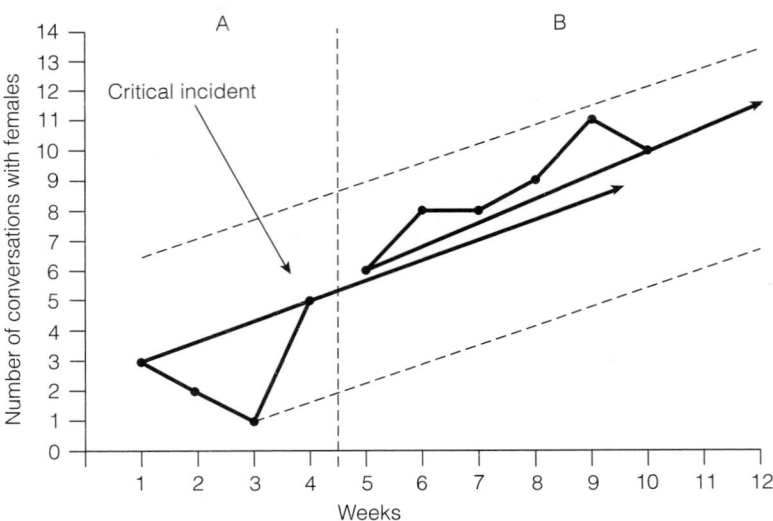

FIGURE 6.16 Hypothetical data from Figure 6.15 when final baseline data point is not treated as "unusual."

the importance of gathering as much information as possible to use in the interpretation of the outlying final baseline data point. Information such as that contained in critical incident recording can be crucial to the proper interpretation of unusual data points at the end or beginning of a phase and the appropriate method to be used in drawing in the phase trend line.

In this hypothetical case, the critical incident information provides a clear rationale for using the moving average technique to smooth out the extra variability introduced by the last baseline data point. However, if necessary, you can do the analysis both ways and thereby explicitly show the differences in your results that are due to the method you use to represent trend. This way the consumer of your evaluation report can have the clearest picture possible of the outcomes experienced by your clients. In this hypothetical case, the data suggest, regardless of the method the practitioner used to draw in the baseline trend, that the young man benefited from treatment. The major difference in this case would be in the clarity with which the effects of treatment are shown.

Illustrative Analysis Number Six

This example shows a situation in which the treatment first used has a small, but significant effect and so the practitioner adds a new component to the intervention to increase its potency. In this case, the client is a young woman who has self-esteem problems and is exceedingly self-critical. She does not like herself, and very frequently engages in self-critical statements about her looks, behavior, and the quality of the work that she does. As a part of her work with

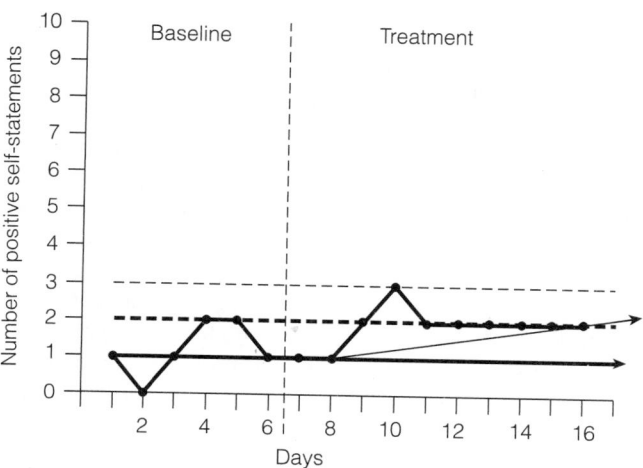

FIGURE 6.17 Hypothetical AB data for a young woman who has self-esteem problems.

this client, a social worker has the young woman count the number of *positive* self-statements she makes each day and record these numbers on a 3-inch by 5-inch note card. The young woman's baseline data are shown in Figure 6.17. Also shown in Figure 6.17 is the baseline trend arrow (the heavy solid arrow), the upper bound of the region of baseline phase background variability (the heavy dashed horizontal line), and the upper bound of the estimated two sigma band (the lighter dashed horizontal line).

The social worker and the young woman collaboratively develop a list of three positive self-statements that the woman agrees are true about herself. The young woman is then given the homework assignment of making these positive self-statements to herself as many times as possible each day. The young woman also continues to count and record the number of positive self-statements she makes to herself each day during this treatment. The data for the first ten days of treatment phase are shown in Figure 6.17. As can be seen in Figure 6.17, there is a small increase in the trend of the number of positive self-statements the young woman makes each day. The social worker notes that 8 out of 10 of the treatment-phase data points are on the same side of the extended baseline-phase trend line. By detection rule 4, described earlier, this indicates the presence of significant change. However, the change is rather small, so the social worker decides to continue with the intervention *but plans an addition that she hopes will increase the potency of the effect of treatment on her client.* She decides to make use of the Premack principle (Sundel & Sundel, 1999) and has the young woman identify behaviors of hers that occur with relatively high frequency. After some discussion of these behaviors, the social worker and the young woman decide to make use of her gum chewing. The young woman chews gum on a fairly frequent basis. Thus, the social worker instructs the young woman to make at least one positive self-statement from the list of three immediately prior to putting a piece of gum into her mouth. The young woman agrees to do this and again keeps count of the number of positive self-statements she makes to herself each day.

The data for the next nine days of treatment are shown in Figure 6.18. In this figure, the first treatment phase has been labeled "treatment I," while the second treatment phase has been labeled "treatment I + II." The extended treatment I phase trend arrow (the solid arrow) is shown in this figure, as are the upper bounds of the extended treatment I phase region of background variability (the heavy dashed line parallel to the extended trend line) and the estimated two sigma band (the lighter dashed line parallel to the extended trend line). The treatment I + II phase trend arrow is the dashed arrow in this figure. As can be seen in Figure 6.18, the final eight treatment I + II phase data points are beyond the extended region of treatment phase I background variability, and five of the last seven are beyond the estimated two sigma bound. The trend in this second treatment phase is greater than in the previous phase. Clearly the young woman is more frequently making positive self-statements about herself, and this change in the second treatment phase is significant relative to the first treatment phase.

Illustrative Analysis Number Seven

This example illustrates the analysis of an A/B/A/B design. As we discussed in earlier chapters, this type of design can be used to provide more compelling evidence in terms of internal validity. In this hypothetical case, the practitioner implements an intervention with a young boy (Johnny) in an effort to decrease the frequency with which he yells at his little sister. The outcome measure is a count of the number of times Johnny yells at his sister each day. The practitioner implements an intervention called "response cost" in which Johnny loses the privilege of playing with one of his favorite toys for a week each time he yells at his sister (Sundel & Sundel, 1999). The baseline trend line is shown by the solid black arrow, the extended region of baseline background variability is shown by the heavy dashed lines, and the lower estimated two sigma bound is shown by the lighter dashed line in Figure 6.19.

As you can see in Figure 6.19, the data in the first treatment (B) phase trend away from the extended baseline trend line, and all treatment phase data points fall below both the extended region of baseline background variability and the lower estimated two sigma bound. There is, by detection rule 2, discussed earlier, very clearly a meaningful decrease in the frequency with which Johnny yells at his sister during the first B phase relative to baseline. As soon as the treatment is stopped during the second A phase, the frequency with which Johnny yells at his sister increases greatly relative to the frequency during the first treatment phase. (The reader is encouraged to draw in the trend line, extended region of background variability, and the estimated two sigma bounds for the data in the first treatment phase.) When the response cost

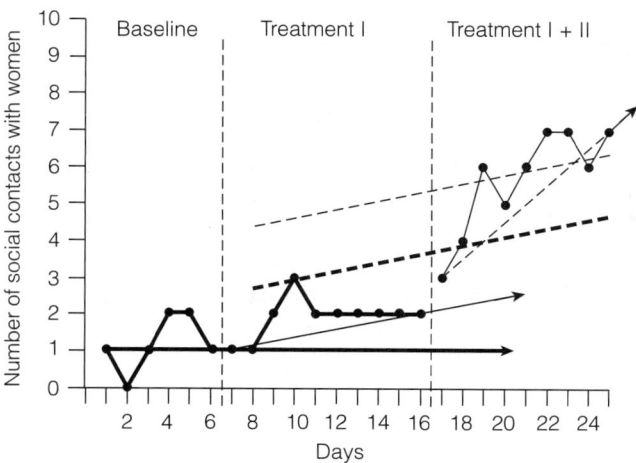

FIGURE 6.18 A/B/BC single-case data for the young woman with self-esteem problems.

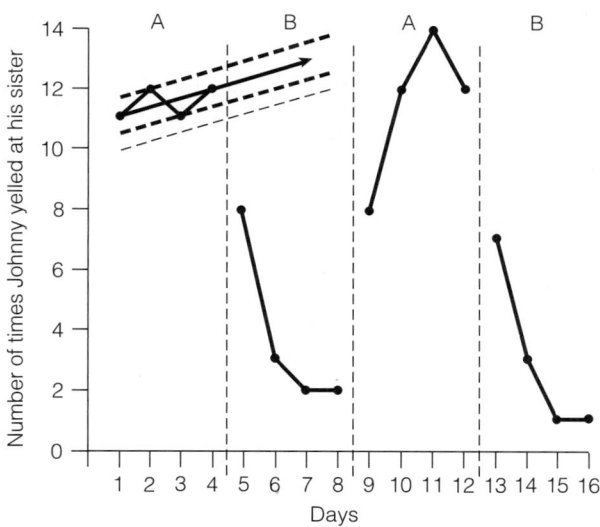

FIGURE 6.19 Hypothetical A/B/A/B single-case design data from an evaluation of an intervention to decrease the frequency with which a young boy yells at his sister.

procedure is reimplemented during the second treatment (B) phase, the data in the second B phase trend away from the extended trend line for the data in the second A phase, and all of the data in the second B phase fall below both the extended region of background variability and the lower estimated two sigma bound from the second baseline phase. Thus, the data in the second treatment phase clearly appear to be meaningfully different from the data in the second baseline phase.

The data in Figure 6.19 show an important pattern. Johnny's yelling behavior decreases when the response cost intervention is used, and increases to higher levels when it is not used. The pattern is analogous to a switch being turned "on" (and an effect occurring) and "off" (and the effect disappearing). When the treatment is "off," Johnny yells much more frequently at his sister than when the treatment is "on." This pattern in the A/B/A/B design strongly suggests that the decreases in Johnny's yelling behavior were caused by the intervention. This evidence is not only clinically compelling, but also scientifically compelling. This is the great advantage of using an A/B/A/B single-case design if you must show that your intervention was responsible for your client's improvement.

The "switch on—effect present/switch off—effect disappears" pattern in Figure 6.19 is necessary for the A/B/A/B design to clearly and unambiguously suggest that the treatment caused the observed change in Johnny's yelling behavior. Suppose that instead of the data pattern in Figure 6.19, the practitioner obtained the data pattern shown in Figure 6.20. Notice that during the second A phase, the data do not indicate that Johnny's yelling behavior increases in frequency (i.e., the effect disappears) when the intervention is turned "off." Instead, the data in the second A phase indicate that Johnny's yelling behavior remains at the low frequency found at the end of the first treatment phase. This pattern in which the data in the second baseline phase appears to be, in some form, a continuation of the data pattern in the first treatment phase is called a *carryover effect* (Bloom et al., 1999; Kazdin, 1982). The problem with a carryover effect is that it does not show the clear "switch on—effect present/switch off—effect disappears" change pattern that is seen in Figure 6.19. The data in Figure 6.20 clearly show that Johnny's yelling behavior decreased during treatment, but the design now more closely approximates an A/B design in terms of the clarity with which a causal connection has been demonstrated between treatment and the observed change (Kazdin, 1982). The data are compelling from a clinical perspective, but much less so from a scientific perspective.

Illustrative Analysis Number Eight

Sometimes it is not possible to have a baseline period in practice. In such a circumstance, you can still use a design that has a rather high degree of internal validity, the B/A/B design that we described earlier. This example illustrates such a design. Suppose that the practitioner and/or Johnny's parent(s) decide that a baseline period is not desirable. Instead, the practitioner immediately has Johnny's parent(s) implement the response cost procedure at home. The outcome measure is the same as in illustrative analysis number seven. The practitioner evaluates the response cost intervention using a B/A/B design with a follow-up and obtains the data shown in Figure 6.21. In this figure, the baseline trend line is shown by the solid black arrow, the extended region of

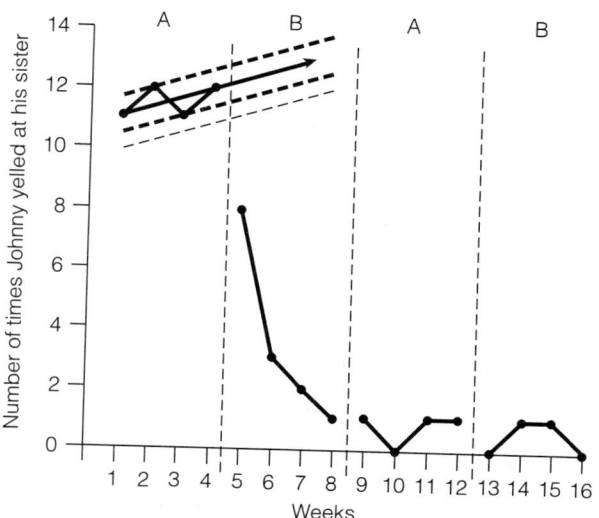

FIGURE 6.20 A/B/A/B design data that show a carryover effect.

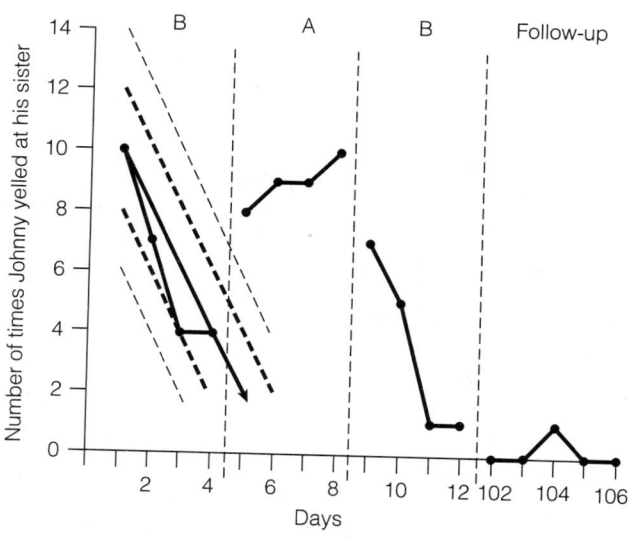

FIGURE 6.21 Hypothetical data in a B/A/B design with a follow-up phase starting 90 days after the final measure in the second B phase.

baseline background variability is shown by the heavy dashed lines, and the estimated two sigma bounds by the lighter dashed lines. You can see that the data in the first treatment, first baseline, and second treatment phases all follow the "switch on—effect present/switch off—effect disappears" pattern described earlier. When treatment is "on," Johnny's yelling behavior decreases to low frequencies, and when the intervention is "off," it increases to substantially higher frequencies relative to the treatment phases. This pattern suggests that the response cost intervention caused the decrease in Johnny's yelling at his sister. The follow-up phase that started 90 days after the end of the second B-phase measure serves to demonstrate that the change in Johnny's behavior has generalized across time.

Illustrative Analysis Number Nine

This example again illustrates the way in which critical incident recording can help inform your analysis of single-case design data. Let us suppose that, when assessing the frequency with which Johnny yells at his little sister, the practitioner obtained the baseline data in Figure 6.22. Notice how the data appear to be rather stable for the first five days, but then jump and nearly double in frequency starting on the sixth day of baseline. The practitioner investigates this sudden change, looking for possible explanations for the change, and finds that on the sixth day of baseline, Johnny's cousin Mack is visiting and staying with Johnny's family. It turns out that Mack is rather unruly and encourages Johnny's yelling behavior. This sudden deterioration can therefore be explicitly represented as shown in Figure 6.23. At this point, the practitioner implements the response cost intervention, while monitoring Mack's visitation to Johnny's home, and obtains the A/B single-case data shown in Figure 6.24. The trend lines for each phase are shown as solid black arrows, the extended region of baseline phase background variability is marked by the heavy dashed lines, and the estimated two sigma bounds by lighter dashed lines in this figure. As you can see in Figure 6.24, the single-case design is best described as an A/A$^{critical\ incident}$/B$^{critical\ incident}$/B single-case design. The A$^{critical\ incident}$ phase represents baseline conditions during Mack's visit with Johnny's family, while the B$^{critical\ incident}$ phase represents treatment phase during Mack's visit. The A phase represents baseline before Mack's visit, while the B phase represents treatment phase after Mack's visit has ended.

As you can see in Figure 6.24, Mack's visit, the critical incident in this case, appears to be associated with a significant deterioration in Johnny's baseline yelling behavior. The data in the B$^{critical\ incident}$ phase suggest that Johnny's yelling behavior improves back to A-phase levels when the intervention is initiated and appears to improve further as the intervention continues. This is suggested by the improving trend during the B$^{critical\ incident}$ phase, a trend that is away from the extended baseline trend line. The B-phase data suggest that Johnny's yelling behavior continues to improve significantly beyond the baseline pattern (A), and substantially beyond the pattern in the A$^{critical\ incident}$ phase. The data in Figure 6.24 suggest that (1) Mack appeared to be a negative influence on Johnny and (2) Johnny's yelling behavior decreased in frequency during treatment. There was an immediate decrease as soon as the intervention was initiated, and this decrease appeared to be significantly different from the data pattern in the A$^{critical\ incident}$ phase, though the decrease in frequency was

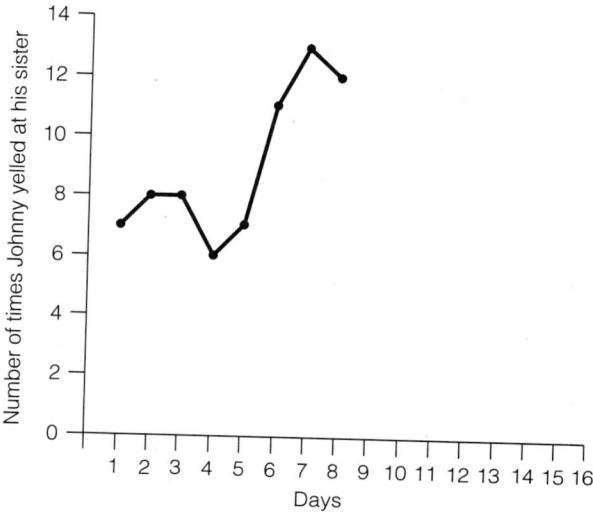

FIGURE 6.22 Baseline data for Johnny which shows a sudden deterioration on the sixth day of baseline.

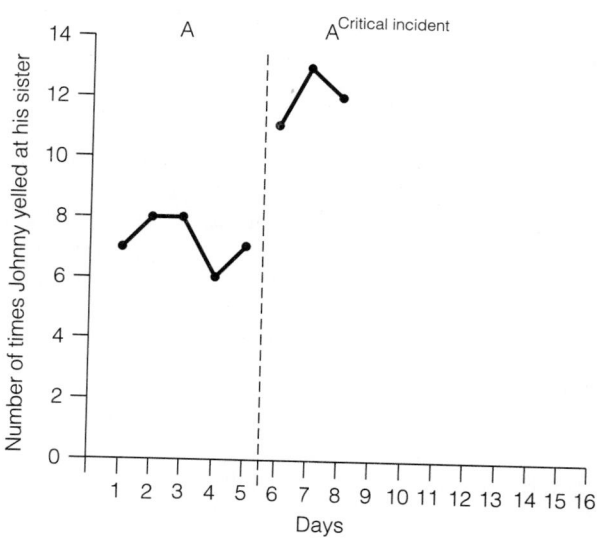

FIGURE 6.23 Baseline data for Johnny in which the sudden deterioration associated with a critical incident is explicitly represented.

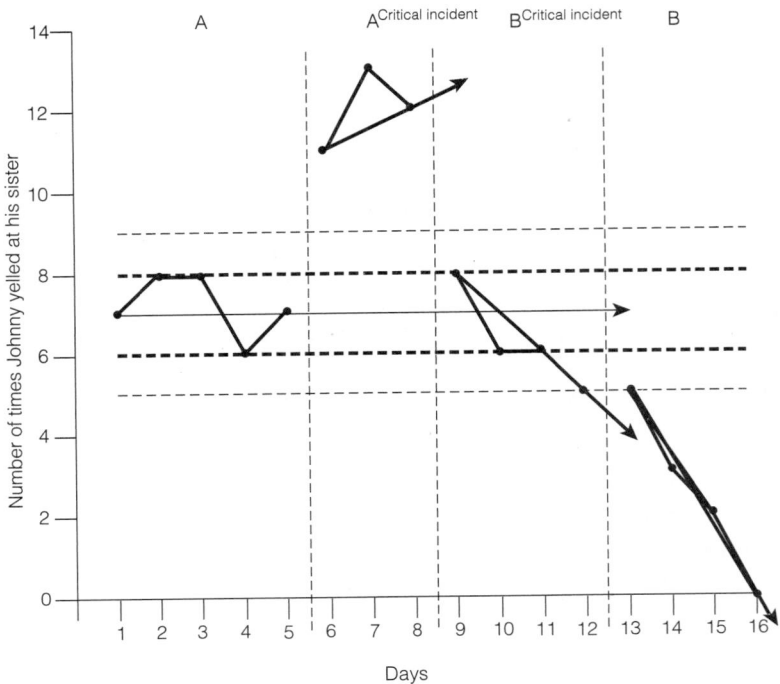

FIGURE 6.24 A/B single-case design data for Johnny in which Mack's visit is explicitly represented.

only back to A-phase levels. The decrease in frequency of yelling behavior continued throughout the period that the intervention was used. The data further suggest that (3) the decrease in Johnny's yelling behavior concomitant with the start of the intervention occurred within the context of Mack's apparent negative influence on Johnny, and (4) the intervention may have been responsible for the decreased frequency of Johnny's yelling behavior, though the evidence for this supposition is not as compelling as it would be if a design stronger in terms of internal validity had been used.

Illustrative Analysis Number Ten

This final example illustrates the use of an ABAB design in which the outcome variable is qualitative as well as quantitative. In this hypothetical example, a client named Bill C. is undergoing treatment for "road rage." Bill C. was cited by a highway patrol officer for driving aggressively, and Bill acknowledged that he was angry at the driver he was tailgating for "driving too slow." As a part of the evaluation being conducted, the social worker has Bill C. speak out loud his feelings and thoughts as he is driving and encounters a driving situation that displeases him. The social worker has Bill place a tape recorder in his car on the seat next to him so that these spoken thoughts and feelings can be recorded as he speaks them. These recorded feeling and thought statements are then placed onto a "feelings and thoughts list," as shown in Table 6.1. The social worker also has Bill rate the intensity of his feelings on a 0 to 10 scale, with a 0 indicating "zero intensity" and a 10 indicating "the most intense the feeling could possibly be." This rating of feeling intensity is commonly used in cognitive-behavioral therapy (see, for example, Burns, 1990). This measurement procedure is a combination of the "feeling listing" described by Nugent (1992), the "thought listing" methods described by Cacioppo and Petty (1981) and Goldberg and Shaw (1989), and the rating of feeling intensity described by Burns (1990). In this measurement technique, the practitioner has a client list (or speak out loud) the thoughts and feelings that he or she has in response to specific situations. The reliability and sensitivity to change of such listings has been investigated by Cacioppo and Petty (1979); Cacioppo, Sandman, and Walker (1978); Cullen (1968); Petty and Cacioppo (1979); and Petty, Wells, and Brock (1976).

The list of thoughts, feelings, and feeling intensities for the first baseline phase, seen in Table 6.1, shows a theme of rather intense anger and aggression whenever Bill C. encounters a driving situation that displeases him. Note the types of thoughts and feelings that Bill has, and note especially the intensity of the angry feelings that Bill experiences during baseline. The mean intensity ratings for anger are shown in the bar graph in Figure 6.25. Note the high mean intensity rating for anger levels during the driving incidents that Bill recorded during baseline.

After a baseline phase of one week, the social worker teaches Bill anger control techniques described by Goldstein and Glick (1987). Bill is taught to recognize when he is angry, to talk to himself and instruct himself to take control, to take a deep breath and hold it for a count of three before letting it out, and to engage in "consequential thinking." Consequential thinking involves anticipating the consequences of engaging in specific behaviors by completing the blanks in the following format: "If I _____, then _____ might happen." Bill C. is instructed to fill in the first blank with whatever impulsive action he feels like engaging in as a response to something that another driver does, and then to fill in the second blank with the potential consequences of his behavior. For example, if he feels an impulse to smash his car into the other driver's car, he might complete the fill-in-the-blank format as follows: "If I smash my car into his car, then I might cause a serious accident and be killed."

The listed thoughts and feelings, and feeling intensities, in the first B phase of this hypothetical evaluation can be seen in Table 6.1, and the mean anger intensity rating for this treatment phase can be seen in Figure 6.25. Notice two things: (1) the different feelings listed in this phase relative to the first A phase (as well as the feelings and thoughts that were in the first A phase but are absent in the B phase), and (2) the different intensities of feelings in the B phase, especially the mean anger intensity rating during this B phase. These differences suggest that Bill's road rage has taken a turn for the better. After two weeks of having Bill use these techniques, the social worker instructs Bill to stop using them for three days to determine whether or not they are responsible for the

Table 6.1 Bill C.'s ABAB Data During Treatment for His Road Rage Problem

A	B	A	B
Angry (level 10)		Angry (level 6)	
Frustrated (level 7)		Angry (level 7)	
Want to tell him off		Angry (level 7)	
Revengeful (level 8)	Annoyed (level 4)	Felt like "flipping finger" at other driver (did it)	Annoyed (level 4)
Hot	Anger decreases when I take deep breath	Felt like yelling at other driver (did it)	Annoyed (level 3)
Put upon		Felt like cussing at other driver (did it)	Annoyed (level 3)
Anger increases as I yell at driver	Angry (level 3)	Felt like ramming my car into other car (didn't do it)	Felt tension lower as I took deep breath
Have urge to "flip the finger" at other driver	Less tense	Angry (level 6)	Felt relaxed after deep breath
Feel angry for long time after event	Cool down pretty quickly	Anger increases as I cuss out other driver	Annoyed (level 3)
Very tense	Angry (level 2)	Anger (level 7)	Felt brief urge to slam on brakes but it went away when I did the "If _____ then _____" thinking
Angry (level 9)	Angry (level 4)		Anger (level 3) that went away when I took deep breath
Urge to slam on brakes	Frustrated (level 3)		Felt more in control
Urge to "flip finger" at other driver (actually did it)	Felt tension lower after deep breath		Relaxed after deep breath
Angry (level 8)	Relaxed (level 3)		Annoyed (level 2)
Angry (level 9)	Annoyed (level 4)		Anger (level 2) that went away when I took deep breath
Felt like cussing at other driver (did it)	Annoyed (level 2)		
Angry (level 9)			
Felt like slamming my car into other car (didn't do it)		Note: Client stated that he felt some residual control from just knowing the anger control techniques, but that not using them made him lose control	
Urge to "flip finger" at other driver (did it)			
Felt like hitting other driver in mouth			

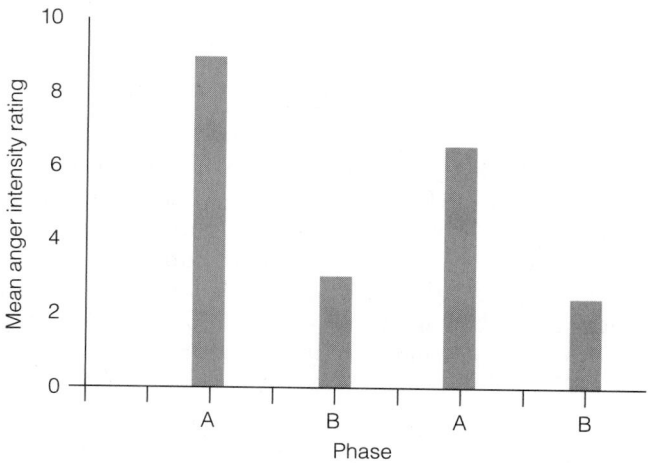

FIGURE 6.25 Bill C.'s mean anger intensity ratings for each phase of the evaluation of the anger control intervention.

changes that are apparent between the first A and B phases. (Please note that many social workers would elect to *not* go to a second A phase in a case such as this, and we would support such a treatment decision. We are using this hypothetical example to illustrate the use of an ABAB design with qualitative and quantitative outcome measures.) The thoughts, feelings, and feeling intensities recorded by Bill C. for this second A phase can be seen in Table 6.1, and the mean anger intensity rating is shown in Figure 6.25. Note the differences in types of thoughts, feelings, and feeling intensities between the first B and the second A phases. At this point, the social worker has Bill go back to using the anger control techniques in a second B phase, with the results shown in Table 6.1 and Figure 6.25.

The data shown in Table 6.1 and Figure 6.25 would be a compelling demonstration that the anger control training had a positive impact on Bill's road rage problem. We urge you to look carefully at the thought and feeling lists, and feeling intensities, shown in Table 6.1 and to note the qualitative changes that occur between phases. An example of a design such as is shown in this hypothetical example can be found in Nugent (1992).

EXAMPLES FROM THE LITERATURE

We encourage you to find examples of the various single-case designs used to evaluate interventions that have been published in the literature. Reading published examples of single-case design evaluations can help you understand the great utility and versatility of this methodology. You can find a surprising range of interventions targeted at a very wide range of problems (personal, interpersonal, and social) that were evaluated using single-case methodology in the journal *Applied Behavior Analysis*. As you read these published accounts, you can also practice analyzing the single-case design data that you find in these articles using the methods we have discussed in this chapter.

We have already given some examples of AB designs with flat, stable baselines. There are other examples of baselines that are very similar. Several of the single-case designs in Cheung (1999) show remarkably flat and stable baselines. Examples of AB designs used to evaluate a variety of interventions for a range of problems are given by Lindsay, Marshall, Neilson, Quinn, and Smith (1998) (treatment of exhibitionism); Lewin, Cowan, Ganzini, Gonzales, and Rasmussen (1997) (working with nursing home residents); Roderick, Pitchford, and Miller (1997) (reducing aggressive behavior on a playground); and Wertkin (1985) (the use of stress inoculation training). Neufeld and Fantuzzo (1987) used an ABC design to evaluate the effects of an intervention for self-injurious behavior by the mentally handicapped.

An excellent example of an ABAB single-case design used to evaluate an intervention is provided by Kelley, Gregory, Middlebrook, McNeer, and Drabman (1984). They evaluated an intervention to reduce the pain experienced by children undergoing hydrotherapy for severe burns. Cheung (1999) used ABAB designs to evaluate the effects of massage therapy with nursing home clients. Murphy, Hutchison, and Bailey (1983) used an ABAB design to evaluate the effects of organized games on aggressive behavior on a school playground. Heard and Watson (1999) used an ABAB design to reduce the wandering behavior of persons with dementia. Rose (1978) and Ayllon and Azrin (1965) present good examples of the use of BAB designs. Ferguson and Rodway (1994) used an ABA design to evaluate the effects of a cognitive-behavioral intervention for perfectionism. Lavelle, Hovell, West, and Wahlgren (1992) used an ABA design to evaluate a community intervention to promote the use of child safety seats in cars. Nugent (1993a) used an ABCB design to assess the impact of a clinical intervention. There are numerous other examples of single-case designs in the literature, with many appearing in the journal *Applied Behavior Analysis*. Other journals in which you can find examples of single-case design evaluations include *Research on Social Work Practice, Behavior Therapy,* and *The Journal of Behavior Therapy* and *Experimental Psychiatry*.

7

Integrating Single-Case and Group-Comparison Designs for Evaluating Practice

s we have discussed at length, single-case design methodology is a powerful tool for evaluating the effects of the services provided to clients. Single-case design methodology is so useful because it focuses on the individual person: single-case designs are used to determine how individual clients fare during their receipt of services. The designs available in the repertoire of single-case designs allow the practitioner to match the design to his or her evaluation purpose. For example, if the purpose is to provide evidence that a client improved during service provision, then the B design is ideally suited to the purpose of the evaluation and, at the same time, is very easy to implement. On the other hand, if the practitioner needs to provide evidence that service provision was *responsible* for the client's improvement, then a design that is stronger in its ability to control threats to internal validity is required. In this case, an ABAB or multiple baseline design may be better suited. In any case, the focus remains on the individual client, and single-case designs were created to focus on the individual (Barlow & Hersen, 1984; Kazdin, 1982; Sidman, 1960).

However, evaluation questions can be much broader than a focus on a specific individual client. The agency in which a practitioner works may be required to provide evidence that the agency's clients, *as a group*, improve during the provision of services. In this case, while the individual client is still the critically most important basic point of focus, that focus has been enlarged to encompass a collection of individual clients. It is also possible that the agency may be required by a funding source to provide evidence that, as a group, all clients who were provided services for a specific type of problem (such as depression, medical noncompliance, etc.) improved *because of the services the agency provided*. Again, the individual client is the critically most important basic point of focus, but the evaluation question has been broadened to encompass a specific collection of individuals. A group design can be used to address these broader questions, while a single-case design cannot (Kazdin, 1982, 1998).

Here we see, however, a situation in which each methodology has both important limitations and significant advantages. Single-case design methods provide a picture of how specific individuals improve, remain the same, or get worse over time, yet fail to provide data on collections of individuals (Kazdin, 1982). Group designs, in contrast, give a picture of group-level responses yet fail to provide detailed information on specific individuals (Barlow & Hersen, 1984). These two methodologies, however, complement one another. The strengths of one addresses the limitations of the other. Thus, combining single-case and group methods creates an evaluation methodology that can be very flexible and powerful for answering evaluation questions such as those posed here (Nugent, 1996).

ADVANTAGES OF INTEGRATED DESIGNS

There are a number of advantages to integrating single-case and group designs. Table 7.1 highlights some of the methodological limitations of single-case and group designs and illustrates how an integrated approach can overcome these weaknesses. First, the single-case design components of an integrated design provide temporal profiles of each client's problems. This is a great advantage when compared with the information provided by group designs, which most often employ measurement strategies in which client problems are measured at only one or two points in time (Barlow & Hersen, 1984). Consider the situation shown in Figure 7.1. In this figure, a hypothetical client's severity of depression (as measured by scores on the GCS) at week 1 is shown by point A, while the client's depression severity at week 9 is shown by point B. The two points A and B are those that would be obtained in a pretest/posttest group design (Kazdin, 1998). Using just these two measures, however, misses the critically important information as to what happened to the client's depression between weeks 1 and 9. If a pretest/posttest design was used, then the practitioner would have no information as to which "path" this client's depression took in getting from point A to point B. While the beginning and end points are the same, paths I and II in Figure 7.1 are dramatically different. In path I, the client's problem with depression *deteriorates* beyond the point (a score of 70) suggesting a possibly suicidal level of depression for five weeks before it drops below its initial level. However, path II shows that the severity of the client's problem with depression drops in one week to a clinically nonsignificant level, and then remains constant at this nonsignificant level. The extra data

Table 7.1 Advantages of Integrating Single-Case and Group-Comparison Methodologies

Methodological Limitations	Integrated Approach
Single-Case Designs	
Inability to generalize from a single case	Aggregation of single-case designs can be conducted as a direct, clinical, or systematic replication series, providing a basis for generalization.
	Sampling methods, such as simple random sampling, can be used to further establish a basis for generalization.
Limited ability to compare relative effectiveness of different interventions	Sets of single-case designs can be aggregated so as to compare the relative effects of different treatments.
Limited ability to identify client/environment-by-treatment interactions	Statistical methods can be used to find systematic variation in response patterns associated with different client and/or environmental factors.
No means of controlling threats to internal validity at the level of a replication series	Random assignment can be used to control threats to internal validity at the replication series level.
Group Designs	
Only one or two measurement occasions	Repeated measurement in single-case designs provide individual client response profiles.
No information provided about which individual clients changed, or how they changed	Response profiles give information on how individual clients changed (or failed to change) across time.
No control over threats to internal validity at the level of the individual client	Some single-case designs provide control over threats to internal validity at the level of the individual client.

given by the repeated measures in single-case design methodology allow the practitioner to know which path the client's problem takes through time as it changes from point A to point B. This information is fundamentally important (Nugent, 1996).

Integrating single-case and group methods also allows us to control threats to internal validity at the level of the individual client *and* at the group level simultaneously. Group-comparison designs do not allow us to make causal inferences about the effects of interventions with individual clients, while single-case designs do (Kazdin, 1998). Similarly, single-case designs do not provide control over threats to internal validity at a group level, while group-comparison methods allow us to compare group means and, with appropriate designs, to make causal inferences about the effects of an intervention on the group as a whole, via the group mean (Barlow & Hersen, 1984). A funding source, or combination of sources, may request (or require)

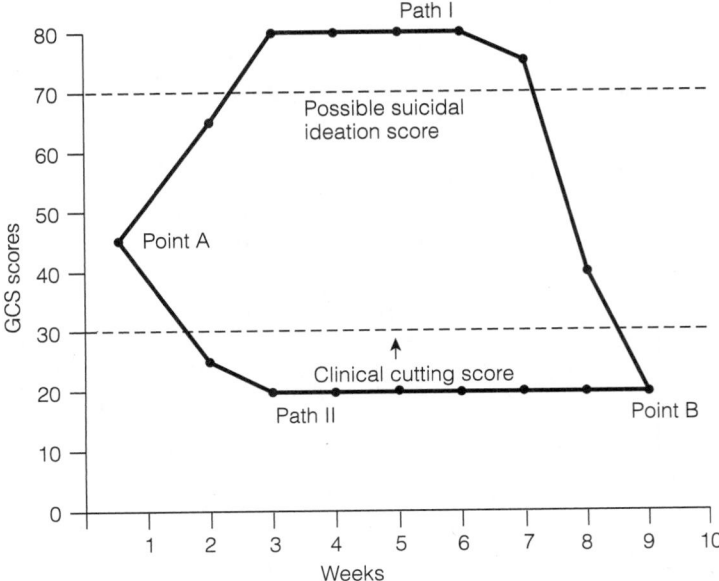

FIGURE 7.1 Two different paths for a client's problem with depression, but with the same starting and ending points.

data that demonstrate positive outcomes due to treatment at both the individual client and group levels. For example, a funding source may require an agency to show that specific clients (such as Joe, Mary, Tom, etc.) improved because of a particular service (such as psychotherapy for depression). The funding source may simultaneously require the agency to show that some collection of clients (such as all those who received psychotherapy for depression) benefited from a particular service. By carefully and thoughtfully combining single-case and group methods, we can conduct an evaluation that will simultaneously meet both of these information needs.

The value of this complementarity between single-case and group designs should not be underestimated. We can simultaneously answer questions at two levels: the level of the individual client, and the level of an aggregation of clients. This means that we can, in addition to answering questions about the progress (or lack thereof) of specific individuals, answer questions about treatment outcomes across specific groups, about the variability in treatment outcomes, and about the relative efficacy of two or more different treatment approaches. This latter evaluation question—the relative efficacy of two different treatment approaches—is actually a general question that can take many different forms, including the comparison of two different interventions, or the comparison of different combinations of intervention components, such as in the so-called "treatment components analysis" evaluation in which the elements of a multicomponent intervention are compared individually and in combination in order to find the active ingredient (or ingredients) in the multielement intervention (Kazdin, 1998).

Another advantage of using integrated designs is that we can search for systematic variation between individual clients' temporal profiles that is associated with personal characteristics, context, and/or environmental variables. For example, let us suppose that path I in Figure 7.1 was "Joe's" response to a specific intervention for depression, while path II was "Mary's" response to the same intervention. Integrated design approaches allow us to search for answers as to why Joe's response to treatment took path I, while Mary's response to the same treatment took path II. Knowledge of the particular variables that function to produce such differences in shape between individual clients' temporal profiles would be critically important for optimally matching clients with treatments or programs. These variables can be thought of as treatment moderators, treatment catalysts, treatment accelerators (those things that make clients respond to treatment more quickly), or treatment decelerators (those things that function to slow down or prevent clients' responses to treatment). You can see how useful such information would be for deciding which intervention, or intervention package, we need to use with a particular client.

A final advantage of integrated designs concerns the generalizability of results. Single-case design methodology relies on replication for establishing the generalizability and replicability of results (Johnston & Pennypacker, 1980; Kazdin, 1982; Sidman, 1960). The successful replication of results across different persons, settings, service providers, and so on provides an empirical basis for inferring the applicability of treatments to new clients, in new settings, and so on (Johnston & Pennypacker, 1980). In contrast, group-comparison designs rely on the sampling component of a research design to support generalizability at the statistical level (Cook & Campbell, 1979; Kazdin, 1998; Scheaffer, Mendenhall, & Ott, 1996). The sampling methods used will ideally produce a sample that is representative of the population to which we wish to generalize (Cook & Campbell, 1979). An integrated design will allow us to flexibly use *both* logical bases, replication and sampling method, to build a case for generalizability and applicability.

A CONCEPTUAL LINK BETWEEN SINGLE-CASE AND GROUP DESIGNS

An important conceptual link between single-case and group designs is the notion of *replication*. Replication is a critically important activity in science, especially in the social sciences (Kazdin, 1998; Neuliep, 1991). Replication concerns our ability to duplicate the evaluation of a particular intervention used to treat a specific problem and to reproduce the original results. The ability to successfully reproduce the original results serves to demonstrate that the original results are less likely to be a fluke. The more times a finding is replicated, the stronger the evidence that the results accurately reflect an out-come that may be expected when using the intervention to treat the same problem with a new client who is similar to those involved in the previous evaluations. As we will discuss, under certain circumstances replication can also increase the confidence with which we can infer that the intervention being evaluated was actually responsible for the changes we observed (Barlow et al., 1984; Barlow & Hersen, 1984).

Replication is an important activity in single-case design methodology (Barlow & Hersen, 1984; Kazdin, 1982; Sidman, 1960). It is impossible to generalize from a single case, and this inability has been noted as a critical lim-itation in conducting an evaluation using a single-case (Barlow & Hersen, 1984). However, the replication of single-case design results can provide a sound basis for generalization (Barlow et al., 1984; Johnston & Pennypacker, 1980). Three forms of replication have been identified in the single-case design literature: direct replication, systematic replication, and clinical replication.

Direct Replication

Direct replication is the name given to the process whereby a specific clinician or researcher reproduces the evaluation of use of the same intervention (such as in vivo exposure) for the same problem (such as agoraphobia) across differ-ent persons who are as much alike as possible (Barlow & Hersen, 1984). The purpose of the direct replication series—that is, the set of replications of single-case evaluations of the particular intervention applied to a specific prob-lem across persons as identical as possible—is to demonstrate that *in each instance the same outcome is obtained*. If the outcomes are the same, then the repli-cation series provides a basis for generalizing the use of the intervention with other clients *with the same characteristics* in order to treat the same problem. The basis for this generalization has been called *logical generalization* (Barlow & Hersen, 1984). The successful direct replication series also demonstrates that the results obtained are unlikely to be a fluke, since the probability is low that we would have the same lucky happenstance occur several times in a row. The successful replication series therefore speaks to the dependability of the results that we have obtained.

Systematic Replication

Now suppose that we have done a direct replication of an evaluation of an intervention for a particular problem, and that in each case we have obtained the same outcome. For example, suppose that we have used a simple B design to evaluate the effects of in vivo exposure to treat agoraphobia with five very similar clients. Each of the clients was, say, a white male, 30 years old, married, who had a bachelor's degree, and who was employed as an engineer. Further suppose that in each case the client's problems with agoraphobia had dimin-ished to a nonsignificant level by the end of 12 treatment sessions. This suc-cessful direct replication series provides compelling evidence that clients *with these characteristics* improve while receiving this intervention.

Our next step is to try the same intervention with *African-American* males, 30 years old, married, who have a bachelor's degree, and who are employed as engineers. Replications of this type are referred to as *systematic replications*. We systematically change the characteristics of the clients with whom we use the intervention. We may also change systematically the characteristics of the treatment setting or the person administering the intervention. We make these systematic changes in the type of client, treatment setting, and/or change agent in an effort to demonstrate that the same results are obtained with persons with different characteristics, under different circumstances, and when the treatment is administered by different persons. If we successfully replicate the original outcomes, then we have provided a further basis for generalizing the use of the intervention. We are able to show that the same results can be expected with different clients, different social workers, in different settings, and so forth. The results are, therefore, invariant across these different conditions and so, on the basis of logical generalization, are likely to be obtained with new clients.

Clinical Replication

Clinical replication refers to the process in which a clinician *in a practice setting* replicates the use of a specific intervention for a specific problem with several different clients (Barlow et al., 1984). The set of evaluations of the effects of the intervention with these clients is called a clinical replication series. This type of replication fits very nicely within the practice setting. The practitioner simply employs (and evaluates) the same intervention procedure with clients who have the same problem. We can learn a lot from a clinical replication series while simultaneously providing evidence that can be useful for program evaluation demands. A clinical replication series can be used to simultaneously provide data that show (1) that specific individual clients have improved while receiving services, and (2) that a specific collection of clients, as a group, has improved (or failed to improve) during service provision. The replication series can also, as discussed earlier, provide a logical basis for generalizing the application of a particular intervention for treating a specific problem with clients having certain characteristics. The replication series can therefore provide an empirical basis for treatment selection or matching.

A replication series can also be used to help build a case that an intervention *caused* clients to improve (Barlow et al., 1984; Kazdin, 1982). This can be done by building a replication series with certain characteristics. First, the series should focus on the application of the same intervention to treat the same client problem, such as the use of in vivo exposure to treat agoraphobia. Second, each client's problem should be measured repeatedly, using objective measures. There should be evidence that the measures used have produced valid and reliable scores. Repeated measures should be obtained before intervention starts as well as during the application of the treatment. Thus, in this evaluation context, at a minimum, an AB single-case design should be used with each client in the replication series. The replication series should include a number of clients with rather heterogeneous characteristics. Under these conditions, *if* (1) each client's problem has a history of stability that suggests that it is unlikely to change without some intervention, and (2) there is a clear, immediate, and large magnitude improvement in each client's problem *immediately* upon implementation of the intervention, then the replication series provides a level of internal validity that approaches that of a controlled experiment (see Barlow et al., 1984; Kazdin, 1981, 1982). Thus, properly conducted and with the right set of outcomes, the clinical replication series offers an option for providing evidence that clients have improved *because of* the services that the practitioner or the agency provided.

Replication series can also be useful in helping to determine why some clients improve, some remain the same, and (unfortunately) some get worse because of a particular intervention procedure. One way this can be done is through a *failure analysis*. In a failure analysis, the evaluator analyzes the cases in a replication series to determine the common characteristics possessed by those who improved, by those who did not change at all, and by those who deteriorated during treatment. Such an analysis can lead to the identification of client characteristics, therapist characteristics, and/or setting characteristics that make some persons amenable to the treatment and likely to benefit, that make others less amenable and not likely to benefit or to get worse, and that make even others distinctly nonamenable to the treatment and likely to get *worse* when the treatment is used with them. Excellent examples of failure analyses are given by Foa and Emmelkamp (1983) and Foa, Grayson et al. (1983).

Linking Single-Case and Group Designs

We are now in a position to describe the conceptual link between single-case and group methods. As we have seen, replications of single-case design evaluations can play a major role in the development of knowledge about the effects of interventions. *A replication series can be thought of as a way of aggregating single-case designs, and the use of group-comparison methods can be thought of as providing strategies for aggregating single-case design evaluations. The various group-comparison methods can be used to impose structure on a replication series.*

Thus, we can use single-case designs to answer questions about individual clients, and we can replicate single-case designs to answer questions about collections of clients. This complementarity of single-case and group designs makes evaluations in which we integrate single-case and group design methods very powerful approaches to evaluating practice. Viewed in this manner, our principal evaluation tools then become (a) single-case designs, and (b) aggregations of single-case designs. We can list the evaluation questions that need to be answered, and then plan the appropriate single-case design evaluation(s) necessary to answer the evaluation questions. If one or more of the evaluation questions concern a collection of clients—or if the evaluation question can be better answered by providing data on a collection of clients—then a replication series can be planned in which group-comparison design methods are used to structure the clinical replication series so as to provide answers to our evaluation questions.

GENERAL PROCEDURES FOR INTEGRATING SINGLE-CASE AND GROUP METHODS

The first step in designing an integrated evaluation is deciding upon the purpose of the evaluation at the level of individual clients. This will typically be one of two things: demonstrating that specific clients have improved during service delivery, and/or demonstrating that specific clients have improved *because of* the services they received. The first of these purposes requires us to provide temporal profiles of each specific client's problems that show that each client's problem changes in an improving direction. If this is the purpose of our evaluation at the individual client level, then a simple B design is all that is necessary to use with each client. There is no need to be concerned about the number and temporal spacing of measures in the B designs (Nugent, 1996). The number and spacing of repeated measures of clients' problems can be tailor-made to fit the unique requirements and context of each individual case.

The second possible evaluation purpose at the level of the individual client concerns a question of causality: were the services received by the client (or clients) a causal factor in her or his (or their) improvement? If this is the focus of our efforts at the individual client level, then our client(s) must be monitored using a single-case design that has the maximum control possible over threats to internal validity given the practice context and the client with whom we are working. *The design used should maximally facilitate, and minimally interfere with, the provision of services* (Thomas, 1978). Thus, at a minimum, AB designs would need to be used with each client. If possible, stronger designs such as the ABAB design, or the multiple baseline design, should be used with each client if compatible with the practice context. Regardless of the single-case design selected for use, we need not be concerned with the number and spacing of repeated measures of the clients' problems. As discussed earlier, the number and spacing of repeated measures of clients' problems can be tailor-made to fit the unique requirements and context of each individual case (Nugent, 1996).

We must also decide the purpose(s) of the evaluation at the group level. There are several possible purposes of an evaluation at this level: demonstrating the replication of results (either improvement or causality) across a group, or across several groups, of clients; providing evidence of generalizability; comparing two (or more) different interventions; providing evidence for the causal effect of a program or intervention; and/or searching for systematic variability in clients' temporal profiles that is associated with personal characteristics, context, and/or environmental factors. Dependent upon the purpose (or purposes) of the evaluation, we will need to employ group design methods that are appropriate to the purpose of the evaluation at the group level. Thus, for example, we may need to use specific sampling methods, types of comparison groups, random assignment, and/or particular statistical analysis procedures.

Once the purposes of the evaluation at both individual client and group levels have been determined, then the appropriate single-case design and group-comparison methods are selected and integrated into an evaluation design that meets the needs of the evaluation at both individual client and group levels. Examples, both hypothetical and real, of integrated designs are discussed in the sections that follow.

HYPOTHETICAL EXAMPLES OF INTEGRATED DESIGNS

Hypothetical Example Number One

Suppose that a funding source asks an agency to provide evidence that the mental health of some clients served by the agency improved. The funding source paid (in part) for the services of a number of clients referred to the agency to be treated for depression. Thus, the funding source wants to know, first of all, whether or not these specific clients improved—did each client's level of depression decrease? The funding source also asks the agency to provide some assessment of the *overall benefit* that these clients obtained while receiving services. Finally, the funding source requests that the agency identify any clients who failed to improve and to provide evidence concerning why they did not improve.

The first of these two needs concerns individual clients; the second concerns the collection of clients whose services were paid for by the funding source; and the third concerns a subset of individual clients. Thus, the first of these information needs requires methods focused on the individual client. The second of these information needs requires methods that focus on the group level, in this case on the collection of clients whose services were paid for by the funding source. The third of these information needs will require methods at both levels. The agency will need data on each of the individual clients, and at the same time data at the group level so that it can try to identify patterns in the responses of the clients to treatment. Thus, in this case, the agency must do three things: (1) provide evidence concerning the depression of each of the specific clients over the course of treatment; (2) provide some measure of the overall outcome for these clients; and (3) identify clients whose depression did not improve during services, and provide some tentative evidence as to why they did not improve.

The agency might elect to have the social workers who work directly with each of these clients monitor their levels of depression during service provision using B single-case designs. The social workers would use the same measure of depression (say the GCS), but obtain repeated measures at time points best-suited to the individual clients with whom they work. These B designs will provide the evidence the agency needs to demonstrate how each client improved, or failed to improve. The B designs will give the agency the evaluation data it needs to meet the first information requirement of the funding source. These B designs can also be aggregated across the clients whose services were paid for by the funding source. In this case, the group-level design is nothing more than massing data on a single group of clients. All of the B design data for these clients can be plotted on a single graph, as shown in the next chapter. This will provide the funding source with a clear picture of how these clients fared during treatment. Whatever variability in client response there is will be readily apparent on this graph of aggregated single-case data. The agency could also include a graphic plot of the average response profile for these clients. This average response profile is a good way of representing the overall benefit these clients received during treatment.

The clients could also be separated into two groups: those whose depression improved during the course of treatment, and those whose depression did not improve (or even got worse). Then the practitioners could search for commonalities within each group, and differences between these groups, that might explain why some clients improved, while others did not. Such explanatory variables might be such things as gender, age, severity of initial depression, type of treatment received, the social worker who provided services, and so on. We will use this hypothetical example again in the next chapter to illustrate the analysis of aggregated single-case design data.

The agency would now be in a position to provide the funding source with the results of this evaluation. It could provide the funding source with: (1) the B design data for each individual client, along with a narrative discussing each case; (2) the graph containing the aggregated B design data for all of these clients, along with a narrative discussing the data; and (3) a graph that highlights the differences between those clients who improved and those who did not. The agency might, for example, plot the data for clients who improved with black solid lines on the graph, and that for clients who did not improve with red dashed lines. This graph would be accompanied by a narrative that would present the results of the failure analysis, with speculations as to why some clients did not improve.

Hypothetical Example Number Two

Now suppose that some source requests information from an agency about the efficacy of the agency's residential program for the hearing impaired. This residential program is designed to increase the independent living skills of hearing-impaired young persons older than 18 and to prepare them for living independently in the community.

The program involves a token economy system (Kazdin, 1983; Sundel & Sundel, 1999) that is used to shape and reinforce the use of specific independent living skills by clients. Clients are required to show counselors that they have successfully done the required independent living skills, such as preparing a balanced meal (breakfast, lunch, and dinner), showering before going to work, leaving the residence in time to get to work or school, completing any of a number of chores (for example, cleaning one's room), and any of a number of other activities that have been identified by program staff as living skills needed by clients in order to successfully live independently in the community. When a client shows a counselor that he or she has completed the independent living skill, then the counselor gives the client a number of "points" that are recorded in the client's "points book." The goal for clients is to get a certain number of points that can be used to move the client through a number of hierarchical steps toward independent living.

For example, once a client has amassed 500 points, then he or she can move from "step 1," which is a set of house rules that give the client very little in the way of independence (e.g., must be in bed by 9:00 P.M.; cannot watch television past 8:00 P.M.; and so forth), to "step 2," which is a set of house rules with fewer restrictions and greater freedom of activity (e.g., must be in bed by 10:00 P.M.; can watch television until 9:30 P.M.; and so forth). Once a client reaches "step 5," he or she has the privilege of living semi-independently in a transitional living apartment. If the client fails to show the counselor successful completion of the activity, does not complete the activity at a required level of quality (such as preparing a dinner with no vegetables), or engages in any of a number of defined "inappropriate behaviors" (such as fighting, cursing, etc.), then the client is "fined" so many points. A fine involves taking so many accumulated points away from the client's points book, and can result in clients being lowered from, say, step 3 to step 2, or even lower depending upon the behavior fined. The staff believes and operates on the assumption that this token economy is the main active ingredient in the residential program.

The funding source requests evidence that the residential program is responsible for increases in the independent living skills of clients who participate in the program. If the agency cannot show that the program is actually responsible for improvement in the clients' independent living skills, then the source may pull its funding.

In this case, the agency must provide evidence of two things: (1) that participation in the program caused an increase in the independent living skills of specific clients, and (2) that, at a group level, the program appeared to cause an increase in the independent living skills of participants. The agency could, therefore, conduct an evaluation such as the following. First, as in hypothetical example number one, the agency could monitor each client's progress through the program using a single-case design. Second, the agency could evaluate the program as a whole by conducting a BCB design *with the residential program as a whole as the "single system."* There could be two outcome measures in this evaluation: (1) the mean percentage of required daily independent living skills successfully completed by the clients in the residence each day; and (2) the total number of inappropriate behaviors (such as fighting, cursing, etc.) occurring each day in the facility. The single-case design used with each individual client, however, would depend on when the client goes through the residential program, since the entire program will be evaluated in a BCB design. This evaluation design is shown in Figure 7.2.

In this evaluation design, the agency would assess the impact of the program using a BCB design, with the residential program as the "single system" of focus. The B element of the design would involve monitoring the progress of clients in the program with all elements of the program operative. The B component of the design is, therefore, the "program as usual." The C element

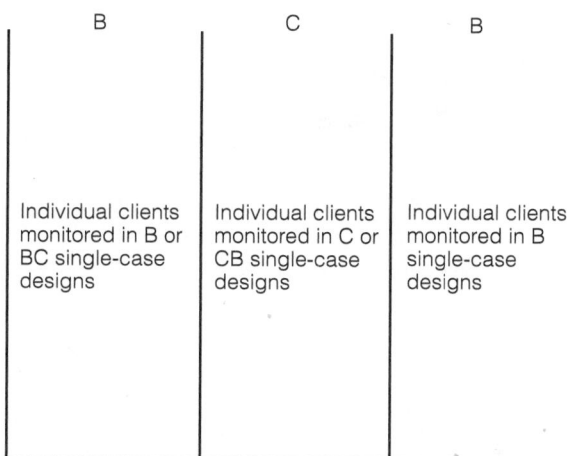

FIGURE 7.2 Illustration of evaluation design for hypothetical example number two. The group-level design is a BCB design. The single-case designs used with specific individual clients would depend upon when the clients enter the residential program.

would entail monitoring the progress of clients in the program *with the token economy system removed.* The token economy system is "turned off" in this part of the design, since the agency wants to determine the extent to which the token economy system causes changes in its clients. In the second B phase, of course, the token economy system in the residential program would be reinstated. The logic of the BCB evaluation design is that if the token economy system is, in fact, the principal active ingredient in the program, then clients should (a) complete a greater percentage of required independent living activities and (b) engage in fewer inappropriate behaviors during B phase than during C phase, when the token economy system has been turned off.

The single-case designs that the agency would use to monitor individual clients in the program would depend upon when the clients enter the residential program. Those who enter during the first B phase would be monitored with either B or BC single-case designs. A client whose stay in the residence occurred in total during the first B phase of the group-level evaluation would have her or his progress monitored in a simple B design. A client whose stay encompassed a time period that overlapped with both the B and C phases of the group-level evaluation would be monitored in a BC single-case design. Similarly, clients whose stays occurred entirely during the C phase of the group-level design would have their progress monitored using a C single-case design—that is, a single-case design with only a treatment phase during which the clients were living in the residence during the C phase of the group-level single-case design evaluation. Those clients whose stays overlapped with both the C and the second B phase of the group-level design would have their progress monitored using CB single-case designs. Those clients whose stays in the facility occurred entirely during the second B phase would be monitored using B single-case designs. Finally, any clients whose stay extended across all three phases would be monitored in BCB designs.

Once these evaluations were completed, the agency would be in a position to give to the funding source an evaluation that included the following. First, the agency could provide a graph of the BCB data at the group level. These data could provide evidence that the token economy system implemented in the residential program was a causal factor in residents' engaging in the required independent living activities. Second, the agency could provide the graphed single-case design data for each client who resided in the facility during the BCB group-level evaluation. These data could show the extent to which each client's performance of the required independent living skills improved, remained the same, or deteriorated during the course of her or his stay in the residence. Taken together, these two forms of data could offer very compelling evidence for the effectiveness of the residential program for increasing the independent living skills of the hearing impaired who go through the program.

EXAMPLES FROM THE LITERATURE

Illustrative Example Number One

Nugent, Champlin, and Wiinamaki (1997) conducted an evaluation of an anger control training (ACT) program in a residential facility for adolescents in state custody. The purpose of the evaluation was to determine the extent to which an anger control training program that is used as a part of aggression replacement training (Goldstein & Glick, 1987), a multicomponent intervention for aggressive and antisocial youths, was related to a reduction in antisocial behavior in the residential program. The design they used included elements similar to those described in hypothetical example number two. They used an interrupted time-series design (Cook & Campbell, 1979), resembling an ABA single-case design, at the group (or residential program) level; and they used ABA, AB, and BA single-case designs to monitor individual clients who resided in the facility during the course of the ABA group-level evaluation.

The outcome variable in this evaluation was the rate of acting-out incidents per client for a number of adolescents who were resident in the facility over the course of a 14-month period. The first phase of the group-level component of the evaluation covered a six-month period prior to the implementation of the ACT program in the facility. The second phase covered a six-month period during which each adolescent in the facility participated in the ACT program. The second no-treatment phase of the interrupted time-series design was unplanned. An incident at the agency led to the unplanned cessation of the ACT program. Data on clients who had participated in the ACT program, and who were still resident in the facility, were obtained for two months during this second no-treatment phase. The mean monthly rate of acting-out incidents per client during the first no-treatment phase was 1.2, while the mean rate during the ACT treatment phase was .60. This change represented a 51 percent decrease in the rate of acting-out incidents per client. During the unplanned second no-treatment phase, the mean rate of acting-out incidents per client increased to 2.3 per month, a 370 percent increase relative to the B phase rate. These results suggested that the ACT program may have been a factor in the decrease in the rate of antisocial behavior in the facility (see Figure 1 in Nugent et al., 1997).

Nugent et al. (1997) also presented single-case design data on three clients who were in the facility and who met specific criteria for the severity and/or deterioration of their antisocial behavior. One of these clients was in the group home for the entire period of the evaluation, and so this client's progress was monitored in an ABA single-case design. A second client was in the group home for three months of the first no-treatment phase, and two months of the treatment phase, so this client's progress was monitored in an AB single-case design. A third client was in the facility for five months of the treatment phase, and two months of the unplanned second no-treatment phase, so this client's progress was monitored in a BA single-case design. In each of these three cases, the single-case design data suggested that the ACT program may have reduced the adolescents' antisocial behavior (see Figure 2 in Nugent et al., 1997).

The evaluation conducted by Nugent et al. (1997) illustrates how group and single-case design methodology may be integrated and used in a complementary manner to evaluate the services received by clients. The results show very nicely how such an integrated methodology can provide information at both the group level and at the level of specific individual clients. The reader is urged to look carefully at this illustrative evaluation.

Illustrative Example Number Two

Ascher (1981) reports the results of an investigation of the use of "graduated exposure" and "paradoxical intention" for ameliorating the travel restrictions of agoraphobic clients. In the Ascher study, "graduated exposure" consisted of having clients enter anxiety-provoking situations (specific to each client), where they were to travel as far as possible without experiencing discomfort. Upon experiencing any discomfort, they were to return home immediately. In contrast, "paradoxical intention" required the clients to enter the anxiety-evoking situations and, upon experiencing any anxiety symptoms, to try to increase the intensity of the symptoms while remaining in the anxiety-evoking situation. They were to return home only after becoming calm.

The outcome variable in the Ascher (1981) study was a client's score on a behavioral approach test involving specific places and situations avoided because of anxiety. Scores on this test could range from 0 (unable to leave home) to 20 (able to travel to target locations and remain until comfortable).

In this study, Ascher (1981) used both group-comparison and single-case design methods. At the group level, he created two comparison groups by randomly assigning five clients into each of the two treatment groups (a total of ten clients). Then, single-case design methods were used to monitor the effects of the different treatments on each of the clients involved in this evaluation. The five clients in each treatment group were studied in multiple baseline, across-subjects, single-case design evaluations of the effects of the interventions they received. After baseline periods of variable length (4, 5, 6, 7, and 8 weeks), each client in Group A received a standard 6-week in vivo graduated exposure treatment (a B phase). Subsequent to the 6-week in vivo program, each client in Group A then received the paradoxical intention treatment (a C phase). Following baseline periods of variable length (4, 5, 6, 7, and 8 weeks), clients in Group B received the paradoxical intention treatment (a B phase). Thus, the Ascher study also nicely illustrates the use of a methodological approach in which group comparison and single-case design methods were used to study the effects of interventions at both aggregate and individual client levels. In this case, the purpose of the evaluation was to compare the relative effects of two different approaches to treating agoraphobia. This design is shown in Figure 7.3.

The results of this study clearly suggested that the paradoxical intention intervention was superior to the graduated exposure. The results also clearly showed that each client involved in the study benefited from treatment. Although practitioners may never have the opportunity to use random assignment in a practice setting, this study of two different interventions is an excellent example of the manner in which group-comparison and single-case design methods can be integrated into a powerful evaluation methodology. Closely scrutinize the Ascher (1981) investigation, and imagine the different ways in which group-comparison and single-case methods might be integrated to meet the needs of practice evaluation efforts.

Illustrative Example Number Three

This final example is that of an evaluation of an anger control training program implemented in a school setting (Whitfield, 1999). In this evaluation, which involved sixteen students in the school, eight students were assigned at random to a group that would receive anger control training, and eight were

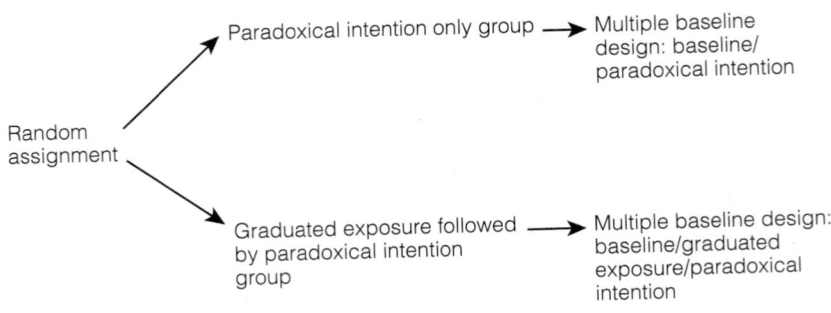

FIGURE 7.3 The design used by Ascher (1981).

randomly assigned to a no-treatment control group. This comprised the group-comparison component of Whitfield's integrated design. The progress of the eight students who received the anger control training was monitored in a multiple baseline design across subjects. This comprised the single-case design component of Whitfield's design. This design is illustrated in Figure 7.4.

Whitfield (1999) analyzed the resulting data at both the group and individual student level. The results suggested that the students who received the anger control training fared better than did those who did not receive the treatment. As with the previous examples, we recommend that the reader read this evaluation study and examine the manner in which the investigators used combinations of single-case and group-comparison design methods to look at the effects of the interventions in which they were interested.

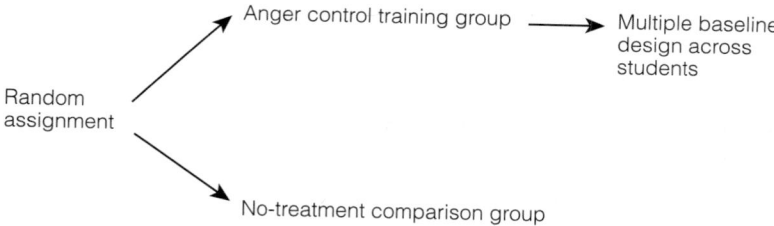

FIGURE 7.4 The integrated design used by Whitfield (1999).

8

Analyzing Aggregated Single-Case Data

A complete analysis of aggregated single-case design data will include analyses done at two levels: at the level of the individual client, using methods described in Chapter 6, and at the aggregate level. The reason for this is that aggregated single-case design data will contain information about individuals and about groups of individuals, and the information at each level of analysis (individual client and aggregation of clients) is important and complements that at the other level (Nugent, 1996). The degree to which the aggregated data will be analyzed at both levels will depend upon the information required in an evaluation. If a complete analysis is done, the evaluator will include in her or his report, first of all, a section that contains graphs of single-case data for each client involved in the evaluation. For example, if there were 10 clients and each client's treatment was monitored using a B design, this section of the report would include the B design data for each client. Each client's B design data would be accompanied by a brief narrative describing the results of a visual analysis of the clients' single-case data.

The aggregate-level analysis may involve either graphical or statistical methods, or both, as are appropriate for the purposes of the evaluation. The statistical procedures that can be used range from the very simple, involving, for example, nothing more complex than means (Nurius & Hudson, 1993) or percentages, to the very complex. An example of a more complex analysis would be the use of hierarchical linear model (HLM) techniques (Bryk & Raudenbush, 1992; Nugent, 1996) to assess the impact of treatment and to determine what factors (if any) were responsible for some clients improving while others stayed the same or got worse.

In this chapter, we discuss graphical methods and only the simpler statistical techniques that might be used to analyze aggregated single-case data. The use of more complex statistical methods has been discussed by Nugent (1996). We begin our discussion in this chapter by focusing on some simple, yet very useful, graphical procedures. We also discuss some very simple statistical methods that can be used in conjunction with graphical procedures or by themselves. We then illustrate the use of both types of procedures by conducting an analysis of hypothetical data from a hypothetical program evaluation.

GRAPHICAL METHODS

One simple yet powerful way to analyze aggregated single-case design data is through the use of graphs. One reason graphical procedures can be so useful and powerful is the ability of the human eye to detect patterns in graphed data (Parsonson & Baer, 1992). There are several ways that graphs can be used to assist in the analysis of aggregated single-case design data: a set of single-case design graphs can be aggregated onto a single graph; single-case design graphs can be aggregated by using different colors or other forms of differential visual representation to highlight distinctions between client groups; simple statistical procedures such as the mean can be used to produce summary graphs; and various combinations of these procedures can be used. When a comprehensive evaluation is being done, these methods of representing and analyzing aggregated single-case design data will be complemented with analyses of each individual single-case design that makes up the aggregation.

The Graphic Representation of Aggregated Data

In the previous chapter, we discussed a hypothetical evaluation (hypothetical example number one) in which an agency was required by a funding source to report on the outcomes for clients served by the agency for problems with depression. There were three things the agency needed to do in this evaluation: provide evidence concerning each client and whether he or she improved during services, provide some assessment of the clients' overall benefit, and provide some possible reasons for the failure of some clients to improve. Say the agency has (for simplicity) a set of B single-case design data for six clients. These hypothetical single-case results are shown in Figures 8.1 through 8.6. The dependent variable in each of these hypothetical cases is the client's scores on the Generalized Contentment Scale (GCS). It will be remembered that higher scores on the GCS are indicative of more severe problems with depression, and lower scores of less severe problems with depression. Further, scores at or above 30 are indicative of a clinically significant problem with depression.

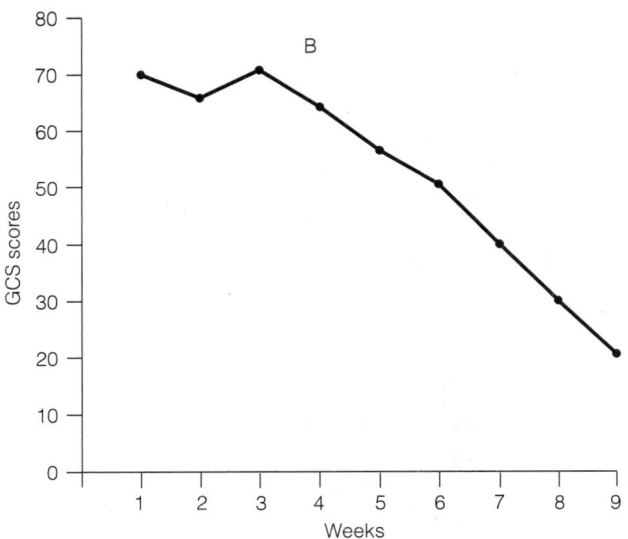

FIGURE 8.1 B design data for a hypothetical female client.

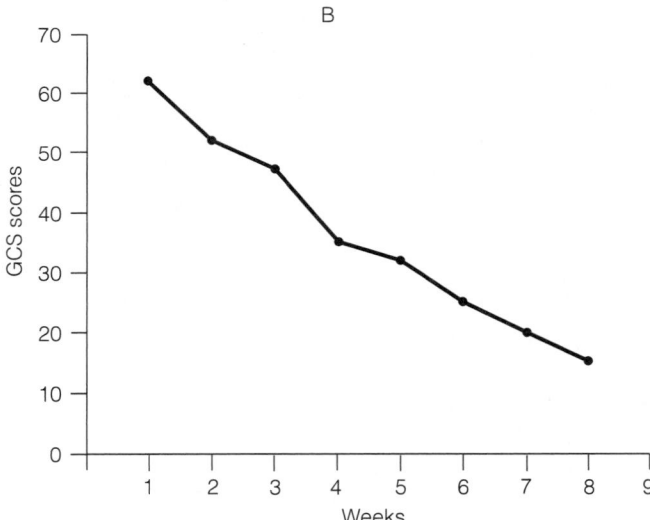

FIGURE 8.2 B design data for a hypothetical female client.

As can be seen in each of these graphs, the GCS scores for the clients in Figures 8.1 through 8.4 declined over time to levels below the clinical cutting score of 30. These results provide evidence, at the level of the individual client, that each client's depression levels improved during the course of treatment to

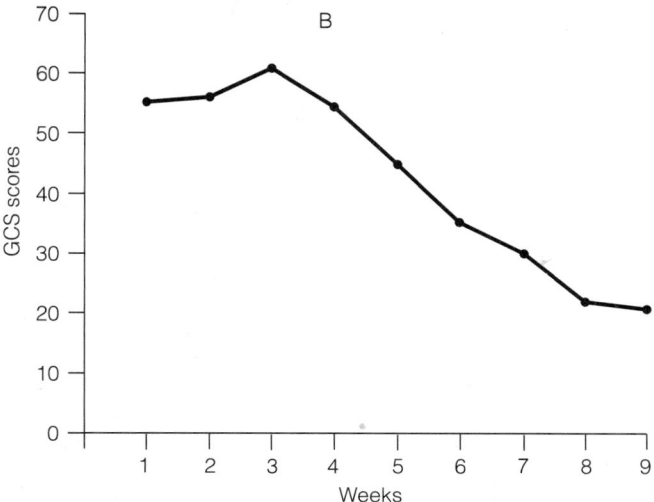

FIGURE 8.3 B design data for a hypothetical female client.

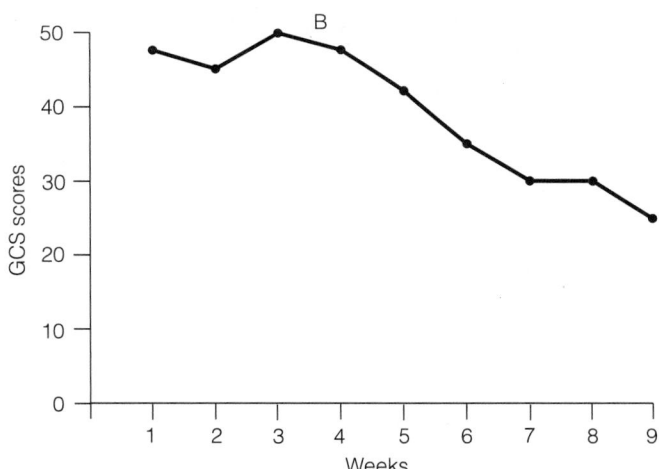

FIGURE 8.4 B design data for a hypothetical female client.

the point that the clients were no longer clinically depressed. However, the GCS scores for the clients in Figures 8.5 and 8.6 fail to show any improvement during the course of treatment. These six single-case design graphs provide the evidence to satisfy the first requirement of the evaluation the agency must do for the funding source.

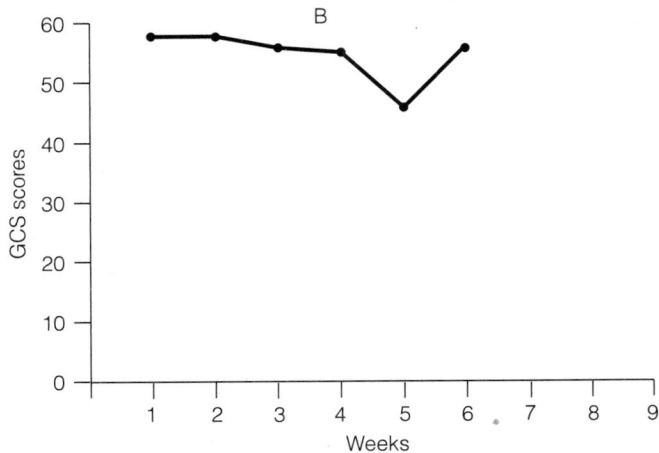

FIGURE 8.5 B design data for a hypothetical male client.

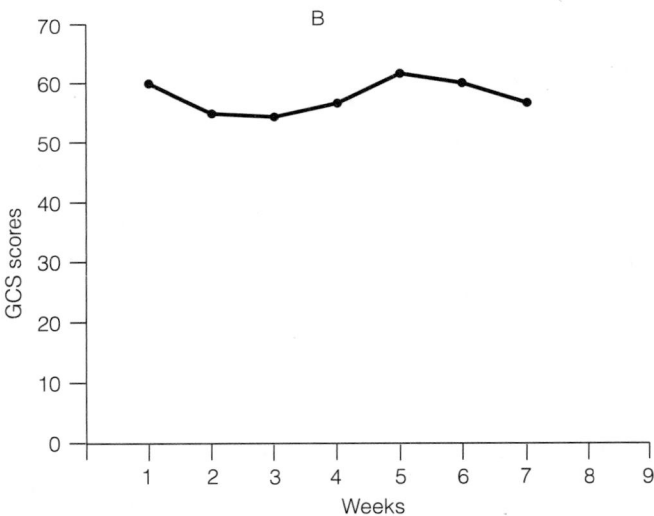

FIGURE 8.6 B design data for a hypothetical male client.

The agency might then place the data for all clients on the same graph, as is done in Figure 8.7. In Figure 8.7, all the data for the six hypothetical clients whose B design data are shown in Figures 8.1 through 8.6 have been placed onto the same graph. As shown later, aggregating single-case design data onto a single graph enables the evaluator to provide evidence that can satisfy the third requirement of the agency's funding source.

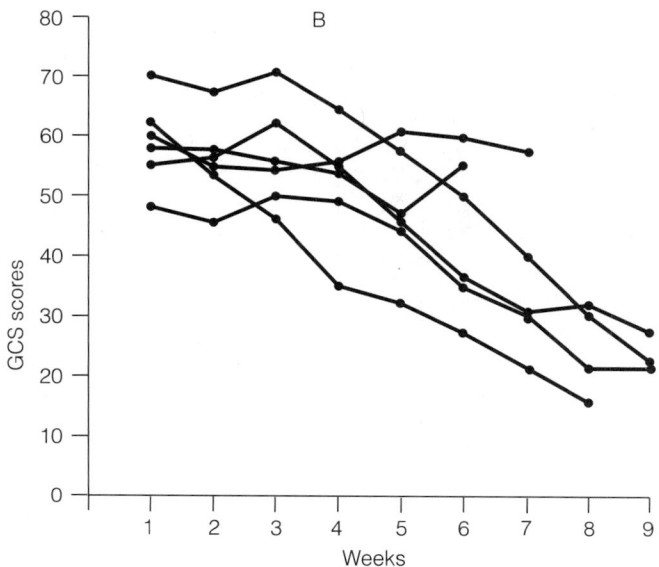

FIGURE 8.7 Aggregated B design single-case data for six hypothetical clients.

Making Distinctions Between Client Groups

Some evaluation questions may require that distinctions be made between client groups. For example, it may be useful to make distinctions between male and female clients in an evaluation report. It may also be important to make distinctions between clients treated with different interventions. There are numerous client characteristics (such as gender, ethnicity, etc.) and/or context factors (such as program, agency, direct service worker, treatment type, etc.) that may be important in an evaluation. In such cases, individual single-case designs can be aggregated onto the same graph, and at the same time, such distinctions can be emphasized by the use of different visual representations for the cases that belong to a particular group. The data in Figure 8.7 can be treated this way by representing the single-case design data for males by solid lines and black circles, and the data for females by dashed lines and squares, as in Figure 8.8. Now a pattern can be readily detected in the data: males' GCS scores declined during the course of treatment, while those of female clients did not. This suggests that one possible reason that some clients improved during service provision, while others did not, was gender. These results suggest, though do not prove, that the treatment used by the social workers in the agency to treat depression may be more appropriate for males than females. Notice how the aggregated data in Figure 8.8, along with a narrative discussing the graph, would be compelling evidence to offer the funding source about the differential outcomes for the clients whose single-case design data are shown in Figures 8.1 through 8.6.

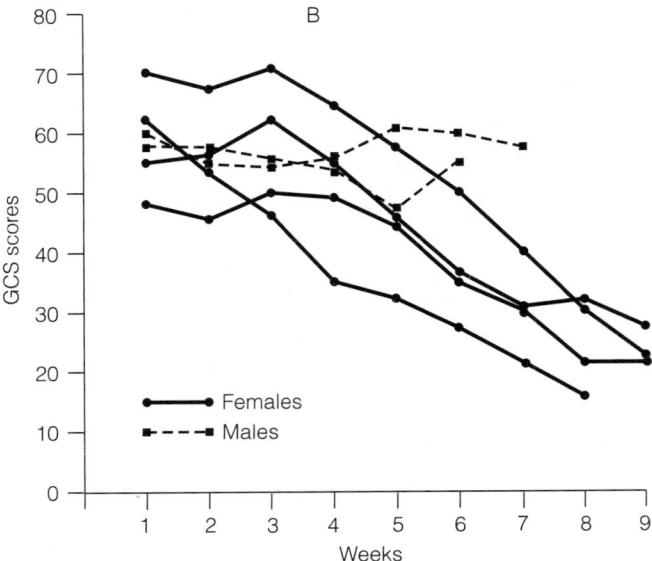

FIGURE 8.8 Aggregated B design single-case data for six hypothetical clients with the data for females in solid lines and black circles, and for males in dashed lines and black squares.

There are other ways of representing graphically the distinctions between groups of clients. For example, suppose that it is important to include in an evaluation the distinction between the responses of males and females, and between couples, to an intervention implemented by direct service workers in an agency for marital problems. Let us also suppose, again for simplicity of presentation, that over a specified period of time, the agency has treated four couples (Couple A, Couple B, Couple C, and Couple D) for marital distress, that each partner in these couples completed the Index of Marital Satisfaction (IMS) during service provision, and that each couple's progress was monitored in a B design. Higher scores on the IMS are indicative of more intense marital distress, and vice versa; scores at or above 30 are indicative of a clinically significant level of marital distress. The B design data for each of these four couples are shown in Figures 8.9 through 8.12, and the aggregated single-case data for these four couples are shown in Figure 8.13. In these figures, the clinical cutting score of 30 is indicated by the dotted line. As can be seen in Figures 8.9 through 8.12, the IMS score for each partner in each couple is at or below the clinical cutting score at the end of 10 weeks of intervention. The aggregated data in Figure 8.13 show the data for each partner in each of the couples. The different types of lines (solid represents females, dashed represents males) preserve the distinction between males and females, and the differently shaped data points preserve the distinctions between the four couples. Thus,

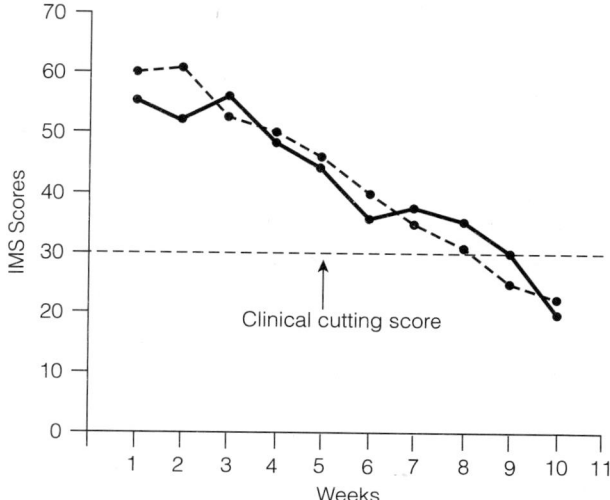

FIGURE 8.9 Single-case data for Couple A.

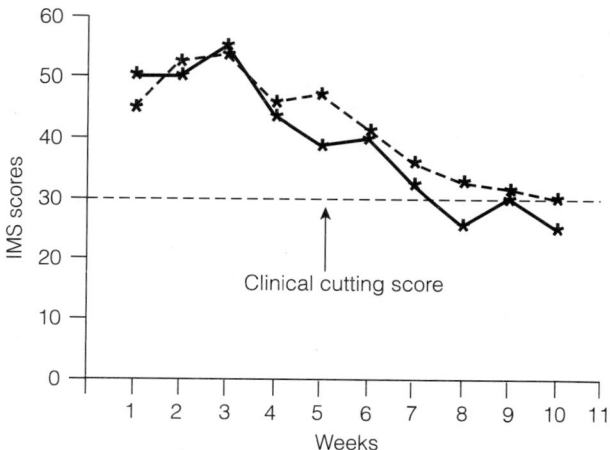

FIGURE 8.10 Single-case data for Couple B.

the graph shown in Figure 8.13 conveys in a simple manner the single-case design data for the couples served by the agency during the specified time period, using the specific intervention method, and can be used as compelling evidence that these couples' relationships improved during the course of service provision.

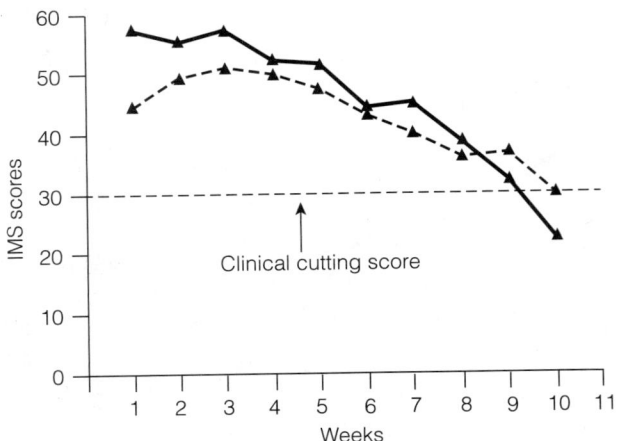

FIGURE 8.11 Single-case data for Couple C.

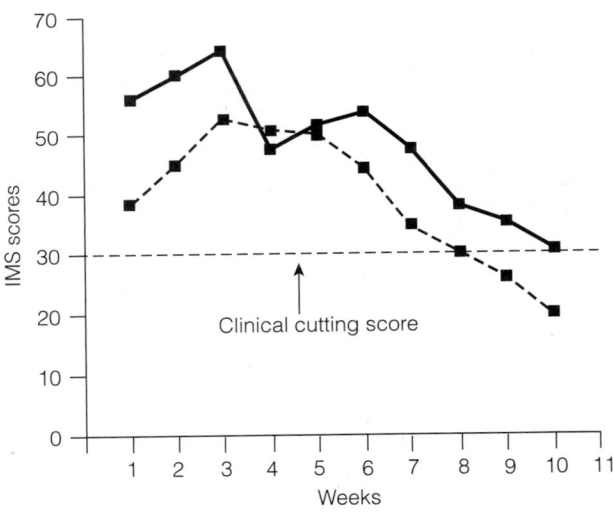

FIGURE 8.12 Single-case data for Couple D.

Comparing Different Context Variables

The methods described previously can be used to compare different context variables. For example, one might want to compare the apparent effects of two different treatments for the same problem or the outcomes for clients treated for the same problem using the same treatment but in different sites. To do this,

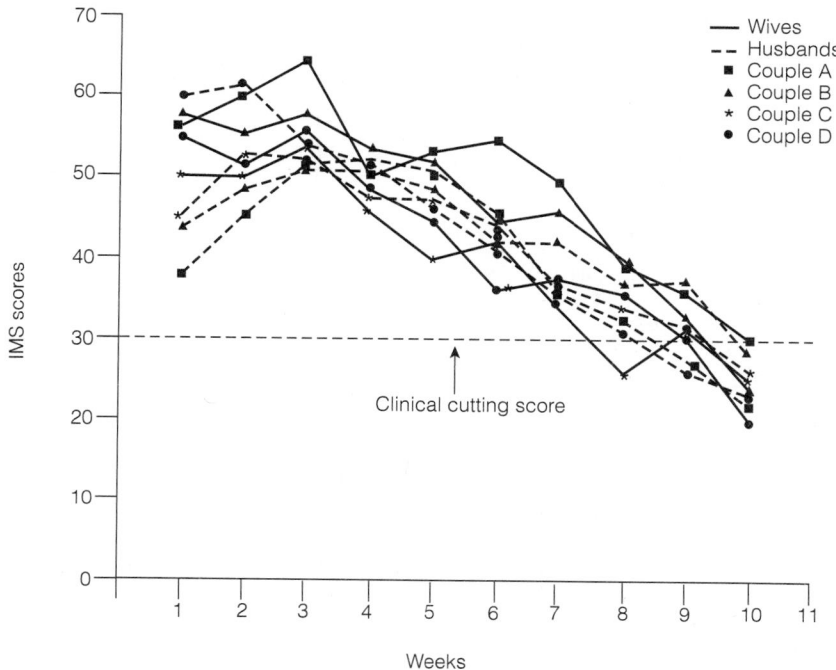

FIGURE 8.13 Aggregated single-case data for four couples, with distinctions made both between males and females and between the four couples.

one could, for example, simply aggregate the single-case designs for the clients and represent treatment or site by using different kinds of lines. Suppose that one wants to compare the apparent relative effects of two different treatments for decreasing clients' problems with self-esteem. The first treatment is, say, "insight therapy," which consists of talking with the client about why he or she has low self-esteem. The second treatment is "cognitive-behavioral bibliotherapy" for self-esteem (Burns, 1999), a variation on the bibliotherapeutic self-help intervention for depression (Burns, 1990, 1992) that has been shown to reduce depression (Jamison & Scogin, 1995; Scogin, Hamblin, & Beutler, 1987; Scogin, Jamison, & Davis, 1990; Scogin, Jamison, & Gochneaut, 1989; Smith, Floyd, Jamison, & Scogin, 1997). Suppose that there were four clients who received cognitive-behavioral bibliotherapy; the results of AB single-case design evaluations of this intervention are shown in Figures 8.14 through 8.17. In these figures, the B phase represents the time during which each client implemented the self-help intervention. Further suppose that there were four clients who received insight therapy (C phase in Figures 8.18 through 8.21) followed by the cognitive-behavioral bibliotherapy (B phase in Figures 8.18 through 8.21). The outcome measure in each of these cases is the Index of Self-Esteem (ISE). Higher scores on the ISE are indicative of more severe

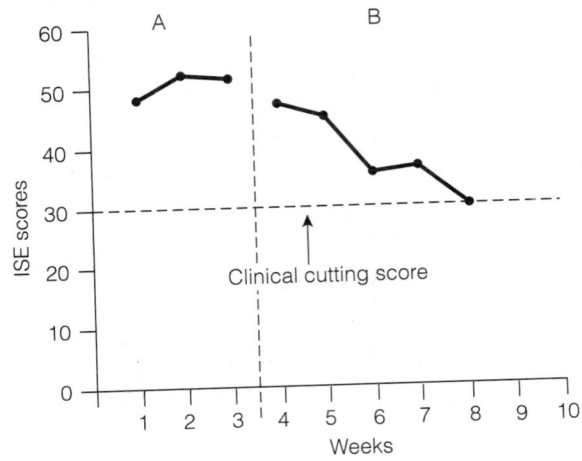

FIGURE 8.14 AB single-case data for client number one receiving cognitive-behavioral bibliotherapy for self-esteem problems.

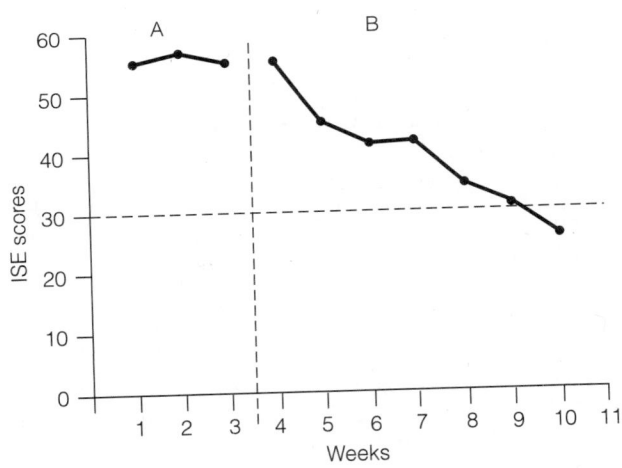

FIGURE 8.15 AB single-case data for client number two receiving cognitive-behavioral bibliotherapy for self-esteem problems.

problems with self-esteem, and vice versa. Further, scores at or above 30 on the ISE are indicative of a clinically significant problem with self-esteem.

The data in Figures 8.14 through 8.17 show that each of the four clients receiving the cognitive-behavioral bibliotherapy improved during treatment, and that their ISE scores at the end of treatment were at or below the clinical cutting score of 30 on the ISE. The data in Figures 8.18 through 8.21

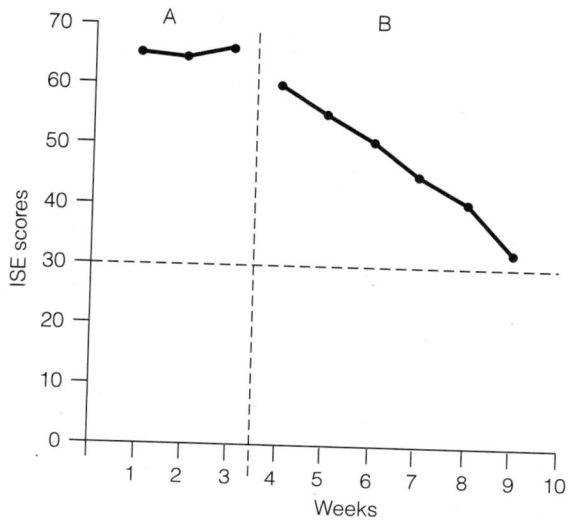

FIGURE 8.16 AB single-case data for client number three receiving cognitive-behavioral bibliotherapy for self-esteem problems.

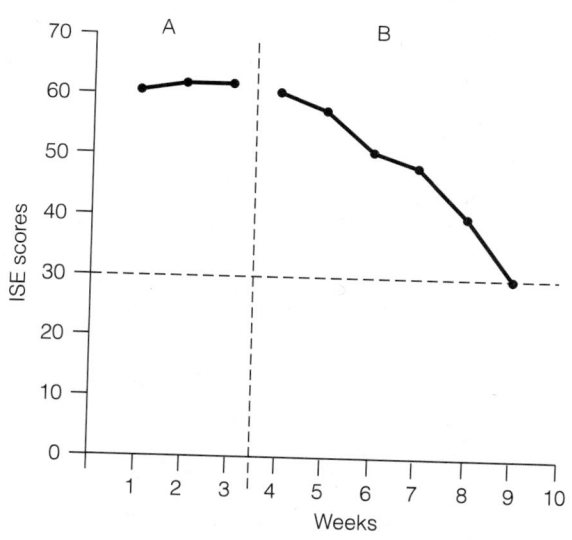

FIGURE 8.17 AB single-case data for client number four receiving cognitive-behavioral bibliotherapy for self-esteem problems.

show that none of the clients appeared to improve with insight therapy, but did show improvement with the cognitive-behavioral bibliotherapy. The evaluator can directly compare the insight therapy with the cognitive-behavioral bibliotherapy by placing all eight clients' baseline data, the B phase data for

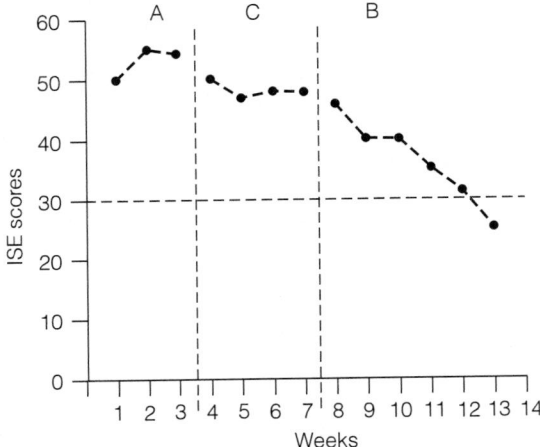

FIGURE 8.18 ACB single-case data for client number one receiving insight therapy followed by cognitive-behavioral bibliotherapy for self-esteem problems.

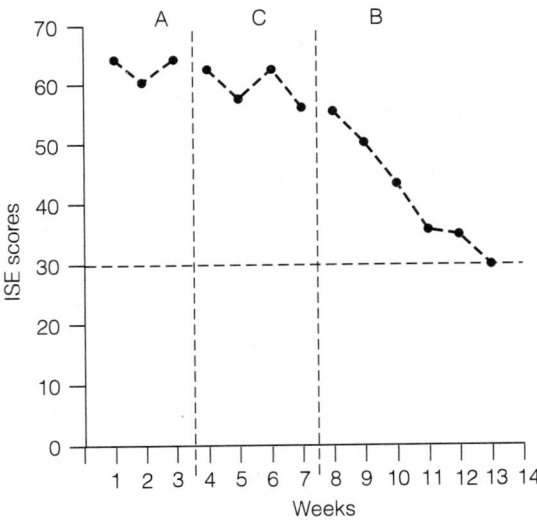

FIGURE 8.19 ACB single-case data for client number two receiving insight therapy followed by cognitive-behavioral bibliotherapy for self-esteem problems.

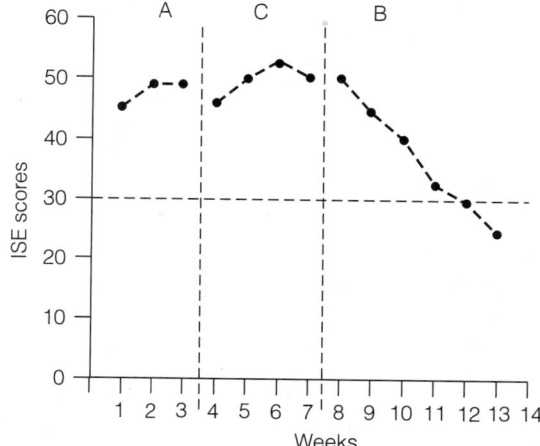

FIGURE 8.20 ACB single-case data for client number three receiving insight therapy followed by cognitive-behavioral bibliotherapy for self-esteem problems.

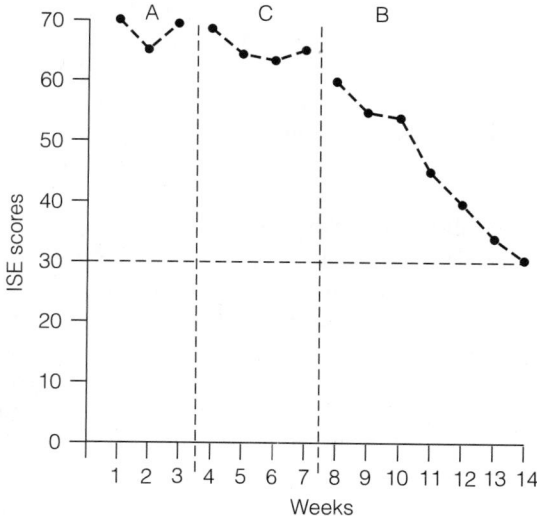

FIGURE 8.21 ACB single-case data for client number four receiving insight therapy followed by cognitive-behavioral bibliotherapy for self-esteem problems.

the clients in Figures 8.14 through 8.17, and the C phase data for the clients in Figures 8.18 through 8.21 on the same graph, as in Figure 8.22. The data for clients who received the cognitive-behavioral bibliotherapy immediately after baseline are shown with solid lines, while the data for clients who received the insight therapy immediately after baseline are shown with dashed lines in Figure 8.22.

As you can see from Figure 8.22, the baseline data for all eight clients overlap. This is apparent from the manner in which the solid and dashed baselines intermingle completely. This feature of the baseline data in Figure 8.22 suggests that the clients who received the cognitive-behavioral bibliotherapy and those who received insight therapy started out very much alike in terms of their problems with self-esteem. However, the treatment-phase data for the two groups of clients (insight therapy shown with dashed lines, cognitive-behavioral bibliotherapy shown with solid lines) look different. The treatment-phase trends for cognitive-behavioral bibliotherapy clients are all in an improving direction, and all have endpoints at or below the clinical cutting score of 30. In contrast, the treatment-phase trends for insight therapy clients show no systematic improving trend, and the final treatment-phase data points for insight therapy clients are all well above the clinical cutting point. The aggregated data in Figure 8.22 clearly support the cognitive-behavioral bibliotherapy over the insight therapy. The individual client level data in Figures 8.14 through 8.21 also support the superiority of cognitive-behavioral bibliotherapy over insight therapy for treating self-esteem problems, at least with these eight clients. This example is a good illustration not only of the use of aggregated single-case data and the use of graphical techniques, but also of how aggregated single-case data and the individual single-case data from specific clients complement one another in terms of helping the evaluator to answer important evaluation questions.

The simple methods illustrated previously can be extended to more complex evaluation problems. Different visual means of representing the distinctions between client characteristics and/or context variables can be used in graphs that contain the aggregated data from a number of single-case designs. Although we have used single-case designs with the same number of, and spacing between, phase measures, this is not necessary. One can aggregate single-case designs in which there are different numbers of, and different temporal spacing between, measurements. Thus, the methods discussed here are rather flexible.

There are, of course, limitations to these methods. The same outcome measure should be used in each case that is included in a graph of aggregated single-case designs. The problems associated with attempts to aggregate single-case design data over different outcome measures have been discussed by Nurius and Hudson (1993), so we will not discuss those problems here. If there are a large number of clients whose single-case data are to be aggregated onto the same graph, then the resulting representation can become quite littered with information, and important distinctions between client characteristics and/or context variables can be obscured by the sheer number of data points

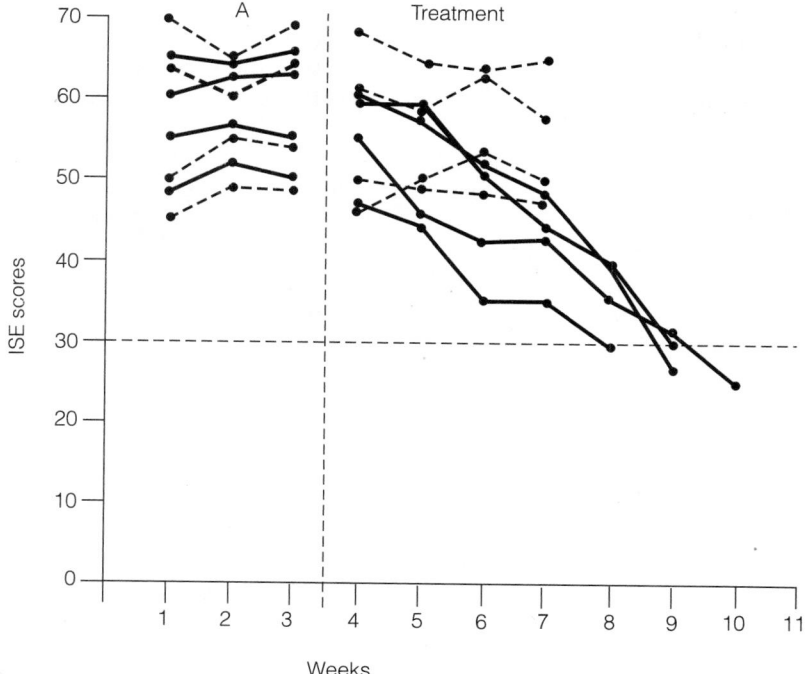

FIGURE 8.22 Aggregated single-case data comparing insight therapy with cognitive-behavioral bibliotherapy. Solid lines show data for clients receiving cognitive-behavioral bibliotherapy; dashed lines show data for clients receiving insight therapy.

and lines on the graph. In a similar vein, by trying to include too many distinctions between client characteristics and/or context variables on the aggregated graph, the evaluator may obscure the information he or she is trying to convey by the complexity of the graph. It is here that the use of some simple statistical methods can help to clarify the analyses.

STATISTICAL METHODS

There will be times when the use of statistical methods can help the evaluator to represent and analyze aggregated single-case data. One such time is when the evaluator has a large number of single-case designs to aggregate. As noted earlier, in such cases, the graphical methods we have outlined may produce graphs of aggregated data that are complex and difficult to interpret because of the large numbers of lines and data points. In cases such as this, it can be useful to use the "mean time path" to represent a set of aggregated single-case design data. The mean time path is simply the across–time profile that is composed of the mean scores across clients at each time point. Nurius and Hudson (1993) have discussed the issues involved in the use of mean scores across clients at each time point as a means of representing aggregated single-case data.

Let us again return to hypothetical example number one from the previous chapter. We have shown how the agency could provide evidence to meet the first (how did each client fare?) and third (why did some clients not improve?) evaluation needs. The agency could use mean scores to address the second evaluation need, that of providing some measure of the overall benefit of services for the six clients whose services were paid for by the funding source. The simplest way to do this would be to provide a graph showing the mean response profile across the six clients whose single-case design data are shown in Figures 8.1 through 8.6. Figure 8.23 shows the mean response of these six clients to the treatment for depression.

The mean response, and other simple statistics, can be useful when one has large sets of data. Suppose, for example, that 56 clients have been served by the agency for problems with self-esteem, that the services provided to these clients were monitored using the simple B design, and that the outcome variable for each client was her or his score on the ISE. A single graph showing the data from all 56 cases might be difficult to interpret due to the large numbers of lines and data points. An alternative method would be to (1) compute the mean ISE score at each time point across clients, (2) plot the resulting mean time path, and (3) plot on the same graph the single-case data from the client who improved most quickly and the single-case data for the client who improved most slowly and/or the least. The resulting graph would show the mean response to treatment across the 56 clients and would also show the best and worst responses to treatment. An example of such a graph is shown in Figure 8.24. The value of this graph is that it summarizes the data from 56 cases and shows very nicely not only the typical response to treatment, but also the range of responses to treatment. Since the worst response is shown on the graph, the evaluator knows that everyone else did better than this client. A graph such as that in Figure 8.24 might be used rather than, or in addition to, one such as those shown in Figures 8.8, 8.13, and 8.22.

Let us go through the process of constructing such a graph for the data in Figures 8.14 to 8.21. The raw data are shown in Table 8.1. The mean time paths are shown in bold italics in this table and are shown plotted in Figure 8.25. A look at Figure 8.25 shows that (1) the mean baseline phase time paths for the two groups of clients are identical, and (2) the mean treatment–phase time path for cognitive-behavioral bibliotherapy clients shows an improving trend to clinically nonsignificant ISE scores, while the treatment–phase mean time path for insight therapy clients shows no trend, either improving or deteriorating, and is, apparently, a continuation of the baseline mean time path for these clients. The data in Figure 8.25 clearly supports the efficacy of cognitive-behavioral bibliotherapy over insight therapy for self-esteem problems.

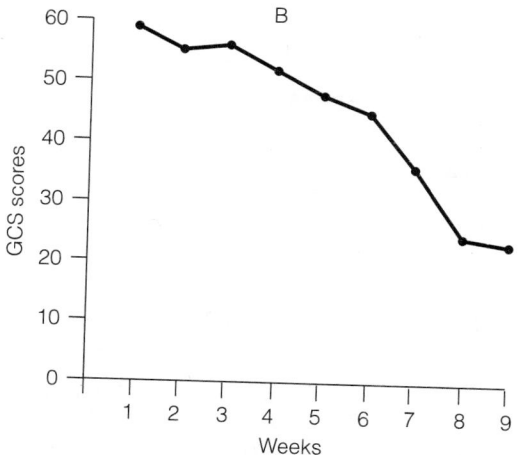

FIGURE 8.23 The mean response to treatment of the clients whose single-case data are shown in Figures 8.1 thorough 8.6.

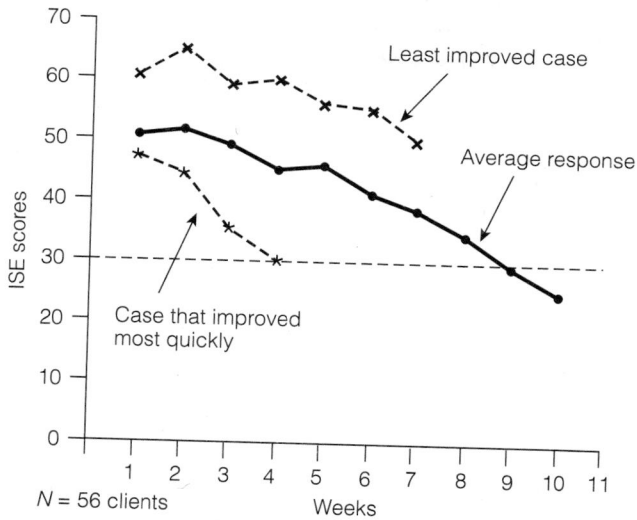

FIGURE 8.24 A graph showing the mean time path for a set of aggregated single-case B design data, along with the worst and best responses to treatment.

The mean time paths for each single-case design phase can be placed on a graph that also shows the single-case data for each client. Thus, we might add the mean time paths from Figure 8.25 to the data shown in Figure 8.22, as shown in Figure 8.26. In Figure 8.26, the heavier dashed lines (equally spaced

Table 8.1 Raw Data for Clients Whose Single-Case Design Data Are Shown in Figures 8.14–8.21

COGNITIVE-BEHAVIORAL BIBLIOTHERAPY CLIENTS									
A Phase			*B Phase*						
Time 1	Time 2	Time 3	Time 4	Time 5	Time 6	Time 7	Time 8	Time 9	Time 10
48	52	51	47	44	35	35	29		
55	57	55	55	46	42	42	35	31	26
65	64	66	60	59	50	44	40	30	
61	63	63	61	57	51	48	39	29	
57	*59*	*59*	*56*	*51*	*45*	*42*	*36*	*30*	*26*

INSIGHT THERAPY CLIENTS						
A Phase			*C Phase*			
Time 1	Time 2	Time 3	Time 4	Time 5	Time 6	Time 7
50	55	54	50	49	48	48
64	61	64	62	58	62	57
45	49	49	46	50	53	50
70	65	69	68	64	63	65
57	*57*	*59*	*57*	*55*	*57*	*55*

Note: Means across clients at each time point shown in **bold italics**.

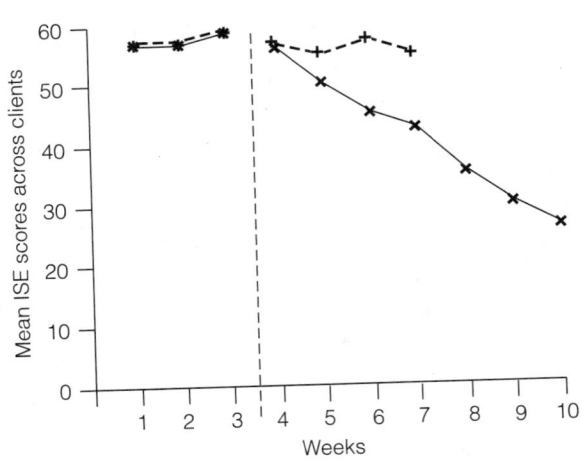

FIGURE 8.25 Mean time paths for data from clients whose single-case design data are shown in Figure 8.22. Solid lines are for cognitive-behavioral bibliotherapy clients, while dashed lines are for insight therapy clients.

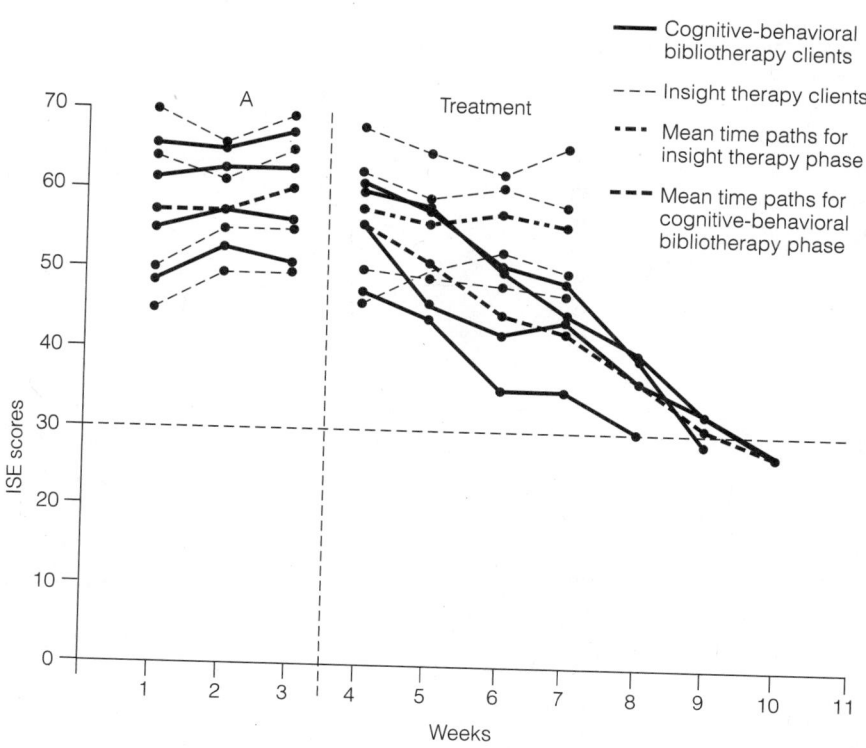

FIGURE 8.26 Aggregated single-case data with mean time paths comparing insight therapy with cognitive-behavioral bibliotherapy.

dashes show cognitive-behavioral bibliotherapy clients, alternating short and long dashes show insight therapy clients) in each phase show the mean time paths for clients in each group. The advantage of a graphic illustration such as that shown in Figure 8.26 is that not only are the mean time paths for clients who received both forms of treatment shown, but the variability of client responses around these mean time paths is also illustrated.

The data from the cognitive-behavioral bibliotherapy phases for clients who had first received insight therapy (B phases in Figures 8.18 through 8.21) could also be added to a graph like that in Figure 8.26. The raw scores for B phases for these hypothetical clients, and the mean ISE scores at each time point, are shown in Table 8.2. These data have been added to Figure 8.26, as shown in Figure 8.27. The graph in Figure 8.27 provides compelling evidence that the cognitive-behavioral bibliotherapy was an effective intervention for self-esteem problems. It shows both the mean time paths for baseline data for both groups of clients, as well as the spread of individual clients' baseline profiles around the mean time paths. These data suggest that both groups of clients

Table 8.2 Cognitive-Behavioral Bibliotherapy Phase Data for Clients Who First Received Insight Therapy

time 8	time 9	time 10	time 11	time 12	time 13	time 14
46	40	40	35	31	24	
55	50	43	36	35	30	
50	45	40	33	30	25	
61	54	53	45	40	34	30
53	*47*	*44*	*37*	*34*	*28*	*30*

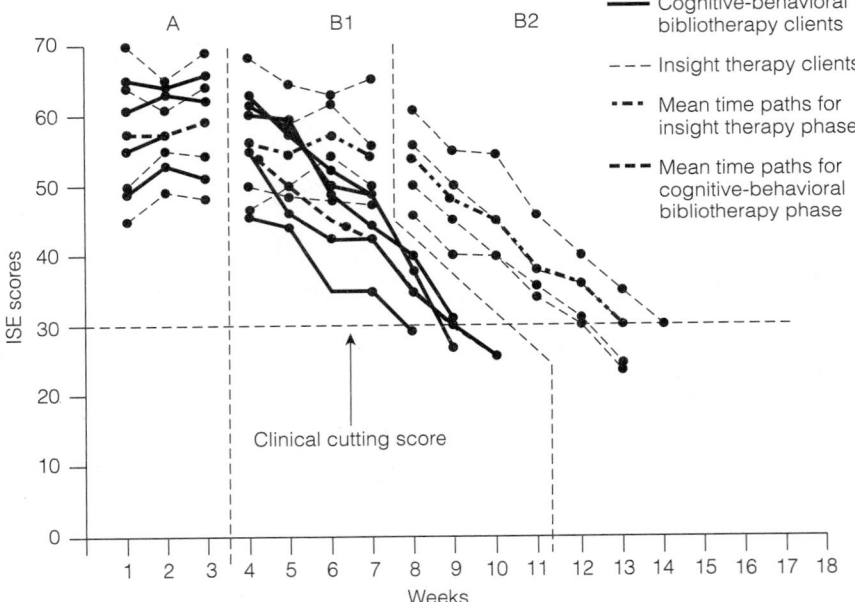

FIGURE 8.27 Aggregated single case data with mean time paths comparing insight therapy with cognitive-behavioral bibliotherapy.

started out with similar problems with self-esteem. The graph also shows clearly the changes that clients who received cognitive-behavioral bibliotherapy experienced relative to both their baseline profiles and to the treatment-phase profiles for the clients who received insight therapy. The graph further shows the changes that the clients who first received insight therapy experienced as soon as they received the cognitive-behavioral bibliotherapy. The combination of Figures 8.14 through 8.21 together with Figure 8.27 would comprise a strong case for the effectiveness of services that these clients received for their self-esteem problems.

Additional Statistical Aids

Other simple statistical methods can be used to aid in the analysis of aggregated single-case design data. One might report, along with graphs such as those shown previously, the percentage of clients whose treatment phase outcome measures reached some criterion of success, such as a clinical cutting score or a previously agreed-upon goal. For example, one could report in a narrative accompanying Figures 8.14 through 8.21 and Figure 8.27 that 100 percent of clients receiving the cognitive-behavioral bibliotherapy had final treatment-phase ISE scores below the clinical cutting score, while 0 percent of those receiving insight therapy had final treatment-phase scores below the clinical cutting score on the ISE. One might also report the percentages (or numbers) of clients who improved, who remained at baseline levels of functioning, and who deteriorated. The important point to recognize here is that virtually any statistical procedure can be used as an adjunct to the graphical methods we have discussed.

More Advanced Statistics

Those with the expertise and the computer software to do it can also complement graphical analyses with advanced statistical methods, such as those discussed by Nugent (1996). It is unlikely, however, that most agencies or practitioners will routinely use such methods. However, at some point it may be profitable to form a linkage with an academic institution in the area and get to know persons there who have the necessary expertise to conduct such analyses. Including the results of such analyses with graphically displayed information would be a powerful format for presenting the results of an evaluation effort.

A SIMPLE EXAMPLE

In the previous chapter, we gave an example of a hypothetical evaluation of a program that teaches independent living skills to hearing-impaired clients. In this example, we described an integrated design in which an interrupted time-series design was used to evaluate the effect that the use of a token economy system had on the performance of required independent living skills by residents in the program. We noted that this group-level design was analogous to a BCB single-case design. We also described in this example how single-case design methods could be used to simultaneously monitor the progress of each individual client through the program, and that the specific single-case design used would depend upon when the particular client entered and participated in the program. Let us briefly consider how the data from such an evaluation might look. The group-level data are shown in Figure 8.28. The data shown in this figure are the aggregated data for all clients who participated in the program during the course of this evaluation. As you can see in this figure, there

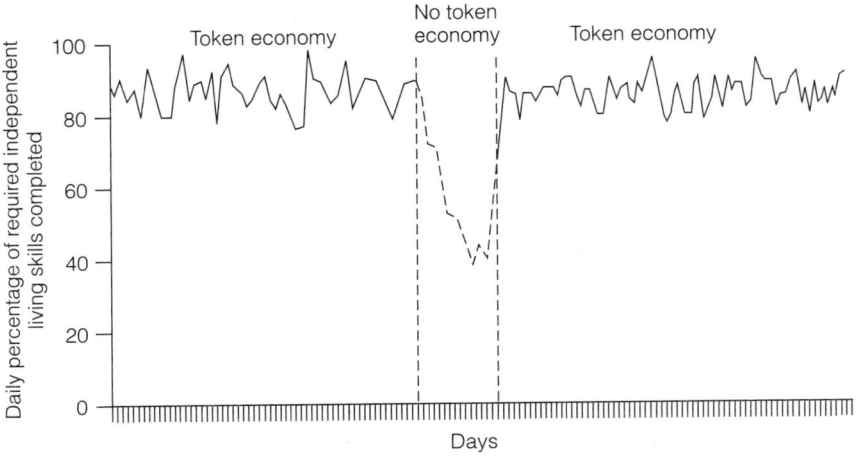

FIGURE 8.28 Group-level data from interrupted time-series design.

is a clear and obvious decrease in the performance of the required independent living skills when the token economy is removed from the program. The performance of the required independent living skills immediately improves when the token economy is reinstated in the residential program. As we noted in the previous chapter, this interrupted time-series design is analogous to a BCB single-case design with the residential program as the "single system." The data in Figure 8.28 would function as compelling evidence that the token economy had a positive effect on the performance of the required independent living skills by clients participating in the program.

   In the interest of brevity and space, we will show and discuss the single-case data for only two hypothetical clients who went through this program during the evaluation. Figure 8.29 shows the data from a B design evaluation of one client's progress through the independent living skills program during the first token economy phase of the interrupted time-series design evaluation. The single-case design graph in Figure 8.29 has been annotated with critical incidents that occurred during the course of this client's involvement in the program. As you can see in this figure, this client made good progress through the program until the end of the second week, at which point the client got into a fight with another resident. At this point, the client was moved down a step. The client then began a steady improvement and quickly regained step 3 status. This client then continued on a steady course through the program and, after a successful stay in a transitional living facility, graduated from the program.

   Figure 8.30 shows the single-case design data for a second hypothetical client who participated in the program during the course of the evaluation. In this case, the client entered the program about two weeks before the start of the "no token economy phase" of the interrupted time-series design, remained

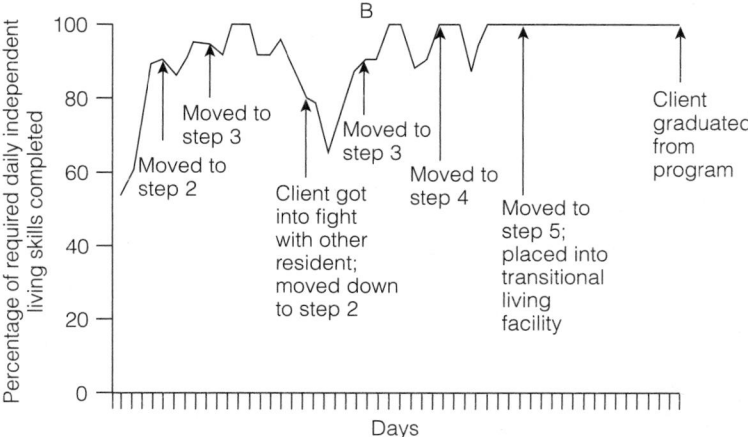

FIGURE 8.29 B data for hypothetical client in the independent living skills program.

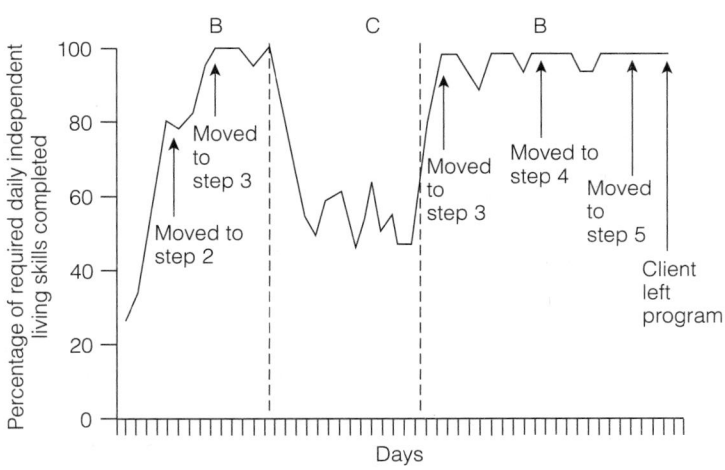

FIGURE 8.30 BCB data for hypothetical client participating in the independent living skills program.

in the program through the entire two weeks of this phase of the evaluation, and then remained in the program for several weeks after the token economy was reinstated. Thus, this client's progress through the program was monitored in a BCB single-case design. As you can see in Figure 8.30, this client was progressing well during the first token economy phase (the B phase) of the evaluation. Just before the token economy was stopped, this client had reached step 3 in the program and was performing nearly 100 percent of the required independent living skills every day. However, when the token economy was stopped, this client's performance of the required independent living skills deteriorated rapidly, reaching an approximate 50 percent daily level after about a week. This client's performance of the required independent living skills again improved with the reinstatement of the token economy, quickly reaching a near 100 percent daily performance. The data in Figure 8.30 not only suggest that this client improved in her or his performance of the required independent living skills during the course of the program, but also suggest that the token economy was a causal factor in this client's improvement.

An evaluator would, of course, have single-case design data for each client who was involved in the independent living skills program during the course of this evaluation. Therefore, the evaluator would be able to: (1) inform the funding source on the extent to which each and every client improved, or failed to improve, during the course of her or his involvement in the program; and (2) provide very compelling evidence to the funding source suggesting that the token economy component of the program was a cause of the improvement in the clients' functioning. We hope that this hypothetical example further demonstrates the powerful evaluation methodology that can be created by integrating single-case and group-design methods.

SUMMARY

We have described a number of graphical procedures for analyzing aggregated single-case design data. We have also described how these graphical procedures can be augmented with simple statistical methods. Which methods a practitioner elects to use will depend upon the evaluation question that needs to be answered and on the audience for whom the evaluation report is intended.

9

≈⋙❁⋘≈

Quality Management: Process and Outcome

This chapter concludes Part I of this book, Using Single-Case Time-Series Designs. By this point, we hope that the reader has become comfortable with the logic, language, and techniques of the single-system designs used to evaluate practice. We firmly believe that the empirical practice model, or EPM, offers a complete system for evaluating client problems, assisting with diagnosis and treatment planning, monitoring client progress over time, and conducting evaluation of practice on both case-by-case and program levels.

No discussion of practice evaluation and single-system designs, however, would be complete without attention to a force that is changing the face of practice more quickly than any other ever encountered in the human services. This force is the juggernaut created by managed care. Over the last two decades, managed care has changed the very nature of health care provision in the United States. In the 1990s, managed care also made remarkable inroads into other forms of care, most notably in mental health. The result of this growth has forced fundamental restructuring in the way human service practice is organized, delivered, monitored, and improved. The benefits clients obtain through health or mental health insurance are very different than those seen only a decade ago, often "carved out" or separated into multiple, confusing components. Practitioners are being asked to rethink the ways in which they provide services, and the rewards for delivering such services are changing rapidly. Soon all practitioners will be forced to become familiar with concepts such as capitation, carve-outs, risk adjustment, and utilization management. At the same time, they will be forced to become much more adept at establishing the accountability of their practice.

Managed care in both medicine and mental health services is first and foremost a business strategy designed to deliver services of a high quality for the lowest financial inputs. It is thus a cost containment system as much as it is anything else. At the same time, however, managed care is also a way to optimize quality management of those services (always with costs in mind, though). Some professionals and client advocates express concerns about the potential impact of such a strong focus on cost containment. These include concerns about the overall quality of care, professional autonomy in managed care structures, and patients' right to choose (Borenstein, 1990; Felty & Jones, 1998; Hughes & Luft, 1998; Miller, 1996; Rogers, Wells, Meredith, Sturm, & Burnam, 1993; Wineburgh, 1998). The focus on quality management, however, also offers potential benefits for better targeting resources to those clients who most require services, and in terms of making mental health care more rational in its orientation, more effectively coordinated, and more outcome-driven.

Regardless of our opinions about managed care, if there is any emerging agenda for human services in the 21st century, it is the one now being shaped by managed care. Growth of managed care in human services demands that professionals become more accountable. We must do so by demonstrating the ability to deliver services that demonstrably help clients solve or alleviate the problems for which they seek help. In the past, we did not know how to do that, because we did not have an effective evaluation technology. Now we do with the EPM. Nor were there, in the past, particularly compelling imperatives to routinely evaluate practice. With managed care, that too has changed.

This chapter focuses on providing a brief description of managed care, its growth, its key principles, and some current issues surrounding managed care in mental health services. We also examine the role of quality management and utilization management in managed human services, and suggest how the empirical practice model can fit into a quality management framework. Finally, we present a brief case example to show how practitioners can use single-system designs to help establish their professional effectiveness as part of a quality management process. First, let us take a look at managed care.

THE EMERGENCE OF MANAGED CARE

Managed care first developed out of early group practice prepayment plans that arose during the first half of the 20th century in the United States. These early plans were based on a belief that health care could be improved by having potential patients prepay for health services. This could be accomplished by eliminating financial barriers many people faced during periods of health difficulties, while at the same time sharing information and expertise among personnel who formed the medical group (Friedman, 1996). These prepayment health programs focused on increasing the quality of care through public health and prevention activities. It was not until the 1970s, however, that evidence emerged to show that prepayment plans actually delivered comparable levels of health care at a substantially lower cost than traditional health programs. This fuelled the growth of such plans, and by the 1980s, health maintenance organizations (HMOs) emerged. These HMOs incorporated both the notion of prepayment of health services and the use of health professionals associated into a single group of health providers. It was also in the 1980s that the term *managed care* came to be applied to HMOs and any other insurance initiative to control health care utilization through selective contracting with smaller panels of health providers (Hughes & Luft, 1998).

Despite its current prevalence in the United States, there is still no common or accepted definition of managed care (Dziegielewski, 1998; Edinburg & Cottler, 1995). This is because managed care has quickly evolved into a collection of practice models and strategies that almost defy common description. Managed care programs can focus on very different objectives, and include a diverse range of practices that can be combined in numerous ways to form almost unrecognizable cousins.

Hughes and Luft (1998), however, suggest that managed care refers to a variety of financing and delivery arrangements for health or mental health services that do share a single characteristic. This characteristic is that those enrolled in a managed care plan are either encouraged or required to obtain care through predefined service providers. These providers are selected and contracted by the managed care organization and, once part of the provider network, are required to follow the rules and procedures established by the contracting managed care organization (Hughes & Luft, 1998; Miller & Luft, 1994). If there is a second common denominator among managed care strategies, it may be that such strategies are designed to balance quality of care with cost containment, allowing the managed care organization to survive and progress (Dziegielewski, 1998).

Perhaps the easiest way to understand managed care is to compare it to a fee-for-service model of care. In a fee-for-service arrangement, the client or patient selects a care provider freely from any of those available to provide such service. Once the service is delivered, a fee is paid, sometimes by the patient, often by the government or a public agency, or perhaps by some combination of the two. Health care in Canada, for example, still follows this model. In contrast, managed care refers to a wide variety of insurance plans that more rigidly finance and deliver health care. Individuals enrolled in a managed care plan make regular prepayments to the insurance company in anticipation of required service. When a health problem does arise, the patient is usually required to seek care from a predetermined set of care providers who are selected by the insurance company. This combination of prepayment and restrictions on patient mobility serves three purposes. First, it restricts patient access to services defined by the insurance company. Second, it more closely monitors service delivery decisions and behaviors on the part of providers. Third, the combination of restricted patient access and control on health providers serves to contain the costs of health care delivery for the insurance company.

Felty and Jones (1998) have suggested that managed care includes three fundamental features. The first is that contracting organizations must agree to provide stipulated services to populations that are predefined, and to do so at a fixed cost. The second is a corollary to the first, in that those organizations must provide contracted services regardless of the eventual costs they incur. In other words, the contracting organization assumes the risk of exceeding budgeted services through miscalculation in the numbers of clients or the severity of issues that must be dealt with. Finally, to minimize risk, managed care organizations must enroll sufficient volumes of clients to ensure that random fluctuations in service demands do not overburden the services budgeted for.

There are a number of easily recognizable types of managed care programs that commonly employ social work professionals (Wagner, 1993). These include the following:

- *Managed indemnity plans.* These are essentially health insurance plans that offer traditional insurance coverage for consumers. Costs borne by consumers in such plans, however, can vary greatly, as they increase directly in proportion to the frequency, intensity, and duration of usage likely to be shown by the consumer.

- *Health maintenance organizations (HMOs).* HMO plans were among the first managed care plans developed in the United States. They provide both insurance coverage and service delivery to consumers. Service delivery is based on a prepaid, fixed fee, and must be obtained from the contracted network of providers. Consumers typically have no insurance coverage for out-of-network services. In addition, providers often bear much of the financial risk of health care usage. This gives HMO providers strong incentives to encourage efficient use of the health care system, to substitute less costly services wherever possible, and to encourage preventive health techniques. Some would also argue, however, that these incentives also lead HMO providers to select or restrict enrollees so that already healthy consumers are given preference over less profitable consumers.

- *Preferred provider organizations* (PPOs). PPO plans negotiate discounted financial rates with a select group of health care providers. In this way, they do not capitate per-client reimbursements as HMOs do. Instead, health care providers are paid on a fee-for-service basis. Clients have choice over whom to obtain services from among the preferred providers, and can obtain out-of-network services if they so wish. Should they choose to obtain out-of-network services, however, clients are required to make significantly higher copayments than they would pay within the network.

- *Exclusive provider plans.* These are among the most restrictive of managed care plans, as clients are required to obtain services *only* from within the network of contracted providers. If they go outside the network, clients must bear the financial costs of the service being delivered

(Wagner, 1993). This type of plan is popular among employers concerned about cutting the costs of health care plans.

- *Point of service* (POS) plans. In POS plans, enrollees can choose to obtain services from outside of the contracted network of providers. In exchange for this freedom, however, they almost always pay significantly higher premiums than those in more traditional plans (such as HMOs).

The growth of these major managed care plans and organizations was staggering in the 1990s. During the early 1990s, health care reform was a major focus of U.S. politicians, especially for the Clinton administration. With the failure of significant health care reform, however, a significant shift in health care provision slipped by largely unnoticed and unscrutinized by the American people. This shift was the increasing dominance of all forms of managed care in the area of health provision. In 1993, only about half (51 percent) of Americans who received health insurance through their employer were enrolled in a managed care plan. In a short two years, this number grew by a remarkable 22 percent, such that 73 percent of these Americans were now part of a managed care health plan (Jensen, Morrisey, Gaffney, & Liston, 1997). At the same time, the last decade of the 20th century witnessed conversion of state Medicaid programs from traditional fee-for-service programs into managed care programs. Most states now enroll most of their Medicaid beneficiaries into managed care programs.

THE SPREAD OF MANAGED CARE
TO MENTAL HEALTH SERVICES

Increasingly, managed care plans also include provisions for mental health care, usually called behavioral health plans in the language used by the insurance industry. The managed care juggernaut, in fact, made unprecedented inroads into mental health care during the last decade of the 20th century. In 1987, Xerox was the first national company to contract with a managed behavioral health company (MBHC), but in the time since, almost all large corporations and mid-sized employers have contracted with specialized behavioral health plans (Findlay, 1999). During the same time period, the majority of states adopted the use of MBHC plans to serve populations covered by Medicaid and other publicly financed programs. In the mid-1990s, from 1994 to 1998, the number of Medicaid recipients enrolled in Medicaid HMOs or state-contracted MBHC organizations doubled, from 23 percent to 54 percent (Medicaid Fact Sheet, 1999). As of 1996, Medicaid spending on mental health and substance abuse treatments accounted for about 14 percent of all national spending on such issues (McKusick, Mark, King, & Harwood, 1998).

This growth is matched in the general American population. In 1992, it was estimated that 44 percent of all people in the United States with health insurance had their mental health benefits covered by a specialty program within a managed care system (Oss, Drissel, & Clary, 1997). By 1997, it was estimated that 75 percent of people in the United States who had health insurance were covered by a behavioral health program within a managed care package (Oss et al., 1997). This estimate means that over 168 million people received mental health benefits through a managed care system.

It should be no surprise, then, that managed behavioral health care has already had an impact on most aspects of mental health care in the United States. In the future, it promises to shape the structure and delivery of mental health services as profoundly as managed care has in the domain of health care. Some of the most powerful impacts are, not surprisingly, cost-related. As inpatient care is the most expensive form of care, managed mental health care will further the trend toward deinstitutionalization and also place great emphasis on reducing admissions to and lengths-of-stay in inpatient settings. Use of short-term treatment models that are limited to periods of less than six months or treatment sessions that number less than twenty will become prevalent, as limits to reimbursements are set by third-party payers (Reid, 1997).

Other impacts are not as obvious. The linkages between acute, institutional settings and community-based mental health services will become increasingly important, something that is sorely lacking at this point. We will also probably see increasing use of carve-outs that break insurance coverage into smaller categories (such as substance abuse) and manage both the insurance and service delivery as a separate entity. This may make the mental health system more fragmented and uneven in its nature (Mechanic, 1998). In addition, carve-outs may be used as a risk management tool through use of selective criteria for determining coverage and targeting of specific client populations (Mechanic, 1998). There are arguments that mental health services simply cannot be "managed" in the same way that other forms of health care are, due to the complexity of mental illness and substance abuse problems, the ideological and conceptual debates about diagnosis and treatment, vague or nonexistent outcome criteria, confidentiality issues, and the stigma attached to mental illness (Wineburgh, 1998).

One potential impact of managed care in both health and mental health is particularly relevant to this book. It is the impact of quality management initiatives inherent in managed care. Managed care certainly imposes strong incentives for human service workers to adopt empirical practice (Corcoran & Gingerich, 1994; Reid, 1997; Thyer, 1996). Thyer (1996), for example, believes that in the near future, managed care providers, insurance companies, and third-party vendors will require the use of empirically derived standards of care in the human services. This will create a situation in which these organizations define the approved therapies for which they will provide reimbursement. In effect, these organizations will demand the use of empirical practice as a way of establishing which treatments may be considered "effective." Corcoran and Gingerich (1994) argue that the growth of managed care will further demands for the three essential elements of practice evaluation—specifying client problems and treatment goals, using suitable measurements, and analyzing client change.

The increasing pressure to establish accountability in managed care programs is so pervasive that the remainder of this chapter discusses the role of quality management in managed care. We focus in particular on one aspect of quality management—utilization management. It is here that the role of EPM may be most relevant to managed care programs and to the professionals who work within those settings.

THE ROLE OF QUALITY MANAGEMENT IN MANAGED CARE

There are many terms used to describe the process of increasing quality in programs. They include, for example, *quality assurance, quality improvement, quality management,* and *performance improvement.* Quality assurance has been somewhat replaced as a concept, since quality cannot be "assured," but simply strived for. In its place, particularly in health care, we have seen the emergence of quality improvement and quality management as concepts that are often used interchangeably.

In its current incarnation, quality management (or improvement) may be defined as "an umbrella term for all the activities that occur within an organization to assess and improve the quality of care, reengineer the process of care, and report information to internal and external customers" (Genovich-Richards, 1997). This definition includes two aspects of quality that are both critical. The first is *clinical quality,* which incorporates peer review of the structures, processes, and outcomes of professional care. This inherently maintains a client or consumer focus. The second focuses on *internal or organizational quality,* which uses traditional monitoring and evaluation techniques to focus on the organization itself. The organizational focus facilitates critical examination of the organization's operations, making judgments about the organization's processes and outcomes, and redesigning organizational processes when necessary.

The process of ensuring quality management in health or mental health settings can seem to be deceptively simple and frustratingly complex at the same time. On a basic level, quality management asks a simple question: Are our services meeting basic standards of care? These standards are set by a variety of sources, such as the Joint Commission on Accreditation of Healthcare Organizations, the National Committee for Quality Assurance, federal and state regulators, and various professional organizations (Byron Smith & Parsons, 1997). Applicable standards exist to judge almost every component of service delivery: quality of clinical care; accessibility and availability of service; utilization and management of resources; credentialing of professional staff; structures to ensure enrollees' rights and responsibilities; nature and quality of preventive services; and quality of clinical and treatment documentation.

Conducting quality review procedures, however, can be frustrating in the complexity of conceptualizing, operationalizing, collecting, analyzing, and reporting across multiple levels of service delivery. There are often whole departments in managed care organizations that strive to measure quality on different dimensions, and then to integrate these into a "picture" of quality for the organization. These departments may be named after and examine factors such as risk management (determining potential service usage and capitation rates on the basis of client characteristics like age, sex, and previous utilization of services); utilization management (monitoring of the necessity and appropriateness of services); and systems administration (responsible for areas such as accounting, marketing, enrollment, or claims). Often these various departments are overseen by a Total Quality or Quality Coordinating department or committee.

Utilization Management

Of all the quality management functions described, probably the one most relevant to practitioners, and this book, is that of utilization management. As noted, utilization management refers to the collection of techniques used by managed care companies to routinely monitor and evaluate the necessity and appropriateness of the care they provide insurance and reimbursement for (Winegar, 1992). These techniques are based on peer review processes and can be grouped into four general categories: (1) pretreatment reviews; (2) second opinion reviews; (3) continued-treatment reviews; and (4) high-cost case management (Tischler, 1990). The first two techniques occur prior to approval of client services, while the latter two occur once treatment has been started or completed.

Utilization management has developed into a critical component of any quality management program, especially in managed care. It incorporates a number of core functions that must be accomplished by every managed care plan. These include:

- Eligibility determination to determine if a client seeking service is indeed an enrolled member and is eligible for services offered by the plan

- Benefit interpretation to determine if the presenting issue is one covered by the plan

- Precertification for admission to make a decision to admit the client to inpatient or outpatient services, authorize reimbursement for care, and recommend alternative care if deemed necessary (often less costly alternatives)

- Concurrent review to facilitate case management, authorize a fixed number of care sessions, assess the need for continued treatment, and engage in discharge planning (Winegar, 1992)

Utilization management activities revolve around the appropriateness and timeliness of clinical decisions. It should be no surprise, then, that utilization management activities are increasingly being expected of, and conducted by, human service professionals such as psychologists, social workers, and other counselors. This only makes sense, as the questions addressed by the peer review mechanisms of utilization management are clinical in nature. What diagnosis is made regarding the potential client? What is the severity of the problem being presented? What concrete measures are used to make this determination? Are there safety or self-harm issues for that person or others? What treatment history does this client bring with him or her? What are the specific goals of this particular treatment episode? What treatment is being recommended for this client's problem? What alternative treatments may exist? How many sessions or visits are expected to resolve this issue? How will successful amelioration of the client's problem be recognized or measured? At what level of success is termination of this case reasonable?

One other aspect of utilization management is critical to human service professionals. The strength of utilization management lies in its emphasis on documenting the reasons for and the progress of treatment. Details regarding each of the questions listed in the previous paragraph (and others) are recorded and routinely reviewed. In fact, routine reviews are conducted for all aspects of a case, including the need for services, assessment of the client's problems, formal diagnoses of the difficulties, and the plan for treatment. This obviously includes as well the monitoring of client progress as treatment ensues. In order to facilitate decision making about issues such as client termination (as well as serve as another cost containment tool), each case is required to have concrete, measurable targets or client goals that are specified in advance. Such information is usually recorded on standard pen-and-paper or computerized forms upon which the practitioner records pertinent case details. Information gathered often includes specific descriptions and diagnoses of the client's problem, short- and long-term goals for change described in measurable terms, description of the treatment to be applied, and indicators of client progress to date. Many of the forms also include an area for general case notes and a chart or graph upon which the client's progress can be visually displayed (Corcoran & Gingerich, 1994; Tischler, 1990).

The Role of EPM in Quality and Utilization Management

Our discussion of managed care and its quality management mechanisms should make one fact clear. In the coming decades, human service professionals will be faced with much stronger demands for accountability. They will require reliable, valid assessment tools to perform the diagnoses demanded within managed care plans. They will need to better operationalize the nature and intensity of interventions applied to clients' situations. They will also need to show that their services make efficient use of resources. Most of all, they will need to show that short- and long-term client outcomes are positive and lasting.

These demands are directly related to the two types of effectiveness outlined in Chapter 1 of this book. One meaning of effectiveness focuses entirely on *what we do*—process. Assessing this form of effectiveness involves examining what services were provided, how many cases we served, what interventions were applied, how much time we spend with the average client, and so on. This is a view of effectiveness that focuses entirely on practitioner, agency, and service delivery system interventive behavior. The second meaning of effectiveness relates to *client change*—outcomes. Did we in fact observe a positive change in the targeted problems for this particular client? If not, effectiveness cannot be established.

Like those responsible for quality management programs, we believe that both process and outcome are critical for measuring effectiveness. We must know what interventive behaviors are likely to produce desired change for our clients and be able to track how such interventions are applied. At the same time, however, it really does not matter what interventions are applied if we are unable to detect or measure positive change in client problems. In short, the definitions of effectiveness inherent in the empirical practice model are fully compatible with the need for quality and utilization management programs to demonstrate effectiveness.

The three definitions of accountability offered in Chapter 1 are also fully compatible and useful within a managed care framework. For example, Kazandjian (1996) states that there are three types of measures useful for monitoring and evaluating accountability. These include: (1) structural measures that examine resources, equipment, staff numbers, certification of staff, and other inputs; (2) process measures that examine the assessment, planning, and treatment functions of care providers; and (3) outcome measures that examine the short- and long-term results, client satisfaction, and adverse effects of care. These categories closely resemble the forms of accountability identified by the empirical practice model.

In the EPM, there are three definitions of accountability. The first is focused on *commercial resource accountability*, which closely resembles the structural accountability described by Kazandjian (1996). Unlike managed care administrators, however, we are not that concerned about structural or commercial resource accountability (remember, they pay very careful attention to financial issues and cost containment). It is not that such accountability is not important; it is just that techniques for demonstrating commercial resource accountability are well established and not the focus of most human service practitioners.

The second and third sources of accountability in managed care, however, are important to us. The *service resources accountability* included in the EPM closely reflects the notion of process accountability that forms part of managed care and quality management. Like managed care administrators, human service practitioners should be concerned with their professional behaviors. Exactly what *did they do* to facilitate client change? Here again, though, extensive quality management procedures have been developed to monitor process or service resources accountability. Most computerized information systems in health care, for example, have traditionally focused on the inputs of health care providers to monitor and evaluate the inputs offered by professionals in those systems.

The final form of accountability inherent to the EPM is *service outcome accountability*, which parallels the outcome accountability in managed care. It is here that we agree with those responsible for quality management programs.

What matters in terms of service outcomes is whether we can demonstrate desired change for our clients. This also happens to be the area that both managed care and human service practitioners have struggled with the most.

This is where the EPM has the most to offer human service professionals and those who administer managed care programs. As outlined in Chapter 1, the fundamental equation of the EPM is one designed to get at the heart of effectiveness and accountability—the detection of change in a client's problem. In order to show that human service practice is effective, we must show that the service behaviors we engage in actually produce observable, measurable change in the targeted problem. Secondly, we must be able to show that the desired change is related to, or a function of, the behaviors we have performed. Again, this fundamental equation reads:

$$\Delta CP = f(X_i) + e \quad i = 1, n$$

The left side of this equation defines our dependent variable in any practice situation—the client problem. The Δ stands for "change," meaning that we seek to observe a positive difference in the client's problem when measured at two or more points in time. This side is the heart of the service outcome accountability. The right side of the equation denotes what we do to effect change in our client's problem. Our service behaviors or interventions can be symbolized as $X_1, X_2, \ldots X_n$, to signify the fact that there are potentially many different service behaviors in which to engage for just one client. And once again, the e stands for "error" and merely reminds us that perfect prediction or explanation is simply not possible when dealing with any clinical situation.

This equation has much to offer managed care providers. It offers a simple way of describing the conceptual linkages between process and outcome of care. In order to fully understand outcomes and to be able to achieve them with any kind of regularity or intensity, we need to measure and control our behaviors (process). At the same time, to measure only interventive behaviors is not enough. The fundamental criteria in assessing quality of human services is that of client change. Did the client's problem actually improve when we intervened? Did we observe an outcome?

We know that within managed care and quality management programs there are already extensive mechanisms and procedures for capturing information about the services delivered to clients. This information forms the right side of the EPM equation (ignoring the effects of error for the moment). We simply need to become adept at routinely asking critical questions about such information. As for the left side of this equation—showing client change—the techniques and tools detailed in this book offer one powerful way of showing positive client outcomes. The use of single-system techniques and standardized assessment tools should become much more common as managed care and quality management spread further into human services.

In short, managed care demands that human service professionals learn and use the fundamental procedures of empirical practice evaluation. These procedures are relatively simple:

1. Measure the client's problem.

2. Measure the client's problem repeatedly over time.

3. Assess the extent to which positive change in the client's problem (or problems) is associated with the intervention.

We firmly believe that use of these three procedures offers a powerful practice evaluation and quality management tool. The procedures involve practical and simple routines that practitioners can use to evaluate their own practice. At the same time, they offer a way of answering the questions posed by utilization management. This makes the EPM an attractive option for demonstrating accountability in the era of managed care.

The remainder of this chapter presents an example of how the EPM can be used to demonstrate accountability. It also shows a sample utilization management form that can be used to document the essential components of the practice evaluation and utilization management models.

EXAMPLE OF EMPIRICAL PRACTICE MODEL IN QUALITY MANAGEMENT PROCESS

Susan M. is a successful 46-year-old teacher in an urban public school system. She has two children, Nathan aged 17, and Erica aged 12. About two years ago she separated from her husband, and two months ago a petition for divorce was filed. Susan has been experiencing a number of difficulties of late. The relationship with her estranged partner is strained, and the pending divorce has increased the frequency and intensity of conflicts between them. There are also persistent worries about the effects of the divorce on Nathan and Erica. At the same time, Susan is experiencing financial difficulties. She is concerned that without an equitable settlement from the divorce and adequate child support from her former partner, bankruptcy could be a real possibility. All of these difficulties have had a dramatic impact on Susan. Her drinking has increased considerably in the past few months, and she is experiencing intense bouts of hopelessness. She also experiences a very strong sense of being trapped, and she feels stressed most of the time.

Susan decides to ask for help in dealing with the issues facing her. After contacting a representative of the managed care plan she belongs to through the school system, she is directed to a counseling service attached to a local hospital. The admissions worker at the hospital first conducts an initial assessment interview with Susan, and gathers details of her insurance coverage. The worker then contacts the utilization management clinician at the health care plan to which Susan belongs. The clinician consults with both Susan and the hospital admissions worker, and also speaks to another member of the utilization management team. All parties agree that initial indicators of Susan's difficulties are significant and that counseling may be in order. The admissions worker proposes that Susan be seen by a mental health therapist at the hospital for further assessment and that intervention be delivered through outpatient counseling. This is agreed to by Susan. The utilization management representative from the health care plan concurs, and authorizes initial coverage of three visits or sessions for such services.

Susan's case is referred to Ajay V., a very experienced social worker at the mental health clinic. Ajay is able to see Susan for an intake interview within a week of her first visit to the hospital. Due to a waiting list for further services, however, Susan will have to wait approximately two weeks before treatment can really begin. During the intake interview, Ajay and Susan discuss the range of issues she is facing. There are certainly a number of issues—conflict with her estranged husband, financial pressures, growing concerns about drinking, depression, and stress. Together they decide that the first issues to be tackled will be to help Susan cope with the stress she is facing and to work toward alleviating her depression. Ajay administers the Generalized Contentment Scale (Hudson, 1982) and the Index of Clinical Stress (Abell, 1991) while Susan is in the office. Scores on both scales (54 and 48 respectively) show that Susan is indeed experiencing clinically significant problems with both depression and stress. Her level of depression is a particular concern, and the therapist probes to ensure that self-harm is not a possibility. Once he determines that it is not, Ajay asks Susan if she would be willing to complete each scale two more times before they meet to begin treatment. Susan agrees to do so.

Two weeks later they have their second session. Ajay collects the scales completed by Susan at home and scores them. The results of these scores are shown in Figure 9.1. The feedback provided by the two scales and the visual representation of scale scores offer Ajay a great deal of important information. They show that while Susan's stress scores seem to have decreased somewhat, her level of depression has risen substantially. The depression scores are approaching very serious levels; the depression needs to be dealt with immediately. The fact that scores on both scales remain substantially above the clinical cutting score also shows Ajay that no improvement has occurred for either problem in the absence of treatment. Both problems certainly continue to warrant professional intervention.

During this session, Ajay and Susan set a target of lowering scores from both scales to below the clinical cutting score. An initial treatment plan is outlined for Susan. It includes three components: (1) arranging for Susan to work with a publicly funded center that provides information and assistance for divorcing parents; (2) individual counseling sessions with Ajay; and (3) having Susan learn techniques of progressive muscle relaxation so that she develops effective strategies for dealing with stress.

As discussed earlier in this chapter, a critical component of utilization management is that of concurrent reviews of the treatment provided. This, of course, happens in Susan's case as well. Even though initial authorization is received to deliver services for three sessions, the therapist must communicate with the utilization management worker to assess the need for continued

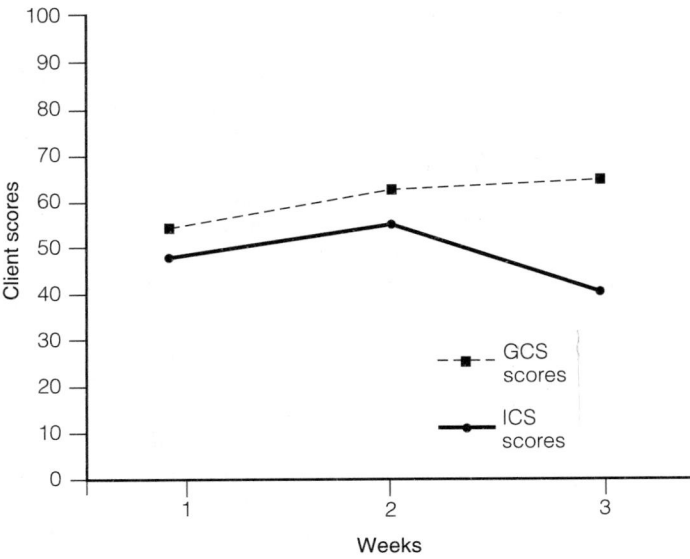

FIGURE 9.1 Initial assessment of Susan M.

treatment. Details of the treatment goals and treatment plan are shared and discussed, and the projected number of service sessions is estimated. In Susan's case, the utilization management worker suggests the incorporation of biofeedback equipment into the progressive muscle relaxation routine, equipment that is available through another office within the health care plan. Susan's projected discharge date is set, and authorization is given for another six sessions.

Treatment begins as planned. A meeting is arranged for Susan to see an information officer at the Center for Mediation and Child Support, which provides separating and divorcing parents with information about the rights, laws, court services, and other supports that apply to them. She and Ajay also begin the individual counseling sessions, and training in progressive muscle relaxation is started using biofeedback equipment. The counseling and progressive muscle relaxation sessions occur for another four-week period, with sessions at the mental health clinic every week. At each session, Ajay administers the GCS and ICS scales. He maintains regular documentation regarding Susan's case, knowing that written updates and summaries will be expected by the health care plan. He also has one phone contact with the utilization management worker after the four weeks of intervention.

Unfortunately, but not surprisingly, the news is not completely positive. Figure 9.2 shows that Ajay has charted Susan's GCS and ICS scores at regular intervals during the month of intervention. Susan's level of depression does seem to be decreasing substantially, though it is still obviously an issue. Her level of stress, however, seems to be staying high; it has not decreased at all.

The feedback offered by this graph is confirmed by the verbal feedback shared by Susan. The Center for Mediation and Child Support has been very helpful, and she feels much more secure about her rights and financial future. In fact, she admits to feeling pretty positive and hopeful at times. Nor is she drinking as much. Moreover, the sessions with Ajay have proven useful, and she values the therapy he is offering. At the same time, however, things are still stressful for her. Susan reports that the progressive muscle relaxation seems to work while Ajay is leading her through it, but she is having a hard time making it work for her at home. Perhaps just as importantly, levels of conflict with her estranged husband have actually worsened, as issues regarding custody/access and child support have arisen. They argue more often, particularly when the children are being picked up and dropped off. There are also strong disagreements emerging around issues like discipline and general rules for the children.

After interpreting the feedback offered by Susan and the graph, Ajay again contacts the utilization management worker. They agree that individual counseling should continue. As for the progressive muscle relaxation, there is considerable discussion about whether to continue such training. It has not yet proven effective. The health plan worker suggests that Ajay provide Susan with audiotapes specifically designed to help lead people through the relaxation process, so that she can continue to practice the technique at home. They agree that going through the process at the clinic, however, will be discontinued. Her stress levels will, of course, continue to be monitored over the coming weeks.

Treatment continues for the final four weeks of authorized service delivery. Susan continues to make progress toward the targeted goal of decreasing her depression. By the end of this period, her GCS scores suggest that depression is no longer a clinically significant issue. Her level of stress also drops, even though it is not yet consistently below the cutting score. This occurs despite the fact that Susan, as she reports, has discontinued practicing the progressive muscle relaxation at home. She simply feels that it does not work for her. Ajay is, of course, surprised by the decrease in stress levels, given that the prescribed treatment has not been continued during the period of improvement. Susan, however, reports that issues surrounding the divorce have been for the most part resolved, and that arguments regarding the children have been far fewer. In fact, there is now very little contact between the two parents.

One week before Susan's authorized treatment is scheduled to be discontinued, the utilization management worker contacts Ajay to inquire about Susan's progress. Together they discuss with Susan the progress of treatment. Given that Susan's depression levels are below clinical levels and that she feels her stress levels are close to the same cutting point, Susan feels that treatment is no longer required. They concur, and the case is closed after the last session.

The final documentation forwarded by Ajay to the utilization management worker and the health care plan is shown in Figure 9.3. This figure shows a fairly typical recording form used in managed care and utilization management (this one happens to be a computerized form). It incorporates areas to record both process and outcome information for the case being referred to, and details the key information required to conduct a utilization review. This includes a record

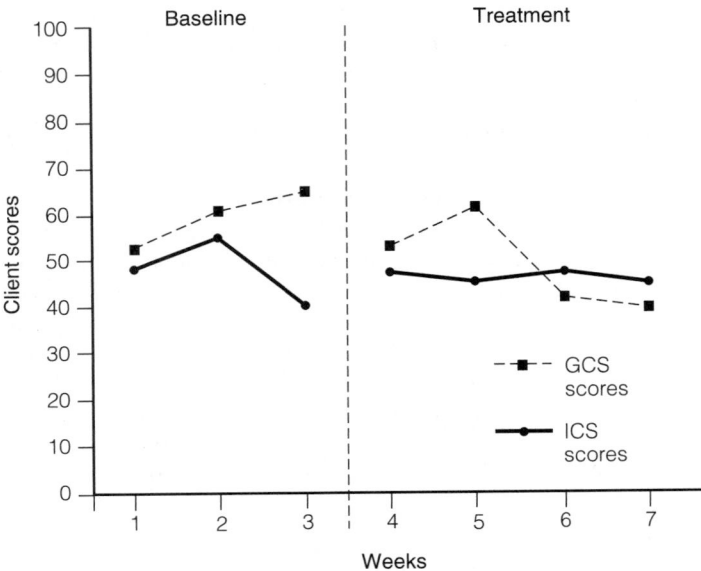

FIGURE 9.2 Baseline and treatment for Susan M.

of the assessment tools used to conduct diagnoses of the client's targeted problems, scores that address the issue of problem severity, specific and concrete treatment goals, a plan for intervention, and even estimates of the number of sessions anticipated for this client. The form also includes areas to record the dates of each client contact, client scores on the selected measures over time, and the length of service provided by the practitioner. Finally, the utilization management form includes a computerized client chart (as depicted in Figure 9.2) that can be used to record a visual representation of the client's progress over time. This chart is generic enough that it can be used to record scores from most measures. Numeric labels for the vertical axis can be added by the practitioner, and scores from multiple measures can be graphed on the same chart.

Figure 9.3 shows the complete history of Susan's case. It shows her initial diagnosis, the goals set for intervention, the treatments planned, and the number of sessions planned and implemented in her case. It also includes a few brief case notes made by Ajay and a record of the amount (duration) of service he has delivered. Finally, Susan's progress is portrayed visually on the single case graph, showing that she has indeed made significant progress. In effect, this one form together with the AB single case design graph has recorded both the process and outcomes appropriate to Susan's treatment.

The case presented here is admittedly a simple one. It does, however, show how utilization management personnel fit within managed care plans. Utilization management personnel fulfill a variety of functions within managed care. First and foremost, they serve a cost containment function for

Client: Susan M.　　　**Case ID:** 2694-99　**Worker:** Ajay V.

Intake date (mm/dd/yy): 10/16/99　　　**Referral source:** Self-referred

Targeted problems:

#1. Depression—situational in nature

#2. Clinical stress (global)

Identified measures:

#1. Generalized Content Scale

　(Hudson, 1990) Scores: 0–100

#2. Index of Clinical Stress

　(Abell, 1996) Scores: 0–100

Treatment goals:

#1. Lower level of depression to below clinical level (GCS score of 30 or lower)

#2. Lower clinical stress to below clinical level (ICS score of 30 or lower)

Treatment plan:

#1. a) Refer to Mediation and Child Support Center　b) Individual counseling

#2. a) Training in progressive muscle relaxation, use of biofeedback

Planned # of sessions: 11　　　　**Actual # of sessions:** 10

Date	Case notes	Score #1	Score #2	Length of service (min)
10/15/99	Initial session. GCS and ICS administered, and given as homework.	54	48	60
10/29/99	2nd baseline measure. Done at client's home on 10/20/99.	62	55	—
10/29/99	3rd baseline measure. Treatment goals and plan set.	65	39	90
11/01/99	Telephone referral made to Joan Davies, Mediation & Child Support Ctr.	—	—	15
11/05/99	Affect improved today. S. upbeat, through very angry with husband.	55	47	60
11/12/99	S. much more depressed, difficult to engage today. Finances are pressing.	63	45	60
11/19/99	S. thrilled with help of Joan Davies. Depression score markedly lower. Tentative child support agreed to. Concerned about no reduction in stress.	43	47	90
11/29/99	Continued conflict with husband. Disputes common regarding children.	39	40	60
12/06/99	Heated argument with husband. Stress higher. S. says PMR not working.	29	44	90
12/13/99	Divorce issues almost settled. S. discontinued PMR, audiotape provided.	26	33	60
12/20/99	Both scores near cutting score. S. very upbeat today.	28	29	60
01/06/00	S. wishes to stop treatment. Overall functioning well, stress still a bit high.	26	33	45

FIGURE 9.3 Quality management form for Susan M.

managed care companies by identifying and resolving usage patterns that can result in excessive resource expenditures or inefficient practices. They do so by reviewing and assessing proposed use of professional services; suggesting alternatives when deemed necessary or beneficial; assisting with scheduling; facilitating discharge planning; offering a vehicle for consultation to clinicians; and monitoring the continuity of care delivered to clients. Finally, they also provide input on referrals and other services available in the community. All of these functions essentially offer a dual focus on *commercial resource accountability* and *service resources accountability*. They define precisely what resources, of what size or intensity, and at what cost are being brought to bear on the problem being addressed.

At the same time, however, utilization management personnel also fulfill a service outcome function by monitoring and assessing whether professional services appear to bring about the desired change for the client. In managed care, such personnel are the ones who often ask if observable client change has occurred. This is where quality management and utilization management have the most in common with the empirical practice model. Utilization management demands concrete definitions of client problems, clearly identified and operationalized client goals, systematic measurement, and the analysis of change over time. These are, in fact, the hallmarks of the EPM. As such, the EPM offers a practical and powerful way for practitioners to answer the accountability demands being placed upon them.

The example provided describes a practitioner who engages in empirically based practice evaluation. Ajay V. applied a basic AB design using two standardized measures to track client outcomes and to obtain some form of evidence regarding his effectiveness. The final quality management form submitted to the managed care plan does indeed suggest, from a clinical perspective, that the individual counseling and progressive muscle relaxation *may* have been a causal factor in the decrease in Susan's depression and stress. From a scientific perspective, this may certainly be incorrect. The services offered by the Mediation and Child Support Center may have been the key factor in Susan's improvement. Indeed, it is likely that resolution of many issues surrounding the divorce had as much to do with Susan's lower depression and stress levels as any other factor. The evidence for Ajay's effectiveness is, therefore, not compelling from a *scientific* perspective. However, given the realities of many practice situations, this may be the best evidence that Ajay or any of us could expect. After all, the EPM is meant to be a practice activity that provides empirical feedback to practitioners—not a strictly followed scientific endeavor.

Measurement Tools

10

The Role of Measurement in Practice

This is the first chapter in Part II of this book. Since Part II focuses on measurement tools suitable for 21st century practice evaluation, it only makes sense that we begin by looking at the role of measurement in practice. In this chapter, therefore, we discuss the nature and utility of measurement in more detail than we have in earlier chapters of this book. This chapter provides the conceptual underpinnings required for determining what makes a good measurement procedure and for selecting measurement procedures for use in practice. We discuss the practical functions of measurement, as well as positive and negative attitudes that practitioners display toward the process of measurement. Finally, we explore how two critical measurement concepts—reliability and validity—affect the measures selected to monitor and evaluate practice. Let us begin by discussing the nature of measurement.

THE NATURE OF MEASUREMENT

Imagine a young girl named Nyako S. walking down a sidewalk. She is playing that age-old game of trying to jump over the sidewalk cracks. Upon getting to a particularly long unbroken section in the sidewalk, she pauses, makes a quick mental calculation, and then makes a longer jump than usual to get over the next crack. The jump is successful, and her feet land nimbly on the other side. Quite pleased with herself, Nyako continues along, skipping happily toward her destination.

Most of us have performed countless acts that are very similar to Nyako's accomplishment. We speculate about whether we can pick up a heavy object, should adjust the heat under a simmering pot, need to slow down upon seeing a speed limit sign, or need to try on a different pair of trousers. Like Nyako's jump, all of these acts involve measurement. Like Nyako, however, we rarely use the language of measurement when we think about such common occurrences. We also rarely think about the tools or indicators that we use to make decisions while we engage in these daily activities, such as tape measures, the smell of burning food in the kitchen, speedometers, or even a tag in a pair of pants. All such aids are really just measuring devices that help us describe, assess, and understand some aspect of a current situation, object, or phenomenon and then make necessary changes in our behavior or activities.

These very basic notions also apply to the conduct of professional practice. Social workers engage in the measurement process every day. This is true in almost every aspect of practice. For example, assessing a client's problem is really just measurement by a different name. On a broader level, every human service agency must measure the resources available to it, the number and type of clients being served, the need for new services, and so on. None of these functions could be achieved without some form of measurement.

The critical role of measurement in practice and in life in general lies in its ability to help us observe, describe, understand, infer, compare, and analyze the world around us. This does not mean that we always require highly specific and systematic ways of measuring this world. In both daily life and professional practice, we often rely on rather unsystematic, subjective means of measurement. In practice, for example, we often use subjective and unsystematic procedures to work our way through an initial interview with a client. An unstructured, free-style interview is an example of a more unsystematic measurement (assessment) method (Groth-Marnot, 1990).

We firmly believe, however, that more formal, structured measurement tools can serve to enhance and deepen our ability to assess, describe, and understand various aspects of our clients' problems and of our practice endeavors. In some practice endeavors, the use of standardized measurement tools is even considered to be a part of the requisite standard of care we must provide for our clients (Bongar et al., 1998; Fremouw, de Perczel, & Ellis, 1990).

MEASUREMENT DEFINED

With the principle discussed in the last section in mind, let us take a closer look at specific definitions of measurement. In a technical sense, measurement is the assignment of numbers, words, or other symbols to persons, objects, or phenomena according to well-specified rules in order to represent attributes and characteristics of these persons, objects, or phenomena (Crocker & Algina, 1986; Lord & Novick, 1968; Nunnally, 1978). In simple terms, though, measurement is a process of representation or description. Anytime we seek to describe or represent something, we are seeking to measure it in some way, shape, or form. A measurement procedure produces a "score" that is composed of words (as in a DSM-IV diagnosis, for example), numbers (such as temperature in degrees Celsius or Farenheit), or both. Blythe and Tripodi (1989) characterize measurement as a translation process that involves:

1. Identifying a concept to be measured
2. Specifying an indicator (or indicators) of the concept
3. Operationally defining relevant data and a way of ordering the data (such as determining how to assign degrees from low to high, and so on)
4. Determining the validity and reliability of the scores produced by the resultant measurement procedure

Two aspects of these definitions need to be highlighted. Measurement is a process of (a) identifying and evaluating properties or characteristics (b) by the use of indicators. By this we mean, first of all, that measurement involves looking at particular "characteristics" of persons, objects, or phenomena. In many cases, the property or characteristic is not directly observable in the same way that something like "height" or "eye color" would be. For example, depression is a problem commonly experienced by clients, yet "depression" is not a thing that can be seen running down the street or sitting in a chair next to the client. We cannot directly observe it in quite the same way that we can observe and study a chemical in a beaker. Depression involves, to a great extent, a set of private events experienced by the client, though it is also manifested in some behaviors that are directly observable by others. In such cases, we must look for the presence of behaviors or physiological states that point to the presence and severity of depression. These behaviors or physiological states that point to the presence and severity of depression are called indicators (Ghiselli, Campbell, & Zedeck, 1981). When asking clients directly about their problems, we ask questions about, and look and listen for, various indicators that will help us to pinpoint the nature and severity of the issues the client faces.

The implication of this fact for using measurement in practice is that we must clearly define, nominally and observationally, the concept(s) of interest. To nominally define means to specifically name the concept (characteristic or property) that is to be measured and to give a verbal definition. To observationally define the concept means to specify (1) the things, behaviors, or events that will serve as indicators of the broader concept defined in the verbal definition, and (2) the procedures we will use to observe the indicators and to summarize our observations into a final product—the "score" produced by the measurement procedure. The final product of the measurement procedure—the "score"—can be a verbal description or classification, such as a written psychosocial assessment or a diagnosis, or a numerical index, such as a score from a short-form scale. For example, suppose that we are interested in knowing if a client is depressed and, if so, to what degree. We would first need a verbal definition of depression. We would also need a complete specification of the entire set of indicators of depression. This process has been called "domain specification" (Messick, 1989). Such indicators might be a sad affect, change in sleeping patterns, change in appetite, anhedonia, and so on. Finally, we would need a complete specification as to how we will combine our observations of the indicators of depression into a final product, or score.

Levels of Measurement

Measurement can be further understood by considering the so-called levels of measurement. The most fundamental level of measurement is called nominal or categorical. In nominal or categorical measurement, we assign the person, object, or phenomenon to one of several mutually exclusive and exhaustive categories dependent upon the particular characteristic, or set of characteristics, possessed by the person, object, or phenomenon. These categories are qualitatively distinct in nature, and differences between categories do not imply any differences in quantity. For example, we can assign persons, on the basis of their "gender," to the categories of *male* and *female*. We can measure marital status by assigning a person to the categories of *single, married, divorced, in a common-law relationship, widowed*, and so forth. A geologist will assign rocks to one of three categories: sedimentary, metamorphic, or igneous. The key notion in nominal or categorical measurement is that we are using it to describe—and we are describing by assigning the person, object, or phenomenon to a specific category dependent upon the possession of a specific characteristic or set of characteristics. We cannot, however, perform any useful mathematical operations on nominal data other than counting the number of persons, objects, or phenomena in each category.

The second level of measurement is ordinal. In ordinal measurement, we are able to rank-order persons, objects, or phenomena in terms of which ones possess more of or less of the characteristic being measured. However, with an ordinal measure, we cannot specify how much more of or less of the characteristic that a particular person, object, or phenomenon has relative to another. For example, an ordinal measure of depression would allow us to rank-order persons from least depressed to most depressed; but it would not allow us to specify how much more or less depressed one person is relative to another.

Goal attainment scaling is sometimes used to assess client progress (Bloom et al., 1999). If the extent to which a goal is reached is scaled "complete," "partial," "minimal," or "zero attainment," then the measurement is ordinal. Each of these categories, respectively, indicates a lesser degree of goal attainment, though we cannot determine how much less attainment is accomplished between any of the categories, such as between the "partial" and "minimal" rankings. The permissible mathematical operations with ordinal data are also limited. For example, we cannot use division with ordinal rankings, and it is meaningless to try to interpret the mean and standard deviation of a set of scores from an ordinal scale (Nunnally, 1978).

The next level of measurement is interval. With interval-level measurement, we are not only able to rank-order individuals in terms of whether one person (or object or phenomenon) possesses more or less of the characteristic being measured relative to another person (or object or phenomenon), but we also are able to specify how much more of or less of the characteristic one possesses relative to another. This is because an interval-level measure has a metric that is scaled into equal-interval, or equally spaced, units. Interval measures, though, have no absolute zero point to anchor these scales. An absolute zero point is a scale point that indicates the complete absence of the characteristic being measured. Perhaps two of the more familiar interval-level measures are the Fahrenheit and Celsius scales for measuring temperature. Each of these systems makes use of a scale that is broken into equal intervals and that is numbered sequentially. Both systems also have a point on their scale called "0 degrees." These zero points do not, however, indicate the complete absence of "temperature"; they are simply arbitrary points assigned on the scales. For example, the zero point (i.e., 0 degrees) on the Celsius (or Centigrade) scale is the freezing point of water.

In human services, the most common interval-like measures are the scores produced by standardized scales, such as those in the CASS software, described later in this book. The CASS scales produce scores that range from 0 to 100, with higher scores indicative of a greater degree or severity of some problem in personal, interpersonal, or social functioning. There is some debate about whether standardized scales such as those in the CASS software produce scores that are "truly interval." However, for all practical purposes, the scores on these scales can be considered to be interval-level (Crocker & Algina, 1986; Nunnally, 1978).

The next, and final, level of measurement is called ratio. A ratio scale is an interval-level measure that possesses an absolute zero point. An absolute zero point is a scale point that represents the complete and total absence of the characteristic being measured. The Kelvin (or absolute) scale for measuring temperature is an example of a ratio scale. The zero point on this scale—called absolute zero—indicates the complete absence of temperature (or heat). Other examples of ratio measures are "the number of times a person has been married" and "number of children." In each of these cases, a zero indicates the complete absence of the characteristic being measured. In the first case, a zero indicates that a person has never been married, while in the second it indicates that a person or couple has absolutely no children. We can use the full range of mathematical operations with ratio measures.

THE FUNCTIONS OF MEASUREMENT

Measurement is fundamental to practice. It is a powerful tool that can be used to enhance the conduct of professional practice. It can help to expand the comprehensiveness and improve the accuracy of assessments, interventions, and general decision making. In fact, it is impossible to adequately gauge the nature and severity of a client's problem without some form of measurement. It is also impossible to apply an intervention, or to stop it, without measurement. Neither the practitioner nor the client can tell how far the client has progressed without some form of measurement. Measurement can be, and often is, conducted in some informal, subjective manner. We argue, though, that more formal measurement routines make all the processes better. Let us take a few minutes to explore these statements in more detail by examining the various functions of measurement.

The Axioms of Treatment

A number of years ago, one of the authors proposed four axioms of treatment (Hudson, 1978). These axioms, which explicitly state the critical role that measurement plays in practice, were quite controversial at the time (and probably still are for some folks). These axioms are: (1) If you cannot measure a client's problem, it does not exist; (2) If you cannot measure a client's problem, you cannot treat it; (3) If you cannot measure an intervention, it does not exist; and (4) If you cannot measure an intervention, you cannot administer it. Let us consider these axioms in light of our discussion about the role of measurement in practice.

The first axiom states that if we cannot measure a client's problem, it does not exist. Let us think about this assertion. The most fundamental level of measurement is nominal, or categorical. At this most basic level, then, we should be able to measure the client's problem as a categorical variable: it is either happening now, or it is not. It is either occurring at a particular point in time, or it is not. If it is not possible to measure a client's problem at this fundamental level, it means that we cannot tell when, or even if, the client's problem is occurring. If we, the client, or anyone else cannot tell when, or if, the client's problem is occurring, then we are in no position to be able to determine if the problem is more or less intense, or worse or better, now than it was at some other point in time. In this case, our client's problem is, therefore, "something" whose occurrence no one is able to specify; that is, no one is able to specify when the problem is occurring, or when it is not occurring. Thus, we cannot tell when the client is experiencing this "something" more (or less) intensely (or frequently) relative to some other point in time. In a very real and important sense, then, the client's problem does not exist.

The second axiom states that if we cannot measure a client's problem, it cannot be treated. This assertion simply follows from the first. If it is impossible to even know when (or if) the client is experiencing the problem, there is certainly no way to intervene.

The third axiom states that if we cannot measure an intervention, it does not exist. Again, the most fundamental level of measurement is categorical. The categorical measurement of an intervention implies, at a minimum, that we can tell when, or if, an intervention is "on" or "off." It implies that we can, at a minimum, describe the intervention in such a manner that it is possible to determine if the procedure has (or has not) been implemented. If we cannot tell when a treatment procedure has started, or even if it has started, then we are in a sorry situation indeed. In a very real sense, if we cannot even tell if a "treatment" has started, or if it has been implemented at a particular point in time, then the treatment does not exist.

The fourth axiom follows immediately from the third. It is just not possible to do something—an intervention—when it is not possible to tell whether it has been implemented. Just imagine trying to do something when it is impossible to know when you are (or are not) doing it. In fact, this axiom suggests the following important corollary: If you cannot measure an intervention, you cannot teach anyone else how to implement it. Just imagine trying to teach others to do something when it is impossible to know when the "something" is occurring.

Refining Description

A practitioner's first task is to determine the exact nature of the client's problem. This task is often far more complex than it appears at first glance. Many times clients present general statements such as "I hate my son," "I just feel like giving up," or "I can't seem to control my temper anymore." Our challenge is to turn these vague statements into concrete knowledge about our client's problem and to develop educated suppositions about how to intervene.

What makes this assessment process even more difficult is that each client can experience and express the same issues in very unique ways. When dealing with chronic pain sufferers, for example, we know that there are cultural and gender differences in the expression of pain (Melzack & Wall, 1988). Some individuals openly voice the extent and location of their pain, while others seem to stoically suffer in silence. The same pattern is true for many other personal and social issues. Each client will have unique aspects in her or his ability to communicate and the manner in which this is done.

Given these complexities, it should be no surprise that we face challenges in estimating the presence and/or magnitude of our clients' personal and interpersonal problems. We cannot "crawl inside the client's head" to fully understand how issues such as stress, depression, or anger are manifested or experienced for that specific individual. Even very common problems, having many common indicators across persons, develop one or more subtle dimensions or aspects depending upon the unique character and life circumstances of that client.

Measurement helps us to tap into these subtle and varied dimensions of client problems. Good measures, particularly standardized measures, help us to more thoroughly and accurately describe client problems. This is accomplished in a number of ways. Good measures, for example, offer rapid assessment techniques that are comprehensive, yet easily applied throughout the assessment process. The domain sampling model allows us to define a concept or construct comprehensively by including aspects of the concept that are both common and unique to persons, and yet actually employ only a small sample of these indicators on our measurement tools. This becomes critical because we usually have limited opportunities to conduct assessment procedures before intervention must be started. The growth of managed care initiatives is a cogent reminder of this fact. We also need to keep in mind that the environment into which clients are placed during assessment is usually at least a little (if not a lot) foreign to them. They are asked to enter a strange environment, sit down with someone they barely (or do not) know, and talk about sensitive and troubling aspects of their lives. These factors can sometimes lead clients to give misleading self-reports, either consciously or unconsciously. Numerous factors can also bias our perceptions and questions in such a way as to lead us to erroneous conclusions (Dawes, 1994; Garb, 1998; Gilovich, 1991; Meier, 1994). Measurement tools provide additional pieces of information that cannot be obtained in any other way. In this sense, they give us a more rounded picture of our client's situation by allowing us to compare verbal self-reports with the information obtained on standardized measures. This multimethod assessment process helps us to triangulate—to corroborate and correct—information that we obtain through any of the methods (interview, questionnaire, etc.) we use in our work with clients.

This point was clearly illustrated for one of the authors several years ago. He was helping a family service agency incorporate the Multi-Problem Screening Inventory (MPSI), one of the CASS scales, into the agency's routine assessment procedures. One of the agency's caseworkers worked with a young female adolescent brought to the agency by her mother. The young woman had been in a residential facility while being treated for suicidal depression. The residential facility had just released the teenager as "cured" on the same day that her insurance benefits had expired. The young woman's mother brought her to the family service agency because she was (justifiably) concerned that her daughter might still be depressed and suicidal.

The caseworker interviewed the teenager and her mother. The main purpose of the interview was to determine whether the young woman was still suicidal. During the interview, the teenager repeatedly and convincingly denied that she was still suicidal. She told the caseworker that she had made progress on her problems while in the residential facility, felt much better, and was no longer thinking about killing herself. The teenager convinced both the caseworker and her mother that she was feeling much better and that she was certainly not suicidal. The caseworker had her complete the MPSI and then sent her home with her mother.

After the teenager and her mother left, the caseworker scored the MPSI and was both horrified and confused. The MPSI contains a suicidal ideation subscale, and the young woman's score on this subscale was 96—nearly the highest score possible (100) on this subscale. The score suggested that she was extremely suicidal, contrary to her verbal self-reports. The caseworker immediately called the young woman on the telephone, informed her of her score on the suicidal ideation subscale, and asked her to help him resolve his confusion: her words said that she was fine, while her score on the suicidal ideation subscale told a dramatically different story. What was going on? The teenager told him that she was, indeed, still very suicidal but that she had not wanted to reveal this in the interview because she had not wanted to upset her mother. The use of the standardized measure as a source of information backing up the interview allowed the caseworker to obtain critical information that the interview had failed to gather. This is by no means the only situation of this type that the authors (and their colleagues) have encountered through the years. The use of standardized measures is very critical and beneficial for augmenting the information obtained in the traditional client-worker interactions;

indeed, in some circumstances, it is considered a critical component of an adequate standard of care (Fremouw et al., 1990).

One other aspect of description should be mentioned. We often focus on the issues and problems that our clients face. Our clients' problems do not have to be the only things we focus on. Measurement can also help to describe the assets, strengths, and accomplishments that clients bring to the therapeutic process. For instance, we could monitor emotionally withdrawn clients' ability to express their feelings to their partners. This could be done during both baseline and intervention phases. In both phases, the act of measuring strengths can be very empowering and exciting for clients.

Enhancing Precision

Suppose we are working with a family in which both parents express discontent with their adolescent son. They both suggest that his behavior is destructive around the home, and that he has regular outbursts when asked to do chores or his homework. They also offer reports of stolen money, repeated lies, and broken curfews. As practitioners, we face a number of key questions. Is this child's behavior as bad as his parents say? If not, how bad is it? The parents obviously believe that their child demonstrates severe behavior problems. But should some extreme intervention be used, or is the boy's behavior problems moderate enough so that a less extreme intervention is appropriate? To adequately answer these questions, we would need a firm sense of how severe the boy's problems really are. We need precision in our assessment.

Now consider a measure that is available to deliver more precision in the assessment, the Children's Behavior Rating Scale, or CBRS (Hudson, 1997). This instrument requires parents to rate the kinds of behavioral problems their child is experiencing. The product of the CBRS is a score that ranges from 0 to 100, with a score of 0 representing the relative absence of behavioral problems and 100 representing severe behavioral problems.

If we asked these parents to complete the CBRS, the father might produce a score of 32, and the mother a score of 61. What do these results tell us? They would suggest that both parents perceive clinically significant behavioral problems from their child, since scores above 30 are clinically significant (Hudson, 1997). This is important. The results also tell us, however, that the mother believes these problems are much more severe than her partner does. Clearly there are differing perceptions, and these differences are important issues to explore. By using the CBRS for an initial assessment, we have accomplished a number of things. We have obtained a more refined sense of the magnitude of the boy's behavior problem. At the same time, however, we have also identified familial contexts and differing perceptions that need to be explored. Together all of this information forms the basis for further questioning, dialog, issue clarification, and comparisons about progress.

Many client problems are, of course, not as simple as the previous example suggests. This child's behavioral problems may be related to a number of other concerns—depression, low self-esteem, substance abuse, or dysfunctional family relationships, for example. As skilled practitioners we would obviously want to take a multidimensional approach to fully explore the complexities of this case. This multidimensional approach, however, poses a difficult challenge of integrating and interpreting large amounts of information. Even in these complex situations, though, there are helpful tools available in the form of well-developed multidimensional measurement scales, as we discuss later.

Facilitating Practice Decisions

Measures and other forms of information are useless if they do not facilitate important practice decisions. Every step of the helping process requires us to make decisions. Is this client eligible for services here? Is the client facing an emergency or crisis that requires immediate intervention? What issues do we need to explore in more depth? What should the client's treatment goals be? Which collateral contacts need to be made in this case? Is our intervention working, or do we need to make changes? Has the client made sufficient progress for us to consider the termination of treatment?

The principles and techniques of measurement help practitioners organize the information needed to answer these kinds of questions. Thinking about measurement forces us to ask, "What information is really necessary to understand and intervene in this case?" It also makes us ask, "How does this information specifically relate to the client goals we have agreed upon?" Answering both of these questions is essential for effective practice. This is true because for any one case, there are many possible diagnoses, client objectives, interventions, and outcomes. The information provided by measurement helps to focus our efforts and provide boundaries for good decision making.

Improving Information Feedback

We have stated that the greatest strength of single-system designs is their ability to provide immediate and relevant feedback to practitioners. This could not be accomplished without the use of measurement. Good measurement makes it easier to determine whether the target of intervention has improved, remained the same, or deteriorated. It also helps to determine how much improvement has been made, and how far the client still has to go in order to reach her or his goals.

All practitioners regularly assess their client's progress subjectively, usually through interview techniques. Sometimes the subjective assessment is quite effective. Monitoring is a very complex process, however. Practice situations often involve dealing with multiple problem areas simultaneously. Even if the subjective assessment is accurate, monitoring all of these problem areas subjectively can be very time-consuming. Complicating the process even more is the fact that change in client problems is rarely a steady, continual progression. Clients typically face highs and lows that can produce unstable patterns during the course of assessment and intervention.

The regular use of measurement tools helps to simplify the process of monitoring client change. By repeatedly measuring the client's problems and/or positive achievements, we obtain current and relevant information. It is such information that helps us to judge the client's progress, make decisions about the rate and direction of change, and make alterations to treatment if necessary. This process is much more than just looking at the client's outcomes to determine if he or she has reached the point at which he or she no longer requires our assistance. Measurement as information feedback is much broader, and provides critical information on a regular and routine basis that is used incrementally to refine our practice efforts.

Ensuring Legal Accountability

There are two aspects of legal accountability that make measurement increasingly important. The first is the trend toward using human service practitioners as expert witnesses and valued professionals in judicial settings. That is, practitioners are frequently called upon to present the results of their home visits, in-depth consultations, direct observations, and collateral interviews in courts-of-law. Practitioners are also asked to provide expert opinions about the implications of these processes. In such cases, measurement offers at least a couple of benefits for practitioners. It offers a means for them to triangulate their findings and opinions with a data source or sources that are known to produce reliable and valid scores. Triangulation is very important in judicial circumstances, as it permits practitioners to combine diverse sources and types of information to demonstrate the thoroughness of their information gathering as well as the consistency in their interpretations and judgments (Bongar, 1991; Fremouw et al., 1990). The use of formal measurement procedures also provides a framework and language that lawyers and jurists can easily understand. This assists the practitioner in fully explaining the case at hand and gives others a deeper appreciation of the case. For these reasons, the use of measurement adds another layer of professional accountability for the practitioner who must appear in court.

The second aspect of legal accountability is not as positive and remains (thankfully) relatively rare. This is the growing possibility that practitioners might face liability suits challenging the validity of their professional decisions, actions, and lack of actions. There are already a few cases of this unhappy occurrence. We know, for example, of a case in which a child welfare worker faced legal consequences for allegedly failing to protect a child who died at the hands of his parents. In such cases, the use of formal measurement procedures offers practitioners a stronger foundation on which to argue that they have provided an adequate standard of care. It is much more difficult to argue neglect, inadequate assessments, inappropriate treatment, or lack of professional judgment when the practitioner is backed by information that came from a variety of methods and sources, and that includes valid and reliable data from formal measurement tools (Bongar, 1991; Woody, 1997).

We do not want to overemphasize the possibility that a practitioner will be taken to court by a dissatisfied client. The risk may be greater, however, in times of fiscal retrenchment, when caseloads and administrative pressures increase for human service workers. At such times, it can be tempting to let the process of comprehensive assessment and measurement slide in the face of such pressures. It should be recognized, however, that well-documented and data-supported practice offers a powerful tool for ensuring legal accountability and promoting positive judicial outcomes (Woody, 1997).

Attitudes About Measurement

Discussing the role of measurement in practice would not be complete without a few comments about the attitudes that practitioners display toward measurement. Practitioners display a remarkable diversity of opinions about measurement. At one end of the spectrum are those who are completely enamored with the measurement process and sometimes bend the therapeutic process to fit the requirements of rigorous measurement routines. At the other end of the spectrum are those who decry the use of any formal measurement, arguing that it imposes artificial and superficial labels to phenomena that cannot, in principle, be objectively quantified (see, for example, the letters to the editor in response to Hudson, 1978).

A reasoned approach, of course, falls somewhere between these two extremes. The complete rejection of measurement on philosophical or ideological grounds simply robs practitioners of a tool that is indispensable to practice. Since measurement is description, it is simply impossible to outright reject it. Practice cannot occur without description. It is more likely that the most strident critics of measurement procedures will reject formal measurement methods that produce quantitative scores in favor of unsystematic procedures that produce verbal descriptions, such as free-style interviews (Groth-Marnat, 1990; Meier, 1994). However, the quality of practice suffers as a result of such a narrow view. By the same token, the blind advocacy of formal, standardized measurement is also a narrow and damaging position. Imposing a rigid, unjustified, and irrelevant measurement regimen with a client may seriously undermine the collaborative nature of the client-worker relationship. It also detracts from developing a full understanding of the client's problems by making the administration of standardized scales the principal goal and by discounting the value inherent in other information-gathering methods, such as interview techniques.

A more reasoned approach to using measurement in practice is one that sees formal measurement procedures as a necessary tool for effective practice, but a tool that must be used with caution and sensitivity as well as with other information-gathering methods. It must be remembered that the events and client characteristics that we try to measure are the things that clients find most sensitive and personal. Client problems are inherently sensitive and involve intimate details that deserve to be treated with respect and dignity. This means that, as professionals, we have ethical and moral obligations to ensure that our measurements are relevant, detailed without being overly obtrusive, and accurate without becoming the be-all-and-end-all of service provision.

It is this last point that perhaps poses the greatest danger for those who possess a blind faith in the act of measurement and attribute some form of infallibility to measurement, whether the measurement procedure produces quantitative or qualitative scores. We all know of persons who have, at some point in their lives, been given a label that was produced by some measurement process. Practitioners need to recognize that labels can become self- or other-fulfilling prophecies in many ways. Labels such as "codependent," "narcissistic," "schizophrenic," "learning impaired," or "antisocial" need to be viewed within the context of their demonstrated utility, and in all cases as artificial constructs, not as reality (Dawes, 1994). We can measure characteristics that are thought to be useful in practice, but it needs to be recognized that these measures are not a priori valid. Validation is a necessary and ongoing process (Messick, 1989). In any event, the products of these measurement procedures are not the client. They are descriptions of characteristics of the client that will have greater or lesser utility in helping the practitioner to conduct practice. In other words, measurement, just like interventions or other practice tools, can harm clients if not used with sensitivity and knowledge.

The thoughtful and skillful use of formal measurement tools in practice is essential to becoming a good practitioner. There are substantial dangers to the excessive reliance upon purely subjective means of assessment (see Dawes, 1994; Garb, 1998; Gilovich, 1991; Meier, 1994). Because subjective measurement is essentially a process of internal comparison and judgment, it is vulnerable to the many mental processes that lead us to "know what isn't so" (Gilovich, 1991). Subjective assessment methods are also unique to each individual practitioner, which introduces variability in the results of these subjective assessments due to differences between practitioners, not to the characteristics of clients and their problems (Cronbach et al., 1972). Pure subjective measurement can lead to unintended consequences, such as labels that are even less grounded than those based on some more formal measure. Since purely subjective measures are based upon unique individual processes, there is no way to verify the reliability and validity of these assessments. This can make it difficult to communicate the nature of the measurement, understand its complexities, or replicate its processes. The use of more formal measures in practice can provide these benefits. Such measures should become part of the practice repertoire.

CHARACTERISTICS OF GOOD MEASURES

There are a range of characteristics that must be considered when selecting a measure for use in practice. Some of these are general attributes that make certain measures more appropriate or easier to use in particular situations. Others are more specific and relate to the psychometrics of the measure. *Psychometric* is a term that refers to the science of measuring psychological, behavioral, and social phenomena.

We believe first and foremost that any measure used to monitor and evaluate practice should be easy to use. This has a number of implications for selecting measures. Measures should be as short as possible. They should be easy to administer. They should be easy for clients to understand and complete. They should be easy for the practitioner to understand and explain to clients. Good measures also provide good referents so that the practitioner can anchor his or her interpretations consistently. The measure needs to be sufficiently sensitive to detect meaningful changes in the problem being measured. Most of all, however, measures selected to monitor and evaluate practice need to meet two key criteria. First, they need to be appropriate for the type of client being assessed in terms of age, cognitive functioning, language capabilities, cultural background, and so on. Second, good measures must focus directly on the client objectives collaboratively established by the practitioner and client. Without meeting these two criteria, all others are meaningless.

The best measures also facilitate one other aspect of monitoring and evaluation. They allow for repeated measurements over time without undue distortion or bias. This is important because the power of single-system designs cannot be realized without the ability to detect change and emerging patterns in client functioning. This suggests the necessity for instruments to fit easily into existing practice paradigms. Practitioners should be able to integrate the measure into normal assessment and monitoring procedures without adding too much extra work for either themselves or their clients. Some instruments are simply too large to fit into this framework. This is particularly true if regular, repeated measurement is desired over a relatively short period of assessment and intervention.

Practitioners are sometimes limited by instruments that demand specialized training or certification. This is most often true of disciplines other than social work. Many of these instruments are also limiting in that they use complex scoring procedures. Some even require practitioners to submit completed instruments to a remote location for scoring and return.

For all of these reasons, we advocate the use of short-form instruments that are quickly and easily administered, scored, and interpreted. Such instruments are often called *rapid assessment instruments*, or RAIs (Edelson, 1985; Levitt & Reid, 1981). Many of the instruments presented later in this book are typical of RAIs in that they fit the desirable characteristics we have already discussed.

There are two other specific criteria for judging the worth of measures that must be discussed. These are the psychometric properties of reliability and validity. A good measure will produce scores that possess both reliability and validity.

Reliability

Reliability concerns the ability of a measure to produce scores, whether qualitative or quantitative, that have very little measurement error. A highly reliable measure administered repeatedly to the same person, under the condition that the level of the characteristic possessed by the person and measured by the instrument remains constant, will produce very nearly the same score every

time (Lord & Novick, 1968). This means the instrument must resist the influence or contamination of random factors external to the phenomenon being
measured that might influence results from one application to another. The
central concept in classical reliability theory is the "reliability coefficient." The
reliability coefficient is a number ranging from 0 to +1.0 that tells us the extent
to which a distribution or set of observed scores matches the distribution or
set of true scores (Crocker & Algina, 1986; Ghiselli et al., 1981; Lord &
Novick, 1968; Nunnally, 1978). An observed score is simply a score that we
have obtained from the administration of a measurement procedure. The true
score is a theoretical concept that is defined as the score we would obtain if the
measurement process were error-free. The true score is an error-free score. The
reliability coefficient, then, tells us how good a job a set of observed scores
does in representing the set of scores we would have if we had error-free measurement. As the reliability coefficient approaches 0, any correspondence (correlation) between observed and true scores vanishes. As the reliability
coefficient approaches +1.0, the correspondence (correlation) between
observed and true scores becomes perfect. There are a number of methods that
can be used to estimate the reliability coefficient, and there are a number of
good reference sources for those who wish to read about these in more detail
(Allen & Yen, 1979; Anastasi, 1976; Crocker & Algina, 1986; Cronbach, 1951;
Kyte & Bostwick, 1997; Lord & Novick, 1968; Nunnally, 1978).

Issues of reliability are central to good practice. An unreliable set of scores
is infused with variability that is unrelated to the construct being measured.
The product of an unreliable set of scores is, therefore, a flawed client assessment. We have an ethical obligation to avoid such risks by using instruments
known to produce a reliable set of scores.

Practitioners who avoid the use of formal measures in their practice still
must deal with the issue of reliability. All practitioners engage in processes of
observation, interpretation, judgment, and decision making (Garb, 1998).
Client assessments and intervention cannot happen without these processes.
The results of unsystematic, subjective measurement approaches can be (and
often are) unreliable (Dawes, 1994; Garb, 1998). This is due, in part, to the
same biasing factors that affect clients (fatigue, distraction, memory loss, etc.).
In addition, practitioners must also deal with flaws in the cognitive maps
(Ingram, 1986) they develop to guide their practice. These cognitive maps
serve as conceptual templates and can be biased by previous training, personal
beliefs in specific theoretical frameworks, past experiences with similar
clients, and so on. These factors can make client assessment remarkably unreliable (Dawes, 1994; Garb, 1998; Gilovich, 1991; Meier, 1994). Different
practitioners can come up with very different assessments of the exact same
client at the exact same point in time. The message should be clear.
Reliability concerns all forms of measurement, from subjective first impressions drawn from the body language of a client to finely developed standardized instruments.

As discussed earlier, the conceptual foundation of reliability lies in the theoretical notion of true scores and their relation to observed scores. Again, true

scores are the scores we would obtain in error-free measurement. For example, if we were trying to assess a child's fear of the dark, a true score obtained by a particular measure would be able to tell us the exact nature and extent of that child's fear. An observed score, on the other hand, is the actual score we obtain from using a particular measurement method. Error scores are just what their name suggests; they are the difference between what we actually observe (the observed score) and the true score: the error score (E) is equal to the observed score (O) minus the true score (T):

$$E = O - T$$

Let us use an example. Suppose that we had a practitioner complete a new scale called the Measurement Skepticism Scale, or MSS (fictional, we assure you). This scale measures the degree to which people are open to the use of measurement in professional practice. Its scores range from 0 to 100, with higher scores signifying increased levels of skepticism toward measurement, and vice versa. Now suppose that a perfect estimate of the practitioner's skepticism would produce a true score of 33. When we had the practitioner complete the MSS, however, the score we actually obtained was 42. This was the observed score. The instrument erred by overestimating the practitioner's degree of skepticism by 9 points; the error score is equal to the observed score minus the true score: $42 - 33 = 9$. This difference of 9 points is called the error of measurement. This example illustrates one of the fundamental equations of classical measurement theory: the observed score (O) is equal to the true score (T) plus the error score (E). Symbolically, this reads as $O = T + E$.

Let us extend the example of the Measurement Skepticism Scale (MSS). Again we will use 33 as the true "skepticism score." In this example, we will assume (1) that we had the practitioner complete the MSS five times in a row, (2) that the skepticism true score remained constant at 33 across all five times the practitioner completed the MSS, and (3) that after each time the practitioner completed the MSS, we used some magical method to make sure that he or she forgot that he or she had completed it (so that what the practitioner did on one occasion could not influence what he or she did on another). The results of this thought experiment are shown in Table 10.1.

In Table 10.1, notice the substantial variability in the observed scores even though the true score remains constant. Also notice that the error scores are rather large, indicating that we have a great deal of measurement error and that the scores are certainly not reliable. There is no consistency at all in the MSS scores from one administration to the next. One consequence of this is that the observed MSS score tells us very little about the practitioner's true level of measurement skepticism.

When developing instruments, we strive to design them in such a manner that they produce reliable sets of scores over as wide a range of conditions as possible (Cronbach et al., 1972). This is accomplished by reducing the amount of error introduced into scores by ambiguous items, items that contain words that are easily misunderstood, and overly complex items, and by being as sure as possible that the items on the scale adequately represent both common and unique aspects of

Table 10.1 Results of a Thought Experiment: Measurement
Skepticism Scale (MSS) Scores

Observed Score	=	True Score	+	Error Score
59		33		26
21		33		−12
69		33		36
45		33		12
15		33		−18

the construct to be measured. If a newly developed measurement instrument
fails to produce reliable scores, it is revised and tinkered with until it does.

Let us return to our MSS example. Suppose that after obtaining the results
shown in Table 10.1, the instrument was subjected to a series of revisions.
Feeling much more confident, we again ask the practitioner to complete the
new version of the MSS five successive times, just as we did earlier. Table 10.2
shows the scores obtained in this second experiment. Notice that there is a
much greater consistency in the observed scores across the repeated measurements. Also notice that the errors of measurement are much smaller. These
examples illustrate the basic ideas behind the notion of reliability.

So how high does the reliability coefficient have to be for a set of scores to
be considered reliable? Remember, reliability coefficients can range from 0.0
to 1.0. Also remember that as the reliability coefficient approaches 0, any correspondence between observed and true scores vanishes; and as the reliability
coefficient approaches 1.0, the correspondence between observed and true
scores becomes perfect (there is no error). Appropriate reliability levels really
depend upon the purpose of the measurement being undertaken and the
scores obtained. When conducting large-sample studies, researchers can rely on
the capacity of well-drawn samples to average out errors of measurement. This
averaging in essence reduces the distorting effects of extreme errors of measurement. Thus, researchers can get away with reliabilities between, say, .70 and
.80 (Nunnally, 1978). Researchers also have data analytic techniques that enable
them to take measurement error into account (Nugent, White, & Basham, 2000).

When applying measurement procedures in practice, however, reliability
estimates must be higher. This is particularly true when measures are applied
to assessments of individuals or small groups of individuals—the very heart of
clinical practice. The reason for such stringent reliability demands should be
obvious. We want any clinical assessment to be as accurate as possible. Mistakes
are very costly in terms of potential client harm, misdirected interventions,
wasted resources, and so on. Therefore, when using a measure for clinical
work, we must have a strong faith in its ability to consistently measure the construct of focus with a minimal amount of error. This means that a measure
being applied to professional practice should be capable of producing scores
that have a reliability coefficient in excess of .80, and preferably in excess of
.90 (Hudson, 1982; Nunnally, 1978).

Table 10.2 Results of a Second Thought Experiment:
Measurement Skepticism Scale (MSS) Scores

Observed Score	=	True Score	+	Error Score
32		33		−1
31		33		−2
34		33		1
33		33		0
34		33		1

Validity

Validity is at the same time a simple and yet complex concept. At its core, validity refers to a simple question: Is the instrument in question measuring what it is supposed to be measuring? In other words, is the instrument providing scores that allow us to accurately make the inferences we want to make (Messick, 1989)? If the answer is no, then the scores produced by the measure are not valid. For example, if we want to know how depressed a client is, we need a measure that produces scores that allow us to accurately infer the client's level of depression. In this case, we want to make inferences from the client's score to her or his level of depression. It is important to realize that this simple notion refers to more than just pencil-and-paper scales. The concept of validity applies to any act of assessment or measurement. Questions of validity are as applicable and critical to practitioners' observations, interview questions, judgments, and so on, as they are to any standardized measure (see Groth-Marnot, 1990; Meier, 1994; Messick, 1989). If we fail to obtain information that allows us to make accurate inferences to the characteristic that we believe is being measured, the result is a misdirected and potentially dangerous understanding of the phenomenon in question.

That is the simple aspect of validity. The complex aspect is that we require multiple types of evidence to support claims that the scores produced by a measurement instrument are valid for making specific inferences. These forms of evidence have often been conceptualized as "types" of validity (Messick, 1989). We speak about such things as "face validity," "content validity," "predictive validity," "concurrent validity," "convergent validity," and "divergent validity." Each of these types of validity is actually a form of evidence used to support a claim that the particular measurement procedure produces scores allowing the user to make a specific inference. To validate a measurement tool means to gather evidence that bears upon the appropriateness of the use of the scores produced by the measure to make specific inferences. The validation of a measurement tool is an evolving and ongoing process that, in a sense, never ends (Messick, 1989). It is critical to note that the best measures will have all of the types of evidence supporting the validity of specific uses of the scores they produce (Messick, 1989). Perhaps most important of all the types of evidence is that for convergent and divergent validity (Meier, 1994).

It is beyond the scope of this chapter to give a full and detailed discussion of validity. The reader is referred to the very detailed treatment of validity given by Messick (1989). Other excellent references are Anastasi (1976), Crocker and Algina (1986), Nunnally (1978), Cook and Campbell (1979), Hudson (1982), and Kyte and Bostwick (1997). Meier (1994) gives an excellent overview of critical measurement issues. Also important is the issue of differential validity, or bias, in measurement. Differential validity concerns the extent to which the manner in which we interpret scores from a measurement procedure *for different types of persons (male and female; majority and minority; etc.) remains invariant.* This topic is discussed in depth by Cole and Moss (1989), and Nugent (1993b) discussed this topic in the context of social work research and practice.

Before we discuss specific standards for judging validity, two related points must be made. First, there is an important relationship between reliability and validity. A set of scores can be highly reliable without being valid. A set of scores cannot be valid, however, without being reliable. This should make sense if one considers the meaning of both reliability and validity. In a reliable set of scores, there is a strong correspondence between observed and true scores. This strong correspondence says nothing, however, about what characteristic or concept the set of scores reflects. We could easily be measuring the wrong characteristic or concept, but doing so in a consistent manner. We could, for example, administer an instrument that measures self-esteem to a number of persons, all the while thinking that we were measuring "marital distress." We might get consistent scores, but the scores would not allow us to make accurate inferences about marital distress. A measure that produces a valid set of scores will have two characteristics: (1) it provides a set of scores that are reliable; and (2) it provides a set of scores that allow us to make accurate and appropriate inferences from the scores to a specific construct. This brings us to the second of the two related points: validity is more important than reliability.

Setting standards for validity is not as easy as it is for reliability. Since there is a variety of types of evidence necessary to support validity claims, it is not possible to give a single number that can be used as a standard for comparison. The situation is further complicated by the fact that validation is an ongoing, ever-evolving process. This makes any determination of the "better validated measure" a comparative process. At the risk of oversimplifying a complex process, the best measure to use is the one that currently has the best and most complete evidence supporting its use for making the type of inference one needs to make.

Evidence for validity is often (though by all means not always) given in the form of a correlation coefficient. A correlation coefficient is a numerical index that ranges from -1 to $+1$ and that tells us the extent to which the scores from two measures are related. A correlation of $+1$ tells us that the scores from the two measures are perfectly related, and that high scores on one of the measures are accompanied by high scores on the second (and vice versa). A correlation of -1 tells us that the scores are perfectly related, but that high scores on one of the measures are accompanied by low scores on the second (and vice versa). As the correlation coefficient approaches 0, it tells us that the scores are unrelated; knowing a person's score on one measure tells us nothing about her or his score on the second measure.

When evidence for validity is reported using correlation coefficients, these correlations are called validity coefficients. Reliability and validity coefficients are closely related. For any set of scores, the absolute upper limit of their validity is considered to be the square root of their reliability coefficient, as calculated by the simple inequality

$$V \le \sqrt{r_{tt}}$$

where V is the validity coefficient, and r_{tt} is the reliability coefficient. The actual value of a validity coefficient will most often be less than the square root of the reliability coefficient. For example, suppose that the reliability coefficient for a set of scores is .81. The upper limit of a validity coefficient for this set of scores will be the square root of .81, or .90. Most actual validity coefficients would, in this case, be less than .90.

In the last two decades, we have seen greatly improved knowledge and procedures related to the construction of clinical measures. This enhanced ability has led to evolving validity standards. Practitioners looking for valid instruments should find those for which the full range of evidence supporting validity has been reported. There should be evidence for face validity; content validity; if appropriate, predictive validity; concurrent validity; convergent validity; and divergent validity. The most demanding form of evidence for validity is the combination of convergent and divergent validity. The prudent practitioner will make sure that evidence for the convergent and divergent validity of scores produced by a measurement procedure exists before using the measure in practice.

SUMMARY

In this chapter, we have discussed the role of measurement in practice. We believe that measurement is already a core function performed by all practitioners. We support a conscious, systematic approach to thinking about measurement, however. All practitioners must describe and understand the issues that their clients face and make critical decisions based upon their descriptions. Such a process requires timely and complete information. Formal measurement procedures and the use of short-form scales provide one method of obtaining reliable and valid feedback for use in making sound practice judgments.

It is important to select measures that are easy to use and that fit within the parameters of good practice. This stance is somewhat different than that of traditional science, but it is essential to making measurement a part of practice instead of an intrusion into practice. It is also important to select measures that have been shown to produce reliable and valid scores. Although we have discussed both reliability and validity in this chapter, there is much more to be learned about the psychometrics of instruments. We encourage the reader to further his or her understanding by reading more in this area.

11

A Sampler of Short-Form Measures for Use in Practice

U ntil now, the discussion in this book has focused on building the foundation for 21st century practice evaluation. This discussion started with developing a conceptual framework useful for evaluating practice and clarifying the role of single-system designs in science and practice. We also presented detailed explanations of single-system designs that can be used to support and enhance treatment planning, as well as to evaluate service effectiveness. Methods for analyzing and aggregating single-system data have been explicated, and the critical role of measurement in practice has been elaborated. By this point it should be obvious that there are powerful techniques available to support the task of establishing accountability in practice. So what is left? In order to make these techniques workable, it is important to have access to reliable and valid measures to assess and monitor client functioning. We, therefore, turn now to presenting one set of such measurement tools—the CASS short-form scales.

The short-form CASS scales are standardized, relatively brief scales specifically designed as clinical measurement tools. They can be used for a number of clinical purposes. One of the CASS scales might be used to screen clients for the potential to commit acts of domestic violence, for example. They can also be used to perform initial client assessments and to monitor progress made with any clinical case. In addition, these scales are well-suited for use as part of a broader program evaluation strategy or as instruments to be used when researching the effects of clinical practice. Just as importantly, they meet an essential criterion for useful practice evaluation; that is, they fit the realities of everyday practice by offering an easy-to-use and understandable technology.

This chapter outlines the range of short-form CASS scales available and explains the clinical problem each is intended to measure. Because it is important to know that such scales are reliable and valid, we also discuss the basic psychometric characteristics of each scale. This discussion should provide the information necessary to select an appropriate scale to use with clients. It also sets the stage for the following chapter, which provides instructions on administering, scoring, and interpreting these short-form scales.

THE CASS SCALES

The short-form CASS scales consist of 25 self-report questionnaires designed to measure the severity of a specific problem across a number of potential problem areas: (1) personal adjustment issues; (2) dyadic relationship issues; (3) family adjustment issues; and (4) difficulties in organizational or work settings. The latter category of CASS scales includes instruments that are not specifically clinical measurement scales. It does, however, include scales that measure problems that practitioners might encounter in working with clients; therefore, the scales in that category have been included in this summary of the short-form CASS scales. All of the scales from each of these categories are available in a paper-and-pencil version, as well as a computerized version within the CASS computer program.

Using the computerized version of CASS does offer a number of advantages over using the paper-and-pencil versions of the scales. The computer can easily make copies of the scales, score the scales, graph the scores, and record the scores over time as part of a single-system design. The computerized version also provides more options for administrating the scales, such as allowing the client to complete the scales right on the computer. In general, the CASS software decreases the burden of doing the paperwork associated with practice evaluation, and makes such efforts more efficient.

The CASS scales all share the same general format and structure. Almost all are comprised of 25 items that describe a client perception, behavior, attitude, or belief. Clients are asked to use a Likert-type scale to rate their agreement with the statement or to indicate the frequency of the situation being described. This format and structure provides a consistent administration routine for the scales. It also allows the use of a single scoring formula for all of the scales. These administration routines and the scoring formula are described in the next chapter.

A principal advantage of utilizing a single scoring formula is the ease of interpreting the CASS scales. Each scale can result in client scores that range from 0 to 100, with low scores indicating the relative absence of the problem being measured. Alternatively, higher scores on the scales indicate the presence of the problem being measured. As scores increase, the problem being measured is considered to be more and more severe.

Most of the scales also share one other useful characteristic. They have clinical cutting scores of 30 (a few have different cutting scores, and clinical cutting scores have yet to be established for a few others). A clinical cutting score is used as a general guideline to indicate whether the problem being assessed should be considered a clinically significant problem. If a client scores well below the clinical cutting score—say a score of 12 on the Index of Self-Esteem, for example—we would conclude that self-esteem is not a problem requiring treatment for this individual. If, on the other hand, the client scores a 59 on the ISE, treatment would certainly be called for.

Table 11.1 shows the full names, labels, and measurement constructs for the 25 short-form CASS scales appropriate for clinical measurement. Samples of the paper-and-pencil versions of these scales are provided in Appendix B.

Establishing the reliability and validity of any standardized measure is critical for generating confidence that the tool will actually measure what it purports to measure. The CASS scales are no different. Each of the scales has undergone a range of psychometric tests to ensure that it produces valid scores. All of the scales have produced sets of scores with a reliability coefficient of .90 or higher and have demonstrated content, concurrent, factorial, discriminant, and convergent and divergent validity. The psychometric characteristics of each of the short-form CASS scales are shown in Table 11.2. For each scale, the table presents the relevant reliability coefficient (alpha), the standard error of measurement (SEM), and known-groups validity coefficients. The standard error of measurement, or SEM, estimates the standard deviation of error scores. Large SEM values are problematic, as they indicate declining levels of reliability for the measure being tested. Conversely, small SEM values suggest that the measure being tested displays high levels of reliability. Known-groups validity refers to the ability of a measure to produce scores that differentiate accurately between persons who have a clinically significant problem and those persons who do not (Hvelson, 1982). A "good" known-groups validity coefficient should be greater than .60.

As Table 11.2 indicates, psychometric testing of some of the short-form CASS scales is not complete. Research to further establish these characteristics is continuing. Readers who wish to obtain the most recent psychometric results of this testing can contact either of the first two authors of this book or the publisher of the CASS scales (WALMYR Publishing).

The remainder of this chapter presents a brief discussion of each of the short-form CASS scales. We discuss them in sections, focusing in turn on scales that address personal adjustment issues, dyadic relationship issues, family adjustment issues, and difficulties in organizational or work settings.

PERSONAL ADJUSTMENT ISSUES

Many of the short-form CASS scales focus on issues of personal adjustment for clients. These are issues that tend to be internalized problems in functioning, such as self-esteem, depression, anxiety, and so on. While it is true that these problems can be shaped by our environment and interactions with others, the actual experience of dealing with these problems is an individualized, internal process. One other point should be made about these measures of personal adjustment. These

Table 11.1 The Short-Form CASS Scales

CASS Scale	Scale Label	Construct Measured
Personal Adjustment Issues		
Clinical Anxiety Scale	CAS	Anxiety
Generalized Contentment Scale	GCS	Depression
Index of Alcohol Involvement	IAI	Alcohol abuse
Index of Clinical Stress	ICS	Personal stress
Index of Drug Involvement	IDI	Drug abuse
Index of Homophobia	IHP	Homophobia
Index of Peer Relations	IPR	Peer discord
Index of Self-Esteem	ISE	Self-esteem
Sexual Attitude Scale	SAS	Sexual conservatism
Dyadic Relationship Issues		
Index of Marital Satisfaction	IMS	Marital discord
Index of Sexual Satisfaction	ISS	Sexual discord
Non-physical Abuse of Partner Scale	NPAPS	Non-physical abusiveness
Partner Abuse Scale: Non-physical	PASNP	Non-physical abuse
Partner Abuse Scale: Physical	PASPH	Physical abuse
Physical Abuse of Partner Scale	PAPS	Physical abusiveness
Family Adjustment Issues		
Child's Attitude Toward Father	CAF	Discord with father
Child's Attitude Toward Mother	CAM	Discord with mother
Index of Brother Relations	IBR	Discord with brother
Index of Family Relations	IFR	Intrafamilial stress
Index of Parental Attitudes	IPA	Discord with child
Index of Sister Relations	ISR	Discord with sister
Organizational Assessment Issues		
Client Satisfaction Inventory	CSI	Satisfaction with service delivery
Index of Job Satisfaction	IJS	Satisfaction with employment
Index of Managerial Effectiveness	IME	Managerial ability
Index of Sexual Harassment	ISH	Sexual harassment

scales are designed as measures of personal functioning or problems in living. They are not, however, to be regarded as measures of psychopathology.

Clinical Anxiety Scale (CAS)

The Clinical Anxiety Scale (CAS) measures the problems that clients have with anxiety (Thyer & Westhuis, 1989; Westhuis & Thyer, 1989). Anxiety can be defined in many different ways, including both global anxieties and more specific anxiety in relation to particular situations. The CAS focuses on a behavior-oriented definition of anxiety. As such, it directly focuses on phobic

Table 11.2 Psychometric Evidence for Scores from Short-Form CASS Scales

Scale Name (Numbers in parentheses refer to references at end of table)	Reliability (Alpha)	Standard Error of Measurement (SEM)	Known-Groups Validity	Clinical Cutting Score
Personal Adjustment Issues				
CAS(1)	.94	4.20	.77	30
GCS(2)	.92	4.26	.74	30
IAI(3)	.90	4.43	*	*
ICS(3)	.90	5.02	*	*
IDI(4)	.97	2.86	.90	30
IHP(5)	.90	4.75	*	50
IPR(6)	.94	4.44	.66	30
ISE(3)	.93	3.70	.52	30
SAS(7)	.94	4.20	.73	50
Dyadic Relationship Issues				
IMS(2)	.96	4.00	.82	30
ISS(2)	.92	4.24	.76	30
NPAPS(3)	.93	3.37	*	15
PASNP(3)	.94	3.78	*	15
PASPH(3)	.93	1.51	*	2
PAPS(3)	.85	0.81	*	2
Family Adjustment Issues				
CAF(2)	.95	4.56	.87	30
CAM(2)	.94	4.57	.86	30
IBR(3)	.97	3.50	*	30
IFR(2)	.95	3.65	.92	30
IPA(2)	.97	3.64	.88	30
ISR(3)	.96	3.35	*	30
Organizational Assessment Issues				
CSI(8)	.90	3.16	*	*
IJS(9)	.93	3.67	*	*
IME(9)	.96	3.53	*	*
ISH(10)	.90	2.97	*	*

*Currently unavailable

SOURCES: (1) Thyer & Westhuis (1989); (2) Hudson (1982); (3) Hudson, MacNeil, & Dierks (1993); (4) Faul & Hudson (1997); (5) Hudson & Ricketts (1980); (6) Hudson, Nurius, Daley, & Newsome (1988); (7) Hudson, Murphy, & Nurius (1983); (8) Hudson & McMurtry (1997); (9) Hudson, Lewis, & Faul (1998); (10) Hudson & Decker (1998).

and anxiety reactions that arise from well–identified and specific events or situations that may arouse anxiety for the client.

The scale has produced scores with a reliability of .90 or greater, and it has evidence for good content, factorial, and construct validity. A clinical cutting score of 30 has been established for the CAS. This means that a client who scores above 30 is nearly always found to have a clinically significant problem with anxiety.

Generalized Contentment Scale

The Generalized Contentment Scale (GCS) is a measure of depression. It has been extensively used and tested for two decades (Hontanosas, Cruz, Kaneshiro, & Sanchez, 1979; Hudson, Acklin, & Bartosh, 1980; Hudson, Hamada, Keech, & Harlan, 1980; Hudson & Murphy, 1980; Hudson & Proctor, 1976; Murphy, 1978; Murphy, Hudson, & Cheung, 1980; Nugent, 1994; Nurius, 1983; Nurius & Hudson, 1987). As with the other short-form CASS scales, a higher score on the GCS indicates an increasing severity of the problem. Thus, a high score on the GCS indicates the client has a problem with depression. The GCS has been shown to produce scores with reliability of .90 or greater, and it displays good validity coefficients. It has a clinical cutting score of 30, which means that a client who scores above 30 is nearly always found to have a clinically significant depression.

The GCS is one of the scales for which very high scores become a serious concern for practitioners. In fact, clients who score above 50 on the GCS often experience suicidal ideation. While the GCS is not a test of suicidal ideation, experience with the scale suggests that practitioners should certainly be concerned about the possibility of suicide for clients who score above 70. These statements should not be taken to mean that the GCS predicts suicidal attempts. Rather, it has been found that for a number of persons who did attempt suicide, the GCS score exceeded 70 immediately preceding the suicidal episode (Hudson, 1982, 1997).

The GCS can be used with clients who are diagnosed as having situational or endogenous depression, but caution should be employed when using it with clients diagnosed as having bipolar depression. If the client is in the depressed phase of a bipolar depression, the scale should perform quite well. If the client moves into the manic phase, the GCS would be expected to perform as well as other depression measures, all of which are susceptible to potentially misleading results due to phase-related factors such as impression management by clients.

Index of Alcohol Involvement

The Index of Alcohol Involvement (IAI) measures the severity of alcohol abuse among clients. It asks clients to report details of their alcohol consumption, symptoms of alcohol use, and the impact of alcohol use on their personal and social functioning. High scores indicate more serious problems in the use and abuse of alcohol.

This instrument has been partially validated; it has been shown to produce scores with a reliability of .90 or greater; and it has evidence for content, factorial, and construct validity (Hudson, MacNeil, & Dierks, 1993; MacNeil, 1991). At present, a known clinical cutting score is not available.

Index of Clinical Stress

The Index of Clinical Stress (ICS) is a measure of personal stress (Abell, 1986, 1991). As with constructs such as anxiety or self-esteem, there are many ways to define stress. It can be defined as a global phenomenon, or it can be tied to specific personal or social situations or stressors. Many people, for example, experience relatively little stress in their relationships among family members. At the same time, however, they may experience very high levels of stress while on the job. Practitioners can use the ICS flexibly. They can simply ask clients to consider their stress levels on an overall basis if they wish to target global stress levels for the client, or they can, alternatively, ask clients to think about specific stressors (such as their job) when completing the scale.

The ICS has produced scores with reliability of .90, and it has good validity coefficients. The clinical cutting score has not yet been finalized for the ICS, but it is expected that the cutting score will be close to 30.

Index of Drug Involvement

Like the IAI, the Index of Drug Involvement (IDI) is meant to be used as a measure of substance abuse among clients (Faul & Hudson, 1997). This scale, however, measures the extent to which clients have problems with drugs, not alcohol specifically. For the IDI, drugs can be defined as any kind of medication or illegal drugs that are consumed by the respondent. It is important to note that item content for this scale was selected based on behaviors and emotions that have been associated with extensive drug use in the literature. The scale was not developed with the intent to represent or develop theory about the origin or causes of drug abuse.

The IDI has produced scores with a high level of reliability (.97 or better) and a low SEM. It also shows strong validity coefficients, with a known-groups validity of .90. The clinical cutting score for the scale has been established at 30.

Index of Homophobia

The Index of Homophobia (IHP) measures the degree of problems clients have with homophobia—the fear of being in close quarters with homosexuals (Hale, 1989; Hudson & Ricketts, 1980; Pain & Disney, 1996). The scale is meant to reflect the degree of comfort respondents feel when associated with or being in the presence of homosexuals. As such, the scale is slightly different in intent than most of the other CASS scales. It does not measure a personal or social problem per se; it does not reflect a clinical problem or dysfunction. Rather, the scale simply reflects the feelings clients may have about working or associating with homosexuals.

The IHP has produced scores with reliability of .90, and strong validity coefficients. It does not, however, have a clinical cutting score in the same sense as most of the other scales. The listed cutting score of 50 does not reflect a "clinically significant" problem. Instead, a score below 50 reflects a degree of comfort with homosexuals, while scores above 50 represent an increasing fear of being in close proximity with homosexuals.

Index of Peer Relations

The Index of Peer Relations (IPR) measures the degree of problems clients have in relationships with peers (Forte & Green, 1994; Hudson, Nurius, Daley, & Newsome, 1988; Klein, Beltran, & Sowers-Hoag, 1990). It may be used to assess client problems with specific reference or peer groups, such as particular friends or work colleagues. The IPR can also be applied to more than one peer group. Practitioners can ask clients to report on their peer relations with more than one group simultaneously, again say friends and work colleagues. Such a contrast can be a valuable comparison to isolate the dynamics of peer relationship problems for the client. The IPR can certainly be used as a global measure to assess the client's general peer relationships as well.

The scale has produced scores with reliability of .90 or greater, and it has good validity coefficients. The IPR has a clinical cutting score of 30, which means that a client who scores above 30 is nearly always found to have a clinically significant problem with peer relationships.

Index of Self-Esteem

The Index of Self-Esteem (ISE) measures the severity of problems clients have with self-esteem (Abell, Jones, & Hudson, 1984; Hontanosas, Cruz, Kaneshiro, & Sanchez, 1979; Hudson & Murphy, 1980; Hudson & Proctor, 1976; Hudson, Wung, & Borges, 1980; Murphy, 1978; Murphy, Hudson, & Cheung, 1980; Nugent, 1994; Nurius, 1983; Nurius & Hudson, 1987). In this scale, the definition of self-esteem focuses on evaluative perceptions of self held by respondents. This draws upon two distinct components of self-evaluation. The first is self-concept, which is the image a person has of his or her own identity. A client may perceive himself or herself as bold and aggressive, for example; but this is different from the evaluation the client makes of these attributes. If the client values characteristics such as aggressiveness, he or she will likely hold a positive self-evaluation, that is, high self-esteem. If, however, the client does not value these characteristics, the result will likely be a negative self-evaluation, that is, low self-esteem. It is this self-evaluation that the ISE measures. As with many of the other short-from scales, the ISE can be administered globally or in reference to specific situations in which clients might find themselves.

This scale has produced scores with reliability of over .90. It also shows strong validity coefficients. Low scores on the ISE indicate that the client holds high self-esteem, and high scores indicate that the client experiences low self-esteem. The ISE has a clinical cutting score of 30.

Sexual Attitude Scale

The Sexual Attitude Scale (SAS) measures the degree of conservatism clients hold in their attitudes toward human sexual expression (Hudson, Murphy, & Nurius, 1983). Like the Index of Homophobia, this scale is not designed to measure a personal problem per se. Rather, the scale measures the values clients hold about sex. For this reason, high scores on the SAS should not be considered indicative of a clinically significant problem. High scores on the scale simply indicate a conservative orientation to sexuality, while low scores reflect a liberal orientation toward sexuality. Those who score closest to 0 will be very liberal in their values about sex, and those who score closest to 100 will be the most conservative about sex.

Studies of the reliability of scores from the SAS have produced alpha estimates at .94. The scale also has strong validity coefficients. The cutting score for the scale is 50, although it is important to emphasize that scores above this point are not indicative of a clinical problem. The SAS score merely provides a general guideline to distinguish between liberal and conservative value positions about human sexual expression.

DYADIC RELATIONSHIP ISSUES

The second category of short-form CASS scales focuses on problems in dyadic relationships, or the relationships between couples. These scales represent a shift from the intrapersonal assessments offered by the CASS personal adjustment scales, measuring instead problems in the interpersonal relationships between two individuals. The dyadic relationship scales can be used to measure relationship problems between any couple, regardless of the marital status or genders of the couple involved.

Index of Marital Satisfaction

The Index of Marital Satisfaction (IMS) measures the severity of problems experienced by spouses or partners in their marital or partner relationships (Cheung & Hudson, 1981; Hontanosas, Cruz, Kaneshiro, & Sanchez, 1979; Hudson & Glisson, 1976; Hudson, Harrison & Crosscup, 1981; Hudson & Murphy, 1980; Murphy, 1978; Murphy, Hudson, & Cheung, 1980; Nurius, 1983; Nurius & Hudson, 1987). More specifically, it measures the magnitude of marital discord or dissatisfaction that is perceived by the respondent. Two important points arise from this definition. First, the scale is not a global measure of marital adjustment. Over time, couples may make adjustments in their relationships that lead to a set of common understandings, behaviors, routines, and so on. This does not mean that both partners in the relationship are satisfied, however. The second point to make, therefore, is that each partner in a relationship can obtain a score that is very different from that of the other partner. The scale measures the marital satisfaction of each partner individually, rather than acting as a global measure of marital adjustment.

The scale has produced scores with reliability of over .90, and it offers strong validity coefficients. It has a clinical cutting score of 30. Clients who score above 30 are considered to be experiencing clinically significant levels of dissatisfaction in their relationships with their partners.

Index of Sexual Satisfaction

The Index of Sexual Satisfaction (ISS) measures the severity of problems in the sexual component of the relationship between spouses or partners (Hontanosas, Cruz, Kaneshiro, & Sanchez, 1979; Hudson, Harrison, & Crosscup, 1981; Hudson, Wung, & Borges, 1980; Murphy, 1978; Murphy, Hudson, & Cheung, 1980; Nurius, 1983; Nurius & Hudson, 1987). The scale includes items that tap into client perceptions of sexual compatibility, enjoyment of sex, and contributions that sex makes to the relationship. As such, the scale is able to assess the degree of sexual discord that is perceived by a client with respect to the relationship with a spouse or partner.

This scale has a produced scores with estimated reliability of over .90, and strong validity coefficients. It has a clinical cutting score of 30. Clients who score above 30 are considered to have a clinically significant problem with the sexual component of a dyadic relationship.

Non-physical Abuse of Partner Scale

This is the first of four short-form CASS scales that focus on abuse issues within the relationship between couples. The Non-physical Abuse of Partner Scale (NPAPS) measures the degree of nonphysical abuse that a client may have committed against a spouse or partner. It is intended to assess clients who are known to be abusive with their partners, and thus is completed by the abuser in a relationship. High scores on the scale suggest that the practitioner needs to introduce treatment that will modify the abusive behavior demonstrated by the client who has completed the scale.

This scale has produced scores with high reliability (.93). It also has good content, factorial, and construct validity, though its known-groups validity is not known at this point (Hudson, MacNeil, & Dierks, 1993). The clinical cutting score for this scale has been set at 15 to reflect the gravity of abuse issues within relationships. This means that any score above 15 is indicative of abusive behaviors (nonphysical) that warrant intervention on the part of practitioners.

It is important to note here that the short-form CASS scales are self-report instruments that do not include lie-detection items or techniques. This means that practitioners should use their professional judgment and collateral sources of information to protect against impression-management responses on the respondent's part. Domestic violence of any description is understandably a sensitive topic that may lead some clients to make attempts to mislead. Practitioners must be careful.

Partner Abuse Scale: Non-physical

The Partner Abuse Scale: Non-physical (PASNP) is completed by clients who may be experiencing nonphysical abuse from their partners (Attala, Hudson, & McSweeney, 1994). The scale measures the degree of perceived nonphysical abuse that clients receive from their partners. This scale is a good complement to the Non-physical Abuse of Partner Scale. When the practitioner suspects that one partner is being abused or victimized by the other, it is useful to have both partners complete the respective scales. This helps to establish the existence of any nonphysical abuse, as well as capturing the dynamics experienced by both partners in the relationship. The PASNP was developed for use with almost any couple, whether the couple is dating, living together, married, heterosexual, or homosexual.

The PASNP has produced scores with reliability of over .90, and displays strong content, factorial, and construct validity (Hudson, MacNeil, & Dierks, 1993). Known-groups validity coefficients are not known for this scale at the present time. It has a clinical cutting score of 15. Any scores higher than 15 should be considered indicative of a client who is experiencing serious levels of nonphysical abuse imposed by his or her partner.

Physical Abuse of Partner Scale

The Physical Abuse of Partner Scale (PAPS) measures the degree of physical abuse that a client may have committed against a spouse or partner. It is intended to assess clients who are suspected or known to be physically abusive toward their partners. Thus, it is completed by the abuser in a relationship.

This scale has produced scores with an estimated reliability of .85. Initial research suggests that it has good content, factorial, and construct validity (Hudson, MacNeil, & Dierks, 1993). Known-groups validity coefficients are not known at the present time. The clinical cutting score for the scale is 2. Any score above this value should be considered a serious indication of the potential for physical violence on the part of the respondent. In such cases, immediate intervention should be considered.

Partner Abuse Scale: Physical

The Partner Abuse Scale: Physical (PASPH) is a complementary scale to the Physical Abuse of Partner Scale (Attala, Hudson, & McSweeney, 1994). Instead of being completed by the potential abuser, however, it is completed by the partner suspected or known to have experienced physical abuse in the relationship. The scale measures the perceptions of physical abuse that a client receives from the spouse or partner.

This scale has produced scores with a high level of reliability (estimated at .93). Research also suggests strong content, factorial, and construct validity (Hudson, MacNeil, & Dierks, 1993). At present, known-groups validity has not been established. It has a clinical cutting score of 2. Scores higher than 2 indicate that the respondent perceives serious physical abuse in the relationship.

FAMILY ADJUSTMENT ISSUES

This next category of short-form CASS scales has been developed to measure problems in family relationships. Most of these scales measure the severity of discord between two members of a family—parents and children, or siblings.

The scales also include a global measure of discord within a family. Each of these scales is described in the following text.

Child's Attitude Toward Father

The Child's Attitude Toward Father (CAF) measures children's perceptions of problems experienced in relation to their fathers (Giuli & Hudson, 1977). As the title of the scale suggests, it focuses on the attitudes that a child holds toward his or her father. This means that the CAF scale does not measure parental behavior per se, or ask children to describe any problematic behaviors on the part of the parent. Rather, it asks children to reflect on the relationship they share with their fathers and to rate the attitudes they hold about this relationship. In this sense, the scale is considered a measure of the quality of the relationship, as perceived by the child.

The CAF has produced scores with a reliability of over .90 and strong validity coefficients. Its clinical cutting score has been established at 30. Clients who score above 30 are nearly always found to have clinically significant problems in their relationships with their fathers. The CAF scale can be used with adolescent and adult children, but it is not recommended for use with children under the age of 12.

Child's Attitude Toward Mother

The Child's Attitude Toward Mother (CAM) is a parallel scale to the Child's Attitude Toward Father scale. It measures children's perceptions of problems experienced in relation to their mothers (Giuli & Hudson, 1977). It, too, is a scale that assesses attitudes toward the parent, rather than parental behaviors per se. A child may respond very differently to the CAM and CAF, thereby offering evidence of genuine differences in the quality of the relationship between the child and the two parents.

The CAM has produced scores with a reliability of over .90 and strong validity coefficients. Like its counterpart scale, the clinical cutting score has been established at 30. Clients who score above 30 are nearly always found to have clinically significant problems in their relationships with their mothers. The CAM scale can be used with adolescent and adult children, but it is not recommended for use with children under the age of 12.

Index of Parental Attitudes

This is the short-form CASS scale that allows parents to assess the quality of their relationship with a specific child (Hamilton & Orme, 1990; Hudson, Wung, & Borges, 1980). It measures the degree of a problem in a parent-child relationship, as seen by the parent. The child may be an infant, young child, adolescent, or adult. The Index of Parental Attitudes (IPA) enables a parent to reflect the extent to which the child, and the parent's relationship to the child, is a source of distress to the parent. Although it does include items that allow the parent to describe the child's behavior, the IPA is not a behavioral rating scale. It does not focus specifically on the child's problematic behavior, but instead on the parent's attitude about the child and these behaviors.

The IPA has produced scores with a high level of reliability (over .90) and strong validity coefficients. Its clinical cutting score is 30. A score above this point is indicative of a clinically significant problem between the parent and child.

Index of Brother Relations

The Index of Brother Relations (IBR) measures the severity of relationship problems respondents experience with their brothers. It is primarily an attitudinal scale rather than a behavioral rating scale. The scale has produced scores with a reliability of .90 or greater, and it has good content, factorial, and construct validity (Hudson, MacNeil, & Dierks, 1993). Known-groups validity coefficients are not known at the present time. The scale has a clinical cutting score of 30.

Index of Sister Relations

The Index of Sister Relations (ISR) scale is a parallel scale to the Index of Brother Relations. It is very similar in format, structure, and psychometric characteristics. The scale measures the severity of relationship problems respondents experience with their sisters. The scale has produced scores with a reliability of .90 or greater, and it has good content, factorial, and construct validity (Hudson, MacNeil, & Dierks, 1993). Known-groups validity coefficients are not known at the present time. The scale has a clinical cutting score of 30.

Index of Family Relations

The Index of Family Relations (IFR) is a global measure of discord within a family. It measures the degree of a problem that family members have in their relationships with one another, as perceived by the client completing the scale (Hamilton & Orme, 1990; Hudson, Acklin, & Bartosh, 1980; Hudson, Hamada, Keech, & Harlan, 1980; Tutty, 1995). It is another scale that can be used flexibly. When completed by a single client, it offers a picture of the individual's sense of discord or stress within the family. When completed by two or more clients from the same family, it can also provide practitioners with therapeutically valuable information about differing perspectives of intrafamilial functioning.

The IFR has produced scores with high levels of reliability (over .90) and strong validity coefficients. It has a clinical cutting score of 30. Scores above this point are considered indicative of the presence of a clinically significant problem within the family's familial relationships.

ORGANIZATIONAL ASSESSMENT ISSUES

This last category of the short-form CASS scales consists of scales that are not clinical scales in the traditional sense of the term. We have included them in this book, however, because they do touch upon issues that routinely arise for practitioners. The category includes scales that measure issues of client satisfaction, job satisfaction, managerial effectiveness, and sexual harassment. Each of the scales is described in the following text.

Client Satisfaction Inventory

The Client Satisfaction Inventory (CSI) was designed to measure consumer satisfaction with multiple types of services, with service integration and coordination, and with the capacity of services to affect the client's interactions with family members and others (Hudson & McMurtry, 1997). As such, it is useful as a measure of general satisfaction with services among clients of human service agencies. Because the scale was intended for use in diverse settings, wording in each item that relates to the program or service being evaluated is nonspecific. For example, respondents are asked to rate the "services" or "help" they were given, but this may apply to many forms of assistance. Similarly, clients are asked to rate the services received "here" or at "this place," which leaves open the option to use the scale in agencies, private practices, or other venues. Each item is also worded so that it may be used by clients whose services are continuing, as well as those for whom services have ceased.

The CSI has been partially validated. Initial evidence suggests the scale can produce scores with reliability of .90 or greater; and the scale has strong content and construct validity. Known-groups validity coefficients and a clinical cutting score have not yet been established.

Index of Job Satisfaction

The Index of Job Satisfaction (IJS) measures the degree or magnitude of satisfaction a respondent experiences with his or her job (Hudson, Lewis, & Faul, 1998). Items on the scale ask about the individual's job satisfaction, problematic situations, and behaviors with regard to job satisfaction. It is important to recognize that the scale is not directed toward determining the origin or cause of job satisfaction problems for the respondent. It is directed instead to measuring the extent to which job satisfaction is present or absent, as perceived by the respondent.

The IJS has been partially validated. Initial evidence suggests the scale has produced scores with a reliability of .90 or greater; and the scale has strong content and construct validity. Known-groups validity coefficients and a clinical cutting score have not yet been established.

Index of Managerial Effectiveness

The Index of Managerial Effectiveness (IME) measures the managerial effectiveness of a supervisor or manager as seen by employees who observe his or her performance (Hudson, Lewis, & Faul, 1998). Items on the scale ask about the manager's behavior and about problematic situations or behaviors with regard to the person's performance as a manager. High scores on the scale are indicative of strong ability as a manager, and lower scores indicate the relative absence of ability to perform as a manager. Like the Index of Job Satisfaction, this scale is not directed toward determining the origin or cause of problems. It is directed instead to measuring the extent to which managerial ability is present or absent, as perceived by the respondent.

The IME has been partially validated. Initial evidence suggests the scale has produced scores with a reliability of .90 or greater; and the scale has strong content and construct validity. Known-groups validity coefficients and a clinical cutting score have not yet been established.

Index of Sexual Harassment

The Index of Sexual Harassment (ISH) measures the presence and severity of sexual harassment, as perceived by respondents, in relationship to peers or supervisors (Hudson & Decker, 1998). Sexual harassment is broadly defined for this scale, and includes verbal, nonverbal, and physical harassment problems. In addition, peers and associates can be defined in several ways and would include those with whom one works, friendship groups, recreational associates, and many others.

The scale was not developed with the aim of representing or developing an extant theory about the origin or cause of sexual harassment. Rather, the aim for using a scale like the ISH is to measure the extent to which harassment behaviors are present or absent, as seen by the respondent. It is also important to note that the item content of the scale identifies behaviors and events that have been adjudicated as illegal and that are potentially punishable as criminal offenses. Low scores on the scale indicate the presence of little or no harassment experiences, while higher scores indicate the presence of a greater degree or number of such problems.

The ISH has been partially validated. Initial evidence suggests the scale has produced scores with a reliability of .90 or greater; and the scale has strong content and construct validity. Known-groups validity coefficients and a clinical cutting score have not yet been established.

SUMMARY

This chapter has described the short-form assessment scales included in the CASS package. We have described the nature and psychometric properties of each short-form scale in enough detail to facilitate selection of an appropriate measure for evaluating practice.

The scales presented in this chapter are by no means the only short-form scales that are useful for evaluating practice. There are many other published instruments that have been shown to possess solid reliability and validity properties. The CASS scales, however, are worth considering as part of a practitioner's evaluative strategies. They are appropriate for a number of purposes, from some client-screening applications, to client assessments, to use as part of a broader program evaluation strategy. They also are easy for clients to complete and can be quickly scored. This ensures that the scales fit within the time and workload demands of practice.

Now that we have discussed what short-form CASS scales are available for evaluating practice, the next step is to describe how to administer, score, and interpret these scales. The next chapter is dedicated to showing how to use the short-form CASS scales with clients, how to calculate scores from their responses, and how to interpret the results.

12

Administering, Scoring, and Interpreting the Short-Form Scales

I n this chapter, we discuss the procedures for administering, scoring, and interpreting the scores from the CASS short-form scales described in Chapter 11.

STRUCTURE AND SCORING

Each of the short-form scales in CASS is a multi-item summated category partition scale (Stevens, 1968). Most of the short-form scales have 25 items, though a few of them have more or less than 25. Most of the short-form scales have a scoring system that allows item scores to range from 1 to 7. A few, however, only allow item scores to range from 1 to 5. The numbers of items and the range of possible item scores for each scale are shown in Table 12.1. All items in these scales were placed in the scales in random order. The items in all of the scales contain a mixture of positively worded and negatively worded statements. The mixture of positively and negatively worded statements and descriptions was used to help control for response set biases (Hudson, 1997; Nunnally, 1978).

Although each of the short-form scales is multi-item, all of the scales were designed to be *unidimensional*. This means that each scale was designed to measure a single dimension, that is, a single personal or social problem. Most of the scales (see next paragraph on the two exceptions) were designed to measure

Table 12.1 The CASS Scales—Numbers of Items and Range of Item Scores

Scale	Number of Items	Range of Possible Item Scores
Personal Adjustment Issues		
Clinical Anxiety Scale	25	1–5
Generalized Contentment Scale	25	1–7
Index of Alcohol Involvement	25	1–7
Index of Clinical Stress	25	1–7
Index of Drug Involvement	25	1–7
Index of Homophobia	25	1–5
Index of Peer Relations	25	1–7
Index of Self-Esteem	25	1–7
Sexual Attitude Scale	25	1–5
Dyadic Relationship Issues		
Index of Marital Satisfaction	25	1–7
Index of Sexual Satisfaction	25	1–7
Non-physical Abuse of Partner Scale	25	1–7
Partner Abuse Scale: Non-physical	24	1–7
Partner Abuse Scale: Physical	25	1–7
Physical Abuse of Partner Scale	25	1–7
Family Adjustment Issues		
Child's Attitude Toward Father	25	1–7
Child's Attitude Toward Mother	25	1–7
Index of Brother Relations	25	1–7
Index of Family Relations	25	1–7
Index of Parental Attitudes	25	1–7
Index of Sister Relations	25	1–7
Organizational Assessment Issues		
Client Satisfaction Inventory	25	1–7
Index of Job Satisfaction	35	1–7
Index of Managerial Effectiveness	30	1–7
Index of Sexual Harassment	19	1–7

the severity or magnitude of a specific personal or social problem. In a sense, then, each scale can be thought of as a type of thermometer. It will provide a measure of the degree or magnitude of a personal or social problem, but it will provide no information about the cause, source, or origin of the problem. This is just like a thermometer, which provides information about how "hot" something is and yet gives no information about the source of the heat that has brought about the temperature in the object.

As mentioned in the previous paragraph, two of the short-form scales do *not* measure the magnitude or severity of a clinical problem. As noted in Chapter 11, the Index of Homophobia (IHP) measures the degree or magnitude of a client's problem with *homophobia*: the fear of being in close quarters with homosexuals. The IHP, therefore, is not designed to measure a personal or social problem per se. Similarly, the Sexual Attitude Scale (SAS) is designed to measure liberal versus conservative attitudes toward human sexual expression. Thus, the SAS reflects a value position and is not designed to measure a personal or social problem per se.

Since each scale (with the two exceptions just discussed) has been designed as a measure of the magnitude or severity of a particular personal or social problem, each is scored in such a manner that higher scores are indicative of greater magnitude, or more severe, problems, and lower scores indicative of the relative absence of such problems.

The first step in scoring any one of the scales is to *reverse-score each of the positively worded items*. The formula for this process is

$$y = (k + 1) - x \tag{12.1}$$

where y is the reversed score, k is the highest possible score for the item, and x is the original item score. For example, suppose that the highest possible score for an item is 7, and that the person responding to the item marked it with a 5. The reverse score would then be

$$y = (k + 1) - x = (7 + 1) - 5 = 8 - 5 = 3 \tag{12.2}$$

For items whose highest possible score is 7, this scoring procedure changes item scores as follows: a 7 becomes a 1; a 6 becomes a 2; a 5 becomes a 3; a 4 stays a 4; a 3 becomes a 5; a 2 becomes a 6; and a 1 becomes a 7. For items whose highest possible score is 5, this scoring procedure changes items scores as follows: a 5 becomes a 1; a 4 becomes a 2; a 3 stays a 3; a 2 becomes a 4; and a 1 becomes a 5. This illustrates how the term *reverse-score* came about. In reverse-scoring, each item score is "flipped" around the middle score (the 3 for item scores ranging from 1 to 5, and the 4 for item scores ranging from 1 to 7) so that it is transformed into its corresponding opposite on the other side of the middle score.

The specific items that must be reverse-scored differ from scale to scale. For this reason, the items that need to be reverse-scored are listed on each of the short-form scales on the lower left-hand side of the scale directly underneath the copyright. For example, underneath the copyright on the Generalized Contentment Scale (GCS), the following set of numbers is listed: 5, 8, 9, 11, 12, 13, 15, 16, 21, 22, 23, 24. These numbers identify the items that must be reverse-scored on this scale.

After reverse-scoring each item that needs to be reverse-scored, the total score, S, on any of the short-form scales is computed by the formula

$$S = \frac{100[sum(y) - N]}{N(k-1)} \tag{12.3}$$

Where y is the item responses, N is the number of items properly completed by the client, and k is the largest possible item score on the scale. Any item that is left blank, or is given a score by the client other than one of the possible item scores (such as a number outside the allowable range or some other response such as the word *yes* written in the item blank), is given a score of 0. There are two important advantages of using the scoring formula in Equation 12.3. First, the formula produces a total score on the scale that ranges from 0 to 100. This score range helps make it easier to interpret the client's score. Second, this formula will produce a score ranging from 0 to 100 regardless of the number of items the client fails to respond to or completes in an improper manner. The effect of the scoring formula is to replace omitted or improperly scored items with the mean of the items the client properly completed.

Let us provide an example. Suppose that the client responds to the 25 GCS items as follows:

Item 1: 6	Item 6: 3	Item 11: 3	Item 16: 2	Item 21: 2
Item 2: 5	Item 7: 6	Item 12: yes	Item 17: 5	Item 22: 2
Item 3: 3	Item 8: 1	Item 13: 3	Item 18: 5	Item 23: 2
Item 4: 6	Item 9: 2	Item 14: 4	Item 19: 5	Item 24: 3
Item 5: 2	Item 10: 4	Item 15: 3	Item 20: 6	Item 25: 5

First notice that item number 12 has been responded to in an improper manner, so this item is scored with a zero (0). Next, the positively worded items must be reverse-scored. These are identified on the GCS under the copyright, as noted earlier. So these items are scored as follows: item number $5 = 8 - 2 = 6$; item number $8 = 8 - 1 = 7$; item number $9 = 8 - 2 = 6$; item number $11 = 8 - 3 = 5$; item number $12 = 0$ because it was improperly responded to; item number $13 = 8 - 3 = 5$; item number $15 = 8 - 3 = 5$; item number $16 = 8 - 2 = 6$; item number $21 = 8 - 2 = 6$; item number $22 = 8 - 2 = 6$; item number $23 = 8 - 2 = 6$; and item number $24 = 8 - 3 = 5$. The sum of these reverse scores is 63, and the sum of all the nonreverse-scored item scores is 63. Thus, the total sum of item scores is 126. The highest possible item score on the GCS is 7, and 24 of the items were properly responded to. Thus, this client's score on the GCS is

$$S = \frac{100[sum(y) - N]}{N(k - 1)} = \frac{100(126 - 24)}{24(7 - 1)} = \frac{100(102)}{24(6)} = \frac{10200}{144} = 70.83 \cong 71$$

Our experience over the years has suggested that if the client agrees to complete one or more of the CASS scales, it will be a rare event if he or she responds improperly (or fails to respond) to more than five items. The omission of five or fewer items on any of the short-form scales will have a negligible effect on the reliability or validity of the score produced by the scale. This is a consequence of the fact that all of the scales were built on the domain sampling model of measurement (Nunnally, 1978). The omission of a few items will not appreciably threaten the content validity of the items on any particular scale. However, if the client fails to respond to, or improperly responds to, 20 percent or more of the items on any of the short-form scales, then the entire completed scale should be discarded. In this situation, the practitioner would need to discuss the situation with the client and find out why he or she failed to respond to (or responded improperly to) so many of the items on the scale.

When used in applied settings, the short-form scales can be completed by the vast majority of clients in less than five minutes, and can be scored in about the same amount of time. The scales can, of course, also be administered and/or scored using the CASS software. If one elects to hand-score one of the short-form scales, it is good practice to circle each item that must be reverse scored, and then cross out the original score and write next to the crossed-out score the reverse score for the item. This process will help the practitioner to accurately score the scale.

INTERPRETING THE SHORT-FORM SCALE SCORES

Each of the short-form scales (except for the SAS and IHP) were designed to measure the degree or severity of a personal or social problem, and the scores on these scales were conceived as reflecting a magnitude continuum. Higher scores are indicative of greater magnitude problems, and lower scores are indicative of problems of lesser severity. Thus, if Joe scores a 65 on the GCS on September 10th, and then a 50 on October 10th, it is proper to infer that Joe is less depressed on October 10th than he was on September 10th. A similar interpretation can be made with each of the short-form scales, except for the IHP and SAS. Thus, in practice, one of the principal goals of service delivery will be to lower clients' scores on the short-form scales.

Scores on the IHP should be interpreted as follows. The IHP has a "cutting" score of 50. As scores increase above 50, they are reflective of an increasing fear of being in close proximity with homosexuals. As scores decrease from 50, they are reflective of an increasing degree of comfort with being in close proximity with homosexuals. Scores on the SAS should be interpreted as follows. The SAS also has a "cutting" score of 50. As scores increase above 50, they are reflective of an increasingly conservative orientation toward human sexual expression. As scores decrease from 50, they are reflective of an increasingly liberal orientation toward sexual expression.

Each of the short-form scales has a *clinical cutting score*. The clinical cutting score is a criterion that allows the practitioner to make a specific type of inference. Specifically, the clinical cutting scores allow the practitioner to infer the presence (or absence) of a clinically significant problem. If the client scores at or above the clinical cutting score, this is prima facia evidence that he or she has a clinically significant problem in the area the scale measures. For example, if the client scores at or above the clinical cutting score on the GCS, this is prima facia evidence that he or she has a clinically significant problem with depression. If the client scores below the clinical cutting score on the GCS, this suggests that he or she does *not* have a clinically significant problem with depression. The clinical cutting scores for each of the short-form scales are shown in Table 11.2 in Chapter 11.

The clinical cutting scores enable the practitioner to make tentative diagnostic decisions. If a client scores at or above the clinical cutting score, the practitioner can make the tentative diagnostic decision that the client has a clinically significant problem in the area measured by the scale. However, this decision should be merely tentative; the score should be interpreted as an indication that further assessment is needed in this area in this case. No inference made from the scores from a measurement tool will be error-free, and this includes decisions about diagnostic classifications, such as "clinically depressed" or "not clinically depressed." When making such decisions, there are four possible outcomes, as shown in Figure 12.1.

The first possible outcome is shown in the box in the upper left corner of Figure 12.1. In this case the practitioner decides, based on the fact that the client's score is below a clinical cutting score, that he or she does *not* have a significant problem in this area. In "reality," the client does *not* have a clinically significant problem in the area reflected by the scale scores. In this case, the decision process has resulted in a *true negative*; the practitioner has decided that the client does *not* have a significant problem in this area when the client, in fact, does *not*. This is a correct decision.

The second possible outcome is shown in the lower right corner of Figure 12.1. In this case the practitioner decides, based on the fact that the client's score is above a clinical cutting score, that the client *does* have a significant problem in this area. In "reality," the client *does* have a clinically significant problem in the area reflected by the scale scores. In this case, the decision process has resulted in a *true positive*; the practitioner has decided that the client *does* have a significant problem in this area when the client, in fact, *does*. This is, again, a correct decision.

The third possible outcome is shown in the box in the lower left corner of Figure 12.1. In this case the practitioner decides, based on the fact that the client's score is below a clinical cutting score, that the client does *not* have a significant problem in this area. In "reality," the client *does* have a clinically significant problem in the area reflected by the scale scores. In this case, the decision process has resulted in a *false negative*; the practitioner has decided that the client does *not* have a significant problem in this area when the client, in fact, *does*. This is an incorrect decision.

The fourth, and final, possible outcome is shown in the upper right corner of Figure 12.1. In this case the practitioner decides, based on the fact that the client's score is above a clinical cutting score, that the client *does* have a significant problem in this area. In "reality," the client does *not* have a clinically significant problem in the area reflected by the scale scores. In this case, the decision process has resulted in a *false positive*; the practitioner has decided that the client *does* have a significant problem in this area when the client, in fact, does *not*. This is also an incorrect decision.

Many of the decisions practitioners make can be modeled in this manner, and one of the important jobs faced in practice is maximizing the true positives

**Decisions based on
clinical cutting scores**

	Client does *not* have a clinically significant problem	Client has a clinically significant problem
Client, in fact, does *not* have a problem	True negative	False positive
Client, in fact, *does* have a problem	False negative	True positive

"Reality"

FIGURE 12.1 The decision matrix showing the types of errors that can be made in decision making about client's problems.

and true negatives, while minimizing the false negatives and false positives (Garb, 1998). In this spirit, we strongly recommend that practitioners use the clinical cutting scores to make *tentative* decisions. These decisions must be backed up with additional information before the practitioner moves the decision from the "tentative" category into a category with more certainty attached. Our experience and research has suggested that most often, the decision made based on the relationship between the client's score and the clinical cutting score will be correct. However, there is enough uncertainty that practitioners should always strive to accumulate additional information before making final, important decisions about a client's care. This is especially true when making decisions with life-or-death implications, such as decisions about suicide risk or risk-of-harm to others (Bongar et al., 1998).

The clinical cutting scores can also be used as criteria to mark "success" in working with clients. If a client starts out with scores on a particular scale above the clinical cutting score on that scale and then, after service provision, obtains scores that are below the clinical cutting score, the practitioner has evidence that the client has improved to the point that he or she no longer has a clinically significant problem in the area measured by the scores on the scale. This is a second, very useful way in which the clinical cutting scores can be used. However, again, practitioners need to obtain other evidence that is consistent with the decision made using the clinical cutting scores before deciding that a client has, in fact, reached a point where her or his problem is no longer clinically significant.

There are three basic reasons that a client's score may be such that it suggests a clinically significant (or clinically nonsignificant) problem and yet all other evidence suggests the opposite. Because of these reasons, which are discussed in the text that follows, practitioners should always investigate discrepancies between the various forms of evidence obtained from clients. If a client scores above the clinical cutting score on one of the short-form scales, and yet all other information points to the absence of a clinically significant problem in the problem area reflected by the scale scores, then the practitioner should ask the client to help resolve the inconsistency.

The first reason for inconsistencies concerns the possibility that the client has responded to the items on the scale in order to give a particular type of impression. He or she may be responding to the items out of a "social desirability" mindset and may be attempting to try to make him- or herself "look good." He or she may also be trying to make him- or herself "look bad" for some reason.

The second possibility is that the manner in which the practitioner administered the scale may have created a set of "demand characteristics" that led the client to respond to items on the scale in a manner that does not reflect the problem area being assessed. For example, suppose that a practitioner has a client complete one of the short-form scales while sitting in the waiting room at the agency. Suppose further that the chairs in the waiting room in the agency are set up to be very close to one another, and that they are so close that the client recognizes that her or his responses might be read by the person sitting next to him or her. In such a circumstance, if there is, indeed, someone sitting next to the client, he or she may *not* respond accurately to the items on the scale.

The third reason for contradictory evidence between a client's scores (and their relationship with a clinical cutting score) and other forms of information is measurement error. The standard error of measurement (SEM) for each of the short-form scales is given in Table 11.2 in Chapter 11. The SEM reported for the scales in Table 11.2 can be used to decrease false-positive and false-negative rates. The SEM can be thought of as a rough guideline as to the amount of error in a client's score; and therefore, it can be used to put an error band around the client's score. The best way to do this is as follows. First, find the SEM for the particular short-form scale in Table 11.2 that is being used. Next, multiply that SEM value by 2, and then round that number to the next whole integer. Finally, add and subtract this value from the client's score in order to obtain upper and lower bounds for the client's score. These upper and lower bounds reflect the uncertainty that is in the client's score due to measurement error.

For example, suppose that the GCS is being used and the client obtains a score of 35. The SEM for the GCS, found in Table 11.2, is 4.26. We next multiply this value by 2, obtaining 4.26 times 2 equals 8.52, which rounded to the next whole integer is 9. Finally, we add and subtract 9 from the client's score of 35:

$$35 + 9 = 44$$
$$35 - 9 = 26$$

Thus, the upper bound for the client's score is 44, and the lower bound is 26.

These upper and lower bounds can be used to make decisions about a client with lower likelihoods of false negatives and false positives. Here is how it is done. Suppose that a practitioner wants to be really sure that a client does *not* have a clinically significant problem. That is, the practitioner wants to make a decision that has a low likelihood of being a false negative (i.e., deciding that the client does *not* have a clinically significant problem when, in fact, he or she *does*). A practitioner might want to do this when making an initial assessment with a client or when providing evidence that a client has reached a point where he or she no longer has a significant problem. To decrease the likelihood of a false negative in this case, the practitioner would *use the lower bound as a clinical cutting score*. By using the lower bound as the clinical cutting score, the measurement error most likely to exist in the client's score is taken into account, thereby decreasing the likelihood of making a decision that is a false negative. It is important to note that as one lowers the likelihood of a false negative, one simultaneously *increases* the likelihood of a false positive.

Now suppose that a practitioner wants to be really sure that a client *does* have a clinically significant problem. That is, the practitioner wants to make a decision that has a low likelihood of being a false positive (i.e., deciding that a client *does* have a clinically significant problem when, in fact, he or she does *not*). To decrease the likelihood of a false positive in this case, the practitioner would *use the upper bound as a clinical cutting score*. By using the upper bound as the clinical cutting score, the measurement error most likely to exist in the client's score is taken into account, thereby decreasing the likelihood of making a decision that is a false positive. It is important to note that as one lowers the likelihood of a false positive, one simultaneously *increases* the likelihood of a false negative.

Anytime a client produces a score of 70 or higher on the short-form scales, the practitioner needs to be concerned about the possibility of violence (except, of course, in the case of the SAS or IHP). Clients who score 70 or above may be at risk of doing violence to themselves and/or others. It has been our experience that few people will score this high on the short-form scales; and when they do, they almost invariably are experiencing very severe levels of personal or social problems. For example, one of the authors who was conducting research on the GCS had a respondent in a day-treatment facility score 87 on the GCS. It turned out that the respondent was severely depressed and was actively suicidal; the agency staff were unaware of this.

Scores of 70 or above on the GCS and/or ISE should alert practitioners to the possibility of suicidal ideation and/or intent. Scores of 70 or above on the CAM, CAF, and IPA scales should alert practitioners to the possibility of violence toward a child or parent, while scores of 70 or above on the IMS or ISS scales should alert practitioners to the possibility of violence toward a partner or spouse. In addition, a score of 70 or above on the IMS or ISS may also indicate that a divorce or separation is a distinct possibility.

The short-form scales were not designed to make predictions of violence. Because of this fact, practitioners should use the interpretive guideline in the previous paragraph with due caution. When making decisions about violence potential, practitioners can make decisions that are false positive or false negative. In the case of violence prediction, however, practitioners will almost always want to make decisions with a low likelihood of committing a false negative error—that is, practitioners want to minimize the chances of deciding that a person is *not* going to be violent when, in fact, he or she *will* be violent. The judicious use of the scores on the short-form scales, along with the use of information from interviews with the client as well as collateral information, can help practitioners to make the most defensible decisions possible (Bongar et al., 1998; Fremouw et al., 1990).

ADMINISTERING THE SCALES

We have discussed some of the ways in which error can appear in the interpretation of scores obtained from clients on the short-form scales. The likelihood of error can be reduced through the ways in which the scales are administered. The following text presents a few guidelines to help in the administration of the short-form scales. These practices will increase the likelihood that a client will respond to the items on the scales in an honest and accurate manner.

Present the Scales with Confidence

One of the worst things a practitioner can do is to present the scale he or she wishes to use to a client in anything other than a matter-of-fact, confident manner. For example, imagine a practitioner approaching a client in the following manner and requesting that the client complete a particular scale. The following is said in a hesitant, apologetic manner: "Joe, I hate to have to ask you to do this, and I know it will take away from our talk time and that you will probably not like doing this, but I would like for you to complete this scale. After you have completed it, I will just put it away and you won't have to worry about it. Now you don't have to do this if you don't want to, Joe. Do you want to fill it out?" Compare and contrast this approach with one in which the practitioner says the following in a confident, matter-of-fact manner: "Joe, one of the most important things I need to do is to determine what problems we need to work on and how severe they are. In order to accomplish these things, I would like for you to complete this scale. The scores from this scale will assist me in deciding how to best help you, and they will help us to know whether or not I am succeeding in helping you. After you complete it, I will score it, and we can discuss what the score means. It should only take you about five minutes to complete. Do you have any questions about it?"

The first approach style is very likely going to convey to the client that the use of the scale is unnecessary and a waste of time. It is also unlikely to elicit the client's confidence. The second approach style is more likely to convey that the use of the scale is an integral, normal, and important part of service provision. It is also likely to elicit the client's confidence and agreement to complete the scale.

It is also important to convey to the client that the short-form scales are *not* tests and that there are no right or wrong answers. Instead, the items on the scales are designed to assist the practitioner in evaluating and monitoring the client's problems. In addition, it is important to share the client's scores with the client. This will help reduce any suspicions that the client may have about the scales, the scores that they produce, and how the practitioner intends to use the scores.

Be Familiar with Scale Performance

Practitioners should be familiar with the scales they plan to use. They should know how the scales read, what it is like to complete them, as well as how they are scored and how the scores should be interpreted. Thus, *practitioners should take the time to complete any of the scales that they intend to use with clients*. This will help practitioners to gain a greater familiarity with each of the scales. Practitioners should score the scales they have completed and compare the scores with how they are feeling in the area the scores reflect. It is also useful for practitioners to remember a time when they had a meaningful problem in the areas measured by the scales. For example, suppose that a practitioner remembers a time a couple of years ago when he or she was feeling depressed. By completing the GCS while recalling how he or she felt and thought during that time and responding to the items as if he or she were back in that time, the practitioner can then compare a current GCS score with the score obtained while recalling the feelings and thoughts from a couple of years ago. This can help the practitioner gain some insight into how the short-form scales work, as well as some understanding of how clients might be feeling when they obtain similar scores. This can aid in the development of accurate empathy.

Explain the Purpose of the Scales

It is important that practitioners clearly explain how they intend to use the scores from the scales. Doing so can greatly reduce any suspicions that clients have about the scales and the scores they get. Clients' concerns can be further reduced when their scores are shared with them. It is also useful to plot a client's scores and share the plot with the client. The practitioner can use this as a means to double-check his or her assessments of how the client is progressing.

Avoid Excessive Administration

Practitioners should not administer the scales too frequently. It is probably best to administer any of the scales no more than once a week.

Check Out Inconsistent Responses

If any inconsistent responses appear on the scale, the practitioner should check them out with the client. Sometimes the client will simply make a mistake. If an inconsistency is caught and pointed out to the client, he or she can immediately correct it. This will help to ensure that accurate information is obtained from clients. If the inconsistent response is *not* an error, the reason for the inconsistency will be important clinical information for the practitioner to have.

Consider Social Desirability, Demand Characteristics, and Misleading Responses

Finally, practitioners should think carefully about the circumstances under which they have their clients complete the scales. They should put themselves "in the client's skin" in the same circumstances and imagine completing the scales. What unintended pressures do the circumstances create that might lead the client to feel a need to respond to items in a misleading manner? By minimizing psychological and social pressures that are created by the circumstances under which the client is completing the scale, practitioners can increase the likelihood that the client will respond accurately and honestly to the items on the scale.

For example, suppose that a practitioner wants a client to complete the IMS at home during the week between appointments. Having the client complete the IMS like this could create some real problems for the client, as well as lead to inaccurate responses. The client may be concerned that his or her partner might see him or her completing the IMS, or that his or her partner might find the completed IMS and read it. Such concerns may lead the client to respond in a manner that he or she believes would please the partner rather than in a manner that accurately reflects how the client feels.

If practitioners put themselves in their clients' shoes and carefully imagine how the clients might feel, and what they might think, in the circumstances in which they are completing the short-form scale, practitioners can often identify social and/or psychological pressures that can lead clients to answer items inaccurately. By then altering the circumstances under which clients complete the scale, such pressures can be minimized. Doing this will help to ensure that the information obtained from clients is accurate.

13

Multidimensional Assessment Tools

Rarely do clients come to practitioners with a single problem. In most instances, clients describe situations that entail multiple problems of personal functioning and with social relationships. The short-form scales described in earlier chapters are unidimensional—they were designed to measure only one problem area, such as depression or marital discord. As such, the short-form scales are extremely useful tools for helping to assess a client's problem in a single specific area of personal or social functioning. They are also very valuable as repeated-measures tools for monitoring a client's progress (or lack thereof) during treatment. However, unidimensional tools are not useful for simultaneously assessing a client's functioning in multiple areas of personal and social functioning.

In this chapter, we discuss *multidimensional assessment tools*. These are measurement devices that allow practitioners to simultaneously assess clients' functioning in multiple areas. Multidimensional assessment tools measure more than one dimension—that is, they provide measures of multiple constructs—and, as opposed to producing a single score, as is the case with the short-form scales, they produce multiple scores, or score profiles. Thus, multidimensional assessment tools can be extremely valuable as an aid in conducting a comprehensive assessment of a client's personal and social functioning in as short a time as possible. Multidimensional tools are also congruent with an ecological or systems perspective of clients' problems.

In this chapter, we discuss two multidimensional assessment tools: the Multi-Problem Screening Inventory, or the MPSI, and the Family Assessment

Screening Inventory, or the FASI. Both the MPSI and the FASI can be scored and administered using the CASS software.

THE MULTI-PROBLEM SCREENING INVENTORY (MPSI)

The Multi-Problem Screening Inventory (MPSI) is a paper-and-pencil self-report measure that can be used to assess client problems in 27 different areas of personal and social functioning. The MPSI contains 334 items and requires 30 to 45 minutes to complete. It can be manually scored in about 30 minutes. It can be scored more quickly using the CASS software. One advantage of the MPSI is that it produces a graphic profile that shows, at a glance, the magnitude or severity of a client's problems in each of the 27 areas of personal and social functioning.

The MPSI should be used primarily at intake as an aid in assessment and treatment planning. It can also be used immediately prior to service termination as a means of providing evidence that a client has improved during the course of service provision. It is not well suited as a repeated-measures instrument. The short-form scales we have already discussed are more appropriate for repeated measures. The MPSI is better suited for use as a screening tool that allows practitioners to quickly, and yet objectively and comprehensively, assess a wide range of areas in which a client may be having problems. It is very likely that no practitioner, using a typical free-style interview, could obtain as much information from as many areas of personal and social functioning in as short a time as can be obtained by using the MPSI.

The MPSI is a problem-focused assessment tool. It is *not* a personality inventory, such as the well-known Minnesota Multiphasic Personality Inventory (the MMPI). Earlier we described the short-form scales as a type of thermometer. Each short-form scale was metaphorically described as a thermometer that allows the practitioner to quickly assess the magnitude of a client's problem in a particular area of personal or social functioning. The MPSI can be thought of as a *collection* of 27 thermometers in a single package. Each of the 27 thermometers will give the practitioner a reading of the severity and magnitude of a client's problem in a specific area of personal and social functioning. Another way of thinking about the MPSI is as a collection of 27 short-form summated rating scales. Each subscale produces an overall score, just like the short-form scales. In addition, the MPSI produces an overall, multidimensional "score" in the form of the profile briefly mentioned earlier. An example of this profile is shown in Figure 13.1.

The MPSI Items

Each subscale of the MPSI contains between 7 and 20 Likert-type items and is scored on a category partition (just like the short-form scales) that ranges from 1 to 7. The numbers of items on each subscale were selected for three reasons: (1) to produce acceptable reliability estimates for subscale scores;

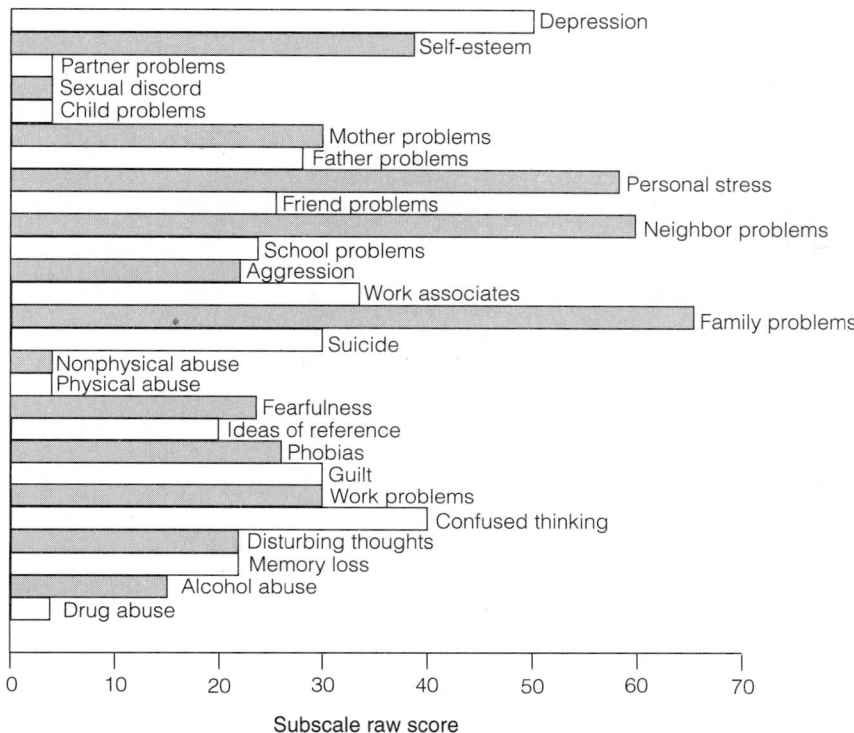

FIGURE 13.1 Example of graphic profile of MSPI subscale scores for a fictitious client.

(2) to keep the subscales short enough to keep client fatigue when responding to the MPSI items to an acceptable level; and (3) to make the scoring procedures simple and quickly accomplished.

The MPSI Subscale Scores

Each subscale is scored in the same manner, as we discuss in detail in the next chapter. Practitioners only need to learn one scoring procedure. As will be seen shortly, the scoring method for the MPSI subscales is the same as that already described for the short-form scales. Also similar to the short-form scales, each MPSI subscale produces a score that ranges from 0 to 100, with higher scores indicative of greater magnitude problems, and vice versa. There are also clinical cutting scores on each of the MPSI subscales. These are discussed in greater detail in the following text.

Restrictions on Use of the MPSI There are few specific restrictions on the use of the MPSI subscales. One concerns age. The MPSI should not be used with persons younger than 12 years of age. The literacy skills, cognitive development, and ability to integrate affective responses with the item content and meaning of each of the subscales demand a level of maturity not usually found in children under 12 years of age. That said, however, it is important to recognize that the decision to use (or not to use) the MPSI with any given client should be made on a case-by-case basis. If it is the practitioner's best clinical judgment that a 10- or 11-year-old child can accurately complete (some of) the MPSI subscales, then the practitioner should use them. One of the authors has experimented with administering the MPSI to children as young as 10 and has found that many can complete at least some of the MPSI subscales in an accurate and meaningful manner. As with any other client, however, practitioners will want to make sure that any children younger than 12 years old whom they have complete the MPSI understand the meaning of the subscales and the items to which they respond.

A second restriction is that the MPSI should not be used with persons who have severe cognitive impairment (such as active psychosis, brain damage, etc.). Severely impaired individuals rarely give valid responses to the MPSI items. Keep in mind, however, that the term *cognitive impairment* is not an all-or-nothing categorization. There may be persons with some degree of cognitive impairment who will be able to accurately and validly complete one or more of the MPSI subscales. Again, clinical judgment must be brought to bear on the making of such decisions.

A third restriction is that practitioners should use the MPSI (or any other clinical tool, including interviews) with great caution in situations in which they are in a position to give or withhold important or valued social rewards or sanctions for a client, and when a client's responses to MPSI items can be seen as having a possible influence on the practitioner's decisions regarding the rewards or sanctions. For example, suppose that a practitioner is in a position to have the power to release a client from a residential facility and the client has the idea that her or his responses to the MPSI can influence the practitioner's decision about her or his possible release. Depending on whether or not the client wants to be released, he or she may purposely try to make him- or herself look better or worse than he or she is actually functioning in an attempt to influence the practitioner's decision. In such circumstances as these, practitioners need to look at the MPSI results, as well as any other data on the client, very closely and judge the results in the context of the situation and all of the evidence available as to how the client is doing. This is the type of situation in which the practitioner will want to closely inspect the consistency of the client's responses, both within and across the MPSI subscales as well as across forms and types of evidence.

A final limitation on the use of the MPSI is that it should be used only with persons who have grown up in, or lived in for a reasonable period of time, what would be regarded as a "western" culture. The psychometric research and development that has gone into the creation of the MPSI has relied predominantly on those who have grown up in the United States, or who have lived in the United States for a very long time. We are not sure how well the MPSI will perform with persons from cultures markedly different from the western culture in the United States.

The MPSI Subscales

In the following text, we briefly describe each of the 27 MPSI subscales. As will be seen, some of them are just shorter versions of the short-form scales we described earlier. Others are unique and specific to the MPSI. Each of the subscales has a clinical cutting score, and these are described in the text that follows.

Depression The MPSI depression subscale contains 12 items from the GCS. The depression subscale is created to assess the severity and magnitude of a client's problem with depression. This subscale has a clinical cutting score of 30, so a score of 30 or above on the depression subscale should be taken as preliminary evidence that the respondent has a clinically significant problem with depression. A score at or above 70 should be taken as an indicator of the possibility of suicidal ideation and/or potential.

Self-Esteem The MPSI depression subscale contains 12 items from the ISE. The self-esteem subscale is created to assess the severity and magnitude of a client's problem with self-esteem. This subscale has a clinical cutting score of 30, so a score of 30 or above on this subscale should be taken as preliminary evidence that the respondent has a clinically significant problem with self-esteem. A score at or above 70 should be taken as an indicator of the possibility of suicidal ideation and/or potential.

The self-esteem subscale can be used flexibly to target a client's self-esteem problems in specific areas of her or his functioning. Although this subscale can be used to obtain an overall measure of a client's problems with self-esteem, it is important to note that a client might have very positive self-esteem in one area of her or his functioning, such as in her or his professional self-concept, while at the same time having a less-than-positive self-esteem in another area, such as with respect to her or his interpersonal relationship skills. Thus, a practitioner can ask a client to complete this subscale *within the context of her or his sense of her or his interpersonal relationship skills* in order to get a more refined assessment.

Suppose, for example, that a practitioner is working with a very shy young man who is very confident about his professional abilities as an engineer, but who feels very badly with respect to his ability to engage in dating relationships. In this case, the practitioner might elect to have the young man complete the MPSI self-esteem subscale in relation to his sense of himself with regard to his ability to engage in dating relationships. This approach will help practitioners to more sharply focus on self-esteem problems in specific areas in clients' lives.

Partner Relationship Problems The partner relationship subscale is designed to measure the magnitude or severity of a problem a spouse or partner has in a partner relationship. The items on this subscale are a subset of items from the IMS. This subscale is a measure of relationship discord. It is not limited to measuring the discord in a marital relationship; rather, it can be used to measure the magnitude of discord in any partner relationship, including dating relationships and living together relationships, and regardless of whether clients are heterosexual or homosexual.

This subscale has a clinical cutting score of 30, so a score of 30 or above on this subscale should be taken as preliminary evidence that the respondent has a clinically significant problem with in his or her relationship with a partner. A score of 70 or higher should alert the practitioner to the possibility of violence in the client's partner relationship.

Sexual Discord This subscale was designed to measure the magnitude of a problem in the sexual component of a dyadic relationship. It measures the magnitude of discord or dissatisfaction felt or perceived by the client with respect to the sexual relationship with a spouse or partner. The items on this subscale come from the ISS. Although partner relationship problems and sexual discord scales tend to be highly correlated, these subscales measure different problems, and neither of these should used as a substitute for the other.

This subscale has a clinical cutting score of 30, so a score of 30 or above on this subscale should be taken as preliminary evidence that the respondent has a clinically significant problem in the sexual component of her or his partner relationship. A score of 70 or higher should alert the practitioner to the possibility of violence in the relationship.

Problems with My Child This subscale enables the client to describe the magnitude of a problem that he or she has in relating to a specific child. The items on this subscale are drawn from the IPA. However, the items are ambiguous enough that they require a client to decide which, if any, child will be the target of the assessment. If the client does not have any children, then have the client place an X in the answer space for the first item and then draw a line straight down through the remaining item response spaces. This will indicate that the scale is not relevant for the client. If the client specifies a child who is to be the focus of the assessment, then have the client write the child's name beside the subscale name. If the client indicates that he or she is having problems with more than one child, it is possible to use the subscale to render an overall assessment of the magnitude of the problem the client is having with all of the problematic children. If this is the case, then have the client write the names of the children who are the focus of the assessment beside the subscale name.

This subscale has a clinical cutting score of 30, so a score of 30 or above on this subscale should be taken as preliminary evidence that the respondent has a clinically significant problem in her or his relationship with the identified child (or children). A score of 70 or higher should alert the practitioner to the possibility of violence in the client's relationship with the identified child (or children).

Problems with Mother This subscale enables the client to provide an assessment of the magnitude of problems that he or she is having with his or her mother. The items on this subscale come from the CAM. Although in most circumstances there is no ambiguity associated with the relationship of focus for this subscale, there are circumstances in which the target relationship will be uncertain. For example, the client may have a birth mother as well as a step-mother, or he or she may have a mother surrogate (such as an aunt or a foster mother) because the client's birth mother is deceased or no longer a part of the client's "family." In such cases, the client should write the name of the "mother relationship" that the client is assessing next to the subscale name. If this sub-scale is irrelevant for the client, then have her or him mark an X in the space for the first item on this subscale and then draw a vertical line down through the remaining item spaces for this subscale.

This subscale has a clinical cutting score of 30, so a score of 30 or above on this subscale should be taken as preliminary evidence that the respondent has a clinically significant problem in her or his relationship with the identified mother figure. A score of 70 or higher should alert the practitioner to the pos-sibility of violence in the client's relationship with the identified mother figure.

Problems with Father   This subscale enables the client to provide an assess-ment of the magnitude of problems that he or she is having with his or her father. The items on this subscale come from the CAF. Although in most cir-cumstances there is no ambiguity associated with the relationship of focus for this subscale, there are circumstances in which the target relationship will be uncertain. For example, the client may have a natural father as well as a step-father, or he or she may have a father surrogate (such as an uncle or a foster father) because the client's natural father is deceased or no longer a part of the client's "family." In such cases, the client should write the name of the "father relationship" that the client is assessing next to the subscale name. If this sub-scale is irrelevant for the client, then have her or him mark an X in the space for the first item on this subscale and then draw a vertical line down through the remaining item spaces for this subscale.

This subscale has a clinical cutting score of 30, so a score of 30 or above on this subscale should be taken as preliminary evidence that the respondent has a clinically significant problem in her or his relationship with the identified father figure. A score of 70 or higher should alert the practitioner to the pos-sibility of violence in the client's relationship with the identified father figure.

Personal Stress   This subscale is designed to measure the magnitude of prob-lems with stress, across all areas of the client's life, that the client is currently experiencing. However, there may be times when it will be useful to measure the level of stress the client is experiencing in a more specific and narrow part of her or his life, such as at work or in her or his role as a parent. If this is the case, the practitioner will want to have the client write next to the name of the subscale the specific area of her or his life that is being rated in terms of stress.

This subscale has a clinical cutting score of 30, so a score of 30 or above on this subscale should be taken as preliminary evidence that the respondent has a clinically significant problem with stress. A score at or above 70 should be taken as an indicator of the possibility of suicidal ideation and/or potential, especially when accompanied by an elevated depression score and/or an elevated suicidal thoughts score.

Problems with Friends This subscale is designed to measure the magnitude of problems that the client is experiencing with her or his friendships. It can be used as a global measure of problems that the client is having in this area of her or his life, or it can be used to assess problems with a specific group of friends or with a specific friend. In such a case, the practitioner will need to have the client write the name of the friend or friendship group that the client is assessing next to the subscale name.

This subscale has a clinical cutting score of 30, so any scores at or above this level should be taken as preliminary evidence that the client has a clinically significant problem in this area. Scores at or above 70 should alert the practitioner to the possibility of violence.

Problems with Neighbors This subscale is designed to measure the magnitude of problems that the client is having in her or his dealings with one or more neighbors. Problems with neighbors can be very revealing of difficulties the client has in her or his social and community relations. On the other hand, sometimes the client will have, for all practical purposes, no relationships with any of her or his neighbors; in such a case, have the client place an X in the space for the answer to the first item on this subscale and then draw a vertical line down through the remaining item response spaces for this subscale. This will indicate that the subscale is not relevant for the client.

This subscale has a clinical cutting score of 30, so a score of 30 or above on this subscale should be taken as preliminary evidence that the respondent has a clinically significant problem in her or his relationship with one or more neighbors. A score of 70 or higher should alert the practitioner to the possibility of violence in the client's relationship with her or his neighbors.

Problems with School This subscale is very useful when working with adolescents or with adults who are attending school on either a full- or a part-time basis. It is designed to measure the magnitude of problems that the client is having in school. If the client is not attending school, then have him or her place an X in the response space for the first item on this subscale and then draw a vertical line down through the remaining item response spaces for this subscale in order to indicate that the subscale is not relevant for this client.

This subscale has a clinical cutting score of 30, so a score of 30 or above on this subscale should be taken as preliminary evidence that the respondent has a clinically significant problem in school. A score of 70 or higher should alert the practitioner to the possibility of a very serious school problem.

Aggression This important subscale is intended to measure the magnitude of the client's proclivity toward aggressive and possibly violent behavior. It should never be left blank. This subscale has a clinical cutting score of 30, so a score of 30 or above on this subscale should be taken as preliminary evidence that the respondent has a clinically significant problem with aggressive and possibly violent behavior. A score of 70 or higher should alert the practitioner to the possibility of a very serious problem with violence.

Problems with Work Associates This subscale is designed to measure the magnitude of problems the client may be having with work associates. It should be completed by any client who has a job. This subscale has a clinical cutting score of 30, so a score of 30 or above on this subscale should be taken as preliminary evidence that the respondent has a clinically significant problem in her or his relationships with one or more work associates. A score of 70 or higher should alert the practitioner to the possibility that the client has a very serious problem with one or more of her or his work associates, and the practitioner should investigate the potential for violence.

Family Relationship Problems This subscale is designed to measure the magnitude of problems in relationships with members of the client's family. However, the family of focus will often be ambiguous because it could be the client's family of origin or her or his present family. Thus, the client should write the family that is the focus in the assessment next to the subscale name. If the client has no family, then have him or her place an X in the response space for the first item on this subscale and then draw a vertical line down through the remaining item response spaces for this subscale in order to indicate that the subscale is not relevant for this client.

This subscale has a clinical cutting score of 30, so a score of 30 or above on this subscale should be taken as preliminary evidence that the respondent has a clinically significant problem in her or his relationships with members of the family of focus. A score of 70 or higher should alert the practitioner to the possibility that the client has a very serious problem with one or more of her or his family members, and the practitioner should investigate the potential for violence.

Suicidal Thoughts This subscale is designed to measure the extent to which the client is thinking about suicide and should be completed by every client. This subscale has a clinical cutting score of 15, so any client who scores at or above this score on this subscale should be considered a possible suicide risk. Although the clinical cutting score on this subscale is 15, the practitioner should look closely at the client's responses to each individual item on this subscale. While unlikely, it is possible that the client might score below 15 and yet respond to one of the items with a number that should alert the practitioner to suicidal potential. This is especially the case with item number 176: "I have actually decided that I am going to take my own life and I now think about my final plans for doing that." Any client who responds to this item with any response other than a 1 (none of the time) should be considered a possible suicide risk, and an appropriate assessment should be conducted. This cautious and thorough approach to suicide risk assessment is a critical necessity in practice (Bongar et al., 1998; Fremouw et al., 1990).

Nonphysical Abuse This subscale is *not* designed specifically for female clients. It should be completed by all clients and should never be omitted. It is designed to assess the extent to which a client feels that he or she has been treated abusively, albeit without a physical component. This subscale has a clinical cutting score of 15, so any client who scores at or above this score on this subscale should be considered to have a potentially serious relationship problem marked by abusive behavior.

Physical Abuse This subscale is *not* designed specifically for female clients. It should be completed by all clients and should never be omitted. It is designed to assess the extent to which a client feels that he or she has been physically abused. This subscale has a clinical cutting score of 5; however, as with the Suicidal Thoughts subscale, the practitioner will want to closely inspect the client's responses to specific items on this subscale, since a response with any number other than a 1 (none of the time) may suggest the presence of a serious problem. For example, item number 196 reads, "My partner knocks me down and then kicks or stomps on me." Should a client respond to this item with, say, a 2 (very rarely), even though the total score on the subscale might be less than 5, the fact that the client has suggested that the behavior described in item 196 *occurs at all* should alert the practitioner to the possibility of a serious problem.

Fearfulness This subscale is designed to assess the extent to which the client feels afraid or is plagued by a sense of fearfulness. It should be completed by every client. Any hesitation on the part of the client to complete this subscale should be investigated. The clinical cutting score on this subscale is 30, and any score at or above this level should be taken as preliminary evidence that the client has a significant problem in this area. Any scores at or above 70 should alert the practitioner to the possibility of suicidal ideation. Usually elevated depression levels are associated with suicide potential. However, recent research has suggested that problems with anxiety and fear may also be associated with elevated suicide risk (Barlow, 1988). Thus, the practitioner should investigate this possibility with any client who scores very high on this subscale.

Ideas of Reference This subscale is designed to measure the magnitude of problems with paranoid thinking. It should be completed by every client. The clinical cutting score on this subscale is 30, and any score at or above this level should be taken as preliminary evidence that the client has a significant problem in this area. As with some of the other subscales, the practitioner should also look at the client's responses to some of the items on this subscale. For example, item number 234 reads, "Secret agents keep spying on me." This item identifies very unusual thinking patterns, and (except in the most *unusual* cases) any client who responds with anything other than a 1 (none of the time) should be considered to have a potential problem in this area.

Phobias This subscale is designed to measure the client's problems with phobic anxiety and avoidance. Anxiety disorders are common and can be masked
by other problems, such a substance abuse (Barlow, 1988). They have also been
linked with suicide risk (Barlow, 1988; Fremouw et al., 1990). For this reason,
the practitioner should have all clients complete this subscale. The clinical cutting score on this subscale is 15, and any score at or above this level should be
taken as preliminary evidence that the client suffers from problems with phobic anxiety and avoidance. Very high scores, say 50 or above, should alert the
practitioner to the possibility of suicidal potential.

Feelings of Guilt This subscale is designed to assess the extent to which the
client feels guilt in the broadest areas of her or his personal and social functioning. However, like some of the other subscales, it can be more specifically
focused on particular areas of the client's personal and social functioning. For
example, a practitioner might wish to assess the level of guilt that a client feels
with regard to a recent relationship breakup. In a case such as this, the practitioner will need to have the client write the area of focus next to the subscale
name. The clinical cutting score on this subscale is 30, and any score at or
above that level should be taken as preliminary evidence of a clinically significant problem in this area.

Problems with Work This subscale parallels the Problems with Work
Associates subscale described earlier. However, this subscale focuses on the
client's work conditions as opposed to work-related relationships. The clinical
cutting score on this subscale is 30, and any score at or above that level should
be taken as preliminary evidence of a clinically significant problem in this area.
If the client does not work, then have her or him place an X in the item
response space for the first item on this subscale and then draw a vertical line
down through the remaining item response spaces in order to show that the
subscale is not relevant for this client.

Confused Thinking This subscale is intended as a global assessment of the
client's cognitive impairment. High scores on this subscale should be taken as
an indicator that the practitioner needs to have a more detailed assessment of
cognitive functioning conducted. Such impairment can arise from a number
of sources—physical, social, and psychological. The clinical cutting score on
this subscale is 30, and any score at or above that level should be taken as preliminary evidence of a clinically significant problem in this area.

Disturbing Thoughts This subscale is designed to assess the extent to which
the client is troubled with unwanted, disturbing, and possibly obsessive
thoughts. A high score on this subscale should be taken as an indication that
the practitioner needs to do a more comprehensive assessment of the nature
and frequency of the disturbing thoughts. The clinical cutting score on this
subscale is 30, and any score at or above that level should be taken as preliminary evidence of a clinically significant problem in this area.

Memory Loss This subscale is designed to assess the extent to which the client is having memory problems. Such problems can arise from a number of sources—physical, social, and psychological. A high score on this subscale should be taken as an indication that the practitioner needs to do a more comprehensive assessment of the nature of the client's memory problems. The clinical cutting score on this subscale is 30, and any score at or above that level should be taken as preliminary evidence of a clinically significant problem in this area.

Alcohol Abuse This subscale is designed to assess the magnitude of problems the client may be having with the use of alcoholic beverages. The clinical cutting score on this subscale is 15, and any score at or above that level should be taken as preliminary evidence of a clinically significant problem in this area.

Drug Use This scale is designed to assess the magnitude of problems the client may be having with the use of either prescription or nonprescription drugs. The clinical cutting score on this subscale is 15, and any score at or above that level should be taken as preliminary evidence of a clinically significant problem in this area.

Psychometric Characteristics of Subscale Scores

Two studies have provided evidence concerning the reliability of the scores produced on the MPSI subscales. The results of these investigations are shown in Tables 13.1 and 13.2. As can be seen in both of these tables, all of the MPSI subscales have been shown to produce scores with reliabilities (as estimated by coefficient alpha) in excess of .70; the overwhelming majority of them have produced scores with reliability estimates in excess of .85; and many of them have produced scores with reliability estimates exceeding .90. The evidence shown in Tables 13.1 and 13.2 provides strong support for the reliability of the MPSI subscale scores.

Estimates of the standard error of measurement (SEM) for the scores from each subscale are also presented in Tables 13.1 and 13.2. It will be remembered from our discussion of the short-form scales that the SEM is given by

$$SEM = S_o \sqrt{1 - r_{tt}}$$

where S_o is the standard deviation of a set of scores, and r_{tt} is the estimated reliability of the set of scores. The SEM gives an estimate of the uncertainty in the client's score and can be used to put upper and lower bounds on the client's score, just as we illustrated in our discussion of the cutting scores on the short-form scales. The estimated standard errors of measurement shown in Table 13.1 and 13.2 can be used in the same manner with the MPSI subscales. We will discuss this further in the next chapter.

Evidence for Validity of the Subscale Scores As we noted in an earlier chapter, there are multiple forms of evidence necessary to support claims of validity, including evidence for content validity, concurrent criterion validity, convergent validity, and divergent validity. Unfortunately, we do not currently

Table 13.1 Reliability Evidence for the MPSI Subscales

Subscale	Number of Items	Sample Size	Alpha	SEM
Depression	12	306	.88	2.99
Self-esteem	12	303	.86	3.12
Partner problems	13	216	.93	3.50
Sexual discord	12	210	.91	3.47
Child problems	13	96	.87	3.54
Mother problems	12	261	.92	3.83
Father problems	13	216	.92	4.02
Personal stress	12	295	.94	2.76
Friend problems	13	298	.90	3.53
Neighbor problems	13	179	.88	4.89
School problems	10	296	.84	2.94
Aggression	10	241	.71	2.70
Work associates	12	267	.89	2.71
Family problems	13	299	.96	3.27
Suicide	11	284	.95	1.30
Nonphysical abuse	13	174	.92	1.89
Physical abuse	12	218	.96	0.55
Fearfulness	19	294	.96	2.61
Ideas of reference	20	287	.90	2.21
Phobias	20	295	.86	4.56
Guilt	10	301	.93	2.44
Work problems	10	251	.88	3.11
Confused thinking	7	305	.92	1.61
Disturbing thoughts	9	299	.95	1.50
Memory loss	8	298	.84	2.06
Alcohol abuse	15	215	.88	2.82
Drug abuse	10	141	.90	1.66

have all of these types of evidence in support of the validity of the uses of scores for the MPSI subscales. There is ongoing research in this area, and papers should appear in the near future in professional journals concerning evidence for the validity of the uses of the MPSI subscales.

Although the evidential picture for validity is far from complete, there is some evidence that can be offered. One type of evidence for validity concerns content validity. Content validity concerns the extent to which (1) each item on a scale comes from a universe of indicators of the construct to be measured, and (2) the set of items that comprises a scale adequately represents the universe of indicators. One approach to providing evidence for content validity is examining the factorial validity of a set of items. In a multi-item scale, such as any of the MPSI subscales, each item should come from the infinite universe of items that serve as indicators of the construct to be measured. One measure

Table 13.2 Reliability Evidence for the MPSI Subscales

Subscale	Number of Items	Sample Size	Alpha	SEM
Depression	12	1529	.90	4.26
Self-esteem	12	1526	.88	4.17
Partner problems	13	1210	.93	4.48
Sexual discord	12	1176	.91	4.46
Child problems	13	895	.87	3.62
Mother problems	12	1316	.92	4.03
Father problems	13	1073	.93	4.23
Personal stress	12	1528	.95	3.88
Friend problems	13	1450	.93	3.66
Neighbor problems	13	1046	.92	4.89
School problems	10	545	.86	3.70
Aggression	10	1524	.88	4.34
Work associates	12	1240	.94	3.57
Family problems	13	1510	.95	3.82
Suicide	11	1523	.97	2.13
Nonphysical abuse	13	1190	.91	4.11
Physical abuse	12	1181	.84	1.39
Fearfulness	19	1532	.97	4.00
Ideas of reference	20	1528	.95	4.43
Phobias	20	1529	.91	6.14
Guilt	10	1525	.92	3.60
Work problems	10	1174	.79	4.21
Confused thinking	7	1530	.95	2.42
Disturbing thoughts	9	1529	.97	2.37
Memory loss	8	1529	.92	2.86
Alcohol abuse	15	1492	.94	3.86
Drug abuse	10	1453	.96	1.68

of the extent to which each item functions as an indicator of the construct to be measured is the correlation between scores on the item and the total score over all the remaining items on the scale. This correlation is called the "corrected item–total" correlation. The correlation is "corrected" in that the correlation is computed between the item and the total score over all items on the scale *minus the item itself.* If we did not remove the item from the total score on the scale, we would be computing a correlation between an item and a total score that included the score on the item. This would make the correlation larger than it would be if we computed the correlation between the score on the item and the total score over all other remaining items on the scale. The larger the corrected item–total correlation, the stronger the evidence that the item comes from the same universe of indicators as the other items on the scale (Crocker & Algina, 1986; Nunnally, 1978).

Now in a multidimensional instrument, such as the MPSI, there are multiple unidimensional scales. If we claim that each of the subscales on the MPSI is a valid measure of the constructs identified earlier, it implies that if we were to simultaneously compute the corrected item–total correlations for each MPSI item not only within each subscale but across subscales as well, then the corrected item–total correlations for items *within the same subscale* should all be larger in magnitude than the corrected item–total correlations *across subscales*. This kind of analysis can be done using what is called the multiple-group method of factor analysis (Hudson & McMurtry, 1997).

The results of such an analysis are shown in Table 13.3 for the MPSI depression subscale. The top row of Table 13.3 contains abbreviations for each of the 27 MPSI subscales. In the first column are numbers indicating the twelve items on the depression subscale. In the second column, under the heading "dep," is the corrected item–total correlation between the particular MPSI depression subscale item and the total score over the remaining eleven depression subscale items. For example, the correlation between the scores on item number 1 on the depression subscale and the total score over item numbers 2 through 12 is .60; the correlation between the scores on item number 2 on the depression subscale and the total score over item number 1 and item numbers 3 through 12 is .60; and so on. The other columns contain the correlations between scores on the specific depression subscale item and the total scores on the other MPSI subscales. For example, the correlation between scores on item number 1 on the depression subscale and the total scores on the self- esteem subscale is .48; the correlation between the scores on item number 2 on the depression subscale and scores on the self-esteem subscale is .35; and so on.

If the items within each subscale are content valid, then we should see that the corrected item–total correlation between the specific item and the total scores on the subscale the item comes from should be greater in magnitude than the correlations between the item and the total scores on any of the other subscales. For example, look at the first row of correlations in Table 13.3. This row shows the correlations in one sample (Hudson & McMurtry, 1997) between (a) scores on item number 1 on the depression subscale and the total scores over item numbers 2 through 12 on the depression subscale, and (b) scores on the first item on the depression subscale and the total scores on each of the remaining 26 MPSI subscales. If the items on the depression subscale are content valid, then, among other things, the corrected item–total correlation between scores on item number 1 on the depression subscale and the total score over item numbers 2 through 12 on the depression subscale should be larger in magnitude than any of the correlations between scores on item number 1 on the depression subscale and the scores on the other MPSI subscales. In other words, the correlation in the first row, first column of Table 13.3 should be larger in magnitude than any of the other correlations in the first row.

The correlation in the first row, first column of Table 13.3 is .60, while the other correlations in the first row range from −.03 to .48. Thus, the necessary relationships hold for this item. If the depression subscale items are content

Table 13.3 Item–Total Correlations for the MPSI Depression Subscale

item	dep	ses	prp	sex	chl	mom	dad	str	frn	nei	sch	agg	wka
1	.60	.48	.11	.06	.04	.15	.29	.43	.37	−.03	.29	.05	.15
2	.60	.35	.10	−.03	−.04	.15	.13	.43	.20	−.03	.23	.02	.19
3	.37	.26	.10	.01	−.11	.15	.08	.33	.12	.01	.05	.01	.11
4	.60	.45	.15	.05	.11	.06	.15	.35	.13	−.01	.13	−.01	.08
5	.40	.28	−.08	−.18	−.06	.09	.18	.37	.11	.09	.35	.02	.24
6	.66	.43	.10	.04	.05	.18	.22	.50	.14	.02	.24	.12	.15
7	.59	.50	.20	.08	.05	.12	.23	.34	.18	.02	.17	.09	.13
8	.74	.47	.13	−.02	.04	.15	.20	.40	.15	.04	.25	.04	.12
9	.71	.52	.16	.06	.06	.14	.17	.50	.22	.06	.31	.07	.14
10	.67	.54	.12	−.09	−.03	.11	.14	.35	.24	−.01	.29	.01	.20
11	.66	.54	.15	−.02	.01	.07	.21	.33	.20	.02	.18	−.02	.11
12	.65	.43	.16	−.01	.11	.17	.15	.31	.16	.04	.19	.06	.08

item	fam	sui	npa	pha	fea	ref	pho	gui	wkp	con	dis	mem	alc	drg
1	.19	.44	.06	.13	.31	.20	.33	.44	.20	.34	.35	.23	.13	.18
2	.20	.33	−.01	−.01	.26	.19	.24	.41	.14	.29	.32	.14	.18	.13
3	.07	.29	.02	.07	.31	.09	.21	.31	.05	.26	.24	.10	.07	−.01
4	.17	.31	.20	.09	.23	.09	.23	.29	.04	.21	.22	.11	.07	.10
5	.23	.20	−.05	−.02	.25	.18	.27	.26	.19	.31	.19	.25	.11	.04
6	.20	.41	.06	.10	.43	.30	.39	.44	.16	.39	.36	.28	.17	.16
7	.19	.32	.11	−.01	.25	.19	.31	.29	.13	.20	.22	.06	.07	.07
8	.19	.34	.08	.04	.32	.18	.30	.32	.13	.33	.31	.25	.13	.21
9	.23	.43	.11	.10	.43	.22	.38	.47	.13	.37	.38	.35	.17	.25
10	.24	.39	.04	.04	.31	.13	.26	.35	.21	.29	.26	.19	.14	.08
11	.26	.42	.13	.07	.27	.10	.24	.33	.17	.29	.23	.13	.20	.12
12	.19	.32	.11	.05	.30	.17	.27	.24	.12	.28	.26	.20	.13	.11

Note: Item–self correlations have been removed.

SOURCE: Hudson (1990).

valid, then each of the correlations in the first column in Table 13.3 should be larger in magnitude than any of the other correlations in the same row. Looking closely at Table 13.3, we can see that this is, in fact, the case for the items on the depression subscale. Thus, this evidence supports the content validity of the depression subscale. It does not prove it, because there are other forms of evidence needed, but it does support it.

Table 13.4 shows the results of this type of analysis for all of the MPSI subscales. In this table, each of the subscale names appears in the same row with numbers indicating the percentage of "factor-loading failures" and the percentage of "factor-loading successes." A factor-loading success occurs when, as with our evaluation of item number 1 for the depression subscale, the corrected item-total correlation between scores on a specific subscale item and the

Table 13.4 Percentages of Factor–Loading Failures and Successes for MPSI Subscale Item Loadings

MPSI Subscale	Percent Failures	Percent Successes
Depression	0.0	100.0
Self-esteem	0.0	100.0
Partner problems	0.0	100.0
Sexual discord	0.0	100.0
Child problems	15.4	84.6
Mother problems	0.0	100.0
Father problems	0.0	100.0
Personal stress	0.0	100.0
Friend problems	0.0	100.0
Neighbor problems	0.0	100.0
School problems	0.0	100.0
Aggression	0.0	100.0
Work associates	0.0	100.0
Family problems	0.0	100.0
Suicide	0.0	100.0
Nonphysical abuse	0.0	100.0
Physical abuse	0.0	100.0
Fearfulness	0.0	100.0
Ideas of reference	5.0	95.0
Phobias	0.0	100.0
Guilt	0.0	100.0
Work problems	0.0	100.0
Confused thinking	0.0	100.0
Disturbing thoughts	0.0	100.0
Memory loss	0.0	100.0
Alcohol abuse	0.0	100.0
Drug use	0.0	100.0
Total[a]	3.4	96.6

[a]Values based on total number of failures across all items on all subscales.

SOURCE: Reprinted with permission from Hudson and McMurtry (1997).

total scores over the remaining items on the subscale is larger in magnitude than the correlations between the scores on the item and the total scores on the other MPSI subscales. A factor-loading failure occurs when these conditions are not met. The strongest evidence for content validity using this method occurs when there is 100 percent factor-loading successes and 0 percent factor-loading failures. By inspecting Table 13.3 very carefully, we can see that the assessments of the correlations in this table for the first item on the depression subscale result in 100 percent factor-loading successes and 0 percent factor-loading failures.

As can be seen in Table 13.4, 96.6 percent of all of the comparisons of correlations for each item on each of the MPSI subscales resulted in factor-loading successes. In other words, there were only 3.4 percent factor-loading failures in these analyses. This is fairly strong evidence supporting the content validity of the MPSI subscales.

Another way to summarize these findings is to say that the results support the factorial validity of the scores on the MPSI; that is, the subscale items do a good job of correlating with their own subscale scores and of *not* correlating with all of the total scores on other subscales. This also supports the claim that the scores on the MPSI subscales measure the constructs they are claimed to be measuring. However, much more evidence is needed before this claim can be said to be strongly supported.

A very important type of evidence for validity is divergent (or discriminant) validity. This form of evidence demonstrates that the scores from a scale (or subscale) fail to highly correlate with other constructs or variables that, given everything we know about these constructs or variables, the scores *should not, in fact, correlate with*. For example, everything we know about depression tells us that it should not correlate *highly* with such things as age, gender, ethnicity, and other demographic factors. This is in contrast to, say, other measures of depression. Scores on a depression scale should correlate highly with other measures of depression. The ability of a scale to produce scores that do not correlate with variables that the scores should not, in fact, correlate with tells us that the use of the scale allows us to differentiate (or discriminate) between constructs. This form of evidence, together with evidence of convergent validity, tells us that the scores on the scale are pointing at the construct they should be pointing at (and not at some other construct).

Table 13.5 shows the correlations between scores on the MPSI subscales and several demographic variables: gender, ethnicity, marital status, age, education, family income, number of times married, years spent with current spouse, number of children, and family size. Scores on the MPSI subscales should not correlate *highly* with any of these demographic variables. We would expect some of them, of course, to correlate to a slight degree with one or more of the demographic variables, but none of them should correlate highly. This table of correlations, therefore, presents some evidence for divergent validity for the scores on the MPSI subscales.

The evidence presented here is by no means all that is necessary to support the validity of the scores produced by the MPSI subscales. Notably missing from this evidence is evidence for criterion validity and for convergent validity. Ongoing research projects will, we hope, produce further evidence in the future to support the validity of the scores on the MPSI subscales. The evidence provided here should be taken, therefore, as encouraging and supportive of use of the MPSI, but certainly not as the final word on the validity of the MPSI subscale scores.

Table 13.5 Correlations Between MPSI Subscale Scores and Demographic Background Variables

MPSI Subscale	Gender	Ethnicity	Marital Status	Age	Education	Family Income	Times Married	Years with Spouse	Number of Children	Family Size	Mean
Depression	-.00	.02	-.19	-.03	-.03	-.08	-.09	-.08	-.10	-.11	.07
Self-esteem	.01	-.00	-.02	-.05	-.07	-.06	-.08	-.00	-.07	.05	.04
Partner problems	-.07	-.07	.03	.12	.02	.03	.11	.11	.09	.06	.08
Sexual discord	-.07	.14	.24	.16	.04	.15	.19	.23	.10	.08	.14
Child problems	-.01	.05	-.03	.27	.02	.05	-.02	.28	.05	-.03	.08
Mother problems	.05	.05	-.10	.17	-.12	.01	.02	.06	.15	.01	.07
Father problems	.00	-.03	-.00	.08	.02	-.11	.13	-.09	-.02	-.06	.05
Personal stress	.16	.01	-.08	-.03	-.07	-.04	-.04	.01	-.05	-.04	.05
Friend problems	-.04	.02	-.05	-.04	-.00	-.10	-.07	.01	-.01	.03	.04
Neighbor problems	.02	-.00	-.04	-.06	-.16	-.14	-.05	-.03	.01	-.07	.06
School problems	-.01	-.00	-.18	-.17	-.04	-.10	-.20	-.11	-.08	-.03	.09
Aggression	-.20	-.27	.05	.03	-.21	-.05	.00	.01	.02	.06	.09
Work associates	-.03	.03	-.08	-.01	-.02	-.08	-.05	-.03	.01	-.03	.04
Family problems	-.03	.09	-.16	-.04	-.01	-.20	-.06	-.19	-.12	-.16	.11
Suicide	.05	-.06	-.18	.02	-.01	-.12	-.09	-.07	.01	-.10	.07
Nonphysical abuse	-.09	-.01	.07	.10	.02	.05	.11	.08	.15	.17	.09
Physical abuse	.02	-.12	-.04	.01	.01	-.03	.05	-.07	.12	.18	.07
Fearfulness	.10	-.06	-.15	-.11	-.06	-.05	-.16	-.13	-.11	-.02	.10
Ideas of reference	-.09	-.14	-.11	-.05	-.12	-.13	-.08	-.05	.01	-.06	.08
Phobias	.06	-.04	-.08	-.05	-.04	-.08	-.09	-.03	-.04	-.05	.06
Guilt	.10	.15	-.08	-.06	.01	-.08	-.05	-.04	-.13	-.03	.07
Work problems	-.05	-.00	-.09	-.02	.06	-.08	-.09	-.08	-.12	-.05	.06

Table 13.5 Correlations Between MPSI Subscale Scores and Demographic Background Variables (continued)

MPSI Subscale	Gender	Ethnicity	Marital Status	Age	Education	Family Income	Times Married	Years with Spouse	Number of Children	Family Size	Mean
Confused thinking	.03	-.06	-.09	.01	-.05	-.14	-.04	-.05	.03	-.06	.06
Disturbing thoughts	.01	-.07	-.10	-.06	-.06	-.13	-.09	-.07	-.06	-.02	.07
Memory loss	-.04	-.10	-.09	.04	-.04	-.10	-.05	.02	-.01	-.04	.05
Alcohol abuse	-.09	.07	-.06	-.04	-.06	-.04	-.03	-.09	-.06	-.12	.07
Drug abuse	-.33	-.04	-.02	-.10	-.07	-.11	.03	-.16	-.08	.04	.10
Means	*.07*	*.06*	*.09*	*.07*	*.05*	*.08*	*.07*	*.08*	*.07*	*.07*	*.08*

SOURCE: Reprinted with permission from Hudson and McMurtry (1997).

THE FAMILY ASSESSMENT
SCREENING INVENTORY (FASI)

The Family Assessment Screening Inventory (FASI) is a paper-and-pencil self-report measure that contains 265 items and requires 30 to 40 minutes to complete. The 265 items are designed to produce scores on 25 different subscales. These subscale scores can be placed into a graphic profile in the same manner as the MPSI subscale scores. An example of such a profile is shown in Figure 13.2.

This instrument was developed to provide an assessment tool that can be used at intake, as well as at other service points, to measure the magnitude of a variety of problems in family living. Although the major application of the FASI focuses on the early assessment of clients' problems, the FASI can be used for periodic reevaluation by having clients complete it during later phases of service provision. When clients have completed the FASI on more than one occasion, it can be used to assess clients' change across the time that occurred between administrations. The FASI is especially well suited for administration just prior to the termination of services as a means of determining a client's progress over the entire period during which services were provided.

As with the MPSI, the FASI can be thought of as a collection of 25 thermometers that simultaneously give readings on the magnitude of problems the family is facing in 25 areas of family functioning. The scores on these subscales will not, however, give information on the source, cause, or origin of these problems. The FASI subscale scores will do a good job of providing information on how serious the problems are.

The FASI Items and Subscale Scores

Each of the FASI subscales was designed to measure the magnitude of problems in a specific area of family functioning. All but two of the subscales are written so that clients can respond to items with a number ranging from 1 to 7. The items on the remaining two subscales require "yes" or "no" ratings. Subscale scores are computed in such a manner (see next chapter) that they produce scores ranging from 0 to 100, with a higher score indicative of more serious and greater magnitude problems, and vice versa.

The 25 FASI subscales are briefly described in the following text. The FASI is a recently developed measure; as of the time of the writing of this chapter, no clinical cutting scores have been established.

Housing This subscale was designed to measure the magnitude of problems the family is having with housing.

Physical Safety This subscale was designed to measure the magnitude of problems that the family is having with physical safety. It is intended to measure the extent to which hazards to physical safety exist within the family's home and in the family's immediate physical environment.

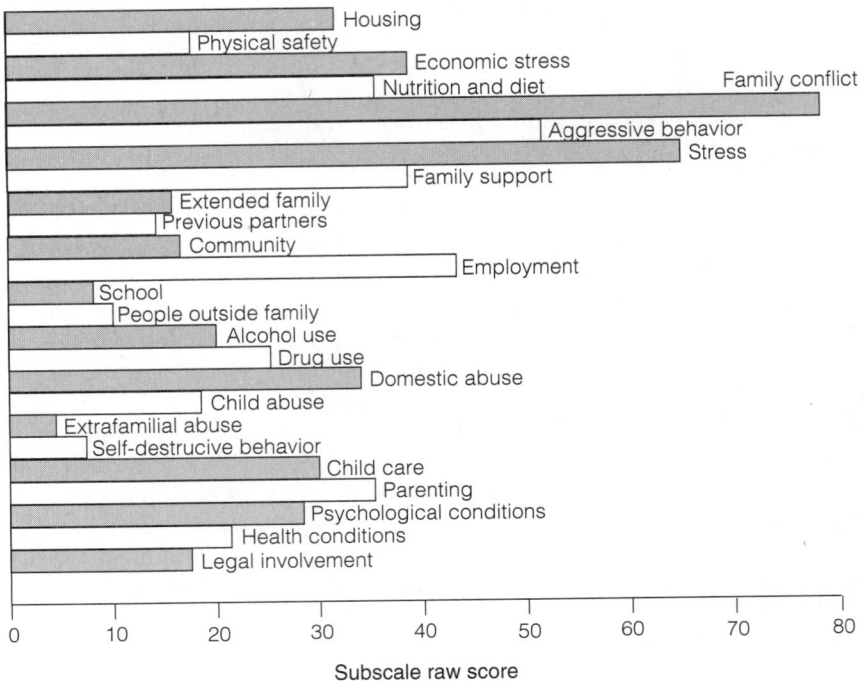

FIGURE 12.2 An illustrative graphic profile of FASI subscale scores. Subscale names are shown next to bars in profile.

Economic Stress This subscale was designed to measure the magnitude of problems that the family is having with financial resources.

Nutrition and Diet This subscale was designed to measure the magnitude of problems that the family is having with food and nutrition.

Family Conflict This subscale was designed to measure the magnitude of problems that the family is having with conflicts and disputes within the family.

Aggressive Behavior This subscale was designed to measure the magnitude of problems with aggressive behavior exhibited by one or more family members.

Stress This subscale was designed to measure the magnitude of problems that family members are experiencing with stress.

Family Support This subscale was designed to measure the magnitude of problems with the support available within the family.

Extended Family This subscale was designed to measure the magnitude of problems that the family is having in its relationships with extended family members.

Previous Partners This subscale was designed to measure the magnitude of problems that the family is having with persons with whom one or more family members have had prior partner relationships.

Community This subscale was designed to measure the magnitude of problems that the family is having with community involvement.

Employment This subscale was designed to measure the magnitude of problems that family members are having within a work environment.

School This subscale was designed to measure the magnitude of problems that family members are having in school.

People Outside the Family This subscale was designed to measure the magnitude of problems that family members are experiencing with persons from outside of the family.

Alcohol Use This subscale was designed to measure the magnitude of problems that the family is having with the use of alcohol.

Drug Use This subscale was designed to measure the magnitude of problems that the family is having with the use of drugs.

Domestic Abuse This subscale was designed to measure the magnitude of problems that the family is having with physical, social, and/or emotional abuse among adult family members.

Child Abuse This subscale was designed to measure the magnitude of problems that the family is having with physical, sexual, and/or emotional abuse of children within the family.

Extrafamilial Abuse This subscale was designed to measure the magnitude of problems that a family member is having with physical, sexual, and/or emotional abuse perpetrated by someone who is outside of the family.

Self-Destructive Behavior This subscale was designed to measure the magnitude of problems that the family is having with the suicidal and/or self-destructive behavior and/or ideation of one of its members.

Child Care This subscale was designed to measure the magnitude of problems that the family is having with meeting the basic needs of children within the family.

Parenting This subscale was designed to measure the magnitude of problems that the family is having with parenting practices within the family.

Psychological Conditions This subscale was designed to measure the magnitude of problems of an emotional or psychological nature experienced by one or more family members.

Health Conditions This subscale was designed to measure the magnitude of health-related problems experienced by family members.

Legal Involvement This subscale was designed to measure the magnitude of legal problems experienced by family members.

Psychometric Characteristics of FASI Subscale Scores

As noted earlier, the FASI is a recently developed scale that is still in the developmental process. As of the time of the writing of this chapter, no studies have been completed in which the psychometric characteristics of the FASI subscale scores have been investigated. We anticipate that there will be research reported in the very near future, however, since several studies are currently in progress.

Note: At the time this book was going to press, a new version of the FASI was being released by Walmyr Press. The interested reader should contact Walmyr Press at the address in the preface for more information about his new version.

14

Administering, Scoring, and Interpreting the MPSI and FASI

In the previous chapter, we discussed the MPSI and the FASI, two recently developed multidimensional measurement tools for use in practice. In this chapter, we briefly discuss the administration, scoring, and interpretation of the MPSI and FASI scales.

ADMINISTERING THE MPSI AND FASI

General Guidelines

Many of the same guidelines that we discussed for administering the short-form scales apply to the administration of the MPSI and the FASI. It is important that practitioners present the MPSI and/or FASI to clients in a confident and matter-of-fact manner. As with the short-form scales, one of the worst things a practitioner can do when administering either of these scales is to convey to the client the impression that the practitioner is uncertain of the value or importance of the scale. The scales should be presented to clients in a manner that clearly conveys to clients that completion of the MPSI or FASI is a routine and critically important part of assessing clients' problems and of monitoring their progress during service provision.

It is also important that practitioners convey to clients that the MPSI or the FASI is not a test. There are no right or wrong answers to the items. The sub-scales are designed to give the client's service provider information about the magnitude and severity of problems in multiple areas of the client's personal, familial, and social functioning. This is an important and legitimate basis on which to request that clients complete either or both of these multidimensional scales.

Unfortunately many persons (both clients and professionals) are wary of so-called "psychological tests." Thus, many clients, and practitioners themselves, may have reservations about taking any "psychological test," especially if the client (or practitioner) is unsure of what the scores will say about her or him, how they will be used, where they will be kept, who will see them, and so on. Because of such (sometimes justified) concerns, it will be important to tell the client that, first of all, neither the MPSI nor the FASI are "psychological tests" in the same sense as such measures as the MMPI, the Rorschach, the MCMI (Milan Clinical Muliaxial Inventory), and other measures used by psychologists to assess a person's personality, psychopathology, and so forth. Instead, the MPSI and FASI were developed for use primarily by social workers (though other appropriately trained human service professionals are encouraged to use them as well) to assess the severity and magnitude of their clients' problems and to monitor their clients' progress (or lack thereof) across time. These scales are, therefore, of fundamental importance to successful practice. Conveying this to clients will help allay any fears that they have. Practitioners can further allay any fears of clients by explaining to them how the scores from these scales will be used and by sharing the clients' scores and the practitioners' interpretations of the clients' scores with the clients.

It will also help practitioners in the use of the MPSI and FASI with clients if practitioners are familiar with both scales. One of the best ways to become familiar with these two scales is for practitioners to complete the scales themselves.. There is no substitute for completing these two scales when it comes to learning about them and to understanding what clients may experience as they complete them. After a practitioner has completed the MPSI and the FASI, he or she should score them and then carefully examine the scores on each subscale in relation to how he or she feels about each area that is measured. For example, the practitioner should examine the score on the depression subscale on the MPSI and consider his or her score in relation to how he or she is currently feeling. A practitioner might want to complete the MPSI (or the FASI) in relation to how he or she felt and thought at some time in the past when he or she was having problems in one or more areas of his or her personal and/or social life. Comparing his or her own scores with his or her sense of how he or she felt and thought at that point in time will not only help the practitioner to learn about scoring the scales, but it will also help the practitioner to understand the depth of information that these two scales are capable of providing.

Practitioners may want to reread the guidelines for administering the short-form scales. These guidelines apply to the administration of the MPSI and the FASI. The guidelines for administering the MPSI and FASI fall within three basic sets of procedures: (1) understand how these scales work; (2) assure clients as to the importance of completing the scales honestly and accurately; and (3) explain how the scores obtained from the clients will be used. Following these procedures can make it easy to administer these scales and can greatly increase the likelihood that valid and reliable information is obtained from clients.

The Nonapplicability of Some Subscales

Some clients may decide that one or more of the MPSI or FASI subscales do not apply to them or to their personal situations. If this is so, just instruct the client to place an *X* in the response space for the first item on the subscale and then draw a vertical line down through the remainder of the item response spaces for the items on the subscale. This will signify that the subscale does not apply to the client. A client may also decide that one or more of the items on a subscale do not apply to his or her situation. If this is so, just have the client place an *X* in the item response space for the particular item.

As noted in the previous chapter, some of the MPSI subscales are to a greater or lesser extent ambiguous as to whom the subscale applies. For example, the Family Relationship Problems subscale can apply to a client's current family or to her or his family of origin. The practitioner and the client must decide which family the client will focus on when completing the subscale; the client should then write the identity of that family next to the subscale name. The same procedure can be used for the other subscales that can have more than one legitimate focus of attention.

Two Administration Models

This brings us to the two administration models that can be used when administering the MPSI: unstructured administration and structured administration. A practitioner who chooses to use an unstructured administration model need only present the MPSI to the client and provide minimal instructions for completing the instrument. Under these conditions, the practitioner leaves it up to the client entirely to decide on the appropriate focus for each of the subscales. The client will then make a choice as to how to complete the ambiguously focused subscales without any influence from the practitioner. The advantage of using this administration model is that the practitioner will discover which individuals and groups are most salient in the client's current life situation. The disadvantage, of course, is that the practitioner may not get the information he or she wants and may lose an early opportunity to engage in planning with the client. The advantages and disadvantages of the unstructured administration model must be weighed before a practitioner decides whether to use it.

If the unstructured administration model is used, the practitioner will need to eliminate the ambiguity about the focus of the client's responses on the different MPSI subscales. To do so, the practitioner can simply ask the client whom he or she was thinking about as he or she completed the various subscales and then write in the names of the persons or groups next to the subscale names.

The second model of administration of the MPSI is the structured approach. In this model, the practitioner reviews each subscale with the client and determines ahead of time the persons or groups that will be the foci of the client's responses on the different subscales. The practitioner will need to write next to each subscale name the specific persons or group of persons that the client will focus on when responding to the items on that subscale. The main advantage to this model of administration is that all ambiguity about the focus of responses on any subscale is removed. It also has the advantage of being an assessment that the practitioner is guiding, so the practitioner will be much more likely to obtain the assessment information that he or she needs.

Neither of these two administration methods should be viewed as "correct" or "incorrect." Rather, they are both legitimate approaches that will serve different assessment purposes, and the choice of methods adds flexibility to the use of the MPSI.

SCORING THE MPSI AND THE FASI

The first step in scoring any of the MPSI or FASI subscales is to reverse-score each of the positively worded items. The items on each subscale that need to be reverse-scored are marked with an asterisk. Items on the MPSI and FASI are reverse-scored in the same manner as on the short-form scales. Equation 12.1 (in Chapter 12) presented the formula used to reverse-score items on the short-form scales:

$$y = (k + 1) - x \qquad (14.1)$$

where y is the item reverse score, k is the highest score an item can receive, and x is the item score given by the client. The highest score that any item on the MPSI or FASI can receive is a 7, so for the MPSI subscales, Equation 14.1 becomes

$$y = (7 + 1) - x = 8 - x \qquad (14.2)$$

Thus, when reverse-scored, a 7 becomes a 1; a 6 becomes a 2; a 5 becomes a 3; a 4 remains a 4; a 3 becomes a 5; a 2 becomes a 6; and a 1 becomes a 7.

As with the short-form scales, when reverse-scoring items, it is a good practice to, for each item to be reverse-scored, (1) circle the score given the item by the client, and then (2) write the reverse score next to the circled score. This practice will help the evaluator to make sure that all items that need to be reverse-scored have been reverse-scored and will help the evaluator to recognize, when adding up the item scores, that the reverse scores for these items need to be added.

Once these items have been reverse-scored, the evaluator is ready to score the subscale. Equation 12.2 (in Chapter 12) demonstrated the formula for scoring the short-form scales:

$$S = \frac{100[sum(y) - N]}{N(k - 1)}$$

where y is the item responses, N is the number of items properly completed by the client, and k is the largest possible item score on the scale. Since k is equal to 7 for each of the MPSI and FASI subscales, Equation 14.3 becomes

$$S = \frac{100[sum(y) - N]}{N(k-1)} = \frac{100[sum(y) - N]}{N(7-1)} = \frac{100[sum(y) - N]}{6N} \quad (14.4)$$

As with the short-form scales, any item that is left blank, scored outside the range of allowable item responses (i.e., 1 to 7), or otherwise answered in an improper manner is given a score of 0 (zero). On page 11 of each MPSI is a scoring blank that can assist practitioners in scoring the MPSI. There is a similar scoring blank at the end of the FASI.

The MPSI scoring blank is illustrated in Table 14.1. Although the entire scoring blank is not reproduced in this table, we do show how this scoring blank looks. It is used as follows. Column B lists the number of items properly completed by the client. In the illustrative blank in Table 14.1, the client properly completed 12 out of 12 items on the depression subscale, 11 out of 12 on the self-esteem subscale, 13 out of 13 on the partner problems subscale, and 10 out of 10 on the drug abuse subscale. These numbers, respectively, were written into column B. Column C shows the sum of item scores (added up after reverse-scoring the necessary items) on each of the subscales. Column D illustrates the difference between the numbers in columns C and B. For example, for the depression subscale, column D indicates the difference $C - B = 66 - 12 = 54$. Column E contains the results from using Equation 14.4 to compute the subscale score. For example, for the depression subscale, the score is

$$\frac{100(66 - 12)}{12 \times 6} = \frac{D \times 100}{B \times 6} = \frac{54 \times 100}{12 \times 6} = \frac{5400}{72} = 75$$

Similarly, for the self-esteem subscale, the score in column E is given by

$$\frac{100(56 - 11)}{12 \times 6} = \frac{D \times 100}{B \times 6} = \frac{45 \times 100}{12 \times 6} = \frac{4500}{72} = 62.5 \cong 62$$

The reader might want to reproduce these numbers, as well as those for the partner problems and drug abuse subscales in Table 14.1.

Once subscale scores on either the MPSI or the FASI have been obtained, it is important to take the time to prepare the MPSI Score Profile Graph or the FASI Score Profile Graph. All one needs to do is plot the subscale scores on the profile graph, using a ruler and a heavy felt-tipped pen, by drawing a line from 0 to the client's score on a particular subscale. The MPSI Score Profile Graph and/or the FASI Score Profile Graph will take their places among the practitioner's most important interpretive tools when using either of these scales with clients.

Table 14.1 An Illustration of the MPSI Subscale Scoring Blank

Subscale Name	A Total Items	B Items Used	C Item Sum	D (C − B) Sum − Used	E D*100/(B*6) Score
Depression	12	12	66	66 − 12 = 54	(54 × 100)/(12 × 6) = 75
Self-Esteem	12	11	56	56 − 11 = 45	(45 × 100)/(12 × 6) = 62
Partner problems	13	13	25	25 − 13 = 12	(12 × 100)/(13 × 6) = 15
....					
Drug abuse	10	10	32	32 − 10 = 22	(22 × 100)/(10 × 6) = 37

INTERPRETING THE MPSI SUBSCALE
AND FASI SUBSCALE SCORES

Each subscale on the MPSI and the FASI produces scores ranging from 0 to 100, with lower scores indicative of less severe problems, and higher scores indicative of more severe problems. All of the MPSI subscales have principal and secondary clinical cutting scores, as shown in Table 14.2. The principal cutting score on most of the subscales is 30. On some of the subscales, the principal clinical cutting score is 15; and on the Physical Abuse subscale, it is 5. Scores at or above these clinical cutting scores should be taken as preliminary evidence that the client has a clinically significant problem in the area measured by the subscale. These cutting scores are based on work that has been done with the short-form scales, most notably the GCS, ISE, IMS, ISS, IPA, CAM, CAF, IPR, and IFR (see Hudson, 1982), and the PASNP, PASPH, NPAPS, and PAPS (see Attala, Hudson, & McSweeney, 1994). However, more research on these MPSI clinical cutting scores is in progress, and until further research is completed and reported, these cutting scores should be taken as suggested guidelines as opposed to hard-and-fast interpretive rules.

The secondary clinical cutting scores are suggested guidelines for inferring the possibility of serious problems in a particular area and the possibility of violence directed against self and/or other. The secondary clinical cutting score on most of the MPSI subscales is 70. However, some of the subscales have suggested secondary clinical cutting scores that are lower. Scores at or above these clinical cutting scores should be interpreted as preliminary evidence of a very serious problem in the area of functioning measured by the subscale. Again, *these scores should be taken as guidelines* as opposed to hard-and-fast interpretive rules. The research data do not yet exist to support these cutting scores as anything other than guidelines.

This is especially important to note for the following subscales: depression, suicidal ideation, nonphysical abuse, physical abuse, alcohol abuse, and drug abuse. Each of these subscales was designed to measure problems that potentially involve a risk of danger to the client and/or to persons in the client's environment. The scores on these subscales must be interpreted within the

Table 14.2 MPSI Subscale Clinical Cutting Scores

Subscale	Principal Clinical Cutting Score	Secondary Clinical Cutting Score
Depression	30	70
Self-esteem	30	70
Partner problems	30	70
Sexual discord	30	70
Child problems	30	70
Mother problems	30	70
Father problems	30	70
Personal stress	30	70
Friend problems	30	70
Neighbor problems	30	70
School problems	30	70
Aggression	30	70
Work associates	30	70
Family problems	30	70
Suicide	15	25
Nonphysical abuse	15	30
Physical abuse	5	10
Fearfulness	30	70
Ideas of reference	30	70
Phobias	15	30
Guilt	30	70
Work problems	30	70
Confused thinking	30	70
Disturbing thoughts	30	70
Memory loss	30	70
Alcohol abuse	15	30
Drug abuse	15	30

context of other information obtained from the client, such as through an in-depth interview and from collateral sources (Fremouw et al., 1990). In these areas, it is better to risk a false positive when assessing the possibility of violence to self and/or others or the possibility of potential health problems for the client than it is to risk a false negative. In this spirit, we strongly recommend that on these subscales, the practitioner not only look at the client's overall score, but also look at the client's responses to each of the subscale items. The content of some of the items is of such serious potential consequences that any response other than a "1" should alert the practitioner to the possibility of a risk of violence and/or adverse health consequences. For example, a response of a "2" or more on item number 126 on the Suicidal Ideation subscale ("I have actually decided that I am going to take my own life and I now think about my final plans for doing that"), or on item number 203 on the Physical Abuse subscale ("My partner tries to suffocate me with pillows, towels, or other objects"), should be taken, by itself, as preliminary evidence of a serious problem in that area. Similarly, a response of "2" or "3" on item number 318 on the Alcohol Abuse subscale ("I drink so much that I pass out") should be taken as preliminary evidence of a potentially serious problem with the use of alcoholic beverages.

Clinical cutting scores have yet to be established for the FASI subscales, though our research to date suggests that a score of 30 will likely be a principal cutting score on many of the FASI subscales. We expect that there will be published research in the very near future that will provide preliminary evidence for the setting of cutting scores on the FASI subscales.

INTERPRETING THE MPSI AND FASI
SCORE PROFILES

The score profiles for the MPSI and FASI are extremely useful tools. Once constructed, these profiles enable the practitioner to, at a glance, obtain information about the client's functioning in each of the areas measured by the subscales on these two multidimensional instruments. If cutting scores exist for the subscales, the practitioner can immediately make note of those areas in which a client's subscale scores are at, or exceed, the appropriate cutting scores. Then valuable interview time can be used to obtain further information regarding the client's problems in those areas.

A client's score profile can also be inspected to see how problems in different areas are interrelated. For example, elevated scores on the MPSI depression, self-esteem, personal stress, aggression, suicidal ideation, and alcohol and/or drug abuse subscales should operate as a red alert to the practitioner for identifying a client at risk for suicidal behavior. Such a constellation of problem areas contains several indicators of suicide risk (Bongar, 1991; Fremouw et al., 1990), and this type of profile provides the multiple measures and indicators that are currently deemed necessary in a defensible assessment of risk.

15

Questions About Using Assessment Scales

The CASS scales are relatively easy and straightforward to use. If one is not familiar with the use of standardized measures, however, many questions about their use can arise. These questions are important, so we have decided to focus one chapter on specific questions that practitioners and administrators often ask about the CASS scales. We cannot possibly answer all the questions that arise, but this chapter answers the most common questions that have been asked about the CASS scales.

The chapter splits common questions into ten specific areas: (1) how to select and use the scales; (2) screening and diagnostic applications; (3) using scales with children and special populations; (4) interpreting and using scale scores; (5) interpreting changes in client scores; (6) client reactions and responses; (7) dependability of client responses; (8) using scales for training and supervision; (9) administrative and logistical questions; and (10) research and technical questions. For each one of these areas, we present questions that many people have about the scales. Along with each question, we provide an answer that is based on our many years of experience in using the CASS program and other standardized scales. From this we hope that practitioners will learn basic questions that can be asked of any standardized scales, or assessment tools and scales developed by practitioners themselves. We also hope to provide the information required to answer these questions so that practitioners will be confident about using standardized scales and self-developed scales in practice.

HOW TO SELECT
AND USE THE SCALES

How do I decide which scales to use?

To some extent, the process of selecting an appropriate scale depends on one's experience as a professional and one's basic approaches to working with clients. Scales should not be applied randomly or in a manner in which the practitioner is fishing for a problem to work on. The decision to use the scales needs to be based, in part, on a set of initial clues or indicators that will direct the practitioner toward the scales that might be appropriate. In some cases, these clues will be provided by other professionals. For example, the next intake might be a client who is referred from a local crisis line for issues related to marital disruption or aggression. The information from this referral will help determine the questions and issues that the practitioner and the client must address. Regardless of the information from other professionals, however, practitioners also need to use their own set of interviewing and assessment skills to obtain information from the client as to the problem, or problems, that he or she wants to address. By opening an honest dialog with the client and conducting a thorough and complete assessment interview, the practitioner will usually be able to identify the major difficulties that the client faces. In addition, the practitioner and client will normally be able to prioritize the problems, selecting one or two to focus on for the beginning of treatment. Once the major problems that the practitioner and client would like to measure are identified, it is simply a matter of determining which available scales will reliably and validly measure the problems being targeted for change.

Many clients present with a set of interrelated problems. This makes selecting a scale a bit more difficult, but by no means impossible. A client might be referred from an EAP program, for example, with problems related to stress, depression, and excessive drinking. If the major focus of intervention becomes treatment related to stress, the Index of Clinical Stress (ICS) would be a good choice as the primary measure to monitor the course of treatment. The other two issues, however, might be monitored through the use of scales such as the Generalized Contentment Scale (GCS) and the Index of Alcohol Involvement (IAI). It would be reasonable to guess that changes in the stressors the client faces, or in the client's ability to cope with stress, might have an impact on depression levels and/or drinking behavior. It might therefore be wise to administer the latter two scales regularly to monitor any progress or deterioration in the secondary problems identified with this client.

How often should I ask the client to complete the scales?

There are no set rules about how often the CASS scales must be administered, though they probably should not be administered more than once a week. Nor are there such rules for most other standardized scales. If a practitioner wants to make effective use of single-system designs, however, it makes sense that the scales must be completed regularly. It is impossible to establish baselines and obtain feedback about the existence and rate of client progress without repeated measurement. Just as importantly, it is difficult to accurately assess any deterioration in a client's situation without regular use of the scales.

The frequency of scale administration may depend on the nature of the intervention. If the client's problem (or the growing limits on service imposed by managed care) requires, the practitioner may develop a short-term treatment plan that covers eight to ten weeks of service delivery. In such instances, it would be wise to administer the scales once a week. If the practitioner has the flexibility and need to structure service delivery over a much longer period, however, he or she might have the client complete the scales every couple of weeks. In cases where service delivery is expected to last beyond several months, completion of the scales might be done only once a month. In general, a good principle to follow is: The practitioner should have the client complete the scales often enough to keep both of them informed about significant changes in the targeted problems, but not often enough to become an intrusion or an ignored piece of information.

Can I have clients complete these scales at home?

It is often useful to have clients complete the scales at home. This is particularly true if the practitioner has already thoroughly assessed the client's problem(s), strengths, and risks and is already using one or more scales to repeatedly measure the client's problem(s) over time. This also implies, however, that it is usually beneficial to have clients complete the scales in the office the first couple of times they are administered. This practice gives the practitioner a chance to make the client familiar with the process of completing the scales, and it allows the practitioner to score the scales immediately and take immediate action if the scales suggest a major clinical difficulty for the client. The implications of having the client complete a particular scale at home also need to be carefully considered; if the practitioner foresees the possibility of this actually causing problems for the client, then the practitioner will not want to have the client do this. For example, suppose that the client is a woman whom the practitioner knows (or suspects) is involved in a relationship with a physically abusive partner. The act of having the client complete a scale such as the Physical Abuse of Partner Scale at home could lead to the client being physically abused. The abusive partner might, upon discovering the client completing the scale, become enraged and assault the client. If the practitioner suspects that there could be some negative consequence to the client (and/or to others) for completing a scale at home, then the practitioner should not have her or him complete the scale at home.

Remember that scales are most useful if they are applied in a flexible manner. If both the practitioner and the client are comfortable with the assignment of "homework," the client can complete paper-and-pencil versions of the scales at regular intervals at home and bring them to the next session. After scoring, the results become a very good starting point for the session.

Should I have clients complete the scales before or after each treatment session?

The previous point brings up another question. If clients complete the scales in the office, is this best done before or after the practitioner–client interaction? Completion before the session is probably a better option for two reasons. The first has already been pointed out. Both the practitioner and the client will benefit from the immediate feedback before a session. It gives the practitioner a solid basis from which to start the session. The second reason is that during any treatment session, it is likely that many issues that are emotionally charged for the client will be discussed. The responses on any scale after an intense session may be distorted somewhat by the experience the client had in interacting with the practitioner during the session.

Can I have the client complete both the computerized and paper-and-pencil versions of these scales? Is there any difference?

Completion of either form of the CASS scales is fine, and the forms may be interchanged in a way that best fits practice. To complete a CASS scale on a computer, the client must be in the office. This precludes the assignment of "homework." Many clients, though, enjoy the experience of working through the CASS scales on a computer and find the immediate feedback interesting and useful. Other clients find the computer intimidating and would rather sit down with a paper-and-pencil scale. Either way, the scores obtained on a scale will be the same. Practitioners should use their best judgment and flexibility to come to an agreement with clients about how best to complete the scales.

SCREENING AND DIAGNOSTIC
APPLICATIONS

Can I use all or most of the CASS scales as a screening or diagnostic tool?

This can be a tricky question. If the practitioner has reason to believe that a client is dealing with a particular set of difficulties upon intake, administration of one or more specific CASS scales can be useful in diagnosis. They can help to confirm the practitioner's initial judgments about the client's situation.

The CASS scales are not meant as a battery of tests, however. It is not a good idea to have an incoming client complete the full range of CASS scales in an attempt to conduct a fishing expedition to find out the client's problem(s). First of all, this would be an extremely time-consuming and tedious exercise that most clients would find very annoying. This would also give clients the sense that they are being diverted away from seeing a real, live professional who is willing and skilled enough to assist them. Either of these situations can delay or detract from the start of a beneficial therapeutic relationship.

We suggest the following set of principles for using CASS or any other scales as a part of a routine intake process. In using the scales as part of intake or background information collection, the practitioner should do so carefully. He or she should consciously and deliberately select scales that are especially focused on the difficulties his or her agency typically deals with (issues surrounding partner abuse in a domestic violence program, for example) or a multidimensional scale such as the MPSI that has been specifically designed to capture a broad range of client problems. In either of these cases, the practitioner must carefully examine the scales to ensure that they will capture the kinds of information that both the practitioner and the client will find useful as a tool to enhance understanding of the problem, or problems, at hand. Most importantly, however, these scales should be applied only after the client has met a professional helper face-to-face and the purpose and importance of the scales have been explained to the client's satisfaction. It is the combination of a caring, skilled interaction with a professional helper and completion of appropriate scales that will offer the best assessment of the problem to be addressed.

Should I have all my clients complete all of the scales?

This question really follows the last one. There is no need to have all clients complete all the scales. This could appear to clients as a fishing expedition type of search for information about their problems, instead of a thoughtful process of client and problem assessment. Practitioners should use the scales selectively by first meeting with clients, and then working with them to identify and prioritize the problems that need to be addressed. Once these priorities are in hand, it becomes much easier to select one or more specific scales that will effectively monitor clients' progress.

Most situations call for the use of only one or two scales at any one time. More complex cases may require the regular administration of up to four scales, but practitioners should try not to go beyond that. Use of more scales than that poses a number of difficulties. First, the client will quickly become tired of regularly completing many scales and might begin to ignore or resent the process. Second, the practitioner might encounter great difficulty in tracking and interpreting client change on many scales at once. To effectively use scales within a single-system design, practitioners need to keep things as simple as possible by targeting specific issues to be assessed and monitored over time. If need be, the use of particular scales can be added or removed as intervention progresses over a prolonged period.

As aids to diagnosis and planning, can I use a larger number of the scales to screen during intake and beginning phases?

This question directly relates to the issue of targeting client change. When clients first enter agencies, they often present with a diverse range of problems and issues. It is not unusual, for instance, to have a client seek help for issues related to marital disruption. Along with that, though, might come related problems such as emotional abuse in the relationship, alcohol abuse, depression, sexual discord, and low self-esteem. Where does one start? One useful way of determining this is to explore these issues in more depth during an initial interview with the client. This might point to the emotional abuse, alcohol abuse, and self-esteem as issues that warrant attention first. By administering the Partner Abuse Scale: Non-physical (PASNP), the Index of Alcohol Involvement (IAI), and the Index of Self-Esteem (ISE), the practitioner has an opportunity to check the severity of these problems and decide if they should indeed become the targets of intervention.

During initial diagnosis and planning of intervention, it is common to use more scales than later on in the intervention process. This make senses, since once a formal treatment plan is implemented, the practitioner must focus on effectively monitoring the impact of treatment on specific areas of client functioning. Once again, however, practitioners must use their judgment to decide how many scales should be used to assist diagnosis and planning, and how few of these should be used to monitor the impact of intervention over time.

USING SCALES WITH CHILDREN
AND SPECIAL POPULATIONS

Can I administer any of the CASS scales to very young children?

The CASS scales are not specifically designed for use with young children, so the answer is no! The CASS scales are intended for use with individuals who have the cognitive ability and maturity to answer scale items thoughtfully. The reliability and validity of the scores produced by each of the CASS scales has also been studied with the use of older populations. As a result, we suggest that the CASS scales not be used for anybody under the age of 12. This is a general guideline, however, and should not be taken as a hard-and-fast rule. We have encountered situations involving youths younger than 12 who were quite capable of completing CASS scales in a thoughtful and accurate manner. We have also encountered youths older than 12 who could not. The practitioner needs to carefully consider the youth's maturity and cognitive ability before asking him or her to complete any of the CASS scales.

Can I use the scales with people who are illiterate?

Obviously individuals who are illiterate cannot complete the CASS scales alone. This does not preclude using the scales for assessment purposes for illiterate individuals, however. The scales can still be used effectively by having somebody reading the scale items to the client, and then recording the responses. The practitioner may have to help the client know how to respond to each item, but a short verbal description or a couple of example items usually makes the process clear to clients.

How do cultural differences affect the use of scales?

Practitioners must be careful about the assumption that the CASS scales (or any other scale) can be used without regard to language and cultural differences. Even reading the scales aloud to clients will not solve misunder-standings created by language problems and cultural differences. Sometimes individuals for whom English is a second language have difficulty understand-ing some of the words in the scales, even if those words are read aloud. There may also be cultural differences that make the meaning of specific words quite different or alien to the client. Take the second item from the Generalized Contentment Scale, for example. It reads, "I feel blue. "Most of us who come from a North American cultural background will recognize what that term means. For people of other cultures, though, the notion of turning "blue" might seem quite strange. That is why it is important for practitioners to read each scale they are considering using and to ask themselves whether it contains wording or imagery that will be understandable to the client. Because the CASS scales were validated using primarily a U. S. population, a basic famil-iarity with western culture is important. Using the CASS scales in situations where cultural differences are significant may invalidate the particular scale being used. This is a caution practitioners must pay particular attention to when using any standardized scales.

Can I use the scales with mentally challenged people?

This depends on the severity of the impairment experienced by the client. Clients who have a mild impairment, say through a brain injury or cerebral palsy, can effectively complete the CASS scales. Other clients who have a severe handicap, however, often do not have the mental functioning to under-stand and appropriately respond to the scale items. Professional judgment and assessment skills must be used to determine whether the client can compre-hend and complete the scales, and whether the scales will provide productive information that will help guide intervention. If the answer is yes to both of these questions, the scales may be of value to use in such situations.

Can I use the scales with psychotic individuals?

A client who is experiencing acute psychosis should not be asked to com-plete the CASS scales. If the client's psychosis is judged to be in remission, though, the CASS scales may provide useful information to help guide inter-vention. This is another area that depends on clinical judgment and assessment skills. The scales should be used with a psychotic individual only if the practi-tioner's best judgment indicates that such use is appropriate.

Can I use the scales with involuntary clients?

The CASS scales do not include items designed to function as lie detec-tors. Nor do we recommend the use of lie scales in conjunction with the CASS scales. For these reasons, we recommend some caution when consider-ing using CASS scales with involuntary clients. Most clients will be open and honest, especially once the practitioner has established a working level of trust and communication. There are some instances, however, when clients may have undue incentives to mislead. Use of the CASS scales with incarcerated clients might be questioned, for example, by the knowledge that inmates can sometimes receive shortened incarcerations or greater freedoms by displaying "good" behaviors. It would be tempting for such a client to provide answers to scale items that would lead the practitioner to believe the client is actually functioning much better than he or she is. When using CASS scales with involuntary clients, practitioners should do so with careful thought and caution, and they should make sure to build a sufficient working relationship with the client first.

INTERPRETING AND
USING SCALE SCORES

My interviews with a client have suggested the presence of a mild or moderate problem. When I administered a CASS scale, though, the score was much higher than I anticipated. Is my assessment wrong?

No, not necessarily. The assessment is probably based on the information that the client provided. Early in the intervention process, clients are often wary of professionals and may not fully disclose the extent or nature of their problems. This is a natural reaction. How many of us like to jump right in and tell a complete stranger about very serious, sensitive, and painful problems in our life? As the working relationship improves, however, the initial assessment will often change. It is in these situations that the CASS scales can be most useful. Both the total scale score and the responses to individual items can be used as starting points to explore the client's problems in much more detail and depth. The scales can also help the practitioner "get inside the client" more effectively by providing clues and indicators that help round out the practitioner's judgment of the severity or nature of the client's problem. The scales should be viewed as a useful tool. They certainly do not replace professional assessment, but they can help establish information and patterns that make assessment more assured.

Can I interpret individual item responses on the scales?

As we have indicated, responses to specific items on the CASS scales can make useful discussion points with clients. This should only be done in the light of the scale's total score and the practitioner's interpretation of that score, though. We do not advise simply going ahead and trying to interpret the scores on individual items from any of the CASS scales. As a single entity, any of the CASS scales usually produces a total score with a reliability of at least .90. The score on any single item from one of these scales, however, will have lower reliability (often .40 or less). As a result, individual item scores will contain more measurement error and may, in fact, be misleading.

It is useful to think of using individual item responses as a balancing act. Discussion of individual item responses often provides clues about the nature and severity of the client's problems. A practitioner might even select to apply a small subset of specific items drawn from a larger scale, say the MPSI. Doing so may help to stimulate client discussion around certain topics, or even provide "red flags" that point to the existence of particularly serious problems. For example, a client might respond to item 195 ("My partner tries to choke or strangle me") on the MPSI Physical Abuse subscale with a response indicating that this occurs "a little of the time." We would take this single-item response very seriously and consider it to be a "red flag" that must be paid attention to and that demands immediate attention.

Practitioners should follow certain procedures to select items or subsets of items from the CASS scales, however. They should follow the instructions provided by the CASS manual to learn how to select out items from existing scales. And they must remember that selecting out individual items or subsets of items from the CASS scales poses the risk of obtaining unreliable and invalid information. Individual items will never have the exact psychometric characteristics shown by the scores obtained from a complete scale, so the total scores remain the best overall assessment of the client's problem.

What do very high scores (over 70) mean?

A high score on any of the CASS scales is a very serious matter. Regardless of the scale, a very high score of 70 or above may be an indicator of violence. This may take the form of either violence against others or acts of self-harm, or both. In either case, quick action may be necessary.

There are particular CASS scales that may point to the potential for violence. These include the Generalized Contentment Scale (GCS), Index of Self-Esteem (ISE), Index of Peer Relations (IPR), Index of Parental Attitudes (IPA), Child's Attitude Toward Mother, and Child's Attitude Toward Father scales. Naturally, they also include the four CASS partner abuse scales, the Non-physical Abuse of Partner Scale (NPAPS), the Partner Abuse Scale: Non-physical (PASNP), the Partner Abuse Scale: Physical (PASPH), and the Physical Abuse of Partner Scale (PAPS).

What do very low scores (0 to 5) mean?

A score of 5 or below is very good news indeed. If the client was open and honest when completing the scale, it means that he or she does not have any difficulties in the area being assessed. Since there is no clinical problem for the client, the practitioner has no reason to treat that specific problem.

How do I interpret scores that are very close to the clinical cutting scores?

There is always a small amount of random error that can create small fluctuations in client scores (about three or four points on the CASS scales). For this reason, scores that fall slightly below or above a clinical cutting score should be interpreted with caution. Consider an example. Suppose a client scores between 27 and 35 over three administrations of the Generalized Contentment Scale (GCS). Would this client be diagnosed as being clinically depressed? Should treatment be introduced? Should it be discontinued?

It is clear that the decisions the practitioner must make in such cases will be difficult. A score of 27 is below the clinical cutting score, but at the same time we know that the client is experiencing some degree of difficulty in this problem area. Otherwise, the scores obtained would be much lower, approaching zero. The question, therefore, is not about the presence of a problem but, rather, focuses on whether the problem is severe enough to warrant professional intervention.

When scores border the clinical cutting score, we strongly recommend that the practitioner seek additional sources of information. The practitioner should interview the client, check with collateral sources, and use these to paint a more complete picture of the client's situation. After all, a situation in which services are offered to a client who does not display a clinically significant problem is wasteful and inappropriate. It is even more important, however, to avoid turning away a client who would benefit from professional intervention.

INTERPRETING CHANGES
IN CLIENT SCORES

What constitutes a dramatic score change?

A sudden change of ten points or more on any of the CASS scales should be considered a dramatic score change. This applies regardless of the change in direction of these scores. The CASS scales show solid stability, with a standard error of measurement of about five points. This means that if a client's problem remains stable, a small degree of random fluctuation in scores might occur. This fluctuation, however, will vary by a small amount, normally around three or four points at most. A change of ten points or more in client scores is therefore not likely the product of a random fluctuation. Some change in the client's situation has occurred, and hopefully this change reflects the effectiveness of the intervention.

How do I interpret these sudden, dramatic changes in scores?

Practitioners should interpret any sudden, dramatic changes in client scores as significant. This is particularly true if the practitioner has had the opportunity to establish stable baseline observations or treatment-phase data. If this occurs, the practitioner can be reasonably assured that some event has occurred that is influencing the client's responses. It is important to explore the change the client has experienced and the range of factors that might have contributed to this change. This process of investigation has been called "critical incident investigation" (Bloom et al., 1999; Hudson, 1982).

Exploring the factors that may have contributed to change will depend on the practitioner's professional skills. Sometimes the reasons for a sudden change in the client's problem will be readily apparent to both the practitioner and the client. Often, though, the reasons for change occur outside of the boundaries of the client-worker relationship. This can make the reasons for change subtle and hidden by the complexities of a client's life. Nor is it unusual for a client to be somewhat reluctant to discuss what is happening in her or his life. Thus, in many cases, practitioners must depend on their interviewing and assessment skills to identify the events that appear to have contributed to client change. There are substantial benefits that can be realized if the practitioner is successful in identifying the factors that may have contributed to client change, however. They might be factors that the practitioner can influence or control, thereby increasing the probability of continued improvement for the client.

If scores increase steadily over time, can I be sure this represents ongoing deterioration for my client?

Almost definitely yes. The CASS scales have demonstrated the ability to detect and measure both deterioration and improvement in client problems. The increase in scale scores must exceed the standard error of measurement of the scale (most have a standard error of measurement of about five points). Assuming that the steady increase exceeds the scale's standard error, the worker can assume that the increase in scores represents a real deterioration for the client. If the scale detects a steady deterioration in the client's problem, the worker needs to consider taking immediate action to reverse this trend.

How do I know that a steady decline in scores represents real improvement for my client?

Steady declines in client scores can be interpreted as a positive sign that real client change is occurring. The decline in client scores must be larger than the standard error of measurement for the scale (around five points for most of the CASS scales). As long as the change exceeds this amount over time, the practitioner can be reasonably sure that the observed change is not a random event. This ability to detect change over repeated administrations of the scales is one of their greatest benefits.

Once again, however, a practitioner cannot be sure that the improvement in the client's scores can be attributed to treatment. There are many other factors that can lead to changes in the client's scores. The client's situation may have changed, a crisis in her or his life may have been resolved, other helpers (professional as well as nonprofessional) may have intervened, and so on. Also, practitioners should bear in mind that a few clients may wish to provide them with the impression of declining scores. They may wish to terminate service delivery, or for some other reason suggest that their problem is improving when in fact it is not. It is therefore important to routinely check the scale responses to ensure they are consistent with other information collected.

Are the scales always right, even if they seem to contradict the practitioner?

Practitioners are not always correct in their assessments, or may be unsure of their assessments. This is because conducting an accurate, thorough assessment of any client is a complex, challenging task. This is true even when complete, reliable information is available about that client. Just think about how challenging the assessment process is in the absence of complete and reliable information. Unfortunately, this is often the case because clients may fail to fill in the blanks when interviewed, important points may be missed, or information may be misinterpreted. Even the best of practitioners can make mistakes (see Garb, 1998, for a review of research on practitioner judgment).

This is not to say that CASS scales are infallible. They may be used to assess problems for which they were not intended, clients may not understand the scales or try to mislead the practitioner, or many items may be skipped when the client completes the scale. These and similar factors may invalidate the scores obtained. One thing we do know, however, is that if the scales are used for the purpose intended, appropriate administration procedures are used, and the client is open and honest, they will usually produce scores that are reliable and valid. As such, they serve to reduce inaccuracies in client assessment and improve the likelihood of detecting and monitoring patterns in the client's problems.

If the client's scores decrease steadily over time, how can I be sure that his or her progress is due to my intervention?

The scores from the CASS scales cannot answer this question. When determining causality in any situation, there are many competing factors to consider. There are many possible explanations for client improvement. The client may have resolved some of the issues on her or his own, a crisis may be over and the client is improving without any intervention at all, or maybe the client is seeking the assistance of nonprofessional helpers. These and other potential explanations have to be ruled out if the practitioner wants to establish that it was her or his intervention that caused change for this client. As we discussed in Chapter 5, establishing causality can be an extremely complex and time-consuming task. If workers want to demonstrate that their intervention caused client improvement, they need to carefully select an appropriate single-system design, and pay careful attention to weeding out alternative explanations that might explain changes in the client's situation. Such practitioners must be prepared for lots of learning, hard work, and some frustration.

What if the client obtains exactly the same score three or more times?

This would be a rare occurrence. In order to obtain exactly the same score three or more times sequentially, a client's situation would have to remain perfectly stable during that time period, and there would have to be no random fluctuations. This is rather unlikely. Most clients seek treatment at a crisis point. Some change would normally occur without any intervention at all (regression to the mean; see discussion in Gilovich, 1991). The client's situation might continue to worsen, and scores would tend to increase over time. In other situations, the crisis might subside, which would be indicated by lower scale scores over time. Of course, with intervention we would hope to see the client's scores decrease as treatment progresses. For these reasons, a pattern of three or more identical scores over time should be carefully examined. The client may be providing responses that he or she sees as socially desirable.

CLIENT REACTIONS
AND RESPONSES

Do clients show resentment or reluctance in completing the scales?

If clients are not well-informed about the nature of the scales and how the worker expects them to aid in the alleviation of the clients' problems, they can become annoyed at the prospect of completing the scales. If the worker takes sufficient time to explain that the scales accurately measure the extent of client problems and that he or she will use scale scores to monitor client progress over time, most clients are quite open to the use of standardized measures. Clients can even become eager to use the scales on a regular basis in order to get immediate feedback and a concrete picture of how they are doing.

This is not to say that all clients are eager to use standardized measures. There are many reasons they may not wish to complete a scale—fear, resistance to sharing personal information, anxiety about the magnitude of their problems, and so on. In these cases, the practitioner should try to be open and honest about the utility of such scales, as well as the limitations they do have. The practitioner should engage in a discussion about their use with the client. It is possible that the client's reluctance to complete a scale may be related to the nature of her or his problem, motivations that are not yet known to the worker, or a lack of readiness for treatment. Discussion may provide valuable information about these issues, and facilitate better assessment and treatment planning. In the end, if the client still wishes to refrain from completing any scale, then the worker should respect her or his wishes. Clients have a right to say "no" to administration of any of these scales.

Should I insist that clients complete the scales I need when they demonstrate reluctance to do so?

This point bears repeating. Again, clients have a right to decline when asked to complete any scale. Practitioners should always explore the reasons underlying such a refusal, though. It is possible that the practitioner was vague when explaining the nature of standardized measures and how they will improve treatment. It is also possible that the client feels the worker has not yet developed the worker-client relationship to an appropriate level of mutual respect and trust. As a result, the client may consider the information obtained through the scales as a threat to his or her privacy or personal boundaries. Of course, as we have suggested, a reluctance to complete scales can often be based on the client's own thoughts, beliefs, fears, motivations, readiness for treatment, and so on. Practitioners should try to explore and understand all of these possibilities. If the client is still unwilling to complete the scales, the worker should not become upset. Rather, the practitioner should use professional skills to adopt alternative assessment strategies so that a thorough assessment can still be accomplished and treatment can begin.

Should I allow clients to see their scores?

By all means! Client scores belong to them. The scores are the product of the client's thoughts, emotions, and commitment to treatment. Practitioners should not only show clients their scores, but also should discuss them thoroughly. The worker should explain what the scores suggest and help the client to understand how the information provided by the scale will be used to improve treatment. We cannot stress enough the power of sharing scores with clients. If a worker were, instead, to hide or ignore the scores, one of two things might happen. First, clients might get the impression that the scales and their scores are not really that important—maybe even useless. Second, clients might react negatively on a personal level. They might think that the worker is trying to hide something from them, which certainly is not the foundation for a good therapeutic relationship. They might think that the worker does not consider them intelligent enough to understand the results. They might even feel that they have somehow failed, and that the results are too bad for them to be shown the "truth." Any of these impressions is very damaging to a good working relationship with the client.

The truth is that clients are almost always very capable of understanding their scores and very interested in what the scores mean. They want to have the results explained, and they find the discussion that emerges very useful. They often provide their own thoughts and insights regarding the results. In short, sharing scores with the client becomes an empowering process for the client, thereby facilitating his or her contribution and commitment to the treatment process.

How should I interpret the scale scores to clients?

Be open and honest with clients. If a practitioner tries to be anything else, clients will certainly detect her or his hesitation or lack of honesty. Workers should explain that the scales are meant to assess the severity of the client's problem and that the scores will get higher as the problem becomes more severe and will go down as the problem improves. The notion of a clinical cutting score and that scores falling above the cutting score usually warrant intervention for the problem should also be explained.

Clients often express a sense of relief when scale scores are presented and interpreted. This is because they sometimes have difficulty explaining the magnitude of their problem verbally. It is very confirming for them to know that a standardized scale, with established validity, has also found their problem to be at a particular level.

DEPENDABILITY OF
CLIENT RESPONSES

How do I know a client has provided truthful and accurate responses on a CASS scale?

There is no definite way to prove a client has provided truthful and accurate responses. The CASS scales do not include items designed as lie detectors. Nor do we recommend the use of lie scales to try to catch any client who might be trying to mislead the practitioner. Routine use of such scales can alienate clients by implying that the practitioner does trust them or their responses.

We favor a different approach, one that relies on the practitioner's professional skills. For most clients, the practitioner has a broad range of information available. There is also the worker–client relationship that is built as the practitioner engages in assessment and works through treatment. These can be used to judge whether the client is likely to be open in disclosing personal, perhaps even painful, information to the practitioner. If the worker's judgment suggests that the client is forthcoming, the client will probably be quite open when completing the scales too. If the client appears resistant, misleading, or dismissive, however, the worker needs to check the client's responses on the scales carefully. In the end, professional assessment of the client must be contrasted with the assessment provided by the CASS scales. In the vast majority of cases, they will be consistent. If not, the worker should proceed with caution and check out inconsistencies.

What do I do if I feel that my client is not being truthful?

Proceed with tremendous caution, and do not place blind faith in the CASS scales. The practitioner should follow the suggestions in the previous section to make judgments about the client's motivation and the consistency between scale scores and the practitioner's professional judgment. A worker who still suspects that the client is not being truthful should consider terminating use of the scales entirely. It is better to have restricted information than to be misled into an intervention that may be misdirected or even harmful.

We also suggest that practitioners be direct with clients and tell them that the scale scores are not consistent with the practitioner's assessment or other available information. This gives the client a chance to clarify her or his responses, explain why the responses may appear to be inconsistent, or let the worker know about some other misunderstanding that may have occurred when the client completed the scales. This kind of frank discussion often highlights some confusion that has occurred in the assessment process. It also provides a means for determining why the client has not been truthful, and acts as a starting point from which to move toward a more trusting and truthful relationship.

What do I do if my judgments radically differ from the scales?

The answer to this question depends on whether the practitioner is using CASS computer software to score the scales or scoring the scales manually. If using the CASS software, the practitioner should discuss the results with the client and clarify that the client understood how to complete the scale and that his or her responses are correct. If the practitioner manually entered the scores into the computer, he or she should check the data entry. If these aspects of the administration process appear to be in order, then the worker should be direct with the client and explore the reasons for the inconsistencies between the worker's clinical impressions and the scores produced on one of the CASS scales. The practitioner should consider the possibility that his or her clinical impressions are flawed in some way, that the treatment is not helping as planned, or that the client is intentionally misleading the practitioner. If the picture still does not make sense, the practitioner should consult with other professionals that he or she trusts. Chances are that exploring one of these possibilities will explain the discrepancy between the practitioner's judgment and the scale scores.

One of the more common reasons that scale scores appear to be inconsistent with the practitioner's judgment occurs when manually scoring the CASS scales. Because there are a number of steps to scoring the scales, it is sometimes easy to make a mistake in calculations. One mistake in calculations can make a large difference in the final scores obtained on the scales. For this reason, practitioners should refer back to Chapter 12 for instructions on scoring the CASS scales and work through the scoring formula again, checking the calculations at each point. If the score does indeed appear to be correct, the previous suggestions can be followed to try making sense of the discrepancy between the scale and the practitioner's judgment.

What if a lot of items are not completed?

In order to obtain a valid score on a CASS scale, the majority of items must be completed. If a client fails to complete a large number of items on one of the scales, the practitioner should not rely on the score that is obtained. As a general rule, clients should complete at least 80 percent of the items on a scale. As long as this level of completion is reached, the scales will still deliver reliable and valid assessment data. This allows for some flexibility when clients do not understand specific items or skip them for some other reason.

If a client does fail to complete the majority of items on a scale, the practitioner should consider the situation carefully. Perhaps the scale is not appropriate for that client's situation, and many items were skipped because the client did not consider them applicable. Failure to complete items may also indicate other barriers, such as literacy problems or cultural differences that make understanding the items difficult. In many cases, skipped items may represent a client reaction to sensitive items that the client finds difficult to discuss. They may even represent client resistance to dealing with specific issues. These situations can serve as useful indicators. The practitioner should ask himself or herself whether the scale is indeed appropriate for the targeted problem and, if it is, whether the client is capable of completing the scale appropriately. If some items are omitted, the practitioner should consider the possibility that these skipped items are indicators of problems that need to be explored with the client.

How do I protect against impression-management responses?

Our first reaction is to say that practitioners need to work hard at developing a productive worker-client relationship. This is the basis for making any progress in the therapeutic relationship. It is the working relationship that is formed that will allow the worker to explain the purpose and role of scales and allow the client to respond positively. Perhaps just as importantly, however, the worker must be clear with the client that accurate information is needed in order to help the client with his or her targeted problem. Our experience suggests that once clients understand that there is a legitimate reason for asking them to complete the scales, they will try to be as helpful as possible. This means that clients will tend to be candid in their responses rather than trying to provide the practitioner with socially desirable or other impression-management responses.

Do clients ever falsify responses?

Yes, certainly. We believe that most clients are candid and honest, however, If there is reason to suspect that a client is falsifying responses, the practitioner's focus should turn to the reasons why the client might want to mislead the practitioner. Perhaps the client is reluctant to share the full extent of her or his problem, fears the treatment process, or does not trust the practitioner enough to share personal information. In some cases, clients may wish to terminate treatment prematurely and are trying to suggest significant improvement when, in fact, it does not exist. If this seems to be the case, the practitioner needs to explore why the client does not wish to continue treatment. In rare cases, some clients may even alter their responses so that their problem appears to persist over time. This allows them to continue on in the therapeutic relationship. If this seems to be happening, it is important to analyze the dynamics inherent in the worker-client relationship. What is the client seeking by trying to maintain ongoing contact with the worker?

I am concerned about reactivity in the scales. Should I be concerned?

Reactivity occurs when the actual process of measuring the client's problem functions to change the client's problem. In a sense, the act of measurement functions as an intervention. Think of a client who is emotionally abusive to his partner, for example. The practitioner has the client complete the Non-Physical Abuse of Partner Scale (NPAPS) as part of the initial assessment process. The client may obtain a relatively high score, suggesting that he is indeed emotionally abusive toward his partner. The very act of completing the scale, however, may help the client develop a deeper understanding of his behavior. This newfound perception might function as a cognitive restructuring and may help to spark changes for the client, thereby facilitating a movement toward lower scores on the scale.

Reactivity is a problem if the practitioner is a researcher trying to establish causal relationships as part of a research study. For the average practitioner, though, reactivity should not be a major concern. If reactivity does occur, and the client's problem seems to be improving due to the act of measurement, then the practitioner can be glad, since it is something that is helping. Most of the time reactivity will not have a large impact on the scores obtained, nor will the changes due to reactivity persist over a prolonged period of time. Of course, if there is evidence that reactivity is making the client's problem *worse*, then the practitioner will want to determine the reasons that the act of measurement is having this effect and, if necessary, discontinue the measurement process.

USING SCALES FOR
TRAINING AND SUPERVISION

Can I use the scales in supervision?

The CASS scales make excellent aids to the supervisory process. They are at their most powerful when the supervisor wishes to discuss a particular case with the practitioner. If the practitioner has used the scales to assess and monitor the client over time, the scores and charts effectively summarize the whole case and facilitate discussion of what has transpired. When combined with other case materials such as case notes and information from other professionals, the benefit is multiplied. Single-system designs and the scales provide a common framework and language that both the supervisor and practitioner can use to carefully reflect on what has or has not worked with that particular case.

Can I use the scales as a teaching aid in the classroom?

Yes, the scales have often been used as class handouts or overhead presentations. They make a valuable starting point from which to discuss the nature of client assessment and to challenge students to think about the importance and complexities of determining practice effectiveness. Perhaps most of all, the scales offer a mechanism to teach students the techniques they need to know to apply single-system designs to their practice, particularly if students have the opportunity to apply the scales to case planning and treatment with clients in their practicum settings. These students come back into the classroom excited about the potential for empirical practice and display great creativity in applying single-system designs to their practice.

If I use the scales for training, how and when is this best done?

As we discussed in Chapter 3, single-system designs can make powerful contributions to social work practice. They aid every stage of practice, from initial data collection and assessment of clients through making decisions about termination and evaluation. This also means that the CASS scales can be useful tools through this entire process. The implication is that students should start to learn about single-system designs and the use of scales early in their educational process. As students engage in their first learning efforts, gaining knowledge about basic communication skills, interviewing, assessment models, and so on, they can also learn the fundamentals of assessment and client monitoring technologies. This means that students should not learn only about the CASS scales. They should also learn about the wide range of measurement tools that they can apply to their burgeoning practice.

Can field practicum instructors use the CASS program in the context of training students?

Yes, most definitely. Field instructors often find that using the CASS scales facilitates discussion of a case with students. They are able to compare the student's initial assessment of the client with the assessment provided by the CASS scales. They are also able to discuss the progress of treatment over time, particularly if the scales have been used to routinely monitor the client's improvement. In short, the scales help to paint a concrete, visual picture for the student.

Field instructors can easily obtain the student version of the CASS program free of charge to use for such training purposes. They can also distribute this software freely to students and other field instructors in their agencies. Chapter 17 provides details about obtaining and installing the CASS software.

ADMINISTRATIVE AND
LOGISTICAL QUESTIONS

These scales might be very useful to me, but I'm already overloaded. How do I handle the extra work that comes with completing the scales?

Conducting effective practice is always a balancing act. It is true that administering, scoring, and interpreting the CASS scales will take some time if it is to be done thoroughly. Using the CASS system on the computer can make this a much more efficient process, especially for things like calculating total scale scores. The practitioner must still be willing to commit the time and resources necessary to effectively use the CASS system, however.

The time spent on using standardized scales must be thought of as an investment in the practitioner's ability to perform effectively. The use of reliable and valid scales can make the assessment process more efficient by allowing practitioners to more quickly focus on specific problems to be addressed, while decreasing the likelihood of inaccurate assessments. Regular monitoring of client change can also highlight deterioration in the client's problem or suggest that intervention is not leading to client improvement as quickly or strongly as hoped. Using CASS in these circumstances can actually save time and resources by more clearly identifying and tracking change in a targeted problem. In the end, we think the benefits of establishing the effectiveness of practice far outweigh the time and effort required.

If I want to acquire the CASS program for use by all of our staff, how would I do that and what would it cost?

The publisher of the CASS scales has made the system available through several mechanisms. Chapter 17 of this book details these mechanisms and explains how to install the CASS system. If you have any further questions, check out the website described in Chapter 17 or write to the publisher using the address shown in that chapter.

From an administrative perspective, what are the principal benefits of using CASS?

CASS is inherently a tool that facilitates accountability. This means that it offers benefits for supervision and case management, as well as a means for evaluating the effectiveness of practice. Using the techniques outlined in this book, CASS scales can also provide data that can be aggregated and analyzed to conduct evaluation on a program level. Perhaps the greatest benefit offered by the use of CASS is more subtle. It helps to reinforce the value of an effectiveness orientation to administrative practice and to quickly infuse the everyday functioning of a human service agency with that orientation.

Can I aggregate single-case data across service units or programs in order to examine performance effectiveness and service outcomes?

As we have already indicated, single-system data can be aggregated across service units or programs to get a broader perspective on the effectiveness of practice. Chapters 7 and 8 in this book describe techniques for conducting such outcome reviews, and the CASS system is designed to assist such work.

RESEARCH AND TECHNICAL
QUESTIONS

If I use the CASS scales in a research project, can I assume the scale scores will be normally distributed?

No. The CASS scales do not produce normally distributed scores in the general population. Nor are they expected to. This is because at any one point in time, most people do not have a clinically significant problem that requires professional intervention. Therefore, if we were to administer the CASS scales to a general population, most of the scores would fall below the clinical cutting score on any of the scales. In statistical terms, this means that the scales have score distributions that are right-skewed.

The fact that CASS scales are not normally distributed in the general population poses no real problem for most practical purposes. The scales can be used with confidence in their ability to consistently and accurately assess the problems they purport to measure. If the plan is to use statistical tests that are based on the normal curve, however, some caution is required. For hypothesis testing, it is recommended that procedures be followed to reduce the impact of skewed data. Square root, logarithmic, or logit transformations work well and are thoroughly described by Neter, Wasserman, and Kutner (1983).

Can I factor analyze the CASS scale items for any specific scale in order to determine what types of problems clients are having in each of the areas being measured?

No. The CASS scales were not designed as multidimensional scales, and they should not be treated as such. For a detailed discussion of this, we refer the reader to a publication entitled *The Clinical Measurement Package: A Field Manual* (Hudson, 1982).

Can I use the CASS program and scales in research applications?

The CASS scales have been effectively used as research tools for a couple of decades. The CASS computer program can administer research questionnaires, measures designed by practitioners, formal scales that practitioners build into the system, and, of course, the CASS scales. Those who wish to take advantage of all of these capabilities must purchase the full professional version of the CASS program. Chapter 17 provides information about how this version of the software can be acquired.

SUMMARY

This chapter has tried to anticipate some of the many questions that might arise about the use of assessment scales. We cannot provide all the answers, and much more detail is available for some of the topics covered. Practitioners will undoubtedly come across many other questions as they gain experience in using such measures. The authors of this book and the publisher of the CASS scales would be very interested in knowing about other questions that are generated. We hope that readers will not hesitate to contact us should they want to ask other questions.

16

Developing One's Own Measurement Scales

In earlier chapters, we discussed the numerous reasons for using formal measures in practice. We also discussed the use of the short-form scales and the multidimensional scales contained in the CASS system for assessing clients' problems and for monitoring clients' progress during service provision. These measures should be useful for many clients. However, there will be times when the measures we have already discussed will not meet the practitioner's needs, and alternative measures will have to be found.

Numerous measures have been developed for use in practice. Many of these measures have been described in Fischer and Corcoran's *Measures for Clinical Practice* (1994). Other sources of assessment and measurement procedures are Beere (1979); Buros (1972, 1998); Butterfield (1977); Chun, Cobb, and French (1975); Ciminero, Calhoun, and Adams (1977); Comrey, Barker, and Glaser (1975); Cone and Hawkins (1977); Goldman and Saunders (1974); Shaw and Wright (1967); and Zung (1965). If at all possible, the evaluator should use instruments and procedures that have already been developed and validated, since it is time-consuming and can be expensive to develop and validate a new instrument. Valid and reliable measurement is a critical foundation upon which the evaluator's efforts rest. Poor measurement can render useless an otherwise well-conceived and conducted evaluation study (Nunnally & Bernstein, 1996). This is especially true if the measurement strategy produces scales that are not valid (Messick, 1989).

However, there may be times that the measurement tool appropriate for a particular program or evaluation effect does not exist. In this case, the evaluator must develop one that meets his or her needs. In this chapter we discuss the process of developing a variety of measurement tools, including the development of standardized scales like the short-form measures discussed earlier. We also illustrate this latter process through a description of the development of a scale to measure self-esteem, the Self-Esteem Rating Scale (SERS), developed by one of the authors (Nugent & Thomas, 1992).

CONCEPTUAL FUNDAMENTALS

Ways of Measuring Clients' Problems

There are essentially two ways to determine whether a client has a problem: by observing the client, or by asking the client. The first of these procedures refers to *direct observation*, while the second refers to *self-report*. Of course, collateral information (i.e., information from others) can be obtained from the client's parents, spouse or partner, children, or some other person or persons familiar with the client. Each of these other reporters, however, has obtained this information by either direct observation or self-report from the client (or both of these). This distinction helps in determining which form of information collection is most appropriate for the measurement task that is faced with a client.

There is another distinction we can make between measurement procedures. This distinction concerns the manner in which the client's problem can be described in a measurement procedure. There are four basic dimensions of the client's problem that the practitioner's measurement process can tap

1. Its binary status; that is, whether it is present or absent;

2. Its frequency; that is, how often the problem occurs during some specified interval of time;

3. Its duration; that is, how long the problem lasts from its onset to some other point in time;

4. Its magnitude; that is, how severe, intense, or serious the problem is.

The first of these methods—binary measures—forms the basis for such things as symptom checklists or problem checklists. A checklist consists of a number of *items*, in the form of statements or questions, that some observer, or the client, will respond to by checking either "yes" or "no." These checklists can be set up for direct observation or self-report. For example, a direct observation checklist for symptoms of depression might contain an item in the form of a question, such as, "Does your client appear dejected?" It could also contain a statement, such as, "Client appears dejected." A "yes" response, of course, would indicate that this characteristic is present in the client, while a "no" response would indicate that this characteristic is absent in the client. Notice that in this measurement procedure, it is the social worker who is directly observing the client and then responding to the items. A self-report checklist for depression might contain an item in the form of a question, such as, "Do you feel dejected?" It might also contain an item in the form of a statement, such as, "I feel dejected." A "yes" response would indicate that the client perceives this characteristic to be true (present) for her or him, while a "no" response would indicate the characteristic is absent. Checklists can be designed as summated scales in which each "yes" response is scored with a 1, while each "no" response is scored with a 0. The total score over all of the items on the checklist is an overall measure of the client's problem.

A frequency measure is designed to assess the repeated occurrence of a problem. For example, a single-item frequency measure might be used to obtain an assessment of how frequently the client curses at other drivers while driving. This could be done by having the client (or some observer, such as the client's partner) keep count on a 3-inch by 5-inch index card the number of times the client becomes angry while driving. A self-anchored, or individualized rating, scale (Bloom et al., 1999) can also be used as a form of single-item measurement, as we describe later. Another option is to develop a multi-item frequency measure in which several items assess the frequency of occurrence of a number of different behaviors, thoughts, or feelings. An example of an item on such a measure that would be completed by an observer other than the client might be, "My husband or partner gets angry when driving." An example of a self-report item on such a scale might be, "I feel angry when driving." The respondent could respond to either of these items with a 1 (meaning "never happens"), a 2 (meaning "happens rarely"), a 3 (meaning "happens often"), a 4 (meaning "happens very often"), or a 5 (meaning "happens all of the time"). Notice that the larger the numerical response to the items, the more frequently the identified behavior occurs. Such a scale could be designed as a summated rating scale (someone other than the client completes it) or a summated self-report scale (the client completes it) in which the item scores are summed to obtain an overall numerical indicator of the frequency of occurrence of the problem, in this case the client getting angry when he or she drives. The short-form scales discussed earlier are examples of summated self-report scales.

Duration captures information on how long something happens. Duration can be measured in any increment of time, such as minutes, days, months, and so on. For example, the client may complain of headaches. One measure of the client's problem with headaches would be how long each headache lasts. This could be measured by having the client record the time of onset of the headache, and then record the time at which the headache is no longer felt. Such measures can, of course, be obtained either through some other person observing the client or through the client's self-report.

Finally, magnitude or intensity captures information on the perceived level of some problem. For example, a practitioner might have the client who has headaches rate each headache in terms of its intensity on a scale from 0 to 10, with a 0 indicating no pain whatsoever, and a 10 indicating the most intense pain a person could feel. An example of a frequently used intensity measure is the so-called Subjective Units of Discomfort, or SUDS, scale (Thyer, 1987). This measure is used to assess the intensity of subjective anxiety experienced by a person. On this scale, a 0 indicates complete calm and relaxation, while a 100 indicates complete and abject panic. Intensity measures can be designed to be direct observation or self-report. The SUDS scale is an example of a self-report intensity measure.

In developing their own measures, practitioners first need to address two core questions: (1) Will the new instrument be designed for direct observation or for self-report? and (2) Which of the four ways of measuring clients' problems—binary, frequency, duration, or intensity—will be used?

Classifying Measurement Tools

There are also some criteria that can be used to classify and describe various measurement tools. Two major ways of describing measures are in terms of *items* and *dimensions*. A measurement item can be considered as any single indicator (question, statement, task, behavior, etc.) that points to the construct, problem, or characteristic that is being measured. The items on the short-form scales are good examples of the types of statements that can be used as items. Other examples of items are:

- What is your age as of your *nearest* birthday?
- How many times have you been married?
- Rate your level of anxiety on a scale from 0 to 100.

An item can be thought of as the smallest possible, or most basic, device for gathering information about the client. It consists of a question, statement, or some other stimulus to which the client, or some observer, responds. Given the notion of the item as the basic measurement device, we can classify measurement tools as being either *single-item* or *multi-item*. A single-item scale is a measurement tool that consists of only one item. Any measurement tool that contains more than one item is called a multi-item scale or device. The short-form scales and the MPSI and FASI described earlier are examples of multi-item devices.

Another useful notion is that of *dimension*. A dimension is any single specific construct (a purposely created concept, such as "depression") that may be indicated by one or more items. "Depression" is an example of a single specific construct. "Anxiety" is an example of another single specific construct. Items may be written that serve as indicators of depression, and other items may be written that serve as indicators of anxiety. A measurement tool that consists of one or more items that indicate, or point to, a single construct is called a *unidimensional* measurement tool. A measurement device that consists of items that measure more than one construct is called a *multidimensional* measurement device. The short-form scales described earlier are examples of unidimensional measurement tools. The MPSI and FASI are examples of multidimensional tools.

Given these characteristics of measurement tools, we can place measurement devices into one of four classifications:

1. *Single-item unidimensional measures.* These are devices that use a single item to measure a single specific construct.
2. *Single-item multidimensional measures.* These are devices that use the same, single item to measure multiple constructs. This is a poor way to conduct

measurement, and these types of measurement devices should be avoided. An example of a measurement tool of this type is the so-called "double-barreled question" (Nurius & Hudson, 1993; Rubin & Babbie, 1989).

3. *Multi-item unidimensional measures.* These are devices that use more than one item to measure a single specific construct. The short-form scales described earlier are examples of this type of measurement device.

4. *Multi-item multidimensional measures.* These are devices that use more than one item to measure more than one specific construct. The MPSI and FASI are examples of this type of measurement device.

Of these four types of measures, the one to avoid is the single-item multidimensional device. The problem with such measures is that the response to the item is usually a single number that is supposed to serve as an indicator of more than one construct; however, the interpretation of this single number in terms of information about the different constructs is extremely problematic. There is no way to disentangle the information about each construct from the single numerical response.

Standardized Scales

A standardized scale is a measurement device that has been developed to measure a specific construct, or set of constructs, and is designed to be used, scored, and interpreted in a very specific manner. The standardized scale is fixed in terms of its content, its response options and methods, its scoring, and the manner in which scores on the measure are to be interpreted.

Standardizing a measure goes a long way toward minimizing the error that is contained in scores produced by the scale. Any time a measurement device contains items or a range of response options that can change from one administration to the next, be scored differently from one administration to the next, or be interpreted differently from one use to the next, there will be differences between scores that have nothing to do with the construct (or constructs) the practitioner is endeavoring to measure. In technical terms, these differences that carry no information about the construct being measured introduce *irrelevant variance* into the variance in the scores obtained from the measurement device. This means that there will be a lot of error in the scores, and this error will mean that whatever inferences are made from the scores will be more flawed than necessary. Making the items, item response options, scoring methods, and interpretation guidelines constant—that is, standardizing them— eliminates this extraneous irrelevant variance in the scores obtained from the measurement tool.

Items

As noted earlier, the item is the basic measurement device. Given this fundamental role that items play in measurement, it goes without saying that good item writing is fundamental and critical to good measurement. We present some specific item writing guidelines later in this chapter. These guidelines should be followed in the creation of any item a practitioner writes and plans to use in any measurement device she or he develops. Other sources of item writing guidelines include Allen and Yen (1979), Crocker and Algina (1986), Mehrens and Lehmann (1984), Nunnally and Bernstein (1994), Popham (1984), and Rubin and Babbie (1989).

When developing an item, a practitioner must also design a method for scoring the item. The methods for scoring items are called *item scaling techniques*. We will discuss four item scaling techniques: binary scoring, frequency counts, category partition scales, and relative frequency estimation.

Binary Scoring One of the simplest ways to score an item is with a 0 (or "no") or a 1 (or "yes"). The 0 indicates that the characteristic or indicator contained in an item is *not present*, or is *absent*, for the client. The 1 indicates that the characteristic or indicator contained in an item is *present* for the client. The item may also be designed so that a check mark serves the same purpose as a 1 or a "yes."

A strength of the *binary scoring* method is its simplicity. It is easy to use, and it is relatively easy to write items that can be scored using the binary method. If the presence or absence of one or more indicators is the only type of information needed, then this is the scoring method to use. It can be very powerful as a means of obtaining information that is based on the presence or absence of certain indicators of the construct being measured.

Its strength is also its limitation, however. This scoring method only gives information as to the presence or absence of the indicator contained within the item. If a practitioner is interested in frequency, duration, or intensity information, the binary scoring method will not provide the information needed.

Frequency Counts A practitioner may want to obtain more than just information about the presence or absence of certain indicators. If so, then one option is the use of *frequency counts*. Consider the following item: "_____ My child hits her or his siblings." If the client responds to this item with a 1, indicating that her or his child engages in this behavior, then the item has a binary scoring procedure. Suppose, however, that the client places a 1 (or a check mark) in the item response space *every time her or his child engaged in this behavior over the course of a week*. This would provide a count of the number of times this behavior occurred during that time interval—that is, a frequency count. Virtually any item designed to be scored in a binary manner can also be used to obtain a frequency count. This form of scoring provides information not only about the occurrence or nonoccurrence of the behavior, but also about how often the behavior occurs.

There are other ways in which frequency counts can be obtained. One is to have someone observe the client and count the number of times a particular behavior occurs on a sheet of paper, a 3-inch by 5-inch note card, or some other suitable medium. A practitioner can also have the client self-observe her or his own behavior and count the number of times the behavior occurs during a specified time period. An example of this is provided by Nugent (1993a). In this evaluation of a clinical intervention, the client recorded the frequency of panic attacks she experienced each day. This was done by simply placing a mark on a 3-inch by 5-inch note card that she carried around with her at all times. This measurement procedure actually combined a frequency count with an intensity measure. The client not only placed a mark on the note card to indicate the occurrence of a panic attack on a given day, but she also rated the severity of the panic attack on a 0 to 10 intensity scale, with a 0 indicating that the panic attack, in essence, did not occur, and a 10 indicating that the panic attack was the most intense possible.

There are some types of problems, behaviors, and/or situations that practitioners would like to count but cannot because it is overly difficult, if not impossible, to obtain an accurate count. In such cases, practitioners can use what is called relative frequency estimation (see the discussion of this method in the subsection after the following one).

Category Partition Scales   How might we scale (i.e., score) something that is manifested along a continuum, such as the intensity of pain or the intensity with which a person feels angry? Obviously, frequency counts will not work. Binary scoring methods could be used, but they will only tell us whether or not the "thing" we are trying to measure, such as pain or anger, is present. One very useful approach is what Stevens (1968) referred to as *category partition scaling*. This is more commonly known as *Likert scaling* because Rensis Likert (1932) wrote an article (considered now to be a classic) discussing the uses and properties of category partition scaling. In category partition scaling, a continuum is broken into a small number of equal intervals or categories. For example, we might think of anger as being an emotion that a person can experience anywhere along a continuum of intensity, ranging from "no intensity" (the emotion is *not* being felt) to a very, very high intensity that we might call "rage." We might then break this continuum into ten equal intervals, or categories, and number these categories or intervals from 0 at the lowest end to 10 at the highest end. This is shown in Figure 16.1. The client merely needs to circle the number of the category that reflects how intensely he or she is experiencing anger, or how intensely he or she experienced anger during some recent situation or event. This approach allows us to measure subjective phenomena such as feeling states and emotions, pain, and other things that constitute "private events" (i.e., things that only the client directly experiences) that can be difficult to measure.

To use the category partition method, we must define (or anchor) the endpoints of the continuum. For example, we could anchor the lower end of the continuum by the number 0, and define it to indicate that none of the phenomenon is being experienced. For example, in the category partition in Figure 16.1, the number 0 would indicate that the respondent was *not* angry. We might also anchor the upper end of the continuum with the number 10 (as in Figure 16.1), and define it to indicate that the respondent is experiencing the most intense anger possible. The numbers in between 0 and 10

```
|-----|-----|-----|-----|-----|-----|-----|-----|-----|-----|
0     1     2     3     4     5     6     7     8     9    10
```

0 = no anger at all

10 = most intense anger a person could possibly feel

FIGURE 16.1 A category partition of an anger intensity continuum with the endpoints anchored.

are meant to break the continuum, or to partition the continuum (and hence the name "category partition"), into equal intervals, so that higher numbers indicate more intense levels of the phenomenon than lower numbers, and vice versa.

Any subjective phenomenon that can be seen as occurring in terms of intensity or magnitude can be subjectively estimated by use of the category partition method. We first define the continuum, and then partition it into equal intervals, such as was done in Figure 16.1. We can anchor and define only the endpoints, or we can anchor and define both the endpoints as well as a number of middle points, as is shown in Figure 16.2. We need not use ten intervals, as in Figures 16.1 and 16.2, but instead may use only five intervals as in Figure 16.3.

How many intervals we partition the continuum into depends upon the degree of sensitivity to differences we are interested in finding. If only large distinctions are needed, then three intervals (and four numbers) might be used, as in Figure 16.4. On the other hand, if finer distinctions are desired, then the ten interval partition, as shown in Figures 16.1 and Figure 16.2, can be used. This takes us back to the beginning of this chapter. The answers to questions about how to construct a measurement tool depend upon the practice task for which the tool is intended and the practice context in which the social work practitioner works.

Although we focused our examples of category partitions on the measurement of anger, this type of scaling can be used to represent many different continua and to measure many different subjectively experienced phenomena. Possibilities include not only feelings, but also beliefs, attitudes, preferences, and so on. For example, a client's attitudes toward something can be thought of as being scaled on a continuum from the strongest disagreement to the strongest agreement. The midpoint of such a continuum could be labeled "neither disagree nor agree." This type of scaling could be used, for example, to develop a measurement tool to assess a client's satisfaction with the services he or she received from a practitioner or the agency.

Category partition scales can be used singly, as with the "self-anchored" (or "individualized rating") scales we discuss in the following text, or as part of a multi-item summated scale. In the latter case, we would add all of the client's ratings on the items to obtain an overall score that could help in making very fine distinctions between clients, or between scores obtained by a single client at multiple points in time.

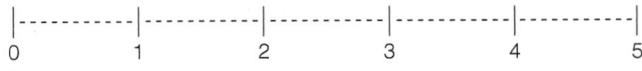

0 = no anger at all

5 = an intensity of anger halfway between 0 and 10

10 = most intense anger a person could possibly feel

FIGURE 16.2 A category partition of an anger intensity continuum with multiple points anchored.

0 = no anger at all

5 = most intense anger a person could possibly feel

FIGURE 16.3 A category partition of an anger intensity continuum with only five intervals.

```
|------------------|------------------|------------------|
0                  1                  2                  3
```

0 = no anger at all

1 = low intensity of anger

2 = moderate intensity of anger

3 = most intense anger a person could possibly feel

FIGURE 16.4 A category partition with only three intervals and four numbers.

Relative Frequency Estimation Sometimes it is very difficult, if not impossible, to obtain actual counts of the occurrence of certain problems, phenomena, or behaviors. It may even be that we are not interested in the actual count of the number of times that a particular problem, phenomenon, or behavior occurs. Instead, we may be more interested in a relative assessment of the frequency with which a problem, phenomenon, or behavior occurs. In such cases, it is useful to use *relative frequency estimation*.

Look, for example, at the sample copy of the GCS in Appendix B. Each of the 25 items represents some indicator of depression. When assessing depression, however, it is very likely that the client will not want to keep detailed counts of the occurrence of each of the feelings, behaviors, and thoughts represented by the items on the GCS. We would, however, very likely be quite interested in the frequency with which each of the feelings, behaviors, and thoughts represented by the items on the GCS occurs over a week's time, since such a count would give us a good assessment as to the magnitude of the client's problem with depression. This is where relative frequency estimation is useful. Relative frequency estimation is a blend of counting and making subjective judgments (Nurius & Hudson, 1993). It consists of estimations of counts, conceiving frequency of occurrence as a continuum, and then using the category partition method to break the continuum of frequency of occurrence into meaningful intervals. For example, the GCS shown in Appendix B defines the frequency continuum in terms of seven categories: 1 = never; 2 = very rarely; 3 = a little of the time; 4 = some of the time; 5 = a good part of the time; 6 = very frequently; and 7 = all of the time.

We refer to this technique of item scaling as relative because the categories are not defined in terms of actual frequency counts. Instead, the client is asked to render a judgment—an estimate if you will—as to how frequently the specific feeling, behavior, or thought referred to by the item occurs. In many ways, and for many applications, this may not be as good as knowing exactly how often the feeling, behavior, or thought occurs. Given the practical considerations involved in conducting assessments in practice, however, the relative frequency count is an excellent compromise. Further, if multiple items are used, and both items and rating levels are clearly and specifically operationalized, then the reliability of the summated score over all of the items, and the validity of the inferences we make from this summated score, can be excellent. This makes relative frequency estimation a very useful and powerful method of measuring clients' problems.

Now that we have described a number of concepts critical to measurement, and a number of techniques for scaling items, we can turn to descriptions of how to develop measures for use in practice. We will discuss in detail two types of measurement methods: standardized summated scales (like the short-form scales described earlier), and self-anchored (or individualized rating) scales.

THE DEVELOPMENT OF STANDARDIZED SUMMATED SCALES

The Scale Blueprint

The first step in the process of developing a new standardized measure is the creation of a scale blueprint, or what some refer to as a test blueprint. The scale blueprint is a detailed plan for the measure and includes such details as a definition of the construct to be measured, the number of items to be on the scale, the numbers of items that will be included to measure specific subdimensions of the construct, the types of items (Likert, semantic differential, etc.), the range of scores to be produced by the scale, and what high and low scores are supposed to indicate. The scale blueprint is a document that, once created, serves as the guide for much of the development activity. A well-thought-out blueprint can also serve as a basis for ensuring the content validity of the measure.

A number of years ago one of the authors was evaluating a training program for direct care staff who worked in a residential program for adolescents. One of the effects expected from participation in the program was an increase in the self-esteem of those who had completed it. Hudson's Index of Self Esteem (ISE; Hudson, 1982) was chosen because of its excellent psychometric properties. However, upon analyzing data from one group of participants in the program, it was found that participants had not shown any significant changes in self-esteem as measured by the ISE. A close inspection of the ISE data showed that there was a floor effect associated with ISE scores; that is, most of the scores clustered near 0 on the scale. There were very few scores that were above 20, and even fewer above 30.

This characteristic of the distribution of the ISE scores suggested that the scale did not have a sufficient range of scores at the lower end to capture changes in nonproblematic levels of self-esteem. This was not surprising, after a little reflection, given that the ISE was created to measure the degree or magnitude of *problems* in self-esteem (Hudson, 1982). It had not been designed to detect improvements in nonproblematic self-esteem, and this was why there was an inadequate range of scores at the low end of the ISE. This floor effect is shown in the distribution of ISE scores shown in Figure 16.5.

It was then decided to develop a new measure of self-esteem, based upon the ISE, that would be better suited to detecting change in nonproblematic self-esteem. Such a scale would produce scores that were less skewed than those shown in Figure 16.5. One way to stretch the distribution out would be to increase the range of scores at the low end; that is, to increase the range of scores in the nonproblematic self-esteem area. Thus, it was decided that the new scale would have more than 25 items (the number on the ISE). It was also decided that the overall range of scores on the instrument would be greater than 100, the range of possible scores on the ISE. Since a Likert scale format was to be used, a good way to increase the range of possible scores (in addition to more than 25 items) was to increase the number of response options on the scale. The ISE allows persons to respond to items with the numbers 1, 2, 3, 4, or 5. It was decided that the scale to be developed would allow persons to respond with the numbers 1, 2, 3, 4, 5, 6, or 7. This increased range of response options could also lead to an increase in the reliability of scores produced by the new measure (Crocker & Algina, 1986; Nunnally, 1978).

It was also decided that high scores on the new scale should indicate "positive" or nonproblematic levels of self-esteem, and low scores should indicate "negative" or problematic levels. This representation of self-esteem was the inverse of the ISE. On the ISE, high scores are indicative of larger problems with self-esteem (i.e., more negative self-esteem), and low scores are indicative of less severe problems with self-esteem (Hudson, 1982). It was also decided that scores from the new scale should range from negative values (to indicate more negative self-esteem) to positive values (to indicate more positive self-esteem).

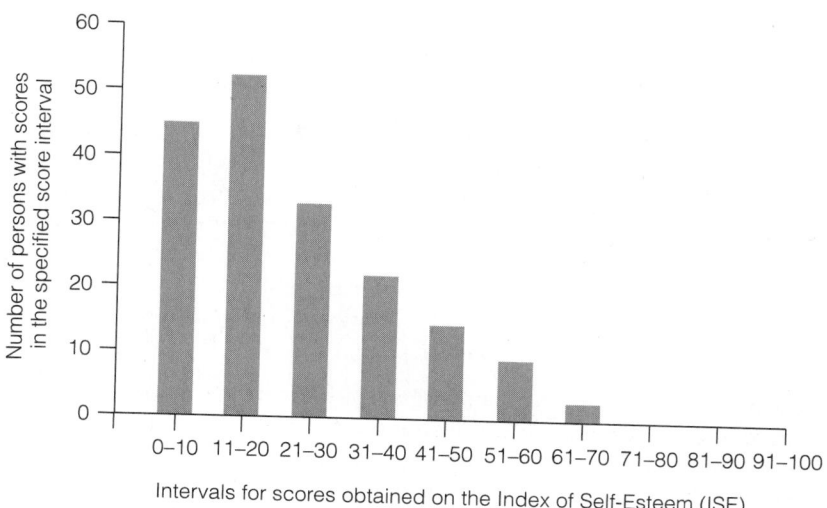

FIGURE 16.5 Frequency distribution of scores on the ISE showing a floor effect.

At this point, the scale blueprint contained the following information:

- Purpose of scale: to produce numerical scores that differentiate between persons with different levels of problematic self-esteem and between persons with different levels of nonproblematic (or positive) self-esteem

- Scale type: Likert

- Number of items: more than 25

- Range of scores: more than 100, going from negative values to positive values

- Intended meaning of scores: high indicates functional, nonproblematic or positive self-esteem; low indicates problematic or negative self-esteem

The blueprint at this point implied that some items would need to be scored in such a manner as to produce positive numbers, while others would need to be scored in such a manner as to produce negative numbers. This would be necessary to lead to a total score on the scale that could range from negative to positive values. For reasons of symmetry, it was decided that there should be equal numbers of positively and negatively scored items. Thus, the part of the blueprint that described the number of items to be on the scale was amended to read:

- Items: More than 25, with equal numbers of positively and negatively scored items. Items with high positive scores should reflect more positive self-esteem, while low scores on these items should reflect less positive (and more negative) self-esteem. Items with high negative values should reflect more negative, more problematic self-esteem, while lower negative scores should indicate less problematic or better self-esteem.

It was now necessary to define self-esteem. Before any items could be developed, a nominal (word) definition of self-esteem had to be written. This is always a necessary step in the development of a new measure (Crocker & Algina, 1986; Nunnally, 1978). Self-esteem has been previously defined as the evaluative component of self-concept (Hudson, 1982). It refers to how persons judge various aspects of their concept of their personhood. Thus, the following definition of self-esteem refers to the results of an evaluation one does of the various aspects of one's self-concept:

> Self-esteem is the evaluative component of self-concept. It consists of the sum total of assessments and evaluations that a person does across numerous occasions of the various components and aspects of her or his self-concept. The assessments and evaluations are of a "good-bad," "positive-negative" character, are conducted on numerous occasions across time, and can vary from occasion to occasion in terms of the "negativeness-positiveness" assigned by the person to the component of self-concept being evaluated. Since the person's self-esteem is the sum total of assessments across numerous occasions, the "level" of a person's self-esteem can be represented by the typical frequency with which they assign a particular "negative-positive" value to the self-concept component. For example, one aspect of self-concept is the person's view of her or his physical attractiveness. If the person endorsed an item that reads, "I feel good about how I look" with a response option that says, "most of the time," then the person has more positive self-esteem relative to that self-concept component than if the person responded with the option, "rarely."

The self-evaluation that leads to self-esteem results in positive or negative, good or bad assessments of each part of the self-concept. The total, or average, evaluation across all evaluations of all components of the self-concept is the "level" of a person's self-esteem.

This definition implied that more problematic self-esteem would be indicated by negative assessments about aspects of a person's understanding of herself or himself, while better self-esteem would be indicated by more positive evaluations. This definition further implied that there are no major subdimensions that make up self-esteem and that self-esteem is the sum total of evaluations made of all aspects of one's self-concept, with no unique subgroupings of evaluations. This is in contrast to a construct such as "anxiety." There is good reason to believe that anxiety is manifested subjectively, behaviorally, and physiologically (Barlow, 1988). Thus, any definition of anxiety would need to explicitly recognize this breakdown, and the scale blueprint for a measure of anxiety would need to include a delineation of the numbers of items to be included on the scale to cover each response component. Given the definition of self-esteem, however, it was decided that it was not necessary to delineate subgroups of items that should appear on the instrument in order to cover all the necessary aspects of self-esteem.

A final issue to be determined concerned the number of items to be on the new measure. Although more than 25 were required, if too many items were on the scale, it could make the measure unwieldy in practice. A very long scale would take a long time to complete and be more of a chore for persons to go through. Thus it was decided that 40 items would be an initial target. If 40 items produced scores that did a good job of differentiating between persons with different levels of nonproblematic self-esteem, while retaining the ability that ISE scores had for differentiating between persons with problematic levels of self-esteem, then the number would be adequate. The extent to which a 40-item scale would do this could only be determined by later validation research. These considerations led to the final scale blueprint shown in Table 16.1.

The foregoing illustrates the first step in the development of a new measurement scale. The scale blueprint serves to structure the development process and should include at least the following: the purpose for which the scores from the scale will be used; the type of scale; the construct to be measured and a nominal definition of that construct; the number of items; the numbers of different types of items; the number of response options for each item; the range of scores produced by the scale; and how the scores are meant to be interpreted. A discussion of scale blueprints (under the term *test content specifications*) can be found in Millman and Greene (1989) and Popham (1984).

Item Development

Once the scale blueprint has been completed, it is time to write items. The numbers and types of items to be written will be dictated by the scale blueprint. There are a number of guidelines for writing good items, and these will be discussed here. In general, items *must* be indicators of the construct to be measured and, therefore, must come from a hypothetical universe of indicators defined by the nominal definition in the scale blueprint. This is essential for the scale to have content validity. Thus, the scale blueprint should be used as a guide for all items that are created, always referring to the nominal definition of the construct.

There are several rules to follow when writing items. Following these rules will help to reduce the amount of extraneous variance unrelated to the construct to be measured that is introduced into score variance. This extraneous variance in scores will reduce the reliability and validity of scores, so good item writing is important.

Rule 1. Stems should be short. Shorter items are easier to understand than long items. For example, the self-esteem item "I feel good about how I do the most menial, routine, and common kinds of things that I have to do each and every day on my job" is long and potentially confusing. In contrast, the item "I feel I do my job well" is shorter and less likely to be confusing to those who must respond to it.

Rule 2. The words in the items should be readable and understandable by the *lowest* functioning reader in the population with which the scale is used.

Table 16.1 Test Blueprint for Self-Esteem Rotary Scale (SERS)

Purpose of Scale: to produce numerical scores that differentiate between persons with different levels of problematic (negative) or with different levels of nonproblematic (positive) self-esteem.

Definition of Self-Esteem: Self-esteem is the evaluative component of self-concept. It consists of the sum total of assessments and evaluations that a person does across numerous occasions of the various components and aspects of her or his self-concept. The assessments and evaluations are of a "good-bad," "positive-negative" character, are conducted on numerous occasions across time, and can vary from occasion to occasion in terms of the "negativeness-positiveness" assigned by the person to the component of self-concept being evaluated. Since the person's self-esteem is the sum total of assessments across numerous occasions, the "level" of a person's self-esteem can be represented by the typical frequency with which they assign a particular "negative-positive" value to the self-concept component. For example, one aspect of self-concept is the person's view of her or his physical attractiveness. If the person endorsed an item that reads, "I feel good about how I look" with a response option that says, "most of the time," then the person has more positive self-esteem relative to that self-concept component than if the person responded with the option, "rarely."

Type of Scale: Likert (category partition), with relative frequency estimation.

Number of Items: 40, with 20 positively scored and 20 negatively scored items. Positive items should be worded such that endorsement with a large magnitude positive number indicates the respondent evaluates him- or herself positively with regard to the aspect of self-concept represented by the item. Endorsement of the item with a low magnitude number indicates the respondent evaluates him- or herself less positively. Negative items should be worded such that endorsement with a negative number that is large in absolute value indicates the person evaluates him- or herself negatively with regard to the aspect of self-concept represented by the items. A negative number of smaller absolute value would indicate the respondent evaluates him- or herself more positively.

Number of Response Options: Seven, ranging from 1 to 7.

Range of Scores: –120 to +120. This range of scores comes from the number of items and the possible range of scores for each item. If a person responds to each of the 20 positively worded items with a 1, and to each of the negatively worded items with a 7 (which is then scored by changing the response to a –7), then the total score would be $(20 \times 1) + (20 \times -7) = 20 + (-140) = -120$. If a person responds to each of the 20 positively worded items with a 7, and to each of the negatively worded items with a 1 (which is then scored by changing the response to a –1), then the total score would be $(20 \times 7) + (20 \times -1) = 140 + (-20) = 140 - 20 = 120$.

Intended Meaning of Scores: High scores indicate the respondent evaluates him- or herself generally positively and therefore has high positive (nonproblematic) self-esteem. Low scores indicate the respondent evaluates him- or herself generally negatively or poorly and therefore has low (problematic) self-esteem.

Complex words should be avoided. For example, the item "I feel that others would say that I have winsome looks" contains a word—*winsome*—that some in the target population may not understand. A better item would be, "I feel that others would say that I have good looks."

Rule 3. The items should be grammatically simple. Items that are grammatically complex and therefore difficult to understand should be avoided. For example, the item "I feel, regardless of how tired I am, or even who I am with, regardless of whether it is a person in authority or just a friend, that I can be assertive with others" is grammatically complex. A better item would be, "I feel I can be assertive with others."

Rule 4. The use of negatives, such as *not* and *no*, in items should be avoided. If a negative must be used, then it should be capitalized and in bold print so it is obvious to the respondent. It is easy for a respondent to overlook a negative in an item. An example of an item with a negative is, "I do not like myself." This item, if it must be used, is better written, "I do **NOT** like myself." Notice how the word *not* is highlighted to make it obvious to the person reading the item.

Rule 5. The use of the double negative must *absolutely* be avoided. Items such as "I never do not feel sad" must be avoided at all costs.

Rule 6. Language that people may find offensive or insulting should not be used in items. For example (and please excuse our graphic example), the item "I feel shitty about myself" may offend some persons responding to the item; this should be avoided.

Rule 7. The words that are used should be understandable to all ethnic groups who might be members of the population with which the scale will be used. If this rule is not followed, the scale developer may introduce cultural bias into the instrument.

Rule 8. Double-barreled items should be avoided. Double-barreled items are those that contain two (or more) indicators of the construct to be measured that are connected by the words *or* or *and*. For example, the item "I feel sad or lonely" is a double-barreled item. There are two indicators (*sad* and *lonely*) of the construct to be measured that are connected by the word *or*. The problem with this item is that the respondent can score the item based on being *sad*, being *lonely*, or being *both*; there is no way to determine what the response to this item means. Double-barreled items should be broken down into two separate items, one for each indicator in the original item. For example, the double-barreled item containing both *sad* and *lonely* could be broken into the following two items: "I feel sad," and "I feel lonely."

Rule 9. Words and phrases contained in the verbal descriptors that define the meaning of numerical response options should not be duplicated in any of the items. For example, suppose the numerical response "3" is defined at the top of a Likert scale as follows:

3—some of the time

Then the phrase *some of the time* should *not* appear in any items. In this case, an item such as "I feel sad some of the time" would be a poor item. Similarly, suppose that the response option "4" is defined to mean:

4—rarely

Then the word *rarely* should *not* appear in an item, such as in the item "I rarely feel good about myself." Violating this rule leads to confusing items and increased error variance in scores.

Rule 10. The use of absolutes, such as *always* or *never*, should be avoided in items that are written. For example, the item "I never feel sad" violates this rule. It is probably true that people never (excuse our use of this word, but it is appropriate here) feel exclusively one way, and using an item with absolutes will probably lead to low item variance; therefore, the item will not add to the reliability and validity of the scores produced by the scale.

Rule 11. The items must match the response categories. For example, suppose that we have a 7-point response scale, which ranges from 1 = rarely to 7 = most of the time. An item such as "I cry a lot of the time" does not match well with the verbal anchors attached to the numerical response options. An item such as "I cry a lot" would fit better with verbal anchors ranging from *NOT at all like me* to *very much like me*.

Initial Review of Items

After the items have been written and a first draft of the instrument constructed, the next step is to have a small number of persons from the population the instrument is to be used with read and respond to the measure. These respondents should be given the scale in much the same way it is intended to be used in actual practice. After these persons have completed the scale, the developer should review the scale with the respondents. Each part of the measure, from directions to items, should be inspected to ensure that the scale is readable and understandable. The scale developer needs to determine if the directions are clear and unambiguous, if the items are understandable and free of offensive or culturally biased language, if there is any aspect of the scale that is confusing, and if the scale looks "on the face of it" like it measures what it is intended to measure.

The scale developer then takes the feedback from these persons and revises the scale to eliminate confusing words, directions, items, and so on. This revision should make the scale more user-friendly and reduce the error variance introduced into scores by poor directions, scale formatting, and poorly written items.

Content Validity

The new scale is now ready to be reviewed by content experts to judge its content validity. Content experts are persons who, by virtue of their training and experience, can be considered experts in terms of their knowledge about the construct the scores from the scale are supposed to measure. For example, at this point in the development of the SERS, the scale was reviewed by several faculty members in a social work graduate program. These faculty had practice expertise as well as research experience.

These content experts review the scale, referencing it against the scale blueprint, and make content judgment at two levels by answering the following two questions:

1. *Does each item come from the universe of indicators implied by the construct definition?*
2. *Does the set of items that comprises the scale adequately represent the universe of indicators implied by the construct definition?*

The scale developer takes the feedback given by the content experts relative to these two questions and makes the necessary revisions.

Once the scale has passed the review of content experts, the developer has evidence for the new measure. Content validity is a necessary but not a sufficient form of evidence to support the validity of scores produced from the scale.

Pilot Test and Item Analysis

The next step is to conduct a small pilot study in which the scale is administered to a sample of persons from the population with which the instrument is intended to be used. The purpose of this pilot study is to obtain a sample of responses on the scale in order to conduct an *item analysis*. The number of responses needed will be larger than that used in the review of the instrument discussed earlier. While there is no clear rule that determines the number of responses needed for the item analysis, a "rule of thumb" suggested by Nunnally (1978) is about five responses for each item on the scale. Thus, for example, with the SERS, the scale developer would need at least 5 times 40, or 200, persons to respond to the items on the scale in order to conduct an item analysis. Ideally, there would be even more persons so that the results of the item analysis could be trusted, and the sample used would include persons with a wide range of levels of the construct the scale is being constructed to measure.

For example, with the SERS, the scale developer would want to have in the sample of 200 or more persons a number with very low (or highly negative) self-esteem, a number with moderate (or equally negative and positive) self-esteem, and a number with high (or highly positive) self-esteem. This inclusion of a wide range of levels of self-esteem would give the scale developer an optimal opportunity to assess the extent to which each item works the way it should be working. The topic of item analysis is somewhat complex and will not be discussed in detail here. Several books contain good coverage of item analysis, including Crocker and Algina (1986), Nunnally (1978), and Nunnally and Bernstein (1994).

Once the scale developer has data from an item analysis, the results are used to make further revisions, as necessary, to the scale. Items that are not working as they should are either revised or replaced. Items that are working well are left alone. Once this revision is completed, any new or revised items should be subjected to review by a small number of persons from the target population as well as to a content validity review by content experts. When the revised scale has passed these inspections, the scale developer is ready to conduct reliability and validity studies.

Reliability and Validity Studies

The scale developer is now at the point where he or she can conduct reliability and validity studies. This process will entail large numbers of respondents and may require rather complex statistical analysis procedures. We have described reliability and validity in an earlier chapter, and the methods used in reliability and validity studies have been discussed in detail by Crocker and Algina (1986), Nunnally (1978), Nunnally and Bernstein (1996), and, perhaps most comprehensively, by Messick (1989). We will not duplicate these descriptions here. It should be noted, however, that the scale developer cannot dismiss the importance of these studies in the development of the new measure. Without the evidence to support the inferences that are to be made from the scores produced by the scale, the new measure is useless at best. At worst, the interpretations and inferences made from the scale scores may lead the user of the scale to make erroneous conclusions about her or his clients. Decisions based on these erroneous conclusions may cause harm to the clients.

By now it should be apparent to the reader that the development of a new measure should not be taken lightly. It requires a lot of time and resources. For these reasons, it is best that already existing measures be used, assuming that the requisite evidence for reliability and validity exist.

CLIENT-SPECIFIC MEASURES:
SELF-ANCHORED SCALES

In contrast to standardized measures, client-specific measures are developed for use with a specific client. The GCS, for example, is a standardized scale for measuring the magnitude of a client's problem with depression. The GCS is used "as is" with clients. In contrast, a practitioner might decide to develop a self-anchored scale (or individualized rating scale [Bloom et al., 1999], target complaint scale [Mintz & Kiesler, 1982], or individual problem rating scale [Gillespie & Seaberg, 1977]) in order to assess a client's problem with depression. Self-anchored scales get their name from the anchoring of points on the scale (usually one or both endpoints) with definitions that are unique and specific to the client. Thus, self-anchored scales are tailor-fitted to the client. Self-anchored scales are easy to develop and can be used easily and quickly in practice.

Probably the easiest way to develop a self-anchored scale is to ask the client to imagine that the practitioner has a special thermometer that is designed to measure her or his problem, say problem X. The special thermometer has readings that can range from 0 to 10 (or, if you wish, 0 to 100), with lower readings indicating lower magnitudes of problem X, and higher readings indicating greater magnitudes of problem X. Furthermore, a reading of 0 indicates the lowest magnitude possible for problem X, while a reading of 10 indicates the greatest magnitude possible for problem X. A reading of 5 indicates the point halfway between 0 and 10. The practitioner then asks the client to remember a time in her or his life when problem X was either nonexistent, or if problem X has been lifelong, then a time when problem X was the lowest ever. Once the client identifies such a time, the practitioner has her or him describe the time period and how she or he was thinking and feeling. This specific experience of the client then becomes the anchor point for a 0 on the self-anchored scale.

Once an anchor point for 0 has been obtained, the practitioner does the same thing for the highest point on the scale, which is usually 10. Reminding the client that a 10 indicates the greatest magnitude problem X possible, the practitioner asks the client if there has ever been a time when problem X was that severe. If so, the client is asked to describe that time period, and how he or she felt and thought, and then the practitioner uses that unique experience of the client's as the anchor point for a 10 on the self-anchored scale. If the client cannot remember a time at which problem X was the most intense it could possibly be, the practitioner asks her or him to remember the time when problem X was the most intense, and then have her or him rate the magnitude of problem X at that point in time in terms of the numbers between 0 and 10. Suppose that the client says that problem X at its most intense level so far has been an 8. The practitioner has the client describe that time period when problem X was at a magnitude of 8 and then defines an 8 on the self-anchored scale using this experience of the client. If desired, one or two other points on the scale can be similarly defined by using specific experiences the client reports.

The practitioner has now created a self-anchored scale for measuring the magnitude of problem X as experienced by the client. Each time the practitioner meets with the client, he or she need only ask the client to rate the magnitude of problem X at this point in time using the special thermometer the practitioner and client have developed. For example, the practitioner might say, "Remember a while back we developed a special thermometer for measuring problem X. On this thermometer, a 0 indicates the lowest possible level of problem X, and that time when you _____ is an example of a level of 0 on the thermometer. A 10 on the thermometer is the most intense problem X could possibly be, and you defined an 8 to be how problem X was at the time when you _____. How does the thermometer read today in terms of the magnitude of problem X?" The client can choose any number between 0 and 10, including fractions or decimals, such as 7 1/2 or 5.75. The number the client gives then serves as a measure of the magnitude of problem X at that point in time. The practitioner can also have the client rate her or his problem in between her or his meetings with the practitioner using the self-anchored scale. As Bloom et al. (1999) noted, the practitioner can even have the client rate her or his problem using the self-anchored scale several times a day.

Self-anchored scales can be developed in a short period of time and can be built to measure any problem a client desires to work on. This is one of the great strengths of self-anchored scales. They can be used to measure anything. They are especially useful for measuring a client's subjective sense of the problem with which he or she is dealing. The SUDS scale (Subjective Units of Discomfort Scale) described earlier is an example of a "near" self-anchored scale. The only difference between the SUDS scale and a self-anchored scale is that the SUDS scale does not contain any client-specific anchor points. Self-anchored scales can also be created for use by someone other than a client. For example, one might develop a self-anchored scale that is to be used by a woman to rate her perception of her child's confidence when interacting with other children. In such a case, the person who will be using the scale to rate someone else would supply the definitions of anchor points on the scale.

One problem with self-anchored scales is the paucity of research on the psychometric properties of the scores they produce. There have been precious few studies on the reliability and validity of scores from self-anchored scales. There is evidence reported on the test-retest reliability of scores from self-anchored scales (Battle et al., 1966; Morrison, Libow, Smith, & Becker, 1978), inter-rater agreement (Reid, 1978), and on various types of validity evidence (Battle et al., 1966; Bond, Bloch, & Yalom, 1979; Dasberg, van der Kleijn, Guelen, & van Praag, 1974; Farkas, Sine, & Evans, 1979; Liberman & Smith, 1972; Mintz, Luborsky, & Christoph, 1979; Nugent, 1992, 1993b; Rosen & Zytowski, 1977; Thyer, Papsdorf, Davis, & Vallecorsa, 1984; Wincze, Hoon, & Hoon, 1977). Some of this evidence is promising. For example, Nugent (1992) obtained, in a clinical setting, a correlation of .82 between scores on self-anchored scales for depression and scores on the GCS. Nugent (1993b) also obtained, in a more general sample, a correlation of .74 between scores on self-anchored scales for self-esteem and scores on the Self-Esteem Rating Scale (Nugent & Thomas, 1993). However, Nugent (1993b) noted that the self-anchored scale scores for self-esteem potentially had a low reliability (.56), and found evidence for differential validity in the self-anchored scale scores (Nugent, 1993c). These findings suggest caution in the use of self-anchored scales. Self-anchored scales may produce reliable and valid scores for some client problems, such as depression, while for other client problems the reliability and validity may not be as good, for example, with self-esteem problems. The interpretation of self-anchored scale scores may also, in some cases, be dependent upon the level of other problems the client is experiencing (see Nugent, 1993c). We hope that more research will be done in the future that will give practitioners more guidance in how to use and interpret the scores from self-anchored scales used to measure a variety of client problems.

In spite of these cautions, it seems at this time that self-anchored scales are a useful measurement tool that can easily and quickly be used in practice to measure a wide range of client problems. Self-anchored scales often have high face validity because the client was involved in the creation of the scale. These scales can also get "at" problems that no other measure can (Bloom et al., 1999). For these reasons, self-anchored scales represent a flexible, client-specific, and easy-to-implement measurement strategy for use in practitioners' work with clients.

SUMMARY

There are other client-specific measures that can be developed, including client logs and behavioral counts and observations (Bloom et al., 1999) and goal attainment scales (Nurius & Hudson, 1993). These methods, together with the short-form scales, the multidimensional scales in the CASS system, self-anchored scales, and standardized scales that practitioners might develop for their own work, offer a wide range of methods for measuring clients' problems and the targets for change that practitioners and clients decide upon. This variety of measurement approaches should meet most (if not all) practice needs.

PART III

The CASS Software

17

✦✦✦✦✦

Acquiring and Installing
the CASS Software
on a PC or LAN

I n Chapter 1 you learned that we would provide detailed information about
the *Computer Assisted Social Services*, or CASS, software. This is the first of
several chapters that provide information about access to the CASS software
and how you can get the most out of it. This chapter is very small and aims
only at explaining what the software is designed to do, how you can acquire
the software, and how to install it on a personal computer or local area network (LAN).

THE ROLE OF CASS IN PRACTICE

As previous chapters have shown, most of the tasks that are involved in using
the empirical practice model are not difficult. Perhaps some or all of them
were new to the reader at the beginning, but once learned, none are very difficult. It is a simple matter to use a short-form standardized measurement scale
to evaluate a client's problem or to use a multidimensional assessment scale to
obtain a more comprehensive evaluation of the client's problems in numerous
areas of personal and social functioning. Previous chapters and exercises have
explained how to use standardized assessment scales—how to administer them,
how to score them, and how to interpret the results.

It is also not difficult to prepare a simple time-series graph and to plot the
client's scores so that the client's progress can be monitored over time. When

using multidimensional assessment scales, it is not difficult to manually produce what we have described as a multidimensional profile graph so that one can obtain a visual aid in the interpretation of both the client's problems and strengths in many areas of personal and social functioning. Although the intellectual underpinnings of our empirical practice model are rich, varied, and often quite detailed, the actual *doing* of empirical practice is quite simple and basically involves the use of simple measurement tools and rather simple graphs. The reader now knows how to do all of these tasks.

Although the core tasks for using the empirical practice model are quite simple when a practitioner is working with *one* client, the matter changes dramatically when a practitioner wishes to use the model on a regular or routine basis with 30 (or perhaps many more) clients per week. The scope of a practitioner's practice workload changes dramatically if he or she is seeing, for example, 30 clients each week and wants each of them to complete even one assessment scale so that their progress can be monitored over time. In this example, the practitioner must locate 30 different assessment scales ("Now where did I put my supply of scales?"), and these scales may take upwards of five hours per week to administer if they are used with each client (10 minutes each for 30 clients). Moreover, if each of those 30 scales was scored by hand using a pocket calculator, it would likely take another 10 minutes for each of them (another five hours per week for scoring), and when doing scoring by hand, the practitioner likely would make some mistakes. Once all the scores were obtained, the practitioner would need to pull each client's case record, locate the time-series graph within it, and then post the score on the graph in order to update the effort to monitor the client's progress over time. Then the chart must be returned to the case record, and the case record must be returned to the filing cabinet. This, at a minimum, would take at least another five hours of the workweek, so use of the simplest of our empirical practice methods has added something like 15 to 20 hours of paperwork to the practitioner's already busy, perhaps overloaded, professional life.

If these simple tasks must be manually carried out with a caseload of 30 or more clients a week, it simply is not going to happen—or the practitioner will become seriously overburdened if such an empirical practice model is imposed upon him or her by those to whom he or she must be accountable. *Something has to give!* The empirical practice model presented in this book simply cannot be considered to be a deliverable technology (Nurius & Hudson, 1987, 1993) if it must be implemented using traditional paper-and-pencil methods.

The CASS software and a personal computer can help enormously. Suppose, for example, that a practitioner sees 30 clients a week and asks each of them to complete one short-form assessment scale each time the client comes in. It may take a half hour to train clients to complete the assessment scale in the intake office by having them come in 15 minutes early for each appointment so that they can pick up the scale from the receptionist and complete it in the waiting room. That alone will save five hours a week because the practitioner will not have to personally administer the scales. However, the scales must still be scored, and the practitioner must pull each client record, locate the time-series graph, update the graph, and then return the record to storage. By using a computer and the CASS software, however, it will take about five minutes to locate the client's computer record and enter the scale item responses into the CASS software. Then the computer will score the scale, store the results in the client's record, automatically update the time-series graph, and automatically return the client's record to the electronic filing cabinet on the hard drive or on the network. In short, the practitioner merely enters the client's responses to the scale. Now another 10 to 15 hours per week have been saved over what would be required by traditional paper-and-pencil methods.

But has the practitioner gotten away with using no additional time? Certainly not. If it takes five minutes to enter the scale responses for a single client, a hypothetical caseload of 30 clients per week will require an investment of about two and a half hours per week to score and process the short-form assessment scales that are used with the clients. Moreover, it is so simple to do that the practitioner can enter the responses in the client's presence, obtain the numerical score, and graph the results immediately so that the information can be used during the session! In summary, the core ingredients of our empirical practice model can be implemented with virtually every client; the practitioner and the client can obtain the informational benefits described in previous chapters; and the practitioner will have a time- and cost-effective way to improve practice and increase the likelihood of a more positive outcome for clients. A computer and the CASS software transform our empirical practice model into a truly deliverable technology (Nurius & Hudson, 1987, 1993).

Naturally, there is much more to practice than what we have described here, and the CASS software can help greatly with such things as case note recording, task definition and monitoring, client assessment, diagnosis, and treatment or service delivery planning in addition to problem monitoring, practice evaluation, and program-level evaluation. In subsequent chapters, we shall describe all of these and other functions and tasks. For now, we only want to provide the reader with a brief introduction to CASS before turning to its acquisition and installation.

The CASS system consists of several different computer programs that are often referred to collectively as CASS. The first of these programs is CASS itself—the *Computer Assisted Social Services* (CASS) program—that is designed for the exclusive use of the human services practitioner, supervisor, administrator, and program evaluator. Bundled with CASS is the *Computer Assisted Assessment Package* (CAAP) program that is designed for use by clients. The CAAP program will actually administer assessment scales to clients, and in doing so, it automatically scores the scales, updates the client's record, and updates the appropriate time-series or multidimensional profile graphs that result from use of the selected assessment scales. The CAAP program enables clients to review their assessment scale scores and produce their own graphs so that they can monitor and evaluate their own progress in treatment. Finally, the CASS system includes the *CASS Utility* software, or CASSUTIL program, that enables one to export data for use in other software packages.

ACQUIRING A COPY OF CASS

There are several ways to obtain a copy of the CASS software; the reader may use the method that best suits him or her. The first way to obtain the CASS software is to open the back jacket to this book and remove the three diskettes. If the diskettes are in the back of the book, the reader can skip ahead to the next section and install the software on a computer. If the three CASS diskettes are not in the book (it might be a secondhand purchase or a gift from someone who lost the diskettes), the software can be obtained using one of the following methods.

The second way to obtain the CASS software is to download a copy from the World Wide Web through an Internet account and a Web browser such as Netscape. To download a copy from the Web, the following URL is entered into the Web browser—**http://www.syspac.com/~walmyr/**—then the Enter key is pressed. You can also download CASS from the publisher at the URL address given on page xviii in the preface. We recommend this method because there are no costs involved with purchasing the software. It is provided by the publisher of CASS as free customer support software for those who use the CASS assessment scales.

Those who do not have an Internet account can obtain a copy of the CASS software by writing to the WALMYR Publishing Company at PO Box 12217, Tallahassee, FL 32317. The publisher requires that a check in the amount of $14 be enclosed to cover the cost of materials and shipping and handling, even though the software itself is free.

Another alternative is to find a friend or colleague who has a copy of the CASS software and ask her or him to make a duplicate copy of the three original CASS diskettes; then that copy can be used to install the software on a computer. Even though the CASS software is copyrighted and owned by the WALMYR Publishing Company, the company grants permission to duplicate and distribute the software provided that users make exact copies of the diskettes as they are produced and distributed by the publisher.

Finally, instructors who wish to order multiple copies of the software for distribution to students may obtain such copies by writing to the publisher at the address shown earlier. Community-based consultants also may obtain multiple copies from the publisher for distribution to trainees.

HARDWARE AND SOFTWARE
REQUIREMENTS FOR CASS

The free customer support version of CASS is designed for use with Microsoft Windows 3.11 or Windows 95 (Win95). It is very compact and very fast, so it will not take up a great deal of space on a hard drive. However, the size of the entire system will grow in proportion to the number of client records that is entered into the database and the amount of information included within each client record.

Requirements, in addition to Microsoft Windows 3.11 or Win95, are a VGA color board and monitor, a mouse or pointing device such as a track ball, and a printer. To get the most from the graphs that are produced by CASS and CAAP, we recommend the use of a color printer. We also recommend a minimum of 16 megabytes of memory, although CASS and its companion programs will function with 8 megabytes of memory. There are no other hardware requirements for use of the CASS system.

INSTALLING CASS ON
A PERSONAL COMPUTER

There are basically two methods for installing CASS on a free-standing personal computer. One is to install it by using the three diskettes obtained from this book, from the publisher, or from a colleague; the other is to download a copy from the World Wide Web. Both methods are very simple, but we shall describe them separately.

Installing CASS From Diskettes

If you are installing the CASS system by using diskettes, first make sure that you have three of them. The first one is the diskette that bears the label *Computer Assisted Social Services*, and we refer to it as the CASS disk. The second diskette bears the label *Borland Database Engine*, and we refer to it as the BDE disk. The third diskette bears the label *Computer Assisted Assessment Package & MAG Design Kit*, and we refer to it as the CAAP disk. Once you have those three diskettes, you are ready to install the software by following these steps.

Step 1. Insert the CASS disk in Drive A (or Drive B) of your computer, and close the drive door.

Step 2. From within Windows 3.11, press Alt-F-R (Alternate, Files, Run), then type the command A:\SETUP (or B:\SETUP), and press the Enter key. From within Win95, click the Start button, then the Run button, then type A:\SETUP (or B:\SETUP), and press the Enter key. Be sure to select all the defaults that are recommended to you by the installation program (more about this later).

Step 3. When the CASS disk has been installed, the program will ask you to insert the BDE disk in Drive A (or Drive B). Do that, and then press the Enter key. Once the BDE disk has been installed, you are ready to begin using the CASS program. The installation program will create a new program group named the *WALMYR Suite* and store the program icons within that group.

Step 4. Insert the CAAP disk in Drive A (or Drive B) of your computer, and close the drive door.

Step 5. From within Windows 3.11, press Alt-F-R (Alternate, Files, Run), then type the command A:\SETUP (or B:\SETUP), and press the Enter key.

From within Win95, click the Start button, then the Run button, then type A:\SETUP (or B:\SETUP), and press the Enter key. Be sure to select all the defaults that are recommended to you by the installation program (more about this later). Once the CAAP disk has been installed, you are ready to begin using the CAAP program.

Installing CASS From The Web

If you wish to download CASS from the World Wide Web, use your Web browser to go to the **http://www.syspac.com/~walmyr/** URL and click the option that reads, "Download CASS." When you have reached the CASS download page, carry out the following steps. Note: Make sure you have an empty directory such as C:\TEMP before you begin.

Step 1. Select the option to download the CASS16.EXE file and store it in your empty C:\TEMP directory.

Step 2. From within Windows 3.11, press Alt-F-R (Alternate, Files, Run); from Win95, click the Start button and then click the Run button. Then type the command C:\TEMP\CASS16, and press the Enter key or click the OK button to decompress the software.

Step 3. From within Windows 3.11, press Alt-F-R (Alternate, Files, Run); from Win95, click the Start button and then click the Run button. Then type the command C:\TEMP\SETUP, and press the Enter key or click the OK button. Respond to the instructions that appear on the screen, and the software will be installed on your computer. The installation program will create a new program group named the *WALMYR Suite* and store the program icons within that group.

Step 4. Delete all files in the C:\TEMP directory.

Step 5. Select the option to download the CAAPWIN.EXE file and store it in your empty C:\TEMP directory.

Step 6. From within Windows 3.11, press Alt-F-R (Alternate, Files, Run); from Win95, click the Start button and then click the Run button. Then type the command C:\TEMP\CAAPWIN, and press the Enter key or click the OK button to decompress the software.

Step 7. From within Windows 3.11, press Alt-F-R (Alternate, Files, Run); from Win95, click the Start button and then click the Run button. Then type the command C:\TEMP\SETUP, and press the Enter key or click the OK button. Respond to the instructions that appear on the screen, and the software will be installed on your computer. The installation program will store the program icons within the *WALMYR Suite* program group.

WHERE THINGS ARE STORED

Once you install the CASS software, it is important for you to know where it will be stored on your computer. The CASS installation procedure will create a new directory on your hard drive that will be named \CASSWIN. All of the

CASS software will be placed inside the \CASSWIN directory and any necessary subdirectories. When you install the CAAP program, it will be installed in the \CAAPWIN directory along with any needed subdirectories.

The CASS software cannot function without the Borland Database Engine (BDE) software, and the installation procedure installs and configures the BDE for you. However, you should know that the software creates the \IDAPI directory and stores the BDE software in that directory. You can execute the BDECFG.EXE program should you ever need to reconfigure the BDE. It is not likely you will ever need to do that.

CHANGING THE DEFAULT INSTALLATION PARAMETERS

When you install CASS and CAAP on your computer, the installation program will permit you to store the software anywhere on your hard drive that you like. We recommend that you never change the default directories, which are C:\CASSWIN, C:\CAAPWIN, and C:\IDAPI, unless you have a truly urgent reason for doing so. If you decide to ignore this advice, you will then have to make several other changes in order to make the software function properly; you will have to make those changes manually; and you will have to consult the online Help in order to learn how to do that. Worse yet, every time the software is upgraded or enhanced, you will have to account for your changes in order to install the upgrades. Again, do not change any of the installation defaults unless you are prepared to deal with a great deal of unnecessary work. The installation procedures are designed to make your computing life simple and easy, and we urge that you take advantage of that.

LOADING THE SHARE.EXE PROGRAM

If you are using Win95, you do not need to use the DOS SHARE.EXE program. However, if you are using Windows 3.11, it is very important that the DOS SHARE.EXE program be loaded in order for the CASS software to function properly. The SHARE program is normally loaded from within your AUTOEXEC.BAT file. If you do not know whether this has been done, you should attend to this matter before you attempt to use the CASS software.

If you need to modify your AUTOEXEC.BAT file to cause loading of the SHARE program, we recommend you place the load command immediately after the last reference to your DOS PATH command. If your DOS system files are located in the C:\DOS directory, the line should read as:

```
C:\DOS\SHARE.EXE /F:4096 /L:40
```

If your DOS system files are located in the C:\BIN directory, the line should read as:

C:\BIN\SHARE.EXE /F:4096 /L:40

Once you have changed your AUTOEXEC.BAT file, be sure to reboot your computer so that the change will take effect. We recommend that you install the CASS software only after you are certain that the SHARE program has been loaded. Please consult your DOS manual for further information about installation and use of the SHARE.EXE program. If you are not familiar with DOS and the proper use and maintenance of the AUTOEXEC.BAT file, we urge that you obtain expert advice and consultation from your local computer vendor.

Note: Windows 3.11 can mislead you about the status of the SHARE.EXE program. Suppose, for example, that the SHARE.EXE program is not loaded into memory. If, from within Windows, you open a DOS window, type the word SHARE, and press the Enter key, Windows 3.11 will tell you that the SHARE program is loaded even though it is not.

INSTALLING CASS ON A NETWORK

The entire CASS system is designed to function on a free-standing personal computer and on a *local area network*, or LAN, system. The only essential difference between a PC and a LAN installation is that all of your data tables are stored on the LAN's file server disk rather than on the PC's hard disk in the C:\CASSWIN\DATA directory. Although a network installation of CASS is not difficult, we recommend that the software be installed on a network only by a trained network administrator. The first step is to install the software on your personal computer as described earlier. Then open the *WALMYR Suite*, double click the *CASSNET* icon which is an ordinary text file, and then print the CASSNET.TXT file. It contains detailed instructions for installing the software on a LAN.

CALLING UP AND USING THE SOFTWARE

Now that you have successfully installed the CASS and CAAP software on your computer, you are ready to call up the programs and use them. To do that, open the *WALMYR Suite* program group (or folder if you are using Win95), and then double click the CASS icon. When the program appears on screen, it will require that you enter your UserID and your Password. In order to begin using the software, enter the word *walmyr* as your UserID (be sure to use all lowercase letters), and press the Tab key. Then enter the word *scales* as your Password (again, be sure to use all lowercase letters), and then press the Enter key or click the OK button. If you enter the proper UserID and Password, you will be admitted into the program and you can then begin using it in your practice.

FREE CASS UPDATES

Before leaving this chapter, you should know that the Windows version of the CASS and CAAP software is a young product and that both programs are frequently upgraded to include new features or to improve the ones that are present. Any such updates to the software are available to you without fee, and we want you to know how to obtain them. However, we also want you to know that you should *never* attempt to upgrade your copy of the software by reinstalling it because to do so will destroy all of your client records. You should install the full version of CASS one time and never again install the original CASS diskettes. When you wish to upgrade your copy of the software, it is essential that you do that by obtaining the *Free CASS Upgrade* disk, which can be used to upgrade the software but which will never disturb your data files. If you have access to the World Wide Web, you can go to the URL shown earlier in this chapter and download a free upgrade to the CASS software. If you do not have access to the Web, you should write to the publisher to obtain a free upgrade for the software.

NEXT STEPS

This chapter has explained the basic purpose of the CASS and CAAP software and the role these programs can play in helping human services practitioners do their work. It has also explained how to install the software on a computer and how to call it up to begin using it. The next step is to learn how to use the CASS software and how to get the most out of it. The next chapter will help the reader to do that.

18

Using CASS in Practice

In the previous chapter, we discussed the role that the CASS software could play in practice and explained how to install the software on a computer. We will assume that the reader has installed the CASS software so that this chapter can focus on helping the reader to get the most out of the software. The CASS program is very easy to use and has many different features to help practitioners do their work. It will take some effort to learn all of them. However, every feature of the system does not need to be mastered in order to begin using it with clients. Only a few features need to be learned in order to make good use of the software. We go through them one at a time and provide examples to follow so that practitioners can easily learn how to use the software in their work with clients.

The online Help that is provided with the CASS software is very important and must be read. We urge that the reader prepare to do that now. The best way to do that is to call up and log onto the CASS software, press Alt-H-C to open the online Help system, put plenty of paper in the printer, and then *print every topic!* We recommend that the printed copy of the CASS Help topics be bound and that the bound printed copy be kept handy until one has mastered the entire system. We do not reproduce the Help system in this chapter, but we do build on that information. Thus, reading the Help topics is essential in order to make best use of the material contained in this chapter. The Help topics can be read on screen, but we have found that a printed copy of the Help information is very useful when learning a new system.

SETTING UP THE
CASS SOFTWARE

The work done to install CASS, as described in the previous chapter, is all that is needed in order to begin using the software. However, there are two very important setup tasks that should be performed before one begins using the software with clients.

Change the UserID and Password

In the previous chapter, you saw how easy it is to log onto the CASS system by entering *walmyr* and *scales* as the UserID and Password. This means that anyone who reads this book or the README.TXT file that CASS presents on screen during installation of the software can log onto your personal copy of CASS and gain immediate access to your client records. You must change your UserID and Password if you want to ensure the confidentiality of your client records. When you change your UserID and Password, it is critical that you write them down and store them in a secure place. If you forget them, you will not be able to gain access to your client records!

Let us change the UserID and Password now so that you can follow along with us. Call up your copy of CASS and log on using the default UserID and Password of *walmyr* and *scales*, respectively. Now press Alt-F-M to call up the CASS Manager module. Once you are in that module, press Alt-U-U to call up the CASS Userlist Facility. There you will see that the first entry is a "person" whose Employee Number is 1 and that this person has a UserID and password of *ChangeMe* and *ChangeMeToo*, respectively. You must replace these values to reflect the ones you wish to use.

Now hold your mouse pointer over the icon at the top of the page that looks like a small pyramid. In a second or two, a balloon message will appear that explains that this tool bar button is used to edit one of the records in this file. Since the record pointer in the far left margin is pointing to the first record (that pointer also looks like a little pyramid), clicking the "edit record" icon will allow you to edit the first record. Click the Edit button in the toolbar. Now click your mouse in the field containing the *ChangeMe* UserID. You can now type the information that you wish to use as your personal UserID. Enter your new UserID, and then press the Tab key. When you do that you see that your new UserID has been entered and that you are now in the Password field of the first record in the table. Type in the new Password that you wish to use, and again press the Tab key. Now type your name as you want it to appear and press the Enter key. Be sure to leave the Employee Number as 1, and be sure to leave the Security code as 5. Now write down your new UserID and Password. Once you have done that, click the *Cancel* button.

These next steps are very important, so do not skip them. First, exit the CASS software completely. Then call it up again, and be sure to log on by using your new UserID and Password. If you are successful in doing that, you know that you have properly entered your own master UserID and Password.

You can now go back into the CASS Userlist Facility and delete Employee 9999, which contains the default UserID and Password of *walmyr* and *scales*. You are now the only person who can log onto your personal copy of the CASS software.

Install the Service Codes

CASS enables you to create and use your own service codes that are used to identify the primary, secondary, and tertiary services that your clients sought when they first came to you for help. However, it is up to you to define your service codes, and their definition requires very careful thought on your part. We recommend that you use a four-digit service code where the first two digits represent a major category of service and the last two digits represent subcategories of the same broad service. A four-digit code will provide you with 99 major service categories, and each of them can then contain up to 99 different subcategories. For example, if 1000 represented the broad category of Family Services, you could then define 1010 as Family Planning, 1011 as Anger Management, 1012 as Family Violence Counseling, and so on. You might design a better coding scheme, so please treat this one as merely a suggestion; the point is that you should design your service codes and enter them into the system before you begin creating and using new client records.

These are the only two tasks that you need to deal with before beginning to use the CASS software with your clients. They are not difficult, but both are very important—you should not ignore them.

CLIENT RECORDS
AND SERVICE PERIODS

An especially useful feature of CASS is that a practitioner can create a client record only once and then have that record forever! This is also true of paper records that are kept in file folders in filing cabinets; however, CASS is different in one respect that practitioners should know about before they begin creating their own client records. In most agency settings, it is common to speak of the actions taken when one "opens a case" or when one "closes a case." When CASS is used to manage client records, the practitioner does not open and close cases. Instead, he or she opens and closes *service periods*, which are defined in terms of the dates the service periods are opened and closed. For example, suppose that a practitioner has a client named John Q. Public. The practitioner can create a record for John Q. Public as follows. First, open your copy of CASS. Next, click on *File* on the main tool bar, then click on *Create New Client Record,* and then just enter the client information requested. Then click *Save.* That's it! You have created a permanent client record and it has been saved in the CASS software. You can then select a service code for your client by highlighting one of the service codes presented on the screen and then clicking OK. You have now created and saved a new service period for your client! It's that simple. You can, then, enter specific tasks that must be completed for your client if you wish, or you can just click cancel and your new case is stored in CASS. If you want to enter new data for this client, you can just open the case by clicking on *File,* then on *Get a Client Record.* Then double click on the client's record as it appears in the client records window. You will then be asked which service period you want to work with, and you select that period by just double clicking on it. Do this now as an exercise: create a client record for John Q. Public, create a new service period for this client, and then save it. Just follow the series of steps as they appear in this paragraph.

When you have completed a particular service period for a client, you can close the period of service by entering a closing date for it. *Practitioners must be careful! They should never close an open service period before checking all the information in it to ensure that the information is accurate.* The reason is that once an open service period is closed, practitioners can never edit or change any of the information in it. The information for any service period can be read and reviewed, but the information in a closed service period cannot be changed. In other words, once a service period for a client is closed, it becomes a permanent record that cannot be changed.

Now that the reader has installed CASS on a computer and has done the required setup tasks, we are ready to begin using the software and to talk in some detail about how it can be put to work in practice. We will begin with a brief tour of CASS to get acquainted with some of the features that are used most frequently, and then move progressively into discussions of how best to make the system work for practitioners and their clients.

A FIRST TOUR OF CASS

One of the best ways to get acquainted with new software is to call it up and play with it. Let us do that now. Call up your copy of CASS and log on with the default UserID and Password or with your own if you have made those changes. Now click *File/Get Client Record . . .* and you will see a dialog box appear on screen that lists three client records. Double click on the John Q. Public record you created earlier, and you will then be presented with another dialog box that lists all of his service periods. Now double click the first service period, which is the one that is currently open. You will then be returned to the CASS Main Menu where you will see John's record noted at the top of the screen. This is now your active case record, and we are ready to work on his case.

Conducting a First Case Review

One of the great advantages of using computerized client records is the ability to conduct rapid and frequent case reviews—a task that is a central feature of human services practice. Case review has many different uses, and it often is based on the review of several types of information, possibly in several different forms.

Entering and Reviewing Scale Scores As a first step in conducting a case review, let us enter and review assessment scale scores for John Q. Public. To do that, click on *Assessment,* then click *Score Assessment Scale,* then click on *Unidimensional Client Scale,* and, finally, double click on *GCS,* the *Generalized Contentment Scale.* You will then see a window asking for a date and for the client's item scores on the GCS. Enter 11/14/00 for the date, and then enter the following 25 GCS item scores: 4, 5, 4, 5, 3, 6, 2, 1, 7, 5, 6, 4, 3, 2, 5, 6, 7, 3, 4, 5, 2, 3, 3, 2, and 5. Then click on *Compute.* You will see that John Q. Public's GCS score for this date was 55.3. Now click on *Save.* You have now saved this score in John's permanent file. Do this exercise again, only enter the date 12/14/00 and the following GCS item scores: 3, 4, 5, 4, 5, 3, 4, 5, 6, 5, 3, 4, 2, 3, 1, 4, 5, 4, 3, 4, 2, 3, 4, 5, and 6. Now click *Compute* and you will see that John's GCS score for this date was 53.3. Now click *Save,* and you have saved this score into John's permanent file.

Now you can review John Q. Public's file by clicking on *Assessment,* then on *Show Scale Scores.* You will now see John's scores for the two dates you have entered and saved. It is really just that simple. You now have created an open case period for a client, and then scored two assessment scales for this hypothetical client for two different dates, saved the scores into his permanent record, and then reviewed these scores. You might want to do this exercise again for a different fictitious client just for the practice.

Viewing Time-Series Graphs The ability to examine the scores obtained on each of many different assessment scales is an important feature of any case review. However, it is often very difficult to comprehend the degree of change that takes place in a range of scores for any particular assessment scale, and it is often difficult to comprehend the meaning of those scores. Most of us are more visually than numerically oriented; when working with numbers, a picture often tells much more than does a group of numerical scores. CASS allows you to graph client scores with considerable ease, and it presents two different kinds of graphs: time-series graphs and multidimensional profile graphs.

Use the main menu and click *Assessment/Time-Series Graphs . . .* to bring up a menu of assessment scales that can be used in preparing time-series graphs. Since you noted earlier that John has completed the GCS scale two times, double click the GCS scale in the menu. You will then see John's GCS scores, which confirm that he did complete that scale two times during the current service period. Now click the OK button and you will see a time-series graph of John's GCS scores.

Now let us play a little more with John Q. Public's file. Click on *Assessment,* then on *Score Assessment Scale,* and then double click again on *GCS.* Enter the date as 01/22/01, and enter the following item scores: 3, 4, 3, 4, 3, 5, 4, 3, 5, 4, 3, 2, 5, 4, 5, 3, 4, 5, 2, 3, 4, 5, 6, 5, and 4. Now click on *Compute* and you will see that John's GCS score for January 22nd of 2001 was 47.3. Click again on *Assessment,* then on *Score Assessment Scale,* and double click again on the *GCS.* Now enter the date as 02/09/01, and enter the following item scores: 2, 2, 2, 2, 6, 1, 1, 4, 6, 2, 6, 6, 6, 1, 4, 6, 2, 1, 1, 2, 6, 6, 6, 6, and 1. Click on *Compute* and you will see that John's GCS score for February 9th of 2001 was 15.3. You have now completed a B design single-case design evaluation of John Q. Public's treatment for depression. Now click on *Assessment,* then on *Time Series Graphs,* and then double click on *GCS.* You will see the four GCS scores for John, from November 14th of 2000 through February 9th of 2001. Click on *OK* and you will see a graph of John's four scores. This graph is, of course, a B design evaluation of the services provided to John for alleviating his depression. Notice that the final GCS score is less than 30, below the clinical cutting score for the GCS. This graph, therefore, provides compelling evidence that John improved during the receipt of services for his problem with depression. We told you it was easy! Using the EPM is also very compatible with the practice context. The use of CASS, and the short-form CASS scales, makes the implementation of the EPM a simple task.

We encourage you to spend a bit more time playing around with the CASS software. Create a new client record for a client named Mary M. Whomever. Create an open service period for this fictitious client for the treatment of depression, and then use the sample copy of the GCS in the back of this book to create a series of eight responses that Mary makes to the GCS items. *Make sure that each of the dates you enter represents a PAST date relative to the date you actually do this on your computer.* Imagine that the first time Mary responds to the GCS items, she is very depressed. Then, for each of the next three times, imagine that she is a bit less depressed. For the last four times, imagine that she is not depressed at all and responds to the GCS items from that frame of reference. Save Mary's scores each time, and then, when you are done, use CASS to make a graph of Mary's eight GCS scores. You have done it again! You have created a B design single-case evaluation of the services that this fictitious client received for depression. You can easily print this graph by clicking on the print icon at the top of the screen on the tool bar. Do this so that you can see how easily it is done.

There is much to learn here, so play with the graph and experiment with its various features. You can do anything you wish with the graph and you will not damage any of the information. For example, hold your mouse cursor over one of the icons in the tool bar, and then press and hold down the right button on your mouse or pointing device. You will see a balloon message pop up that explains what the tool does. Do that for the 3D icon and you will see that you can use it to toggle from a 3D to a 2D view of the graph. Use the left button on your mouse to click the 3D icon; do it several times. You can even change the type of graph with a couple of mouse clicks. Spend some time working with the various graphing features until you become familiar with them. When you are finished, click the Close button to return to the main CASS screen.

Exercise 18.1. Use the CASS main menu and click *Assessment/ Time-Series Graphs . . .* and then double click the IHP scale from the menu. No scores appear because the client has not completed the IHP during this service period. Click the Close

button or press the Esc key to terminate production of a time-series graph. What did you learn by doing this exercise?

Reviewing Tasks   Another very powerful feature of CASS consists of the ability to define specific tasks that we must do in order to provide services or treatment to our clients. We will have more to say about this later, but for the moment we want to stick close to the task of simply reviewing the case for Mary Test. In this regard, it will be important to quickly review the specific tasks that have been defined for this case and to examine the status of their completion. To do this, use the CASS main menu and click *Service Tasks/Task Completion Review . . .*; you will then be shown a table containing all the tasks that have been set up for this case. You will see that only two tasks have been set up for this client during the current service period. In addition, you will see that neither of them have been completed.

As you can see, it is a simple matter to quickly view all of the tasks that have been defined for this case and service period; and since there are only two tasks, it is also an easy matter to check their due dates and whether they have been completed. Suppose, however, that the case has been very active and that the practitioner has defined 50 or more tasks for this service period. You can still use these features to examine each task and determine whether it has been completed or is perhaps overdue. There is yet another way that you can review the tasks for this case, however, and that is to conduct an analysis of the tasks.

> **Exercise 18.2. Using the CASS main menu, click *Service Tasks/Task Analysis . . .* and study the information that is presented to you on screen. Can you see how this feature will help you to examine the progress you are making in providing services to your clients? What have you learned by doing this exercise?**

Reviewing Case Notes   Case note recordings have traditionally been an important device for recording information about a client—what is needed to assist the client, and what was done to provide the needed assistance. It is therefore important to have a quick and simple way to review the case notes for a particular client. You can see how this is done by using the CASS main menu and clicking *Casenotes/Read A Case Note . . .* in order to pull up a menu of case recordings that are identified by topic and date. Then double click the case note you wish to review.

Reviewing the Case History   As you can see, there may be many ser-vice periods for a particular client, and there is potentially a great deal of informa-tion available for each client. We will soon show you how to review all of that information, but it is very useful to have a rapid means of obtaining a quick overview of the entire case. You can obtain that by clicking the *File/Show Case History . . .* options in the main menu. That will produce for you a dialog box that reports basic information about each service period for this client begin-ning with the first period when the case was originally created.

Exercise 18.3. Click the buttons in the navigator bar at the top of the service history dialog box. That will enable you to cycle through each service period to see what kinds of help the client was seeking during each of them. What have you learned about this client by doing this review of her service periods?

Reviewing Client Background Information   You now know how to review all of the major items of information that are stored in the client's record. This covers assessment scale scores, graphic displays of measured client problems, service tasks, case notes, and a brief overview of the case history. However, every client record provides for the recording of basic background information about the case, and you will want to know how to access that information. You need only click *File/Display Current Case . . .* in order to view the background information about the client. Do that now for John Q. Public to learn more about who he is.

Reviewing a Caseload

The hallmark of any human services practice is doing things for your clients, doing things with your clients, or doing things on behalf of your clients. Another way to put it is to recognize that practice consists almost exclusively of defining and completing tasks. That is why CASS gives you the ability to work with and manage the tasks that make up your practice activities. In the foregoing discussion of task management, the focus was given to task management for a single case, but each one of your cases will likely consist of many defined tasks. Naturally, this means that you will have defined a truly enormous number of tasks for your entire caseload (across all of your cases that have open service periods). It would be convenient if you had a way to review your entire caseload from a task management perspective. And you do. Just click the menu option *Service Tasks/Caseload Task Analysis . . .* and you will see the same task analysis described earlier, but this time it is conducted for all cases assigned to you, and not just for the active case that is shown on screen.

Try it now and you will likely obtain a report showing a value of zero for every item in the task analysis report. The reason is that you likely logged onto CASS with a UserID and Password to which no cases have been assigned. If so, do not worry. You need only consult the online Help to learn how you can assign cases to your caseload. Once you begin to assign cases to your caseload, you can use this feature to quickly see how you have performed with respect to your caseload task management.

Note: If CASS has been installed on a network and you have logged on with supervisory privileges, your caseload is defined as all of the cases that have been assigned to your unit. In that case, the caseload task analysis will include all of the cases assigned to you personally as well as all the cases assigned to the practitioners whom you supervise.

Learning About the Tool Bar

Now that you have learned about conducting a case review for a client, we want to call your attention to the tool bar at the top of the main screen. You can learn about the functions in the tool bar by holding your mouse cursor over any of the icons without clicking it. After a couple of seconds, a balloon message will appear that explains what the icon does when you do click it. Once you have done this a few times, you will remember what each icon in the tool bar does, and using these icons will give you more rapid access to the features that you will most often use when working with your clients' records.

Ending the First Quick Tour of CASS

You have covered a lot of ground, and you have done it rather quickly. By now we hope you have seen how CASS can give you very rapid access to a great deal of high-quality information about each of the cases assigned to you. You have also learned how to navigate among some the most frequently used features of the software, and we urge you to explore the many other features that are available. Again, you must consult the online Help in order to learn about the remaining features.

In this first quick tour of CASS, you have done little more than examine data and information that have been previously stored in the two sample cases that are shipped with the software, which are used only to learn about the software and how to use it. In the remainder of the chapter, we shall turn to the features that enable you to enter data so that you can use the software to enhance the conduct of practice with your clients. However, the major emphasis will be on making the most of the system rather than on learning how to use the software. We shall begin with a discussion of the case note recording facility in CASS because that is such a traditional and important feature of human services practice and documentation.

WORKING WITH CASE NOTES

When you begin working with the case notes facility within CASS, you will quickly discover that you are working with a blank page text editor. That is, when you wish to create a new case note for a client, you will begin with a blank page on which you can write anything you like. Many will find this to be the most useful and the preferred format for creating and writing case note information. On the other hand, others will prefer to use a highly structured and preconfigured outline so that the content and organization of case notes are consistent from one client to the next.

If you prefer the use of a structured case note format, you can easily create the case note outline or structure that you wish to use and then save it as a template. Once you do that, you will be presented with your case note template each time you create a new case note for a client. You may even find the use of such a template to be the best of both worlds—structured and unstructured case note recording. That is, you can begin with a preconfig-ured template that can be easily erased in those few cases where you wish to use a blank page format. In those instances, you can create a new case note and then erase the template before you begin writing. When the template appears on screen, you need only hold down the Shift and the Ctrl key and then press the End key. That will highlight the entire template. Once you have done that, press the Del key to erase the template. In short, press Ctrl-Home to go to the top of the page, then press Shift-Ctrl-End to highlight all of the template text, and then press the Del key to delete the entire template.

Creating a Case Note Template

Creating a case note template is very easy. From the CASS main screen, click the main menu option *Casenote/Plain Text Editor* to call up the CASS editor (or press Alt-C-P), and then write the case note structure that you wish to use with every new cas note. When you have finished writing your structured case note outline, save your work by pressing Alt-F-A and using the filename of TEMPLATE.NOT. Your template will thereafter be presented on screen each time you choose the options to create a new case note for a client. You also can edit your template any time you wish by using the plain text editor. If you wish to edit your template, call up the editor by pressing Alt-C-P, then press Alt-F-O, and type TEMPLATE.NOT. Your case note template will then appear on screen so that you can revise it.

Naming Each Case Note

Whenever you create a new case note for a client, you will be required to describe that case note at the time you save it and exit the case note editor by pressing Alt-F-X. The description you enter at that time will become a menu item when you next call up any of the case note options. This means that you should give each case note a content focus so that it can easily be described in your case notes menu for each client. Suppose, for example, that you meet with a client and that the purpose of the interview is to help locate employment. When you write a case note to describe that interview, you could then describe the case note with an entry such as *Employment Counseling*. CASS was designed with the belief that every client contact should have a purpose and that case notes should be written to reflect the purpose of the contact with the client. Thus, your contact purpose can be used as the description of each case note.

Dating Case Notes

Each time you write and save a new case note, CASS automatically records the date you wrote the case note. You have no control over that, and the date that you write each case note will appear in the case note menu when you use the case note facilities of CASS. It is therefore important to stay on top of your case note recording. Otherwise, the dates shown in your case note menu will not correspond very well with the dates you have in the content of each case note. Moreover, it is important that you include dates within your case notes and that you do not depend on the automatic case note dating that is performed by CASS. Every case note should prominently begin, or end, with the date of contact with the client if the case note reflects such a contact.

Keeping Case Notes Brief

There was a day when practitioners were taught that they must write pages and pages of material to describe every interview or contact with a client. Those days are largely gone, and one hallmark of good case note recording today is brevity. Stick to the facts—which consist of essential information and observations—and write nothing that will not be of interest to a reviewer five years after the case is closed. Especially in an electronic case record, it is far better to have a large number of brief and well-focused case notes than it is to have a small number of lengthy, rambling case notes.

Writing "To Do" Notes

It may be tempting for some to use the case notes facility of CASS to write "to do" lists as a planning device. "To do" notes are very handy as planning tools, but we urge that you not use the case notes facility for such purposes. It is much better to put your "to do" lists in the Task Management facilities of CASS because "things to do" are, by definition, tasks.

Case Note Accountability

Never forget that you are accountable for what you write in a case note file. In some locations, clients have a right to see anything that you have written about them. If you are working with children, their parents may have a right to see anything that you have written about their child. Thus, write your case notes with the idea in mind that your client, or one of your client's significant others, may one day read what you have written. Equally important, everyone who works with the client's record will also be able to read your case notes, and the notes could become legal documents in some cases if litigation ever becomes an issue. And remember, once you close a service period for a client, you cannot then go back and edit your case notes. You can read them for review purposes, but you cannot change them once the service period has been closed.

Editing Case Notes

Interruptions are the common fare of daily practice, and it happens all too frequently that you will be called away when you are in the midst of writing a case note for one of your clients. You need not worry about that. Merely press Alt-F-S to save your partially written note, give it a title or description when asked to do so, and you can then leave to deal with the interruption. When you are able to return to the task at hand, it is a simple matter to call up your partially written case note and finish your work. The case note facility includes an option to edit any case note for any open service period.

Case Note Limitations

It is important to know that you can write only one case note each day for a specific client because case notes are tracked by date. In addition, you can write a maximum of 32,000 characters in a single case note file. That is approximately 10 pages of material. Thus, the built-in limitations of the case note facility encourage brevity. If you really must write a truly lengthy case note, you can always divide it into two or more segments and write each of them on separate days.

TASK MANAGEMENT

In Chapter 1 we presented some definitions of accountability and drew attention to the notion of *service resources accountability*, or SRA for short. There we noted that SRA is vitally concerned with professional *behavior*—what services we provide, how many cases we carry, how many visits we make, what theories or service delivery protocols we use, and so on. Also, in Chapter 1 we defined the concept of *service outcome accountability*, or SOA, which is a form of accountability that depends on the detection and measurement of desired change. We continued that discussion by noting that these two forms of accountability must be related to one another such that desired change in a client's problem or situation is at least in part a function of the services we provide and the professional behaviors in which we engage. Ultimately, we must be able to show that what we *do* as professional caregivers really does matter in terms of improving the problems that clients bring to us. In order to make such demonstrations, we must be able to measure positive change, and we must be able to capture systematic information about the professional activities we use in our efforts to help clients solve their problems. We shall deal elsewhere with the task of measuring the client's problems and of measuring positive change in those problems. Here we focus on the task of measuring our own behaviors. Before turning to the specifics of how we do that, however, we should attend to some issues that have great bearing on our professional lives.

Quality Assurance Monitoring and Managed Care

We dare not forget that we now live and work in the age of managed care and quality assurance monitoring. These concepts have emerged with considerable force in the field of medical practice, but they are spilling over into the non-medical human services disciplines and professions. In medical practice, the concept of managed care is often a euphemism for cost reduction and profit maximization, and the concept of quality assurance refers less often to patient improvement (measuring positive change) than it does to the monitoring of physician behavior. Even so, nonmedical human service providers are increasingly being called upon to describe and account for the behaviors (services) that they employ in their efforts to solve the problems for which clients seek help.

Strangely enough, we have never before developed a routine or systematic method for gathering information about and describing the services we provide. The task management features of CASS represent one way to do that, although they are only a partial solution to the problem of fully describing what we mean by service delivery. Limited though they may be, they can help considerably to close this informational deficit and help us to deal more effectively with the mandates of managed care and quality assurance monitoring to which we must respond.

Goal Attainment and Task Completion Scaling

Goal attainment scaling has occupied considerable attention in the past. Task completion scaling has received far less attention. Yet, the heart and soul of service delivery in the human services is the definition and completion of tasks. As Nurius and Hudson (1993) noted, goals are defined as aims or objectives, whereas tasks are defined as something that we must *do*. This is an exceedingly important distinction because we can define goals in a rather endless fashion but they come to naught unless we engage in specific behaviors—unless we do something—to accomplish those goals. Stated differently, goals can never be achieved directly; instead, goals are achieved through the completion of one or more different tasks.

The things that we must do, the behaviors in which we must engage, are the completion of very specific tasks that constitute the services we provide to our clients. A task can be defined as a behavior we plan to carry out and which should or must be performed by a specific date. The current version of CASS provides no means for defining or monitoring goals, but it *does* have the facility for defining and monitoring the completion of behaviorally specific tasks. For some agencies and practitioners, this can be the *sine qua non* of service delivery and quality assurance monitoring.

Making the Most of Task Management

One of the best ways to miss a terrific opportunity is to ignore the task management facilities of CASS. A second way to miss that opportunity is to use the facility poorly. We think the task management capability of CASS can be a powerful aid in helping the practitioner to deal with several important issues and tasks and with virtually every case that is assigned to him or her.

Defining Treatment/Service Delivery

First and foremost, specifying service tasks is a way to literally define the concept of treatment or service delivery. Moreover, that can be done in terms of the specific and detailed things that the practitioner will do (the tasks that he or she will define and complete) that represent the practitioner's conception of what needs to be done for each and every client. This is service resource accountability at its best, and we have never before seen such a facility because we did not have the conceptual and computer tools to do it. Now we do, and the use of the task management features of CASS will enable practitioners to define, document, and demonstrate the delivery of service or treatment in a way that can be very comprehensive, very detailed, and very convincing. And this can be done for every case that is assigned to a practitioner.

Developing New Conceptual Tools

Task definition and management can become an efficient and rapid way to define and document the delivery of services. We nearly always think in terms of "things to do" for every client. However, we have not always focused our attention on the need to be systematic about the way we define and complete the tasks that we do for our clients. We often do them and do not even bother to record what we have done. In beginning to use the task management features of CASS, it is very important to engage in treatment planning from the (perhaps new) perspective of devising a carefully thought out list of specific tasks that operationalize the treatment plan. The treatment plan then becomes the specific list of tasks that the practitioner has put together. It becomes the all-important "to do" list for the case at hand.

Understanding and Reducing Risks

When using the task management tools of CASS, there are definite risks that must be understood and either minimized or eliminated. The first thing to avoid is writing a long list of tasks that others would see as being "trivial." If a practitioner writes and completes such tasks, others could see this as an effort to pad the record, and that could cause external evaluators and managers to raise questions about the practitioner's ability to develop an effective treatment or service plan.

A complementary risk is that of failing to record very important tasks that represent the core actions of a sound treatment plan for a client. If a practitioner has done, or will do, something that moves the treatment along with clarity, it is critical that he or she capture that information. Though it is important to avoid padding the record, it is also important to avoid the underreporting of those tasks that truly are central to the practitioner's conception and definition of treatment or service delivery. In this regard, it is probably better to risk over- rather than underreporting of the case-relevant actions that the practitioner takes on behalf of the client.

It bears repeating that practitioners should, at all costs, avoid writing goal statements in the task manager. Goals are always things that are achieved by defining and completing specific tasks, so practitioners should stick to tasks and avoid goals completely. A practitioner who wishes to state and record treatment or service delivery goals should do that in the case notes facility, but never in the task manager. Frequently practitioners have little control over whether or not a client reaches a goal, and that is one reason to avoid writing goal statements in the task manager. For example, it would be folly of the highest order for a practitioner to state that he or she will "improve the client's social skills by one-third" and record a due date of November 30. What could be done is provide, say, six sessions of social skills training by the end of November. The practitioner can control his or her task behavior by actually providing the social skills training, but he or she has no way of knowing to what extent the client will actually use that training to improve his or her social skills. Tasks are things the practitioner will do, not things the client will do, and these two things should never be confused.

Finally, it is very important to specify reasonable and realistic due dates for tasks and then be sure to stay on top of that. If one becomes too ambitious and specifies due dates that cannot possibly be met, one will consistently appear to fall behind in one's work. On the other hand, by writing due dates that are too distant in the future, one risks giving the impression that one is not very efficient in dealing with one's caseload. Regardless of how due dates are dealt with, the practitioner should make sure every task is completed before or on the date that it is due. The last thing a practitioner wants is for a supervisor to run a case task analysis or a caseload task analysis that reports a high percentage of overdue tasks.

CLIENT ASSESSMENT
AND PROGRESS MONITORING

We turn now to the most important features of CASS, which are the ability to administer, score, and graph standardized assessment scales. It is through use of these features that practitioners will have a full and complete implementation of what was described in Chapter 1 as service outcome accountability. It is through these features that practitioners can demonstrate that their clients do improve with respect to the specific problems for which they seek help. Moreover, it is incredibly easy to use CASS, and the assessment scales described in Part II to completely and totally meet the most demanding quality assurance mandates ever encountered.

There is no doubt that the CASS software, the WALMYR assessment scales, and other assessment tools that can be used in practice are extremely important in helping practitioners deal with accountability issues and mandates. As practitioners, however, external accountability to others can and should be the least of our concerns. It will come quite naturally through the simple process of using the CASS features to help us conduct and improve our efforts to help clients.

Stated differently, our first accountability concerns are never to external auditors, though they are very important and cannot be ignored. Instead, the most important accountability issues for practitioners are those that relate to the conduct of practice. The first is to find improved ways of describing the degree or severity of clients' problems. The second is to monitor those problems over time to determine whether clients are making progress in reducing the severity of those problems. The third is to find (and use) the intervention procedures that have the greatest likelihood of alleviating clients' problems. The CASS software and the assessment scales described in this book were specifically designed to help practitioners carry out the first two of these tasks.

Initial Assessment

In Part II of this book, you learned about several multidimensional assessment tools that can be used with clients to measure the severity of their problems in many different areas of personal and social functioning. If one or more of those measurement tools are used during the intake phase, or very early in the treatment or service delivery phase, the practitioner will have an excellent picture of the problems to be dealt with. He or she will also obtain good information about areas in that the client has strengths or areas that do not need intervention. This information will be enormously useful in helping to render both a differential diagnosis and a treatment or service plan. Equally important, it is the minimally adequate first step in defining and measuring change as described in Chapter 1.

Once a multidimensional assessment scale has been administered to a client, it is quite easy to then enter the client's responses into the CASS software to produce the subscale scores that are provided by the instrument. The software will do all the scoring and store the results as a permanent part of the client's record. Then an instant multidimensional profile graph that depicts the scores obtained by the client can be produced.

Final Assessment

When the practitioner decides to terminate services and close the current service period, it is all but essential to ask the client to once again complete the same multidimensional assessment scale that was used for the initial assessment of the client's problems. This becomes the second minimally adequate step in defining and measuring change as described in Chapter 1. The score differences from the initial to the final assessment provide all but unassailable evidence of the progress that clients have made in dealing with the problems for which they sought help. Once again, the practitioner can enter the client's item responses to the instrument into the CASS software and produce powerful graphic evidence of the client's initial and final problem status as well as solid graphical evidence of the amount of change that took place over the course of treatment or service delivery.

The mere act of conducting an initial and final multidimensional assessment of the client's problems provides the practitioner with the ability to address all but the most demanding requirements of accountability that will be imposed on the practitioner by external auditors, which may include the supervisor and other administrative personnel within the practitioner's organization. It cannot get any simpler than this. And it is vitally important.

Interim Assessment

An early initial assessment is extremely useful as an aid to understanding the kinds and severity of problems for which the client seeks help. The final assessment is essential in order to determine whether and how much positive change has occurred over the entire course of service delivery or treatment. Neither are of much use in helping the practitioner to determine early on whether the treatment plan is doing the intended job. By the time the treatment ends, it is too late to adjust the treatment if it does not perform as hoped or as expected. The only way to obtain information that will help in evaluating the treatment plan is to conduct interim-level assessments. At a minimum, practitioners need to conduct at least one interim-level assessment about halfway through the treatment or service period so that they can make adjustments to the treatment plan before it is too late to correct any deficiencies in the plan—that is, change the plan if it is not producing desired positive change.

It now becomes an important judgment call as to how many and what kinds of interim assessments to make and how to use the information. This becomes an important issue if the initial and final assessments are based on a comprehensive instrument such as the Multi-Problem Screening Inventory (MPSI), which contains 334 items. Obviously, it would be very time-consuming for the practitioner and the client to employ the MPSI in multiple interim assessments. In fact, it is likely not at all feasible, and there is a better alternative available.

Problem Monitoring with Short-Form Scales

If an instrument such as the MPSI is used for initial, interim, and final assessments, the practitioner should be able to identify one to four major problems that will become the central focus of service delivery or treatment. Once the problems that will occupy the central focus of the intervention are identified, at least initially, the practitioner should be able to locate the one or two (never more than four) short-form assessment scales that can be used as interim assessment tools. These can be used once a week or once every two weeks to determine whether and how much change is taking place with respect to the targeted problems that constitute the major focus of treatment. Such instruments can be scored easily with the CASS software, and the software will produce updated time-series graphs so that the practitioner can quickly determine whether the client is improving, experiencing little or no change, or deteriorating.

Short-form assessment scales are far more efficient and cost-effective as monitoring devices to determine whether the client is making progress in the area that is the principal target of change, treatment, or service delivery. In order to illustrate this point, let us call up the Mary Test case and prepare a time-series graph of her scores obtained from use of the Index of Clinical Stress, or ICS, scale. When we do that, we see that Mary initially had very high levels of stress but that over the period of treatment, her stress levels declined considerably.

Seeing Real Change

In Chapter 1 and earlier in this chapter, we placed great emphasis on the detection and measurement of change in the client's problem severity or status. It is now very important to note that there is a "Change" button at the bottom of the time-series graph that was prepared for Mary Test. If we click that button, we see a dramatic picture of the very positive change in Mary's level of stress as compared, each week, with her very first measured stress level.

Now we can prepare a time-series graph of Mary's GCS scores. When the graph appears on screen, we can click the "Change" button and see a picture of Mary's GCS scores. When we viewed the changes with respect to Mary's ICS scores, it appeared that the treatment (whatever it might have been) was working quite well, and perhaps there would be no need to make changes in the treatment plan. On the other hand, when we view the same information for Mary's GCS scores, we see very little evidence of positive change. Does that strongly suggest that there needs to be some modification to the treatment plan? Whatever is being done to help Mary with her depression, the change graph strongly suggests that it is not helping.

MEASUREMENT AS A CENTRAL PRACTICE TASK

We come now to the central theme of this book. Measurement used to monitor client problems can be one of the most powerful practice tools that practitioners can use. What practitioners do to help their clients will always be the central and most important element of practice. And the goal, always, is to help clients reduce or even eliminate the problems for which they seek help. The use of measurement tools as described here is the very best way for practitioners to determine that what they are doing really does matter in terms of achieving positive outcomes for their clients. Even more important, practitioners can now see that measurement of problem severity (and change in problem level) provides them the best means possible for detecting early treatment failures so that they can make appropriate changes to the initial treatment plan. In short, the detection and measurement of change on a regular basis becomes one of the best ways possible to increase the likelihood of a more positive change for your clients.

SUMMARY

Measurement, evaluation, and quality assurance monitoring all have different purposes depending on those who use them. None of us can ignore the increased demands for accountability to external observers and decision makers. However, from our perspective as practitioners, these can and should be the least of our concerns. The truly important concern, given our service delivery role, is to ensure that what we do to help our clients really does get the job done. By using the tools described in this chapter, we can do precisely that. Then we can focus our efforts on the actual doing of practice and stop worrying about external accountability for a very simple reason: by focusing on the doing of practice with the measurement aids described here, we can also provide responsible and convincing evidence of effectiveness at any time that it is requested. What others may regard as the tools of evaluation we have made into the tools for doing improved practice.

19

Making CAAP
Available to Clients

The *Computer Assisted Assessment Package*, or CAAP, program is an integral part of the CASS system, but it is designed for use by clients. In a nutshell, the CAAP program enables clients to perform two major tasks. First, it will administer and score any or all of the assessment scales that are available on the CASS system. Second, it enables clients to prepare time–series and multidimensional profile graphs whenever they wish. If practitioners make full use of the CAAP software, they can almost completely eliminate the need to use paper-and-pencil assessment scales. Since a few clients may not be able to use a computer or may not wish to do so, practitioners may need to use paper-and-pencil assessment scales with a small number of clients; however, assessment scale administration and scoring tasks may be reduced by as much as 90 percent or more by making the CAAP software available to clients and teaching them how to use it.

The automation of scale administration is no doubt a great advantage in the practical affairs of working with clients and obtaining improved measures of their personal and social problems. However, we believe that programs such as CAAP have a much greater positive impact on the conduct of practice than achieving improved efficiency in administering and scoring assessment scales. In this regard, it is important to look at all of this from the client's point of view. One of the first and very powerful implications of providing CAAP to clients is that the practitioner is including them in the single most important aspect of the helping relationship—evaluating the nature and severity of the problem to be treated or solved. Once the practitioner has explained the use of measurement scales as described in previous chapters, the client will understand that the practitioner is not keeping secrets and that the practitioner and client will be working as partners in an effort to help the client deal with and solve his or her problems. Clients' use of the CAAP program to complete the assessment scales that the practitioner and clients agree to use will enhance their sense of empowerment and strengthen the collaborative relationship they have with the practitioner.

An even greater advantage comes when clients begin to use the graphics capabilities of the CAAP program. Each time they come in for an appointment, they can call up the CAAP program, log into their own record, and prepare a graph of the scores for the problem for which they are seeking help. In short, they can see at a glance whether they have improved and how much progress they have made. Suppose, for example, that a client has sought help with a troubled relationship. The practitioner and the client might agree that each week the client will come to the office a few minutes before the appointment and complete the *Index of Marital Satisfaction*, or IMS, scale. Since the practitioner will have explained how to interpret obtained IMS scores, the client will immediately see how much, if any, progress he or she has made during the week since his or her last appointment. Moreover, with the click of a mouse, the client can prepare an updated graph of his or her IMS scores, print it, and bring the updated graph with him or her for discussion during the appointment.

CALLING UP CAAP

Once the practitioner knows how to call up and use the CASS software, it is very easy to call up and use the CAAP software. We recommend that readers work with the CAAP software until they are thoroughly familiar with it. This is very important, since practitioners need to be able to comfortably explain to clients how they can call up and use the CAAP software. Although use of the CAAP software is very simple, we want to offer a few pointers or suggestions that may help the reader in getting the most out of this part of the system.

Calling up the CAAP program is as easy as calling up the CASS program. Just double click the CAAP icon in the WALMYR Suite program group or folder. Once the CAAP program appears on screen, you will see that you must log on by entering a client record number and a password. Naturally, this means that you must supply a client record number and a password to your client if he or she is to use the CAAP program. The online Help in the CASS software explains how to assign a unique password to each client record so that your clients can use the CAAP software.

Exercise 19.1. Call up the CAAP program and enter *SAMPLE1* and *NELLIE* as the record number and password, respectively. Be sure to enter both in all uppercase letters. When you are finished exploring CAAP and this case record, call up the CASS

program, change the client's password, and then repeat the previous steps using the new password. What have you learned by conducting this exercise?

LEARNING THE CAAP ROPES

Once you have successfully logged onto the CAAP program, you should play with and explore every feature that is available. Be sure to read all of the material in the online Help in the CAAP program. After all, this is the material that your clients will see when they use the CAAP software; therefore, you need to be thoroughly familiar with it so that you can answer any questions that may be raised by your clients.

TRAINING CLIENTS

Clients need to understand why the practitioner is using measurement scales, and practitioners need to show them how to use the CAAP software. Previous chapters provide a great deal of information that will help in introducing clients to the use of measurement in the treatment of their problems. Once the reason for using measurement scales in practice is explained, it will be a simple matter to then show clients how to use the CAAP software.

When practitioners are ready to show clients how to use the CAAP software, we recommend that they work with the clients at the keyboard for the first two or three times that the clients actually use the software. Once the clients are comfortable with the software, they can use it independently in the reception room or other locale where a computer and the CAAP software have been made available for their use. The fictitious Mary Test case can also be used to illustrate what the CAAP program will do and how clients can use it to monitor and evaluate their own problems in personal and social functioning.

When clients are comfortable with the use of the CAAP program, it can assist greatly in the sessions practitioners plan with them. For example, a client could arrive a few minutes early for an appointment, call up the CAAP software in the reception room, complete one or two scales used to monitor his or her problems, prepare and print a graph, and bring a fresh copy of the graph into the session for discussion and planning.

TRAINING RECEPTIONISTS

If the proper equipment is available in the reception room, it will not be difficult to teach the receptionist how to use the CAAP software so that he or she can help clients gain access to and use the CAAP program. Once the client and the receptionist are familiar with the software, it may prove to be an enormous aid to the practitioner in his or her efforts to help clients. That is, the receptionist could provide all of the client training on the use of measurement scales and problem monitoring. On the other hand, the practitioner may want to have the receptionist do little more than ensure that the CAAP software is available and help clients use it should they have questions or problems.

USING CAAP ON A PERSONAL COMPUTER

The CASS and CAAP software are designed specifically for use on a local area network (LAN), and in that environment they work together in a seamless fashion. If CASS and CAAP are installed on a single personal computer, they will also work together very smoothly. This implies, however, that practitioners and clients will be using the same personal computer to do work. And this is a very important assumption.

Many will want to install CASS on one computer for use by the practitioner and install the CAAP software on a different computer, say, in a reception area, for use by clients. This arrangement is ideal if both computers are part of a LAN. However, if these are two independent personal computers, this can create a very large problem because all of the data tables will be on the computer containing CASS, and the CAAP program will not function unless it has access to the client data tables that are installed and maintained by the CASS software.

It may seem like an easy solution would be to install CASS and CAAP on both computers, but this can create some major problems and frustrations. This would mean that two independent sets of client records would be on two independent computers. This arrangement will work well only if the practitioner ensures that the client records on the two computers are never intermingled.

INSTALLING A NETWORK

If a practitioner has two to ten different computers and wants them all to work together in using the CASS and CAAP software, there is only one good solution: installing a network system. It is not as expensive as one might think. With only two computers, a small network installation can be created for an expense that is quite trivial. Then one common database can be used for all clients, so it will not matter on which computer or computers the CAAP software is installed for use by clients. We urge the reader to consult a local computer dealer concerning the installation of an inexpensive network if the CASS and CAAP software will be used on two or more computers.

USING TWO
INDEPENDENT COMPUTERS

Despite the difficulties in using CASS and CAAP on two independent computers, some practitioners may need to do precisely that. And it can be done. However, it is tricky, and the practitioner must be extremely careful. In order to illustrate what is involved, we shall describe a scenario and a solution that we hope will explain how to accomplish this application and use of the software.

Suppose you have a personal computer in your office and that will be the computer that you use for all of your professional work. We shall denote this as *Computer A*. Let us now suppose that you have a second computer, *Computer B*, that is located in your reception room, and you wish to make it available to your clients so that they can use the CAAP program. You can do this with the CASS and CAAP software, but it is not a very good solution. We provide the information about how to handle this in the hope it will be a temporary solution while you install a modest network. Here are the steps and procedures you must use in order to successfully use the software under such an arrangement.

Step 1. Install CASS on both computers and be sure to use the default installation options.

Step 2. Install the CAAP software on *Computer B* only.

You can now use the CASS software on *Computer A* in your office to create all of your client records and to manage all of your case notes and other tasks that you wish to perform with the software. Thus far, nothing is unusual or unique, and this is a quite normal arrangement.

Now suppose you have a client coming in for an appointment and you wish to have the client do some work with the CAAP program on *Computer B* in your reception room. It cannot be done yet because all of your client records are stored on *Computer A* in your office. In a sense, the solution is quite simple. Here is what you can do.

Step 1. Put a blank floppy disk in Drive A of *Computer A* and copy all of the files in the C:\CASSWIN\DATA directory onto the floppy disk. Use the DOS command

COPY C:\CASSWIN\DATA A: <Enter>

Step 2. Put the same floppy disk in Drive A of *Computer B* and issue the DOS command

COPY A:\ C:\CASSWIN\DATA <Enter>

Once you have carried out these steps, the CAAP program on *Computer B* will have access to your data files and your client can make full use of the software. However, you must never forget that you now have two exact copies of your data files stored on two different computers. This means that you absolutely cannot use CASS on *Computer A* to do any work with your client records until your client has finished working with the CAAP program and you have restored your master copy of your data records back onto *Computer A*. Here is the way to do that.

Step 1. Put a blank floppy disk in Drive A of *Computer B* and copy all of the files in the C:\CASSWIN\DATA directory onto the floppy disk. Use the DOS command

COPY C:\CASSWIN\DATA A: <Enter>

Step 2. Put the same floppy disk in Drive A of *Computer A* and issue the DOS command

COPY A:\ C:\CASSWIN\DATA <Enter>

These procedures will work if you must use them. However, they are clumsy at best, and at worst they expose you to the risk of contaminating your data files. Again, we urge that you do not do this. It is neither difficult nor expensive to install a network that will meet your data-sharing needs.

SUMMARY

The CAAP software can be used for many purposes, as indicated at the beginning of this chapter. It is a relatively simple program to use, and it can provide an enormous service to practitioners and clients. Once the appropriate equipment and the CAAP software are installed, practitioners can be completely free from the administration of assessment scales and the management of critical assessment tasks. Equally important, it helps clients to become full partners with practitioners in monitoring their progress and in engaging the planning and treatment that will help them solve the personal and social problems for which they seek help.

20

The Manager's
Use of CASS

So far we have discussed how practitioners can use CASS to help them provide services to their clients, to help evaluate their practice efforts, and to manage their client records. In this chapter, we briefly discuss how CASS can be used by the manager. The CASS software can also be thought of as a tool to help manage the complex and difficult task of running a human services agency. We first discuss how the CASS software can help to standardize some aspects of agency functioning and to conduct program evaluations. We then discuss some of the critical tasks that the person assigned to be the CASS manager must carry out.

STANDARDIZING PRACTICE

The CASS software can help the manager to standardize certain parts of the functioning of the agency. It can do so, in part, by defining the manager's record-keeping procedures. The CASS software saves all client records and scale scores in a record file for each client. The CASS features, such as Casenotes, provide a framework that constrains the manner in which direct service workers record their contacts with clients and the activities they engage in on behalf of their clients. The CASS software also contains a wide range of standardized scales, as well as any scales the manager elects to add, that are used to assess and monitor clients' progress. This feature provides a set of measures, used by all practitioners, that standardizes the assessment activities in which all practitioners engage. This has the advantage of making program evaluations much easier to conduct. This latter advantage is, in our estimation, of significant value.

The CASS software also makes it possible to create a "paperless" record-keeping system. All client records can be kept on the computer system on which CASS has been installed. Further, old client records can be kept on computer diskettes or CD-ROMs instead of being kept in paper files. Of course, if a manager does not feel comfortable trusting client records to an electronic system, he or she can back it up with paper files. The electronic system will have the advantages of taking up less physical space and of requiring less paper.

Managing Service Codes

The CASS system also enables the manager to define and install service codes so that the manager can better track and define different types and frequency of services that are sought by clients and provided to them by the direct service workers. Because CASS incorporates end-user service codes, the manager must define his or her own service codes and then install them into the manager's copy of CASS. By far the easiest part is installing the service codes into the copy of the software, as we describe in the following text. The hard part is defining the codes the manager wishes to use in his or her agency or practice.

Entering and managing service codes is simple. The manager need only log onto the system and, from the main menu screen, press Alt-F-M to enter the CASS Manager's Module. From that screen, pressing Alt-U-S will present the Service Codes Management Module. From that point on, the manager can enter the desired service codes and their descriptions. Once the manager is ready to begin work, he or she just clicks on the Help button in the Service Codes facility to obtain specific and detailed instructions.

Once a manager has defined the service codes, he or she can track clients over many years while keeping an extensive historical record of the services they sought over an unlimited number of service periods. There is no limit on the number of service codes that can be used with CASS.

HELPING WITH PROGRAM EVALUATION

The CASS system can help managers to conduct program evaluations, and we believe that this is one of the greatest advantages CASS offers to the manager. As noted earlier, it can help in program evaluations by providing a standardized set of client assessment tools to be used by all practitioners in the agency. This standardization provides the manager with a set of outcome measures for clients that can be placed in single-case designs and aggregated and analyzed in the program evaluation efforts using the procedures described in Chapters 6, 7, and 8. The CASS system can also be linked with other software to assist managers in program evaluation efforts.

The CASS Utility Kit

The *CASS Utility Kit*, or CASSUK, is a separate software package that is designed for use only by program managers. It gives the manager the ability to delete client records and to purge client records that have been closed for a specified period of time. The CASSUK also enables the manager to export unidimensional and multidimensional client scores as both comma separated or CSV files, or as dBase or DBF files. This ability enables managers to download information for program evaluators or researchers. This information can then be uploaded into a spreadsheet program, a database manager, or a statistical package for analysis. The CASSUK is not a standard feature of the CASS or CAAP programs. Managers can obtain more information by writing to WALMYR Publishing.

The CASS Program Evaluator

The *CASS Program Evaluator*, or CASSPE, program provides the manager with access to a completely automated means for conducting program evaluations in terms of client outcome measures. The CASSPE enables managers to aggregate individual client record data so that they can conduct evaluations of their overall program of service delivery or of any component of the overall program. It enables managers to categorize clients according to any defining characteristic (such as age, gender, ethnicity, treatment received, etc.) and then evaluate the differences in outcome relative to these characteristics. The CASSPE will allow managers to aggregate clients' single-case design data in a computer-driven, automated manner, as opposed to doing so by hand.

The CASSPE analyzes the relationship between two variables. The first variable is always a categorical independent variable, and the second is a dependent variable that consists of a set of time-series scores from any assessment scale that has been used with CASS or CAAP. For example, suppose that a manager wants to determine whether his or her agency does a better job of treating depression with male than with female clients (or vice versa). The CASSPE program will aggregate all of the data from the clients the agency has treated for depression into two time-series graphs—one for males and one for females. Each of the time-series graphs, the one for males and the one for females, will be based on the assessment scale that agency uses to assess each client's level of depression (for example, the GCS). The manager can then compare these two graphs, visually and/or statistically, and make a determination as to the relative effectiveness of his or her services for males and females suffering from depression. Many of the techniques described in Chapter 8 can be used to conduct this form of evaluation.

If a manager has used the CASS and CAAP software to monitor clients' progress (or lack thereof) over time, then he or she will have collected all of the data needed for many program evaluations that he or she may want or need to conduct. All that will remain will be for the manager to classify clients according to virtually any categorical variable that the manager or some external agent finds important. These categorical variables can be used for program evaluation with any of the short-form assessment scales that the agency has used to monitor clients' progress.

The categorical variables that will be used for independent variables are created through the development and use of a simple questionnaire that the manager constructs using the CASSPE software. This questionnaire can contain up to 25 questions. Here are some sample questions that might be created for use in the questionnaire:

A. Is this person 18 years old or less?

> 1 = yes
>
> 2 = no

B. What is this client's gender?

> 1 = male
>
> 2 = female

C. Was this client referred from the state EAP program?

> 1 = yes
>
> 2 = no

It should be apparent from these examples that a manager can create a questionnaire that will enable him or her to conduct a very wide range of analyses based on the simple "yes/no" or "true/false" question format. If a manager created a questionnaire with 25 such questions and used 20 different short-form assessment scales in CASS, he or she could conduct up to 500 different analyses for use in a program evaluation study.

Managers are not restricted, however, to the use of dichotomous independent variables. They can, instead (or in addition to the dichotomous variables), use polytomous independent variables by developing questions that have more than two (but less than ten) categories. For example, a question could be created that reads:

> What treatment procedure did this client receive?
>
> 1 = psychopharmacological
>
> 2 = cognitive-behavioral
>
> 3 = insight therapy
>
> 4 = group therapy
>
> 5 = psychopharmacological plus cognitive-behavioral
>
> 6 = psychopharmacological plus insight therapy
>
> 7 = psychopharmacological plus group therapy
>
> 8 = cognitive-behavioral plus group therapy
>
> 9 = insight therapy plus group therapy

If one were to use such a question on a questionnaire, the CASSPE program would produce nine different time-series graphs, one for each of the treatment categories. The use of such polytomous questions will enable managers to conduct much richer comparisons in their program evaluation.

From the foregoing it is apparent that two steps are involved in using the CASSPE program to conduct program evaluations. The first is to develop a questionnaire and to distribute it to all workers who provide direct services to clients. The second is for the direct service workers to complete the questionnaire for each client who has a currently open service period. Once these two steps have been completed, the manager can use the CASSPE program to aggregate the data and produce graphical and/or statistical results that need to be placed into a program evaluation report. The final graphs can be copied to the Windows clipboard and pasted into the report that the manager is creating using his or her favorite word processing program.

More than one questionnaire can be created for use in carrying out many different program evaluations. The CASSPE program, therefore, enables the manager to create and use an unlimited number of different questionnaires and then organize them as separate evaluation projects. Once that is done, the manager can call up any project, send the associated questionnaire(s) to his or her practitioners, have them complete it (them) or update it (them), and then conduct an initial or follow-up study based on the selected questionnaire(s).

The CASSPE program is not a standard part of the CASS system. Anyone who is interested in using it should write to or call WALMYR Publishing.

MANAGING THE
CASS SOFTWARE

There is a critical task that must be accomplished by someone who serves as the CASS manager: managing the access that agency personnel have to the CASS software.

Managing Passwords

The CASS Userlist Facility consists of a single table of information that contains all of the essential information about those persons who will be permitted to use the CASS software. It is the heart and soul of the security system for the CASS software. If the CASS software is used on a single personal computer, the manager will need to enter and use the Userlist Facility only once. However, if the manager has installed the CASS software on a network for use by many different persons, he or she will need to use the Userlist Facility on a regular basis.

When calling up and logging onto the CASS software, the manager can access the Userlist Facility by pressing Alt-F-M. This will call up the Manager's Module, which enables the CASS manager to regulate key features of the software. Once into the Manager's Module, pressing Alt-U-U will bring the Userslist Facility up on the screen. It is important to note that one can access the Manager's Module only if one has a security clearance of 4 or 5 (see the following discussion).

Once the Userslist Facility has been called up, the first thing to look for is the navigator bar at the top of the screen. It has ten buttons across the top, though some have been greyed out. The function of each button can be seen by holding the mouse pointer over any button. A balloon message will appear that will define the button's function. The first four buttons will locate, respectively, the *First, Previous, Next,* and *Last* record in the table. The first four buttons allow the manager to move through the table quickly. One can also move through the table using the vertical scroll bar on the right. The button with the plus (+) sign enables the manager to add a new employee to the list. The minus (–) sign allows the manager to delete an employee from the list. The button with the pyramid allows the manager to edit the record on which the pointer in the left margin is sitting. To edit a record, go to the record you want to edit, click the edit button, and tab to the field you want to change. Then type in the information you want to place in that field. When you want to post the change, click on the button with the check mark. To cancel the change you made, just click on the button with the *x*.

The first time you call up the Userlist Facility you will see that it contains only two employees. The first one has an employee number of 1, a UserID of "ChangeMe," and a password of "ChangeMe Too." It is very important that you, the CASS manager, change these fields and assign yourself a unique UserID, Password, WorkerName, and Security Level. Do not change your security level because it has been preset to 5. Be certain that you write down your UserID and Password and put this information in a safe and secure place so that you can refer to it if you forget your UserID and/or Password! If you forget and do not have the information someplace where you can find it, then you will not be able to gain access to the Userlist Facility, and no one will be able to help you do that. There is no "back door" into this system. If you fail to take care of these essential details, you run the risk of losing your entire security system and the need to completely rebuild it.

Once you have assigned yourself to be the CASS Manager, exit the CASS software completely. Then call it up again and attempt to log on using your UserID and Password. If you get on successfully, go back to the CASS Userlist Facility and delete employee number 9999. This will ensure that others will not be able to log onto your copy of the software by using the default UserID and Password of *walmyr* and *scales*, respectively. Make sure, however, that you do *not* delete employee number 9999 until you have confirmed that your CASS Manager's UserID and Password are properly functioning.

When the Userlist Facility appears on the screen, you will see that it contains several items of information about each employee who is granted access to the CASS software. The data fields of the Userlist Facility are defined as follows:

Employee Number: Every employee who is to have access to CASS needs to have an employee number that is unique. We suggest a simple numbering system from 1 to *n*. For example, if you have 10 employees who are to have access to CASS, then your employee numbers would be 1, 2, 3, 4, 5, 6, 7, 8, 9, and 10.

UserID: Every CASS user must also have a unique UserID. As you have seen, anyone who logs onto the CASS software is asked to enter the UserID that was assigned to him or her.

Password: Every CASS user must also have a unique Password. As you have seen, anyone who logs onto the CASS software is asked to enter the unique Password that was assigned to him or her.

WorkerName: The WorkerName field contains the complete name of the employee. This is the name that is displayed at the top of the main CASS screen after a successful logon.

Security: Each employee must be given a security level that can range from 1 to 5. These security levels define the privileges that each user will be given when working with the CASS software. The security levels are defined as follows:

5 = CASS manager privileges

4 = CASS assistant manager privileges

3 = Administrator privileges

2 = Supervisor privileges

1 = Practitioner privileges

CASS Manager Privileges If someone is assigned a security level of 5, that person has complete and unrestrained access to all features of the CASS software. A manager should only assign this level of security to one or two persons who will serve the key function of maintaining the CASS software.

CASS Assistant Manager Privileges The CASS assistant manager is anyone who has been given a security level of 4. This person will have the same access to CASS as the CASS manager except for one thing: The CASS assistant manager cannot alter the CASS manager's password. It is important to note that only CASS managers and CASS assistant managers can delete client records from the CASS system.

Administrator Privileges Persons who function as administrators are given a security level of 3. A person with a security level of 3 can do anything with CASS except gain access to the Manager's Module. Administrators can open new client records, but they cannot delete client records.

Supervisor Privileges Supervisors are given a security level of 2. Persons with this security level can work with all client records assigned to their unit or program. They can also close current service periods for clients as well as open new ones.

Practitioner Privileges Practitioners are given a security level of 1. They can only work with those client records that are assigned to them. A person with this security level can review previous service periods but cannot open a new service period or close a current one.

21

Concluding Remarks

We sincerely hope reading this book has been a valuable learning exercise for the reader. More importantly, we hope the discussion has inspired the reader to begin evaluating his or her own practice using the principles and techniques presented. This hope comes at a uniquely challenging time in the human services. The demands of clients, funders, governments, communities, professional associations, and the general public are quickly changing the very way we conceptualize and deliver human services. All of these constituencies are demanding that human service organizations and practitioners demonstrate accountability. Although the exact definitions of accountability among these constituencies may differ, two common threads bind the calls for accountability together.

First is the call for effectiveness. After many decades in which the human services have had difficulty showing practice and program efficacy, a sense of skepticism has emerged for many with whom we relate. Increasingly we are told to prove that what we do makes a difference—for clients, for communities, for broader social justice issues. Thus, the call for accountability includes a strong and consistent focus on demonstrating positive outcomes. This is a tremendous challenge for a profession as diverse as social work, but one that we must and can attend to.

The second thread common to accountability demands is drawn from the process of selection of appropriate interventions. Because our profession is so diverse, the models of intervention available are also very diverse. We draw upon theoretical foundations from a wide variety of disciplines, and from these derive and implement ever-growing methods of practice. Unfortunately, however, we have long experienced frustration and limited success in developing techniques to select appropriate practice methods. In far too many cases we still cannot say which interventions work with which clients, under what conditions. As accountability demands increase, we can expect to see corresponding pressures to produce practice evidence that provides guidance about the selection of interventions across a wide range of clients, problems, and helping situations.

The dual thrust of accountability demands—demonstrating outcome and refining process—is at the heart of 21st century practice. These are also the issues that form the core of this book. In this book, we have introduced the empirical practice model (EPM), a model that can help to address the two primary questions of accountability. We strongly believe this model provides a complete and powerful assessment and evaluation technology for use by all human services professionals in service delivery, educational, and research settings. We have tried to be thorough in describing it principles and techniques. We have also tried to make recommendations and offer suggestions that make the model practical and relevant to practice evaluation. If we have done so successfully, the model has been shown as a complete system for evaluating client problems, assisting with initial diagnosis and treatment planning, monitoring client progress over time, evaluating the effectiveness of practice or service delivery on a case-by-case basis, conducting program-level evaluations of organizational service delivery efforts, and conquering all of the most demanding outcome-oriented quality management problems.

In this final chapter, we do two things. First, we summarize some of the major themes woven throughout the pages of this book. Second, as we describe the themes, we also comment on emerging trends and patterns in the human services. These are important for understanding the future role of empirical practice models and helping social workers become proficient users of such models.

PRACTICE EVALUATION
THEMES AND FUTURE DIRECTIONS

The Integration of Practice and Evaluation

The central theme of this book is that practice and evaluation are not only compatible, but necessarily linked by an orientation toward effectiveness. This means that effective practitioners routinely conduct evaluation of what they do, and evaluation in turn offers invaluable information to guide effective practitioners. Such is the nature of an "effectiveness orientation."

Historically there have been tensions between the art of practice and the science of evaluation. Evaluations were often conceptualized and implemented as large-scale explorations of outcome, designed by external consultants and implemented using a "top-down" approach. This made evaluations a foreign and intimidating process to most practitioners, who would see evaluations implemented without much input from the front lines, and who would naturally be suspicious or at least ambivalent toward the evaluations. In addition, the data collected might not be directly relevant to how *they* practiced. Even if the data was appropriate and relevant, the feedback derived from it would often arrive far too late to offer useful guidance for practice with the clients from whom the data came. All of these factors ensured that evaluations were often considered a project that practitioners simply had to survive in order to get back to the real work of conducting practice.

These perceptions were unfortunate, but were certainly understandable. The resulting myths developed about evaluation, and poorly integrated evaluation efforts, have had a lasting impact on the social work profession. Use of scientific methods, research in general, and evaluation techniques failed to gain wide acceptance in social work in the last few decades of the 20th century. Among other criticisms, such endeavors were often accused of being based on an obsolete scientific paradigm, ignorant of multiple, subjective realities, and blindly focused on causality and generalization. Consequently, many social workers have concluded that evaluation offers little to facilitate good practice.

As we enter the 21st century, however, models of evaluation are changing. So, too, are professional attitudes toward evaluation. We are developing models of evaluation meant not as time-limited projects, but as a mechanism to facilitate regular feedback and guidance for practice. These models are based on practitioner decision making, not external expertise of consultants. They seek to understand and improve both process and outcome, not just judge whether intervention or programs "work." The emerging model of practice evaluation is, therefore, integrative in nature. It integrates simple evaluation methods with the decision-making needs and practical realities of practice. The focus is truly on using evaluation techniques to *do* and *enhance* practice. By necessity, the "new" practice evaluation forces evaluation techniques to adapt to practice, rather than the other way around.

Moving to integrated practice evaluation models requires a tremendous shift in the way we think about decision making and information. All data collected in practice evaluation must be directly relevant to improving practice—on either a process or outcome level. It must fit within the workload issues imposed by the realities of practice, and be simple enough to use without months or years of specific training. It must also help practitioners make routine decisions about the way they conduct practice, not just help make decisions about the fate of programs. These requirements call for evaluation models that integrate continuous collection, analysis, and reporting of data seamlessly into practice routines. In other words, the foundation of relevant practice evaluation models lies in ongoing monitoring and decision making at the case level of practice. It is, in essence, a focus upon quality improvement in practice!

In this book we have presented a practice evaluation model based on the principles just described. This model is the empirical practice model, or EPM. The EPM requires three basic steps that together address both the issues of process and outcome:

1. Measure the client's problem.
2. Measure the client's problem repeatedly over time.
3. Assess the extent to which positive change in the client's problem (or problems) is associated with the intervention.

Beyond these basic steps, the EPM offers tremendous freedom to structure practice in a way that suits individual needs and skills. Practice evaluation can be a simple task. A practitioner might, for example, adopt a basic AB single-system design (Chapter 4) to monitor a client's progress on two practice objectives. These objectives could be measured at regular intervals using a standardized short-form assessment scale, and the results graphed on a simple chart. Analysis of the data could consist of simple visual inspection, or calculation of simple weighted means across the A and B phases using any common calculator (Chapter 6). Such procedures can be conducted by *any* practitioner, and do not require either extensive training or undue additional effort. At the same time, practice evaluation can be conducted on a very sophisticated level. Using the same case just described, the practitioner may be able to implement a reversal or ABAB single-system design (Chapter 5). Using the same assessment scales as measures and charting the data over time, the practitioner would be able to portray on a practical level the likely impact of intervention. For sophisticated analysis, the practitioner might choose to conduct an ordinary least squares (OLS) regression analysis to determine how much variance in the client's outcome measures can be explained by the practitioner's intervention. Such techniques, of course, require a bit more training and technical expertise.

The point we are trying to make is that practice evaluation can no longer be considered a foreign, "scientific" process. Science is not practice. Nor is practice science. The tools of science and evaluation, however, can help practitioners *do* practice. The features of practice evaluation—setting measurable client objectives, selecting valid and reliable outcome measures, and assessing these measures over time—can contribute to the entire helping process. If these are guided by practitioners and used in ways that fit into practice, the product is a new and far more powerful form of evaluation. Such evaluation is first and foremost a practice tool, not a scientific or purely administrative endeavor.

Managed Care and Quality Management

There is no question that managed care and its quality management procedures will continue to weave their way into human service delivery. Despite professional concerns about managed care—concerns about the overall quality of care, professional autonomy in managed care structures, patients' right to choose, and so on—managed care is much like a tube of toothpaste. The cap has been removed, and the contents of that tube (managed care plans and procedures) will be impossible to put back.

The impact of managed care on human services in the 21st century will be profound and widespread. On an agency or program level, managed care will likely fuel trends toward consolidation and integration of human services, particularly in areas of mental health care. This is to be expected on a number of fronts. For-profit managed care companies are steadily expanding into areas traditionally served by nonprofit organizations as they build capital, experience, and contracts in such areas. This expansion will include provision of formerly public-based services, and much more direct service delivery than we have seen in the past. At the same time, competitive pressures and scarce resources will force existing nonprofit organizations to place greater emphasis on marketing, niche-building, and development of joint initiatives.

Managed care will also change the very ways in which we conceptualize and implement service delivery. We can expect to see a continued movement away from any form of institutional care, as such care tends to be more costly than other forms of service. This promises to increase the use of various group and community-care models. It also encourages the use of short-term treatment models wherever possible, unless empirical evidence is produced that shows more intensive treatment is the only option for resolving a client difficulty.

Regardless of the treatment option selected for a case, many practitioners will become very familiar with the supervision of utilization managers. These managers employ peer review techniques to review proposed treatments, offer second opinions about service options, review ongoing treatment, and take steps to contain expenditures for high-cost cases. This is, thus, a process of examining the appropriateness and timeliness of clinical decisions. As such, it inherently focuses on questions of process and outcome.

It is here, in satisfying quality management and utilization management demands, that practice evaluation offers a tremendously powerful tool to professionals. By adopting practice evaluation as a routinely conducted part of practice, professionals can equip themselves with the conceptual framework and techniques necessary to function in the new "accountability era." As an example of a practice evaluation framework, the EPM is one set of tools ideally suited to meeting the accountability demands created by managed care. The EPM is designed to get at the heart of effectiveness and accountability—the detection of change in a client's problem. Its use of short-form assessment scales and time-series designs offers a powerful way for practitioners to show that the service behaviors we engage in actually produce observable, measurable change in clients' objectives.

The Role of Technology

Increased demands for accountability at both the practice and program levels inevitably increase corresponding demands for flexible, quickly processed information. In addition, the information being asked for is more complex, and focused more directly on performance assessment—that is, outcomes. Such pressures require transformation of the ways we conceptualize information needs and the ways in which we manage information. Traditionally, information management in our organizations relied on pen-and-paper files. More recently, we (usually support staff and administrators) adopted the use of simple word processing programs, spreadsheets, and databases to record and report on professional activities. Soon, however, *all* human service personnel will play critical roles in information management. Information management no longer fits into the domain of support services, but squarely in the middle of the domain we call practice.

The shift in information management roles poses two direct challenges for human service organizations. First is the basic challenge of structuring the daily tasks and providing organizational resources so that frontline practitioners *can* effectively manage their information. For example, we must answer questions about how practitioners can best build record keeping into their practice without being overly burdened by "paperwork" and overwhelmed by volumes of data. The second challenge is one of building upon case-level data. How does one effectively aggregate and manage information from unique cases in ways that offer valid pictures of overall program functioning? As our information needs evolve, so too will the complexity of managing such aggregated information.

The considerable challenges posed by emerging information needs will necessarily advance the use of computer hardware and software in human service organizations. The advantages of computerized information management are substantial. It permits storage of volumes of data that was unfathomable just a few years ago. Moreover, this data can be retrieved at will in a matter of seconds. User-friendly software allows anybody to manipulate and analyze the data in countless ways, and then produce automated, sophisticated reports. Relational databases also allow us to link seemingly random or sundry data in ways that forge new understanding and knowledge. We might, for example, link data collected for client intakes, professional interventions, and case closures to gain a better understanding of the factors that contribute to effective service.

The task of processing information when using empirical practice is not difficult. Any competent professional can use a short-form standardized measurement scale to evaluate a client's problem or use a multidimensional assessment scale to obtain a more comprehensive evaluation of multiple client problems. Nor is it difficult to chart client data in a simple time-series graph to monitor the client's progress over time. What we have described as the actual *doing* of empirical practice is quite simple and basically involves the use of simple measurement tools and rather simple graphs. The reader now knows how to do all of these tasks.

All of these practice evaluation components can be completed manually. The volume of information processed by routine practice, however, demands a more efficient and powerful technology. Part III of this book presented a computer program—the CASS system—that helps to manage the large volumes of information that accompany practice evaluation models and helps to aggregate these on programmatic levels. As such, it can be used by all those concerned with practice effectiveness—human services practitioners, supervisors, administrators, and program evaluators.

The CASS system described in this book is one example of the emerging technologies that offer sophisticated functions to manage the information of practice. CASS software can help greatly with most components of practice. It includes functions to record client histories, administer assessment scales, keep case notes, prepare time-series charts, set and review practice activities and tasks, conduct case reviews, and summarize caseloads.

The CASS system is representative of the new technology that is becoming infused into human service practice. It offers a complete software package to perform all practice and program-level evaluation tasks. And because the empirical practice model presented in this book cannot be considered to be a deliverable technology without the use of computer technology, we urge the reader to learn and experiment with the CASS system.

The Impact of Consumerism

As human services are being transformed, so too are the reactions and demands from clients. Even though social work has long proclaimed the rights of clients to self-determination, many services in the past valued professional expertise and decision making above client decision making. Clients assumed a passive role in the helping process. This role included a process of diagnosis, labeling, and prescriptions about what services were needed. Even success was often defined in the language of experts. In extreme cases, such a framework created a sense of client subordination and dependence. Of course, there were (and are) many examples of excellent programs and practitioners who did not fit into this negative description. There were, however, too many who did.

One of the strongest voices for professional accountability is now from the "client." As client advocacy groups become more active, we are increasingly seeing client "bills of rights" being drafted to ensure that professional service delivery is accountable. In relation to managed care, for example, the National Alliance for the Mentally Ill (NAMI) has developed a strong set of principles for structuring such plans. These principles argue for provisions such as continuing state responsibility for mental health services, meaningful participation of consumers and their families in every phase of managed care, and rigorous training and credentialling for service providers.

Similar patterns of growing awareness and advocacy are being felt in most areas traditionally served by human service professionals. It is at the front line, however, that the product of increased client consumerism will be most felt. In coming decades, the "expert-client" relationship will likely fade from prominence, replaced by a new practitioner-client duality. This duality is one in which the client will assume a far more equal role in defining the nature of his or her difficulties, take a more active role in defining the shape and progress of treatment, and play as large a role in interpreting outcomes as the practitioner. In effect, practitioner and client will become equal partners in the treatment process to an extent never before experienced.

One particularly important trend in client rights and empowerment is related to the ease of access and use of information. Through widespread information dissemination, tools such as the Internet are rapidly transforming clients' ability to learn about the difficulties they face and the services available to assist them. A client who seeks information about aggression in adolescents, for example, can, in a matter of minutes, search, sort, and print volumes of information about the topic. In addition, this same client is likely to be able to identify various services that are available locally to help him or her deal with the aggression being experienced. This ability to self-inform and learn, along with the ability to track down professional services, provides clients with an ever-increasing capacity for exercising choice. Conflicts are likely to emerge, however, as clients try to exercise that choice within the frameworks imposed by managed care plans. A question therefore remains about the extent to which clients will have the flexibility to "choose" the kinds of services they access and support.

The authors of this book believe strongly in the right of clients to informed, full participation in the helping process. Clients should know what assessment scales practitioners propose to use, why these scales have been selected, and how practitioners intend to use the results. They have a right to know what training and experience practitioners have in the kinds of treatment they are about to embark upon. As well, clients have a right to know what other resources and services might be available to them inside the agency or in the community. In fact, clients have a right to know about the entire process of assessment, treatment, and evaluation. Practitioners can expect clients to more frequently ask questions about such things in the future.

An essential component of this emerging client consumerism is the desire to take part in and fully understand the assessment and intervention process. This is one reason the CASS system has been included as a core part of this book. Within the system is a program called the Computer Assisted Assessment Package (CAAP). The CAAP program is the part of the CASS system designed for use by clients. It enables clients to perform two major tasks while they sit at a computer. First, it administers and scores the entire range of assessment scales included in the CASS system. Second, it enables clients to prepare time-series and multidimensional profile graphs whenever they wish. The implications of these two steps are profound. The client is immediately drawn into the single most important aspect of the helping relationship—evaluating the nature and severity of the problem to be treated or solved. This sends a critical message, one that says that the practitioner respects the client's rights to full disclosure. It also lets the client know that the practitioner is not keeping secrets and that both the client and practitioner are equal partners in the helping process. We strongly encourage this approach to practice as a way of enhancing client empowerment and strengthening the collaborative relationships that practitioners form with clients.

New Models of Professional Practice

The essential nature of work is rapidly evolving in our society. In the coming decades, workers are likely to be employed in more jobs over the span of their working career, and more likely to make radical shifts in the type of work in which they engage. It is probable that this work will tend to be part-time, contract work, and less oriented toward manual or service jobs. The ability to manage information and apply sophisticated technology will also become far more critical to successful employment.

A critical impact of the trend toward a flexible (or transient) workforce will be the need for continuing, lifelong education. No longer will advanced training be contained only within postsecondary institutions. Instead, successful workers will continue to seek out new learning experiences in order to remain relevant and competitive in the workforce. These individuals will likely abandon "mass production," degree-based models of education in favor of "mass customization" of education. By this we mean that education will increasingly focus on being portable, flexible, and managed as much in the home and workplace as in educational institutions. In this way, workers of the future will likely develop lifelong learning portfolios that extend far beyond the notion of traditional education.

These trends apply just as much to human service professionals as to any other member of our society. We are already seeing, for example, the development and implementation of new models of professional practice. Consider a couple of examples. In the area of health care, for instance, we have recently seen the implementation of technology-based interventions that negate the barriers of geography. These "telemedicine" models use video, audio, and computer technology to connect professionals to clients at remote locations. The professional is thus able to conduct a complete health or mental health therapeutic session through the technology linkage. The growth of such practice is likely, as it offers a cost-effective form of care particularly suited for delivering services to remote and traditionally underserved populations.

Another example is also "distance" based. One of the authors is familiar with an employee assistance program (EAP) that is delivered on a national basis. This service is managed in one central office, but delivered through a network of contracted employees who function very independently. The employees are all equipped with laptop computers. Every aspect of their practice—communicating with the central office through e-mail, performing client assessments, entering case notes, recording daily activity logs, and performing client assessments—is done using the computer. At regular intervals, reports of these worker activities and client progress are submitted electronically to the national office. There the reports are aggregated and processed to form a single, "virtual" organizational information base. This information base is used to supervise the contracted workers, plan future service delivery, and establish overall organizational effectiveness levels for reporting to those who pay for the EAP.

As professional practice and human service organizations adapt to these new realities, there will be considerable pressure for the kinds of skills discussed in this book. Human service professionals will need to possess higher levels of technical skill, knowledge of information management, and familiarity with technology. In fact, these professionals will likely not find employment in human services without at least basic expertise in these areas. At the same time, retrenchment of public services, economic pressures, and consolidation of the service industry will likely increase competition in human services. This will raise the skill levels required on the part of practitioners in order to be competitive for fewer jobs. It will also require those professionals who are employed to demonstrate that they are indeed effective. This would be particularly true for those workers employed in contract or fee-for-service arrangements with third-party payers. In short, successful professionals will soon require the kinds of skills discussed in this book. They will need to be able to structure their practice using an effectiveness orientation, and possess the technical skills to use practice-enhancing technologies. We hope that this book has offered some direction and skills to assist in this emerging process.

SUMMARY

Some may bemoan the growing importance of evaluation to practice as a movement away from professional autonomy and a blow to the "art" of intervention. We strongly disagree. The emerging integration of practice and evaluation offers a timely and powerful tool that will facilitate dramatic changes in the profession of social work. New and strengthened models of evaluation, data collection strategies, and tools for information storage, processing, and reporting will change the very way we think about practitioner effectiveness. Rather than making the demonstration of effectiveness a solitary or ad hoc procedure, these will make demonstrating effectiveness a routine and expected process. Similarly, new methods of collecting and analyzing aggregate information will improve our efforts to evaluate human service programs.

The 21st century is bringing many challenges to professionals in the human services. We have tremendous confidence in the capacity and ability of these professionals to respond to those challenges. They have the skills and creativity to quickly understand and adapt to the kinds of trends discussed in this chapter. They also have the skills and creativity to easily learn how to use practice evaluation models. Together this bodes very well for the future of our profession and the conduct of effective practice.

Appendix A
Some Technical Details

In Chapter 6, we claimed that a line connecting the first and last data points in a phase will produce the weighted mean trend across the phase. We also claimed that the distance between the trend line and the data point in the phase farthest from the phase trend line serves as a reasonable estimate of one sigma unit (relative to the trend line), and that the presence of autocorrelation acts to attenuate whatever bias exists in this estimate. These claims need to be justified in order for the reader to be able to defensibly use these procedures. In this appendix, we will prove these claims. The material in this appendix is *not* easy, and it is not for the reader who is willing to accept our assertions at face value. However, this appendix is important for the researcher or academic who will be using and/or teaching these methods and needs to assure her- or himself that our claims have merit. The details in this appendix will probably be mathematically challenging to some, and the reader will require knowledge of multivariable calculus to follow our argument. The reader who does not wish to read this appendix can ignore it without any loss of continuity.

PROOF THAT LINE CONNECTING
FIRST AND LAST PHASE DATA
POINTS GIVES WEIGHTED MEAN
TREND ACROSS PHASE

Let Y_i be the value of the dependent variable (i.e., the measure of the client's problem) obtained at time t_i. If there are k measures of the client's problem in the single-case design phase, then the values of the index i range from 1 to k, that is:

$$Y_i = \text{measure of client's problem at time } t_i, \; i = 1, 2, 3, \ldots k$$

The change in the client's problem between measures taken at time t_1 and t_2 will be

$$\Delta Y_1 = Y_2 - Y_1 \tag{A.1}$$

where ΔY_1 is change in the client's problem across the first time interval in the phase. In general, the change in the client's problem between two successive measures in the phase will be

$$\Delta Y_i = Y_{i+1} - Y_i, \; i = 1,2,3, \ldots k-1 \tag{A.2}$$

Similarly, the time interval during which the client's problem changes by ΔY_i will be

$$\Delta t_i = t_{i+1} - t_i, \; i = 1,2,3, \ldots k-1 \tag{A.3}$$

This is just a formal way of saying that there are k measures taken during the phase,

$$Y_1, \; Y_2, \; Y_3, \ldots Y_k.$$

and that these measures were taken at, successively, times,

$$t_1, \; t_2, \; t_3, \ldots t_k.$$

This also says that the change in the client's problem from time t_i to time t_{i+1} is given by $Y_{i+1} - Y_i$

By definition, the trend in the client's problem from time t_i to time t_{i+1} is given by

$$T_i = \Delta Y_i / \Delta t_i = (Y_{i+1} - Y_i) \, / \, (t_{i+1} - t_i), \; i = 1,2,3, \ldots k-1. \tag{A.4}$$

This trend might be called the "local trend," meaning the trend over a specific small portion of a single-case design phase that covers the time interval $\Delta t_i = t_{i+1} - t_i$. This local trend $\Delta Y_i \, / \, \Delta t_i$ also gives the ordinary least squares (OLS) regression estimate of the trend between the two time points t_i and t_{i+1} (Neter, Wasserman, & Kutner, 1983). Now the weighted average trend in the client's problem across the single-case design phase is given by

$$T_{wm} = [\sum_{i=1}^{k-1} w_i T_i] \, / \, \sum_{i=1}^{k-1} w_i, \qquad (A.5)$$

(Ash, 1993), where T_i is local trend i, and w_i is the weight given to local trend T_i.

One important weight that might be used in the above mean is the time interval, Δt_i, that a particular local trend covers. Local trends that are based on longer time intervals should carry more weight than local trends based on shorter intervals. If the time interval Δt_i is used as the weight w_i, then the term

$$\sum_{i=1}^{k-1} w_i$$

in equation A.5 for the weighted mean is nothing more than the total length of time between the first and the last phase measures, because

$$w_i = \Delta t_i = t_{i+1} - t_i,$$

so

$$\sum_{i=1}^{k-1} w_i = \sum_{i=1}^{k-1} (t_{i+1} - t_i) = (t_2 - t_1) + (t_3 - t_2) + (t_4 - t_3) + \ldots + (t_k - t_{k-1}) \quad (A.6)$$

$$= t_2 - t_1 + t_3 - t_2 + t_4 - t_3 + \ldots + t_k - t_{k-1}$$

$$= t_2 - t_2 + t_3 - t_3 + \ldots + t_{k-1} - t_{k-1} + t_k - t_1$$

$$= t_k - t_1$$

Thus:

$$T_{wm} = \left[\sum_{i=1}^{k-1} w_i T_i\right] \, / \, \left[\sum_{i=1}^{k-1} w_i\right] = [\sum_{i-1}^{k-1} \Delta t_i(\Delta Y_i \, / \, \Delta t_i)] \, / \, (t_k - t_1) \quad (A.7)$$

$$= [\sum_{i=1}^{k-1} \Delta Y_i] \, / \, (t_k - t_1) = [\sum_{i=1}^{k-1} (Y_{i+1} - Y_i] \, / \, (t_k - t_1)$$

$$= [(Y_2 - Y_1) + (Y_3 - Y_2) + (Y_4 - Y_3) + \ldots + (Y_k - Y_{k-1})] \, / \, (t_k - t_1)$$

$$= (Y_k - Y_1) \, / \, (t_k - t_1).$$

Thus, the weighted mean trend in the client's problem is given simply by dividing the difference between the final phase measure and the first phase measure by the length of time between the first and last phase measures. The ratio

$$(Y_k - Y_1) \, / \, (t_k - t_1)$$

in Equation A.7 is also the OLS estimate of the trend based upon the two data points Y_1 and Y_k (Neter, Wasserman, & Kutner, 1983). Since this ratio also gives the weighted mean trend across the phase, the expression for the weighted mean trend is also an unbiased estimate of the mean trend across the phase.

It should be noted that this holds true even as $k \rightarrow \infty$ and the profile of the dependent variable across the single-case design phase approaches a continuous function. If the number of observations between the initial phase measurement, taken at time $t_{initial} = a$, and the final phase measurement, taken at time $t_{final} = b$, approaches an unlimited number, then the set of phase measures becomes a graph of a function $f(t)$ between a and b. In this case, the trend at any time t_k is given by the value of the derivative of $f(t)$, $f'(t)$, at t_k (Swokowski, 1988). Thus, the sum of trends across the time interval a to b will be given by

$$\text{Sum of values of } f'(t) \text{ between } a \text{ and } b = \int_a^b f'(t)dt = f(b) - f(a)$$

(Swokowski, 1988). Since the total length of time between the measurement $f(a)$ and the measurement $f(b)$ is $t_{final} - t_{initial} = b - a$, then the mean trend between $t_{initial}$ and t_{final} is

$$T_{wm} = \left[\int_a^b f'(t)dt \right] / [b - a] = [f(b) - f(a)]/(b - a) \tag{A.8}$$

This is part of the statement of the mean value theorem for derivatives (Swokowski, 1988).

If all of the phase measures are equally spaced temporally, then the weighted mean reduces to the simple mean of the local trends across the phase.

USE OF POINT FURTHEST FROM TREND LINE AS A MEASURE OF BACKGROUND VARIABILITY

As noted earlier, the trend line is a natural frame of reference against which to compare data in an adjacent phase (Parsonson & Baer, 1986), and the procedure described earlier for representing background variability models variability relative to the trend line. It is as if we were "riding on" the trend line, noting how far data points fluctuate away from the trend line, our frame of reference. We will see data points above, below, and/or on the trend line.

The following transformation, called a "linear filter" (Gottman, 1981), removes the trend from the phase data and produces a representation of variability relative to the trend line:

$$y'_i = y_i - T_{wm} \Delta \tau_i \quad i = 1, 2, \ldots n \tag{A.9}$$

where y'_i is the transformed value of the data point y_i; T_{wm} is the weighted mean trend, trend adjusted for outlying data points, or local trend over the second part of the phase; and $\Delta\tau_i$ is the time interval between the measures y_1 and y_i. For example, suppose that there are six measures in the phase: 1, 3, 2, 5, 4, and 6, taken at times 1, 2, 3, 4, 5, and 6. The weighted mean trend, by Equation 6.3, is $(6 - 1)/(6 - 1) = +1$. Thus, the transformed data points are, using Equation A.9:

$$y'_1 = y_1 - 1(0) = 1 - 0 = 1$$

$$y'_2 = y_2 - 1(1) = 3 - 1 = 2$$

$$y'_3 = y_3 - 1(2) = 2 - 2 = 0$$

$$y'_4 = y_4 - 1(3) = 5 - 3 = 2$$

$$y'_5 = y_5 - 1(4) = 4 - 4 = 0$$

$$y'_6 = y_6 - 1(5) = 6 - 5 = 1$$

This transformation from the original to the trend line frame of reference is illustrated in Figure A.1. In this new frame of reference, the trend is, by Equation 6.3, $(1 - 1)/(6 - 1) = 0$. Notice that the distance of each transformed point from this flat trend line is, in the metric of the dependent variable, the same as the distance the data point is from the trend line in the original frame of reference. This transformation has removed the trend while preserving the variability of the data points relative to the trend line (Gottman, 1981). Let us therefore consider how to estimate one sigma unit for the data within the trend line frame of reference.

Consider Figure A.2. This figure shows single-case design phase data within the trend line frame of reference. The moving range from the first data point (Y_1) to the second data point (Y_2) is $|Y_1 - Y_2|$; from the second data point to the third $|Y_2 - Y_3|$; and so on. The mean moving range will be

$$\bar{R} = (1/n - 1) \sum_{i=1}^{n-1} |Y_1 - Y_{i+1}|, \, i = 1, 2, \ldots n - 1 \qquad (A.10)$$

Now each data point in Figure A.2 lies a distance $c_i k$ from the trend line, where k is the distance between the farthest data point and the trend line, and $-1 \leq c_i \leq +1$. The absolute value of c_i is the proportion of the distance k that the data point y_i lies from the trend line, while the sign of c_i tells whether the data point is above (+) or below (−) the trend line. The end points in the phase, y_1 and y_n, fall on the trend line, so $c_1 = c_n = 0$. Thus, $\bar{R}$ will be, in terms of the $c_i k$ values:

$$\bar{R} = \frac{\displaystyle\sum_{i=1}^{n-1} |c_i k - c_{i+1} k|}{n-1} \qquad (A.11)$$

$$= \frac{|c_1 k - c_2 k| + |c_2 k - c_3 k| + \ldots + |c_{n-1} k - c_n k|}{n - 1} \qquad (A.12)$$

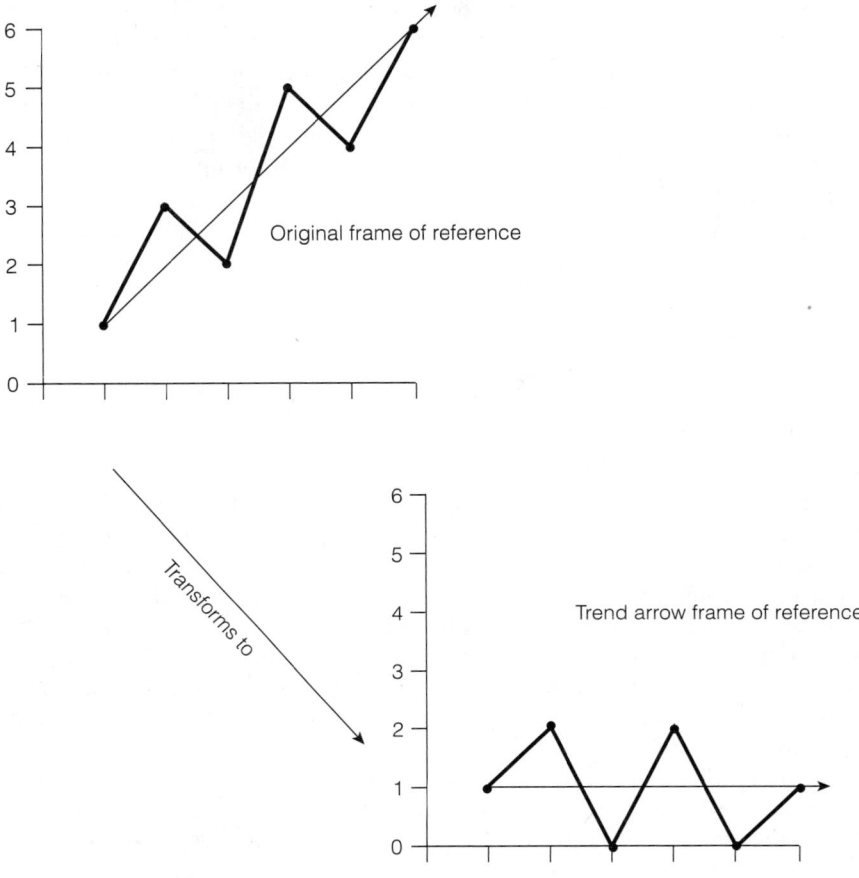

FIGURE A.1 Visual representation of transformation from original frame of reference to trend arrow frame of reference.

Since $c_1 = c_n = 0$, then

$$\overline{R} = \frac{|0k - c_2k| + |c_2k - c_3k| + ... + |c_{n-1}k - 0k|}{n - 1} \quad \text{(A.13)}$$

$$= \frac{c_2k + |c_2k - c_3k| + |c_3k - c_4k| + ... + |c_{n-2}k - c_{n-1}k| + c_{n-1}k}{n - 1} \quad \text{(A.14)}$$

Now there are $n - 1$ pairs of data points in the phase, y_1 and y_2, y_2 and y_3, and so on, so there are $n - 1$ pairs of c_ik values: c_1k and c_2k, c_2k and c_3k, and so on. These pairs of c_ik values are the elements of the mean moving range, since each part of the sum in the numerator of Equation A.12 is the absolute value of the difference between these data point pairs. If the two data points in a pair,

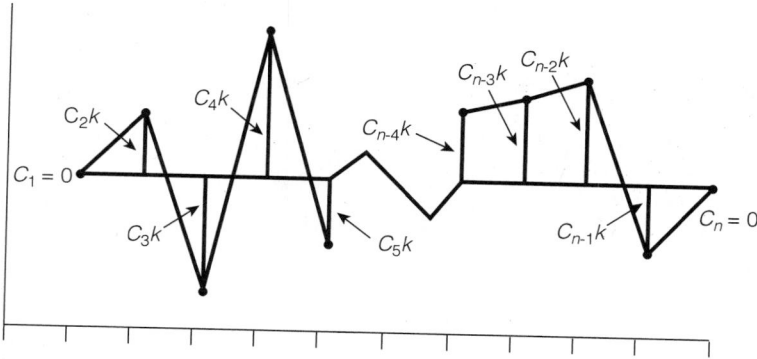

FIGURE A.2 Single-case design data within trend arrow frame of reference.

y_i and y_{i+1}, are on opposite sides of the trend line, then either $c_i > 0$ and $c_{i+1} < 0$, or $c_i < 0$ and $c_{i+1} > 0$; that is, either y_i is above the trend line (a distance of $c_i k$) and y_{i+1} is below the trend line (a distance of $c_{i+1} k$), or y_i is below the trend line (a distance of $c_i k$) and y_{i+1} is above the trend line (a distance of $c_{i+1} k$). If $c_i > 0$ and $c_{i+1} < 0$, then

$$|c_i k - c_{i+1} k| = |c_i k - (-c_{i+1} k)| = |c_i k + c_{i+1} k| = c_i k + c_{i+1} k$$

and if $c_i < 0$ and $c_{i+1} > 0$, then

$$|c_i k - c_{i+1} k| = |(-c_i k) - c_{i+1} k| = |-(c_i k + c_{i+1} k)| = c_i k + c_{i+1} k$$

If both of the data points fall on the same side of the trend line, then they are either both above or both below the trend line. If they are both *above* the trend line, then either $c_i > c_{i+1}$ or $c_i < c_{i+1}$. If $c_i > c_{i+1}$, then

$$|c_i k - c_{i+1} k| = [\max(|c_i|, |c_{i+1}|) - \min(|c_i|, |c_{i+1}|)] = c_i k - c_{i+1} k$$

and if $c_i < c_{i+1}$ then

$$|c_i k - c_{i+1} k| = [\max(|c_i|, |c_{i+1}|) - \min(|c_i|, |c_{i+1}|)] = c_{i+1} k - c_i k$$

where $\max(|c_i|, |c_{i+1}|)$ is c_i or c_{i+1}, whichever is *greater* in absolute value, and $\min(|c_i|, |c_{i+1}|)$ is c_i or c_{i+1}, whichever is *lesser* in absolute value. If both data points are *below* the trend line, then either $|c_i| > |c_{i+1}|$ or $|c_i| < |c_{i+1}|$. If $|c_i| > |c_{i+1}|$, then

$$|c_i k - c_{i+1} k| = [\max(|c_i|, |c_{i+1}|) - \min(|c_i|, |c_{i+1}|) = c_i k - c_{i+1} k$$

and if $|c_i| < |c_{i+1}|$ then

$$|c_i k - c_{i+1} k| = [\max(|c_i|, |c_{i+1}|) - \min(|c_i|, |c_{i+1}|)] = c_{i+1} k - c_i k$$

Thus, when both data points are on the same side of (whether above or below) the trend line, then the order of the terms in the difference

$[\max(c_i, c_{i+1}) - \min(c_i, c_{i+1})]$ depends on which of the two data points in the pair has the largest absolute value of c.

The mean moving range can, therefore, be written

$$\bar{R} = \frac{1}{n-1}[c_2k + \{(c_2k + c_3k) \text{ or } \langle\max(|c_2|,|c_3|) - \min(|c_2|,|c_3|)\rangle\} \quad (A.15)$$

$$+ \{(c_3k + c_4k \text{ or } \langle\max(|c_3|,|c_4|) - \min(|c_3|,|c_4|)\rangle\} + \cdots$$

$$+ \{(c_{n-2} + c_{n-1}) \text{ or } \langle\max(|c_{n-2}|,|c_{n-1}|) - \min(|c_{n-2}|,|c_{n-1}|)\rangle\} + c_{n-1}k]$$

where in any particular instance the specific term that will be in the brackets $\{\ \}$, that is, either $\{(c_ik + c_{i+1}k)\}$ or $\{\langle\max(|c_i|,|c_{i+1}|) - \min(|c_i|,|c_{i+1}|)\rangle\}$, in the sum in Equation A.15 depends upon whether the data points y_i and y_{i+1} are on opposite sides of, or on the same side of, the trend line.

The sum in the numerator of Equation A.15 will be a maximum when all of the data points between y_1 and y_n are (1) on alternating sides of the trend line, and (2) equidistant from the trend line—that is, they all fall k units from the trend line. Under these circumstances, the mean moving range will be

$$\bar{R} = \frac{2(n-2)k}{n-1} \quad (A.16)$$

and the maximum value of one sigma unit will be

$$\sigma = \left(\frac{2.66}{3}\right)\bar{R} = \left(\frac{2.66}{3}\right)\frac{2(n-2)k}{n-1} = \frac{1.77(n-2)k}{n-1} \quad (A.17)$$

The minimum value of the mean moving range will occur when all of the data points between y_1 and y_n are (1) on the same side of and equidistant from (i.e., k units from) the trend line, or (2) only one data point falls off of the trend line, and it is k units away. Under these circumstances, the mean moving range will be

$$\bar{R} = \frac{2k}{n-1} \quad (A.18)$$

and the minimum value of one sigma unit will be

$$\sigma = \left(\frac{2.66}{3}\right)\left(\frac{2k}{n-1}\right) = [\frac{1.77}{n-1}]k \quad (A.19)$$

Thus, all values of one sigma unit will fall between

$$\sigma = \frac{1.77(n-2)}{n-1}k \quad (A.20)$$

and

$$\sigma = \frac{1.77}{n-1}k \quad (A.21)$$

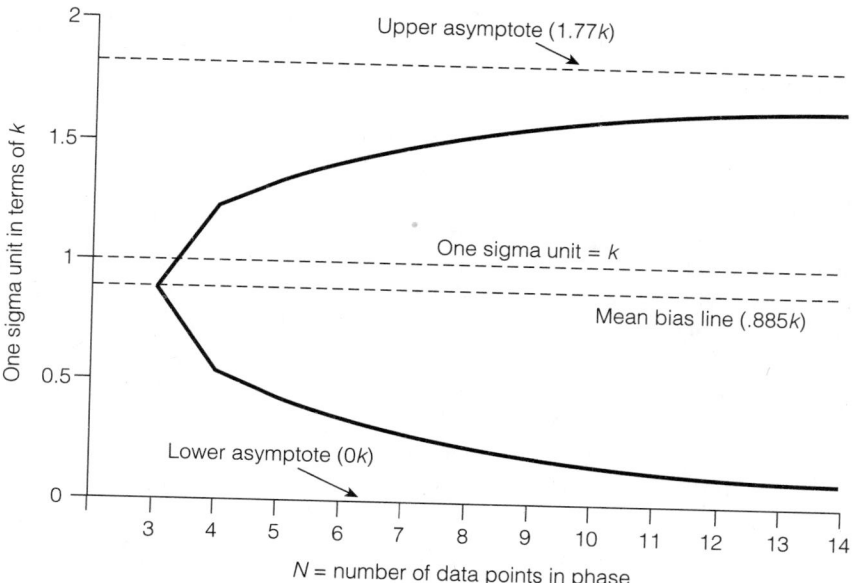

FIGURE A.3 Bias in use of *k* (distance between trend arrow and data point farthest from trend arrow) as an estimate of one sigma unit for *n* = 3 to *n* = 14 phase data points.

The graph in Figure A.3 shows the bias in the use of *k* as an estimate of one sigma unit for phase lengths of $n \geq 3$; that is, from $n = 3$ to $n \to \infty$ phase measures. The upper asymptote of the curve in Figure A.3 is 1.77, since

$$\lim_{n \to \infty} \left[\frac{1.77(n-2)}{n-1}\right] = 1.77$$

and the lower asymptote will be 0, since

$$\lim_{n \to \infty} \left[\frac{1.77}{n-1}\right] = 0$$

On the horizontal axis in Figure A.3 is the number of data points in a phase, while the value of one sigma unit in terms of *k* is shown on the vertical axis. The dashed horizontal line at $\sigma = 1k$ is the "no bias" line; it is the line indicating that *k* is an exact estimate of one sigma unit. The region beneath the dashed horizontal line indicates that *k* overestimates one sigma unit, while the region above the dashed line indicates that *k* underestimates one sigma unit.

The centroid of the region encompassed by the curves in Figure A.3 can be calculated using procedures described by Swokowski (1988). The vertical axis component of the centroid of the region shown in Figure A.3, which will give the mean one sigma unit estimate over all possible estimates of one sigma unit, is given by

$$\overline{\sigma}_{est} = \frac{M_n}{A}k = \frac{\iint_R \sigma_{est}\, dA}{\iint_R 1\, dA}k \qquad (A.22)$$

(Swokowski, 1988), where M_n is the "moment" of the region in Figure A.3 about the horizontal (i.e., the n) axis, A is the area enclosed by the curves in Figure A.3, and $\overline{\sigma}_{est}$ is the vertical axis component (i.e., the mean estimate of one sigma unit over all possible estimates) of the centroid of the region in Figure A.3. Following Swokowski (1988), the "moment" M_n will be

$$M_n = \int_3^\infty \int_{\frac{1.77}{n-1}}^{\frac{1.77(n-2)}{n-1}} \sigma_{est}\, d\sigma_{est} dn = \int_3^\infty [\tfrac{1}{2}\sigma_{est}^2]_{\frac{1.77}{n-1}}^{\frac{1.77(n-2)}{n-1}}\, dn \qquad (A.23)$$

$$= \frac{1}{2}\int_3^\infty [\frac{1.77^2\,(n-2)^2}{(n-1)^2} - \frac{1.77^2}{(n-1)^2}]dn = \frac{1.77^2}{2}\int_3^\infty [\frac{(n-2)^2}{(n-1)^2} - \frac{1}{(n-1)^2}]dn$$

$$= \frac{1.77^2}{2}\int_3^\infty [\frac{(n-2)^2 - 1}{(n-1)^2}]dn = \frac{1.77^2}{2}\int_3^\infty [\frac{(n^2 - 4n + 4) - 1}{(n-1)^2}]dn$$

$$= \frac{1.77^2}{2}\int_3^\infty [\frac{n^2 - 4n + 4 - 1}{(n-1)^2}]dn = \frac{1.77^2}{2}\int_3^\infty [\frac{n^2 - 4n + 3}{(n-1)^2}]dn$$

$$= \frac{1.77^2}{2}\int_3^\infty [\frac{(n-3)(n-1)}{(n-1)(n-1)}]dn = \frac{1.77^2}{2}\int_3^\infty \frac{n-3}{n-1}dn$$

The area encompassed by the curves in Figure A.3 will be

$$A = \int_3^\infty \int_{\frac{1.77}{n-1}}^{\frac{1.77(n-2)}{n-1}} 1\, d\sigma_{est}\, dn = \int_3^\infty [\frac{1.77(n-2)}{(n-1)} - \frac{1.77}{(n-1)}]dn \qquad (A.24)$$

$$= 1.77\int_3^\infty [\frac{(n-2)}{(n-1)} - \frac{1}{(n-1)}]dn = 1.77\int_3^\infty [\frac{(n-2) - 1}{(n-1)}]dn$$

$$= 1.77\int_3^\infty [\frac{n-2-1}{n-1}]dn = 1.77\int_3^\infty \frac{n-3}{n-1}dn$$

(Swokowski, 1988). Thus, the mean estimate of one sigma unit over all possible estimates will be

$$\overline{\sigma}_{est} = \frac{M_n}{A}k = \frac{\frac{1.77^2}{2}\int_3^\infty \frac{n-3}{n-1}dn}{1.77\int_3^\infty \frac{n-3}{n-1}dn}k = \frac{1.77^2}{2(1.77)}k = \frac{1.77}{2}k = .885k \qquad (A.25)$$

This means that if we were to compute the mean estimated value of one sigma unit, using the distance of the data point farthest from the phase trend line as the estimate of one sigma unit, over all possible values of $\bar{z}$ (i.e., over all values between 0 and 1) and over all possible numbers of phase measures greater than or equal to 3 (i.e., $n \geq 3$), the value we would obtain is $.885k$. This means that, on the average, the use of k as an estimate of one sigma unit will result in an overestimate of sigma by about 13 percent. These results suggest that the use of k, the distance between the trend line and the data point farthest from it, as a general rule for estimating one sigma unit, and for representing the region of background variability, will on average be conservative and is certainly reasonable.

THE EFFECTS OF AUTOCORRELATION

The presence of autocorrelation in time-series data can bias estimates of variability. Autocorrelation exists when successive data points y_i and y_{i+1} are correlated. If the autocorrelation is positive, then formulas for estimating variability underestimate the actual variability; if the autocorrelation is negative, then formulas for estimating variability overestimate the actual variability (Gottman, 1981). For example, if the lag-1 autocorrelation in a time series is positive, then the one sigma bands created using statistical process control procedures must be expanded by an approximate factor of

$$\frac{1}{\sqrt{1 - r_1^2}}$$

where r_1 is the sample lag-1 autocorrelation (Wheeler, 1995). Wheeler (1995) has argued that this bias does not become substantial until $r_1 \geq .70$, and that when the autocorrelation reaches a positive value this large, then the graphed data will show a very coherent pattern. In the context of the scatter of data points about a trend line, a large positive autocorrelation will usually be associated with a data pattern in which all, or nearly all, data points are on the same side of the trend line. As discussed earlier, such a pattern may well suggest the presence of a nonlinear trend; and if a nonlinear trend is modeled using the procedures described earlier, then the autocorrelation that is due to the nonlinear trend will, in essence, be subtracted out (Gottman, 1981).

Even if the positive autocorrelation due to a systematic pattern of data points about a trend line is not subtracted out by representing nonlinear trend, the biasing effects of autocorrelation on the use of the data point farthest from the trend line as an estimate of one sigma unit will work *opposite* to the overestimation/underestimation patterns represented immediately above in Figure A.3. The autocorrelation in the pattern of data points relative to a trend line will most often be at a maximum positive value when all (or most all) of the data points are on the same side of the trend line. As can be seen in the lower curve in Figure A.3, when all of the data points are on the same side of the trend line, the use of the data point farthest from the trend line as an estimate of one sigma unit will result in an *overestimate* of the actual value of one sigma unit. The presence of positive autocorrelation will lead to an *underestimate* of one sigma unit using the usual formulas for estimating sigma (Wheeler, 1995). Thus, the two procedures counteract one another.

For example, suppose that there are 14 data points in a phase, and that the values of the data points relative to the weighted mean trend line are 0, 1, 3, 5, 4, 6, 7, 6, 4, 5, 3, 1, and 0. The values of the data points at the ends of the phase, relative to the trend line, are 0 because they lie on the trend line. The autocorrelation between these data points is $+.72$, and one sigma unit will be equal to about $.20k$. However, taking autocorrelation into account gives an adjusted estimate of one sigma unit as

$$\frac{.20k}{\sqrt{1 - .72^2}} = .29k \qquad\qquad (A.26)$$

Thus, the presence of positive autocorrelation has improved the estimate of one sigma unit by reducing the overestimate.

A similar line of argument can be made for negative autocorrelation. A large negative autocorrelation will occur when the data point pairs all fall on opposite sides of the trend line (Gottman, 1981). As can be seen in the upper curve in Figure A.3, when this occurs, the use of the data point farthest from the trend line as an estimate of one sigma unit results in an underestimate. Thus, the presence of large negative autocorrelation will reduce this underestimate since, in the presence of negative autocorrelation, the formulas for variability (such as the formula for $\overline{R}$) result in an overestimate of the actual variability. Once again, the biasing effect of autocorrelation works in an opposite direction to the overestimation/underestimation pattern in the use of the data point farthest from the trend line as an estimate of one sigma unit. Once again, the results of this analysis suggest that the use of k, the distance between the trend line and the data point farthest from it, as a general rule for estimating one sigma unit, and for representing the region of background variability, is certainly reasonable.

Appendix B
Sample Copies of
the CASS Scales

GENERALIZED CONTENTMENT SCALE (GCS)

Name: _____   Today's Date: _____

This questionnaire is designed to measure the way you feel about your life and surroundings. It is not a test, so there are no right or wrong answers. Answer each item as carefully and as accurately as you can by placing a number beside each one as follows.

    1 = None of the time
    2 = Very rarely
    3 = A little of the time
    4 = Some of the time
    5 = A good part of the time
    6 = Most of the time
    7 = All of the time

1. ____ I feel powerless to do anything about my life.
2. ____ I feel blue.
3. ____ I think about ending my life.
4. ____ I have crying spells.
5. ____ It is easy for me to enjoy myself.
6. ____ I have a hard time getting started on things that I need to do.
7. ____ I get very depressed.
8. ____ I feel there is always someone I can depend on when things get tough.
9. ____ I feel that the future looks bright for me.
10. ____ I feel downhearted.
11. ____ I feel that I am needed.
12. ____ I feel that I am appreciated by others.
13. ____ I enjoy being active and busy.
14. ____ I feel that others would be better off without me.
15. ____ I enjoy being with other people.
16. ____ I feel that it is easy for me to make decisions.
17. ____ I feel downtrodden.
18. ____ I feel terribly lonely.
19. ____ I get upset easily.
20. ____ I feel that nobody really cares about me.
21. ____ I have a full life.
22. ____ I feel that people really care about me.
23. ____ I have a great deal of fun.
24. ____ I feel great in the morning.
25. ____ I feel that my situation is hopeless.

5, 8, 9, 11, 12, 13, 15, 16, 21, 22, 23, 24.

CLINICAL ANXIETY SCALE (CAS)

Name: _____ Today's Date: _____

This questionnaire is designed to measure how much anxiety you are currently feeling. It is not a test, so there are no right or wrong answers. Answer each item as carefully and as accurately as you can by

1 Rarely or none of the time
2 A little of the time
3 Some of the time
4 A good part of the time
5 Most or all of the time

1. ____ I feel calm.
2. ____ I feel tense.
3. ____ I feel suddenly scared for no reason.
4. ____ I feel nervous.
5. ____ I use tranquilizers or antidepressants to cope with my anxiety.
6. ____ I feel confident about the future.
7. ____ I am free from senseless or unpleasant thoughts.
8. ____ I feel afraid to go out of my house alone.
9. ____ I feel relaxed and in control of myself.
10. ____ I have spells of terror or panic.
11. ____ I feel afraid in open spaces or in the streets.
12. ____ I feel afraid I will faint in public.
13. ____ I am comfortable traveling on buses, subways or trains.
14. ____ I feel nervousness or shakiness inside.
15. ____ I feel comfortable in crowds, such as shopping or at a movie.
16. ____ I feel comfortable when I am left alone.
17. ____ I feel afraid without good reason.
18. ____ Due to my fears, I unreasonably avoid certain animals, objects or situations.
19. ____ I get upset easily or feel panicky unexpectedly.
20. ____ My hands, arms or legs shake or tremble.
21. ____ Due to my fears, I avoid social situations, whenever possible.
22. ____ I experience sudden attacks of panic which catch me by surprise.
23. ____ I feel generally anxious.
24. ____ I am bothered by dizzy spells.
25. ____ Due to my fears, I avoid being alone, whenever possible.

1, 6, 7, 9, 13, 15, 16.

INDEX OF ALCOHOL INVOLVEMENT (IAI)

Name: _____

Today's Date: _____

This questionnaire is designed to measure your use of alcohol. It is not a test so there are no right or wrong answers. Answer each item as carefully and as accurately as you can by placing a number beside each one as follows.

    1 = None of the time
    2 = Very rarely
    3 = A little of the time
    4 = Some of the time
    5 = A good part of the time
    6 = Most of the time
    7 = All of the time

1. ____ When I have a drink with friends, I usually drink more than they do.
2. ____ My family or friends tell me I drink too much.
3. ____ I feel that I drink too much alcohol.
4. ____ After I've had one or two drinks, it is difficult for me to stop drinking.
5. ____ When I am drinking, I have three or fewer drinks.
6. ____ I feel guilty about what happened when I have been drinking.
7. ____ When I go drinking, I get into fights.
8. ____ My drinking causes problems with my family or friends.
9. ____ My drinking causes problems with my work.
10. ____ After I have been drinking, I cannot remember things that happened when I think about them the next day.
11. ____ After I have been drinking, I get the shakes.
12. ____ My friends think I have a drinking problem.
13. ____ I drink to calm my nerves or make me feel better.
14. ____ I drink when I am alone.
15. ____ I drink until I go to sleep or pass out.
16. ____ My drinking interferes with obligations to my family or friends.
17. ____ I have one or more drinks when things are not going well for me.
18. ____ It is hard for me to stop drinking when I want to.
19. ____ I have one or more drinks before noon.
20. ____ My friends think my level of drinking is acceptable.
21. ____ I get mean and angry when I drink.
22. ____ My friends avoid me when I am drinking.
23. ____ I avoid drinking to excess.
24. ____ My personal life gets very troublesome when I drink.
25. ____ I drink 3 to 4 times a week.

5, 20, 23.

INDEX OF CLINICAL STRESS (ICS)

Name: _____   Today's Date: _____

This questionnaire is designed to measure the way you feel about the amount of personal stress that you experience. It is not a test, so there are no right or wrong answers. Answer each item as carefully and as accurately as you can by placing a number beside each one as follows.

1 = None of the time
2 = Very rarely
3 = A little of the time
4 = Some of the time
5 = A good part of the time
6 = Most of the time
7 = All of the time

1. ____ I feel extremely tense.
2. ____ I feel very jittery.
3. ____ I feel like I want to scream.
4. ____ I feel overwhelmed.
5. ____ I feel very relaxed.
6. ____ I feel so anxious I want to cry.
7. ____ I feel so stressed that I'd like to hit something.
8. ____ I feel very calm and peaceful.
9. ____ I feel like I am stretched to the breaking point.
10. ____ It is very hard for me to relax.
11. ____ It is very easy for me to fall asleep at night.
12. ____ I feel an enormous sense of pressure on me.
13. ____ I feel like my life is going very smoothly.
14. ____ I feel very panicked.
15. ____ I feel like I am on the verge of a total collapse.
16. ____ I feel that I am losing control of my life.
17. ____ I feel that I am near a breaking point.
18. ____ I feel wound up like a coiled spring.
19. ____ I feel that I can't keep up with all the demands on me.
20. ____ I feel very much behind in my work.
21. ____ I feel tense and angry with those around me.
22. ____ I feel I must race from one task to the next.
23. ____ I feel that I just can't keep up with everything.
24. ____ I feel as tight as a drum.
25. ____ I feel very much on edge.

5, 8, 11, 13.

INDEX OF DRUG INVOLVEMENT (IDI)

Name: _____   Today's Date: _____

This questionnaire is designed to measure your use of drugs. It is not a test so there are no right or wrong answers. Answer each item as carefully and as accurately as you can by placing a number beside each one as follows:

1 = None of the time
2 = Very rarely
3 = A little of the time
4 = Some of the time
5 = A good part of the time
6 = Most of the time
7 = All of the time

1. _____ When I do drugs with friends, I usually have more than they do.
2. _____ My family or friends tell me I take too many or too much drugs.
3. _____ I feel that I use too much drugs.
4. _____ After I've begun using drugs, it is difficult for me to stop.
5. _____ I do not use drugs.
6. _____ I feel guilty about my use of drugs.
7. _____ When I do drugs, I get into fights.
8. _____ My drug use causes problems with my family or friends.
9. _____ My drug use causes problems with my work.
10. _____ After I have been using drugs, I cannot remember things that happened.
11. _____ After I have been using drugs, I get the shakes.
12. _____ My friends think I have a drug problem.
13. _____ I do drugs to calm my nerves or make me feel better.
14. _____ I do drugs when I am alone.
15. _____ I do drugs so much that I pass out.
16. _____ My drug use interferes with obligations to my family or friends.
17. _____ I do drugs when things are not going well for me.
18. _____ I can stop using drugs whenever I want to.
19. _____ I do drugs before noon.
20. _____ My friends think my level of drug use is acceptable.
21. _____ I get mean and angry when I do drugs.
22. _____ My friends avoid me when I am using drugs.
23. _____ I avoid excessive use of drugs.
24. _____ My personal life gets very troublesome when I do drugs.
25. _____ I use drugs several times a week.

INDEX OF ATTITUDES TOWARD HOMOSEXUALS (IAH)

Name: _____ Today's Date: _____

This questionnaire is designed to measure the way you feel about working or associating with homosexuals. It is not a test, so there are no right or wrong answers. Answer each item as carefully and as accurately as you can by placing a number beside each one as follows.

       1 = Strongly agree
       2 = Agree
       3 = Neither agree nor disagree
       4 = Disagree
       5 = Strongly disagree

1. ____ I would feel comfortable working closely with a male homosexual.
2. ____ I would enjoy attending social functions at which homosexuals were present.
3. ____ I would feel uncomfortable if I learned that my neighbor was homosexual.
4. ____ If a member of my sex made a sexual advance toward me I would feel angry.
5. ____ I would feel comfortable knowing that I was attractive to members of my sex.
6. ____ I would feel uncomfortable being seen in a gay bar.
7. ____ I would feel comfortable if a member of my sex made an advance toward me.
8. ____ I would be comfortable if I found myself attracted to a member of my sex.
9. ____ I would feel disappointed if I learned that my child was homosexual.
10. ____ I would feel nervous being in a group of homosexuals.
11. ____ I would feel comfortable knowing that my clergyman was homosexual.
12. ____ I would be upset if I learned that my brother or sister was homosexual.
13. ____ I would feel that I had failed as a parent if I learned that my child was gay.
14. ____ If I saw two men holding hands in public I would feel disgusted.
15. ____ If a member of my sex made an advance toward me I would be offended.
16. ____ I would feel comfortable if I learned that my daughter's teacher was a lesbian.
17. ____ I would feel uncomfortable if I learned that my spouse or partner was attracted to members of his or her sex.
18. ____ I would feel at ease talking with a homosexual person at a party.
19. ____ I would feel uncomfortable if I learned that my boss was homosexual.
20. ____ It would not bother me to walk through a predominantly gay section of town.
21. ____ It would disturb me to find out that my doctor was homosexual.
22. ____ I would feel comfortable if I learned that my best friend of my sex was homosexual.
23. ____ If a member of my sex made an advance toward me I would feel flattered.
24. ____ I would feel uncomfortable knowing that my son's male teacher was homosexual.
25. ____ I would feel comfortable working closely with a female homosexual.

3, 4, 6, 9, 10, 12, 13, 14, 15, 17, 19, 21, 24.

INDEX OF PEER RELATIONS (IPR)

Name: _____   Today's Date: _____

Peer Group: _____

This questionnaire is designed to measure the way you feel about the people you work, play, or associate with most of the time; your peer group. It is not a test, so there are no right or wrong answers. Place the name of your peer group at the top of the page in the space provided. Then answer each item as carefully and as accurately as you can by placing a number beside each one as follows.

    1 = None of the time
    2 = Very rarely
    3 = A little of the time
    4 = Some of the time
    5 = A good part of the time
    6 = Most of the time
    7 = All of the time

1. ____ I get along very well with my peers.
2. ____ My peers act like they don't care about me.
3. ____ My peers treat me badly.
4. ____ My peers really seem to respect me.
5. ____ I don't feel like am "part of the group".
6. ____ My peers are a bunch of snobs.
7. ____ My peers understand me.
8. ____ My peers seem to like me very much.
9. ____ I really feel "left out" of my peer group.
10. ____ I hate my present peer group.
11. ____ My peers seem to like having me around.
12. ____ I really like my present peer group.
13. ____ I really feel like I am disliked by my peers.
14. ____ I wish I had a different peer group.
15. ____ My peers are very nice to me.
16. ____ My peers seem to look up to me.
17. ____ My peers think I am important to them.
18. ____ My peers are a real source of pleasure to me.
19. ____ My peers don't seem to even notice me.
20. ____ I wish I were not part of this peer group.
21. ____ My peers regard my ideas and opinions very highly.
22. ____ I feel like I am an important member of my peer group.
23. ____ I can't stand to be around my peer group.
24. ____ My peers seem to look down on me.
25. ____ My peers really do not interest me.

1, 4, 7, 8, 11, 12, 15, 16, 17, 18, 21, 22.

INDEX OF SELF-ESTEEM (ISE)

Name: _____ Today's Date: _____

Context: _____

This questionnaire is designed to measure how you see yourself. It is not a test, so there are no right or wrong answers. Please answer each item as carefully and as accurately as you can by placing a number beside each one as follows.

        1 = None of the time
        2 = Very rarely
        3 = A little of the time
        4 = Some of the time
        5 = A good part of the time
        6 = Most of the time
        7 = All of the time

1. ____ I feel that people would not like me if they really knew me well.
2. ____ I feel that others get along much better than I do.
3. ____ I feel that I am a beautiful person.
4. ____ When I am with others I feel they are glad I am with them.
5. ____ I feel that people really like to talk with me.
6. ____ I feel that I am a very competent person.
7. ____ I think I make a good impression on others.
8. ____ I feel that I need more self-confidence.
9. ____ When I am with strangers I am very nervous.
10. ____ I think that I am a dull person.
11. ____ I feel ugly.
12. ____ I feel that others have more fun than I do.
13. ____ I feel that I bore people.
14. ____ I think my friends find me interesting.
15. ____ I think I have a good sense of humor.
16. ____ I feel very self-conscious when I am with strangers.
17. ____ I feel that if I could be more like other people I would have it made.
18. ____ I feel that people have a good time when they are with me.
19. ____ I feel like a wallflower when I go out.
20. ____ I feel I get pushed around more than others.
21. ____ I think I am a rather nice person.
22. ____ I feel that people really like me very much.
23. ____ I feel that I am a likeable person.
24. ____ I am afraid I will appear foolish to others.
25. ____ My friends think very highly of me.

3, 4, 5, 6, 7, 14, 15, 18, 21, 22, 23, 25.

SEXUAL ATTITUDE SCALE (SAS)

Name: _____ Today's Date: _____

This questionnaire is designed to measure the way you feel about sexual behavior. It is not a test, so there are no right or wrong answers. Answer each item as carefully and as accurately as you can by placing a number beside each one as follows.

1 = Strongly disagree
2 = Disagree
3 = Neither agree nor disagree
4 = Agree
5 = Strongly agree

1. ____ I think there is too much sexual freedom given to adults these days.
2. ____ I think that increased sexual freedom undermines the American family.
3. ____ I think that young people have been given too much information about sex.
4. ____ Sex education should be restricted to the home.
5. ____ Older people do not need to have sex.
6. ____ Sex education should be given only when people are ready for marriage.
7. ____ Pre-marital sex may be a sign of a decaying social order.
8. ____ Extra-marital sex is never excusable.
9. ____ I think there is too much sexual freedom given to teenagers these days.
10. ____ I think there is not enough sexual restraint among young people.
11. ____ I think people indulge in sex too much.
12. ____ I think the only proper way to have sex is through intercourse.
13. ____ I think sex should be reserved for marriage.
14. ____ Sex should be only for the young.
15. ____ Too much social approval has been given to homosexuals.
16. ____ Sex should be devoted to the business of procreation.
17. ____ People should not masturbate.
18. ____ Heavy sexual petting should be discouraged.
19. ____ People should not discuss their sexual affairs or business with others.
20. ____ Severely handicapped (physically and mentally) people should not have sex.
21. ____ There should be no laws prohibiting sexual acts between consenting adults.
22. ____ What two consenting adults do together sexually is their own business.
23. ____ There is too much sex on television.
24. ____ Movies today are too sexually explicit.
25. ____ Pornography should be totally banned from our bookstores.

21, 22.

INDEX OF MARITAL SATISFACTION (IMS)

Name: _____ Today's Date: _____

This questionnaire is designed to measure the degree of satisfaction you have with your present marriage. It is not a test, so there are no right or wrong answers. Answer each item as carefully and as accurately as you can by placing a number beside each one as follows.

1 = None of the time
2 = Very rarely
3 = A little of the time
4 = Some of the time
5 = A good part of the time
6 = Most of the time
7 = All of the time

1. ____ My partner is affectionate enough.
2. ____ My partner treats me badly.
3. ____ My partner really cares for me.
4. ____ I feel that I would not choose the same partner if I had it to do over again.
5. ____ I feel that I can trust my partner.
6. ____ I feel that our relationship is breaking up.
7. ____ My partner really doesn't understand me.
8. ____ I feel that our relationship is a good one.
9. ____ Ours is a very happy relationship.
10. ____ Our life together is dull.
11. ____ We have a lot of fun together.
12. ____ My partner does not confide in me.
13. ____ Ours is a very close relationship.
14. ____ I feel that I cannot rely on my partner.
15. ____ I feel that we do not have enough interests in common.
16. ____ We manage arguments and disagreements very well.
17. ____ We do a good job of managing our finances.
18. ____ I feel that I should never have married my partner.
19. ____ My partner and I get along very well together.
20. ____ Our relationship is very stable.
21. ____ My partner is a real comfort to me.
22. ____ I feel that I no longer care for my partner.
23. ____ I feel that the future looks bright for our relationship.
24. ____ I feel that our relationship is empty.
25. ____ I feel there is no excitement in our relationship.

1, 3, 5, 8, 9, 11, 13, 16, 17, 19, 20, 21, 23.

INDEX OF SEXUAL SATISFACTION (ISS)

Name: _____ Today's Date: _____

This questionnaire is designed to measure the degree of satisfaction you have in the sexual relationship with your partner. It is not a test, so there are no right or wrong answers. Answer each item as carefully and as accurately as you can by placing a number beside each one as follows.

1 = None of the time
2 = Very rarely
3 = A little of the time
4 = Some of the time
5 = A good part of the time
6 = Most of the time
7 = All of the time

1. ____ I feel that my partner enjoys our sex life.
2. ____ Our sex life is very exciting.
3. ____ Sex is fun for my partner and me.
4. ____ Sex with my partner has become a chore for me.
5. ____ I feel that our sex is dirty and disgusting.
6. ____ Our sex life is monotonous.
7. ____ When we have sex it is too rushed and hurriedly completed.
8. ____ I feel that my sex life is lacking in quality.
9. ____ My partner is sexually very exciting.
10. ____ I enjoy the sex techniques that my partner likes or uses.
11. ____ I feel that my partner wants too much sex from me.
12. ____ I think that our sex is wonderful.
13. ____ My partner dwells on sex too much.
14. ____ I try to avoid sexual contact with my partner.
15. ____ My partner is too rough or brutal when we have sex.
16. ____ My partner is a wonderful sex mate.
17. ____ I feel that sex is a normal function of our relationship.
18. ____ My partner does not want sex when I do.
19. ____ I feel that our sex life really adds a lot to our relationship.
20. ____ My partner seems to avoid sexual contact with me.
21. ____ It is easy for me to get sexually excited by my partner.
22. ____ I feel that my partner is sexually pleased with me.
23. ____ My partner is very sensitive to my sexual needs and desires.
24. ____ My partner does not satisfy me sexually.
25. ____ I feel that my sex life is boring.

1, 2, 3, 9, 10, 12, 16, 17, 19, 21, 22, 23.

 **NON-PHYSICAL ABUSE OF PARTNER SCALE (NPAPS)**

Name: _____ Today's Date: _____

This questionnaire is designed to measure the non-physical abuse you have delivered upon your partner. It is not a test, so there are no right or wrong answers. Answer each item as carefully and as accurately as you can by placing a number beside each one as follows.

1 = Never
2 = Very rarely
3 = A little of the time
4 = Some of the time
5 = A good part of the time
6 = Very frequently
7 = All of the time

1. _____ I make fun of my partner's ability to do things.
2. _____ I expect my partner to obey.
3. _____ I become very upset and angry if my partner says that I have been drinking too much.
4. _____ I demand my partner to perform sex acts that he or she does not enjoy or like.
5. _____ I become very upset if my partner's work is not done when I think it should be.
6. _____ I don't want my partner to have any male friends.
7. _____ I tell my partner he or she is ugly and unattractive.
8. _____ I tell my partner that he or she really couldn't manage without me.
9. _____ I expect my partner to hop to it when I give him or her an order.
10. _____ I insult or shame my partner in front of others.
11. _____ I become angry if my partner disagrees with my point of view.
12. _____ I carefully control the money I give my partner.
13. _____ I tell my partner that he or she is dumb or stupid.
14. _____ I demand that my partner stay home.
15. _____ I don't want my partner to work or go to school.
16. _____ I don't want my partner socializing with his or her female friends.
17. _____ I demand sex whether my partner wants it or not.
18. _____ I scream and yell at my partner.
19. _____ I shout and scream at my partner when I'm drinking.
20. _____ I order my partner around.
21. _____ I have no respect for my partner's feelings.
22. _____ I act like a bully towards my partner.
23. _____ I frighten my partner.
24. _____ I treat my partner like he or she is a dimwit.
25. _____ I'm rude to my partner.

PARTNER ABUSE SCALE: Non-physical (PASNP)

Name: _____ Today's Date: _____

This questionnaire is designed to measure the non-physical abuse you have experienced in your relationship with your partner. It is not a test, so there are no right or wrong answers. Answer each item as carefully and as accurately as you can by placing a number beside each one as follows:

      1 = None of the time
      2 = Very rarely
      3 = A little of the time
      4 = Some of the time
      5 = A good part of the time
      6 = Most of the time
      7 = All of the time

1. _____ My partner belittles me.
2. _____ My partner demands obedience to his or her whims.
3. _____ My partner becomes surly and angry if I say he or she is drinking too much.
4. _____ My partner demands that I perform sex acts that I do not enjoy or like.
5. _____ My partner becomes very upset if my work is not done when he or she thinks it should be.
6. _____ My partner does not want me to have any male friends.
7. _____ My partner tells me I am ugly and unattractive.
8. _____ My partner tells me I couldn't manage or take care of myself without him or her.
9. _____ My partner acts like I am his or her personal servant.
10. _____ My partner insults or shames me in front of others.
11. _____ My partner becomes very angry if I disagree with his or her point of view.
12. _____ My partner is stingy in giving me money.
13. _____ My partner belittles me intellectually.
14. _____ My partner demands that I stay home.
15. _____ My partner feels that I should not work or go to school.
16. _____ My partner does not want me to socialize with my female friends.
17. _____ My partner demands sex whether I want it or not.
18. _____ My partner screams and yells at me.
19. _____ My partner shouts and screams at me when he or she drinks.
20. _____ My partner orders me around.
21. _____ My partner has no respect for my feelings.
22. _____ My partner acts like a bully towards me.
23. _____ My partner frightens me.
24. _____ My partner treats me like a dunce.
25. _____ My partner is surly and rude to me.

PARTNER ABUSE SCALE: Physical (PASPH)

Name: _____   Today's Date: _____

This questionnaire is designed to measure the physical abuse you have experienced in your relationship with your partner. It is not a test, so there are no right or wrong answers. Answer each item as carefully and as accurately as you can by placing a number beside each one as follows:

1 = None of the time
2 = Very rarely
3 = A little of the time
4 = Some of the time
5 = A good part of the time
6 = Most of the time
7 = All of the time

1. _____ My partner physically forces me to have sex.
2. _____ My partner pushes and shoves me around violently.
3. _____ My partner hits and punches my arms and body.
4. _____ My partner threatens me with a weapon.
5. _____ My partner beats me so hard I must seek medical help.
6. _____ My partner slaps me around my face and head.
7. _____ My partner beats me when he or she drinks.
8. _____ My partner makes me afraid for my life.
9. _____ My partner physically throws me around the room.
10. _____ My partner hits and punches my face and head.
11. _____ My partner beats me in the face so badly that I am ashamed to be seen in public.
12. _____ My partner acts like he or she would like to kill me.
13. _____ My partner threatens to cut or stab me with a knife or other sharp object.
14. _____ My partner tries to choke or strangle me.
15. _____ My partner knocks me down and then kicks or stomps me.
16. _____ My partner twists my fingers, arms or legs.
17. _____ My partner throws dangerous objects at me.
18. _____ My partner bites or scratches me so badly that I bleed or have bruises.
19. _____ My partner violently pinches or twists my skin.
20. _____ My partner badly hurts me while we are having sex.
21. _____ My partner injures my breasts or genitals.
22. _____ My partner tries to suffocate me with pillows, towels, or other objects.
23. _____ My partner pokes or jabs me with pointed objects.
24. _____ My partner has broken one or more my bones.
25. _____ My partner kicks my face and head.

PHYSICAL ABUSE OF PARTNER SCALE (PAPS)

Name: _____ Today's Date: _____

This questionnaire is designed to measure the physical abuse you have delivered upon your partner. It is not a test, so there are no right or wrong answers. Answer each item as carefully and as accurately as you can by placing a number beside each one as follows.

1 = Never
2 = Very rarely
3 = A little of the time
4 = Some of the time
5 = A good part of the time
6 = Very frequently
7 = All of the time

1. _____ I physically force my partner to have sex.
2. _____ I push and shove my partner around violently.
3. _____ I hit and punch my partner's arms and body.
4. _____ I threaten my partner with a weapon.
5. _____ I beat my partner so hard he or she must seek medical help.
6. _____ I slap my partner me around his or her face and head.
7. _____ I beat my partner when I'm drinking.
8. _____ I make my partner afraid for his or her life.
9. _____ I physically throw my partner around the room.
10. _____ I hit and punch my partner's face and head.
11. _____ I beat my partner in the face so that he or she is ashamed to be seen in public.
12. _____ I act like I would like to kill my partner.
13. _____ I threaten to cut or stab my partner with a knife or other sharp object.
14. _____ I try to choke or strangle my partner.
15. _____ I knock my partner down and then kick or stomp him or her.
16. _____ I twist my partner's fingers, arms or legs.
17. _____ I throw dangerous objects at my partner.
18. _____ I bite or scratch my partner so badly that he or she bleeds or has bruises.
19. _____ I violently pinch or twist my partner's skin.
20. _____ I hurt my partner while we are having sex.
21. _____ I injure my partner's breasts or genitals.
22. _____ I try to suffocate my partner with pillows, towels, or other objects.
23. _____ I poke or jab my partner with pointed objects.
24. _____ I have broken one or more of my partner's bones.
25. _____ I kick my partner's face and head.

CHILD'S ATTITUDE TOWARD FATHER (CAF)

Name: _____ Today's Date: _____

This questionnaire is designed to measure the degree of contentment you have in your relationship with your father. It is not a test, so there are no right or wrong answers. Answer each item as carefully and as accurately as you can by placing a number beside each one as follows.

1 = None of the time
2 = Very rarely
3 = A little of the time
4 = Some of the time
5 = A good part of the time
6 = Most of the time
7 = All of the time

1. ____ My father gets on my nerves.
2. ____ I get along well with my father.
3. ____ I feel that I can really trust my father.
4. ____ I dislike my father.
5. ____ My father's behavior embarrasses me.
6. ____ My father is too demanding.
7. ____ I wish I had a different father.
8. ____ I really enjoy my father.
9. ____ My father puts too many limits on me.
10. ____ My father interferes with my activities.
11. ____ I resent my father.
12. ____ I think my father is terrific.
13. ____ I hate my father.
14. ____ My father is very patient with me.
15. ____ I really like my father.
16. ____ I like being with my father.
17. ____ I feel like I do not love my father.
18. ____ My father is very irritating.
19. ____ I feel very angry toward my father.
20. ____ I feel violent toward my father.
21. ____ I feel proud of my father.
22. ____ I wish my father was more like others I know.
23. ____ My father does not understand me.
24. ____ I can really depend on my father.
25. ____ I feel ashamed of my father.

2, 3, 8, 12, 14, 15, 16, 21, 24.

CHILD'S ATTITUDE TOWARD MOTHER (CAM)

Name: _____ Today's Date: _____

This questionnaire is designed to measure the degree of contentment you have in your relationship with your mother. It is not a test, so there are no right or wrong answers. Answer each item as carefully and as accurately as you can by placing a number beside each one as follows.

        1 = None of the time
        2 = Very rarely
        3 = A little of the time
        4 = Some of the time
        5 = A good part of the time
        6 = Most of the time
        7 = All of the time

1. ____ My mother gets on my nerves.
2. ____ I get along well with my mother.
3. ____ I feel that I can really trust my mother.
4. ____ I dislike my mother.
5. ____ My mother's behavior embarrasses me.
6. ____ My mother is too demanding.
7. ____ I wish I had a different mother.
8. ____ I really enjoy my mother.
9. ____ My mother puts too many limits on me.
10. ____ My mother interferes with my activities.
11. ____ I resent my mother.
12. ____ I think my mother is terrific.
13. ____ I hate my mother.
14. ____ My mother is very patient with me.
15. ____ I really like my mother.
16. ____ I like being with my mother.
17. ____ I feel like I do not love my mother.
18. ____ My mother is very irritating.
19. ____ I feel very angry toward my mother.
20. ____ I feel violent toward my mother.
21. ____ I feel proud of my mother.
22. ____ I wish my mother was more like others I know.
23. ____ My mother does not understand me.
24. ____ I can really depend on my mother.
25. ____ I feel ashamed of my mother.

INDEX OF BROTHER RELATIONS (IBR)

Name: _____   Today's Date: _____

Brother's Name: _____

This questionnaire is designed to measure the way you feel about your brother. It is not a test so there are no right or wrong answers. Answer each item as carefully and as accurately as you can by placing a number beside each one as follows.

1 = None of the time
2 = Very rarely
3 = A little of the time
4 = Some of the time
5 = A good part of the time
6 = Most of the time
7 = All of the time

1. _____ I get along very well with my brother.
2. _____ My brother acts like he doesn't care about me.
3. _____ My brother treats me badly.
4. _____ My brother really seems to respect me.
5. _____ I can really trust my brother.
6. _____ My brother seems to dislike me.
7. _____ My brother really understands me.
8. _____ My brother seems to like me very much.
9. _____ My brother and I get along well together.
10. _____ I hate my brother.
11. _____ My brother seems to like having me around.
12. _____ I really like my brother.
13. _____ I really feel that I am disliked by my brother.
14. _____ I wish I had a different brother.
15. _____ My brother is very nice to me.
16. _____ My brother seems to respect me.
17. _____ My brother thinks I am important to him.
18. _____ My brother is a real source of pleasure to me.
19. _____ My brother doesn't seem to even notice me.
20. _____ I wish my brother was dead.
21. _____ My brother regards my ideas and opinions very highly.
22. _____ My brother is a real "jerk".
23. _____ I can't stand to be around my brother.
24. _____ My brother seems to look down on me.
25. _____ I enjoy being with my brother.

1, 4, 5, 7, 8, 9, 11, 12, 15, 16, 17, 18, 21, 25.

INDEX OF FAMILY RELATIONS (IFR)

Name: _____ Today's Date: _____

This questionnaire is designed to measure the way you feel about your family as a whole. It is not a test, so there are no right or wrong answers. Answer each item as carefully and as accurately as you can by placing a number beside each one as follows.

1 = None of the time
2 = Very rarely
3 = A little of the time
4 = Some of the time
5 = A good part of the time
6 = Most of the time
7 = All of the time

1. ____ The members of my family really care about each other.
2. ____ I think my family is terrific.
3. ____ My family gets on my nerves.
4. ____ I really enjoy my family.
5. ____ I can really depend on my family.
6. ____ I really do not care to be around my family.
7. ____ I wish I was not part of this family.
8. ____ I get along well with my family.
9. ____ Members of my family argue too much.
10. ____ There is no sense of closeness in my family.
11. ____ I feel like a stranger in my family.
12. ____ My family does not understand me.
13. ____ There is too much hatred in my family.
14. ____ Members of my family are really good to one another.
15. ____ My family is well respected by those who know us.
16. ____ There seems to be a lot of friction in my family.
17. ____ There is a lot of love in my family.
18. ____ Member of my family get along well together.
19. ____ Life in my family is generally unpleasant.
20. ____ My family is a great joy to me.
21. ____ I feel proud of my family.
22. ____ Other families seem to get along better than ours.
23. ____ My family is a real source of comfort to me.
24. ____ I feel left out of my family.
25. ____ My family is an unhappy one.

1, 2, 4, 5, 8, 14, 15, 17, 18, 20, 21, 23.

INDEX OF PARENTAL ATTITUDES (IPA)

Name: _____ Today's Date: _____

Child's Name: _____

This questionnaire is designed to measure the degree of contentment you have in your relationship with your child. It is not a test, so there are no right or wrong answers. Answer each item as carefully and as accurately as you can by placing a number beside each one as follows.

1 = None of the time
2 = Very rarely
3 = A little of the time
4 = Some of the time
5 = A good part of the time
6 = Most of the time
7 = All of the time

1. ____ My child gets on my nerves.
2. ____ I get along well with my child.
3. ____ I feel that I can really trust my child.
4. ____ I dislike my child.
5. ____ My child is well behaved.
6. ____ My child is too demanding.
7. ____ I wish I did not have this child.
8. ____ I really enjoy my child.
9. ____ I have a hard time controlling my child.
10. ____ My child interferes with my activities.
11. ____ I resent my child.
12. ____ I think my child is terrific.
13. ____ I hate my child.
14. ____ I am very patient with my child.
15. ____ I really like my child.
16. ____ I like being with my child.
17. ____ I feel like I do not love my child.
18. ____ My child is irritating.
19. ____ I feel very angry toward my child.
20. ____ I feel violent toward my child.
21. ____ I feel very proud of my child.
22. ____ I wish my child was more like others I know.
23. ____ I just do not understand my child.
24. ____ My child is a real joy to me.
25. ____ I feel ashamed of my child.

2, 3, 5, 8, 12, 14, 15, 16, 21, 24.

INDEX OF SISTER RELATIONS (ISR)

Name: _____ Today's Date: _____

Sister's Name: _____

This questionnaire is designed to measure the way you feel about your sister. It is not a test so there are no right or wrong answers. Answer each item as carefully and as accurately as you can by placing a number beside each one as follows.

1 = None of the time
2 = Very rarely
3 = A little of the time
4 = Some of the time
5 = A good part of the time
6 = Most of the time
7 = All of the time

1. ____ I get along very well with my sister.
2. ____ My sister acts like she doesn't care about me.
3. ____ My sister treats me badly.
4. ____ My sister really seems to respect me.
5. ____ I can really trust my sister.
6. ____ My sister seems to dislike me.
7. ____ My sister really understands me.
8. ____ My sister seems to like me very much.
9. ____ My sister and I get along well together.
10. ____ I hate my sister.
11. ____ My sister seems to like having me around.
12. ____ I really like my sister.
13. ____ I really feel that I am disliked by my sister.
14. ____ I wish I had a different sister.
15. ____ My sister is very nice to me.
16. ____ My sister seems to respect me.
17. ____ My sister thinks I am important to her.
18. ____ My sister is a real source of pleasure to me.
19. ____ My sister doesn't seem to even notice me.
20. ____ I wish my sister was dead.
21. ____ My sister regards my ideas and opinions very highly.
22. ____ My sister is a real "jerk".
23. ____ I can't stand to be around my sister.
24. ____ My sister seems to look down on me.
25. ____ I enjoy being with my sister.

1, 4, 5, 7, 8, 9, 11, 12, 15, 16, 17, 18, 21, 25.

CLIENT SATISFACTION INVENTORY (CSI)

This questionnaire is designed to measure the way you feel about the services you have received. It is not a test, so there are no right or wrong answers. Answer each item as carefully and as accurately as you can by placing a number beside each one as follows.

1 = None of the time
2 = Very rarely
3 = A little of the time
4 = Some of the time
5 = A good part of the time
6 = Most of the time
7 = All of the time
X = Does not apply

1. _____ The services I get here are a big help to me.
2. _____ People here really seem to care about me.
3. _____ I would come back here if I need help again.
4. _____ I feel that no one here really listens to me.
5. _____ People here treat me like a person, not like a number.
6. _____ I have learned a lot here about how to deal with my problems.
7. _____ People here want to do things their way, instead of helping me find my way.
8. _____ I would recommend this place to people I care about.
9. _____ People here really know what they are doing.
10. _____ I get the kind of help here that I really need.
11. _____ People here accept me for who I am.
12. _____ I feel much better now than when I first came here.
13. _____ I thought no one could help me until I came here.
14. _____ The help I get here is really worth what it costs.
15. _____ People here put my needs ahead of their needs.
16. _____ People here put me down when I disagree with them.
17. _____ The biggest help I get here is learning how to help myself.
18. _____ People here are just trying to get rid of me.
19. _____ People who know me say this place has made a positive change in me.
20. _____ People here have shown me how to get help from other places.
21. _____ People here seem to understand how I feel.
22. _____ People here are only concerned about getting paid.
23. _____ I feel I can really talk to people here.
24. _____ The help I get here is better than I expected.
25. _____ I look forward to the sessions I have with people here.

INDEX OF JOB SATISFACTION (IJS)

Job Title/Description: _____

The IJS scale is designed to measure the way you feel about your job or place of employment. It is not a test, so there are no right or wrong answers. Answer each item as carefully and as accurately as you can by placing a number beside each one as follows.

1 = None of the time
2 = Very rarely
3 = A little of the time
4 = Some of the time
5 = A good part of the time
6 = Most of the time
7 = All of the time

1. _____ My job is very boring.
2. _____ I hate my job.
3. _____ I cannot stand my boss.
4. _____ My boss is a fool.
5. _____ I really like my job.
6. _____ I think I am good at my job.
7. _____ If I won a lottery, I would quit this job.
8. _____ I get to work on time.
9. _____ I like to "goof off" on the job.
10. _____ The best part of my job is coffee breaks, lunch, and vacations.
11. _____ I work very hard at my job and I am very conscientious about doing it well.
12. _____ I enjoy thinking about my job when I'm not at work.
13. _____ I don't like to think about work when I'm at home.
14. _____ The work I do is important to me, personally.
15. _____ My job is just a way to make a living.
16. _____ I enjoy taking on new responsibilities in my job.
17. _____ My job is more than just a way to make a living.
18. _____ I enjoy thinking of ways to improve the work I do in my job.
19. _____ The best part of my day is leaving work.
20. _____ I get personal rewards from the work I do.
21. _____ My organization provides the resources and tools I need to do my job.
22. _____ I get through the day by planning what I'll do when I retire.
23. _____ I think about looking for another job.
24. _____ My job is interesting to me.
25. _____ I don't have enough to do in my job.
26. _____ I have more work than I can do in my job.
27. _____ My boss doesn't appreciate the work I do.
28. _____ My organization does not support my work.
29. _____ My organization makes it easier to accomplish my work.
30. _____ I can depend on my boss to back me up.
31. _____ My boss doesn't support me when my work is challenged by others.
32. _____ I believe I have job security.
33. _____ My pay is adequate for the work I do.
34. _____ Organizational rewards are distributed fairly.
35. _____ Management supports my work efforts.

1, 2, 3, 4, 7, 9, 10, 13, 15, 19, 22, 23, 25, 26, 27, 28, 31.

Further reproduction prohibited without permission.

INDEX OF MANAGERIAL EFFECTIVENESS (IME)

Manager's Name: _____

The IME scale is designed to measure the way you perceive your manager or administrator with respect to his or her managerial and leadership effectiveness. It is not a test, so there are no right or wrong answers. Answer each item as carefully and as accurately as you can by placing a number beside each one as follows.

1 = None of the time
2 = Very rarely
3 = A little of the time
4 = Some of the time
5 = A good part of the time
6 = Most of the time
7 = All of the time

1. _____ The manager places a great deal of confidence in me and my coworkers.
2. _____ The manager listens to and appreciates subordinates' views about their job.
3. _____ The manager seeks out my ideas and makes good use of them.
4. _____ The manager uses threats, fear, or punishment to extract compliance with directives.
5. _____ The manager does a good job of sharing responsibility for achieving organizational goals.
6. _____ The manager is very skillful in communicating the organizational goals to be achieved.
7. _____ The manager does an excellent job of stimulating and nurturing a cooperative work environment.
8. _____ The manager's superiors are very well informed about problems faced by subordinates.
9. _____ The manager attempts to impose his or her ideological perspectives onto subordinates.
10. _____ The manager engages in excessive amounts of micromanagement.
11. _____ The manager relies heavily on subordinates' expertise in shaping the direction of the program.
12. _____ The manager relies heavily on a collaborative model of decision making about the work unit.
13. _____ The manager uses excellent judgment concerning spending priorities for the work unit.
14. _____ The manager tends to rely on autocratic rule as a basis for decision making about the work unit.
15. _____ The manager adequately meets the needs of subordinates for access to equipment and supplies.
16. _____ The manager is skilled at creating an atmosphere of trust and openness.
17. _____ The manager does a good job of trying to retain competent personnel.
18. _____ The manager is skilled in encouraging subordinates' participation in decision making.
19. _____ The manager does a good job of supporting and encouraging subordinates' work agendas.
20. _____ The manager appears eager to solicit and use subordinates' views and suggestions.
21. _____ The manager does a good job of seeking subordinates' input in recruitment of new personnel.
22. _____ The manager appears quick to blame others for program failures or shortcomings.
23. _____ The manager provides the kind of leadership that stimulates cooperation and enthusiasm.
24. _____ The manager uses the program largely to promote his or her personal esteem and status.
25. _____ The manager appears to care a great deal about the individual accomplishments of subordinates.
26. _____ The manager appears to be very skilled at setting appropriate budgetary priorities.
27. _____ The manager is very sensitive to the needs, views, and wishes of subordinates.
28. _____ The manager gives an excess of attention to appearances at the expense of substance.
29. _____ The manager is admirable as an effective leader of this organization or program.
30. _____ The manager is vindictive toward those who might disagree with his or her views.

4, 9, 10, 14, 22, 24, 28, 30.

INDEX OF SEXUAL HARASSMENT (ISH)

Name: _____ Today's Date: _____

This questionnaire is designed to measure the level of sexual harassment in the workplace. It is not a test, so there are no right or wrong answers. Answer each item as carefully and as accurately as you can by placing a number beside each one as follows.

1 = None of the time
2 = Very rarely
3 = A little of the time
4 = Some of the time
5 = A good part of the time
6 = Most of the time
7 = All of the time

1. ____ My peer or supervisor tells sexually explicit jokes at work.
2. ____ My peer or supervisor describes me or a coworker using sexually explicit terminology.
3. ____ My peer or supervisor creates offensive rumors concerning the appearance or sexual behavior of me or a coworker.
4. ____ My peer or supervisor uses subtle questioning to determine my or my coworker's sexual behavior or availability.
5. ____ My peer or supervisor repeatedly asks me or a coworker for a date.
6. ____ My peer or supervisor asks me or a coworker for sexual favors.
7. ____ My peer or supervisor places obscene phone calls to me or a coworker.
8. ____ My peer or supervisor offers me or a coworker compensation or work benefits in exchange for sexual favors.
9. ____ My peer or supervisor demands sexual favors from me or a coworker to maintain job security.
10. ____ My peer or supervisor displays sexually explicit photographs and pictures at work.
11. ____ My peer or supervisor produces sexually explicit graffiti for display at work.
12. ____ My peer or supervisor shows pornographic videotapes at work.
13. ____ My peer or supervisor sends sexually explicit letters, cards or other written material to me or a coworker.
14. ____ My peer or supervisor uses gestures or staring considered sexually offensive by me or a coworker.
15. ____ My peer or supervisor stalks me or a coworker to pressure a personal relationship.
16. ____ My peer or supervisor blocks my or a coworker's pathway to force physical contact.
17. ____ My peer or supervisor touches self sexually in the presence of me or a coworker.
18. ____ My peer or supervisor touches me or a coworker in a sexually offensive manner.
19. ____ My peer or supervisor initiates unwelcome sexual activity with me or a coworker.

MPSI

WALMYR Publishing Company

Post Office Box 12217
Tallahassee, FL 32327

THE MULTI-PROBLEM SCREENING INVENTORY

INSTRUCTIONS

This questionnaire is designed to obtain information about a wide range of possible problem areas. Answer each item as carefully and as accurately as you can by placing a number beside each one as follows:

1 = None of the time
2 = Very rarely
3 = A little of the time
4 = Some of the time
5 = A good part of the time
6 = Most of the time
7 = All of the time
x = Does Not Apply

You may discover that some of the items do not apply to you or your personal situation. For any such item, please enter an x or X but *do not leave any item blank*.

When you begin to complete the items on this questionnaire you will see that you can very easily make yourself look as good or as bad as you wish. *Please do not do that*. It is extremely important for you to provide the most accurate answers possible even though you may feel embarrassed or uncomfortable. If you provide incorrect or misleading information to those who are trying to assist you, it will be very difficult to provide you with the help that you are seeking.

Please Print Your

Name: _____

Address: _____

City:_____ State: _____ Zip: _____

Age: _____ Gender: ___ Male ___ Female Race: _____

SSAN: _____ Today's Date: _____

ANSWER KEY	
1 = None of the time 2 = Very rarely 3 = A little of the time 4 = Some of the time	5 = A good part of the time 6 = Most of the time 7 = All of the time X = Does not apply

1

SUBSCALE: DEPRESSION

1. _____ I feel powerless to do anything about my life.
2. _____ I feel blue.
3. _____ I have crying spells.
4. _____ It is easy for me to enjoy myself. *
5. _____ I have a hard time getting started on things that I need to do.
6. _____ I get very depressed.
7. _____ I feel there is always someone I can depend on when things get tough. *
8. _____ I feel that the future looks bright for me. *
9. _____ I feel downhearted.
10. _____ I feel that I am needed. *
11. _____ I feel that I am appreciated by others. *
12. _____ I enjoy being active and busy. *

SUBSCALE: SELF-ESTEEM

13. _____ I think my friends find me interesting. *
14. _____ I think I have a good sense of humor. *
15. _____ I feel very self-conscious when I am with strangers.
16. _____ I feel that if I could be more like other people I would have it made.
17. _____ I feel that people have a good time when they are with me. *
18. _____ I feel that people do not enjoy my company.
19. _____ I feel I get pushed around more than others.
20. _____ I think I am a rather nice person. *
21. _____ I feel that people really like me very much. *
22. _____ I feel that I am a likable person. *
23. _____ I am afraid I will appear foolish to others.
24. _____ My friends think very highly of me. *

SUBSCALE: PARTNER RELATIONSHIP PROBLEMS

25. _____ My partner is affectionate enough. *
26. _____ My partner treats me badly.
27. _____ My partner really cares for me. *
28. _____ I feel that I would not choose the same partner if I had it to do over again.
29. _____ I feel that I can really trust my partner. *
30. _____ I feel that our relationship is breaking up.
31. _____ My partner really does not understand me.
32. _____ I feel that our relationship is a good one. *
33. _____ Ours is a very happy relationship. *
34. _____ Our life together is dull.
35. _____ We have a lot of fun together. *
36. _____ My partner does not confide in me.
37. _____ Ours is a very close relationship. *

2

SUBSCALE: SEXUAL DISCORD

38. _____ I feel that my partner enjoys our sex life. *
39. _____ Our sex life is very exciting. *
40. _____ Sex is fun for my partner and me. *
41. _____ Sex with my partner has become a chore for me.
42. _____ I feel that our sex is dirty and disgusting.
43. _____ Our sex life is monotonous.
44. _____ When we have sex, it is too rushed and hurriedly completed.
45. _____ I feel that our sex life is lacking in quality.
46. _____ My partner is sexually very exciting. *
47. _____ I enjoy the sex techniques that my partner likes or uses. *
48. _____ I feel that my partner wants too much sex from me.
49. _____ I think that our sex life is wonderful. *

SUBSCALE: PROBLEMS WITH MY CHILD

50. _____ My child gets on my nerves.
51. _____ I get along well with my child. *
52. _____ I feel that I can really trust my child. *
53. _____ I dislike my child.
54. _____ My child is well behaved. *
55. _____ My child is too demanding.
56. _____ I wish I did not have this child.
57. _____ I really enjoy my child. *
58. _____ I have a hard time controlling my child.
59. _____ My child interferes with my activities.
60. _____ I resent my child.
61. _____ I think my child is terrific. *
62. _____ I hate my child.

SUBSCALE: PROBLEMS WITH MOTHER

63. _____ My mother is very patient with me. *
64. _____ I really like my mother. *
65. _____ I like being with my mother. *
66. _____ I feel like I do not love my mother.
67. _____ My mother is very irritating.
68. _____ I feel very angry toward my mother.
69. _____ I feel violent toward my mother.
70. _____ I feel proud of my mother. *
71. _____ I wish my mother was more like others I know.
72. _____ My mother does not understand me.
73. _____ I can really depend on my mother. *
74. _____ I feel ashamed of my mother.

3

1 = None of the time	5 = A good part of the time
2 = Very rarely	6 = Most of the time
3 = A little of the time	7 = All of the time
4 = Some of the time	X = Does not apply

SUBSCALE: PROBLEMS WITH FATHER

75. _____ My father gets on my nerves.
76. _____ I get along well with my father. *
77. _____ I feel that I can really trust my father. *
78. _____ I dislike my father.
79. _____ My father's behavior embarrasses me.
80. _____ My father is too demanding.
81. _____ I wish I had a different father.
82. _____ I really enjoy my father. *
83. _____ My father puts too many limits on me.
84. _____ My father interferes with my activities.
85. _____ I resent my father.
86. _____ I think my father is terrific. *
87. _____ I hate my father.

SUBSCALE: PERSONAL STRESS

88. _____ I feel very panicked.
89. _____ I feel like I am on the verge of a total collapse.
90. _____ I feel that I am losing control of my life.
91. _____ I feel that I am near a breaking point.
92. _____ I feel wound up like a coiled spring.
93. _____ I feel that I cannot keep up with all the demands on me.
94. _____ I feel very much behind in my work.
95. _____ I feel tense and angry with those around me.
96. _____ I feel I must race from one task to the next.
97. _____ I feel that I just cannot keep up with everything.
98. _____ I feel as tight as a drum.
99. _____ I feel very much on edge.

SUBSCALE: PROBLEMS WITH FRIENDS

100. _____ I get along very well with my friends. *
101. _____ My friends act like they do not care about me.
102. _____ My friends treat me badly.
103. _____ My friends really seem to respect me. *
104. _____ I do not feel like I am "part of the group" with my friends.
105. _____ My friends are a bunch of snobs.
106. _____ My friends understand me. *
107. _____ My friends seem to like me very much. *
108. _____ I really feel "left out" by my friends.
109. _____ I hate my present group of friends.
110. _____ My friends seem to like having me around. *
111. _____ I really like my present group of friends. *
112. _____ I really feel that I am disliked by my friends.

4

ANSWER KEY	
1 = None of the time	5 = A good part of the time
2 = Very rarely	6 = Most of the time
3 = A little of the time	7 = All of the time
4 = Some of the time	X = Does not apply

SUBSCALE: PROBLEMS WITH NEIGHBORS

113. _____ I really feel that I am disliked by my neighbors.
114. _____ I wish I had a different group of neighbors.
115. _____ My neighbors are very nice to me. *
116. _____ My neighbors seem to look up to me. *
117. _____ My neighbors think I am important to them. *
118. _____ My neighbors are a real source of pleasure to me. *
119. _____ My neighbors do not seem to even notice me.
120. _____ I wish I were not part of this neighborhood.
121. _____ My neighbors regard my ideas and opinions very highly. *
122. _____ I feel like I am an important member of my neighborhood. *
123. _____ I cannot stand to be around my neighbors.
124. _____ My neighbors seem to look down on me.
125. _____ My neighbors really do not interest me.

SUBSCALE: PROBLEMS WITH SCHOOL

126. _____ I hate school.
127. _____ I enjoy my school work and studies. *
128. _____ I put off studies at school until the last minute.
129. _____ My school homework is very boring.
130. _____ School is not for study, it is for parties and play!
131. _____ I study very hard at school. *
132. _____ I think I am a good student at school. *
133. _____ I think my school work will help my future. *
134. _____ I really do pretty shoddy work at school.
135. _____ I feel I learn a great deal at school. *

SUBSCALE: AGGRESSION

136. _____ When I have to, I really do not mind punching someone out.
137. _____ I get into fights.
138. _____ When I hurt someone physically it really does not bother me.
139. _____ I am quick to let people know they cannot walk all over me.
140. _____ I push others around before they have a chance to push me around.
141. _____ People tell me I have a bad temper.
142. _____ I hurt people before they can hurt me.
143. _____ I threaten people with a fight.
144. _____ I like it when others are afraid of me.
145. _____ If punches are thrown, mine go first!

SUBSCALE: PROBLEMS WITH WORK ASSOCIATES

146. _____ I get along very well with my work associates. *
147. _____ My work associates act like they do not care about me.
148. _____ My work associates treat me badly.

5

1 = None of the time	5 = A good part of the time
2 = Very rarely	6 = Most of the time
3 = A little of the time	7 = All of the time
4 = Some of the time	X = Does not apply

149. _____ My work associates really seem to respect me. *
150. _____ I do not feel like I am "part of the group" with my work associates.
151. _____ My work associates are a bunch of snobs.
152. _____ My work associates understand me. *
153. _____ My work associates seem to like me very much. *
154. _____ I really feel "left out" by my work associates.
155. _____ I hate my present group of work associates.
156. _____ My work associates seem to like having me around. *
157. _____ I really like my work associates. *

SUBSCALE: FAMILY RELATIONSHIP PROBLEMS

158. _____ There is too much hatred in my family.
159. _____ Members of my family are really good to one another. *
160. _____ My family is well respected by those who know us. *
161. _____ There seems to be a lot of friction in my family.
162. _____ There is a lot of love in my family. *
163. _____ Members of my family get along well together. *
164. _____ Life in my family is generally unpleasant.
165. _____ My family is a great joy to me. *
166. _____ I feel proud of my family. *
167. _____ Other families seem to get along better than mine.
168. _____ My family is a real source of comfort to me. *
169. _____ I feel "left out" of my family.
170. _____ My family is an unhappy one.

SUBSCALE: SUICIDAL THOUGHTS

171. _____ I think about ending my life.
172. _____ My life is so grim that I have considered ending it.
173. _____ I think about committing suicide.
174. _____ I feel that everyone would be better off if I were dead.
175. _____ I actually think about different ways that I could kill myself.
176. _____ I have actually decided that I am going to take my own life and I now think about my final plans for doing that.
177. _____ I feel that it is useless for me to continue living.
178. _____ I think about finding relief or peace by taking my own life.
179. _____ I feel that the only way to end my shame is to end my life.
180. _____ I feel that my agony is too great for me to continue living.
181. _____ I feel that my life is over and I may as well end it.

SUBSCALE: NON-PHYSICAL ABUSE

182. _____ My partner belittles me.
183. _____ My partner demands obedience to his or her whims.
184. _____ My partner becomes surly and angry if I say he or she is drinking too much.
185. _____ My partner demands that I perform sex acts that I do not enjoy or like.

6

ANSWER KEY	
1 = None of the time	5 = A good part of the time
2 = Very rarely	6 = Most of the time
3 = A little of the time	7 = All of the time
4 = Some of the time	X = Does not apply

186. _____ My partner becomes very upset if my work is not done when he or she thinks it should be.
187. _____ My partner does not want me to have any friends.
188. _____ My partner tells me I am ugly and unattractive.
189. _____ My partner tells me I really could not manage or take care of myself without him or her.
190. _____ My partner acts like I am his or her personal servant.
191. _____ My partner insults or shames me in front of others.
192. _____ My partner becomes very angry if I disagree with his or her point of view.
193. _____ My partner is stingy in giving me money.
194. _____ My partner belittles me intellectually.

SUBSCALE: PHYSICAL ABUSE

195. _____ My partner tries to choke or strangle me.
196. _____ My partner knocks me down and then kicks or stomps me.
197. _____ My partner twists my fingers, arms or legs.
198. _____ My partner throws dangerous objects at me.
199. _____ My partner bites or scratches me so badly that I bleed or have bruises.
200. _____ My partner violently pinches or twists my skin.
201. _____ My partner hurts me badly while we are having sex.
202. _____ My partner injures my breasts or genitals.
203. _____ My partner tries to suffocate me with pillows, towels, or other objects.
204. _____ My partner pokes or jabs me with pointed objects.
205. _____ My partner has broken one or more of my bones.
206. _____ My partner kicks my face and head.

SUBSCALE: FEARFULNESS

207. _____ I experience a great deal of fear.
208. _____ A sense of terror washes over my entire body.
209. _____ I have frightening nightmares.
210. _____ My dreams are very frightening.
211. _____ I become afraid very easily.
212. _____ I feel panic stricken and terrified.
213. _____ I am stricken with a sense of paralyzing fear.
214. _____ Panic and fear disrupt what I am trying to do.
215. _____ I am frightened very easily.
216. _____ I am very afraid that I will be hurt or damaged.
217. _____ I become afraid for no apparent reason.
218. _____ I am terrified that something awful is going to happen.
219. _____ I break out in cold sweats of fear and panic.
220. _____ I am terrified that something really bad will happen to me.
221. _____ I become so afraid that I feel I am going to die.
222. _____ I become so afraid that I can hardly move.
223. _____ I wake up at night feeling afraid.
224. _____ Fear courses through my body.
225. _____ I wake up at night in a state of terror.

7

ANSWER KEY	
1 = None of the time	5 = A good part of the time
2 = Very rarely	6 = Most of the time
3 = A little of the time	7 = All of the time
4 = Some of the time	X = Does not apply

SUBSCALE: IDEAS OF REFERENCE

226. _____ I think people talk about me behind my back.
227. _____ People are definitely "out to get me".
228. _____ I think people are plotting against me.
229. _____ People keep staring at me.
230. _____ People who are supposed to be my friends are really out to stab me in the back.
231. _____ Various people keep talking about me.
232. _____ I think there are people who are plotting against me.
233. _____ People are out to get me because they are jealous of me.
234. _____ Secret agents keep spying on me.
235. _____ People sneak around and try to cause me trouble.
236. _____ People are trying to hurt me.
237. _____ People who call themselves my friends try to pull me down because they would love to see me fail.
238. _____ People are plotting to kill me.
239. _____ I can feel people watching me.
240. _____ Government agents are plotting my downfall.
241. _____ My boss would really like to see me mess up.
242. _____ People around me really resent my ability and talent.
243. _____ People keep trying to invade my privacy.
244. _____ There are people who would really like to get rid of me.
245. _____ People are trying to make me look foolish.

SUBSCALE: PHOBIAS

246. _____ I feel extremely nervous when I must go to high places or look down from them.
247. _____ I am extremely frightened or nervous when I am in crowds of people.
248. _____ I feel panicked when I must cross over bridges or go through tunnels.
249. _____ I am terrified when I enter small rooms or closed spaces.
250. _____ I am extremely nervous when I fly in airplanes.
251. _____ I am terrified of driving in even moderate traffic.
252. _____ I am extremely nervous when I am in the presence of strangers.
253. _____ I am terrified of being alone.
254. _____ I am extremely nervous, even panicked, when I meet people for the first time.
255. _____ I feel completely incapacitated at the thought of public speaking.
256. _____ I feel afraid to go out of my house alone.
257. _____ I feel afraid in open spaces or in the streets.
258. _____ I feel afraid I will faint in public.
259. _____ I am comfortable traveling on buses, subways or trains. *
260. _____ I feel nervousness or shakiness inside.
261. _____ I feel comfortable in crowds, such as shopping or at a movie. *
262. _____ I feel comfortable when I am left alone. *
263. _____ Due to my fears, I unreasonably avoid certain animals, objects or situations.
264. _____ Due to my fears, I avoid social situations, whenever possible.
265. _____ Due to my fears, I avoid being alone, whenever possible.

8

ANSWER KEY	
1 = None of the time	5 = A good part of the time
2 = Very rarely	6 = Most of the time
3 = A little of the time	7 = All of the time
4 = Some of the time	X = Does not apply

SUBSCALE: FEELINGS OF GUILT

266. _____ I seem to feel guilty for no good reason.
267. _____ When things go wrong, I feel I should apologize even if it is not my fault.
268. _____ When things do not go right I usually accept the blame for them.
269. _____ I am usually the one who apologizes for anything.
270. _____ I have this nagging feeling that I have done something wrong.
271. _____ I have the feeling I should be punished even when I have done nothing for which to be punished.
272. _____ I have the feeling that I have done something terrible.
273. _____ I feel very guilty and ashamed.
274. _____ Deep inside, I feel that I am really a "bad" person.
275. _____ I feel that people would be ashamed of me if they really knew me very well.

SUBSCALE: PROBLEMS WITH WORK

276. _____ My job is very boring.
277. _____ I hate my job.
278. _____ I cannot stand my boss.
279. _____ My boss is a fool.
280. _____ I really like my job. *
281. _____ I think I am good at my job. *
282. _____ I get to work on time. *
283. _____ I like to "goof off" on the job.
284. _____ The best part of my job is coffee breaks, lunch, and vacations.
285. _____ I work very hard at my job and I am very conscientious about doing it well. *

SUBSCALE: CONFUSED THINKING

286. _____ I have difficulty keeping my thoughts straight.
287. _____ My thinking becomes confused.
288. _____ I cannot seem to keep things straight in my mind.
289. _____ There are times when my mind plays tricks on me.
290. _____ Some of the strangest ideas just pop into my mind.
291. _____ There are times when my thinking does not seem to work right.
292. _____ I worry about the way my mind seems strange.

SUBSCALE: DISTURBING THOUGHTS

293. _____ I have ideas and thoughts that disturb me greatly.
294. _____ Some of my thoughts are frightening to me.
295. _____ I think about ugly or horrible things.
296. _____ There are times when I have very strange and disturbing thoughts.
297. _____ I cannot get certain bad thoughts out of my mind.
298. _____ Disturbing ideas come to me and I cannot get rid of them.
299. _____ I worry about the horrible thoughts that I have.
300. _____ Ugly or horrible thoughts rush into my mind.
301. _____ I just cannot get certain bad thoughts out of my mind.

9

SUBSCALE: MEMORY LOSS

302. _____ I forget where I put my keys, glasses, or other objects that I use daily.
303. _____ There are times when I forget my name.
304. _____ I forget what day it is.
305. _____ I forget important dates, addresses, or phone numbers that I should remember with ease.
306. _____ I have difficulty remembering things that I should easily remember.
307. _____ There are times when I actually forget my own address.
308. _____ I forget important things about my work or school.
309. _____ My memory seems to fail me.

SUBSCALE: ALCOHOL ABUSE

310. _____ When I have a drink with friends, I usually drink more than they do.
311. _____ My drinking causes problems with my family or friends.
312. _____ My drinking causes problems with my work.
313. _____ After I have been drinking, I cannot remember things that happened.
314. _____ After I have been drinking, I get the shakes.
315. _____ When I am drinking, I have three or fewer drinks. *
316. _____ I drink to calm my nerves or make me feel better.
317. _____ I drink when I am alone.
318. _____ I drink so much that I pass out.
319. _____ My drinking interferes with obligations to my family or friends.
320. _____ I have one or more drinks when things are not going well for me.
321. _____ I have one or more drinks before noon.
322. _____ My friends avoid me when I am drinking.
323. _____ My personal life gets very troublesome when I drink.
324. _____ I drink several times a week.

SUBSCALE: DRUG USE

325. _____ I take drugs to calm my nerves or make me feel better.
326. _____ When I take drugs with friends, I usually take more than they do.
327. _____ My drug use causes problems with my family or friends.
328. _____ My drug use causes problems with my work.
329. _____ I take drugs when I am alone.
330. _____ My drug use interferes with obligations to my family or friends.
331. _____ I take drugs when things are not going well for me.
332. _____ My friends avoid me when I take drugs.
333. _____ My personal life gets very troublesome when I use drugs.
334. _____ I take drugs several times a week.

10

MPSI SUBSCALE SCORING BLANK

Subscale Name	A Total Items	B Items Used	C Item Sum	D (C - B) Sum-Used	E D*100/(B*6) Score
Depression	12	___	___	___	___
Self-Esteem	12	___	___	___	___
Partner Problems	13	___	___	___	___
Sexual Discord	12	___	___	___	___
Child Problems	13	___	___	___	___
Mother Problems	12	___	___	___	___
Father Problems	13	___	___	___	___
Personal Stress	12	___	___	___	___
Friend Problems	13	___	___	___	___
Neighbor Problems	13	___	___	___	___
School Problems	10	___	___	___	___
Aggression	10	___	___	___	___
Work Associates	12	___	___	___	___
Family Problems	13	___	___	___	___
Suicide	11	___	___	___	___
Non-Physical Abuse	13	___	___	___	___
Physical Abuse	12	___	___	___	___
Fearfulness	19	___	___	___	___
Ideas of Reference	20	___	___	___	___
Phobias	20	___	___	___	___
Guilt	10	___	___	___	___
Work Problems	10	___	___	___	___
Confused Thinking	7	___	___	___	___
Disturbing Thoughts	9	___	___	___	___
Memory Loss	8	___	___	___	___
Alcohol Abuse	15	___	___	___	___
Drug Abuse	10	___	___	___	___

11

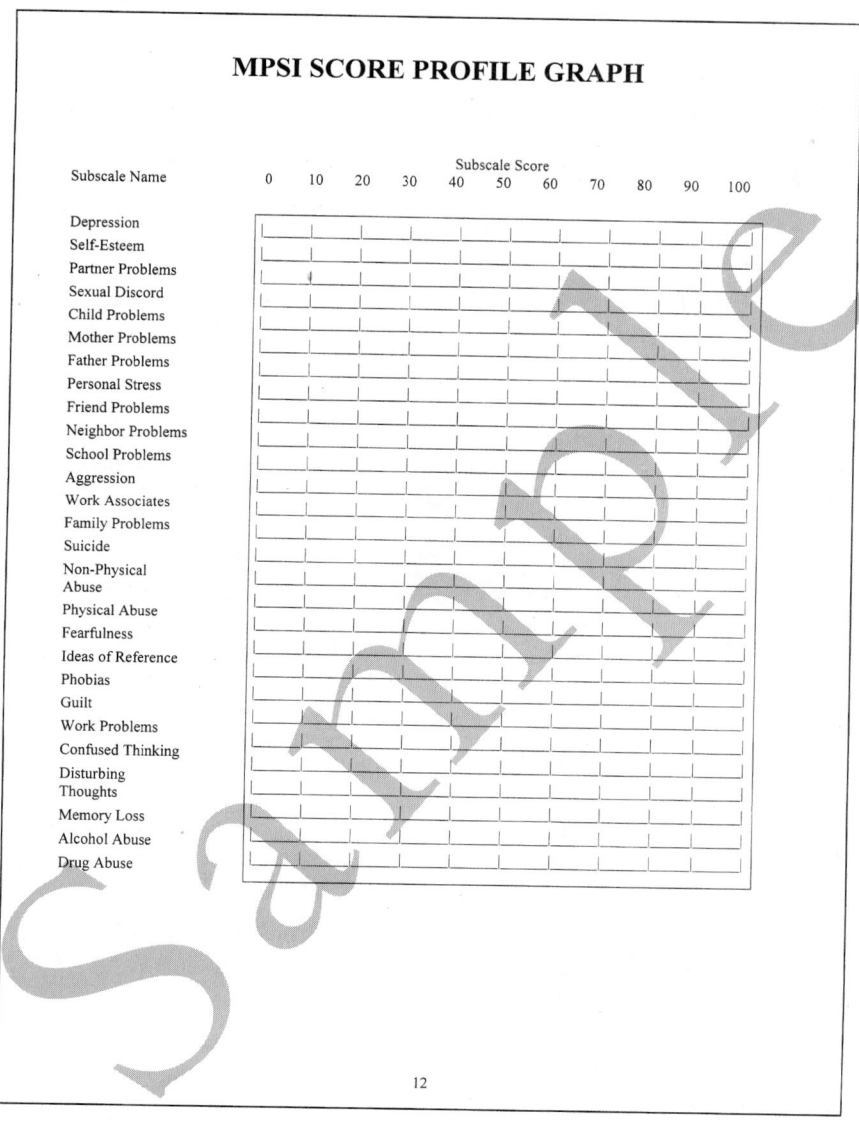

MPSI SCORE PROFILE GRAPH

Subscale Score

| Subscale Name | 0 | 10 | 20 | 30 | 40 | 50 | 60 | 70 | 80 | 90 | 100 |

Depression
Self-Esteem
Partner Problems
Sexual Discord
Child Problems
Mother Problems
Father Problems
Personal Stress
Friend Problems
Neighbor Problems
School Problems
Aggression
Work Associates
Family Problems
Suicide
Non-Physical Abuse
Physical Abuse
Fearfulness
Ideas of Reference
Phobias
Guilt
Work Problems
Confused Thinking
Disturbing Thoughts
Memory Loss
Alcohol Abuse
Drug Abuse

12

FASI

WALMYR Publishing Co.
PO Box 12217
Tallahassee, FL 32317-2217

FAMILY ASSESSMENT SCREENING INVENTORY

This questionnaire is designed to obtain information about a wide range of family strengths, resources, and problem areas. Answer each item as carefully and as accurately as you can by placing a number beside each one, using the answer key below.

1 = None of the time
2 = Very rarely
3 = A little of the time
4 = Some of the time

5 = A good part of the time
6 = Most of the time
7 = All of the time
X = Does not apply

You may discover that some of the items do not apply to you or your family situation. For any such item, please enter an X but *do not leave any item blank*.

You will also note that some items refer to your family as a whole. When this is the case, think of how the item applies to the family as a unit. Other items refer to a member of the family. For such items, answer the question by thinking of the family member to whom the item applies the most.

When you begin to complete the items on this questionnaire you will see that you can easily make your family look as good or as bad as you wish. Please do not do that. It is extremely important for you to provide the most accurate answers possible even though you may feel embarrassed or uncomfortable. If you provide incorrect or misleading information, it will be difficult to provide helpful services to your family members.

Name: _____

Address: _____

City: _____ State/Province: _____ Zip: _____

Age: _____ Sex: _____ Ethnicity: _____

SSN/SIN: _____ Today's Date: _____

FAMILY CONFLICT

1. _____ A member of my family dislikes another member.
2. _____ In my family we respect each other. *
3. _____ A member of my family has conflicts with another member.
4. _____ Our family members get along with each other. *
5. _____ Members of my family are good at resolving conflicts within the family. *
6. _____ Family members cooperate with one another. *
7. _____ Other families get along better than my family does.
8. _____ Members of my family argue and yell, but know when to back off. *
9. _____ Issues and concerns divide our family.
10. _____ There are serious disputes between members of our family.

AGGRESSIVE BEHAVIOR

11. _____ A member of my family throws objects when angry.
12. _____ A member of my family breaks things when upset.
13. _____ A member of my family physically threatens other family members.
14. _____ A member of my family bullies other family members.
15. _____ A member of my family pushes other members around.
16. _____ A member of my family becomes hostile and threatening.
17. _____ A member of my family has a bad temper.
18. _____ A member of my family is afraid of another member.
19. _____ A member of my family is quick to anger.

STRESS

20. _____ A member of my family is experiencing serious stress.
21. _____ A member of my family seems emotionally drained.
22. _____ A member of my family cannot perform his or her household duties because of stress.
23. _____ Our family copes well under stress. *
24. _____ A member of my family appears overwhelmed with household duties or outside work.
25. _____ A member of my family talks about walking out on the family.
26. _____ A member of my family appears near the breaking point.
27. _____ A member of my family seems tense and anxious.
28. _____ Other family members provide support when one of us is under stress. *
29. _____ A member of my family is physically exhausted.

FAMILY SUPPORT

30. _____ In our family we support each other. *
31. _____ Someone in my family can be counted on to provide support to other members. *
32. _____ A member of my family can be counted on to provide encouragement when someone needs it. *
33. _____ A member of my family assists other members in solving problems. *
34. _____ Our family provides a sense of confidence to its members. *
35. _____ A member of my family provides emotional support to other members. *
36. _____ Our family provides practical help to its members. *
37. _____ Members of my family can be counted on to be more helpful than friends. *

- 2 -

38._____A member of my family puts down our efforts.
39._____In our family we listen to each other's problems.*
40._____We turn to others, outside the family, for help or support.

EXTENDED FAMILY

41._____A member of the extended family tries to impose his or her ideas on our family.
42._____A member of the extended family forces one of our members to have sex.
43._____A member of the extended family interferes with our family life.
44._____A member of the extended family criticizes how the children in this family are managed.
45._____Members of the extended family say positive things about our family.*
46._____We like our contacts with members of our extended family.*
47._____Members of my family are close to the extended family.*
48._____Members of the extended family can be depended upon for help and support.*
49._____Members of the extended family visit my family.*
50._____Members of the extended family want little to do with our family.
51._____We look forward to contacts with members of the extended family.*

PREVIOUS PARTNERS

52._____A previous partner threatens to get legal custody of a child in this family.
53._____A previous partner withholds or has been late with child payments.
54._____A previous partner takes a child in this family to unsafe places.
55._____A previous partner returns a child late from visits.
56._____Previous partners approve of the care we provide to children.*
57._____A previous partner pressures or forces a member of this family to have unwanted sex.
58._____A previous partner stalks our family.
59._____A previous partner exposes a child in this family to situations unsuitable for children.
60._____Previous partners approve of our household routines.*
61._____A previous partner tells a child in this family negative things about us.
62._____A previous partner threatens members of this family.
63._____One or more members of this family are afraid of a previous partner.
64._____We maintain good relations with previous partners.*

COMMUNITY

65._____Members of my family have many friends.*
66._____Members of my family feel alone and isolated.
67._____Members of my family can count on getting help and support in the community.*
68._____Members of my family belong to clubs, or groups.*
69._____Our family makes this neighborhood a better place.*
70._____Our neighbors avoid us.
71._____Our family knows where to go for assistance if needed.*
72._____A friend or neighbor is around to help out if needed.*
73._____Members of my family visit other people and families in their homes.*
74._____Our family participates in community events and recreational activities.*
75._____Our family is able to obtain help when needed.*
76._____Our family feels a part of this community.*

- 3 -

1 = None of the time
2 = Very rarely
3 = A little of the time
4 = Some of the time

5 = A good part of the time
6 = Most of the time
7 = All of the time
X = Does not apply

PEOPLE OUTSIDE THE FAMILY

77. _____ Members of my family get along with friends.*
78. _____ A member of my family does not have friends.
79. _____ A member of my family feels "left out" by friends.
80. _____ A member of my family complains that friends dislike him or her.
81. _____ Family members are respected by others.*
82. _____ Members of my family get along with people.*
83. _____ A member of my family has serious conflicts with people outside the family.
84. _____ Members of my family get along with neighbors.*
85. _____ Members of my family are involved in disputes with people outside the family.
86. _____ Our neighbors look down on a member of my family.
87. _____ Our neighbors criticize a member of my family.

ALCOHOL USE

88. _____ A member of my family drinks alone.
89. _____ A member of my family drinks alcohol before noon.
90. _____ A family member's drinking causes problems at work or school.
91. _____ A family member's drinking causes problems within the family.
92. _____ A family member passes out after drinking.
93. _____ As a family, we worry that one of our members drinks excessively.
94. _____ A member of my family becomes aggressive, abusive or violent when drinking.
95. _____ A member of my family neglects his or her obligations at home after drinking.
96. _____ A family member neglects his or her responsibilities at work or at school after drinking.
97. _____ A family member frightens us when he or she has been drinking.
98. _____ When they drink, members of my family drink moderately. *

DRUG USE

99. _____ A family member takes medicine in larger doses than prescribed.
100. _____ A member of my family sniffs or inhales substances like glue and solvents.
101. _____ A member of my family abuses non-prescription drugs.
102. _____ A member of my family over uses prescription drugs.
103. _____ Members of my family use medications as directed. *
104. _____ A member of my family uses illegal drugs.
105. _____ A member of my family uses illegal drugs in the presence of children.
106. _____ Drug use by a family member creates problems for us.
107. _____ Drug use by a family member creates problems at work or at school.
108. _____ Drug use by a family member creates problems in the community.
109. _____ A member of our family neglects his or her obligations within the family when using drugs.

DOMESTIC ABUSE

110. _____ An adult member of our family belittles or ridicules another adult family member.
111. _____ An adult member of our family insults or shames another adult family member in front of others.
112. _____ An adult member of our family threatens another adult family member.
113. _____ An adult member of our family shoves, pushes or scratches another adult family member.

- 4 -

```
                                ANSWER KEY
        1 = None of the time              5 = A good part of the time
        2 = Very rarely                   6 = Most of the time
        3 = A little of the time          7 = All of the time
        4 = Some of the time              X = Does not apply
```

114._____An adult member of our family pinches or bites another adult family member.
115._____An adult member of our family hits, punches or kicks another adult family member.
116._____An adult member of our family uses weapons or instruments to hurt another adult family member.
117._____An adult member of our family forces another adult family member to engage in sexual acts.
118._____An adult member of our family forces another adult family member to engage in sexual intercourse.
119._____Police are called to our home as a result of fights.

CHILD ABUSE

120._____A member of my family belittles or ridicules one of our children.
121._____A member of my family insults or shames one of our children in front of others.
122._____A member of my family yells at or threatens one of our children.
123._____A family member shoves, pushes or scratches one of our children.
124._____A family member pinches or bites one of our children.
125._____A family member hits, punches or kicks one of our children.
126._____A family member hits, chokes or strangles one of our children.
127._____A family member violently shakes one of our children.
128._____A family member uses weapons or instruments to hurt one of our children.
129._____A family member engages in sexual acts with one of our children.
130._____A family member engages in sexual intercourse with one of our children.
131._____A child in this family is present when adults threaten each other.
132._____A child in this family observes acts of physical violence between adults.
133._____A child in this family observes sexual activity between adults.

EXTRA-FAMILIAL ABUSE

134._____Someone outside the family belittles or ridicules a member of my family.
135._____Someone outside the family insults or shames a member of my family in front of others.
136._____Someone outside the family threatens a member of my family.
137._____Someone outside the family shoves, pushes or scratches a member of my family.
138._____Someone outside the family pinches or bites a family member.
139._____Someone outside the family hits, punches or kicks a family member.
140._____Someone outside the family uses weapons or instruments to hurt a family member.
141._____Someone outside the family forces a family member to engage in sexual acts.
142._____Someone outside the family forces a family member to engage in sexual intercourse.

SELF-DESTRUCTIVE BEHAVIOR

143._____A member of my family talks about harming himself or herself.
144._____A member of my family scars or mutilates his or her arms or body.
145._____A member of my family talks about ending his or her own life.
146._____A member of my family says that the family would be better off without him or her.
147._____A member of my family says that his or her situation is hopeless.
148._____A member of my family is seriously depressed.
149._____A member of my family talks about committing suicide.
150._____A member of my family has attempted to commit suicide.
151._____A member of my family has been hospitalized as a result of a suicide attempt.
152._____A member of my family threatens to commit suicide.

- 5 -

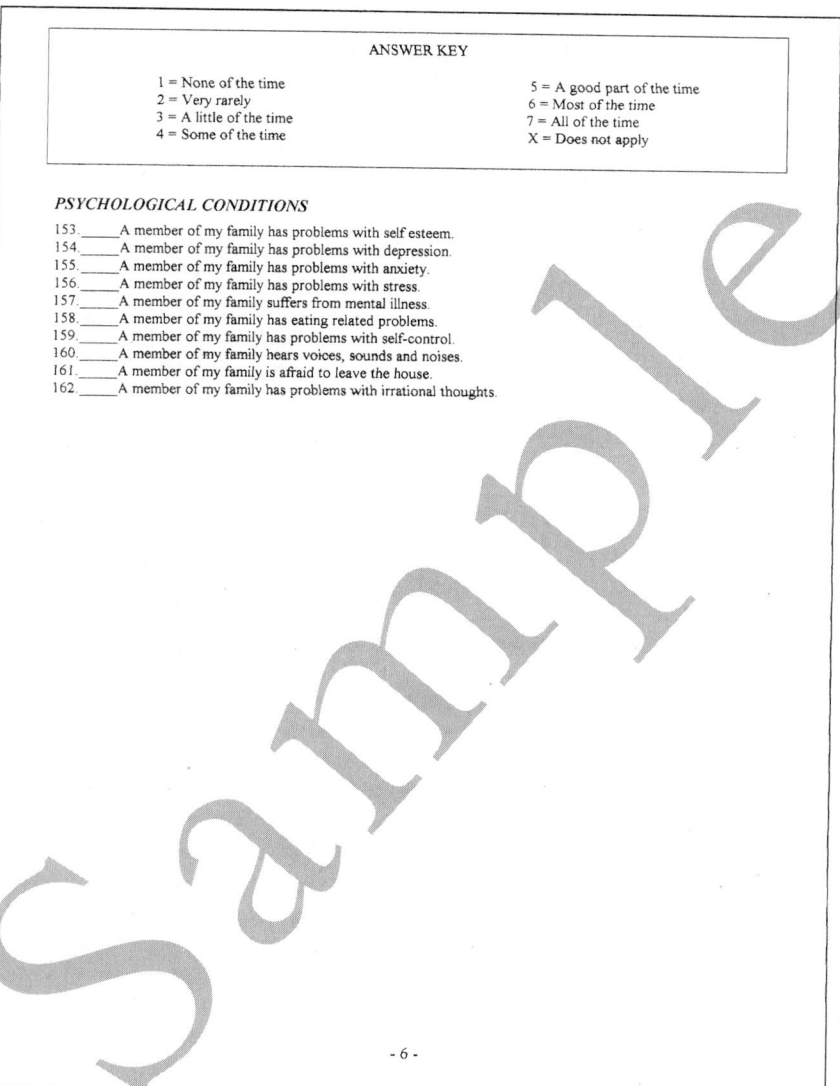

ANSWER KEY

1 = None of the time	5 = A good part of the time
2 = Very rarely	6 = Most of the time
3 = A little of the time	7 = All of the time
4 = Some of the time	X = Does not apply

PSYCHOLOGICAL CONDITIONS

153._____ A member of my family has problems with self esteem.
154._____ A member of my family has problems with depression.
155._____ A member of my family has problems with anxiety.
156._____ A member of my family has problems with stress.
157._____ A member of my family suffers from mental illness.
158._____ A member of my family has eating related problems.
159._____ A member of my family has problems with self-control.
160._____ A member of my family hears voices, sounds and noises.
161._____ A member of my family is afraid to leave the house.
162._____ A member of my family has problems with irrational thoughts.

- 6 -

FASI SUBSCALE SCORING FORM

Prior to calculating subscale scores, adjust the items indicated with (*) by subtracting the entered score from 8. Use the adjusted score in your calculation.

Subscale Name	A Total Items	B Items Used	C Item Sum	D (C - B) Sum-Used	E D*100/(B*6) Score
Family Conflict	10	____	____	_____	_____
Aggressive Behavior	9	____	____	_____	_____
Stress	10	____	____	_____	_____
Family Support	11	____	____	_____	_____
Extended Family	11	____	____	_____	_____
Previous Partners	13	____	____	_____	_____
Community	12	____	____	_____	_____
People Outside Family	11	____	____	_____	_____
Alcohol Use	11	____	____	_____	_____
Drug Use	11	____	____	_____	_____
Domestic Abuse	10	____	____	_____	_____
Child Abuse	14	____	____	_____	_____
Extra-Familial Abuse	9	____	____	_____	_____
Self-Destructive Behavior	10	____	____	_____	_____
Psychological Conditions	10	____	____	_____	_____

- 7 -

Appendix C
Training and
Practice Exercises

ollowing are a number of exercises that practitioners can use to help in learning the ideas and methods we have discussed throughout this book. Some are designed to help in the development of skills needed to use the CASS short-form and multidimensional scales. Others are designed to help in learning how to use single-case designs to monitor and evaluate practice. Doing these exercises will help practitioners enormously in understanding the methods presented in this book. Good luck, and have fun learning!

EXERCISE 1

Choose one of the sample CASS short-form scales from Appendix B and complete it yourself. Respond to the items on the scale as honestly as you can. Then, using the instructions in Chapter 12, compute your score on the scale. How does the score you obtained on the scale compare with your own sense of the magnitude or severity of a problem you might (or might not) have in the area of personal, interpersonal, or social functioning addressed by the scale?

EXERCISE 2

Choose one of the subscales from the sample MPSI in Appendix B and complete it yourself. Respond to the items on the subscale as honestly as you can. Then, using the instructions in Chapter 14, compute your score on the subscale. How does the score you obtained on the scale compare with your own sense of the magnitude or severity of a problem you might (or might not) have in the area of personal, interpersonal, or social functioning addressed by the scale?

EXERCISE 3

Choose three or four of the subscales from the sample MPSI in Appendix B and complete them yourself. Respond to the items on the subscales as honestly as you can. Then, using the instructions in Chapter 14, compute your scores on the subscales. Now use the scoring profile in the sample MPSI to plot your subscale scores on the profile blank. How do the scores you obtained on the subscales compare with your own sense of the magnitude or severity of problems you might (or might not) have in the areas of personal, interpersonal, or social functioning addressed by the subscales? Discuss in class the relative usefulness of a score profile, such as the one you have made from the scores you obtained on the MPSI subscales, versus the single score you obtained from one of the CASS short-form scales.

EXERCISE 4

Pair up with a classmate. Your classmate will be the client, and you will be the social worker. Your job is to introduce one of the CASS short-form scales to your client and to try to get your client to agree to complete the scale. Do this exercise twice. The first time, introduce the CASS scale to your client by being apologetic, uncertain about the usefulness of the scale, and uncertain about whether your client really should take the time to complete it; also, inform your client that he or she cannot see his or her score or know what it means. You might say, for example, in a hesitant voice, "I hate to ask you to do this, but please complete this scale. I don't know if it will be of any help to us, but please do it anyway. I am not sure how long it will take, but I don't think it will take too long. After you complete it, I will score it and put your score in your record. However, please do not ask me what your score was, or what it means. I can't tell you those things." After you have introduced the scale in this manner, have the person in the client role give you feedback. How did he or she feel about completing the scale? How did he or she feel toward you, the social worker? Did he or she feel like completing the scale?

Now repeat the exercise, but this time introduce the scale in a matter-of-fact manner, with confidence about its usefulness in helping you assess your client's problems; also, inform your client that he or she can see his or her score and that you will tell him or her what the score means. Do this in a confident tone of voice, and in a manner indicating that this is a standard part of the assessment process. You might say, for example, in a confident, matter-of-fact voice, "I always have my clients complete one or more of these short assessment scales. They are like thermometers in that they tell me how serious and intense a problem you have in certain areas. The score you obtain on this scale will help me to know what to do to help you and will also help both of us to know how well we are doing with changing your problem. After you complete the scale, which should take only about five minutes, I will score it, show you your score, and tell you what it means." After you have introduced the scale in this manner, again have the person in the client role give you feedback. How did he or she feel about completing the scale this time? How did he or she feel toward you, the social worker? Did he or she feel like completing the scale?

Now reverse roles; you will become the client, and your partner will become the social worker. Complete the exercise again with the roles reversed.

Discuss this exercise as a class. What did you learn from the exercise? What impact does the manner in which you present the CASS scale to your client have on your client's motivation to complete the scale and on your client's attitude toward you, the social worker?

EXERCISE 5

Create a graph of an AB single-case design. Plot the following GCS baseline scores on the graph: 50, 47, 51, and 49. Using the methods in Chapter 6, draw in the baseline trend line, the region of baseline-phase background variability, and the estimated two sigma bounds for baseline data. Extend these into the treatment phase. Now plot the following GCS treatment-phase scores: 47, 45, 45, 46, 42, and 39. Draw in the treatment-phase trend line. Now, using the methods and ideas from Chapter 6, answer the following questions:

a. Compute the baseline trend and the treatment-phase trend. Does the treatment-phase trend line converge on or diverge from, or is it parallel to, the extended baseline trend line?

b. How many of the treatment-phase data points *overlap* with the baseline-phase data pattern?

c. How many treatment-phase data points fall more than two estimated sigma units away from the extended baseline trend line?

d. Which of the four detection rules (if any) given in Chapter 6 suggests that there is significant change between baseline and treatment phases in this AB design? Regardless of whether you decide that any of the detection rules suggest the presence of significant change, tell why you decided what you did.

EXERCISE 6

Following are the data from six B single-case design evaluations of an intervention for anxiety used with six different clients: Joe C., Ashwin R., Sally P., Bill T., Waneta S., and Janice V. The data are scores on the Clinical Anxiety Scale, which was administered each week, and the treatment was intervention *X* for anxiety:

Joe C.: 65, 64, 60, 54, 47, 45, 39, 30, 25

Ashwin R.: 60, 60, 54, 55, 47, 43, 34, 26, 22

Sally P.: 55, 56, 57, 55, 51, 45, 43, 44, 41, 41, 35, 36, 32, 30, 26

Bill T.: 70, 67, 60, 57, 54, 50, 51, 45, 40, 34, 27

Waneta S.: 57, 56, 55, 50, 52, 46, 45, 47, 48, 47, 43, 44, 39, 39, 35, 31, 33, 29, 27

Janice V.: 72, 73, 70, 67, 69, 65, 62, 57, 55, 55, 50, 45, 46, 42, 40, 38, 39, 36, 34, 31, 30

Now do the following:

a. Plot all of these B design results on individual graphs, one for each of the six hypothetical clients. What do the data for each client tell you?

b. Now plot all of the B design data on one graph, as shown in Chapter 8. Plot the data for the males (Joe, Ashwin, and Bill) in black, and the data for the females (Sally, Waneta, and Janice) in blue. (Note: Solid and dashed lines can be used in place of color.)

c. What does the plot of all of the B design data in the aggregated graph tell you? Did these clients get better during treatment? How do you know? Is there a difference between how males and females fared during treatment *X*? How do you know? What does your answer suggest that might be true about the effects of treatment *X*?

EXERCISE 7

Find an example of a single-case design evaluation of an intervention or program of some type in a professional journal. Look in journals such as *Research on Social Work Practice, Social Work Research, Journal of Social Service Research, Applied Behavior Analysis, Behavior Therapy,* and *Journal of Behavior Therapy and Experimental Psychiatry.* Read the article that describes the evaluation, and analyze the data in the single-case design (or designs) presented in the article. Present the evaluation to your class, discussing what the authors of the evaluation did. In your discussion with the class, talk about the steps you would need to take to do a similar evaluation in various practice settings.

EXERCISE 8

Plan how you would conduct a single-case design evaluation of an intervention you might use with a client. Write out your plan, and discuss it with your class.

EXERCISE 9

Plan how you would conduct an evaluation of a program that has served a number of clients. In your plan, include both single-case and group design elements. Write out your plan, and discuss it with your class.

EXERCISE 10

Discuss as a class the policies that an agency might have in place that would actually *inhibit and discourage you from evaluating your helping efforts with your clients using single-case designs and the scales presented in this book.* What policies could an agency have in place that would serve to *encourage and support you in evaluating your work with your clients using single-case designs and the types of measures discussed in this book?* What policies have you encountered in a field placement or in some other setting that functioned to inhibit efforts to evaluate practice? What policies have you encountered that supported (or would have supported) efforts to evaluate practice? How might you work to change agency policies that inhibit and discourage practice evaluation efforts?

EXERCISE 11

A practitioner begins working with a client on February 1st. This client complains of feeling very depressed. The practitioner assesses the client's depression using only her or his subjective impressions of how the client is doing based on the client's behavior and the things that the client says. The practitioner begins treatment almost immediately, uses no objective measures of the client's depression, and uses no single-case design methods to monitor the client's progress. On June 1st, the practitioner decides that the client is "better" and that the treatment the practitioner implemented was responsible for the client getting "better." Discuss this method of evaluating practice in light of the ideas and methods discussed in this book. What can be said about the reliability and validity of the practitioner's assessment of the client's problem with depression as well as the practitioner's assessment that the client is "better" on June 1st? Discuss, within the context of the concept of internal validity, the practitioner's claim that the client is "better" because of the treatment that the practitioner implemented. Assuming that the client is, in fact, "better" on June 1st, what alternative explanations are there for the client's improvement; that is, what things other than the treatment provided might have been responsible for the client's improvement?

EXERCISE 12

This exercise is probably best done as a class exercise, though you can certainly do it individually. Look through several years of articles published in the journal *Applied Behavior Analysis*. Make a list of the various interventions and programs that have been evaluated using single-case design methods and that have been published in this journal. The authors, through the years, have seen evaluations of interventions to help (among other things) "latchkey" children be safe at home alone, to decrease the pain experienced by children undergoing hydrotherapy for serious burn injuries, to reduce vandalism in schools, to teach young children to safely cross the street, and to increase the use of seat belts by children. All of these are problem areas of concern to social workers and interventions that social workers might use. Discuss the range of problem areas addressed, and the interventions used and evaluated, in the journal articles that you find. Brainstorm with your classmates various interventions you might use for a wide range of problems that you might encounter in practice, and discuss how you might evaluate the effects of these interventions using single-case design methods.

References and Suggested Readings

Abell, J. N. (1986). *Assessing the impact of family stress on psycho-social functioning.* Doctoral dissertation, Florida State University School of Social Work, Tallahassee.

Abell, J. N. (1991). The index of clinical stress: A brief measure of subjective stress for practice and research. *Social Work Research and Abstracts, 20,* 11–16.

Abell, J. N., Jones, B. L., & Hudson, W. W. (1984). Revalidation of the index of self-esteem. *Social Work Research and Abstracts, 20,* 11–16.

Allen, M., & Yen, W. (1979). *Introduction to measurement theory.* Monterey, CA: Brooks/Cole.

Alter, C., & Evens, W. (1990). *Evaluating your practice: A guide to self-assessment.* New York: Springer.

Anastasi, A. (1976). *Psychological testing* (4th ed.). New York: Macmillan.

Ascher, M. (1981). Employing paradoxical intention in the treatment of agoraphobia. *Behaviour Research and Therapy, 19*(6), 533–542.

Ash, C. (1993). *The probability tutoring book.* New York: IEEE Press.

Attala, J., Hudson, W. W., & McSweeney, M. (1994). A partial validation of two short-form partner abuse scales. *Women and Health, 21,* 125–139.

Ayllon, T., & Azrin, N. (1965). Measurement and reinforcement of behavior in psychotics. *Journal of the Experimental Analysis of Behavior, 8*(6), 357–383.

Bailey, D., Jr. (1984). Effects of lines of progress and semilogarithmic charts on ratings of charted data. *Journal of Applied Behavior Analysis, 17,* 359–365.

Barlow, D. (1988). *Anxiety and its disorders: The nature and treatment of anxiety and panic.* New York: Guilford.

Barlow, D., & Cerny, J. (1988). *The psychological treatment of panic.* New York: Guilford.

Barlow, D., Hayes, S., & Nelson, R. (1984). *The scientist practitioner: Research and accountability in clinical and educational settings.* New York: Pergamon.

Barlow, D., & Hersen, M. (1984). *Single case experimental designs* (2d ed). New York: Pergamon.

Battle, C., Imber, S., Hoehn-Saric, R., Stone, A., Nash, E., & Frank, J. (1966). Target complaints as criteria of improvement. *American Journal of Psychotherapy, 20,* 184–192.

Beck, A., Rush, A., Shaw, B., & Emery, G. (1979). *Cognitive therapy of depression.* New York: Guilford.

Beere, C. A. (1979). *Women and women's issues: A handbook of tests and measures.* San Francisco: Jossey-Bass.

Benbenishty, R. (1996). Integrating research and practice: Time for a new agenda. *Research on Social Work Practice, 6*(1), 77–82.

Benbenishty, R., & Oyserman, D. (1995). Integrated information systems for human services: A conceptual framework, methodology and technology. *Computers in Human Services, 12,* 311–325.

Bloom, M., & Fischer, J. (1982). *Evaluating practice: Guidelines for the accountable professional.* Englewood Cliffs, NJ: Prentice-Hall.

Bloom, M., Fischer, J., & Orme, J. (1999). *Evaluating practice: Guidelines for the accountable professional* (3d ed). Needham Heights, MA: Allyn & Bacon.

Blythe, B. (1990). Improving the fit between single-subject designs and practice. In L. Videka-Sherman & W. J. Reid (Eds.), *Advances in clinical social work research* (pp. 29–32). Silver Spring, MD: National Association of Social Workers.

Blythe, B., & Tripodi, T. (1989). *Measurement in direct practice.* Newbury Park, CA: Sage.

Blythe, B., Tripodi, T., & Briar, S. (1994). *Direct practice research in human service agencies.* New York: Columbia University Press.

Bond, G., Bloch, S., & Yalom, I. (1979). The evaluation of a "target problem" approach to outcome measurement. *Psychotherapy: Theory, Research, and Practice, 11,* 48–54.

Bongar, B. (1991). *The suicidal patient: Clinical and legal standards of care.* Washington, DC: American Psychological Association.

Bongar, B., Berman, A., Maris, R., Silverman, M., Harris, E., & Packman, W. (Eds.). (1998). *Risk management with suicidal patients.* New York: Guilford.

Borenstein, D. B. (1990). Managed care: A means of rationing psychiatric treatment. *Hospital and Community Psychiatry, 41,* 1095–1098.

Bracht, G. H., & Glass, G. V. (1968). The external validity of experiments. *American Educational Research Journal, 5,* 437–474.

Bradshaw, W. (1996). Structured group work for individuals with schizophrenia: A coping skills approach. *Research on Social Work Practice, 6*(2), 139–154.

Bryk, A., & Raudenbush, S. (1992). *Hierarchical linear models: Applications and data analysis methods.* Newbury Park, CA: Sage.

Burns, D. (1990). *The feeling good handbook.* New York: Plume.

Burns, D. (1992). *Feeling good: The new mood therapy.* New York: Avon.

Burns, D. (1999). *Ten days to self-esteem.* New York: William Morrow.

Buros, O. K. (1972). *The seventh mental measurements notebook.* Highland Park, NJ: Gryphon Press.

Buros, O. K. (1977). *The eighth mental measurements yearbook.* Highland Park, NJ: Gryphon Press.

Buros, O. K. (1998). *Mental measurements yearbook* (13th ed.). Highland Park, NJ: Gryphon Press.

Busk, P., & Marascuilo, L. (1992). Statistical analysis in single-case research: Issues, procedures, and recommendations, with applications to multiple behaviors. In T. Kratochwill & J. Levin (Eds.), *Single-case research design and analysis: New directions for psychology and education* (pp. 159–186). Hillsdale, NJ: Lawrence Erlbaum.

Butterfield, W. H. (1977). Instrumentation in behavior therapy. In E. J. Thomas

(Ed.), *Behavior modification procedures: A sourcebook* (pp. 267–311). Chicago: Aldine.

Byron Smith, G., & Parsons, C. (1997). Improving quality in psychiatric and mental health care. In C. G. Meisenheimer (Ed.), *Improving quality: A guide to effective programs* (2d ed., pp. 569–622). Gaithersburg, MD: Aspen.

Cacioppo, J., & Petty, R. (1979). The effects of message repetition and position on cognitive response, recall, and persuasion. *Journal of Personality and Social Psychology, 37,* 97–109.

Cacioppo, J., & Petty, R. (1981). Social psychological procedures for cognitive response assessment: The thought listing technique. In T. V. Merluzzi, C. P. Glass, & M. Genest (Eds.), *Cognitive assessment* (pp. 308–342). New York: Guilford.

Cacioppo, J., Sandman, C., & Walker, B. (1978). The effects of operant heart rate conditioning on cognitive elaboration and attitude change. *Psychophysiology, 15,* 330–338.

Carrilio, T. E., Kasser, J., & Moretto, A. H. (1985). Management information systems: Who is in charge? *Social Casework, 66,* 417–423.

Cheung, K. (1999). Effectiveness of social work treatment and massage therapy for nursing home clients. *Research on Social Work Practice, 9*(2), 229–247.

Cheung, P. P. L., & Hudson, W. W. (1981). Assessing marital discord in clinical practice: A revalidation of the index of marital satisfaction. *Journal of Social Service Research, 5,* 101–118.

Chow, S. (1996). *Statistical significance: Rationale, validity, and utility.* Thousand Oaks, CA: Sage.

Chun, K., Cobb, S., & French, J. R. (1975). *Measures for psychological assessment: A guide to 3,000 original sources and their application.* Ann Arbor, MI: Institute for Social Research, University of Michigan.

Ciminero, A., Calhoun, K., & Adams, H. (Eds.). (1977). *Handbook of behavioral assessment.* New York: Wiley.

Cohen, J., & Cohen, P. (1983). *Applied multiple regression/correlation analysis for the behavioral sciences* (2d ed.) Hillsdale, NJ: Lawrence Erlbaum.

Cole, N., & Moss, P. (1989). Bias in test use. In R. L. Linn (Ed.), *Educational measurement* (3d ed., pp. 201–220). New York: Macmillan.

Comrey, A., Barker, T., & Glaser, E. (1975). *A sourcebook for mental health measures.* Los Angeles, CA: Human Interaction Research Institute.

Cone, J., & Hawkins, R. (1977). *Behavioral assessment.* New York: Brunner/Mazel.

Cook, T., & Campbell, D. (1979). *Quasi-experimentation: Design and analysis issues for field settings.* Chicago: Rand McNally College.

Corcoran, K. (1985). Clinical practice with nonbehavioral methods: Strategies for evaluation. *Clinical Social Work Journal, 13,* 573–579.

Corcoran, K., & Gingerich, W. (1994). Practice evaluation in the context of managed care: Case-recording methods for quality assurance reviews. *Research on Social Work Practice, 4,* 326–337.

Craske, M., & Barlow, D. (1993). Panic disorder and agoraphobia. In D. Barlow (Ed.), *Clinical handbook of psychological disorders* (2d ed., pp. 1–47). New York: Guilford.

Craske, M., Brown, T., & Barlow, D. (1991). Behavioral treatment of panic disorder: A two-year follow-up. *Behavior Therapy, 22,* 289–304.

Crocker, L., & Algina, J. (1986). *Introduction to classical and modern test theory.* Chicago: Holt, Rinehart, & Winston.

Cronbach, L. J. (1951). Coefficient alpha and the internal structure of tests. *Psychometrika, 16,* 297–334.

Cronbach, L. J., Gleser, G., Nanda, H., & Rajaratnam, N. (1972). *The dependability of behavioral measurements.* New York: Wiley.

Cullen, D. (1968). *Attitude measurement by cognitive sampling.* Unpublished doctoral dissertation, Ohio State University, Columbus.

Dasberg, H., van der Kleijn, E., Guelen, P., & van Praag, H. (1974). Plasma concentrations of diazepam and of its metabolite N-desmethyldiazepam in relation to anxiolytic effect. *Clinical Pharmacology and Therapeutics, 15,* 473–483.

Dawes, R. (1994). *House of cards: Psychology and psychotherapy built on myth.* New York: Free Press.

Downie, N., & Heath, R. (1967). *Basic statistical methods.* New York: Harper & Row.

Dziegielewski, S. F. (1998). *The changing face of health care social work: Professional practice in the era of managed care.* New York: Springer.

Edelson, J. (1985). Rapid assessment instruments for evaluating practice with children and youth. *Journal of Social Service Research, 8,* 17–31.

Edinburg, G. M., & Cottler, J. M. (1995). Managed care. In R. L. Edwards (Ed.), Encyclopedia of social work (19th ed., Vol. 2, pp. 1199–1213). Silver Spring, MD: National Association of Social Workers.

Edwards, R., & Reid, W. (1989). Structured case recording in child welfare: An assessment of social workers' reactions. *Social Work, 34,* 49–52.

Egan, J. (1990). *The skilled helper: A systematic approach to effective helping* (4th ed.). Pacific Grove, CA: Brooks/Cole.

Farkas, G., Sine, L., & Evans, I. (1979). The effects of distraction, performance demand, stimulus explicitness, and personality on objective and subjective measures of male sexual arousal. *Behaviour Research and Therapy, 17,* 25–32.

Faul, A. C., & Hudson, W. W. (1997). The index of drug involvement: A partial validation. *Social Work, 42,* 565–572.

Feindler, E., Marriott, S., & Iwata, M. (1984). Group anger control training for junior high school delinquents. *Cognitive Therapy and Research, 8,* 299–311.

Felty, D. W., & Jones, M. B. (1998). Human services at risk. *Social Service Review, 72,* 192–208.

Ferguson, K., & Rodway, M. (1994). Cognitive behavioral treatment of perfectionism: Initial evaluation studies. *Research on Social Work Practice, 4*(3), 283–308.

Findlay, S. (1999). Managed behavioral health care in 1999: An industry at a crossroads. *Health Affairs, 18,* 116–124.

Fischer, J. (1973). Is casework effective? A review. *Social Work, 18*(1), 5–20.

Fischer, J., & Corcoran, K. (1994). *Measures for clinical practice: A sourcebook.* (2d ed., Vols. 1 & 2). New York: Free Press.

Foa, E., & Emmelkamp, P. (1983). *Failures in behavior therapy.* New York: Wiley.

Foa, E., Grayson, J., Steketee, G., & Doppelt, H. (1983). Treatment of obsessive-compulsives: When do we fail? In E. B. Foa & P. M. G. Emmelkamp (Eds.), *Failures in behavior therapy.* New York: Wiley.

Foa, E., Grayson, J., Steketee, G., Doppelt, H., Turner, R., & Latimer, P. (1983). Success and failure in the behavioral treatment of obsessive-compulsives. *Journal of Consulting and Clinical Psychology, 51,* 287–297.

Foa, E., Steketee, G., Grayson, J., Turner, R., & Latimer, P. (1984). Deliberate exposure and blocking of obsessive-compulsive rituals: Immediate and long term effects. *Behavior Therapy, 15,* 450–472.

Forte, J., & Green R. (1994). The reliability and validity of the Index of Peer Relations with a clinical and nonclinical sample of adolescents. *Journal of Social Service Research, 19,* 49–65.

Fremouw, W., de Perczel, M., & Ellis, T. (1990). *Suicide risk: Asssessment and response guidelines.* New York: Pergamon.

Friedman, E. S. (1996). Capitation, integration, and managed care: Lessons from early experiments. *Journal of the American Medical Association, 275,* 957–962.

Fuchs, D. (1987). Integrated information systems for child welfare agencies: Evolution in two Canadian case studies. In W. LaMendola, B. Glastonbury, & S. Toole (Eds.), *A casebook of computer applications in the social and human services.* New York: Haworth.

Gabor, P.A., Unrau, Y.A., & Grinnell, R. M. (1998). *Evaluation for social workers: A quality improvement approach for the social services* (2d ed.). Boston: Allyn & Bacon.

Garb, H. (1998). *Studying the clinician: Judgement research and psychological assessment.* Washington, DC: American Psychological Association.

Genovich-Richards, J. (1997). Selecting quality initiatives and methodologies. In C. G. Meisenheimer (Ed.), *Improving quality: A guide to effective programs* (2d ed., pp. 569–622). Gaithersburg, MD: Aspen.

Gentile, J., Roden, A., & Klein, R. (1974). An analysis of variance model for the intrasubject replication design. *Journal of Applied Behavior Analysis, 5,* 193–198.

Ghiselli, E., Campbell, J., & Zedeck, S. (1981). *Measurement theory for the behavioral sciences.* San Francisco: Freeman.

Gibbs, L., & Gambrill, E. (1999). *Critical thinking for social workers: Exercises for the helping professions.* Thousand Oaks, CA: Pine Forge Press.

Giere, R. (1988). *Explaining science: A cognitive approach.* Chicago: University of Chicago Press.

Giere, R. (1991). *Understanding scientific reasoning* (3d ed.). New York: Harcourt, Brace, Jovanovich.

Gilovich, T. (1991). *How we know what isn't so: The fallibility of human reason in everyday life.* New York: Free Press.

Gingerich, W. (1984). Generalizing single-case evaluation from classroom to practice setting. *Journal of Education for Social Work, 20*(1), 74–82.

Gingerich, W. (1990). Rethinking single case evaluation. In L. Videka-Sherman & W. J. Reid (Eds.), *Advances in clinical social work research* (pp. 11–24). Silver Spring, MD: National Association of Social Workers.

Giuli, C., & Hudson, W. W. (1977). Assessing parent-child relationship disorders in clinical practice: The child's point of view. *Journal of Social Service Research, 1,* 77–92.

Goldberg, J., & Shaw, B. (1989). The measurement of cognition in psychopathology. In A. Freeman, K. Simon, L. Beutler, & H. Arkowitz (Eds.), *Comprehensive handbook of cognitive therapy* (pp. 37–59). New York: Plenum.

Goldman, B., & Saunders, J. (1974). *Directory of unpublished experimental mental measures* (Vol. 1). New York: Human Services Press.

Goldstein, A., & Glick, B. (1987). *Aggression replacement training.* Champaign, IL: Research Press.

Gottman, J. (1981). *Time series analysis: A comprehensive introduction for social scientists.* New York: Cambridge University Press.

Grant, E., & Leavenworth, R. (1980). *Statistical quality control* (6th ed.). New York: McGraw-Hill.

Grinnell, R. M., Gabor, P., & Unrau, Y. (1997). *Evaluation and quality improvement in the human services.* Needham Heights, MA: Allyn & Bacon.

Grinnell, R., Rothery, M., & Thomlison, R. (1993). Research in social work. In R. M. Grinnell, Jr. (Ed.), *Social work research and evaluation* (4th ed., pp. 2–16). Itasca, IL: Peacock.

Grinnell, R. M., & Unrau, Y. (1997). Group designs. In R. M. Grinnell, Jr. (Ed.), *Social work research and evaluation.* (5th ed., pp. 259–297). Itasca, IL: Peacock.

Groth-Marnot, G. (1990). *Handbook of psychological assessment* (2d. ed.). New York: Wiley.

Hale, A. C. (1989). *Residence hall assistants' attitudes toward homosexual persons as the result of leaders' disclosure of sexual orientation.* Ann Arbor, MI: University Microfilms International No. 8920254.

Hamilton, M. A., & Orme, J. G. (1990). Examining the construct validity of three parenting knowledge measures using LISREL. *Social Service Review, 64,* 121–143.

Harris, F., & Jenson, W. (1985). AB designs with replications: A reply to Hayes. *Behavioral Assessment, 7*(2), 133–135.

Harvey, A. C. (1990). *The econometric analysis of time series* (2d ed.). New York: Phillip Allen.

Heard, K., & Watson, S. (1999). Reducing wandering by persons with dementia using differential reinforcement. *Journal of Applied Behavior Analysis, 32*(3), 381–384.

Heineman, M. (1981). The obsolete scientific imperative in social work research and practice. *Social Service Review, 55,* 371–397.

Henggler, S., Melton, G., & Smith, L. (1992). Family preservation using multisystemic therapy: An effective alternative to incarcerating serious juvenile offenders. *Journal of Consulting and Clinical Psychology, 60,* 953–961.

Hersen, M., & Barlow, D. (1976). *Single-case experimental designs: Strategies for studying behavior change.* New York: Pergamon.

Hojem, M., & Ottenbacher, K. (1988). Empirical investigation of visual inspection versus trend-line analysis of single-subject data. *Journal of the American Physical Therapy Association, 68,* 983–988.

Hontanosas, D., Cruz, R., Kaneshiro, K., & Sanchez, J. (1979). *A descriptive study of spouse abuse at the University of Hawaii at Manoa.* Unpublished masters research project, University of Hawaii School of Social Work, Honolulu.

Hope, D., & Heimberg, R. (1993). Social phobia and social anxiety. In D. Barlow (Ed.), *Clinical handbook of psychological disorders* (2d ed., pp. 99–136). New York: Guilford.

Howard, G., Millham, J., Slaten, S., & O'Donnell, L. (1981). Influence of subject response style effects on retrospective measures. *Applied Psychological Measurement, 5*(1), 89–100.

Hudson, W. W. (1978). First axioms of treatment. *Social Work, 23*(1), 65.

Hudson, W. (1981). Development and uses of indexes and scales. In R. M. Grinnell, Jr. (Ed.), *Social work research and evaluation* (2d ed., pp. 185–205). Itasca, IL: Peacock.

Hudson, W. W. (1982). *The clinical measurement package: A field manual.* Homewood, IL: Dorsey Press.

Hudson, W. W. (1990). *Multi-problem screening inventory.* Tallahassee, FL: WALMYR.

Hudson, W. W. (1996). *Computer assisted social services.* Tallahassee, FL: WALMYR.

Hudson, W. (1997). *WALMYR assessment scales scoring manual.* Tallahassee, FL: WALMYR.

Hudson, W. W., Acklin, J. D., & Bartosh, J. C. (1980). Assessing discord in family relationships. *Social Work Research and Abstracts, 16,* 21–29.

Hudson, W. W., & Decker, A. L. (1998). *The index of sexual harassment: A partial validation.* Tallahassee, FL: WALMYR.

Hudson, W. W., Faul, A., & Sieppert, J. (1996). *Gate control pain management inventory (GC-PMI).* Tallahassee, FL: WALMYR.

Hudson, W. W., & Glisson, D. F. (1976). Assessment of marital discord in social work practice. *Social Service Review, 50,* 293–311.

Hudson, W. W., Hamada, R., Keech, R., & Harlan, J. (1980). *A comparison and revalidation of three measures of depression.* Unpublished manuscript, Florida State University School of Social Work, Tallahassee.

Hudson, W. W., Harrison, D. F., & Crosscup, P. C. (1981). A short-form scale to measure sexual discord in dyadic relationships. *Journal of Sex Research, 17,* 157–174.

Hudson, W. W., Lewis, S. L., & Faul, A. C. (1998). *Managerial effectiveness and job satisfaction: Two measures for use in organizational research and administration.* Tallahassee, FL: WALMYR.

Hudson, W. W., MacNeil, G., & Dierks, J. (1993). *Six new assessment scales: A partial validation.* Tallahassee, FL: WALMYR.

Hudson, W., & McMurtry, S. (1997). Comprehensive assessment in social work practice: The multi-problem screening inventory. *Research on Social Work Practice, 7*(1), 79–98.

Hudson, W. W., & Murphy, G. J. (1980). The non-linear relationship between marital satisfaction and stages of the family life cycle: An artifact of Type I errors? *Journal of Marriage and the Family, 42,* 263–267.

Hudson, W. W., Murphy, G. J., & Nurius, P. S. (1983). A short-form scale to measure liberal vs. conservative orientations toward human sexual expression. *Journal of Sex Research, 19,* 239–254.

Hudson, W. W., Nurius, P. S., Daley, J. G., & Newsome, R. D. (1988). A short-form scale to measure peer relations dysfunction. *Journal of Social Service Research, 13,* 57–69.

Hudson, W. W. & Proctor, E. K. (1976). The assessment of depressive affect in clinical practice. *Journal of Consulting and Clinical Psychology, 45,* 1206–1207.

Hudson, W. W. & Ricketts, W. A. (1980). A strategy for the measurement of homophobia. *Journal of Homosexuality, 5,* 357–372.

Hudson, W. W., Wung, B., & Borges, M. (1980). Parent-child relationship disorders: The parents' point of view. *Journal of Social Service Research, 3,* 283–294.

Hughes, D. C., & Luft, H. S. (1998). Managed care and children: An overview. *The Future of Children, 8,* 25–38.

Huitema, B. (1985). Autocorrelation in behavioral research: A myth. *Behavioral Assessment, 7,* 109–120.

Huitema, B. (1986). Autocorrelation in behavioral research: Wherefore art thou? In A. Poling & R. Fuqua

(Eds.), *Research methods in applied behavior analysis: Issues and advances* (pp. 187–208). New York: Plenum.

Huitima, B. (1988). Autocorrelation: 10 years of confusion. *Behavioral Assessment, 10,* 253–294.

Ingram, R. E. (Ed.). (1986). *Information processing approaches to clinical psychology.* New York: Academic Press.

Jacobs, F. H. (1988). The five-tiered approach to evaluation. Context and implementation. In H. B. Weiss & F. H. Jacobs (Eds.), *Evaluating family programs.* New York: Aldine de Gruyter.

Jamison, C., & Scogin, F. (1995). Outcome of cognitive bibliotherapy with depressed adults. *Journal of Consulting and Clinical Psychology, 63,* 644–650.

Jayaratne, S., Tripodi, T., & Talsma, E. (1988). Methodological observation on applied behavioral science. *Journal of Applied Behavioral Science, 24,* 119–128.

Jensen, G. A., Morrisey, M. A., Gaffney, S., & Liston, D. K. (1997). The new dominance of managed care: Insurance trends in the 1990s. *Health Affairs, 16,* 125–136.

Johnson, J. H., Williams, T. A., Klingler, D. E., & Giannetti, R. A. (1977). Interventional relevance and retrofit programming: Concepts for the improvement of clinician acceptance of computer-generated assessment reports. *Behavior Research Methods and Instrumentation, 9*(2), 123–132.

Johnston, J., & Pennypacker, H. (1980). *Strategies and tactics of human behavioral research.* Hillsdale, NJ: Lawrence Erlbaum.

Jordan, K., & Franklin, C. (1995). *Clinical assessment for social workers: Quantitative and qualitative methods.* Chicago: Lyceum.

Kazandijian, V. A. (1996). Indicators of performance or the search for the best pointer dog. In V. A. Kazandijian (Ed.), *The epidemiology of quality* (pp. 25–37). Gaithersburg, MD: Aspen.

Kazdin, A. (1982). *Single case research designs: Methods for clinical and applied settings.* New York: Oxford University Press.

Kazdin, A. (1983). The token economy: A decade later. *Journal of Applied Behavior Analysis, 15,* 431–445.

Kazdin, A. (1998). *Research design in clinical psychology* (3d ed.). Boston: Allyn & Bacon.

Kazi, M., & Wilson, J. (1996). Applying single-case evaluation methodology in a British social work agency. *Research on Social Work Practice, 6*(1), 5–26.

Kelley, M., Gregory, J., Middlebrook, J., McNeer, M., & Drabman, R. (1984). Decreasing burned children's pain behavior: Impacting the trauma of hydrotherapy. *Journal of Applied Behavior Analysis, 17*(2), 147–158.

Kerlinger, F. (1973). *Foundations of behavioral research* (2d ed.). New York: Holt, Rinehart & Winston.

Klein, W., Beltran, M., & Sowers-Hoag, K. (1990). Validating an assessment of peer relationship problems. *Journal of Social Service Research, 13,* 71–85.

Klein, W., & Bloom, M. (1995). Practice wisdom. *Social Work, 40*(6), 799–807.

Kovacs, M., & Lohr, W. D. (1995). Research on psychotherapy with children and adolescents: An overview of evolving trends and current issues. *Journal of Abnormal Child Psychology, 23,* 11–30.

Kratochwill, T. (1992). Single-case research design and analysis: An overview. In T. Kratochwill & J. Levin (Eds.), *Single-case research design and analysis: New directions for psychology and education* (pp. 1–14). Hillsdale, NJ: Lawrence Erlbaum.

Kratochwill, T., & Levin, J. (1992). *Single-case research design and analysis: New directions for psychology and education.* Hillsdale, NJ: Lawrence Erlbaum.

Kyte, N., & Bostwick, G. (1997). Measuring variables. In R. M. Grinnell, Jr. (Ed.), *Social work research and evaluation* (5th ed., pp. 161–183). Itasca, IL: F. E. Peacock.

Laudan, L. (1990). *Science and relativism: Key controversies in the philosophy of science.* Chicago: University of Chicago Press.

Lavelle, J., Hovell, M., West, P., & Wahlgren, D. (1992). Promoting law enforcement for child protection: A community analysis. *Journal of Applied Behavior Analysis, 25*(4), 885–892.

Levitt, J., & Reid, W. (1981). Rapid assessment instruments for practice. *Social Work Research and Abstracts, 17,* 13–19.

Lewin, L., Cowan, M., Ganzini, L., Gonzales, L., & Rasmussen, J. (1997). Behavioral problem solving, contracting, and feedback with nursing home residents. *Journal of Clinical Geropsychology, 3*(4), 245–255.

Liberman, R., & Smith, V. (1972). A multiple baseline study of systematic desensitization in a patient with multiple phobias. *Behavior Therapy, 3,* 597–603.

Likert, R. (1932). A technique for the measurement of attitudes. *Archives of Psychology, 140,* 55.

Lindsay, W., Marshall, I., Neilson, C., Quinn, K., & Smith, A. (1998). The treatment of men with a learning disability convicted of exhibitionism. *Research in Developmental Disabilities, 19*(4), 295–316.

Lord, F., & Novick, M. (1968). *Statistical theories of mental test scores.* Reading, MA: Addison Wesley.

Lyons, J., Hammer, J., & White, R. (1987). Computerization of psychological services in the general hospital: Collaborative information management in the human services department. *Computers in Human Services, 2,* 27–36.

MacNeil, G. (1991). A short-form scale to measure alcohol abuse. *Research on Social Work Practice, 1*(1), 68–75.

Mandell, S. (1989). Resistance and power: The perceived effect that computerization has on a social agency's power relationships. *Computers in Human Services, 4,* 29–40.

Mattaini, M. (1996). The abuse and neglect of single-case designs. *Research on Social Work Practice, 6,* 83–90.

Matyas, T., & Greenwood, K. (1990). Visual analysis of single-case time series: Effects of variability, serial dependency, and magnitude of intervention effects. *Journal of Applied Behavior Analysis, 23,* 341–351.

McCleary, R., & Hay, R. (1980). *Applied time series analysis for the social sciences.* Beverly Hills, CA: Sage.

McCleary, R., & Welsh, W. (1992). Philosophical and statistical foundations of time-series experiments. In T. Kratochwill & J. Levin (Eds.), *Single-case research design and analysis: New directions for psychology and education* (pp. 41–92). Hillsdale, NJ: Lawrence Erlbaum.

McKusick, D., Mark, T., King, E., & Harwood, R. (1998). Spending for mental health and substance abuse treatment, 1996. *Health Affairs, 17*(5), 147–157.

McMillan, T., Jongen, E., & Greenwood, R. (1996). Assessment of post-traumatic amnesia after severe closed head injury: Retrospective or prospective? *Journal of Neurology, Neurosurgery, and Psychiatry, 60,* 422–427.

McMurtry, S. L., & Hudson, W. W. (2000). The client satisfaction inventory: Results of an initial validation study. *Research on Social Work Practice, 10*(5), 622–643.

Mechanic, D. (1998). Emerging trends in mental health policy and practice. *Health Affairs, 17,* 82–98.

Medicaid fact sheet. (1999). Washington, DC: Kaiser Commission on Medicaid and the Uninsured.

Mehrens, W., & Lehmann, I. (1984). *Measurement and evaluation in education and psychology* (3d ed.). New York: Holt, Rinehart & Winston.

Meier, S. T. (1994). *The chronic crisis in psychological measurement and assessment.* San Diego: Academic Press.

Melzack, R., & Wall, P. D. (1988). *The challenge of pain.* Great Britain: Penguin Group.

Messick, S. (1989). Validity. In R. L. Linn (Ed.), *Educational measurement* (3d ed., pp. 13–104). New York: Macmillan.

Meyer, C. (1996). My son the scientist. *Social Work Research, 20,* 101–104.

Miller, I. (1996). Ethical and liability issues concerning invisible rationing. *Professional Psychology: Research and Practice, 27,* 583–587.

Miller, R. H., & Luft, H. S. (1994). Managed care plans: Characteristics, growth and premium performance. *Annual Review of Public Health, 15,* 437–459.

Millman, J., & Greene, J. (1989). Specification and development of tests of achievement and ability. In R. L. Linn (Ed.), *Educational Measurement* (3d ed.). New York: Macmillan.

Mintz, J., Luborsky, L., & Christoph, P. (1979). Measuring the outcomes of psychotherapy: Findings of the Penn Psychotherapy Project. *Journal of Consulting and Clinical Psychology, 34,* 186–187.

Morrison, J., Libow, J., Smith, F., & Becker, R. (1978). Comparative effectiveness of directive vs. non-directive group therapist style on client problem resolution. *Journal of Clinical Psychology, 34,* 186–187.

Murphy, A., Hutchison, J., & Bailey, J. (1983). Behavioral school psychology goes outdoors: The effects of organized games on playground aggression. *Journal of Applied Behavior Analysis, 16*(1), 29–35.

Murphy, G. J. (1978). *The family in later life: A cross-ethnic study in marital and sexual satisfaction.* Unpublished doctoral dissertation, Tulane University, New Orleans, LA.

Murphy, G. J., Hudson, W. W., & Cheung, P. P. L. (1980). Marital and sexual discord among older couples. *Social Work Research and Abstracts, 16,* 11–16.

Neter, J., Wasserman, W., & Kutner, M. (1983). *Applied linear regression models.* Homewood, IL: Richard D. Irwin, Inc.

Neufeld, A., & Fantuzzo, J. (1987). Treatment of severe self-injurious behavior by the mentally retarded using the bubble helmet and differential reinforcement procedures. *Journal of Behavior Therapy and Experimental Psychiatry, 18*(2), 127–136.

Neugeboren, B. (1995). Organization influences on management information systems in the human services. *Computers in Human Services, 12,* 295–310.

Neuliep, J. (Ed.). (1991). *Replication research in the social sciences.* Newbury Park, CA: Sage.

Nugent, W. (1986). Information gain through integrated research approaches. *Social Service Review, 61,* 337–364.

Nugent, W. (1992). The affective impact of a clinical social worker's interviewing style: A series of single-case experiments. *Research on Social Work Practice, 2*(1), 6–27.

Nugent, W. (1993a). A series of single case design clinical evaluations of an Ericksonian hypnotic intervention used with clinical anxiety. *Journal of Social Service Research, 17,* 41–69.

Nugent, W. R. (1993b). A validity study of a self-anchored scale for self-esteem. *Research on Social Work Practice, 3,* 276–287.

Nugent, W. R. (1993c). Differential validity in social work measurement. *Social Service Review, 67,* 631–650.

Nugent, W. R. (1994). An investigation of the dependability of clinical cutting scores using generalizability theory. *Journal of Social Service Research, 18,* 89–107.

Nugent, W. (1996). Integrating single-case and group-comparison designs for evaluation research. *Journal of Applied Behavioral Science, 32*(2), 209–226.

Nugent, W. (2000). *Single case design visual analysis procedures for use in practice evaluation.* Forthcoming in *Journal of Social Service Research.*

Nugent, W. R., Champlin, D., & Wiinamaki, L. (1997). The effects of anger control training on adolescent antisocial behavior. *Research on Social Work Practice, 7,* 446–462.

Nugent, W., & Thomas, J. (1992). Validation of a clinical measure of self-esteem. *Research on Social Work Practice, 3,* 191–207.

Nugent, W. R., & Thomas, J. (1993). Validation of a clinical measure of self-esteem. *Research on Social Work Practice, 3*(2), 191–207.

Nugent, W., White, L., & Basham, R. (2000). A "devil" hidden in the details: The effect of measurement error in regression analysis. Forthcoming in *Journal of Social Service Research.*

Nunnally, J. C. (1978). *Psychometric theory* (2d ed.). New York: McGraw-Hill.

Nunnally, J., & Bernstein, I. (1994). *Psychometric theory* (3d ed.). New York: McGraw-Hill.

Nurius, P. S. (1983). Mental health implications of sexual orientation. *The Journal of Sex Research, 19,* 119–137.

Nurius, P. S., & Hudson, W. W. (1987). Sexual activity and preference: Six quantifiable dimensions. *Journal of Sex Research, 24,* 30–46.

Nurius, P., & Hudson, W. W. (1993). *Human services: Practice, evaluation, and computers.* Pacific Grove, CA: Brooks/Cole.

Orme, J., & Cox, M. E. (2000). Analyzing single-subject design data using statistical process control charts. Forthcoming in *Social Work Research.*

Oss, M. E., Drissel, A. B., & Clary, J. (1997). *Managed behavioral health market share in the United States (1997–98).* Gettysburg, PA: Open Minds.

Ostrom, C. W. (1990). *Time series analysis: Regression techniques* (2d ed.). Newberry Park, CA: Sage.

Ottenbacher, K., & Cusick, A. (1991). An empirical investigation of interrater agreement for single-subject data using graphs with and without trend lines. *Journal of the Association for Persons with Severe Handicaps, 16,* 48–55.

Pain, M., & Disney, M. (1996). Testing the reliability and validity of the Index of Attitudes Toward Homosexuals in Australia. *Journal of Homosexuality, 30,* 99–110.

Paine-Andrews, A., Fawcett, S., Richter, K., Berkley, J., Williams, E., & Lopez, C. (1996). Community coalitions to prevent adolescent substance abuse: The case of the "project freedom" replication initiative. In J. Wodarski, M. Feit, & J. Ferrari (Eds.), *Adolescent health care: Program designs and services* (pp. 81–99). New York: The Haworth Press.

Palmer, R. J., Tucker, M., & King, J. B. (1991). A diagnostic approach to information management problems in the organization. *Journal of Systems Management, 42,* 13–16.

Parsonson, B., & Baer, D. (1986). The graphic analysis of data. In A. Poling & R. Fuqua (Eds.), *Research methods in applied behavior analysis: Issues and advances* (pp. 157–186). New York: Plenum.

Parsonson, B., & Baer, D. (1992). The visual analysis of data, and current research into the stimuli controlling it. In T. Kratochwill & J. Levin (Eds.), *Single-case research design and analysis: New directions for psychology and education* (pp. 15–40). Hillsdale, NJ: Lawrence Erlbaum.

Patton, M. Q. (1996). *Utilization-focused evaluation: The new century text* (3rd ed.) Thousand Oaks, CA: Sage.

Penka, C., & Kirk, S. (1991). Practitioner's involvement in clinical evaluation. *Social Work, 36,* 513–518.

Perneger, T., Etter, J., & Rougemont, A. (1997). Prospective versus retrospective measurement of change in health status: A community based study in Geneva, Switzerland. *Journal of Epidemiology and Community Health, 51*(3), 320–325.

Persons, J., & Burns, D. (1986). Mechanisms of action in cognitive therapy: The relative contributions of technical and interpersonal interventions. *Cognitive Therapy and Research, 9*(5), 539–551.

Petty, R., & Cacioppo, J. (1979). Issue involvement can increase or decrease persuasion by enhancing message relevant cognition. *Journal of Personality and Social Psychology, 37,* 1915–1926.

Petty, R., Wells, G., & Brock, T. (1976). Distraction can enhance or reduce yielding to propaganda: Thought disruption versus effort justification. *Journal of Personality and Social Psychology, 34,* 874–884.

Pfadt, A., Cohen, I., Sudhalter, V., Romanczyk, R., & Wheeler, D. (1992). Applying statistical process control to clinical data: An illustration. *Journal of Applied Behavior Analysis, 25*(3), 551–560.

Pfadt, A., & Wheeler, D. (1995). Using statistical process control to make data-based clinical decisions. *Journal of Applied Behavior Analysis, 28,* 349–370.

Poertner, J., & Rapp, C. A. (1987). Designing social work management information systems: The case for performance guidance systems. *Administration in Social Work, 11,* 177–190.

Popham, W. (1984). Specifying the domain of content or behaviors. In R. A. Berk (Ed.), *A guide to criterion referenced test construction* (pp. 29–48). Baltimore: Johns Hopkins University Press.

Posavac, E. J. (1998). Toward more informative uses of statistics: Alternatives for program evaluators. *Evaluation and Program Planning, 21,* 243–254.

Ptacek, J., Smith, R., Espe, K., & Raffety, B. (1994). Limited correspondence between daily coping reports and retrospective coping recall. *Psychological Assessment, 6*(1), 41–49.

Reid, W. (1978). *The task-centered system.* New York: Columbia University Press.

Reid, W. J. (1997). Long-term trends in clinical social work. *Social Service Review, 71,* 200–213.

Reinherz, H. (1990). Beyond regret: Single-case evaluations and their place in social work education and practice. In L. Videka-Sherman & W. J. Reid (Eds.), *Advances in clinical social work research* (pp. 25–28). Silver Spring, MD: National Association of Social Workers.

Riggs, D., & Foa, E. (1993). Obsessive compulsive disorder. In D. Barlow (Ed.), *Clinical Handbook of Psychological Disorders* (2d ed., pp. 189–239). New York: Guilford.

Robinson, E., Bronson, D., & Blythe, B. (1988). An analysis of the implementation of single-case evaluation by practitioners. *Social Service Review, 62,* 285–301.

Roderick, C., Pitchford, M., & Miller, A. (1997). Reducing aggressive playground behavior by means of a school-wide "raffle." *Educational Psychology in Practice, 13*(1), 57–63.

Rogers, W. H., Wells, K. B., Meredith, L. S., Sturm, R., & Burnam, M. A. (1993). Outcomes for adult patients with depression under prepaid or fee-for-service financing. *Archives of General Psychiatry, 50,* 517–525.

Roid, G. (1984). Generating the test items. In R. A. Berk (Ed.), *A guide to criterion referenced test construction* (pp. 49–77). Baltimore: Johns Hopkins University Press.

Roid, G., & Haladyna, T. (1982). *A technology for test-item writing.* New York: Academic Press.

Rojahn, J., & Schulze, H. H. (1985). The linear regression line as a judgmental aid in the visual analysis of serially dependent A-B time series data. *Journal of Psychopathology and Behavioral Assessment, 7,* 191–206.

Rose, T. (1978). The functional relationship between artificial food colors and hyperactivity. *Journal of Applied Behavior Analysis, 11*(4), 439–446.

Rosen, D., & Zytowski, D. (1977). An individualized, problem-oriented self-report of change as a follow-up of a university counseling service. *Journal of Counseling Psychology, 24,* 437–439.

Rosen, J. (1991). *Capricious cosmos: Universe beyond law.* New York: Macmillan.

Rossi, P. H., & Freeman, H. E. (1993). *Evaluation: A systematic approach* (5th ed.) Thousand Oaks, CA: Sage.

Rubin, A., & Babbie, E. (1989). *Research methods for social work.* Belmont, CA: Wadsworth.

Rubin, A., & Knox, K. (1996). Data analysis problems in single-case evaluations: Issues for research on social work practice. *Research on Social Work Practice, 6,* 40–65.

Scheaffer, R., Mendenhall, W., & Ott, R. (1996). *Elementary survey sampling* (5th ed.). Belmont, CA: Wadsworth.

Scogin, F., Hamblin, D., & Beutler, L. (1987). Bibliotherapy for depressed older adults: A self-help alternative. *The Gerontologist, 27,* 383–387.

Scogin, F., Jamison, C., & Davis, N. (1990). A two year follow-up of the effects of bibliotherapy for depressed older adults. *Journal of Consulting and Clinical Psychology, 58,* 665–667.

Scogin, F., Jamison, C., & Gochneaut, K. (1989). The comparative efficacy of cognitive and behavioral bibliotherapy for mildly and moderately depressed older adults. *Journal of Consulting and Clinical Psychology, 57,* 403–407.

Shaw, M., & Wright, J. (1967). *Scales for the measurement of attitudes.* New York: McGraw-Hill.

Sheafor, B., Horejsi, C., & Horejsi, G. (1994). *Techniques and guidelines for social work practice* (3d ed.). Needham Heights, MA: Allyn & Bacon.

Shinn, M., Good, R., & Stein, S. (1989). Summarizing trend in student achievement: A comparison of two methods. *School Psychology Review, 18,* 356–370.

Sidman, M. (1960). *Tactics of scientific research.* New York: Basic Books.

Simpura, J., & Poikolainen, K. (1983). Accuracy of retrospective measurement of individual alcohol consumption in men: A reinterview after 18 years. *Journal of Studies on Alcohol, 44*(5), 911–917.

Slonim-Nevo, V., & Anson, Y. (1998). Evaluating practice: Does it improve treatment outcome? *Social Work Research, 22*(2), 66–74.

Smith, N., Floyd, M., Jamison, C., & Scogin, F. (1997). Three year follow-up of bibliotherapy for depression. *Journal of Consulting and Clinical Psychology, 65*(2), 324–327.

Stevens, J. (1968). Ratio scales of opinion. In D. K. Whitla (Ed.), *Handbook of measurement and assessment in behavioral science*. Reading, MA: Addison-Wesley.

Stocks, T., & Williams, M. (1995). Evaluation of single-subject data using statistical hypothesis tests versus visual inspection of charts with and without celeration lines. *Journal of Social Service Research, 20*, 105–127.

Sundel, M., & Sundel, S. (1999). *Behavior change in the human services* (4th ed.). Thousand Oaks, CA: Sage.

Swokowski, E. (1988). *Calculus with analytic geometry* (4th ed.). Boston: PWS Kent.

Tawney, J., & Gast, D. (1984). *Single-subject research in special education*. Columbus, OH: Merrill.

Thomas, E. J. (1978). Research and service in single case experimentation: Conflicts and choices. *Social Work Research and Abstracts, 14*, 20–31.

Thyer, B. (1987). *Treating anxiety disorders: A guide for human service professionals*. Newbury Park, CA: Sage.

Thyer, B. A. (1993). Single system designs. In R. M. Grinnell, Jr. (Ed.), *Social work research and evaluation*. (4th ed.). Itasca, IL: Peacock.

Thyer, B. (1996). Forty years of progress toward empirical clinical practice. *Social Work Research, 20*, 77–82.

Thyer, B., Papsdorf, J., Davis, R., & Vallecorsa, S. (1984). Autonomic correlates of the subjective anxiety scale. *Journal of Behavior Therapy and Experimental Psychiatry, 15*, 3–7.

Thyer, B., & Westhuis, D. (1989). Test-retest reliability of the clinical anxiety scale. *Phobia Practice and Research Journal, 2*, 111–113.

Tischler, G. L. (1990). Utilization management and the quality of care. *Hospital and Community Psychiatry, 147*, 967–973.

Tolson, E. (1990). Why don't practitioners use single subject designs? In L. Videka-Sherman & W. J. Reid (Eds.), *Advances in clinical social work research* (pp. 58–64). Silver Spring, MD: National Association of Social Workers.

Tutty, L. (1995). Theoretical and practical issues in selecting a measure of family functioning. *Research on Social Work Practice, 5*, 80–106.

Wagner, E. R. (1993). Types of managed care organizations. In P. R. Kongstvedt (Ed.), *The managed health care handbook* (2d ed., pp. 12–21). Rockville, MD: Aspen.

Wakefield, J., & Kirk, S. (1996). Unscientific thinking about scientific practice: Evaluating the scientist-practitioner model. *Social Work Research, 20*, 83–96.

Wertkin, R. (1985). Stress-innoculation training: Principles and applications. *Social Casework, 66*(10), 611–616.

Westhuis, D., & Thyer, B. A. (1989). Development and validation of the clinical anxiety scales: A rapid assessment instrument for empirical practice. *Educational and Psychological Measurement, 49*, 153–163.

Wheeler, D. (1995). *Advanced topics in statistical process control*. Knoxville, TN: SPC Press.

Whitfield, G. (1999). Validating school social work: An evaluation of a cognitive-behavioral approach to reduce school violence. *Research on Social Work Practice, 9*(4), 399–426.

Whittaker, J. K., Fine, D., & Grasso, A. (1989). Youth and family characteristics in residential treatment intake: An exploratory study. In E. Balcerzak (Ed.), *Group care of children: Transition toward the year 2000* (pp. 67–87). Washington, DC: Child Welfare League of America.

Wilber, K. (1998). *The marriage of sense and soul: Integrating science and religion*. New York: Random House.

Wincze, J., Hoon, P., & Hoon, E. (1977). Sexual arousal in women: A comparison of cognitive and physiological responses by continuous measurement. *Archives of Sexual Behavior, 6,* 121–133.

Wineburgh, M. (1998). Ethics, managed care, and outpatient psychotherapy. *Clinical Social Work Journal, 4,* 433–443.

Winegar, N. (1992). *The clinician's guide to managed health care.* New York: Haworth.

Witkin, S. (1991). Empirical clinical practice: A critical analysis. *Social Work, 36,* 158–163.

Witkin, S. (1996). If empirical practice is the answer, then what is the question? *Social Work Research, 20,* 69–76.

Wolpe, J., & Lazarus, A. (1966). *Behavior therapy techniques.* New York: Pergamon.

Woody, R. H. (1997). *Legally safe mental health practice.* Madison, CT: Psychosocial Press.

Young, J., Beck, A., & Weinberger, A. (1993). Depression. In D. Barlow (Ed.), *Clinical handbook of psychological disorders* (2d ed., pp. 240–277). New York: Guilford.

Zung, W. W. (1965). A self rating depression scale. *Archives of General Psychiatry, 12,* 63–70.

Index

Domestic Abuse subscale, 283
Doppelt, H., 53, 66
Drabman, R., 150
Drissel, A. B., 198
Drug Use subscale (FASI), 283
Drug Use subscale (MPSI), 272
Duration, 316
Dyadic relationship scales, 241–243
Dziegielewski, S.F., 195

E

Ecology, 58
Economic Stress subscale, 282
Edelson, J., 226
Edinburg, G. M., 195
Edwards, R., 42
Effectiveness, 2–3, 381
    two definitions of, 3, 201–202
Effectiveness-oriented practice, 29, 46–49
    evaluation levels, 30–36
    role of goals, objectives, activities,
        36–45
Efficiency assessment, 36
Egan, J., 84
Ellis, T., 57, 214
Emmelkamp, P., 158
Employee assistance program (EAP), 101,
    389
Employment subscale, 283
Engagement, 60–62
EPM (empirical practice model), 1, 3, 29,
    72, 90–91, 193, 340, 382–385
    and computers, 25
    defined, 7
    example of in quality management
        process, 204–210
    First Rule of, 3
    fundamental equation of, 4–7, 203
    promise of, 20–22
    role in quality and utilization manage-
        ment, 201–204
    Second Rule of, 6
    setting measurable client objectives,
        73–74
    Third Rule of, 12
    three fundamental procedures, 8
Error scores, 228
Espe, K., 80
Etter, J., 80
Evaluability assessment, 32
Evaluating practice, 109
    basic designs for, 98–108
    nature of, 90–92
    single-system designs for establishing
        causality, 92–98
Evaluation, 66–68
    typology, 30–36
Evans, I., 334

Evens, W., 40
Exclusive provider plans, 196
Experimental Psychiatry, 150
Extended Family subscale, 283
External validity, 97–98
Extrafamilial Abuse subscale, 283

F

Factor-loading failures, 276–278
Factor-loading successes, 276–278
Failure analysis, 158
False negative, 254, 257
False positive, 254, 257
Family adjustment scales, 243–245
Family Assessment Screening Inventory
    (FASI), 281, 317–318
    administering, 285–288
    interpreting score profiles, 292
    items in, 281–284
    sample copy, 442–448
    scoring, 288–289
    subscale scores, 281
        interpreting, 290–292
        psychometric characteristics of, 284
Family Conflict subscale, 282
Family Relationship Problems subscale,
    269, 287
Family Support subscale, 282
Fantuzzo, J., 150
Farkas, G., 334
FASI. *See* Family Assessment Screening
    Inventory (FASI)
Faul, A. C., 71, 239, 246
Fearfulness subscale, 270
Feedback
    improving, 222–223
    role of, 14–20
Feelings of Guilt subscale, 271
Felty, D. W., 194, 196
Ferguson, K., 150
Fine, D., 43
Fischer, J., 50–51, 68, 72, 92, 97,
    111–113, 123, 314
Floyd, M., 177
Foa, E., 53, 66, 158
Forte, J., 240
Franklin, C., 51
Freeman, H. E., 40
Fremouw, W., 57, 214, 221, 223, 258,
    270–271, 292
French, J. R., 314
Frequency counts, 319–320
Frequency measure, 316
Friedman, E. S., 194
Fuchs, D., 42

G

Gabor, P. A., 31–37, 40, 43, 73
Gaffney, S., 197
Gambrill, E., 54
Ganzini, L., 150
Garb, H., 63, 70–71, 220, 225, 227, 255
Gate Control Pain Management
    Inventory, 71
Generalized Contentment Scale (GCS), 8,
    76, 96, 107, 169–172, 205, 238, 253,
    259, 265, 294, 322–323, 332, 365,
    405
Generic problem-solving framework, 51
Genovich-Richards, J., 199
Ghiselli, E., 215, 227
Gibbs, L., 54
Giere, R., 55
Gilovich, T., 54, 63, 70, 81, 134, 220,
    225, 227, 304
Gingerich, W., 198, 201
Giuli, C., 244
Glaser, E., 314
Glass, G. V., 97
Glick, B., 147, 164
Glisson, D.F., 241
Goal attainment scaling, 216, 360
Gochneaut, K., 177
Goldberg, J., 147
Goldman, B., 314
Goldstein, A., 147, 164
Gonzales, L., 150
Good, R., 112
Gottman, J., 111–112, 117, 122, 394–395,
    401–402
Graduated exposure, 165–166
Grant, E., 128
Grasso, A., 43
Grayson, J., 53, 66, 158
Green, R., 240
Greene, J., 327
Greenwood, R., 80
Gregory, J., 150
Grinnell, R. M., 31–37, 40, 43, 51, 73,
    94, 97
Groth-Marnot, G., 214, 224, 230
Group-comparison design, 151–152. *See
    also* Integrated designs
Guelen, P., 334

H

Hale, A. C., 239
Hamada, R., 238, 245
Hamblin, D., 177
Hamilton, M. A., 244–245
Harlan, J., 238, 245
Harris, F., 53, 72, 88
Harrison, D. F., 241–242

Harvey, A. C., 111
Harwood, R., 197
Hawkins, R., 314
Hay, R., 111
Hayes, S., 72, 122, 131
Health care reform, 197
Health Conditions subscale, 284
Health maintenance organizations
    (HMOs), 195–196
Heard, K., 150
Heineman, M., 52
Henggler, S., 78
Hersen, M., 81, 106, 122, 126, 151–153,
    156
History, 94–95
Hontanosas, D., 238, 240–242
Hoon, E., 334
Hoon, P., 334
Horejsi, C., 60
Horejsi, G., 60
Housing subscale, 281
Hovell, M., 150
Howard, G., 80
Hudson, W. W., 21, 46, 71, 79, 85, 128,
    168, 184, 205, 218, 224, 231,
    238–247, 275, 290, 302, 313, 318,
    323, 334, 360
Hughes, D. C., 194–195
Huitema, B., 111
Human problem theory, 22–24
Hutchison, J., 150

I

Ideas of Reference subscale, 270
Index of Alcohol Involvement (IAI), 81,
    104, 238, 294, 298, 407
Index of Attitudes Toward Homosexuals
    (IAH), 410
Index of Brother Relations (IBR), 245,
    422
Index of Clinical Stress (ICS), 86,
    102–103, 205, 238–239, 294, 408
Index of Drug Involvement (IDI), 239,
    409
Index of Family Relations (IFR), 85, 245,
    423
Index of Homophobia (IHP), 239,
    250–251, 253, 257
Index of Job Satisfaction (IJS), 246, 427
Index of Managerial Effectiveness (IME),
    246–247, 428
Index of Marital Satisfaction (IMS), 174,
    241, 257, 260, 265, 414
Index of Parental Attitudes (IPA),
    244–245, 257, 266, 424
Index of Peer Relations (IPR), 101, 240,
    411